Entrepreneurship and Small Business

Second Edition

Paul Burns

First edition 2001
Reprinted 8 times
Second edition 2007

Published by
PALGRAVE MACMILLAN
Houndmills, Basingstoke, Hampshire RG21 2XS and
175 Fifth Avenue, New York, N.Y. 10010
Companies and representatives throughout the world

PALGRAVE MACMILLAN is the global academic imprint of the Palgrave
Macmillan division of St. Martin's Press, LLC and of Palgrave Macmillan Ltd.
Macmillan is a registered trademark in the United States, United Kingdom
and other countries. Palgrave is a registered trademark in the European
Union and other countries.

ISBN-13: 978–1–4039–4733–8
ISBN-10: 1–4039–4733–3

This book is printed on paper suitable for recycling and made from fully
managed and sustained forest sources. Logging, pulping and manufacturing
processes are expected to conform to the environmental regulations of the
country of origin.

A catalogue record for this book is available from the British Library.

A catalog record for this book is available from the Library of Congress.

Library of Congress Catalogue Card Number – 2006051367

10   9   8   7   6   5   4   3
16   15   14   13   12   11   10   09   08

Printed and bound in China

Entrepreneurship and
Small Business

To my friend, my lover and my wife, Jean
She makes every day of my life happy
and the prospect of tomorrow a joy

Contents Overview

Contents

Case Insights and Quotes: the Businesses

Web addresses for these companies can be found by doing a search on Google.

*   Also a case with questions
➡   at the end of a case or quote indicates that it continues
●   at the end of a case or quote indicates that it does not continue

Case Insights and Quotes: the Entrepreneurs

* Also a case with questions
➔ at the end of a case or quote indicates that it continues
● at the end of a case or quote indicates that it does not continue

Cases with Questions

The businesses

The entrepreneurs

Web addresses for these companies can be found by doing a search on Google.

* Also case insights or quotes

List of Figures

List of Tables

Preface to the Second Edition

The major change to the new edition of this book is the addition of a number of chapters on specific types of entrepreneurship – social, international and corporate entrepreneurship. It is a measure of how the topic of entrepreneurship is maturing that it is being extended into other areas of commercial and public life. It is no longer just about starting up a new business. Entrepreneurship is seen as encouraging two vital qualities – creativity and innovation – but with an extra push that makes things happen. For this reason the section on creativity and innovation has also been expanded to two chapters with extensive new material on creativity.

The popular things remain: the blend of theoretical and practical; the informal style that makes the book so accessible; the quotes from entrepreneurs reinforcing the theory and the case studies linking theory with practice. There are new and updated case studies and most chapters now end with a longer case study with questions. The book remains targeted at a broad range of student readers and market research indicates that it is indeed successfully used at all higher education levels, albeit in different ways.

Nevertheless, for the most part, this book remains about the dominant form of business on this planet – the small firm. It looks at how firms develop from start-up, sometimes to grow, sometimes to fail, but mainly to stagnate. It looks at their contribution to society. It looks at their defining characteristics – how they are not just scaled-down versions of large firms. It looks at how they go about business and the problems they face. It looks at family firms and the added complexity this brings. This new edition also looks at the challenge for this millennium – how entrepreneurship might be encouraged in larger firms and in society generally.

This book is still also about owner-managers and, most interesting of all, entrepreneurs. It is about what motivates them to do what they do – their personal and family influences. It is about how they go about the task of management – making decisions, balancing risk and return – and how they are different from managers in large firms. It is about how they must develop and change as the firm grows. It is about how certain defining characteristics they possess shape and define the business they run – for good or ill. And in this edition it is also about developing entrepreneurial leadership in any organisation.

This book is also a 'how-to-do-it' text, synthesising good management practice for entrepreneurs involved in start-ups and growing firms. It is informed by research and based on thirty years' experience of working with small firms and small firm advisors. Management in small firms is a holistic activity, so the skills developed include marketing, accounting, finance, people management and strategy development. Over 120 cases and case insights are linked to the main text, to illustrate how the concepts are actually used in small, growing and successful firms. Stories of success – and failure – are what makes the study of entrepreneurship so interesting.

Keeping up to date is a problem in any text that sets out to be practical and current. This is achieved by the extensive signposting to websites that offer up-to-date information and practical help and advice. It is an unfortunate sign of the times that the web resource also contains a warning about plagiarism – particularly necessary since business plans of any sort can now be so easily downloaded. The Learning Resources section also contains recommended books for further reading in selected areas and recommended journals for further research.

The book contains extensive teaching materials. Each chapter has essays and discussion topics as well as practical exercises and assignments. However, entrepreneurship is essentially a practical activity so there is a series of business start-up activities that lead to the development of a start-up business plan. There is also a series of activities that enable a growth audit to be undertaken on an existing firm. These are supported by pro formas and checklists. There is also a pro-forma business plan with examples from a retail, service and manufacturing businesses.

The major challenge facing business schools today is how to encourage and develop the entrepreneurial skills of students. This book is designed to address this issue. It is written to motivate students at the same time as providing frameworks to nurture these precious skills in a systematic way.

Courses using this book

The book is written for a range of undergraduate and postgraduate courses with the aim of fostering entrepreneurial talent and developing entrepreneurial skills. These are described below as three pathways. Each pathway is likely to use this book differently, although there is a core of common material.

Pathway 1

First year undergraduate business studies skill-development courses. This is the typical 'introduction to business course'. However, rather than teach each topic in its own 'compartmentalised' session, relevant chapters are designed to act as a holistic introduction to the topic of business studies in the practical context of a business start-up project. In this way students can better see the interconnections and realise that the solutions to business problems require the application of a wide range of business skills. Relevance and practicality can also aid motivation.

Pathway 2

Third-year undergraduate and postgraduate business studies skill-development courses. These develop the themes to a greater depth by looking at growth as well as start-up and can be used by students who have previously studied business by skimming early skills-based chapters. Students can undertake the start-up project or the business growth audit. For students who have previously studied business and management, an entrepreneurship course typically aims to integrate and apply most of the functional areas they have previously studied and give it a creative but practical focus. Again this helps them better see the interconnections in the topics they have already studied and realise that the solutions to business problems require the application of all the areas they have studied.

Pathway 3

Third-year undergraduate and postgraduate specialist courses on entrepreneurship and small business (including MBA). Students can use the book to study this topic in its own right – reviewing research and developing their understanding of the sector. They can rely simply on the essays and discussion topics or exercises and activities or alternatively undertake the business growth audit. For these students, the entrepreneurship course still aims to integrate and apply the functional areas they have previously studied and give it a creative but practical focus, albeit at a higher level, but also to give them an insight into the study of entrepreneurship and small business in its own right. The second edition has been enhanced by the inclusion of chapters on social, international and corporate entrepreneurship.

It would be nice to think that students will find this book sufficiently interesting to read it all, but given the pressure of time and the different skills and backgrounds of these groups, it is more realistic to think that they will dip into it where they find it relevant to their course. The table below attempts to signpost which chapters are most relevant to these three pathway groups. Students may find many of the accounting concepts in Chapters 7 and 11 difficult to grasp. Since many courses may wish to omit some of this material, the more technical aspects have been relegated to appendices in these chapters.

Chapter	Pathway 1	Pathway 2	Pathway 3
1	☆☆☆	☆☆☆	☆☆☆
2	☆☆☆	☆☆☆	☆☆☆
3	☆☆☆	☆☆☆	☆☆☆
4	☆☆☆	☆☆☆	☆☆☆
5	☆☆☆	☆☆☆	☆☆☆
6	☆☆☆	☆	☆
7	☆☆☆	☆	☆
8	☆☆	☆☆☆	☆☆☆
9	☆☆	☆☆☆	☆☆☆
10		☆☆☆	☆☆
11	☆☆	☆☆☆	☆☆
12		☆☆☆	☆☆☆
13	☆☆	☆☆	☆☆☆
14	☆☆☆	☆☆☆	☆☆
15			☆☆☆
16		☆	☆☆☆
17			☆☆☆
18			☆☆☆

Key: ☆☆☆ Core, essential reading
    ☆☆   Relevant and of interest but not essential
    ☆   Dip into as required, depending on interest and/or skill level

Learning styles and the learning resources

Daniel Kim (1993) suggests *effective* learning can be considered to be a revolving wheel (Figure A). During half the cycle you test and experiment with concepts and observe what happens through concrete experience – learning 'know-how'. In the second half of the cycle you reflect on the observations and form concepts or theories – learning 'know-why'. This is often called 'double-loop learning' – the best sort of learning which links knowing how with knowing why, linking theory with practice. So effective learning involves forming concepts, testing concepts, experience and reflection. Traditionally education has focused too much on the second half of the cycle – forming concepts or theories and reflection – and it is difficult to break away from this in a textbook which, inevitably, focuses on the concepts and theories. However, I have tried to do so by including a number of learning resources. Each learning resource is designed to influence a particular learning style. Taken together, they should complete the wheel of learning.

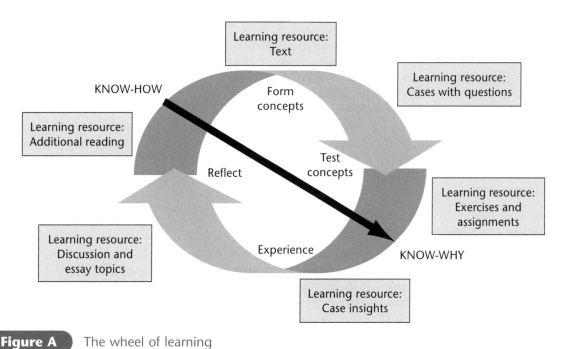

Figure A The wheel of learning

Cases with questions

Embedded in the chapters are 25 cases with questions, designed to make students think about and apply the concepts being discussed in that chapter. This is the testing stage of the wheel of learning. Recommended longer, more complex cases are given in the Learning Resources at the end of the book. The related website (www.palgrave.com/business/burns) also provides longer versions of some of the cases in the book.

Exercises and assignments

In the testing and experimenting phase of the cycle are exercises and assignments, which involve doing something, in the main further research. This research is often desk-based – including visits to websites – but some of the most popular assignments, in my experience, involve students going out to do things – such as interviewing entrepreneurs. This is very much the 'test concepts' part of the wheel of learning.

Case insights and summaries

Spread throughout this book, there are over 120 case insights and quotes from entrepreneurs around the world. They are designed to illustrate and reinforce the theoretical points being made in the text with practical examples and opinions from the real world – there is nothing like an endorsement from an entrepreneur. The summary at the end of each chapter links these cases and quotes to the main points being made in that chapter. This is the experience element of the wheel of learning, linked to the concepts and theories through the summaries and case questions.

Discussion and essay topics

Each chapter has topics for group discussion or essay writing. These can be used as a basis for tutorials. They are designed to make students think about the text material and develop their critical and reflective understanding of it and what it means in the real world. The summary and discussion topics help students discriminate between main and supporting points and provide mechanisms for self-teaching. The discussion and essay topics also form the reflective element of the wheel of learning, forcing students to think through the theories and concepts, often linking them to the real world.

Other learning resources in the book

At the end of the book there are selected international case studies linked to the themes in various chapters. Many of the cases have related videos or DVDs. All these can be obtained from the European Case Clearing House. These are particularly valuable for postgraduate teaching. Use of these case studies forces students to test concepts, and reflect on them in the face of the real-world experience they provide. The shorter cases are more suitable for undergraduate teaching.

   Each chapter has full journal and book references. There are also selected further textbooks, organised by topic, and selected journals at the end of the book. Finally there are selected websites where further learning resources and practical, up-to-date help and advice can be accessed.

Visiting speakers

Courses on entrepreneurship are greatly enriched by visiting speakers, particularly the entrepreneurs themselves. They can tell students what it is really like and often have some wonderful 'derring-do' stories to tell. I shall never forget the incredulity of an MBA class at Cranfield as they were told how a Rolls Royce-driving entrepreneur, who left school at the age of sixteen, made his first million selling meat from open markets across the south east of England. And there was the time Anita Roddick said she would never hire anybody from a business school. That went down well. My experience is that these talks are normally the highlight of the course. No matter how good the teacher, there is no substitute for the real thing – somebody who did it. Cases can help develop skills and illustrate important points in a practical context. Unfortunately entrepreneurs are such a vital part of the entrepreneurial business that, without access to them in person or through a video, they can seem a little flat.

Entrepreneurship exercises

At the end of the book there are exercises to help students evaluate whether they really might have what it takes to become an entrepreneur and set up their own business, to help them plan to set up the business and to evaluate whether a business has growth potential. These exercises can be used in a structured way for student evaluation. They are split into four parts.

1. Are you really entrepreneurial?
Students are asked to evaluate their own entrepreneurial tendency with the aid of questionnaires and to write a report. This exercise is best undertaken very early in the course, shortly after Chapter 2 is covered.

2. Generating the idea
This exercise helps students generate a business idea. It is best undertaken as a group activity and can be incorporated into other creativity exercises detailed in Chapter 4.

3. Evaluating the opportunity
Central to any entrepreneurship course ought to be a practical project. The most commonly used project is the business start-up. This is normally assessed by the development of a business plan. Ideally students should be asked to prepare a plan on an idea of their own that they think has some commercial potential. Preparing the plan forces them to be both creative and practical. It takes them beyond the ideas stage and forces students to crystallise the idea and show how it can be made to happen. This is an excellent management discipline that integrates all the functional areas of management which are too often taught separately. It forces them to think through which strategies are most likely to lead to success in a real situation and evaluate the outcome. A pro-forma business plan is supplied to help students.

Growth audit

An alternative activity, better suited to older, more experienced students, is to write a report on the growth prospects of a small firm. This involves them going out and actually talking to entrepreneurs, finding out what small firms really are like. It gets them to apply theories and concepts to a real situation. If undertaken by mature MBA students, it can often provide the entrepreneur with an invaluable outside view on how the business is doing. Running a small firm can certainly be a lonely, insular affair. This sort of project also provides a much-needed link between university or college and the small business community. The eight-part exercise involves students undertaking a Growth Audit on an existing business. This can be undertaken individually, but my experience is that it is best undertaken in small groups. Because many students may not have much business experience, extensive use is made of checklists and worksheets to help students undertake the audit. Sometimes student reports can provide a basis for case study development. Sometimes the personal links they develop open up research opportunities.

In the final analysis, any course on entrepreneurship must challenge students to think entrepreneurially. It must make them aware of opportunities in the market place and generate a 'can-do' mentality. It must empower them and convince them that they can shape their own destinies. It must make them realise how important the entrepreneur is to the small firm and to society as a whole. It must make them realise how business problems do not come in neatly labelled boxes reflecting the way the subject is taught. But, most of all, it must be interesting and fun.

Website (www.palgrave.com/business/burns)

The website accompanying this book provides further resources:

- An electronic, self-diagnostic version of the General Enterprise Tendency (GET) Test, produced by Durham University Business School, so that students can better understand whether they have the characteristics required to be entrepreneurial;
- Extended versions of some of the cases with questions;
- A print version of the pro-forma Business Plan used in the book;
- A print version of the Entrepreneurial Exercises;
- Web references, with hyperlink;
- Any updates or revisions.

There is a password-protected site for lecturers which contains:

- Overhead slides for each chapter;
- Teaching notes for cases;
- Teaching notes for the specimen business plans.

Learning outcomes

Each chapter has clear learning outcomes that identify the key concepts to be covered. These assume that students will undertake the essays and discussion topics as well as assignments and exercises, at the end of each chapter.

On completing the course based on this book a student should be able to:

1 Write a business plan for a start-up business.
2 Evaluate the growth potential of a small firm.
3 Describe the problems and issues facing small and family firms and how they might be resolved.
4 Describe the nature of entrepreneurship in individuals – character traits and approaches to business and management – and evaluate their own entrepreneurial qualities.

5 Describe the process of creativity and innovation and explain how it might be encouraged in others and in themselves.
6 Explain what is required to become an entrepreneurial leader and manager and how this can be achieved even in a larger organisation.
7 Describe how strategies are developed in an entrepreneurial organisation and explain which strategies are most likely to lead to successful start-up and growth, even in an international context.
8 Describe how the concept of entrepreneurship can be extended to non-commercial fields.

Key and cognitive skills for the course

Having completed a course in entrepreneurship using this book, with the seminar discussion topics, exercises and activities designed around it, a student should have developed a number of important skills:

- Information interpretation, critical analysis and evaluation skills;
- Data analysis and interpretation skills;
- Problem identification and solving skills;
- ICT skills, in particular the use of the internet;
- Independent and/or team-working skills;
- Writing and presentation skills.

Students should also have developed a range of applied business and management skills in a holistic way that can be applied to help a developing or existing organisation become more entrepreneurial.

Acknowledgements

Every effort has been made to trace all the copyright holders, but if any have been inadvertently overlooked the publishers will be pleased to make the necessary arrangements at the first opportunity.

I would particularly like to thank Durham University Business School for permission to reproduce an electronic version of their GET Test on the website accompanying this book. Their work on entrepreneurship over the years has inspired all of us.

I would also like to thank my editor, Ann Edmondson, for her hard work, particularly on the last-minute revisions. Without her diligence this book would be littered with errors and omissions.

Reference

Kim, D.H. (1993) 'The Link between Individual and Organizational Learning', *Sloan Management Review*, Fall.

Guided Tour of the Book …

Cases with questions encourage students to apply theory to real-world situations.

Case insights and **quotes** illustrate theoretical points with practical examples and opinions from the real world.

Learning outcomes identify the key concepts to be covered within the chapter and the key knowledge and skills that students will obtain by reading it.

Case with questions

Ridgeway Primary School and Nursery is a large primary school on the outskirts of Croydon in the UK. It is an unlikely place to find an example of civic entrepreneurship but since 1998 it has defied the UK's national curriculum and not implemented the literacy or numeracy hours required of it. Instead it has followed its own strongly held philosophy that a primary curriculum is only made coherent through making creative links between subjects. The school's vision is to have a creative curriculum that inspires both children and teachers to learn. The school wants to create a real learning community based upon a genuine will to learn that encourages creativity in children and teachers alike. The literacy and numeracy hours did not fit with this philosophy.

Head teacher, **Anna House**, believes creativity is the thread that runs through everything the school does. She believes in motivating people rather than working through hierarchies and structures. Parents, governors and visitors are used as a creative resource. Teachers work in creative teams along with teaching assistants, each learning from the other. Even the school meals organisers are encouraged to think creatively.

There is a detailed 38-page teaching and learning policy which draws on research into effective teaching and learning to justify the school's policies. The school aims to create a holistic curriculum with certain sustained themes like 'spirituality', 'citizenship', 'water' or 'save the planet' running through it so as to create continuity and embed learning, thus avoiding the danger of short-term, easily forgotten experiences. There are three themes each year. The themes build up to provide a view of the world that fire the children's curiosity. There is detailed planning of the curriculum around these themes. Literacy or numeracy is encouraged because of the child's interest in the theme, rather than as an end in itself. So, for example, the theme of 'shoes' was the context in year 6 for learning about materials and developing different shoe designs. This 'enquiry-based learning' provides scope for individual creativity and the development of thinking skills. The curriculum is enhanced by lunchtime clubs in areas such as chess, drama and even Japanese (run by a parent). Creative activity is linked to opportunities to think, so as to turn the experience into learning. So, for example, children are encouraged to think about how and why certain types of shading on a drawing create the effect of texture. There is also an emphasis on developing independence and self-direction in learning. Children assess themselves against their own learning targets. In year 1 children are given their own Inventions Book in which to design creative solutions to problems. At Key Stage 1 (5–7 years old) there are no set playtimes. Children develop their own portfolios showing achievements in learning. One feature of this is the extensive use of digital photographs to record these achievements. Teachers also enjoy much autonomy. For example, they can choose when, and if, to take a playtime.

The risks faced by the school in not following the national curriculum were high. Ultimately, if there had been persistently poor Ofsted (the UK schools' inspectorate) reports the school may have been closed. But the risk has paid off. Not only has it passed all its Ofsted visits but Ofsted has describes the school as having a 'very high quality curriculum'.

Questions
1 Is this an example of civic entrepreneurship? If so, why?
2 Is this an entrepreneurial response to an educational issue? If so, why?
3 What are the risks posed by this form of action?

18

Corporate Entrepreneurship

Contents

- Defining corporate entrepreneurship
- Building an entrepreneurial architecture
- The learning organisation
- Shaping the architecture
- The role of entrepreneurial leadership
- Constructing an entrepreneurial culture
- The role of size and structure
- Management and structure
- Freedom and control
- Summary

LEARNING OUTCOMES

By the end of this chapter you should be able to:

- Explain what is meant by the term 'corporate entrepreneurship' and the basic schools of thought that have contributed to its development;
- Explain what is meant by the term 'entrepreneurial architecture', how it might be shaped and how it might lead to sustainable competitive advantage in the appropriate environment;
- Explain what is meant by the term 'learning organisation' and how it underpins the entrepreneurial architecture in a larger firm;
- Explain what is meant by the term 'entrepreneurial management' and

the differences between it and traditional management;
- List the disciplines that contribute to this new area;
- Explain what an entrepreneurial culture means in an organisation;
- Explain how structures and size can encourage and contribute to the development of corporate entrepreneurship;
- Describe the balance between freedom and control needed in an entrepreneurial organisation and explain the dimensions on which it can be measured.

470

Case insight

Jim Clark is worth about $3 billion. He is now a cross between a serial entrepreneur and a venture capitalist because he realised that he is better at start-ups than running the business in the longer term. He discovered this with his first company, **Silicon Graphics (SGI)**, which he built around a graphic chip called the Geometry Engine that he invented in the 1970s. He spent 13, mainly unhappy, years at SGI where he found he just did not like the discipline of running a successful growing business.

He left in 1994 and invested $3 million of his own money in a primitive web browser called Mosaic and a 22-year-old who helped develop it called Marc Andreesen. **Netscape** went public 18 months later and made Jim Clark a billionaire.

In 1995 he moved on and founded another company called **Healtheon**, which uses the internet to share patient and administrative information between doctors, hospitals, insurance companies and the patients themselves. Again the business was run by somebody else, Mike Long.

Jim Clark has now started up another company, **MYCFO**, this time using the internet to help the wealthy manage their financial affairs. It also satisfies a necessary condition for success: Jim Clark is not planning to run it.

Building the management team

Entrepreneurs will only succeed in growing their company if they get a good management team to work with. Attracting good staff is always difficult for small firms because of perceived lack of job security, uncertainty about promotion prospects and the fact that it is often difficult for new people to fit into an existing team. Hence the need, often, to offer shares in the company.

'Once you have a business up and running the best way to keep in touch is to employ great people and empower them. This brings with it trust, communication and team spirit. When you work as a team you are in touch. My business style is non-aggressive, non-confrontational – it's who I am. It's important to be yourself. It comes from a background where you have to get on with people to get on. I believe that if you treat people like dirt on the way up it will come to haunt you as you find yourself on the way down.'

Jonathan Elvidge
founder of Gadget Shop
The Times 6 August 2002

Selecting a team will depend upon the mix of functional skills and market or industry experience required in the firm, as well as the personal chemistry between its members. For a team to be effective individuals need to have the right mix of a certain set of personal characteristics. Dr Meredith Belbin (1981) identified nine clusters of personal characteristics or attributes which translate into 'team roles'. Individuals are unlikely to have more than two or three of these, yet all nine clusters of characteristics need to be present in a team for it to work effectively.

The leader's role is to select the team and then to build cohesion and motivation. In most cases this involves

Summaries link the in-chapter case insights and quotes to the main points discussed in the chapter.

Exercises and assignments involve students in additional research activities in order to develop their knowledge and skills much further.

Essays and discussion topics encourage students to critically reflect on the material within the text and to link theory to real-world scenarios. They can be used as a basis for tutorials.

Summary

Owner-managers and entrepreneurs are both born and made. They have certain personal character traits that they are born with and are influenced by antecedent factors as well as the culture into which they are born. The issue of linking the character traits of an individual to the success of a business – picking winners – needs to be approached with caution. Success or failure in business comes from a mix of many different things. The character traits of the manager is just one factor in the equation. What is more, there are a number of methodological problems associated with trying to measure personality traits:

- They are not stable and change over time.
- They require subjective judgements.
- Measures tend to ignore cultural and environmental influences.
- The role of education, learning and training is often overlooked.
- Issues such as age, sex, race, social class and education can be ignored.

Owner-managers have the following character traits:

- Need for independence.
- Need for achievement, strongest in entrepreneurs like **Stephen Waring, Chey Garland, Brent Hoberman** and **Charles Muirhead**.
- Internal locus of control, that is, a belief that they can control their own destiny, as with **Jonathan Elvidge**.
- Ability to live with uncertainty and take measured risks, like **David Speakman** and **Jonathan Elvidge** but unlike **Jean Young**.

In addition, entrepreneurs have the following character traits. Some more entrepreneurial owner-managers might also exhibit them, albeit to a lesser degree:

- Opportunistic, creating or exploiting change for profit, like **Richard Branson** and **Simon Woodroffe**.
- Innovative, using innovation as their prime tool to create or exploit opportunity, like **Neil Kelly**.
- Self-confident, like **Richard Thompson** and **Chris Ingram**.
- Proactive and decisive with high energy, like **Tom Farmer** and **Bob Worcester**.
- Self-motivated, like **Martha Lane Fox** and **Wing Yip**.
- Possessing vision and flair, like **Mike Peters**.
- Willing to take greater risks and live with greater uncertainty, like **Anne Notley**.

Education is an important antecedent influence on start-ups but more particularly entrepreneurial growth businesses. Whilst unemployment is a strong push into self-employment, entrepreneurial growth businesses are more likely to be set up for more positive motives. It is possible that having a parent who was previously self-employed is more likely to lead people to set up their own firm. Observation tells us that another influence is immigration to a foreign country. Despite arguments to the contrary, we observe numerous examples of immigrants who establish very successful business (**Navin Engineer, Bharat Shah, Bharat** and **Ketan Mehta, Vijay** and **Bikhu Patel, Ravi Karia** and **Naresh Shah**).

Many start-ups do not undertake formal market research – a risk that **Stephen Hemsley**, founder of **Domino's Pizza**, is unwilling to take. They treat the launch as market research, constantly reviewing customer reaction.

The ability to sell is important at start-up. Selling is about matching the benefits of the product or service to the needs of customers and then convincing them to buy. As with **Goldsmiths Fine Foods**, the benefits customers are looking for are not always obvious, but the sales role is important in finding out what they are. Over time the salesperson can build a relationship of trust and respect that can lead to new customer networks being developed. Selling skills can be developed with practice. There are ways to start a sales interview; there are sales aids that can be used in the interview itself. There are techniques to handle objections and to help close a sale.

The internet offers new opportunities for innovative businesses – such as **eBay** – and new routes to a global market for small firms generally. It increases competitive pressures and emphasises the need to understand what you are selling, to whom and why your customers continue to buy from you.

There are sole traders, partnerships and limited liability companies. Sole traders are easy and quick to set up but, if the business is to grow, it is probably best to form it into a limited company sooner rather than later. Franchise is a popular, low-risk way of setting up in business using the ideas, expertise and systems of an established organisation like **Body Shop**.

Essays and discussion topics

1 Are customers logical?
2 Why are people willing to pay quite high prices for bottled water?
3 Why do owner-managers prefer interactive or personal marketing?
4 Why is it said that the three most important elements of the marketing mix for a retail business are location, location and location?
5 Advertising is the most expensive way of one person talking to another. Discuss.
6 What is marketing?
7 What is the difference between marketing and selling?
8 Why is marketing important?
9 Costs determine prices. Discuss.
10 Is there really a limit to the price you can charge for a product or service?
11 Can you really sell less and make more profit?
12 How can you charge different prices for the same product or service?
13 How different does a product or service have to be to mean that you are following a strategy of differentiation?
14 Every product or service is different. Discuss.
15 Why is branding so important?
16 Is creating a brand easier or more difficult for a small firm?
17 What makes a good brand?
18 Is Carphone Warehouse really different from other shops selling mobile phones? If so, how? If not, why not? Does it matter?
19 We spent most of the twentieth century creating mass markets and will spend most of the twenty-first breaking them down. Discuss.
20 Is market segmentation an art or a science?
21 Is market research worthwhile?
22 Do most small firms set about market positioning in a haphazard sort of way with the result that success or failure is really just luck?

---

23 Business is 90% perspiration and 10% inspiration. Discuss.
24 If you think knowledge is expensive, try ignorance. Discuss.
25 How do you go about undertaking market research prior to starting a business?
26 How do you find out who your customers might actually be?
27 Describe some sorts of customers that might not be interested in the service that Goldsmith's Fine Foods provides. What elements of the marketing mix might they be more interested in?
28 Selling is not an honourable profession. Discuss.
29 What are the advantages and disadvantages of being a small supplier to a large assembler linked through a fully integrated supply chain?
30 What are the particular problems facing a small firm wanting to sell on the internet and how might they be overcome?
31 What are the particular problems facing a purely internet start-up and how might they be overcome?
32 Are there any good business opportunities left using the internet?
33 Why are franchises an attractive business opportunity?
34 What is the best legal form of business?

Exercises and assignments

1 Select five products or services. List their features and translate these into benefits for the customer. Alongside this list any proof that might be needed to convince the customer that the benefit is real.
2 Place the five products or services in each of the four boxes of Porter's Generic Marketing Strategies. Explain why you place them where you do.
3 Select one product or service and write up its history – how it got to be where it is, what strategies the firm followed and how competitors reacted.
4 If a company has fixed costs of £160 000 and sells only one product at £25, with a variable cost of £17, calculate its break-even point. If the same company introduces a second product to increase sales above the break-even point and achieves total sales in this year of £960 000 against total variable costs of £720 000, calculate the new break-even point. Fixed costs remain unchanged. Calculate the profits it makes at this level of sales.
5 List as many generic ways to differentiate a product or service as you can think of. Alongside them jot down what you need to do to sustain these differences.
6 Develop a market research questionnaire to find out what benefits existing customers of a health club are looking for from their membership.
7 Develop a market research plan to evaluate the commercial potential of opening a shop selling sportswear in a small market town.
8 Select a product or service from Exercise 1. Team up with two other students, one as a customer, another as an observer. Conduct a role-playing sales interview with the customer lasting 15 minutes. Make certain each of you understands the role you are playing. Plan your interview using the outline contained in this chapter. When it is finished, get the observer to give you feedback on how you performed.

References

Bayus, B.L. (1985) 'Word-of-Mouth: The Indirect Effects of Marketing Efforts', *Journal of Advertising Research*, 25(3), June/July.
Brady, G. (1999) 'New Rules for Start-ups', *e-business*, December.
Carson, D., Cromie, S., McGowan, P. and Hill, J. (1995) *Marketing and Entrepreneurship in SMEs*, London: Prentice Hall.
Chaston, I. (2000) *Entrepreneurial Marketing: Competing by Challenging Convention*, Basingstoke: Macmillan – now Palgrave Macmillan.

Additional resources . . .

Sources of Information, Help and Advice in the UK

There are many sources of help and advice in the UK. The most comprehensive single source is the British Library Business and IP (Intellectual Property) Centre in London (www.bl.uk/bipc). The free Reader Pass gives you access to the Library's collection of over 150 million items – books, manuscripts, maps, newspapers, magazines, patents, prints and drawings, photographs and more. You can find images and sounds to aid in the creative process, technical literature to aid in scientific discovery and market information to help develop your competitive strategy. There is information on market size, trends, competition and target customers including hundreds of market research reports from companies such as Mintel, Datamonitor and Frost and Sullivan covering a huge variety of industries. They offer free online access to databases giving company, financial and industrial information such as Fame, Amadeus, OnSource, Lexis-Nexis and Dialog. The British Library also houses the most comprehensive collection of patent specifications in the world – currently over 50 million specifications from 40 countries – and provides access to the most up-to-date literature on patents, trademarks, designs and copyright, together with access to

Practical help and advice – support the application of theory to the practice of start-up

...tions such as the local Chamber of ...es them access to certain support and ... largely self-selecting, self-regulating ... developed their own rather onerous ... provided by these associations vary ...ces are predominantly low-cost, low-...her words they can provide you with ...nerally attract a higher proportion of ...iding good opportunities for local

...cottish counterparts, Local Enterprise ...ely private sector boards of manage-...rly in Investors in People), diagnostic ...information and advice on grants and ...s of Scottish Enterprise and Highlands ...consultancy, larger grant aids infra-...nett et al., 1994).

...d through the Business Link network, ...Vales through Business Connect. These ...evral advice on business and grant and ...ich as marketing, exports, innovation ... to offer a greater range of ... mainly by government and ...ess Link has an excellent, ...connections to other relevant

...ncies around the UK. Their ...ents or LSC/LEC contracts,

Checklist of Regulations to be met in Setting up a Business in the UK

The following list summarises some of the main UK regulations. The Business Link website has an interactive tool which tells you what licences and permits your particular business may need in addition to these: www.businesslink.gov.uk/bdotg/action/lfilter. The website also contains hyperlinks to relevant local authorities.

Additional exercises and learning resources – cases, further readings, journals and websites help learning

Entrepreneurship Exercises

1 Are you really entrepreneurial?

1 Go to the electronic version of the GET test that is available on the website accompanying this book (www.palgrave.com/business/burns). Answer the questions and review the analysis provided. Do you have the character traits of an entrepreneur? Append a print-out of the analysis provided and outline why you agree or disagree with it giving concrete examples of your behaviour to support your views.

2 If for any reason you cannot obtain the test, try answering the following questions:

		Yes	No
1	Do you work hard at things that interest you?	☐	☐
2	Are you a self-starter, somebody who does not need pushing?	☐	☐
3	Are you the sort of person who frequently has new ideas?	☐	☐
4	Do these ideas usually get implemented?	☐	☐
5	Do you try to do things differently?	☐	☐
6	Are you willing to put in the extra hours to get things done?	☐	☐
7	Are you willing to do without holidays for the sake of your business?	☐	☐
8	Have you a supportive family that does not object to you putting in those extra hours?	☐	☐
9	Do you usually do your own thing rather than follow the crowd?	☐	☐
10	Do you set yourself goals and gain satisfaction from achieving them?	☐	☐
11	When things go wrong do you press on regardless if you believe in what you are doing?	☐	☐
12	Can you work alone, if you need to?	☐	☐
13	Do you like money?	☐	☐
14	Are you fairly stable – not too many ups and downs?	☐	☐
15	When you don't get your own way, do you shrug it off, not bear a grudge and just get on with life?	☐	☐
16	Can you motivate others to work with you?	☐	☐
17	Are you willing to take measured risks?	☐	☐

508

Learning Resources

Selected case studies

Chapter 3 or 5: Opportunity recognition

Ajay Bam
2 part case 805-009-1 and 805-010-1. Teaching note 805-009-8
Written by W. Bygrave and C. Hedberg, Babson College.

Chapter 3 or 18: Innovation and new product development

Domino Printing Sciences (A & B).
2 cases 602-031-1 and 602-032-1. Video: 602-031-3. Teaching note: 602-031-8.
Written by K. Goffin, D. Walker and M. Sweeney, Cranfield School of Management, Cranfield, England.

Chapters 5, 6 and 14: Business start-up

Fariba (A) and (B).
Cases 803-012-1 and 803-013-1. Video 803-012-3. Teaching note 803-012-8.
Written by P. Clark, D. Molian and R. Brown, Cranfield School of Management, Cranfield University, England.

Michelle Mone and MJM International.
Case 803-044-1. Teaching note 803-044-6.
Written by F. Martin, University of Stirling, Scotland.

Chapter 7: Running a small firm – focus, priorities

Lemmings.
Case 397-033-1. No teaching note.
Written by F. Martin, University of Stirling, Scotland, and C. Craig, Carol Craig Associates.

Chapter 8: Individual entrepreneurs

Richard Branson/Herb Kelleher – Leaders Extraordinaire.
Case 803-005-1. Teaching note: 803-005-8.
Written by V. Sarvai, under the direction of A. Mukund, ICMR Center for Management Research (ICMR), Hyderabad, India.

Richard Branson's Leadership Style.
Case 804-019-1. No teaching note.
Written by D.G. Prasuna and K.B.S. Kumar, ICFAI University Press, India.

Michael Dell – The Man Behind Dell.
Case 402-015-1. Teaching note: 402-015-8.
Written by K. Subhadra, under the direction of A. Mukund, ICFA Center for Management Research (ICMR), Hyderabad, India.

522

. . . Website

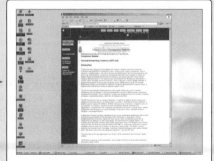

Additional teaching and learning resources on www.palgrave.com/business/burns including the General Enterprise Tendency Test

Part 1

Entrepreneurship and Innovation

1

David and Goliath

Contents

- The stuff of dreams
- The entrepreneurial revolution
- Entrepreneurs and owner-managers
- Defining small firms
- Why small firms are different
- Lifestyle and growth firms
- The UK small firms sector
- Global Entrepreneurship Monitor (GEM)
- The economics of entrepreneurship
- Summary

LEARNING OUTCOMES

By the end of this chapter you should be able to:

- Explain why small firms and entrepreneurs are so important to the economies of modern countries;

- Describe the influences that have contributed to their increasing importance;

- Explain the meaning of the terms entrepreneur and owner-manager and how they are different;

- Explain the differing statistical definitions of small firms;

- Describe the relationship between small firms and entrepreneurship;

- Describe the size and other characteristics of the UK small firms sector compared to other countries and the significant contribution it makes to the economy;

- Explain what data is gathered by the annual GEM surveys;

- Explain some of the economic underpinning for entrepreneurship.

The stuff of dreams

Over the last twenty years the business world has fallen in love with the idea of entrepreneurship. Entrepreneurs have evolved to become super-heroes who valiantly and single-handedly battle to make the most of business opportunities, pulling together resources they do not own, finding willing suppliers and eager customers and, just sometimes, against all the odds, winning out to become millionaires. The entrepreneur has emerged as a new 'cultural hero' (Cannon, 1991; Carr and Beaver, 2002). It is the stuff of dreams. Entrepreneurs are held up as role models. They are said to embody ephemeral qualities that we ought to emulate – freedom of spirit, creativity, vision, zeal. Above all, they have the courage and self-belief to turn their dreams into reality. Is it any wonder that we envy them?

Yet take time to get a perspective on this. Just a century ago, as we entered the twentieth century, the focus was on big. Big was beautiful and size really mattered. Big was respectable, it was political-establishment. Big was the future. It offered economies of scale; mass production that brought well-being, if not wealth, to the masses. It was how the Western democracies would keep the common man, not only in food, shelter and life's necessities, but also in his place. It even spawned its own professional elite – managers. Whilst this has been a fundamental activity throughout history, the recognition and study of it as a discipline and profession is a thoroughly modern, twentieth century phenomenon. Harvard Business School awarded its first Masters degree in the discipline in 1910. And all of this was based upon the best practices in large corporations. Business Schools have reflected the wider establishment view and traditionally eschewed the arts of running a small business and largely ignored the skills of entrepreneurialism (Crainer and Dearlove, 1998).

But have small firms, like David, suddenly triumphed over the Goliath of large firms? In fact small firms, new firms and entrepreneurs never went away. And in the later part of the last century reality began to dawn. In 1974 E. F. Schumacher, in his somewhat romantic book *Small is Beautiful* asserted that giant organisations and increased specialisation resulted in economic inefficiency, environmental pollution and inhumane working conditions and proposed a system of intermediate technology based on smaller working units. Others began to doubt even the hard-nosed economic orthodoxy. In 1983 Jim Dewhurst wrote:

> In all the short history of modern business there is nothing so strange as this. On the one hand we have the traditional belief in the rightness and power of size. Rationalisation, standardisation and concentration are the watchwords. Economies of scale rule the industrial world. And in the UK we have gone further along this road of concentration than any other country in the world. Yet this predilection for economic orthodoxy has not brought us economic success. (Dewhurst and Burns, 1983)

The reality is that large firms were not so much the future of business but the natural consequence of businesses being set up by entrepreneurs and then growing. Unfortunately, like many things in life, they have a natural life expectancy and prolonging this is not always beneficial – to the firm or to society. According to Arie de Geus (1997) large organisations have proved amazingly inept at survival. He quoted a Dutch survey showing the average corporate life expectancy in Japan and

Europe was 12.5 years. 'The average life expectancy of a multinational corporation – the Fortune 500 or equivalent – is between 40 and 50 years.' The reality is that large companies die young, or at least their ownership changes fairly quickly.

In the last twenty years we have come to realise that new firms have done more to create wealth than firms at any time before them – ever! Ninety-five per cent of the wealth of the USA has been created since 1980. When Bill Gates founded Microsoft, IBM dominated the computer market with over 70 per cent of the market and more cash on its balance sheet than the sales of the rest of the industry. Since then its share price has plummeted and its workforce was slashed as it struggled to stay alive, whilst Dell has prospered to become one of the biggest manufacturers and marketers of PCs in the world. By 1997, one in every three households in the USA – 37 per cent or 35 million households – had at least one person who was involved in a primary role in a new or emerging business (*Economic News*, 1997).

Also over the last twenty years people have begun to appreciate the sheer proportion of firms that can be described as small – by any definition, in any country. Small firms, virtually no matter how they are defined, make up at least 95 per cent of enterprises in the European Community. At the same time, their contribution to the economies of their countries began to be appreciated. It was David Birch (1979) who, arguably, started this process with his seminal research which showed that 81.5 per cent of net new jobs in the USA, between 1969–76, were created by small firms (under

Case insight

We start with what is probably the outstanding business success story of a generation. Born in 1955 in Seattle, **Bill Gates** and his friend Paul Allen, 'begged, borrowed and bootlegged' time on his school's computer to undertake software commissions. The two went to Harvard University together, using the University's computer to start their own business. Bill's big break came when he approached Altair, a computer company in Albuquerque, New Mexico, trying to sell it a customised version of BASIC , the programming language for the PC it produced. The only problem was that, at the time, he and Paul Allen had not finished writing it. He had a vision of what it would look like and how it would operate, but no software. That was not finished until some weeks later and with it **Microsoft** came about. The package was later licensed to Apple, Commodore and IBM. IBM then commissioned Microsoft to develop its own operating system and that was how Microsoft Disk Operating System (MS DOS) was born. Founded in the late 1970s, by 1980 Microsoft was seen as a successful start-up with turnover of £8 million from just 38 employees.

Since then Microsoft's growth has been amazing. Microsoft is now the world's largest software company producing a range of products and services, including the Windows operating system and Office software suite. By 2005 Microsoft employed some 61 000 people and made profits of over $12 billion on turnover of just under $40 billion – not bad for a business only 30 years old. And its ambitions are still anything but small. The company has expanded into markets such as video game consoles, interactive television, and internet access. With its core markets maturing, it is targeting services for growth, looking to transform its software applications into web-based services. Microsoft has also reached a settlement to end an ongoing antitrust investigation, agreeing to uniformly license its operating systems and allow manufacturers to include competing software with Windows.

500 employees). The general pattern has been repeated since. Small, growing firms have outstripped large ones in terms of job generation, year after year. At times when larger companies retrenched, smaller firms continued to offer job opportunities. There are now about 10 million self-employed people in the USA and it has been estimated that small firms now generate some 50 per cent of GDP and over 50 per cent of exports now come from firms employing less than 20 people.

Europe lags a little behind the USA. Overall in the EU small firms generate 66 per cent of employment. In Italy the proportion is 79 per cent, in France it is 63 per cent and in Germany it is 60 per cent. In the UK they generate 62 per cent of employment and over 25 per cent of GDP. With some 4 million small firms, the UK now has one of the highest business start-up rates in Europe. By just about any measure the contribution small firms make to the economy of any country is increasing and their importance is now fully recognised.

But the focus is not just on small firms. It is also on high-growth firms. Despite being few in number, high-growth businesses are disproportionately important to national economies. Harrison and Taylor (1996) claim that in the USA it has been estimated that, whilst 15 000 medium sized businesses represent just 1 per cent of all businesses, they generate a quarter of all sales and they employ a fifth of all private sector labour. In the UK, Storey *et al.* (1987) asserted that 'out of every 100 small firms, the fastest growing four firms will create half the jobs in the group over a decade' – an assertion that has stood the test of time.

This book looks at a range of things that make up this whole romanticised, but blurred, vision – entrepreneurs and small business. It looks at entrepreneurs. Who are they? Are they born rather than developed? What do they do? What is their link with the process of innovation, so loved by governments in most countries? Can entrepreneurs manage large firms or do they have to change as the business grows? Are entrepreneurs any different from managers or leaders? Are they any different from owner-managers? Are they any different from managers of small firms generally? And, the important question for this millennium, can entrepreneurship be engendered in larger companies or other sorts of organisations?

The book looks at small firms. Are all small firms the same? Are owner-managed small firms really different from any others? What are the skills you need to manage a small firm and a growing firm? What are the particular problems small firms face and how can they be overcome? This book is now also about big firms. Can corporate entrepreneurship be made to flourish? How are the entrepreneurial leaders of tomorrow to be crafted?

The book looks at start-ups and growing firms. How does the start-up happen? Are some people more likely to start up a business than others? What are the qualities and skills required to ensure a successful start-up? How do you pull together the necessary resources? What sectors do small firms have the best chances in? Should they be encouraged to 'go international' at an early age? What marketing strategies should they use? Are growth businesses different in any way from the 'normal' small firm? Are the particular problems they face as they grow predictable and how can they be overcome? Are international start-ups any different from the traditional sort? How should growth be financed? What skills are needed to grow the firm? Are there business strategies that are more likely to work than others? Can you spot 'winners'?

Case insight

Michael Dell purchased his first computer – an Apple II – in 1980 and immediately took it apart to see how it was built. Only three years later he started a lucrative business selling upgraded PCs and add-on components out of his dormitory room at the University of Texas with capital of only $1000. Michael registered the name **Dell Computer Corporation** in 1984 when he decided to leave college and start selling custom-built computers directly to end-users, ignoring the more normal channel of selling mass-produced computers through computer resellers. This not only eliminated the substantial middleman mark-up, but also the costly inventories required.

'We built the company around a systematic process: give customers the high-quality computers they want at a competitive price as quickly as possible, backed by great service.' (Dell, 1999)

Since then Dell has grown at five times the industry average growth rate to become one of the biggest manufacturers and marketers of PCs in the world. The company's share price has reflected this success, increasing 36 000 per cent in the last decade. Michael is now CEO and Chairman of a $18 billion company.

Michael Dell started life as an entrepreneur, but to grow a successful international organisation of this size in such a short time demonstrates that, like Bill Gates, he has become a truly excellent and exceptional entrepreneurial leader.

→

The book also looks at family firms and the social role they play within the family structure. Does being a family firm make any difference to how they operate? How do families deal with the succession from one owner-manager to another? Are the particular problems they face predictable and how can they be overcome?

Finally this book looks at social entrepreneurship. Can the qualities and skills of the entrepreneur be transferred to the social, public or civic sectors? What does this mean and how can it be achieved? With over thirty years of research into entrepreneurship and small business there are answers to many of these questions. This book will take a conceptual perspective to develop a theoretical framework for understanding the area and, based on this, move forward to show how many of these concepts may be operationalised and developed into practical help in successfully launching and growing a business – indeed any organisation.

The entrepreneurial revolution

What we are seeing now is nothing short of an entrepreneurial revolution. The major factor causing this is change and the pace of change is accelerating. Change itself has changed to become discontinuous, abrupt but all pervasive. And small, entrepreneurial firms are better able to cope. Their flexibility and speed of response to changing market circumstances is well documented. In a turbulent world, full of uncertainties, they seem better able to survive and prosper. This is the essence of their success – their ability to spot an opportunity arising out of change or even create it and then focus resources on delivering what the market wants quickly. In essence they are expert in innovation. And that often means taking risks that larger businesses are unwilling or unable to take. This all boils down to one word – entrepreneurship. It is the entrepreneurial small firms that have been able to capitalise most on the turbulent world we face today – entrepreneurial firms led by founders like Bill Gates, Michael Dell, Richard Branson, and Anita Roddick.

A number of other influences have accelerated this trend towards smaller firms. Firstly there has been the shift in most economies away from manufacturing towards the service sectors where small firms often flourish because of their ability to deliver a personalised, flexible, tailor-made service at a local level. The 'deconstruction' of larger firms into smaller, more responsive units concentrating on their core activities, often sub-contracting many of their other activities to smaller firms, has also contributed to the trend. Large firms and even the public sector became leaner and fitter in the 1980s in a bid to reduce fixed costs and reduce risks. Small firms have benefited, although they may be seen as dependent on large ones.

> 'We now stand on the threshold of a new age – the age of revolution. In our minds, we know the new age has already arrived: in our bellies, we're not sure we like it. For we know it is going to be an age of upheaval, of tumult, of fortunes made and unmade at head-snapping speed. For change has changed. No longer is it additive. No longer does it move in a straight line. In the twenty first century, change is discontinuous, abrupt, seditious.'
>
> **Gary Hamel**, author (2000)

Technology has played its part. It has influenced the trend in three ways. Firstly, the new technologies that swept the late twentieth century have been pioneered by new, rapidly growing firms. Small firms have pioneered innovation in computers and the internet, although only time will tell whether these markets will start to consolidate and amalgamate into larger units as they mature. Secondly, these technologies have actually facilitated the growth of self-employment and small business by easing communication, encouraging working from home and allowing smaller and smaller market segments to be serviced. Indeed information has become a product in its own right and one that can be generated anywhere around the world and transported at the touch of a button. Finally, many new technologies, for example in printing, have reduced fixed costs so that production can be profitable in smaller, more flexible units.

Social and market trends have also accelerated the growth of small firms. Firstly, customers increasingly expect firms to address their particular needs. Market niches are becoming slimmer and markets more competitive – better served by smaller firms. Secondly, people want to control their own destiny more. After periods of high unemployment, they now see self-employment as more attractive and more secure than employment. Redundancy pushed many people into self-employment at the same time as the new 'enterprise culture' gave it political and social respectability. The growth of 'new age' culture and 'alternative' lifestyles have also encouraged the growth of a whole new range of self-employment opportunities.

Entrepreneurs and owner-managers

Before we go much further we need to define some terms. There is no universally accepted definition of the term entrepreneur. The *Oxford English Dictionary* defines an entrepreneur as 'a person who attempts to profit by risk and initiative'. This definition emphasises that entrepreneurs exercise a high degree of initiative and are willing to take a high degree of risk. But it covers a wide range of occupations, including that of a paid assassin. No wonder there is an old adage that if you scratch an entrepreneur you will find a 'spiv' (somebody who makes a living from unlawful work). The difference is more than just one of legality. Therefore a question you might ask is, how do they do it?

Back in the 1800s, Jean-Baptist Say, the French economist, said: 'entrepreneurs shift economic resources from an area of lower productivity into an area of higher productivity and greater yield'. In other words entrepreneurs create value by exploiting some form of change, for example in technology, materials, prices or demographics. We call this process innovation and this is an essential tool for entrepreneurs. We shall examine it in greater detail in Chapter 3. Entrepreneurs, therefore, create new demand or find new ways of exploiting existing markets. They identify a commercial opportunity and then exploit it.

> 'We learned the importance of ignoring conventional wisdom and doing things our way ... It's fun to do things that people don't think are possible or likely. Its also exciting to achieve the unexpected.' (Dell, 1999)
> **Michael Dell**
> ➡

Central to all of this is change. Change causes disequilibrium in markets out of which come the commercial opportunities that entrepreneurs thrive upon. To them change creates opportunities that they can exploit. Sometimes they initiate the change themselves – they innovate in some way. At other times they exploit change created by the external environment. Often in doing so they destroy the established order and complacency of existing social and economic systems. How entrepreneurs manage and deal with change is central to their character and essential if they are to be successful. Most 'ordinary people' find change threatening. Entrepreneurs welcome it because it creates opportunities that can be exploited and often create it through innovation.

Another key feature of entrepreneurs is their willingness to accept risk and uncertainty. In part this is simply the consequence of their eagerness to exploit change. However, the scale of uncertainty they are willing to accept is altogether different from that of other managers. This high degree of uncertainty they are willing to accept reflects itself in the risks they take for the business and for themselves. And for some this can become so addictive they become 'serial entrepreneurs', best suited to continuing to start up businesses and unwilling to face the tedium of day-to-day management.

It is no wonder that entrepreneurship has been described as 'a slippery concept not easy to work into a formal analysis because it is so closely associated with the temperament or personal qualities of individuals' (Penrose, 1959). We shall examine it in more detail in the next chapter where we attempt to differentiate entrepreneurs

---

Case insight

Richard Branson is probably the best known entrepreneur in Britain today and his name is closely associated with all the many businesses that carry the **Virgin** brand name. He is outward-going and an excellent self-publicist. He has been called an 'adventurer', taking risks that few others would contemplate. This shows itself in his personal life with his transatlantic power boating and round-the-world ballooning exploits as well as in his business life where he has challenged established firms like British Airways and Coca-Cola.

Now over 50 years old, his business life started as an 18-year-old schoolboy when he launched *Student* magazine, selling advertising space from a phone booth. He started selling mail-order records but soon decided he needed a retail site. He got his first store, above a shoe shop on London's Oxford Street, rent free on the grounds that it could not be let and would generate more customers for the shoe shop. It was a great success and Richard next branched into the music business with Virgin Records.

Since those early days the Virgin brand has found its way onto aircraft, trains, cola, vodka, mobile phones, cinemas, a radio station, financial services and most recently the internet. In 1986 Virgin was floated but later reprivatised because Richard did not like to be accountable for his actions to institutional shareholders. In 1999 a 49 per cent stake in the airline was sold to Singapore Airlines. Today Virgin describes itself as a 'branded venture capital company', having created over 200 businesses.

'Despite employing over 20 000 people, Virgin is not a big company – it's a big brand made up of lots of small companies. Our priorities are the opposite of our large competitors ... For us our employees matter most. It just seems common sense that if you have a happy, well motivated workforce, you're much more likely to have happy customers. And in due course the resulting profits will make your shareholders happy. Convention dictates that big is beautiful, but every time one of our ventures gets too big we divide it up into smaller units ... Each time we do this, the people involved haven't had much more work to do, but necessarily they have a greater incentive to perform and a greater zest for their work.' (Branson, 1998)

→

from others by their character traits. We shall also address the question of whether entrepreneurs are born or made.

Notice in these definitions that there is no mention of small firms. Indeed, Richard Branson, surely a successful entrepreneur in his own right, said

I am often asked what it is to be an 'entrepreneur' and there is no simple answer. It is clear that successful entrepreneurs are vital for a healthy, vibrant and competitive economy. If you look around you, most of the largest companies have their foundations in one or two individuals who have the determination to turn a vision into reality (Anderson, 1995).

The point is that entrepreneurs are defined by their actions, not by the size of organisation they happen to work within. Any manager can be entrepreneurial. The manager of a small firm may not be an entrepreneur – an important distinction that is often missed in the literature. Equally entrepreneurs can exist within large firms, even ones that they did not set up themselves, and how large firms encourage and deal with this is an important issue for them.

Anita Roddick may have retired as Chairman of what is now an international public company, but when she opened the first, tiny **Body Shop** in a cobbled back street in Brighton, England in 1976 the roof leaked and the ugly unpainted walls were covered with green garden lattice primarily because it was cheap. The shop had lots of pine shelves but stocked only about a dozen inexpensive, natural cosmetics, herbal creams and shampoos, so pot plants were placed between the products.

Anita was the daughter of Italian immigrants who settled in the small town of Littlehampton and ran the Clifton Cafe. Originally a teacher, she spent some time travelling around the world before returning to England where she met her husband, Gordon. They wanted to travel around the world together and then open a pineapple plantation but first the arrival of one and then a second child forced them to change plans. Instead they opened a restaurant and later a small hotel in Littlehampton. About a month after they opened the first shop Gordon left to ride a horse across the Americas from Buenos Aires to New York. He did not get very far because within a few months it was obvious that Body Shop was going to be an enormous success.

Now the Roddicks rank among the top 100 richest people in the UK and are no longer actively involved with Body Shop. They started up a business that became a multinational enterprise with a life of its own and harvested the fruits of their hard work. They have come a long way from that first small shop in Brighton.

➡

The way our notion of entrepreneur has been crafted has a long history, dating back to Cantillon in 1755. These concepts have shifted and developed. Table 1.1 tries to summarise some of the major developments in the concept. Trying to combine these concepts and definitions together with elements of character, I would propose the following definition for this elusive term:

Entrepreneurs use innovation to exploit or create change and opportunity for the purpose of making profit. They do this by shifting economic resources from an area of lower productivity into an area of higher productivity and greater yield, accepting a high degree of risk and uncertainty in doing so.

You do not have to own a firm to manage it. However, some managers do own the firms they manage and these make up the majority of managers of small firms. These are owner-managers. Sole traders are owner-managers. Limited companies, however, have share capital. The term owner-manager, therefore, needs further refinement. An obvious one would be that to qualify as an owner-manager requires ownership (or beneficial ownership) of over 50 per cent of the share capital, thereby controlling the business.

These definitions are, however, restrictive. For example, if a company is owned equally by two managers they would not be called owner-managers. Would this be any different if it were a partnership? Many people would call the managers in both situations owner-managers. But where does this dilution begin and end? How many managers do you need to own part of the business before they cease being called owner-managers? Are all the employees of the John Lewis Partnership owner-managers? The real issue is not ownership, but control. Owner-managers significantly control the operations of their firm on a day-to-day basis. Notice,

Table 1.1 The antecedence of modern entrepreneurship

Date	Author	Concept
1755	Cantillon	Introduced the concept of entrepreneur from 'entreprendre' (ability to take charge).
1803, 1817	Jean Baptist Say	Emphasised the ability of the entrepreneur to 'marshal' resources in order to respond to unfulfilled opportunities.
1871	Carl Menger	Noted the ability of entrepreneurs to distinguish between 'economic goods' – those with a market or exchange value – and all others.
1893	Ely and Hess	Attributed to entrepreneurs the ability to take integrated action in the enterprise as a whole, combining roles in capital, labour, enterprise and entrepreneur.
1911, 1928	Schumpeter	Envisioned that entrepreneurs proactively 'created' opportunity using 'innovative combinations' which often included 'creative destruction' of passive or lethargic economic markets.
1921	Knight	Suggested that entrepreneurs were concerned with the 'efficiency' in economic factors by continually reducing waste, increasing savings and thereby creating value, implicitly understanding the opportunity-risk-reward relationship.
1948, 1952, 1967	Hayek	Continued the Austrian tradition of analytical entrepreneurs giving them capabilities of discovery and action, recognising the existence of information asymmetry which they could exploit.
1975, 1984, 1985	Shapero	Attributed a 'judgement' ability to entrepreneurs to identify 'credible opportunities' depending on two critical antecedents – perceptions of 'desirability' and 'feasibility' from both personal and social viewpoints.
1974	Drucker	Attributed to entrepreneurs a sense to 'foresee' market trends and make a timely response.
1973, 1979, 1997, 1999	Kirzner	Attributed to entrepreneurs a sense of 'alertness' to identify opportunities and exploit them accordingly.

Source: Adapted from Etemad, H. (2004) 'International Entrepreneurship as a Dynamic Adaptive System: Towards a Grounded Theory', *Journal of International Entrepreneurship*, 2.

however, that this is a question of judgement and therefore this term, as with the term entrepreneur, is likely to be used very loosely.

Notice also that, using these definitions, owner-managers need not be entrepreneurs. Indeed, most owner-managers are not entrepreneurial. This book argues that entrepreneurs can be described in terms of their character and judged by their actions and one of the major factors differentiating them from owner-managers is the degree of innovation they practise.

Many managers of small firms do not own or control the firm they are employed by. The firm is controlled by its larger, parent company. The manager is therefore not

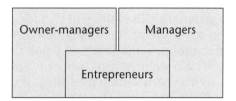

Figure 1.1 Managers, owner-managers and entrepreneurs

an owner-manager. Paradoxically, however, they might be entrepreneurs, depending on the way they act. Figure 1.1 shows these relationships. Managers are different people from owner-managers, but both can be entrepreneurs.

Defining small firms

As with the other terms, there is no uniformly acceptable definition of a small firm. Back in 1971, what is usually held to be a definitive report on the state of small business in Britain at the time, the Bolton Report (Bolton, 1971), made heavy weather of providing a statistical definition. Recognising that one definition would not cover industries as divergent as manufacturing and service, it used eight definitions for various industry groups. These ranged from under 200 employees for manufacturing firms to over £50 000 turnover (in 1971) for retailing, and up to five vehicles or less for road transport. So many definitions clearly cause practical problems. What is more, definitions based on financial criteria suffer from inherent problems related to inflation and currency translation.

Not withstanding this, the 1985 UK Companies Act which has special less stringent reporting requirements for small and medium-sized firms, uses the following definitions:

Criterion	Small business	Medium business
Maximum annual turnover	£2.8 million	£11.2 million
Maximum annual balance sheet total	£1.4 million	£5.6 million
Maximum number of employees	50	250

The European Commission has coined the term 'small and medium enterprise' (SME) and in 1996 defined it as an organisation employing fewer than 250 people. This is disaggregated into three parts and, to qualify as a SME, both the employee and the independence criteria must be satisfied plus either the turnover or balance sheet criteria:

Criterion	Micro business	Small business	Medium business
Maximum number of employees	9	49	249
Maximum annual turnover	–	€7 million	€40 million
Maximum annual balance sheet total (total assets)	–	€5 million	€27 million
Maximum percentage owned by one, or jointly by several, enterprise(s) not satisfying the same criteria	–	25%	25%

Despite the independence criteria, SMEs could still include organisations managed by non-owner-managers. Even so, some of them may be entrepreneurs. We are still, therefore, left with our three groups – managers of small firms, owner-managers and entrepreneurs – without any clear delineation. However, it is likely to be true that the smaller the firm, particularly the owner-managed firm, the more important the personality and influence of the managers, be they entrepreneurial or not.

Being a small firm is not just about size, defined in simple statistical terms. Small firms also have important defining characteristics. The Bolton Committee described a small firm as satisfying three criteria, all of which defy practical statistical application:

1 *Market influence.* In economic terms, the small firm has a small share of the market. Therefore it is not large enough to influence the prices or national quantities of the good or service that it provides. Unfortunately, two fundamental problems arise with this, firstly with the definition of market and secondly with the ability of the small firm to influence price and the quantity sold in that market. Many of the most successful small firms operate in market niches so slim that they dominate that market segment, with no clear competition, and they can and do influence both price and quantity sold. In that respect Bolton's definition looks naïve and dated and was probably influenced by the economists' definition of perfect competition. It is certainly not one that I or most entrepreneurs would agree with.
2 *Independence.* The small firm is independent in the sense that it does not form part of a larger enterprise and that the owner-managers are free from outside control in taking their principal decisions. This means that only owner-managed firms are considered small firms. This is clearly unsatisfactory if you believe, as I do, that there are certain specific characteristics about managing a small firm that mark it out as different from a large one.
3 *Personal influence.* The small firm is managed in a personalised way and not through the medium of a formalised management structure. This person is involved in all aspects of the management of the business and is involved in all major decision-making. Frequently there is little devolution or delegation of authority.

Small firms start to make managerial appointments when they have some 10–20 employees and at this point they start to take on the appearance of more formal structures (Atkinson and Meager, 1994). Nevertheless, this third point is the key to a definition of the real small firm – the one with potential, the one that economists cannot understand, the one that is so different from the large firm. Essentially the real small firm can be described as having '*two arms, two legs and a giant ego*' – in other words it is an extension of a person, be he/she owner-manager or entrepreneur, to the firm. The personality of the manager is imprinted on the way it operates and the personal risks they and their family face if the firm fails influences how business decisions are made.

Why small firms are different

Small firms are not just scaled down versions of large ones. They go about their business in a number of fundamentally different ways. The key to understanding how a particular small firm goes about management and why and how decisions are made is to understand the personality of the owner-manager. Their personality and their behavioural characteristics will strongly influence this. More than large firms, small firms are social entities that revolve around personal relationships. They approach risk and uncertainty in a particular way that sometimes may seem far from rational, which explains why they are so little understood by economists.

There are a number of other characteristics that are typical of small firms and underline their different approach to management and business. The first is that they are typically short of cash. They cannot raise capital in the same way that a large company can. This has major strategic implications. Firstly, it constrains the strategies that they can adopt. For example, they cannot afford to adopt expensive advertising and promotion campaigns, so instead managers develop close relationships with customers and prospective customers, investing their time rather than money. Secondly, it dictates that business decisions must have a quick pay-off and therefore decision-making is short-term. For a growing business it means that raising finance becomes a major strategic issue and relationships with financing institutions such as banks and venture capitalists can become a major resource issue.

The second characteristic is that small firms are likely to operate in a single market, or a limited range of markets, probably offering a limited range of products or services. This means that their scope of operations is, or at least should be, limited. In that sense they face fewer strategic issues than larger firms and often business strategy is synonymous with marketing strategy. However, unlike large firms, they find it difficult to diversify their business risk, which is another reason they find it hard to raise finance.

Related to this is the characteristic that most small firms are over reliant on a small number of customers. This means that they are particularly vulnerable to losing any one customer and the effect on the firm of such a loss will be disproportionately large. This is yet another reason why they are riskier prospects than large firms and find difficulty raising finance.

The final characteristic is the effect of scale on the economics of the business and how that translates into financial evaluation and decision-making. Most Business Finance textbooks are written with large companies in mind; consequently, whilst the principles they espouse are sound, the examples they use and generalisations that result are not. For example, taking on an additional member of staff for a small firm is a major strategic decision involving relatively large sums of money that represent a step increase in their fixed costs. Consequently they are reluctant to do so unless absolutely necessary. Yet in most Business Finance textbooks wage costs are treated as a variable cost, a view that can only be justified when there are a large number of staff. As we shall see later in this book, this error can lead to quite incorrect business decisions being made. It is little wonder that managers of small firms have little faith in professional advisors and accountants. Banks have for some time realised that traditional financial analysis says little about the health of the small firm and have started to broaden their approach.

These characteristics start to combine to distinguish small firms from large ones on a basis other than scale. Wynarczyk *et al.* (1993), strongly influenced by Casson (1982), argue that the much greater role played by uncertainty, innovation and firm evolution is the real defining characteristic of small firms. Small firms face more uncertain markets than large firms. They have a limited customer base and often cannot influence price. The owner-manager's own aspirations and motivations may also be uncertain. The effect of this high degree of uncertainty is to force decision-making to become short-term. Small firms also innovate in a particular way that we shall explore in a subsequent chapter that makes them different to large firms. The final distinguishing characteristic is evolution – the recognition that the nature, style and functions of management change considerably as the small firm grows and evolves. Once more, we shall explore this in detail in a subsequent chapter, in particular looking at the 'stage theories' of how firms grow.

Lifestyle and growth firms

Small firms and entrepreneurship have often been linked together in a very loose fashion. They are broadly overlapping sets. As Storey and Sykes (1996) explained,

> the small firm is less concerned with formal systems and its decision-making process will be more judgemental, involving fewer individuals, and can therefore be quicker. It can be much more responsive to changes in the market-place but, conversely, is much less able to influence such developments. Hence the small firm is likely to adjust more quickly than the large firm to situations of market disequilibrium and, in these senses, embodies the characteristics of the classic entrepreneur.

However, this is a question of scale and, just as it was necessary to distinguish between owner-managers and entrepreneurs, it might be useful to distinguish between two categories of small firms:

1 *Lifestyle firms.* These are businesses that are set up primarily to undertake an activity that the owner-manager enjoys or gets some comfort from whilst also providing an adequate income, for example craft-based businesses. They are not set up to grow and, therefore, once a level of activity that provides the adequate income is reached, management becomes routine and tactical. There is probably little thought about strategic management unless things start to go wrong, and the most likely thing to go wrong is that the market changes without the owner-manager realising it. These firms are rarely managed by entrepreneurs and, if they are, the entrepreneur will be extremely frustrated. Most owner-managed firms fall into this category. Many are sole-traders (un-incorporated businesses). However, a lifestyle business can change if the owner-manager's motivations change and they have the entrepreneurial qualities to see it through.

2 *Growth firms.* These are set up with the intention of growth, usually by entrepreneurs. Occasionally a lifestyle business can turn into a growth business unintentionally. However, if the manager does not have entrepreneurial characteristics they are unlikely to succeed in the long run. Rapid growth is risky and creates major problems that must be addressed within very short time frames. Effective strategic management is vital if the firm is to succeed, indeed possibly survive. Notwithstanding this, these firms will face numerous problems and crises as they grow, some of which are predictable, others that are not. This is the classic entrepreneurial firm so beloved by the financial press.

Case insight

In the late 1980s **Julian Leaver** and **Tim Slade** were looking for ways to finance their lifestyle as 'ski-bums' in the French Alps. They travelled the world financed by selling printed T-shirts out of rucksacks. In 1993 they decided to open a clothes shop in London's Fulham Road selling a range of high quality sports clothing. Named after a famous downhill run in Val d'Isère, **Fat Face** really took off, selling both to fashion conscious young people and a 'niche' technical market.

Find out how they got on in Chapter 11.

➜

It is important to realise that the small firm sector is far from homogeneous. Consider issues of size and age of business, sector, location, growth and decline, economic and market conditions. What is more, the people that manage them are many and varied. You do not have to own a small firm to manage it and you certainly do not have to be an entrepreneur. Consider also issues of age, sex, ethnicity, social origins, family relationships and then you start to realise the scale of the complexity.

Generalisations about small firms and the people that manage them are therefore just that – vast generalisations that are supposed to cover what makes up some 95 per cent of firms in most countries. Small firms are not homogeneous but, notwithstanding this, let us try to paint a broad picture of their nature and role in the UK.

The UK small firms sector

Over the last century, until the 1960s, the UK saw a decrease in the importance of small firms, measured in terms of their share of manufacturing employment and output. The proportion of the UK labour force classified as self-employed was at its lowest point in the 1960s. It was no wonder that the Bolton Committee (*op. cit.*), set up in the late 1960s to investigate the role of small firms in the economy, concluded that 'the small firm sector was in a state of long-term decline, both in size and its share of economic activity'. From the 1970s the situation has been reversed. Since then small firms have increased in importance, measured in terms of their number and their share of employment and turnover. The number of small firms continues to rise, as does the number of people classified as self-employed. In 1979 there were only 2.4 million SMEs in the UK (see preceding definition). By 2004 this had grown to 4.3 million – an increase of almost 80 per cent in 25 years.

In fact the number of small firms is now increasing in most advanced countries, as is their share of employment. 99.7 per cent of enterprises in the EU are SMEs (see definition on page 13), compared to 99.9 per cent in the UK. SMEs are a vital part of all EU economies, accounting for two-thirds of turnover in the EU. In the UK this is 51 per cent. They generate 70 per cent of employment across the EU. In the UK this is 59 per cent. And these percentages are increasing year on year. Small firms dominate many service sectors, particularly hotels, catering, retailing and wholesaling, and are important in construction. In the USA it is estimated that small firms now generate 50 per cent of GDP. Small firms are a vital and growing part of business in all countries.

In the UK a range of SME statistics are produced and are available free on the website of the Small Business Service (www.sbs.gov.uk). These are updated annually. The SME statistics for 2004 show that:

- 72.8 per cent of all firms in the UK had no employees (3.1 million).These comprise sole proprietors, partnerships with only self-employed partners and companies with only an employee/director. By definition these firms generated no employment. They generated 7.9 per cent of UK turnover (£190 billion).
- 99.3 per cent of all firms in the UK were classified as small (0–49 employees). These generated 46.8 per cent of employment (10.3 million) and 37 per cent of UK turnover (£888 billion).
- 99.9 per cent of all firms in the UK were classified as SMEs (0–249 employees). These generated 58.5 per cent of employment (12.9 million) and 51.3 per cent of UK turnover (£1231 billion).

These statistics reinforce the fact that most UK small firms really are small, offering no more than self-employment. Most of these are probably lifestyle businesses. Few firms grow to any significant size. And only 0.1 per cent of firms in the UK are 'large' with 250 employees or more. But employment in small firms varies widely from sector to sector. Over 70 per cent of employment in both construction and agriculture is in SMEs. At the other extreme, less than 10 per cent of employment in financial intermediaries is in SMEs. Small firms are not a homogeneous group.

Table 1.2 summarises some international comparisons. SMEs in Europe generate 69.8 per cent of employment, compared to 58.5 per cent in the UK. The average number of people employed by a SME in the UK was estimated as seven in 2003, compared to an EU average of only five. This in turn compares to five in Japan and only three in the USA (European Commission, 2003). Indeed the USA does not compare too well in these statistics since its SME sector generates only 49.1 per cent of employment.

But aggregate statistics can create some misleading conclusions. One widely held misconception is that Britain has a smaller proportion of middle-sized, or 'mittelstand', companies than Germany. The high level of start-ups since the 1980s has made this seem to be the case but Storey (1998) concludes that 'the size structure of the UK and (pre-unification) Germany is in fact closer than between any other two large countries in the European Community'. However, Storey also concludes – and this is evident from Table 1.1 – that employment in the USA, and to a lesser extent the UK, is still more concentrated in very large companies than in other EC countries or Japan.

In the UK, there are also a range of VAT statistics that inform us about SMEs. These are available free on the website of the Small Business Service (www.sbs.gov.uk). Information about VAT registrations and deregistrations is widely used as the best guide to patterns of change in the small-firm sector – levels of entrepreneurship and the health of the business population. They are also used in regional and local economic planning. The net change in business stocks is a particularly important figure that often gets reported in national newspapers. The net change in stock tends to be highly related to the state of the economy. Small firms are particularly vulnerable to economic changes because of their often precarious financing situation. In times when the economy is in recession there tends to be a net decrease in the

Table 1.2 SME international comparisons

	Total	SMEs				Large
		% micro	% small	% medium	Total	
Number of enterprises (x 1000)						
EU (2003)	19 310	92.3	6.5	0.9	99.7	0.3
Japan (2001)	4 703	n.a.	n.a.	n.a.	99.7	0.3
USA (2000)	21 223	94.2	4.8	0.8	99.8	0.2
Number of occupied persons (x 1000)						
EU (2003)	139 710	39.4	17.4	13.0	69.8	30.2
Japan (2001)	38 277	n.a.	n.a.	n.a.	66.9	33.1
USA (2000)	129 635	21.5	15.5	12.1	49.1	50.9
Average number of occupied people per enterprise						
EU (2003)	7	3	19	98	5	1 052
Japan (2001)	8	n.a.	n.a.	n.a.	5	975
USA (2000)	6	1	20	94	3	1 119

Source: European Commission (2003) *2003 Observatory of European SMEs: 2003/8 Highlights from the 2003 Observatory*; available free online at http://ec.europa.eu.int/comm/enterprise/enterprise_policy/analysis/doc/smes_observatory_2003_report8_en.pdf.

stock of businesses and vice versa. So, the 1980s saw a large increase in the stock of registered companies, whereas the stock decreased between 1991 and 1994. From 1995 until 2004 stocks increased. 2004 saw a net increase of only 2000 firms (181 400 registrations less 179 400 deregistrations), the smallest rise since 1995. These statistics are also broken down by sector and region. So, whilst most sectors saw no or a small net increase, the manufacturing and agriculture and fisheries sectors continued a long decline. At the same time London and the South East of England continued to see the largest net increases. One interesting point is that areas with high registrations tend to also have high deregistrations – an effect called 'churning' – indicating that high economic growth may cause or be caused by more firms coming into existence (register) but the increased competition means that more will cease (deregister).

These VAT statistics have also been used to show that the most dangerous time for a new business is in its first three years of existence. Almost 50 per cent of businesses will cease trading within that period. This does not, of course, mean that the closures represent failure in terms of leaving creditors and unpaid debts. Most are simply wound down. Businesses that cease trading do so for a number of reasons. Some will close because the business ceases to be lucrative. Others because of the death or retirement of the proprietor, or changes in their personal motivations and aspirations. Some will simply close to move on to other, more lucrative opportunities. This 'churning effect' of small firms closing and opening is part of the dynamism of the sector as they respond to changing opportunities in the market place and is why the net change in the stock of businesses is more important than the individual number of failures.

Other studies have given an insight into the UK small firms sector. Small firms tend to have lower productivity than large firms, even in the same industry. Firms with fewer than 200 employees had 55 per cent of the productivity (measured in value added per employee) of firms with 1000 or more employees. In the computer and office machinery sectors SME productivity is only a third of that of larger firms. These differences are largely because of lower capital backing. Not surprisingly therefore, the 1998 Workplace Employee Relations Survey (DTI, 1998) showed that employees in SMEs tend to have lower pay and have less job security than in large firms, with employers making extensive use of dismissal as a disciplinary device. Research also indicates that SMEs have a disproportionately high number of 'bad jobs' (McGovern *et al.*, 2004) and higher accident rates (Walters, 2001). The availability of flexible working practices to encourage family-friendly working appears arbitrary in SMEs (Dex and Smith, 2002) and there is low take-up of training initiatives such as NVQs (national vocational qualifications) and IIP (Investors in People) (Matlay, 2002). However it would be wrong to characterise SMEs as poor employers as there is enormous diversity of practice (Barret and Rainnie, 2002; Ram and Edwards, 2003).

Case insight

Stories of successful entrepreneurs always make good reading. And successful entrepreneurs have been with us for many, many years in Britain. **Joseph Cyril Bamford** gave his initials to the ubiquitous yellow hydraulic excavator and digger seen on just about every building site or road works – the **JCB**. In fact JCB became one of the few post-war British industrial success stories. By the time of his death in 2001 the company employed over 4500 people across three continents and had a turnover of £833 million. Over 70 per cent of JCB production is for overseas markets.

Joseph Bamford came from a prosperous Staffordshire engineering family which had been making agricultural equipment since mid-Victorian times. When he returned to civilian life after the Second World War he decided to start up on his own doing what he knew best. Starting his business with only an electric welder he bought for £2.50, he started producing tipping farm trailers from a garage in Uttoxeter, using materials from old air-raid shelters. These sold well, but in 1948 he decided to branch out into hydraulic equipment and, in 1953, went into partnership to produce a range of earth-moving machines before eventually coming up with the famous backhoe loader that combined the two functions of excavator and shovel and became the visual embodiment of the initials JCB.

Joseph Bamford was a paternalistic employer, who provided a social club and a fishing lake next to his factory in Rochester. He ran a tight ship but rewarded effort. He also knew how to get PR. In 1964, when he famously paid his workers £250 000 in bonuses because the company's turnover had topped £8 million, he personally handed out the bonus to each employee standing on the first farm tractor he had designed in 1947.

Joseph Bamford made JCB into one of the most successful privately owned companies in Britain. Eventually the company diversified from his central control into a group of several operating companies. He gave up his chairmanship of the group in 1975, handing it over to his eldest son, now Sir Anthony Bamford, and retired to Montreux, Switzerland where he enjoyed yacht designing and landscape gardening.

●

Small firms vary widely in the resources they allocate to innovation. Of small firms with over 20 employees, about one in ten spends 10 per cent or more of turnover on new product or process development. However, one-third of manufacturing small firms spend nothing at all.

Global Entrepreneurship Monitor (GEM)

GEM is a research programme which was started in 1999 in 10 countries. By 2005 it had been extended to 39 countries. It is a harmonised assessment of the level of national entrepreneurial activity in each of the countries. In the UK it is based upon an annual survey of 22 500 adults of working age. It asks a number of questions but a central one is whether or not they are starting up a business, or already own or manage a business. From this information a figure for total entrepreneurial activity (TEA) is calculated for each country. In 2003 the TEA index for the UK was 6.4 per cent (5.4 per cent in 2002) – in other words 6.4 per cent of the UK population were engaged in some form of entrepreneurial activity (GEM, 2003). The UK ranked 23 out of the 37 in this survey but it ranked higher than all other EU countries apart from Ireland, Spain and Greece. As you might expect, the USA with a score of 12 per cent was higher.

GEM 2003 came up with some interesting conclusions that, by and large, support other research, much of which we shall return to in the next chapter.

- Not surprisingly given actual start-up rates, the 2003 GEM report found that the UK TEA in males at 8.9 per cent was far higher than in females at 3.9 per cent. 'Women are more likely to fear failure, see fewer opportunities, have a lower perception of their skills to start business and are less likely to know an entrepreneur than men.' (GEM, 2003)
- Ethnic minorities were more likely to be involved in start-ups than white people. By and large they have a more positive attitude to entrepreneurship.
- Entrepreneurs were most likely to be in the age range 25 to 34.
- People with higher incomes and better education were more likely to be entrepreneurs.
- UK business start-ups were predominantly UK focused.
- There was a visible *equity* gap between £150 000 and £1 175 000.
- It also concluded that the culture encouraging entrepreneurship in the UK had improved, with more respondents having a positive attitude to entrepreneurship.

Central to the GEM approach is the hypothesis of a causal relationship between entrepreneurial activity in the economy and the level of economic growth – we shall see the economic justification for this in the next section. The GEM model is shown in Figure 1.2. The demand side is represented by entrepreneurial opportunity and the supply side by entrepreneurial capacity. These are affected in different ways by demography, education, economic infrastructure and culture.

GEM is an enormous research endeavour generating quantitative data that can be used for both cross-sectional analysis and, probably most importantly, longitudinal analysis, allowing us to track individuals from entrepreneurial aspiration (called 'nascent entrepreneurship') to action. However, by its own admission problems

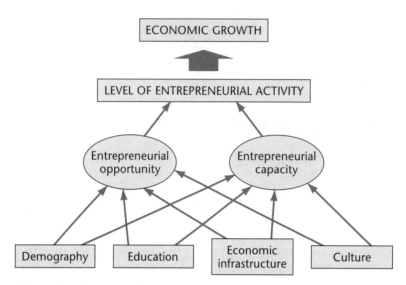

Source: Adapted from *Global Entrepreneurship Monitor (2001) Executive Report*, GEM Project, Babson College/ London Business School, Boston, USA.

Figure 1.2 The GEM approach to measuring entrepreneurial activity

remain in understanding this data and the relationships with 'highly entrepreneurial countries reflecting low economic growth' (GEM, 2003). Obvious methodological problems exist. For example, it does not attempt to measure differences in culture. Also the use of a single questionnaire across all the countries is clearly problematic. Nevertheless data from GEM is increasingly being pored over by econometricians eager to find statistical relationships of any kind, no matter how unsupported by theory or other research. GEM reports can be downloaded free of charge from www.gemconsortium.org/default.asp. There is a range of reports. In 2006, in addition to the 2003 Global Report, there were special reports on Women and Enterprise, High-Expectation Entrepreneurs and a Financing Report, as well as a UK Social Entrepreneurship Report.

The economics of entrepreneurship

The question arises as to whether there are any underlying theories to explain the growth in number and importance of small firms. Marxist theory predicts that capitalism will degenerate into economies dominated by a small number of large firms and society will polarise between those that own them and those that work in them. To a Marxist, the rise of small firms is just another, subtler way for this trend to manifest itself. The small firms are dependent upon larger firms for their custom and well being. They absorb risk and push down pay and conditions for workers as they are rarely unionised. However, the successful growth of so many small firms over the period, the increasing fragmentation of industries and markets and the increasing popularity of self-employment by choice would seem to belie this theory.

People like Fritz Schumacher (1974) would have us believe that the growth of small firms is part of a social trend towards a more democratic and responsive society – 'small is beautiful'. To him the quality of life is more important than materialism. He is very much in favour of 'intermediate technology' – simpler, cheaper and easier to use – with production on a smaller scale and more locally based. However, the technologies that fuelled the growth of small firms at the end of the twentieth century were far from simple and for many quality of life improved alongside materialism. Which leads us on to free-market economics. At one extreme the growth of small firms can be seen as the triumph of the free market and the success of the 'enterprise culture' promulgated by politicians like Ronald Reagan and Margaret Thatcher. Increasing numbers of small firms are the natural result of increased competition and a drive to prevent private and public monopoly. But what exactly does economic theory have to say about small firm creation?

Traditional industrial economists would explain the growth of new firms in terms of industry profitability, growth, barriers to entry and concentration. However, they are more concerned with 'entry' to an industry, rather than whether this is by a new or an existing firm. They assume an endless supply of potential new entrants. They would say that entry to an industry is high when expected profits and growth are high. Entry is deterred by high barriers to entry and high concentration, when collusion between existing firms can take place. However, much of this work does not specifically consider the role of new or smaller firms. Indeed, Acs and Audretsch (1989) show that entry by small, primarily new, firms is not the same as entry by large firms and that small firm birth is lower in highly concentrated industries and ones where innovation plays an important part.

By way of contrast, labour market economists have been more interested in what influences individuals to become potential entrants to an industry by becoming self-employed. Psychologists have also contributed greatly to this work which has focused on the character or personality of the individual, the antecedent influences on them such as age, sex, education, employment status, experience and ethnicity as well as other societal influences. This work has proved far more successful and informative and we examine it in detail in the next chapter.

The link between entrepreneurship – the creation of new firms – and economic growth has until recently been far from clear, as far as economists are concerned. In fact, traditional theories tended to suggest entrepreneurship impeded rather than encouraged growth. Only the recent theories of 'industrial evolution' have linked entrepreneurship and economic growth (Jovanovic, 1982; Lambson, 1991; Hopenhayn, 1992; Audretsch, 1995; Ericson and Pakes, 1995 and Klepper, 1996). These new theories focus on change as the central phenomenon and emphasise the role knowledge plays in charting a way through this. Innovation is seen as the key to entry, growth and survival for an enterprise and the way entire industries change over time. But the information they need to innovate is crucial – being inherently uncertain, asymmetric (one party may have more than another) and associated with high transaction costs. As a result there are differences in the expected value of new ideas and people therefore have an incentive to leave secure employment to start up a new enterprise in order to capitalise on a commercial idea they believe in more than others. Once established, if economies of scale are important (see Chapter 5), the enterprise must grow, simply to survive. In this way the economic performance of nations is linked to how well the potential from innovation is tapped – start-ups encouraged and growth facilitated. And inherent in the process is churning – firms being displaced by newer, more innovative rivals.

These new evolutionary theories, supported by empirical evidence, therefore state that entrepreneurship encourages economic growth for three reasons:

1 It encourages competition by increasing the number of enterprises. Whilst this increases growth in itself, it is a cumulative phenomenon because competition is more conducive to knowledge externalities – new ideas – than is local monopoly. And so entrepreneurship encourages entrepreneurship – a factor we return to in the next chapter.
2 It is a mechanism for 'knowledge spillovers' – transmission of knowledge from its point of origin to other individuals or organisations. Knowledge spillover is an important mechanism underlying endogenous growth and start-ups – entrepreneurs – are seen as particularly adept at appropriating knowledge from other sources. In other words entrepreneurs spot opportunities and innovate – a factor we shall also return to in the next chapter.
3 It generates diversity and variety among enterprises in any location. Each enterprise is in some way different or unique and this influences economic growth.

Summary

In the late twentieth century the focus of business interest shifted from large to small firms. Their contribution to the economy became recognised as did the shortcomings of large companies. Start-up entrepreneurs like **Bill Gates**, founder of **Microsoft**, **Michael Dell**, founder of **Dell Computers**, **Richard Branson**, founder of **Virgin**, and **Anita** and **Gordon Roddick**, founders of **Body Shop**, demonstrated they could become world-class, outstanding successes very quickly, and at the same time they became 'the stuff of dreams' – at least in the financial press.

Entrepreneurs use innovation to exploit or create change and opportunity for the purpose of making profit. They do this by shifting economic resources from an area of lower productivity into an area of higher productivity and greater yield, accepting a high degree of risk and uncertainty in doing so.

Owner-managers own the business they manage. Sole traders are owner-managers. Managers of companies owning over 50 per cent of the share capital, and thereby controlling the business, are owner-managers. However, the term is also used loosely when a small group of managers own and control the business. Not all owner-managers are entrepreneurs, indeed most are not entrepreneurial. Entrepreneurs are defined primarily by their actions although, as we shall see in the next chapter, they can have certain identifiable characteristics. They are the particular type of owner-manager that the financial press love so much. They make 'the stuff of dreams' come true.

A small or medium-sized enterprise (SME) is one with under 250 employees. A micro business has up to 9 employees, a small business up to 49 employees and a medium-sized business up to 249 employees. A defining characteristic of the small firm is the influence of the owner-manager. It is managed in an informal, personalised way and the character and preoccupations of the manager are significant influences on decision-making.

There are a number of other significant characteristics, which include shortage of cash and difficulty in raising finance, limitations in product or service range and markets they operate in, reliance on a small number of customers and the effects of their small scale on financial evaluation and decision-making. But perhaps the other defining characteristics are uncertainty, innovation and firm evolution.

Small firms and entrepreneurship are broadly overlapping sets. However, the two concepts are not necessarily synonymous. We broadly characterised small firms as either lifestyle – set up to allow the owner-manager to pursue an activity they enjoy – or growth – one set up to make money and grow. However, as in the case of **Fat Face**, one can change into the other.

Notwithstanding the success of firms like **JCB**, until the 1960s the UK saw a decrease in the importance of small firms. Since the 1970s this has been reversed and SMEs are now an important part of the UK and EU economies, generating significant employment and wealth. However, most small firms in the UK do not grow to any size.

The increasing number of small firms is a result of many trends – the move from manufacturing to the service sectors, the 'deconstruction' of many large firms and the trend towards sub-contracting, the influence of new technologies, and social and market changes.

Whilst Marxist theory would seem to be able to accommodate the growth of small firms, many politicians would claim that it is a manifestation of the success of free-market capitalism. But whilst industrial economists would have little to say to explain the phenomenon, labour economists and psychologists have been more successful. Recent theories of 'industrial evolution' have linked entrepreneurship and economic growth through their tendency to increase competition, make the most of knowledge spillovers and the increase in diversity they produce.

Essays and discussion topics

1 Are small firms worthy of special treatment? If so, by whom and what form should it take?
2 List the pros and cons of running your own business.
3 Do you think you might have what it takes to be an entrepreneur? Return to this question after you have read the next chapter.
4 Do you think the definition of an entrepreneur is adequate?
5 How does the management of a small firm differ from the management of a large one?
6 What are the characteristics of small firms that distinguish them from large firms and what are their implications? Do these mean that small firms really are sufficiently different to warrant special study?
7 Are small firms sufficiently homogeneous to justify special study? What further segmentation might you suggest and what are the special and different characteristics of these segments?
8 Does your country have a culture that encourages entrepreneurship and business start-ups? Return to this question when you have read the next chapter.
9 From the data in this chapter, how do you evaluate the performance of SMEs in the UK compared to the rest of the EU and the USA?
10 Is it good that so many businesses close in their first three years?
11 Why have the number of small firms been increasing in the UK since the late 1960s?
12 Does Marxism say anything to explain the increasing number of small firms?
13 How does entrepreneurship encourage economic growth?
14 How might entrepreneurship be encouraged?

15 Is small really beautiful?
16 What are the real defining characteristics of a small firm?

Exercises and assignments

1 Research the history and profile of an entrepreneur who set up their own business and grew it successfully.
2 Update the statistics on small firms in Britain (from the Small Business Service website) and in the EU (from the Europa website). Alternatively, obtain similar statistics on the performance of small firms in your country. What does this tell you about recent developments? Summarise your findings in a report.
3 Access the latest GEM report for your country and summarise its findings in a report.

References

Acs, Z.J. and Audretsch, D.B. (1989) 'Births and Firm Size', *Southern Economic Journal*, 55.

Anderson, J. (1995) *Local Heroes*, Glasgow: Scottish Enterprise.

Atkinson, J. and Meager, N. (1994) 'Running to Stand Still: The Small Business in the Labour Market', in J. Atkinson and D.J. Storey (eds), *Employment, The Small Firm and the Labour Market*, London: Routledge.

Audretsch, D.B. (1995) *Innovation and Industry Evolution*, Cambridge: MIT Press.

Barret, R. and Rainnie, A. (2002) 'What's So Special About Small Firms? Developing an Integrated Approach to Analysing Small Firms Industrial Relations', *Work, Employment and Society*, 16(3).

Birch, D.L. (1979) 'The Job Creation Process', unpublished report, MIT Program on Neighbourhood and Regional Change, prepared for the Economic Development Administration, US Department of Commerce, Washington, DC.

Bolton, J.E. (1971) *Report of the Committee of Inquiry on Small Firms*, Cmnd. 4811, London: HMSO.

Branson, R. (1998) *Losing my Virginity*, London: Virgin.

Cannon, T. (1991) *Enterprise: Creation, Development and Growth*, Oxford: Butterworth-Heinemann.

Cantillon, R. (1755) *Essai sur la Nature du Commerce en General*, London and Paris: R. Gyles; translated (1931) by Henry Higgs, London: Macmillan; see also Resources on Cantillon available at cepa.newschool.edu/het/profiles/cantillon.htm.

Carr, P. and Beaver, G. (2002) 'The enterprise culture: Understanding a misunderstood concept', *Strategic Change*, 11.

Casson, M. (1982) *The Entrepreneur: An Economic Theory*, Oxford: Martin Robertson.

Crainer, S. and Dearlove, D. (1998) *Gravy Training: Inside the Shadowy World of Business Schools*, Oxford: Capstone.

de Geus, A. (1997) *The Living Company*, Boston, MA: Harvard Business Press.

Dell, M. (1999) *Direct from Dell: Strategies that Revolutionised an Industry*, New York: Harper Business.

Dewhurst, J. and Burns, P. (1983) *Small Business Finance and Control*, London: Macmillan – now Basingstoke: Palgrave Macmillan.

Dex, S. and Smith, C. (2002) *The Nature and Pattern of Family-Friendly Employment Policies in the UK*, Abingdon: Policy Press.

Drucker, P.F. (1974) *Management Tasks, Responsibilities, Practices*, New York: Harper & Row.

DTI (1998) 'The 1998 Workforce Employee Relations Survey' by M. Cully, A. O'Reilly, N. Millard, S. Woodward, G. Dix, and A. Byson, London: DTI.

Economic News, The Small Business Advocate, February 1997, Washington, DC, Office of Advocacy, SEA.

Ely, R.T. and Hess, R.H. (1893) *Outline of Economics*, New York: Macmillan.

Ericson, R. and Pakes, A. (1995) 'Markov-Perfect Industry Dynamics: A Framework for Empirical Work', *Review of Economic Studies*, 62.

European Commission (2003) *2003 Observatory of European SMEs: Highlights from the 2003 Observatory*, Observatory of European SMEs, 8; available free online at www.europa.eu.int/comm/enterprise/enterprise_policy/analysis/observatory_en.htm.

GEM (2003) *Global Entrepreneurship Monitor 2003*, London: London Business School.

Harrison, J. and Taylor, B. (1996) *Supergrowth Companies: Entrepreneurs in Action*, Oxford: Butterworth-Heinemann.

Hayek, F.A. (1948) 'The Use of Knowledge in Society', in *Studies in Philosophy, Politics and Economics*, Chicago: University of Chicago Press.

Hayek, F.A. (1952) *The Sensory Order*, Chicago: University of Chicago Press.

Hayek, F.A. (1967a) 'Competition as a Discovery Procedure', in Hayek, *New Studies in Philosophy, Politics, Economics and History of Ideas*, Chicago: Chicago University Press.

Hayek, F.A. (1967b) 'The Results of Human Action, but not Human Design', in Hayek, *New Studies in Philosophy, Politics, Economics and History of Ideas*, Chicago: Chicago University Press.

Hopenhayn, H.A. (1992) 'Entry, Exit and Firm Dynamics in Long Run Equilibrium', *Econometrica*, 60.

Jovanovic, B. (1982) 'Favourable Selection with Asymmetrical Information', *Quarterly Journal of Economics, MIT Press*, 97(3).

Kirzner, I.M. (1973) *Competition and Entrepreneurship*, Chicago: University of Chicago Press.

Kirzner, I.M. (1979) *Perception, Opportunity and Profit: Studies in the Theory of Entrepreneurship*, Chicago: University of Chicago Press.

Kirzner, I.M. (1997) 'Entrepreneurial Discovery and Competitive Market Processes: An Austrian Approach', *Journal of Economic Literature*, 35.

Kirzner, I.M. (1999) 'Creativity and/or Alertness: A Reconsideration of the Schumpeterian Entrepreneur', *Review of Austrian Economics,* 11.

Klepper, S. (1996) 'Entry, Exit, Growth and Innovation over the Product Life Cycle', *American Economic Review,* 86(3).

Knight, F. (1921) *Risk, Uncertainty and Profit,* Chicago: University of Chicago Press.

Lambson, V.E. (1991) 'Industry Evolution with Sunk Costs and Uncertain Market Conditions', *International Journal of Industrial Organisations*, 9.

Matlay, H. (2002) 'Training and HRD Strategies in Family and Non-Family Owned Small Business: A Comparative Approach', *Education and Training*, 44.

Menger, C. (1871/1981) *Principles of Economics,* New York: New York University Press.

McGovern, P., Smeaton, D. and Hill, S. (2004), 'Bad Jobs in Britain: Non-standard Employment and Job Quality', *Work and Occupations*, 31.

Penrose, E.T. (1959) *The Theory of the Growth of Firms*, Oxford: Basil Blackwell.

Ram, M. and Edwards, P. (2003) 'Praising Caesar Not Burying Him – What We Know About Employment in Small Firms', *Work, Employment and Society*, 17 (4).

Say, J.B. (1803) *Trait d'economie politique ou simple exposition de la manière dont se forment, se distribuent, et se consomment les riches*; revised (1819); translated (1830) by R. Prinsep, *A Treatise on Political Economy: On Familiar Conversations on the Manner in Which Wealth is Produced, Distributed and Consumed by Society*, Philadelphia: John Grigg and Elliot. See also Resources for Say at cepa.newschool.edu/het/profiles/say.htm.

Say, J.B. (1817) *Catechisme d'economie politique*, translated (1921) by John Richter, *Catechism of Political Economy*, J.A.

Schumacher, E.F. (1974) *Small is Beautiful*, London: Abacus.

Schumpeter J.A. (1911) *Theorie der Wirtschaftlichen Entwicklung*, Munich and Leipzig: Dunker und Humblat; translated (1934) by R. Opie, *The Theory of Economic Development*, Cambridge, MA: Harvard University Press.

Schumpeter J.A. (1928) 'The Instability of Capitalism', *Economic Journal*, 38.

Shapero, A. (1975) 'The Displaced, Uncomfortable Entrepreneur', *Psychology Today*, 8.

Shapero, A. (1984) 'The Entrepreneurial Event', in C. Kent (ed.) *The Environment for Entrepreneurship*, Lexington, MA: DC Health.

Shapero, A. (1985) 'Why Entrepreneurship?', *Journal of Small Business Management*, 23(4).

Storey, D.J. (1998) *Understanding the Small Business Sector*, London: International Thomson Business Press.

Storey, D. and Sykes, N. (1996) 'Uncertainty, Innovation and Management', in P. Burns and J. Dewhurst (eds), *Small Business and Entrepreneurship*, London: Macmillan – now Basingstoke: Palgrave Macmillan.

Storey, D., Keasey, K., Watson, R. and Wynarczyk, P. (1987) *The Performance of Small Firms, Profits, Jobs and Failure*, London: BCA.

Walters, D. (2001) *Health and Safety in Small Enterprise*, Oxford: PIE Peter Lang.

Wynarczyk, P., Watson, R., Storey, D.J., Short, H. and Keasey, K. (1993) *The Managerial Labour Market in Small and Medium Sized Enterprises*, London: Routledge.

2

Heroes and Super-heroes

Contents

- Born and made
- Character traits
- Character traits of owner-managers
- Character traits of entrepreneurs
- Antecedent influences
- Entrepreneurial culture
- Summary

By the end of this chapter you should be able to:

- Explain the influences that help develop owner-managers and entrepreneurs;

- Describe the character traits of owner-managers;

- Describe the character traits of entrepreneurs;

- Explain the methodological problems associated with trying to measure character traits and the linkages with growth businesses;

- Describe the antecedent influences that are likely to influence owner-managers and entrepreneurs;

- Recognise the importance of culture;

- Explain what constitutes an entrepreneurial culture and how it might be measured.

Born and made

Launching and running your own business, even a lifestyle business, is not easy. It requires, amongst other things, hard work, tenacity and a willingness to live with uncertainty in varying degrees. But if owner-managers are the heroes of this book, then entrepreneurs must be the super-heroes. The personal character traits required to launch a business successfully are not sufficient to see it grow to any size. But what are these characteristics? Notwithstanding this, we also know that the role of the entrepreneur needs to change as the business develops and all too often they are not able to make the transition.

Were it not for those who have a vested interest in identifying our super-heroes at an early stage in their business development, it is unlikely that economists, sociologists and psychologists would have paid this area so much attention. Because of this it remains an area of heated academic debate and constant development, not least over the question as to whether entrepreneurs are born rather than made.

Figure 2.1 shows the influences on individuals to start up and grow their businesses. The model proposes that entrepreneurs, and indeed owner-managers, are in fact both born and made. Whilst they do have certain personal character traits that they may be born with, they are also shaped by their history and experience of life. This comprises their antecedent influences – the social environment that they find themselves in, for example, their family, ethnic group, work, education and so on – and the culture of the society they are brought up in. Some cultures encourage entrepreneurial activity, others discourage it. What is more, the situations entrepreneurs find themselves in can influence the decision. For example, if they are thrown out of work they may have little option but to try to start up their own business.

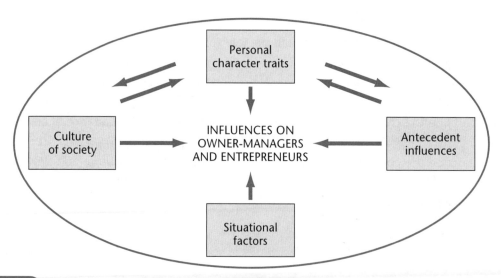

Figure 2.1 Influences on owner-managers and entrepreneurs

All these factors influence the decision whether to start up a business and whether to grow it. If all the factors are favourable the volume of start-ups should increase as, too, should the number of businesses that grow. Indeed both antecedent influences and the dominant culture of the society will almost certainly influence the personal character traits of individuals as they develop over time and vice versa – over time entrepreneurial characters will start to shape society and influence those they come in contact with. These three factors are interrelated.

However, of most interest to many people are the character traits and antecedents of our super-heroes – entrepreneurs. And that has a lot to do with trying to 'pick winners'. Entrepreneurs share certain character traits with owner-managers but they also have certain additional, almost magical, qualities that the average owner-manager does not possess.

Character traits

The issue of linking the character traits of an individual to the success of a business – picking winners – needs to be approached with caution. Even if it is possible to identify personal characteristics of owner-managers and entrepreneurs, it is not always possible to link them directly with a particular sort of business. So far we have considered three types of managers and implicitly linked them to three types of small firm:

	Type of manager	Type of business
1	Owner-manager	Lifestyle firm. Often trade- or craft-based. Will not grow to any size.
2	Entrepreneur	Growth firm. Pursuit of growth and personal wealth important.
3	Manager	Manages a business belonging to someone else. Will build an organisation putting in appropriate controls similar to a large firm.

These were broad generalisations. The linkages are not that simple or direct all of the time. For example, an entrepreneur might manage a business belonging to someone else, at least for a time. Similarly, an owner-manager may find himself with a growth business, quite by accident. Success or failure in business, as we shall see later, comes from a mix of many different things. The character traits of the manager is just one factor in the equation. What is more, it takes time for entrepreneurs to prove that the business they manage is in fact a growth business, so do you measure aspirations or reality?

A further difficulty is that much of the research fails to distinguish between owner-managers and entrepreneurs, assuming anyone who starts their own business is an entrepreneur. However, research into the character traits of owner-managers of growth businesses, who should mainly be entrepreneurs, does allow us to come to some broad conclusions and to paint a picture of the different characters of owner-managers compared to entrepreneurs.

There are also a number of methodological problems associated with attempting to measure personality characteristics (Deakins, 1996):

- They are not stable and change over time.
- They require subjective judgements.
- Measures tend to ignore cultural and environmental influences.
- The role of education, learning, and training is often overlooked.
- Issues such as age, sex, race, social class and education can be ignored.

Clearly the area is an academic minefield. Notwithstanding this, many researchers do believe that, collectively, owner-managers have certain typical character traits, although the mix and emphasis of these characteristics will inevitably be different for each individual. Whether a clearly definable set of entrepreneurial characteristics exists is more controversial. Furthermore, many of the character traits that have been found are similar to those found in other successful people such as politicians or athletes (Chell *et al.*, 1991). Perhaps, the argument goes, it just happens that the individual has chosen an entrepreneurial activity as a means of self-satisfaction. Certainly, even if you believe the character traits can be identified, they do not explain why the individual chose to apply them in an entrepreneurial context. Figure 2.2 summarises the character traits associated with owner-managers and entrepreneurs accumulated from numerous research studies.

Character traits of owner-managers

Notwithstanding these issues, most researchers believe that, collectively, owner-manager entrepreneurs have certain typical character traits, although the mix and emphasis of these characteristics will inevitably be different for each individual. The character traits of the owner-manager might be characterised as an instinct for survival – since most owner-managed businesses never grow to any size – and those of the entrepreneur might be characterised as an instinct for growth.

Owner-managers
Need for independence
Need for achievement
Internal locus of control
Ability to live with uncertainty
and take measured risks

Entrepreneurs
Opportunistic
Innovative
Self-confident
Proactive and decisive with high energy
Self-motivated (intrinsic motivation)
Vision and flair
Willingness to take greater risks and
live with greater uncertainty

Sources: Based on Aldrich and Martinez, 2003; Andersson *et al.*, 2004; Baty, 1990; Bell *et al.*, 1992; Blanchflower and Meyer, 1991; Brockhaus and Horwitz, 1986; Brush, 1992; Buttner and More, 1997; Caird, 1990; Chell *et al.*, 1991; Cuba *et al.*, 1983; de Bono, 1985; Hirsch and Brush, 1987; Kanter, 1983; Kirzner, 1973, 1979, 1997, 1999; McClelland, 1961; Pinchot, 1985; Rosa *et al.*, 1994; Schein *et al.*, 1996; Schumpeter, 1996; Schwartz, 1997; Shapero, 1985; Shaver and Scott, 1992; Storey and Sykes, 1996.

Figure 2.2 Character traits of owner-managers and entrepreneurs

Need for independence

Owner-managers have a high need for independence. This is most often seen as 'the need to be your own boss' and is the trait that is most often cited, and supported, by researchers and advisors alike. However, independence means different things to different people, such as controlling your own destiny, doing things differently or being in a situation where you can fulfil your potential. It has often been said that, once you have run your own firm, you cannot work for anybody else.

Need for achievement

Owner-managers typically have a high need for achievement, a driving force that is even stronger for entrepreneurs. Achievement for individual owners means different things depending what type of person they are. For example, the satisfaction of producing a beautiful work of art, employing their hundredth person, or making the magic one million pounds. Often money is just a badge of achievement to the successful entrepreneur. It is not an end in itself.

Public recognition of achievement can be important to some owner-managers and entrepreneurs. And this can lead to certain negative behaviours or unwise decisions. For example, overspending on the trappings of corporate life – the office, the company car and so on (often called the corporate flagpole syndrome) – or the 'big project' that is very risky but the entrepreneur 'knows' they can do it. These can lead to cash flow problems that put at risk the very existence of the business.

'Money doesn't motivate me. But it's not to say I don't drive a Bentley Continental T2.'
Stephen Waring founder of **Green Thumb**
Sunday Times 2 October 2005

●

'As a child I never felt that I was noticed. I never felt that I achieved anything or that there was any expectation of me achieving anything. So proving myself is something that is important to me and so is establishing respect for what I have achieved.'
Chey Garland founder of **Garlands Call Centres**
Sunday Times 27 June 2004

●

'Most of the pleasure is not the cash. It is the sense of achievement at having taken something from nothing to where it is now.'
Charles Muirhead founder of **Orchestream**, acquired by MetaSolv in 2003 for £8 million
Sunday Times 19 September 1999

●

'We don't feel like millionaires at all. Money doesn't come into it. It's not really why you do it, it really isn't.'

Brent Hoberman co-founder of **Lastminute.com**
Sunday Times 19 September 1999

➜

Internal locus of control

If you believe that you can exercise control over your environment and ultimately your destiny, you have an internal locus of control. If, however, you believe in fate, you have an external locus of control and you are less likely to take the risk of starting a business. Owner-managers typically have a strong internal locus of control, which is the same for many senior managers in large firms.

In extreme cases this trait also can lead to certain negative behaviours. In particular, it can show itself as a desire to maintain personal control over every aspect of the business. That can lead to a preoccupation with detail, over work and stress. It also leads to an inability or unwillingness to delegate as the business grows. Again, in extreme cases it might show itself as a mistrust of subordinates. Kets de Vries (1985) thinks these behaviours lead to subordinates becoming 'infantilised'. They are expected to behave as incompetent idiots, and that is the way they behave. They tend to do very little, make no decisions and circulate very little information. The better ones do not stay long.

> 'I want to take control of my life and achieve something.'
> **Jonathan Elvidge** founder of **Gadget Shop**
> *Sunday Times* 17 March 2002
> ➡

This need for control also shows itself in the unwillingness of many owner-managers to part with shares in their company. They just do not want to lose control, at any price.

Ability to live with uncertainty and take measured risks

Human beings, typically, do not like uncertainty and one of the biggest uncertainties of all is not having a regular pay cheque coming in. That is not to say owner-managers like it. Uncertainty about income can be a major cause of stress. The possibility of missing out on some piece of business that might affect their income is one reason why they are so loath to take holidays.

There are also other commercial aspects of uncertainty that owner-managers have to cope with. Often they cannot influence many aspects of the market in which they operate, for example, price. They must therefore react to changes in the market that others might bring about. If a local supermarket has a special price promotion on certain goods it may well affect sales of similar goods in a local corner shop. A business with a high level of borrowing must find a way of paying interest charges but has no direct influence over changes in interest rates. Many small firms also have a limited customer or product base and this can bring further uncertainty. If, for whatever reason, one large customer ceases buying it can have an enormous impact on a small firm.

> 'When I was made redundant self-employment was my only option and the work with the Business Link made it possible. The money was good, but I don't like the uncertainty – where the money for next month is coming from. It did not help to have three young boys to support. Eventually I went back into teaching.'
> **Jean Young**
> self-employed 1998–99
> ➡

Hand in hand with owner managers' ability to live with uncertainty is their willingness to

'You have to be prepared to lose everything and remember that the biggest risk is not taking any risk at all.'
Jonathan Elvidge founder of
Gadget Shop
Sunday Times 17 March 2002
➡

take measured risks. Most people are risk averse. They try to avoid risks and insure against them. Setting up your own business is risky and owner-managers are willing to take more risks with their own resources than most people. They might also risk their reputation and personal standing if they fail. However, they do not like it and try always to minimise their exposure. Hence, their preference to risk other peoples' money and borrow, sometimes too heavily, from the bank. Another example of this is the way they often 'compartmentalise' various aspects of their business. For example, an owner-manager might open a second restaurant but set it up as a separate limited company just in case it fails and should endanger the other. In this way they sometimes develop a portfolio of individually small businesses and their growth and success is measured not just in the performance of a single one but rather by the growth of the portfolio.

One important characteristic of owner-managers in their approach to dealing with uncertainty and risk is the short-term view they take on all business decisions. It really is a case of not being certain that the business will survive until tomorrow. Therefore decision-making is short-term and incremental. Strategies often evolve on a step-by-step basis. If one step works then the second is taken. At the same time owner-

'The ideal business has no fixed overheads, commission only sales, large volume and low overheads.'
David Speakman founder of
Travel Counsellors
Sunday Times 6 December 1998
➡

managers will keep as many options open as possible, because they realise the outcome of their actions is very uncertain. Prudent entrepreneurs also seek to keep their fixed costs as low as possible, trying to minimise the risk they face. They also see assets as a liability, limiting the flexibility that they need, which is just as well since finding the resources for the business is usually a problem.

Character traits of entrepreneurs

Entrepreneurs share the characteristics of owner-managers. However, they have certain additional traits. Nevertheless, owner-managers can be entrepreneurial in some of their actions and the boundaries between the two are not always clear. Consequently, many of these traits are present in owner-managers, but to a far lesser extent.

Opportunistic

By definition, entrepreneurs exploit change for profit. In other words they seek out opportunities to make money. Often entrepreneurs see opportunities where others see problems. Whereas ordinary mortals dislike the uncertainty brought about by change, entrepreneurs love it because they see opportunity and they do not mind the uncertainty.

'I have always lived my life by thriving on opportunity and adventure. Some of the best ideas come out of the blue, and you have to keep an open mind to see their virtue.'

Richard Branson (Anderson, 1995)
➡

For many entrepreneurs the problem is getting them to focus on just one opportunity, or at least one opportunity at a time. They see opportunity everywhere and have problems following through on any one before becoming distracted by another. This is one reason why some entrepreneurs are not able to grow their business beyond a certain size. They get bored by the routines and controls; they see other market opportunities and yearn for the excitement of another start-up. They probably would be well advised to sell up and do just that. However, others recognise this element of their character and become serial entrepreneurs, moving to set up and sell on one business after another. You see this very often in the restaurant business where an entrepreneurial restaurateur launches a new restaurant and makes it successful, then sells it on so as to move onto another new venture. They make money by creating a business with capital value, not necessarily income for themselves.

Case insight

Simon Woodroffe, founder and CEO of **YO! Sushi**, took a while to home in on his final business idea. His first idea was to drive a van on the hippy trail to India, charging passengers to accompany him, but he did not have enough money to buy a van and his father declined to invest. Soon after this he started producing belts. He put together £100, bought an old sewing machine, some buckles and snakeskin trimmings. The belts sold well. Later he intended to make indoor rock climbing popular – another idea he never got round to pursuing. Then a Japanese man over a sushi lunch suggested what he really needed to do was open a conveyor-belt sushi bar with girls dressed in black PVC mini skirts. The idea stuck. Two years later in 1997 he opened his first YO! Sushi bar in London – but without the girls in mini skirts. He now has over 20 restaurants and bars in the UK and more in France, Dubai and Kuwait.
●

Innovative

The ability to spot opportunities and to innovate is the most important distinguishing feature of entrepreneurs. Innovation is the prime tool entrepreneurs use to create or exploit opportunity. These characteristics set entrepreneurs apart from owner-managers. Entrepreneurs link innovation to the market place so as to exploit an opportunity and make their business grow. Although innovation is difficult to define and can take many forms, entrepreneurs are always, in some way, innovative. We shall explore this in more detail in the next chapter.

'True innovation is rarely about creating something new. Its pretty hard to recreate the wheel or discover gravity; innovation is more often about seeing new opportunities for old designs.'

Neil Kelly owner and managing director of **PAV**
Sunday Times 9 December 2001
●

Self-confident

Facing uncertainty, you have to be confident in your own judgement and ability to start up your own business. Many start-up training programmes recognise this and try to build confidence by developing a business plan that addresses the issue of future uncertainty. As well as a useful management tool, the plan can become a symbol of certainty for the owner-manager in an otherwise uncertain world and some even keep it with them at all times, using it almost like a bible, to reassure them of what the future will hold when the business is successful.

> 'My mother gave me a massive self-belief. I will always try things – there is nothing to lose.'
>
> **Richard Thompson** founder and chairman of **EMS**
> Rupert Steiner, *My First Break: How Entrepreneurs Get Started*, Sunday Times Books, 1999
> ●

Entrepreneurs, therefore, need self-confidence a-plenty to grow their business given the extreme uncertainty they face. If they do not believe in the future of the business, how can they expect others to do so? However, the self-confidence can be overdone and turn to an exaggerated opinion of their own competence, and even arrogance.

Some researchers believe entrepreneurs are actually 'delusional'. In an interesting piece of research, two American academics tested the decision-making process of 124 entrepreneurs (defined as people who started their own firm) and 95 managers of big companies in two ways (Busenitz and Barney, 1997). Firstly, they asked five factual questions, each of which had two possible answers. They asked respondents to rate their confidence in their answer (50 per cent, a guess; 100 per cent, perfect confidence). Entrepreneurs turned out to be much more confident about their answers than managers, especially those who gave wrong answers. Secondly, they were given a business decision. They were told they must replace a broken foreign-made machine and they had two alternatives. The first was an American-made machine, which a friend had recently bought and had not yet broken down, and the second a foreign-built machine, which was statistically less likely to break down than the other; 50 per cent of the entrepreneurs opted for the American machine but 90 per cent of the managers opted for the foreign one. The researchers concluded that the entrepreneurs were more prone to both delusion and opportunism than normal managers. So the question is raised, is entrepreneurial self-confidence so strong as to make them delusional, blinding them to the reality of a situation?

> 'An entrepreneur is unfailingly enthusiastic, never pessimistic, usually brave, and certainly stubborn. Vision and timing are crucial. You have to be something of a workaholic, too. You have to be convinced that what you are doing is right. If not you have to recognise this and be able to change direction swiftly – sometimes leaving your staff breathless – and start off again with equal enthusiasm.'
>
> **Chris Ingram** founder of **Tempus**
> *Sunday Times* 17 March 2002
> ●

Proactive and decisive with high energy

Entrepreneurs tend to be proactive rather than reactive and more decisive than other people. They are proactive in the sense that they seek out opportunities, they do not just rely on luck. They act quickly and decisively to make the most of the opportunity before somebody else does.

'Neither my grandfather nor my father would be surprised if they could see me now. My success didn't just happen As a young boy, I was always working. My parents and my brothers and sisters all had high energy.'

Tom Farmer founder of **Kwik-Fit**
Daily Mail 11 May 1999
➡

'Enthusiasm is my strength. And good health, and energy and endeavour. I love what I do. It's just so interesting, it is new every day, exciting every day. I work 364 days a year. The only day I don't work is Christmas Day, because its my wife's birthday.'

Bob Worcester founder of **MORI**
Financial Times 7 April 2002
●

Entrepreneurs are often seen as restless and easily bored. They can easily be diverted by the most recent market opportunity and often seem to do things at twice the pace of others, unwilling or unable to wait for others to complete tasks. Patience is certainly not a virtue many possess. Many entrepreneurs seem to work 24 hours a day and their work becomes their life with little separating the two. It is little wonder that it places family relationships under strain.

One important result of this characteristic is that entrepreneurs tend to learn by doing. They act first and then learn from the outcomes of the action. It is part of their incremental approach to decision-making, each small action and its outcomes contribute to the learning process.

Self-motivated

Entrepreneurs are highly self-motivated, amounting almost to a driving urge to succeed in their economic goals. This is driven by their exceptionally strong inner need for achievement, far stronger than with the average owner-manager. Running

'I have never had anything to do in my life that provides so many challenges – and there are so many things I still want to do.'
Martha Lane Fox co-founder of **Lastminute.com**
Sunday Times 19 September 1999
●

'I am motivated by my success not money. But success is partly measured by money.'
Wing Yip founder of **W. Wing Yip & Brothers**
Sunday Times 2 January 2000
➡

your own business is a lonely affair, without anyone to motivate and encourage you. You work long hours, sometimes for little reward. You therefore need to be self-motivated, committed and determined to succeed.

This strong inner drive – what psychologists call type 'A' behaviour – is quite unique and can be seen as almost compulsive behaviour. This is not to say that entrepreneurs are not motivated by other things as well, such as money. But often money is just a badge of their success that allows them to measure their achievement. What drives them is their exceptionally high need to achieve. 'A' types tend to be goal-focused, wanting to get the job done quickly. However, they also tend to be highly reactive, focusing on the future and often not in control of the present.

Vision and flair

To succeed, entrepreneurs need to have a clear vision of what they want to achieve. That is part of the fabric of their motivation. It also helps them bring others with them, both employees and customers. The flair comes with the ability to be in the right place at the right time. Timing is everything. Innovation that is before its time can lead to business failure. Innovation that is late results in copy-cat products or services that are unlikely to be outstanding successes. A question constantly asked about successful entrepreneurs is whether their success was due to good luck or good judgement? The honest answer in most cases is probably a bit of both.

'My strength and my weakness is that I am very focused. Some people would describe me as obsessive . . . The secret is to have vision and then build a plan and follow it. I think you have to do that, otherwise you just flounder about . . . You change your game plan on the way, as long as you are going somewhere with a purpose . . . I wouldn't say it was at the cost of everything else, but when I am at work, I work hard and do long hours – and when I am not at work my mind still tends to be there anyway.'

Mike Peters, founder of **Universal Laboratories**
Sunday Times 11 July 2004

Willingness to take greater risks and live with even greater uncertainty

It is worth stressing that, whilst all owner-managers are willing to take risks and live with uncertainty, true entrepreneurs are willing to take far greater risks and live with far greater uncertainty. Often they are willing to put their own home on the line and risk all, so strong is their belief in their business idea.

What is more, growth businesses face rapid change. Even with careful management they are extremely risky. Growth businesses require large amounts of capital and entrepreneurs are, if necessary, willing to risk all they own for the prospect of success. Faced with such extreme uncertainty a high degree of self-confidence is essential.

'You have to have nerves of steel and be prepared to take risks. You have to be able to put it all on the line knowing you could lose everything.'
Anne Notley co-founder of
The Iron Bed Company
Sunday Times 28 January 2001

Antecedent influences

Whilst inherent character traits are important, there are other influences at work and there are other approaches to trying to explain the complicated process of entrepreneurship. Cognitive theory shifts the emphasis from the individual towards the situations that lead to entrepreneurial behaviour. Research has started to distinguish a certain 'antecedent influence' – the entrepreneur's history and experience of life (Carter and Cachon, 1988). We are all born with certain character traits. However, we are also influenced by the social environment that we find ourselves in, for example, our family, ethnic group, education and so on. They influence our values, attitudes and even our behaviours. These are also antecedent influences.

In many ways the academic research in this area is even more confusing, and sometimes contradictory, than with personal character traits. There are a myriad of claimed influences that are difficult to prove, or indeed, disprove. There are simply too many variables to control. A further confusion is between owner-managers and entrepreneurs. Most of the research is about influences on start-ups. But start-ups comprise both owner-managers and entrepreneurs. However, there is a body of research on antecedent influences on managers of growth businesses which can apply, in the main, to entrepreneurs. The problem here is that some of the influences that seem to influence growth are not those that can be proved to influence start-ups. The only really safe conclusion is that, except for a handful of influences, the research is inconclusive.

Education

One influence that comes through on many studies for both start-up and growth is educational attainment. Clearly there are problems measuring educational attainment consistently over studies, however, particularly in the USA, research consistently shows a positive association between the probability of starting up in business and increases in educational attainment (Evans and Leighton, 1990). Similar research in other countries tends to support this result, albeit less strongly and not consistently. However, what is altogether stronger is the relationship between educational attainment and business growth. Storey (1994) reviewed 17 multivariate antecedent studies which gauged the influence of educational attainment (amongst other influences) and found that there was a positive influence in eight. This led him to conclude that there was 'fairly consistent support for the view that educated entrepreneurs are more likely to establish faster-growing firms'. The GEM 2003 UK study suggests that people with higher incomes and better education are more likely to be entrepreneurs.

This is not a widely acknowledged result and perhaps one that is more true of the USA than Britain. It is the stuff of folk lore that the entrepreneur comes from a poor, deprived background and has little formal education. In fact some writers go further and claim that 'anecdotal evidence' suggests that too much education can discourage entrepreneurship (Bolton and Thompson, 2000). But times are changing and if you ask venture capitalists why they think certain firms will grow rather than others, they will tell you that they are looking for background and track record in the firm's management, and education counts. It is also particularly true of the new generation of entrepreneurs pursuing e-commerce opportunities.

The rationale for the relationship might be two-fold. Firstly, educational attainment might provide the basis for better learning through life, enabling entrepreneurs to deal better with business problems and giving them a greater openness and more outward orientation. Secondly, it might give them higher earning expectations that can only be attained by growing the business. What is more it might also give them greater confidence in dealing with customers and other business professionals.

Employment and unemployment

Storey's (1994) review of antecedent literature also came to some important conclusions regarding the influence of employment and unemployment. Reviewing three multivariate studies he found two had statistically significant relationships between unemployment and the probability of starting up in business. However, when he came to look at growth four out of eight studies showed a negative relationship and the other four showed no relationship at all. What is more, four out of seven studies found a positive relationship between positive motives for setting up the business (for example, market opportunity, making money) and subsequent growth. This led Storey to conclude that 'if the founder is unemployed prior to starting a business, that firm is unlikely to grow as rapidly as where the founder is employed'.

It would seem that unemployment gives people a strong push into self-employment. They possibly have limited options open to them. However, they may not have the skills needed to grow the business and may have lower aspirations than those who leave employment to start their own business. It would seem that what is needed to make the firm grow is positive motivation – a real desire, an ambition, almost a need to achieve certain internally generated goals or pursue some market opportunity. Growth does not happen (often) by chance. The entrepreneur must want it.

Research in France also casts doubt on the long-term viability of start-up generated by unemployed people (Abdesselam *et al.*, 1999). They found that firms with the shortest life-spans were set up by the young (under 30) and unemployed. They also found that there was a high probability that they would be female and the business would be in the retail or wholesale sector. These results cast worrying doubt on the wisdom of any government policy to encourage the unemployed to start up their own business.

Other influences on start-ups

There are other influences on start-ups that have been cited, many supported by univariate research, for example the influence of family. In a survey of 600 respondents, Stanworth *et al.* (1989) found that between 30 per cent and 47 per cent of individuals either considering, about to start, or in business had a parent who had been in business. Another factor often cited is that immigrants to a country often go into self-employment. Examples such as the high incidence of self-employment in the Indian, Pakistani and Bangladeshi immigrant communities in the UK are often quoted. However, Storey in his review of multivariate analyses concludes that there is little support for the impact of family, family circumstances, cultural or ethnic influences on self-employment decisions. In countering the issue of immigrant populations he quotes the example of West Indian and Guyanese immigrant communities where the levels of self-employment are low. Other factors that Storey could not prove were influences are shown in Table 2.1. You might at this point reconsider the UK findings of the 2003 GEM study cited in the previous chapter.

It has to be said that Storey's cold analytical approach to the immigrant issue does not stand the test of observation. As Harper (1985) observed:

> The Indians in East Africa, the Armenians in Egypt, the Lebanese in West Africa, the Kikuyu in Masailand, the Mahajans all over India except in their desert homeland of Rajasthan, the Tamils in Sri Lanka, the Palestinians in Arabia and the British almost everywhere except in Britain; all have shown that dislocation and hardship can lead to enterprise. The very experience of living in a difficult environment, and of planning, financing and executing a move and then surviving in a new and often hostile environment requires the qualities of self-restraint, abstinence, hard work and voluntary postponement of gratification which are normally far more severe than those demanded by the lifestyle of those who remain at home, or of the indigenous people of the place in which these refugees relocate.

Starting and running your own business is not easy and immigrants often have the motivation to work the long hours. Often with few options open to them, they have little to lose from failure and much to gain from success.

One further strand of cognitive theory is worthy of note because it reinforces at least two elements of trait theory. Chen *et al.* (1998) set out the idea that successful entrepreneurs possess high levels of 'self-efficacy'. Self-efficacy is 'the strength of an individual's belief that he or she is capable of successfully performing the roles and tasks of an entrepreneur'. Clearly this is part of the self-confidence of entrepreneurs referred to in the last section, but it is also created by their internal locus of control and rooted firmly in their need for achievement and therefore more than just self-confidence. Chen *et al.* argue that it is self-efficacy that motivates entrepreneurs and gives them the dogged determination to persist in the face of adversity when others just give in. With this characteristic entrepreneurs become more objective and analytical and attribute failure to insufficient effort or poor knowledge. They argue that self-efficacy is affected by a person's previous experiences – success breeds success.

One interesting perspective on entrepreneurship is provided by Kets de Vries (1997) who believes entrepreneurs often come from unhappy family backgrounds. This makes them unwilling to accept authority or to work closely with others. He paints the picture of a social deviant or misfit who is both hostile to others and tormented in himself:

> A prominent pattern among entrepreneurs appears to be a sense of impulsivity, a persistent feeling of dissatisfaction, rejection and pointlessness, forces which contribute to an impairment and depreciation of his sense of self-esteem and affect cognitive processes. The entrepreneur is a man under great stress, continuously badgered by his past, a past which is experienced and re-experienced in fantasies, daydreams and dreams. These dreams and fantasies often have a threatening content due to the recurrence of feelings of anxiety and guilt which mainly revolve around hostile wishes against parental figures, or more generally, all individuals in a position of authority.

In reality there is little support for this extreme view.

Table 2.1 Factors that could not be proved to influence start-ups

- Marital status
- Children
- Previous wage

- Experience
- Age
- Ethnicity

- Gender
- Social class
- School type

- Personality
- Manager
  (in previous job)

Case insight

It is an astonishing fact that six of the most successful wholesale companies supplying drugs and medicines to Britain's retail pharmacies and hospitals were founded by Kenyan Asians now in their fifties. All left poverty in Kenya to come to Britain in the late 1960s and early 1970s where they went to College to achieve pharmacy qualifications, generally supporting themselves with menial part-time jobs. Then they set up their own retail pharmacy before building their much bigger wholesale businesses. All are now multi-millionaires.

Bharat Shah has built up the family firm of **Sigma Pharmaceuticals** to a company making profits of £4.8 million on turnover of £190 million. It sells some 100 generic medicines and also deals in parallel imports – whereby drugs are bought in a country where wholesale prices are much lower and repackaged for a country where the price is higher.

Bharat and Ketan Mehta founded **Necessity Supplies** in 1986. It also sells generic drugs and deals in parallel imports and made profits of £15.3 million on turnover of £144 million in 2002.

Vijay and Bikhu Patel have built up **Waymade Healthcare** into a business with 700 employees, turnover of £280 million and profits of £22 million. They have ambitions to turn the company into a 'mini-Glaxo' and in 2003 launched Amdipham to develop medicines that are too small for the big pharmaceuticals.

Ravi Karia founded **Chemilines** in 1986. With profits of £4 million on sales of £60 million, it claims to be one of Britain's fastest growing companies.

Naresh Shah founded **Jumbogate** with his wife Shweta in 1982. Whilst still involved in retailing the business is predominantly wholesale and had a turnover of £97 million in 2003.

Navin Engineer came to London with only £75 in his pocket in 1969 at the age of 16 to live with his aunt. He worked in a Wimpy burger restaurant in Oxford Street in the evenings to support himself through sixth form and then the London School of Pharmacy. On graduation he took a job with Boots, the retail chemist. Eventually he opened his own pharmacy in Chertsey, Surrey, working long hours to make money to buy other pharmacies. By 1999 he had 14 such shops and, when the German group GEHE offered him £12 million for the retail chain, he decided to take it. He invested most of the proceeds in his much smaller wholesale business. He bought a range of small turnover branded pharmaceuticals from bigger companies, switched production to established factories in Eastern Europe and the Far East, and realised cost savings as profit. He then went into generic medicines – copies of branded drugs produced after the expiry of their patent. This involves checking patents and making certain the drug can be developed without infringing the patent. At the same time regulatory authorities have to be satisfied. His company, **Chemidex** is now a wholesaler of both branded and some 42 generic medicines including treatments for gout, depression and an antibiotic for anthrax. The company made profits of £9 million in 2003.

Other influences on growth

Storey's review of the research concludes that there are three further factors that are positively correlated with growth companies:

1 Growth companies are more likely to be set up by groups rather than individuals. This proves the venture capitalist's view that they invest in a management team not in a business and explains why they are so willing to invest in management buy-outs and buy-ins. Managing growth needs a range of different skills with managers able to work as a team. Attracting a strong management team can be a problem for a start-up. How do you tempt successful managers to leave secure jobs and face the risks associated with a start-up? The answer is by offering them a share in the business. In that way they share in the success of the business as well as the risks that it faces.

2 Middle-aged owners are more likely to be associated with growth companies. Middle age does have some advantages. It brings experience, credibility and financial resources. With the family possibly grown up, middle-aged entrepreneurs can devote more time and resources to the business.

   However, as with all research these results must be treated with caution. Findings like these come from looking at what has happened in the past and if situations change, the past may not be a good indication of what might happen in the future. Computing and e-commerce may well be changing the nature of the game of start-up and growth businesses.

   > Forged in the white heat of two great forces: the spirit of free enterprise introduced during their youth by Margaret Thatcher and a technological revolution. Never before have so many millions been made by people so young.

   wrote the *Sunday Times* (17 September 1999). Around this time newspapers carried stories of these young self-made millionaires, usually following up e-commerce opportunities, mainly well educated, often raising many millions in venture capital by giving away some of their equity, with their businesses still in their infancy and not yet breaking even. Among the *Sunday Times* 'Top 100 Internet Tycoons' (3 November 1999), the average fortune amassed was £40.3 million and 20 per cent were aged 30 or less. The youngest was Benjamin Cohen aged 17 who had amassed a modest £5 million from his website aimed at the Jewish community, Jewish.com, started with just £150. However, for many the dot.com boom was to end in failure.

3 Owners with previous managerial experience are more likely to be associated with growth companies. This is likely to be the case because they bring with them both managerial and, probably, market experience. They also know their previous worth which may create salary expectations that can only be satisfied by a growth business.

The factors that Storey could not prove influenced growth are shown in Table 2.2. However, he also concludes that the picture is 'fuzzy' and that what the entrepreneur has done prior to establishing the business 'only has a modest influence on the success of the business'. One factor frequently debated is that of the experience of prior business failure. Whether or not this is a positive experience is still to be adequately researched. Until then no conclusion can be drawn.

Table 2.2 Factors that could not be proved to influence growth

• Gender	• Training	• Family history
• Prior firm size experience	• Social marginality	• Prior self-employment
• Prior sector experience	• Ethnicity	

One curious conclusion is that the influence of training cannot be proved. If you believe that entrepreneurs are both born and made, then you must accept that they can be influenced. Just like an athlete or a musician, if they have the basic ingredients, then training should improve their performance. There are at least two major problems related to this variable. Firstly, there is the question of what constitutes training. Smaller firms are notoriously poor at undertaking formal training but that does not necessarily mean they do not undertake informal training. Secondly, those small firms that do seek out formal training are also likely to seek out other sources of help and so the influence of the formal training becomes more difficult to measure.

These studies of growth businesses allow us to draw an, albeit tentative, identikit picture of the antecedent influences on an entrepreneur which are most likely to result in them successfully growing their business. These are shown in Table 2.3. Remember, however, that they are generalisations. Whilst broadly supportable because of the samples on which they are based, they do not apply to every individual. Just like small firms, entrepreneurs are not homogeneous. They are also based on ex-post research, that is, analysis based on the past. Circumstances do change and sometimes the past is not always a good predictor of the future. What is more, if picking winners were really that easy there would be an awful lot of rich people around.

Table 2.3 Antecedent influences on the entrepreneur

- Well-educated
- Starts business because of positive motivations
- Leaves managerial job to start business
- Middle-aged (or very young?)
- Willing to share ownership of business

Entrepreneurial culture

The final element in the jigsaw puzzle is culture. In his seminal work on the subject, Hofstede (1980) defined culture as the 'collective programming of the mind which distinguishes one group of people from another'. It is a pattern of taken-for-granted assumptions. An entrepreneurial culture is one that fosters positive social attitudes towards entrepreneurship. Cultures can change over time, albeit slowly. So, most people would argue that Britain has developed a more entrepreneurial culture from the 1970s through to today. What is more, there may be subcultures within any dominant culture. So, for example, different ethnic groups in a country may be more or less entrepreneurial.

It has been argued that there is no such thing as one identifiable entrepreneurial culture; what is needed is a favourable environment which combines social, political and educational attributes (Timmons, 1994). However, many would consider the culture in the USA to be the most entrepreneurial in the world. It is an achievement orientated society that values individualism and material wealth. According to Welsch (1998):

> Entrepreneurship is ingrained in the fabric of North American culture. It is discussed at the family dinner table among intergenerational members, practised by pre-school children with their lemonade stands, and promoted every day through personal success human interest stories in the media. Furthermore, entrepreneurship is taught in school from kindergarten through to the twelfth grade, it has been integrated into college and university curricula, and is taught and promoted through various outreach and training programmes including government Small Business Development Centres in every state of the nation. Consequently, through one's life as an American citizen, entrepreneurship as a career option is espoused early and reinforced regularly.

Americans are said to have a 'frontier culture', always seeking something new. They are restless, constantly on the move. They have a strong preference for freedom of choice for the individual. The individual is always free to compete against established institutions. Rebellious, non-conformist youth is the accepted norm. If there is an 'American dream' it is that the humblest of individuals can become the greatest of people, usually measured in monetary terms. Achievement is prized and lauded throughout society. Individuals believe they control their destiny. Americans think big. Nothing is impossible. They prefer the new, or at least the improved. They worship innovation. Time is their most precious commodity. They are tolerant of those who make mistakes as long as they learn from them. Things need to get done quickly rather than always get done perfectly.

Measuring the dimensions of culture in a scientific way is extremely difficult. The most widely used dimensions are those developed by Hofstede (1981) who undertook an extensive cross-cultural study, using questionnaire data from some 80 000 IBM employees in 66 countries across seven occupations. From his research he established four dimensions (Figure 2.3):

1 **Individualism vs collectivism** This is the degree to which people prefer to act as individuals rather than groups. Individualistic societies are loosely knit social frameworks in which people primarily operate as individuals or in immediate families. Collectivist societies are composed of tight networks in which people operate as members of ingroups and outgroups, expecting to look after, and be looked after by, other members of their ingroup. In the individualist culture the task prevails over personal relationships. The atmosphere is competitive. In the collectivist culture the opposite is true. 'Anglo' countries (USA, Britain, Australia, Canada and New Zealand) are the highest scoring individualist cultures, together with the Netherlands. France and Germany just made it into the upper quartile of individualist cultures. South American countries were the most collectivist cultures, together with Pakistan.

High (upper quartile countries)		Low (lower quartile countries)
USA Australia New Zealand UK Canada France Germany	INDIVIDUALISM	South America Pakistan
Malaysia Philippines France South America	POWER DISTANCE	UK USA Scandinavia Germany
Greece Portugal Uruguay Guatemala France	UNCERTAINTY AVOIDANCE	Hong Kong Singapore UK USA
Japan Austria Italy UK USA Germany	MASCULINITY	North Europe

Figure 2.3   Hofstede's dimensions of culture

2 **Power distance**   This is the degree of inequality among people that the community is willing to accept. Low power distance countries endorse egalitarianism, relations are open and informal, information flows are functional and unrestricted and organisations tend to have flat structures. They are more empowered cultures. High power distance cultures endorse hierarchies, relations are more formal, information flows are formalised and restricted and organisations tend to be rigid and hierarchical. Low power distance countries tend to be Austria, Ireland, Israel, New Zealand and the four Scandinavian countries. The USA, Britain and Germany also make it into the lower quartile. High power distance countries are Malaysia, the Philippines and four South American countries, with France also making it into the upper quartile.

3 **Uncertainty avoidance**   This is the degree to which people prefer to avoid ambiguity, resolve uncertainty and prefer structured rather than unstructured situations. Low uncertainty avoidance cultures tolerate greater ambiguity, prefer flexibility, stress personal choice and decision-making, reward initiative, risk-taking and team-play and stress the development of analytical skills. High uncertainty avoidance cultures prefer rules and procedures, stress compliance, punish error and reward compliance, loyalty and attention to detail. The lowest uncertainty avoidance countries are Hong Kong, Ireland, Jamaica, Singapore and two Scandinavian countries. The USA and Britain are in the lowest quartile group. The highest uncertainty avoidance countries are Greece, Portugal, Guatemala and Uruguay, with France also in the highest quartile group. Germany is about halfway.

4 **Masculinity vs femininity**   This defines quality of life issues. Masculine virtues are those of assertiveness, competition and success. Masculine cultures reward financial and material achievement with social prestige and status. Feminine virtues are those such as modesty, compromise and cooperation. In feminine

cultures issues such as quality of life, warmth in personal relationships, service and so on are important, and in some societies having a high standard of living is thought to be a matter of birth, luck or destiny (external locus of control). The most masculine countries are Japan, Austria, Venezuela, Italy and Switzerland. The USA, Britain and Germany all fall into the highest quartile. Four North European countries are the highest scoring feminine countries. France is about halfway.

At a later date Hofstede and Bond (1991) added a fifth dimension – short/long-term orientation. A short-term orientation focuses on past and present and therefore values respect for the status quo, including, for example, an unqualified respect for tradition and for social and status obligations. A long-term orientation focuses on the future and therefore the values associated with this are more dynamic. For example they include the adaptation of traditions to contemporary conditions and only qualified respect for social and status obligations.

Using Hofstede's dimensions, therefore, the USA, our role model for entrepreneurial culture, emerges as a highly individualistic, masculine culture, with low power distance and uncertainty avoidance. It is a culture that tolerates risk and ambiguity, has a preference for flexibility and an empowered culture that rewards personal initiative. It is a highly individualistic and egalitarian culture, one that is fiercely competitive and the home of the 'free-market economy'. Assertiveness and competition are central to the 'American dream'. If there is a key virtue in the USA it is achievement, and achievement receives its monetary reward. It is an informal culture. All men are created equal, however, they also have the freedom to accumulate sufficient wealth to become very unequal. The USA is the original 'frontier culture'. It actually seems to like change and uncertainty and certainly rewards initiative and risk-taking.

Using Hofstede's dimensions, this, then, is the anatomy of an enterprise culture. One that encourages enterprise and entrepreneurship, one where the probability of an entrepreneur being made, rather than just born, is highest. This is the sort of culture that many other countries have been trying to encourage and develop because it seems to encourage the characteristics that are needed for successful management. This culture, combined with the other antecedent influences, is said to be likely to develop the largest number of that most valuable resource – entrepreneurs.

However, notice one thing from Figure 2.3; alongside the USA, at the extreme ends of these dimensions, is the UK and that can hardly have been held up to be the epitome of an enterprise culture at the time these studies were conducted. The explanation may lay in the timing of the study. In the 1970s in both UK and USA political interest focused on enterprise as a means of rescuing their stagnant economies (O'Connor, 1973). It was argued that structural change was needed to achieve an 'enteprise culture' (Carr, 2000; Morris, 1991) and this would have to be accompanied by cultural change at the level of the individual, so much so that it would bring about a revolution that was moral, economic and enduring. And in the UK it was, arguably, the Thatcher government that brought about that change in the 1970s.

It is possible, however, that the dimensions measured by Hofstede are just not relevant to entrepreneurship. Perhaps there are other equally relevant, important but uncharted dimensions. After all, his work was based upon IBM employees and they can hardly be described as the most entrepreneurial in the world, particularly just at

Case with questions

Hilary Andrews comes from a family of entrepreneurs. Her father ran a building and landscaping company and her sister ran a public relations company. Hilary wanted to be a beauty therapist so she left sixth form college to go to a private college ahead of going to work in a beauty salon. However it was not too long before she opened her own salon in Woking, in 1983. But Hilary got bored and felt the insecurity of self-employment, so in 1990 she took a teacher training course and then a degree in education, going on to teach beauty and holistic therapy in Farnborough. She then got a job in a company distributing products to the spa industry, working in their mail order department. It was here that she came upon the idea for her business. Men kept asking for advice on products for them to use on their skin, so she decided to research the emerging market for men's skin care products. She quickly decided there was a real business opportunity in setting up a mail order company selling just men's cosmetics. The market for male grooming products was growing rapidly but, more importantly for her idea, many men preferred not to visit shops.

However Hilary was by now 38 years old and she found the prospect of setting up on her own daunting. Luckily she was able to find a business partner, **Paul Jamieson**, through a mutual friend. She enthused him with her business idea and he decided he was willing to back her. But more money was needed and the banks and private investors were not convinced. They thought the idea untried and untested and did not believe men would buy grooming products in this way. Not to be put off, Hilary remortgaged her house, raising £10 000 and Paul put in £20 000 of his own money. Hilary managed to borrow a further £20 000 from two family members and two friends. With £50 000 of capital **Mankind** was launched in 2000.

First Hilary secured the products she wished to sell by entering into distributor agreements for a range of selected products. Then she bought mailing lists and printed some 100 000 catalogues. Friends and family helped stuff the catalogues into envelopes and mail them out. Sufficient sales came from this first mailshot to establish the business and it quickly developed its own mailing list. But it was through developing a website and exploiting the internet market that the business really took off. This was a key decision that allowed it to grow, just as online shopping was becoming popular.

'We knew there were guys who wanted these products but didn't want the hassle of going to a shop and speaking to a consultant. The internet has made it easy to buy products that were previously difficult to get and enabled us to give people a lot of information about them. About 99 per cent of our sales are through the internet now. We have watched things develop very quickly in both the male grooming and the internet market. But we have tried to control the growth so we don't try to run before we can walk. I'm a cautious person who looks at the downside of things.

It's about being really focused on what you do ... You have to watch the bottom line constantly. Its not about starting a business and getting yourself a nice car; its about starting a business and having a really solid model that works ... What motivates me is being successful in an industry I love. It's a rewarding thing to give people confidence.'

By 2005 Mankind's turnover had grown to almost £3 million – and despite the hard work Hilary had still found time to marry and have a son.

Sunday Times 9 October 2005

Questions
1 Which of the character traits of the entrepreneur does Hilary exhibit?
2 What other influences can you detect?
3 How much of the success of this venture is down to the right idea at the right time?

the time when Microsoft was setting out in business. Whilst other countries try to emulate the enterprise culture of the USA, the jury is out on how precisely the dimensions of their enterprise culture are to be measured.

Notwithstanding this serious reservation about measurement, we know that deep cultures take time to change, if indeed they can be changed. There is little evidence, as yet, of different cultures around the world converging. What is more, we do not understand how best to go about changing national cultures, even if we believe it desirable. Rather than trying to change a nation's culture perhaps the best thing to do may be to ensure that, at the very least, it does not inhibit entrepreneurship.

Culture is, however, something that can be influenced and shaped in an organisational context and we return to this important issue in Chapters 9 and 18.

Measuring Entrepreneurial Personality

The **General Enterprise Tendency** test has been developed by staff at Durham University Business School over several years to measure a number of personal 'tendencies' commonly associated with the enterprising person. The test aims to measure 'tendency' rather than traits and was developed following research into a variety of dimensions used to measure entrepreneurship and enterprise. It was validated with a number of different groups of people and amended accordingly. It is a 54-question instrument that measures entrepreneurial personality traits in five dimensions:

- Need for achievement – 12 questions.
- Autonomy – 6 questions.
- Drive and determination – 12 questions.
- Risk-taking – 12 questions.
- Creativity and potential to innovate – 6 questions.

It is relatively quick and simple to administer – with either agree or disagree questions – and score. Each dimension receives a score of up to 12 points (Autonomy six points) and the final composite score measures inherent entrepreneurial character traits on a scale of 0–54.

Stormer et al. (1999) applied the test to 128 owners of new (75) and successful (53) small firms. They concluded that the test was acceptable for research purposes, particularly for identifying owner-managers. It was poor at predicting small business success. They concluded that either the test scales needed to be refined for this purpose or that the test did not include sufficient indicators of success such as situational influences on the individual or other factors related to the business rather than the individual setting it up. It would seem that, while entrepreneurs are both born and made, success requires more than an ounce of commercial expertise ... oh yes ... and a little luck!

An electronic version of the tool is available online at the website accompanying this book (www.palgrave.com/business/burns). Why not try it and see whether you are entrepreneurial?

Summary

Owner-managers and entrepreneurs are both born and made. They have certain personal character traits that they are born with and are influenced by antecedent factors as well as the culture into which they are born. The issue of linking the character traits of an individual to the success of a business – picking winners – needs to be approached with caution. Success or failure in business comes from a mix of many different things. The character traits of the manager is just one factor in the equation. What is more, there are a number of methodological problems associated with trying to measure personality traits:

- They are not stable and change over time.
- They require subjective judgements.
- Measures tend to ignore cultural and environmental influences.
- The role of education, learning and training is often overlooked.
- Issues such as age, sex, race, social class and education can be ignored.

Owner-managers have the following character traits:

- Need for independence.
- Need for achievement, strongest in entrepreneurs like **Stephen Waring**, **Chey Garland**, **Brent Hoberman** and **Charles Muirhead**.
- Internal locus of control, that is, a belief that they can control their own destiny, as with **Jonathan Elvidge**.
- Ability to live with uncertainty and take measured risks, like **David Speakman** and **Jonathan Elvidge** but unlike **Jean Young**.

In addition, entrepreneurs have the following character traits. Some more entrepreneurial owner-managers might also exhibit them, albeit to a lesser degree:

- Opportunistic, creating or exploiting change for profit, like **Richard Branson** and **Simon Woodroffe**.
- Innovative, using innovation as their prime tool to create or exploit opportunity, like **Neil Kelly**.
- Self-confident, like **Richard Thompson** and **Chris Ingram**.
- Proactive and decisive with high energy, like **Tom Farmer** and **Bob Worcester**.
- Self-motivated, like **Martha Lane Fox** and **Wing Yip**.
- Possessing vision and flair, like **Mike Peters**.
- Willing to take greater risks and live with greater uncertainty, like **Anne Notley**.

Education is an important antecedent influence on start-ups but more particularly entrepreneurial growth businesses. Whilst unemployment is a strong push into self-employment, entrepreneurial growth businesses are more likely to be set up for more positive motives. It is possible that having a parent who was previously self-employed is more likely to lead people to set up their own firm. Observation tells us that another influence is immigration to a foreign country. Despite arguments to the contrary, we observe numerous examples of immigrants who establish very successful business (**Navin Engineer, Bharat Shah, Bharat** and **Ketan Mehta, Vijay** and **Bikhu Patel, Ravi Karia** and **Naresh Shah**).

Growth companies are more likely to be set up by groups rather than individuals often sharing ownership to attract experienced managers. They are more likely to be set up by middle-aged owners with previous managerial experience who leave their job for the start-up. However, observation tells us that this might be changing with computers and e-commerce creating a whole generation of very young millionaire entrepreneurs.

Culture – 'the software of the mind' – also influences the decision whether to set up one's own firm and whether to grow it. Culture can be measured in four dimensions: individualism vs collectivism; power distance; uncertainty avoidance; and masculinity vs femininity. The USA is probably the role model for an entrepreneurial culture. It emerges as a highly individualistic, masculine culture, with low power distance and uncertainty avoidance. Whether or not you accept these dimensions of culture as saying anything about entrepreneurship, what is true is that entrepreneurship is ingrained into the fabric of culture in the USA, part of the 'American dream'.

Essays and discussion topics

1   Are entrepreneurs born or made?
2   Do you think you have what it takes to be an owner-manager or entrepreneur?
3   Which character traits of owner-managers and entrepreneurs might have negative effects on a business?
4   What factors do you think affect the success or otherwise of a business venture?
5   Can you 'pick winners'?
6   How do entrepreneurs cope with risk and uncertainty?
7   What are the defining characteristics of an entrepreneur?
8   Are immigrants more entrepreneurial?
9   Can training help develop entrepreneurship?
10 Has your education, so far, encouraged you to be entrepreneurial? If so, how? If not, how could it be changed?
11 Does this course encourage entrepreneurship?
12 Is entrepreneurship really just for the middle-aged?
13 Are there advantages to setting up your own business when you are young?
14 Why might so many dot.com entrepreneurs be young and well-educated?
15 Is it really better to set up in business with other individuals?
16 Does previous business failure mean that you are more likely to succeed in the future?
17 Have attitudes to entrepreneurs changed in this country over the last twenty years?
18 Does this country have an enterprise culture?
19 How can enterprise culture be encouraged?
20 Why is the USA considered the most entrepreneurial culture in the world?
21 Which other countries would you consider to have an entrepreneurial culture?
22 Are there any other dimensions along which an enterprise culture could be measured?

Exercises and assignments

1   List the questions you would ask an owner-manager or entrepreneur in trying to assess their character traits.
2   Use the list of questions developed in exercise 1 to conduct an interview with an owner-manager of a local small firm. Once you have done this get them to complete the GET test. Summarise the most important observation and insights you have gained from the interview. Write a report describing their character. Make sure you justify your conclusions about their character with evidence from the interview and the GET test.

3   Find out all you can about a well-known entrepreneur and write an essay or report describing their character. Give examples of their actions that lead you to make your conclusions.
4   Using the GET test and the questions developed in exercise 1 as a basis, evaluate your own entrepreneurial character. Write a report describing your character. Give examples of actions or behaviours that support these conclusions.

References

Abdesselam, R., Bonnet, J. and Le Pape, N. (1999) 'An Explanation of the Life Span of New Firms: An Empirical Analysis of French Data', *Entrepreneurship: Building for the Future*, Euro PME 2nd International Conference, Rennes.
Aldrich, H.E. and Martinez, M. (2003) 'Entrepreneurship as a Social Construction: A Multi-Level Evolutionary Approach', in Z.J. Acs and D.B. Audretsch (eds), *Handbook of Entrepreneurship Research: A Multidisciplinary Survey and Introduction*, Boston, MA: Kluwer Academic Publishers.
Anderson, J. (1995) *Local Heroes*, Scottish Enterprise, Glasgow.
Andersson, S., Gabrielsson, J. and Wictor, I. (2004) 'International Activities in Small Firms – Examining Factors Influencing the Internationalisation and Export Growth of Small Firms', *Canadian Journal of Administrative Science*, 21(1).
Baty, G. (1990) *Entrepreneurship in the Nineties*, Englewood Cliffs, NJ: Prentice Hall.
Bell, J., Murray, M. and Madden, K. (1992) 'Developing Expertise: An Irish Perspective', *International Small Business Journal*, 10(2).
Blanchflower, D.G. and Meyer, B.D. (1991) 'Longitudinal Analysis of Young Entrepreneurs in Australia and the United States', *National Bureau of Economic Research*, Working Paper no. 3746, Cambridge, MA.
Bolton, B. and Thompson, J. (2000) *Entrepreneurs: Talent, Temperament, Technique*, Oxford: Butterworth-Heinemann.
Brockhaus, R. and Horwitz, P. (1986) 'The Psychology of the Entrepreneur', in D. Sexton and R. Smilor (eds), *The Art and Science of Entrepreneurship*, Cambridge, MA: Ballinger Publishing Co.
Brush, C.G. (1992) 'Research on Women Business Owners: Past Trends, A New Perspective and Future Directions', *Entrepreneurship: Theory and Practice*, 16(4).
Busenitz, L. and Barney, J. (1997) 'Differences between Entrepreneurs and Managers in Large Organisations: Biases and Heuristics in Strategic Decision Making', *Journal of Business Venturing*, 12.
Buttner, E. and More, D. (1997) 'Women's Organisational Exodus to Entrepreneurship: Self-Reported Motivations and Correlates with Success', *Journal of Small Business Management*, 35(1).
Caird, S. (1990) 'What Does it Mean to be Enterprising?', *British Journal of Management*, 1(3).
Carr, P. (2000) *The Age of Enterprise: The Emergence and Evolution of Entrepreneurial Management*, Dublin: Blackwell.
Carter, S. and Cachon, J. (1988) *The Sociology of Entrepreneurship*, Stirling: University of Stirling Press.
Chell, E., Haworth, J. and Brearley, S. (1991) *The Entrepreneurial Personality*, London: Routledge.
Chen, P.C., Greene, P.G. and Crick, A. (1998) 'Does Entreprenerial Self Efficacy Distinguish Entrepreneurs from Managers?', *Journal of Business Venturing*, 13.
Cuba, R., Decenzo, D. and Anish, A. (1983) 'Management Practises of Successful Female Business Owners', *American Journal of Small Business*, 8(2).
Deakins, D. (1996) *Entrepreneurs and Small Firms*, London: McGraw-Hill.
de Bono, E. (1985) *Six Thinking Hats*, Boston: Little Brown & Company.
Evans, D.S. and Leighton, L.S. (1990) 'Small Business Formation by Unemployed and Employed Workers', *Small Business Economics*, 2(4).
Harper, M. (1985) 'Hardship, Discipline and Entrepreneurship', *Cranfield School of Management*, Working Paper no. 85.1.

Hirsch, R.D. and Brush, C.G. (1987) 'Women Entrepreneurs: A Longitudinal Study', *Frontiers in Entrepreneurship Research,* Wellesley, MA: Babson College.

Hofstede, G. (1980) *Culture's Consequences: International Differences in Work-related Values*, Beverly Hills, CA: Sage.

Hofstede, G. (1981) *Cultures and Organisations: Software of the Mind*, London: HarperCollins.

Hofstede, G. and Bond, M.H. (1991) 'The Confucian Connection: From Cultural Roots to Economic Performance', *Organisational Dynamics*, Spring.

Kanter, R.M. (1983) *The Change Masters*, New York: Simon & Schuster.

Kets de Vries, M.F.R. (1985) 'The Dark Side of Entrepreneurship', *Harvard Business Review*, November–December.

Kets de Vries, M.F.R. (1997) 'The Entrepreneurial Personality: A Person at the Crossroads', *Journal of Management Studies*, February.

Kirzner, I.M. (1973) *Competition and Entrepreneurship,* Chicago: University of Chicago.

Kirzner, I.M. (1979) *Perception, Opportunity and Profit: Studies in the Theory of Entrepreneurship*, Chicago: University of Chicago.

Kirzner, I.M. (1997) 'Entrepreneurial Discovery and Competitive Market Processes: An Austrian Approach', *Journal of Economic Literature*, 35.

Kirzner, I.M. (1999) 'Creativity and/or Alertness: A Reconsideration of Schumpeterian Entrepreneur', *Review of Austrian Economics*, 11.

McClelland, D. C. (1961) *The Achieving Society*, Princeton, NJ: Van Nostrand.

Morris, P. (1991) 'Freeing the Spirit of Enterprise: The Genesis and Development of the Concept of Enterprise Culture', in R. Keat and N. Abercrombie (eds), *Enterprise Culture*, London: Routledge.

O'Connor, J. (1973) *The Fiscal Crisis of the State*, New York: St. Martin's Press.

Pinchot, G. (1985) *Intrapreneuring*, New York: Harper & Row.

Rosa, P., Hamilton, S., Carter, S. and Burns, H. (1994) 'The Impact of Gender on Small Business Management: Preliminary Findings of a British Study', *International Small Business Journal*, 12(3).

Schein, V., Mueller, R., Lituchy, T. and Liu, J. (1996) 'Thinking Manager – Think Male: A Global Phenomenon?', *Journal of Organisational Behaviour*, 17.

Schumpeter, J.A. (1983/1996) *The Theory of Economic Development*, New Brunswick, NJ: Transaction Publishers.

Schwartz, E.B. (1997) 'Entrepreneurship: A New Female Frontier', *Journal of Contemporary Business,* Winter.

Shapero, A. (1985) *Managing Professional People – Understanding Creative Performance*, New York: Free Press.

Shaver, K. and Scott, L. (1992) 'Person, Processes and Choice: The Psychology of New Venture Creation', *Entrepreneurship Theory and Practice,* 16(2).

Stanworth, J., Blythe, S., Granger, B. and Stanworth, C. (1989) 'Who Becomes an Entrepreneur?', *International Small Business Journal*, 8(1).

Storey, D.J. (1994) *Understanding the Small Business Sector*, London: International Thomson Business Press.

Storey, D. and Sykes, N. (1996) 'Uncertainty, Innovation and Management', in P. Burns and J. Dewhurst (eds), *Small Business and Entrepreneurship*, London: Macmillan – now Basingstoke: Palgrave Macmillan.

Stormer, R., Kilne, T. and Goldberg, S. (1999) 'Measuring Entrepreneurship with the General Enterprise Tendency (GET) Test: Criterion-Related Validity and Reliability', *Human Systems Management*, 18(1).

Timmons, J. (1994) *New Venture Creation*, Boston, MA: Irwin.

Welsch, H. (1998) 'America: North', in A. Morrison (ed.), *Entrepreneurship: An International Perspective*, Oxford: Butterworth Heinemann.

3

Opportunity, Innovation and Entrepreneurship

Contents

- Tools of entrepreneurship
- Innovation and invention
- Innovation and entrepreneurship
- Creativity and entrepreneurship
- Sources of opportunity
- Innovation and size
- Innovation and location
- Summary

LEARNING OUTCOMES

By the end of this chapter you should be able to:

- Explain the nature of innovation and why it is so difficult to define;

- Explain the critical role of the entrepreneur in the process of innovation;

- Describe the links between innovation, opportunity and entrepreneurship;

- Describe how opportunity seeking can be stimulated in a systematic way;

- Describe how innovation differs in small and large firms;

- Explain 'innovative milieu' theory and how it explains innovative clusters of small firms;

- Assess whether you are an innovative thinker.

Tools of entrepreneurship

Chapter 1 defined entrepreneurs by their use of innovation to exploit or create change and opportunity for the purpose of making profit. Change creates opportunity and entrepreneurs create value by exploiting or creating change, for example in technology, materials, prices or demographics. They create new demand or find ways of exploiting existing markets. Entrepreneurs are the key to identifying commercial opportunities and then exploiting them and this is why they are so valued in today's society. In this way they innovate. Change, opportunity and innovation are all brought together by the entrepreneur for commercial gain. In *The Competitive Advantage of Nations*, Michael Porter (1990) states that 'companies achieve competitive advantage through acts of innovation'. Cannon (1985) points out that 'the ability of the entrepreneurial mould-maker to break free from bureaucratic rigidities, fan the flames of innovation and create new situations has been the basis of the growth of many of today's great corporations. Ford, Durant, Kellogg, Singer, Krupp, Eastman, Courtauld, Daimler, Biro, Siemens and Daussault all built giant enterprises which are virtually synonymous with their industries'.

The ability to spot opportunities arising from change and to innovate are the two most important distinguishing features of entrepreneurs. Innovation is the prime tool entrepreneurs use to create or exploit opportunity and firms that grow do so because they innovate in some way. However, entrepreneurs are not the only people who try to practise innovation. For all firms, of any size, innovation has become something of a Holy Grail to be sought after and encouraged.

Creativity is also linked to innovation. However, in his review of the literature, Van Grundy (1987) distinguishes between innovation and creativity. Creativity may contribute to innovation, but equally it can be used towards other ends. Indeed creativity is only part of the process of innovation. Kanter (1983) defines innovation as 'the generation, acceptance and implementation of new ideas, processes, products and services ... [which] involves creative use as well as original invention'. Mellor (2005) defines it simply as either 'creativity + application' or 'invention + application'.

So how is innovation to be encouraged? Can it be pursued in a systematic way? Can entrepreneurs learn anything from this? Indeed, can large firms learn anything about the process of innovation by observing how entrepreneurs go about it? Do small firms innovate? What changes in the future will create opportunities for entrepreneurs to pursue?

Innovation and invention

Porter (*op. cit.*) said: 'Invention and entrepreneurship are at the heart of national advantage.' In saying this he implied two things. Firstly, there exists a relationship between invention and entrepreneurship, which must be correct because entrepreneurship is the process that brings invention to the market place. Secondly, he implied a direct and important link between invention and national advantage. This is more questionable since invention is not the only source of innovation which can benefit the individual firm and create national advantage. Invention is the extreme and riskiest form of innovation. It is usually associated with the development

Case insight

James Dyson is the inventor of the revolutionary cyclone vacuum cleaner who challenged established large companies in the market and gained a market share in excess of 50 per cent. Inventor of the 'Ballbarrow', a light plastic wheelbarrow with a ball rather than a wheel, the idea for the cleaner came to him in 1979 because he was finding that traditional cleaners could not clear all the dust he was creating as he converted an old house. Particles clogged the pores of the dust bags and reduced the suction. He had developed a small version of large industrial cyclone machines, which separate particles from air by using centrifugal force, in order to collect paint particles from his plastic-spraying operation for the Ballbarrow. He believed the technology could be adapted for the home vacuum cleaner, generating greater suction and eliminating the need for bags.

Working from home, investing all his own money, borrowing on the security of his home and drawing just £10 000 a year to support himself, his wife and three children, he produced 5000 different prototypes. However, established manufacturers rejected his ideas and venture capitalists declined to invest. In 1991 he took the product to Japan and won the 1991 International Design Fair prize. He licensed the manufacture of the product in Japan where it became a status symbol selling at $2000 a time. On the back of this and twelve years after the idea first came to him, he was able to obtain finance from Lloyds Bank to manufacture the machine under his own name in the UK.

Early sales were through mail order, then followed a deal with John Lewis and later Comet and Currys. There are now 18 different sorts of Dyson cleaner and the company has captured 38 per cent of the UK market. But the Dual Cyclone was nearly never made due to patent and legal costs. Unlike a songwriter who owns his songs, an inventor must pay substantial fees to renew his patent each year. This nearly bankrupted Dyson in the development years.

Dyson's major competitor, Hoover, paid him the ultimate compliment of copying his design with their Vortex range. In 2000 he won his case against them for infringing his patents. James Dyson is chairman and sole shareholder of his company with his personal wealth estimated to be over £700 million. He is in the top 50 richest people in the UK. Dyson is one of that rare breed – inventor, innovator and entrepreneur.

●

of a new or better product or process but, arguably, could be associated with different forms of marketing. However, examples abound of inventions that are not commercially successful. Thomas Edison, probably the most successful inventor of all time, was so incompetent at introducing his inventions to the market place that his backers had to remove him from every new business he founded.

On the other hand, innovation is more than just invention and it is not, necessarily, just the product of research. It can be many things, for example the substitution of a cheaper material in an existing product, or a better way of marketing an existing product or service, or even a better way of distributing or supporting an existing product or service. Entrepreneurial firms in particular are often innovative in their approach to marketing, finding more effective, often cheaper routes to market. Direct Line pioneered the sale of car insurance – a mature, long-established product – to the UK public in a way that was innovative at the time – directly, cutting out insurance brokers. Interestingly it was copying a US firm that had done the same.

It looked at the value chain (see Chapter 9) for insurance and concluded that the broker network added substantial cost but little or no value to the customer. Innovation, therefore, is about doing things differently in some way.

Mintzberg (1983) defined innovation as 'the means to break away from established patterns', in other words doing things really differently. So, simply introducing a new product or service that has customers willing to buy it is not necessarily innovation. True innovation has to break the mould of how things are done. New cars are rarely truly innovative, despite what the marketing hype might say. However, the Mini was innovative because it changed the way cars were designed and changed the way people perceived vehicle size.

Schumpeter (1996) described five types of innovation:

1 The introduction of a new or improved good or service.
2 The introduction of a new process.
3 The opening up of a new market.
4 The identification of new sources of supply of raw materials.
5 The creation of new types of industrial organisation.

In fact there are considerable problems interpreting these criteria for innovation. For example, what constitutes a new product or service? When a sofa manufacturer produces a 'new' sofa, is that a new product? Economists would probably argue that it was not (because the cross elasticity of demand[1] is unlikely to be zero) – but the entrepreneur might disagree. What if the sofa manufacturer starts manufacturing chairs? At what point does the firm start producing genuinely new products? As Porter (1998a) observed, 'much innovation is mundane and incremental, depending more on an accumulation of small insights than on a single major technological breakthrough'. If Schumpeter's description of innovation is inadequate it is because of the myriad forms it can take. What is more, the central role of the entrepreneurial firm in taking the innovation to the market needs to be explicitly acknowledged in any definition.

Morris and Kuratko (2002) expand on Schumpeter's list and talk about the range or continuum of possibilities shown in Figure 3.1. These relate to either the introduction of new products/services or new processes. New processes can be administrative or service delivery systems, new production or financing methods, different marketing, sales, distribution or procurement approaches, new information or supply chain management systems. This is a frequent route to innovation for entrepreneurial firms.

What constitutes innovation in the context of this continuum may be contentious, but what is true is that the sum of many small, incremental innovations can have an enormous impact on competitive advantage (Bessant, 1999). Often these innovations are introduced during the later stages of the life cycle of a product or service so as to

---

[1] Cross elasticity of demand measures the responsiveness of demand for a product to the change in price of other related products. When there is zero elasticity of demand there is no relationship between the products. Thus if elasticity is not zero, customers require some price inducement to try the 'new' product.

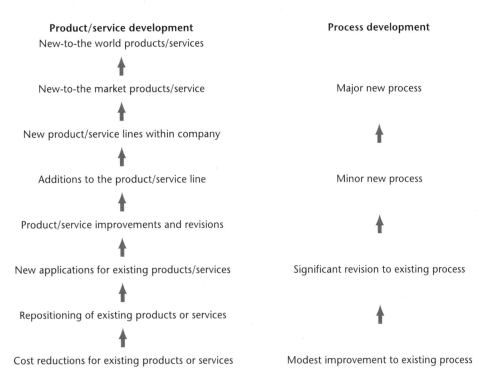

Product/service development

New-to-the world products/services

↑

New-to-the market products/service

↑

New product/service lines within company

↑

Additions to the product/service line

↑

Product/service improvements and revisions

↑

New applications for existing products/services

↑

Repositioning of existing products or services

↑

Cost reductions for existing products or services

Process development

Major new process

↑

Minor new process

↑

Significant revision to existing process

↑

Modest improvement to existing process

Source: Adapted from Morris and Kuratko, *op. cit.*

Figure 3.1 Product/service and processes development: a spectrum

maintain or improve competitive advantage and extend its life. This leads to the idea that the impact of innovation on competitive advantage might be measured on two dimensions – frequency of innovation and scale of innovation. This is shown in Figure 3.2. Frequent small innovations may compensate for the occasional 'big-bang' breakthrough. What is more, frequent small innovations may also be less risky.

One point to note is that Morris and Kuratko's continuum of possibilities (Figure 3.1) does not include innovations in marketing, a form of innovation that is also used very effectively by entrepreneurial firms – for example when Direct Line introduced direct selling of insurance in the UK, doing away with the traditional insurance broker network. Whether a concept or activity may be described as innovative depends on whether it represents a 'departure from what is currently available' – that is, what is unique or different. This is what makes the concept or activity an innovation.

Kirton (1976) distinguishes between an innovator and an adaptor in terms of the *approach* each takes to problem solving, rather than the outcome itself. One engages in divergent thinking aimed at innovation; the other engages in convergent thinking aimed at perfection. These are contrasted in Table 3.1.

But entrepreneurial innovation is even more than this. What is needed to make the innovation successful is for it to be linked to customer demand – existing or in the future – that is, a market opportunity. Whilst some entrepreneurs might achieve this

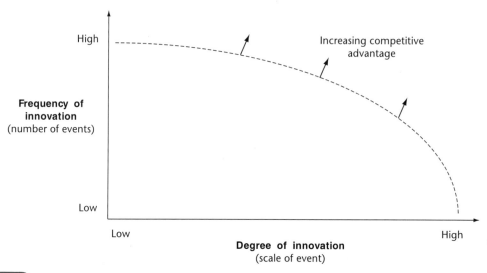

Figure 3.2 Innovation and competitive advantage

link through luck, it is the link between innovation and opportunity in the market place that reduces the risk for the entrepreneurial firm and gives it the competitive advantage it seeks – and that market linkage needs to be developed and embedded in the processes of the firm. Even process innovation, which may involve no change in the product itself, to be successful must be linked to customer demand through cost/ price, quality lead times and so on. Finding opportunities must become a systematic process for the entrepreneurial firm.

Table 3.1 Two approaches to problem solving

Adaptor	Innovator
Employs a disciplined, precise, methodical approach	Approaches task from unusual angles
Is concerned with solving, rather than finding, problems	Discovers problems and avenues of solution
Attempts to refine current practices	Questions basic assumptions related to current practices
Tends to be means orientated	Has little regard for means; is more interested in ends
Is capable of extended detail work	Has little tolerance for routine work
Is sensitive to group cohesion and cooperation	Has little or no need for consensus; often is insensitive to others

Source: Kirton, M. (1976) 'Adaptors and Innovators: A Description and Measure', *Journal of Applied Psychology*, October.

Like it or loath it, **McDonald's**, the ubiquitous hamburger chain, brought true innovation to the food industry. It developed a standardised, high quality hamburger sandwich, produced using entirely new cooking procedures, delivered with the speed of just-in-time preparation by meticulously trained people, in clean surroundings and at a bargain price. This was something entirely new for customers and it spawned a completely new market called 'the fast-food industry'. In doing this not only did they have first mover advantage, they also created the rules for a whole new industry. And if you write the rule book, inevitably you have an incredible competitive advantage. The question today is whether the product has finally come to the end of its life cycle?

●

Video recorders were invented by an American firm called Ampex in 1954. They were reel-to-reel devices, about the size of a juke box, and were used by television networks to record and then transmit programmes in different time zones. However, the real innovators were the Japanese companies Sony (with their Betamax system) and, to a greater extent, JVC (with their VHS system) who realised that the big market for video recorders would be in the home. They succeeded in producing a small video recorder at an affordable price. Like all the best innovations it did not replace an existing product but created its own market. In the 1980s Japanese video-cassette recorders accounted for half of its consumer electronics industry's annual sales of $30 billion and three-quarters of its combined profits. Today they have almost been replaced by DVD recorders, such is the pace of technological change.

Innovation and entrepreneurship

It is the work of Joseph Schumpeter, an Austrian economist, that most strongly links entrepreneurship to innovation. He was the first person to challenge classical economics and the way it sought to optimise existing resources within a stable environment and treated disruptions as a 'god sent' external force. In his primary work, Schumpeter (1934) sets out his overall theory of economic development – an endogenous process within capitalism of wrenching the economy out of its tendency towards one equilibrium position and towards a different one. This fundamental phenomenon entails new combinations of the means of production being carried out, which Schumpeter labels 'enterprise' but we could equally call 'innovation', while the individuals carrying them out are called 'entrepreneurs'. These new combinations 'as a rule ... must draw the necessary means of production from some old combinations'.

Schumpeter was arguing against traditional economic theory which presumed that the economy always tended towards equilibrium and that changes in that equilibrium could only occur through changes in underlying conditions of the economy such as population growth or changes in savings ratios, or what were thought of as external shocks such as wars or natural disasters. The former were thought to change only slowly and the latter only unpredictably. Schumpeter sought to explain the process of economic development as a process caused by enterprise – or innovation – and carried out by entrepreneurs.

For Schumpeter a normal healthy economy was one that was continually being 'disrupted' by technological innovation producing the 50-year cycles of economic activity noticed earlier by the Russian economist, Nikolai Kondratieff. Using data on prices, wages and interest rates in France, Britain and the USA, Kondratieff first noticed these 'long waves' of economic activity in 1925. Unfortunately he was executed by Stalin some ten years later because he (accurately as it turned out) predicted that Russian farm collectivisation would lead to a decline in farm production. It was therefore left to Schumpeter to study these waves in depth.

Schumpeter said that each of these cycles was unique, driven by different clusters of industries. The upswing in a cycle started when new innovations came into general use:

- Water power, textiles and iron in the late 18th century.
- Steam, rail and steel in the mid 19th century.
- Electricity, chemicals and the internal combustion engine in the early 20th century.

These booms eventually petered out as the technologies matured and the market opportunities were fully exploited, only to start again as a new set of innovations changed the way things were done. For the last twenty years of the cycle the growth industries of the last technological wave might be doing exceptionally well. However they are, in fact, just repaying capital that is no longer needed for investment. This situation never lasts longer than twenty years and returns to investors then start to decline with the dwindling number of opportunities. Often this is precipitated by some form of crisis. After the twenty years of stagnation new technologies will emerge and the cycle will start again.

The other factor at work is that innovation – particularly technological innovation – also seems to generate growth that cannot be accounted for by changes in labour and capital. Although the return on investment may decline as more capital is introduced to an economy, any deceleration in growth is more than offset by the leverage effects of innovation. Because of this the rich Western countries have seen their return on investment increasing, whilst the poorer countries have not caught up.

By the time Schumpeter died in 1950 the next cycle of boom was starting, based upon oil, electronics, aviation and mass production. Another started in the 1980s based upon digital networks, software and new media. The internet and e-commerce triggered an even shorter boom in the late 1990s. One reason for this shortening cycle may be the more systematic approach entrepreneurs now have towards exploiting innovation.

But innovation does not happen as a random event. Central to the process are the entrepreneurs. It is they who introduce and then exploit the new innovations. For Schumpeter, 'the entrepreneur initiates change and generates new opportunities. Until imitators force prices and costs into conformity, the innovator is able to reap profits and disturb equilibrium'. By way of contrast, early classical economists such as Adam Smith saw the entrepreneurs as having a rather minor role in overall economic activity. He thought that they provided real capital, but did not play a leading or direct part in how the pattern of supply and demand was determined.

Pulling together these strands, therefore, real innovation might be defined as a single 'mould-breaking' development in new products or services or how they are produced (the materials used, the process employed or how the firm is organised to deliver them) or how or to whom they are marketed that can be linked to a commercial opportunity and successfully exploited. However frequent, incremental small-scale 'innovations' may create similar competitive advantage, with lower associated risk. In reality degree and frequency of innovation combine to produce competitive advantage.

Returning to Michael Porter's issue of national advantage, the link in taking invention to the market place is indeed the entrepreneur or the entrepreneurial firm but what they are really seeking in doing this is innovation – difference – rather than invention, *per se*. It is innovation and entrepreneurship that are at the heart of success for the individual firm and of national advantage.

Creativity and entrepreneurship

Bolton and Thompson (2000) stress the importance of creativity in this process of invention and innovation. They associate invention closely with creativity but also link it with entrepreneurship if the invention is to become a commercial opportunity to be exploited. 'Creativity is the starting point whether it is associated with invention or opportunity spotting. This creativity is turned to practical reality (a product, for example) through innovation. Entrepreneurship then sets that innovation in the context of an enterprise (the actual business), which is something of recognised value'. Like Porter, to them creativity and invention need the entrepreneurial context, including the perception of opportunity, to become a business reality. These links between creativity, invention and innovation, opportunity perception and entrepreneurship are represented in Figure 3.3.

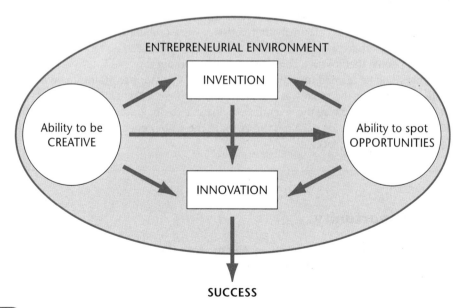

Figure 3.3 Creativity, invention, opportunity and entrepreneurship

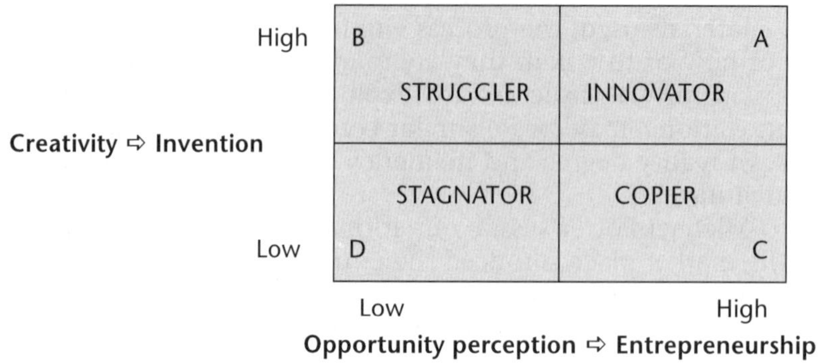

Figure 3.4 Invention and entrepreneurship

Another way of looking at this relationship between creativity and entrepreneurship and its real outcomes is shown in Figure 3.4. Only in quadrant A is there a winning combination of creativity and entrepreneurship. All other quadrants fail to achieve their full potential. In quadrant B there is a firm struggling with too many wasted ideas. It lacks an entrepreneurial orientation with the ability both to see the commercial application of the idea and to exploit it. In quadrant C there is a firm that lacks creativity but can at least copy and perhaps improve on the creative inventions coming from other firms if they have a commercial application. Firms in quadrant D, lack both creativity and entrepreneurship, are certain never to grow and indeed their very survival may be questioned.

Case insight

In 1991 **Trevor Baylis** was watching a TV programme about the Aids epidemic in Africa. It got him thinking about how information about Aids prevention might be broadcast to people in a country where there was no electricity and batteries were prohibitively expensive. He quickly came up with a design for a clockwork radio. Despite being featured on radio and TV he could not convince people that it was a commercially viable product.

It was only when he teamed up with an entrepreneur, **Christopher Staines**, and a company called **Liberty Life** that the radio was produced and marketed. The entrepreneur was able to exploit the innovation in a way the inventor was not able to do. Production began in 1994 and 120 000 radios are now made each month. Without the entrepreneur the invention would not have reached the market place.

●

Sources of opportunity

Valery (1999) believes that 'innovation has more to do with the pragmatic search for opportunity than the romantic ideas about serendipity or lonely pioneers pursuing their vision against all the odds.' Peter Drucker (1985) takes this further. He believes innovation can be practised systematically through a creative analysis of change in the environment and the opportunities this generates. It is not the result of happenstance. Entrepreneurs can practise innovation systematically by searching for

Case insight

Recently *Time* magazine named **RadioScape** as one of the top 50 technology companies in Europe. The company was set up in 1997 by **Peter Florence**, a serial entrepreneur. Aged only 39 at the time, this was his third technology-based start-up. RadioScape designs and develops enabling wireless communication. The technology developed by the company is part of the dominant digital radio brand and has the potential to be incorporated into every third-generation mobile phone. The company started to develop products on a wide front. Texas Instruments is now using its chip as part of a digital radio package, which means that when the medium takes off the royalty payments could be huge. Said Peter Florence:

'We believed that the world was going digital. We could see that, although the US was ahead of Europe in the use and development of the internet, Europe was way ahead in the use of mobiles and the development of digital technology. Like others, we could also see the potential of digital radio, not just in broadcasting quality sound but in receiving and transmitting raw data that can be used in computers. We went for digital radio as the major players were waiting and it was still at an early stage.'

Peter raised £18 million in venture capital in 2001 against this vision. But timing and credibility are all. Peter's first venture was **Digital Pictures**, a film production house specialising in 3D computer graphics. He had identified new technology that worked with the opportunity to generate revenues quickly. Eventually he sold out and moved on to set up **Cambridge Animation**, starting with 3D and expanding into 2D technology. The company grew rapidly, moving to Los Angeles where it worked with studios such as Dreamworks and Warner Bros. He then started looking for the next big technological niche with the help of the technologist behind Cambridge Animation, Gavin Ferris. RadioScape currently has 90 employees and has a turnover of £8 million. Peter continues:

'There was a time if you had good technology in an interesting market and one or two ideas about how it might all end up ok on the night, that was enough. No more. Now you must have proven management, own a pretty solid patent and show that you can generate revenues quickly. Although the UK has been good at inventing technology, we have been poor at marrying the men in white coats with businessmen and entrepreneurs who can make the product work. That is my skill. You need a good chief executive and a good chief technology officer. One without the other is wasted.'

Peter Florence founder and Chief Executive, **RadioScape**
The Times 6 July 2002

change then carefully and creatively evaluate its potential for an economic or social return. Change provides the opportunity for innovation and it is the entrepreneur that makes this generate an economic return.

Drucker said 'innovation is the specific tool of entrepreneurs, the means by which they exploit change as an opportunity for a different business or a different service. It is capable of being presented as a discipline, capable of being learned and capable of being practised. Entrepreneurs need to search purposefully for the sources of innovation, the changes and their symptoms that indicate opportunities for successful innovation. And they need to know and to apply the principles of successful innovation'.

'When I started the Gadget Shop it was from a frustration with the difficulties of finding gifts for family and friends mixed with a love of innovation and gadgets. There are lots of problems in life that could be solved with the right insight leading to a business opportunity; you just have to spot them. Some of the most successful ideas are actually very simple.'

Jonathan Elvidge founder of **Gadget Shop**

The Times 6 July 2002

He lists seven sources of opportunity for firms in search of creative innovation. Four can be found within the firm itself or from the industry of which it is part and are therefore reasonably easy to spot. They are 'basic symptoms' – highly reliable indicators of changes that have already happened or can be made to happen with little effort. They are:

- *The unexpected* – be it the unexpected success or failure or the unexpected event. Nobody can predict the future but an ability to react quickly to changes is a real commercial advantage, particularly in a rapidly changing environment. Information and knowledge are invaluable.
- *The incongruity* – between what actually happens and what was supposed to happen. Plans go wrong and unexpected outcomes produce opportunities for firms that are able to spot them.
- *The inadequacy in underlying processes* – that are taken for granted but can be improved or changed. This is essentially improving process engineering – especially important if the product or service is competing primarily on price and therefore needs to minimise its costs.
- *The changes in industry or market structure* – that take everyone by surprise. Again, unexpected change, perhaps arising from technology, legislation or other outside events creates an opportunity for the entrepreneur and, as is often the case with all these sources of opportunity, first-mover advantage – making the most of the advantage before others do so – is usually worth striving for.

These changes produce sources of opportunity that need to be dissected and the underlying causes of change understood. The causes give clues about how innovation can be used to increase value added to the customer and economic return.

The other three factors come from the outside world:

- *Demographic changes* – population changes caused by changes in birth rates, wars, medical improvements etc.
- *Changes in perception, mood and meaning* – that can be brought about by the ups and down of the economy, culture, fashion etc. In-depth interviews or focus groups can often give an insight into these changes,
- *New knowledge* – both scientific and non-scientific.

Drucker lists the seven factors in what he sees as the increasing order of difficulty, uncertainty and unreliability, which means that he believes that new knowledge including scientific knowledge, for all its visibility and glamour – is in fact the most

> **Case insight**
>
> The internet is an opportunity that many have struggled to make a profit out of. The dot.com boom and bust underlined the fact that the opportunity created was high-risk. **Ebay**, the online auction site, is probably the leading example of a profitable network. But there are others. It all depends on the business model and how revenues are raised.
>
> **Yahoo** have been bundling services together for customers to subscribe to almost since its inception. For example, Yahoo Mail Plus bundles extra storage space for archived e-mails with a forwarding service for those with more than one e-mail address. With over 2 million fee-paying customers, revenues from fee-based services are now growing at five times the growth of advertising revenue.
>
> **NCsoft**, a Korean online gaming company, boasts more than 4 million customers of whom some 250 000 pay subscriptions. Customers 'join swords' in 'massively multiplayer' games such as Lineage, a fantasy role-playing game that can involve thousands of people at a time.
>
> **Friendsreunited.co.uk**, a British website that brings together old friends, started as a hobby working out of a home based website, and now claims 8 million registered users, many of whom pay a £5 annual subscription.
>
> ●

difficult, least reliable and least predictable source of innovation. Paradoxically, this is the area to which government, academics and even entrepreneurial firms pay most attention. He argues that innovations arising from the systematic analysis of mundane and unglamorous unexpected successes or failures are far more likely to yield commercial innovations. They have the shortest lead times between start and yielding measurable results and carry fairly low risk and uncertainty.

One technique for getting to the root cause of these 'unexpected events', 'incongruities' or 'inadequacies' is the 'Why? Why?' exercise. This is used to explore options related to the event. Figure 3.5 shows a 'Why? Why?' diagram exploring the reason for a fall in sales (Vyakarnham and Leppard, 1999). From it you can see there are several possible reasons, although the trails have not been taken to completion. The root cause will lie at the end of the 'why?' trail.

Figure 3.4 addresses a problem, but opportunities also spring from other sources. Bolton and Thompson (*op. cit.*) suggest that three basic approaches to innovation are practised, none of which are mutually exclusive:

1 *Have a problem and seek a solution.* They cite as an example Edwin Land's invention of the Polaroid camera because his young daughter could not understand why she had to wait to have pictures of herself printed.
2 *Have a solution and seek a problem.* They cite 3M's Post-it notes as an example of a product with loosely sticking qualities that was applied to the need to mark pages in a manuscript.
3 *Identify a need and develop a solution.* The example they cite is James Dyson's dual cyclone cleaner that he developed because of his frustration with the inadequate suction provided by his existing vacuum cleaner when he was converting an old property.

Firms with a good track record for innovation, therefore, practise it systematically. It does not happen by chance. They look for small changes that can be made to the

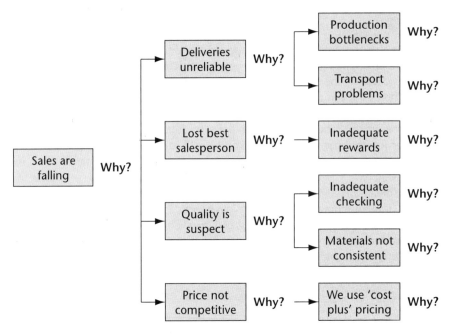

Source: Adapted from S. Vyarkarnham and J. Leppard (1999) A Marketing Action Plan for the Growing Business, 2nd edn, London: Kogan Page.

Figure 3.5 Why? Why? diagram

way they do things. Indeed so systematic can the search for innovation be that some firms have been set up specifically to undertake it. Drucker (*op. cit.*) advocates a five-stage approach to purposeful, systematic innovation:

1 *Start with the analysis of opportunities, inside the firm and its industry and in the external environment.* Information and knowledge are invaluable – from as many sources as possible. Do not innovate for the future, innovate for now. Timing is everything. The right idea at the wrong time is worth nothing.
2 *Innovation is both conceptual and perceptual.* Therefore look at the financial implications but also talk to people, particularly customers, and analyse how to meet the opportunity.
3 *To be effective, an innovation must be simple and has to be 'focused'.* Keep it as simple as possible. Don't try to be too clever. Don't try to do too many things at once. The slightly-wrong-but-can-be-improved idea can always be developed and still earn a fortune.
4 *To be effective, start small.* Don't be grandiose. Take an incremental approach. Minimise the commitment of resources for as long as possible, thus maximising information and knowledge and minimising risk. This is called 'bootstrapping' and we return to it in Chapter 5.
5 *Aim at leadership and dominate the competition in the particular area of innovation as soon as possible.* This marketing strategy is called niche marketing and we return to it in Chapter 5. It is the strategy that is most likely to lead to success.

Oxford Asymmetry International is a British example of a world-class firm that specialises in the systematic development of invention and high technology. When British Petroleum withdrew its financial support for a research project analysing the small-scale manufacturing of certain chemicals, **Stephen Davies**, an Oxford University professor, secured £500 000 backing from two business angels to continue his work and, in 1992, set up the company with only 4 employees.

The company provides a one-stop shop in chemical discovery and promotes itself as a partner to drug manufacturers who are looking to innovate and are willing to out-source this activity. Successful innovation is the result of an effective partnership, each partner bringing different qualities to the relationship.

Over lunch in 1995 at Oxford University's Innovation Centre, Stephen happened to meet a senior manager from Pfizer and this led to the formation of a joint venture company called Oxford Diversity Pfizer, the company that developed Viagra.

Oxford Asymmetry International now works with companies like Astra, Bayer, Eastman Chemicals, Leukosite, Pfizer, Vanguard Medica and Vertex. It was floated in 1998 with a staff of 200 (40 per cent with PhDs) and a market capitalisation of £120 million, a figure that doubled within a year.

How innovations, particularly technical innovations, see the light of commercial day is complex. Scientific discoveries do lead to commercial opportunities which entrepreneurial firms can exploit. However, the linkages are not always as you would expect and they involve a labyrinthine series of inter-relationships and feedback networks that underline the importance of a learning organisation. William Shockley had to invent a theory of electrons and 'holes' in semiconductors to explain why the transistors that he and his colleagues at Bell Laboratories in the USA had invented in 1948 actually worked. Even then, in order for the transistor idea to see the light of day, he and his colleagues had to take it to Palo Alto in California and start a company that eventually became Intel.

Innovation and size

Just as entrepreneurs are not defined simply as owner-managers, entrepreneurial firms are not defined, necessarily, in terms of size. But there are linkages between size and innovation. Few small firms introduce really new products into their product range. Even fewer introduce really new products into the economy as a whole. This role is more likely to be undertaken by larger firms because of the resources they command. However, small firms can, and often do, introduce products or services that are clearly differentiated from those of the 'competition', to the point where one might question whether there is any direct competition. Indeed, this ability to differentiate clearly is a major element in their success. Is this innovation? Perhaps it is, but one would have to stretch Schumpeter's first or even his third criterion (opening up of a new market) to accommodate it.

Small firms are most likely to provide something marginally different from the competition in terms of the product or service, and thus find a gap in the market.

They are also far more likely to innovate in terms of marketing and customer service (often low-cost options). They often find new routes to market first, for example 'direct' selling, via the phone with the growth of call centres located in low-cost areas or via the internet offering similar advantages through the 'virtual' organisation. Small firms are often innovative in their approach to key account management and customer relationships. They find ways of networking with customers and suppliers so as to cut costs and lead times. Which of Schumpeter's categories do these fall into? These are all approaches an entrepreneurial firm of any size can adopt.

Many truly successful innovations, particularly product innovations but certainly the ones involving large amounts of capital, originate from large not small companies. There are few Dysons in this world who successfully struggle to bring a genuinely new product to the market themselves, against all the odds. There are just too many problems to sort out – not least of which is finding the finance. Moreover it is easier for a middle-sized or large company to sort out these problems because it has more resources, more experience ... more of everything to throw at a problem.

This is not to decry the importance of small firms in the process of product innovation. Studies suggest that, although they are much less likely to conduct R&D than large firms, they conduct them more efficiently and introduce new products to the market place faster than big companies. Studies measuring only R&D expenditure must be treated with caution because of the inability of small firms often to separate out this expenditure. However, a US study (Acs and Audretsch, 1990) found that small firms produce 2.4 times as many innovations per employee as large firms. Another UK study (Pavitt et al., 1987) concluded that small firms are more likely to introduce fundamentally new innovations than large firms. In their review of innovation in small firms Deakins and Freel (2003) concluded that 'the innovative contributions of small firms vary across industry sectors and through the industry life cycle, at least with respect to technical innovations. In new industries, where technology is still evolving, small firms have a more significant role to play than in mature industries, where the innovation focus has switched to cost-reducing process innovation and minor product enhancements. However, in mature industries small firms may benefit from innovations in structure, supply or markets.'

What seems clear is that innovative behaviour is not entirely related to firm size. It also relates to business activity, the industry, the nature of the innovation, and the type of company. Large firms outperform small firms where resources are important – because of capital intensity or because of scale of spending on R&D, advertising etc. or simply because of barriers to entry. Rothwell (1989) shows that, where no such prerequisite exists, the share of small firms in innovation is substantial. He concludes that 'innovative advantage is unequivocally associated with neither large nor small firms. The innovatory advantages of large firms are in the main associated with their relatively greater financial and technological resources, i.e. they are material advantages; small firm advantages are those of entrepreneurial dynamism, internal flexibility and responsiveness to changing circumstances, i.e. they are behavioural advantages'. It has also been pointed out that the advantages of large firms are generally the disadvantages of small firms, and vice versa, and therefore collaboration between the two sizes (inside or outside the same corporation) can create powerful synergistic relationships (Vossen, 1998).

Innovation is important if a small firm wants to grow and be successful. In a study of fast-growing small firms matched against slow-growing firms, Storey et al. (1989)

concluded that the owner-managers of the fast-growing firms were much more likely to emphasise competitive advantage as being in areas such as innovation and product or service quality. By way of contrast, the owner-managers of the slow-growing firms emphasised price. Innovation, therefore, is not only the vehicle for faster growth but also a means of fending off competition and being able to charge a higher price.

In fact, Schumpeter said nothing about whether innovation could be best carried out by small or large firms. To him this was irrelevant. An entrepreneur could just as easily work in a large firm as in a small one. However, small firms do have the inherent flexibility needed to spot market opportunities and capitalise on them quickly if, that is, they are run by an entrepreneur. Small firms typically lack the bureaucratic, hierarchical structures of large firms.

Innovation and location

There is evidence that innovation can be geographically concentrated in certain areas, particularly with respect to smaller firms, and this leads to 'clusters' of small firms that form mutually supportive networks. This is often referred to as 'innovative milieu' theory (Camagni, 1991; Keeble and Wilkinson, 1999). This theory is based on the assumption that knowledge is a crucial element in the process of innovation (Simmie, 2002) and, whereas large firms have their own R&D functions to help generate this, small firms have to rely on networking and a process of 'socialisation' that allows them to collect information and accumulate knowledge (Capello, 1999). Geographical proximity facilitates this process of knowledge transfer and hence these clusters of small firms can be observed (Porter, 1998b; Keeble and Wilkinson, *op. cit.*).

Within these clusters, where there is the development and sharing of a common base of knowledge, 'collective learning' is taking place. This allows the firms to coordinate their actions so as to solve the technological and organisational problems they face (Lorenz, 1996 in Keeble and Wilkinson, *op. cit.*). 'Collective learning' can be either conscious – as in research collaborations – or unconscious. Unconscious learning occurs where the skills and knowledge are vested in a workforce that is shared between the small firms. These clusters therefore attract similar small firms because it is a low-cost way of gaining knowledge. It will be interesting to see how far the development of the internet affects the formation of clusters based on geographic proximity in future years.

Cambridge in the UK is home to a number of high technology clusters and is an example of both types of learning. In computing, not only are there research collaborations between the University and the firms in the cluster, but also there is also a skilled workforce graduating from the University and a group of academics willing to work part-time with them. Such is the strength of the cluster and importance of the University that Bill Gates endowed it with sufficient funds to finance new state-of-the-art computer laboratories. These days, universities generally are seen as an important source of knowledge and therefore important to the development of clusters, hence the various initiatives to encourage them to work more closely with industry. Universities generate 'public knowledge' and this 'spills over' into the commercial world through conferences and seminars, consultants, the personal networks of academics and industrial researchers (MacPherson, 1998), and commercial spin-offs (Mitra, 2000).

Case with questions

Peggy Yu studied for an MBA and worked on Wall Street in the USA until she moved back to China in 1997, aged 32. It was at this point, together with her husband Li Guoqing, already in charge of Science and Culture Book Information Co., that she decided to set up her own business. Impressed by the success of Amazon in the USA, she decided to try online bookselling. Launched in November 1999, **Dangdang.com,** is now China's biggest online bookseller and Peggy Yu is one of China's growing breed of successful private entrepreneurs. The company also sells CDs and DVDs.

Despite a 86 per cent literacy rate – compared to 99 per cent in the USA – and a population five times that of the USA, China has only 77 000 bookstores and 10 per cent of these are part of the state-owned Xinhua news agency. However, book sales, at some 43 billion yuan, are only one-eighth that of the USA where they topped $40 billion in 2002. Often there is a limited range of titles particularly of foreign books.

Dangdang is based very much on the Amazon model. However, there are some significant differences in the business model to suit China's particular circumstances. For example, Amazon's key asset is its huge database of titles that it licenses from book wholesalers. No such facility is available in China so Dangdang had to build its own, which currently stands at some 210 000 titles. The company has also faced some big problems. The internet was slow to take off in China and customers are not used to shopping on line. They are not used to paying in advance for goods that arrive later. Nor are they used to paying for delivery. What is more the credit card market is still in its infancy. All of this means that some two-thirds of business is still 'cash-on-delivery', concentrated in 12 large cities where books are delivered by freelance couriers. The balance of business is based on money orders and credit cards.

To keep its capital spending low, Dangdang owns only one warehouse in Beijing that distributes only 15 per cent of its sales. A bricks-and-mortar rival, Xinhua, distributes the other 85 per cent from its warehouses around the country. Dangdang also monitors developments on Amazon's website so it can copy the best ideas. The latest to be introduced were multiple delivery addresses and customer wish lists.

Dangdang claims to take some 4000 orders a day, generating sales of 35 million yuan in 2002 at a gross margin of 25 per cent. However, this represents less than 0.1% of the market. The book market is gradually being deregulated and sales are growing rapidly but Dangdang face stiff competition. One of the fastest growing is the 500-store franchise chain of Xi-Shu. And there are online competitors such as Joyo.com and the German run Bol.com. The question is, when will Amazon enter the Chinese market?

Questions

1 What are the strengths and weaknesses in Dangdang's business model?
2 What are the elements of the company's competitive advantage? Can it be sustained in the face of competition?
3 What are the dangers facing Dangdang?
4 How could it compete against Amazon in the Chinese market?
5 What are the opportunities facing the company?
6 How might it grow?

Summary

Innovation is difficult to define. It is about introducing new products, services or processes, opening up new markets, identifying new sources of supply of raw materials or creating new types of industrial organisation. But real innovaton is more than that. It is about breaking the mould – doing things differently. That might involve invention or developing an innovative processes, as with **McDonald's**. But it must be linked to customer demand. However, competitive advantage can equally be gained by frequent, incremental innovations – a strategy that is also less risky. It is degree and frequency of innovation that combine to produce competitive advantage.

Some inventors, like **Trevor Baylis**, are not necessarily innovators. They need the help of an entrepreneur or an entrepreneurial organisation to link their invention to customer demand. However, others, like **James Dyson**, can be inventor, innovator and entrepreneur all in one. Whilst creativity is at the core of invention and innovation, so too is the ability to spot market opportunities – and this is one very important role of the entrepreneur. When these factors come together you get a successful firm like **RadioScape**.

Historically there have been cycles of innovation that disrupted economies, causing rapid growth. These are usually technology-led but facilitated by entrepreneurial activity. Figure 3.1 shows how invention can be successfully exploited in an entrepreneurial environment.

Using new knowledge, including scientific knowledge, is the most difficult form of innovation. Innovation stemming from the systematic analysis of unexpected successes or failures, or the incongruities between what actually happens and what was supposed to happen, are far more likely to yield commercially viable results. **Jonathan Elvidge** believes that opportunities can be spotted, systematically. **Oxford Asymmetry International** proves this to be the case. However, not all opportunities are profitable, as dot.com businesses have found. **Yahoo, NCsoft** and **Friendsreunited** are examples of companies that have made internet-based opportunities pay through robust business models.

Innovation in one market might involve 'copying' products or services in another, as in the case of **Direct Line**. However, it is likely to require a different approach depending on the customers, competitors and the market – as in the case of **Dangdang.com**.

Small firms produce more than their fair share of innovations and seem to do it more efficiently than large firms. However, they tend to do this in sectors where resources, in particular capital, are less important. **Dyson** would seem to be a notable exception. Innovation is not entirely related to firm size. It also relates to business activity, industry, nature of innovation and the type of company. Small and large firms have advantages in producing different types of innovation.

Geographical proximity facilitates the process of knowledge transfer and hence clusters of small firms can be observed, sharing 'collective learning' either through conscious or unconscious mechanisms.

Are you an innovative thinker?

Innovation is the prime tool entrepreneurs use to create or exploit opportunity and is one of the two most important distinguishing features of their character. The **Innovative Potential Indicator (IPI)** was developed by Dr Fiona Patterson based upon research on employees in established companies. It is published by Oxford Psychologists Press. It claims to be the only psychometric test able to identify those people who have the potential to become innovative thinkers.

Dr Patterson identifies ten types of people:

1 The **Change Agent** who thrives on change and is independent, who conjures up the strangest ways to solve problems and who does not stick to what they were told. This is the innovative thinker who embodies one of the most essential characteristics that differentiate entrepreneurs from owner-managers.
2 The **Consolidator**, whose rigidity and independence militates against innovative thinking but is a safety net because of their preference for the status quo.
3 The **Harmoniser**, who likes the challenge but does not disclose good ideas for fear of upsetting people.
4 The **Firefighter**, who flits from one idea to another in an imaginative but unpredictable way.
5 The **Cooperator**, who likes change but 'goes with the flow'.
6 The **Catalyst**, who is good at thinking up ideas but soon loses interest.
7 The **Inhibited Innovator**, whose brainwaives could be valuable but lacks the confidence to push it forward.
8 The **Incremental Innovator**, who dreams up radical ideas but likes to implement them in a step-by-step way which can appear inflexible.
9 The **Spice-of-Life**, whose dominant characteristic is the need to be doing something, anything, new.
10 The **Middle-of-the-Road**, who is good at blending ideas but is ambivalent about them.

The IPI questionnaire asks for agreement/disagreement to 36 statements about how you approach change, how adaptable you are and how you stand up to others. Based upon your answers, it scores you on four main areas of behaviour which Dr Patterson's research shows can be used to establish whether a person has innovative potential. Scores can be between 20 and 80 on each dimension. The dimensions are:

- Motivation to change (MTC).
- Willingness to behave in a challenging way (CB).
- Willingness to adapt and use tried and tested approaches (AD).
- Consistency of working style which indicates efficiency and orderliness (CWS).

Change Agents have high MTC and CB scores, and low AD and CWS scores. So for example, Trevor Baylis, the inventor of the clockwork radio, had a MTC score of 70, a CB score of 60, an AD score of 25 and a CWS score of 35.

Source: The Times, 14 March 2000.

Essays and discussion topics

1 Is invention good?
2 Do you agree with Michael Porter that 'invention and entrepreneurship are at the heart of national advantage'?
3 What do you think constitutes innovation? Give examples.
4 Can an adaptor also be an innovator?
5 What is the relationship between innovation and change?
6 Why are entrepreneurs interested in innovation?
7 Over the last ten years what was the major commercial opportunity that arose?
   How was it exploited? Was the development technology- or market-led? What were the consequences?
8 Over the next ten years, what are the main commercial opportunities that entrepreneurial firms might be best advised to exploit?
9 What steps would a 'copier' have to take to become an innovator?
10 What steps would a 'struggler' have to take to become an innovator?
11 Do you agree with the comments of Peter Florence in the RadioScape case?
12 Give some examples of new-to-the-world products that have been successful and some that have not. Why have they been successful or unsuccessful?
13 Why is 'time to market' important?
14 Do you have an idea for a new product or service? Explain why it might be successful.
15 List the advantages and disadvantages small firms have over large firms in introducing innovation.
16 What are the main barriers to innovation in large firms?
17 What are the main barriers to innovation in small firms?
18 Large firms are likely to be more innovative than small firms. Discuss.
19 With the development of the internet geographic clusters of small firms sharing 'collective learning' will become a thing of the past. Discuss.
20 If you want to make a big return, you need to take the big risks – that is what entrepreneurship is really about. Discuss.

Exercises and assignments

1 Answer the Innovation Potential Indicator questionnaire and assess your innovative potential. You can get more details of how to obtain it from the website of Oxford Psychologists Press on www.opp.co.uk.
2 Research Dyson. How is the company doing today? Does it continue to grow? Does it continue to innovate? How has its strategy changed over the years?
3 Write up a case study of successful innovation in a small firm. Analyse why it was successful.
4 Research the reasons for the success of VHS rather than Betamax video format. What are the lessons from this?
5 Research the commercial reasons for the success of the Mini. How important is good marketing to the success of an innovation?
6 Write up a case study of a 'creative' firm. Analyse the factors that contribute to them being creative.
7 Find out how Britain performs compared to other countries in terms of its ability to innovate.

References

Acs, Z.J. and Audretsch, D.B. (1990) *Innovation and Small Firms*, Cambridge, MA: MIT Press.

Bessant, J. (1999) 'Developing Continuous Improvement Capability', *International Journal of Innovation Management*, 2.

Bolton, B. and Thompson, J. (2000) *Entrepreneurs: Talent, Temperament, Technique*, Oxford: Butterworth-Heinemann.

Camagni, R. (ed.) (1991) *Innovative Networks: Spatial Perspectives,* London: Belhaven.

Cannon, T. (1985) 'Innovation, Creativity and Small Firm Organisation', *International Small Business Journal*, 4, 1.

Capello, R. (1999) 'Spatial Transfer of Knowledge in High Technology Milieux: Learning versus Collective Learning Processes', *Regional Studies*, 33.

Deakins, D. and Freel, M. (2003) *Entrepreneurship and Small Firms*, London: McGraw Hill.

Drucker, P. (1985) *Innovation and Entrepreneurship*, London: Heinemann.

Hamel, G. and Prahalad, C.E. (1991) 'Corporate Imagination and Expeditionary Marketing', *Harvard Business Review*, 69(4) (July–August).

Kanter, R.M. (1983), *The Change Masters: Innovation and Productivity in American Corporations*, New York: Simon & Schuster.

Keeble, D. and Wilkinson, F. (1999) 'Collective Learning and Knowledge Development in the Evolution of Regional Clusters of High Technology SMEs in Europe', *Regional Studies*, 33.

Kirton, M. (1976) 'Adaptors and Innovators: A Description and Measure', *Journal of Applied Psychology*, October.

MacPherson, A.D. (1998) 'Academic–Industry Linkages and Small Firm Innovation: Evidence from the Scientific Instruments Sector', *Entrepreneurship and Regional Development*, 10(4).

Mellor, R.B. (2005) *Sources and Spread of Innovation in Small e-Commerce Companies*, Skodsborgvej: Forlaget Globe.

Mintzberg, H. (1983) *Structures in Fives: Designing Effective Organisations*, London: Prentice-Hall.

Mitra, J. (2000) 'Nurturing and Sustaining Entrepreneurship: University, Science Park, Business and Government Partnership in Australia', *Industry and Higher Education*, June.

Morris, M.H. and Kuratko, D.F. (2002) *Corporate Entrepreneurship: Entrepreneurial Development within Organisations*, Fort Worth, TX: Harcourt College Publishers.

Pavitt, K., Robinson, M. and Townsend, J. (1987) 'The Size Distribution of Innovating Firms in the UK: 1945–1983', *Journal of Industrial Economics*, 45.

Porter, M. E. (1990) *The Competitive Advantage of Nations*, New York: Free Press.

Porter, M.E. (1998a) *On Competition*, Boston, MA: Harvard Business School.

Porter M.E. (1998b) 'Clusters and the New Economics of Competition', *Harvard Business Review*, Nov–Dec.

Rothwell, R. (1989) 'Small Firms, Innovation and Industrial Change', *Small Business Economics*, 1, 51–64.

Schumpeter, J.A. (1934) *The Theory of Economic Development: An Inquiry into Profits, Capital, Credit, Interest and the Business Cycle* (trans. by Redvers Opie), Oxford University Press.

Schumpeter, J.A. (1983/1996) *The Theory of Economic Development*, New Brunswick, NJ: Transaction Publishers.

Simmie, J. (2002) 'Knowledge Spillovers and Reasons for the Concentration of Innovative SMEs', *Urban Studies*, 39, 5–6.

Storey, D.J., Watson, R. and Wynarcyzk, P. (1989) 'Fast Growth Small Business: Case Studies of 40 Small Firms in North East England', Department of Employment.

Valery, N. (1999) 'Innovation in Industry', *Economist*, 5(28).

Van Grundy, A. (1987) 'Organisational Creativity and Innovation', in S.G. Isaksen, *Frontiers of Creative Research*, New York: Brearly.

Vyakarnham, S. and Leppard, J. (1999) *A Marketing Action Plan for the Growing Business*, 2nd edn, London: Kogan Page.

Vossen, R.W. (1998) 'Relative Strengths and Weaknesses of Small Firms in Innovation', *International Small Business Journal*, 16(3), 88–94.

4

Developing Creativity

Contents

- Understanding creativity
- The creative process
- Barriers to creativity
- Techniques for generating new ideas
- Encouraging creativity
- Summary

By the end of this chapter you should be able to:

- Explain what makes individuals creative;

- Assess your own aptitude to be creative;

- Describe the creative process;

- Describe the barriers to creativity;

- Recognise the barriers to creativity you face;

- Use a range of techniques to help the creative process;

- Explain how individual creativity can be stimulated.

Understanding creativity

Creativity is at the core of any true entrepreneur. Creativity leads to innovation. Innovation is one of the most important distinguishing features of entrepreneurs. Creativity is important in coming up with completely new ways of doing things, rather than looking for adaptive, incremental change. Parkhurst (1999) defined it as 'the ability or quality displayed when solving hitherto unsolved problems, when developing original and novel solutions to problems others have solved differently, or when developing original and novel (at least to its originator) products'. For the entrepreneur the focus for their creativity is commercial opportunity leading to new products, services, processes or marketing approaches. It has been estimated that for every eleven ideas that enter the new product development process, only one new product will be successfully launched (Page, 1993). So new ideas are at a premium and it is a numbers game. The more you generate, the more are likely to see the light of day commercially. So how can you stimulate creativity?

> 'There are so few new ideas, so few new things that have not been done. But although the safe place to be is copying what others are doing, I think the people who succeed will be those with the boldness to do something in a totally different way. They take an idea and reinvent it. We have seen that in airlines, where people said, "It's just a flying bus, why shouldn't tickets cost £29?" And there are still plenty of opportunities.'
>
> **Rachel Elnaugh** founder of
> **Red Letter Days**
> *Sunday Times* 23 May 2004
> ➡

We are now starting to understand how the creative process works on an individual level. The brain has two sides that operate in quite different ways. The left side performs rational, logical functions. It tends to be verbal and analytic, operating in a linked, linear sequence (called logical or vertical thinking). The right side operates intuitive and non-rational modes of thought. It is non-verbal, linking images together to get a holistic perspective (called creative or lateral thinking). A person uses both sides, shifting naturally from one to the other. However, the right side is the creative side. Creative innovation is therefore primarily a right brain activity whilst adaptive innovation is a left brain activity.

Left brain thinkers therefore tend to be rational, logical, analytical and sequential in their approach to problem solving. Right brain thinkers are more intuitive, value-based and nonlinear in their approach. The cognitive styles are also reflected in the preferred work-styles with left brain thinkers preferring to work alone, learn about things rather than experience them and having the ability or preference to make quick decisions. By way of contrast, right brain thinkers prefer working in groups, experiencing things (e.g. learning by doing) and generating lots of options in preference to focusing on making a speedy decision. People have a preference for one or other approach, but can and do switch between them for different tasks and in different contexts.

Normally the two halves of the brain complement each other, but many factors, not least our education, tend to encourage development of left brain activity – logic. Kirby (2003) speculates that this may well explain why so many successful entrepreneurs appear not to have succeeded in the formal education system.

Creative		**Logical**
Seeks questions	⟷	Seeks answers
Diverges	⟷	Converges
Explores different views, seeks insights	⟷	Asserts best or right view
Restructures	⟷	Uses existing structure
Seeks ways an idea might help	⟷	Says when an idea will not work
Welcomes discontinuous leaps	⟷	Uses logical steps
Welcomes chance intrusions	⟷	Concentrates on what is relevant
Open-ended	⟷	Closed

Figure 4.1   Dimensions of creative (lateral) vs logical (vertical) thinking

He argues that entrepreneurs are right brain dominant. But he goes even further by speculating that there may be a link between this and dyslexia, observing that so many entrepreneurs are dyslexic and language skills are left brain activities. This is an interesting but unproved hypothesis.

However, the point is that most people need to encourage and develop right brain activity if they wish to be creative. And this is possible, with training. To overcome the habit of logic you need to deliberately set aside this ingrained way of thinking. Creative or lateral thinking is different in a number of dimensions to logical or vertical thinking. It is imaginative, emotional, and often results in more than one solution. Edward de Bono (1971) set out some of the dimensions of difference. Figure 4.1 is based on his work.

One important aspect of high level creativity is the ability to recognise relationships among objects, processes, cause and effect, people etc. that others do not see, searching for different, unorthodox relationships that can be replicated in a different context. These relationships can lead to new ideas, products or services. So, the inconvenience of mixing different drinks to form a cocktail led to the (obvious?) idea of selling them ready mixed. James Dyson was able to see that a cyclone system for separating paint particles could be used (less obviously?) to develop a better vacuum cleaner. Most creativity skills can be practised and enhanced, but this particular skill is probably the most difficult to encourage. Majaro (1992) believes that, while stereotyping is to be avoided, creative types do exhibit some similar characteristics:

- *Conceptual fluency*   They are able to produce many ideas.
- *Mental flexibility*   They are adept at lateral thinking.
- *Originality*   They produce atypical responses to problems.
- *Suspension of judgement*   They do not analyse too quickly.
- *Impulsive*   They act impulsively on an idea, expressing their 'gut-feel'.
- *Anti-authority*   They are always willing to challenge authority.
- *Tolerance*   They have a high tolerance threshold towards the ideas of others.

Mintzberg (1976) makes the interesting suggestion that the very logical activity of planning is essentially a left brain activity whilst the implementation of the plan, that

How creative are you?

Find out how creative you are by going to *www.creax.com/csa* and answering the 40 questions in their creativity quiz. It is free and the analysis assesses you on eight dimensions against answers from others with similar backgrounds. The dimensions are:

- **Abstraction** – the ability to apply abstract concepts/ideas.
- **Connection** – the ability to make connections between things that do not appear connected.
- **Perspective** – the ability to shift one's perspective on a situation in terms of space, time and other people.
- **Curiosity** – the desire to change or improve things that others see as normal.
- **Boldness** – the confidence to push boundaries beyond accepted conventions. Also the ability to eliminate the fear of what others might think of you.
- **Paradox** – the ability to simultaneously accept and work with statements that are contradictory.
- **Complexity** – the ability to carry large quantities of information and be able to manipulate and manage the relationships between such information.
- **Persistence** – the ability to force oneself to keep trying to more and stronger solutions even when good ones have already been generated.

Case insight

Monorail Corporation is a virtual organisation that could provide a glimpse of the future. Like Dell, it sells computers. Unlike Dell, it owns no factories, warehouses or other assets, operating from a single floor in a leased building in Atlanta, USA. Computers are designed by freelance workers. Customers phone a freephone number connected to the logistics service of Federal Express, which forwards the order to a contract assembler that assembles them from parts supplied by other contract manufacturers. FedEx ships the computer to the customer and sends the invoice to SunTrust Bank, Monorail's agent.

is the act of management, is a right brain activity. He bases this claim on the observation that managers split their attention between a number of different tasks, preferring to talk briefly to people rather than to write, reading non-verbal as well as verbal aspects of the interaction, take a holistic view of the situation and rely on intuition. He argues that truly effective managers are those that can harness both sides of the brain.

The creative process

The creative process has four commonly agreed phases, shown in Figure 4.2. There is wide agreement on their general nature and the relationship between them, although they are referred to by a variety of names (de Bono, 1995).

```
┌─────────────────────────────────────────┐
│  1   Generating knowledge and awareness  │
└─────────────────────────────────────────┘
                     │
                     ▼
┌─────────────────────────────────────────┐
│  2   Incubation process                  │
└─────────────────────────────────────────┘
                     │
                     ▼
┌─────────────────────────────────────────┐
│  3   Generating ideas                    │◄─ ─ ┐
└─────────────────────────────────────────┘     │  feedback
                     │                           │  loop
                     ▼                           │
┌─────────────────────────────────────────┐     │
│  4   Evaluation and implementation       │─ ─ ─┘
└─────────────────────────────────────────┘
```

Figure 4.2   The creative process

Phase 1: Generating knowledge and awareness

A prerequisite to all creative processes is the generation of awareness of different ideas and ways of doing things through reading and travelling widely, talking with different people with different views about the world. This is, of course, to be placed in the context of the issue being addressed. It is not just about being aware of different approaches or perspectives on the problem, but also about getting the brain to accept that there are different ways of doing things – developing an enquiring mind. Many people almost have to give themselves permission to be creative – to think the unthinkable. Carrying a notebook and recording ideas and information can be useful. So too can developing a small library. Some sources of commercial new ideas are shown in Figure 4.3.

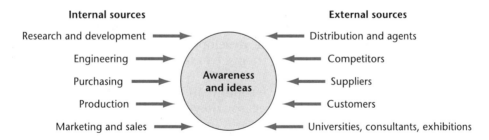

Figure 4.3   Sources of awareness and ideas

Phase 2: Incubation process

People need time to mull over the tremendous amounts of information they generate from Phase 1. This incubation period happens when people are engaged in other activities (the best are those instinctive activities that do not require left brain dominance) and they can let their subconscious mind work on the problem.

Interestingly sleep happens when the left brain gets tired or bored and during this time the right brain has dominance. Incubation therefore often needs sleep. It is little wonder that so many people have creative ideas when they are asleep – the problem is trying to remember them. Creativity therefore can take time and 'sleeping on'.

Phase 3: Generating ideas

Ideas can come up unexpectedly during the incubation period, but often they need encouragement. There are a number of techniques to encourage idea generation. Some of the more widely used ones are explained in the next section.

Phase 4: Evaluation and implementation

The next stage is to select which ideas are the most promising. This is the convergent stage of the process involving discussion and analysis, possibly voting. Some ideas generated in Phase 3 might be easy to discard because they are unrealistic but others might need to be worked up or modified before they can be properly evaluated. Sometimes a return to Phase 3 is required to do this.

Roger von Oech (1986) has a slightly different 'take' on this, focusing on the changing role of the individual as the creative process takes its course. He outlines four sequential roles:

1 *The explorer* – searching for new insights and perspectives by sifting through information, being curious, observing other fields, generating ideas, broadening perspective, following unexpected leads, using difficulties and obstacles and constantly writing things down.
2 *The artist* – turning information and resources into new ideas by imagining, adapting, reversing, linking, parodying, evaluating, discarding.
3 *The judge* – evaluating and assessing the merits of a concept and incorporating ideas through objectivity and looking at assumptions, probabilities and timing.
4 *The warrior* – achieving organisational acceptance and implementation of ideas by being bold, courageous and persistent, developing plans, commanding resources, motivating stakeholders to commit themselves to the project.

In a start-up the entrepreneur may have to fulfil all four of these roles, a not inconsiderable achievement, not least because they require different types of left and right brain activity.

Some organisations have created environments designed to facilitate these stages of the creative process. The Royal Mail Group has its own 'Creativity Laboratory'. This is made up of a number of open areas – facilitating groups forming, breaking up and coming together again – all with very informal seating arrangements. Standing and walking are encouraged. There is background music as well as toys, drinks and other distractions for the left brain. All the walls are 'white walls' which can be written on with felt tip pens when ideas are in free flow. Pens are everywhere. There are computer systems that allow ideas to be posted and voted on anonymously. And records are kept of the whole process – even the white walls are photographed – so agreed actions and outcomes can be followed up back in the workplace.

Barriers to creativity

> We learned the importance of ignoring conventional wisdom ... It's fun to do things that people don't think are possible or likely. It's also exciting to achieve the unexpected.'
>
> **Michael Dell** (1999)
> ➜

People are inherently creative, but most of us stifle it because we find change threatening. We all create rituals and routines that we feel comfortable with and these normally mitigate against questioning the status quo. These routines help us through the day. Being creative often takes people outside of their 'comfort-zone'. They are uneasy with it. Sometimes blocks and barriers need to be attacked. Von Oech (1998) focuses on the blocks to individual creativity. He lists ten that are critical:

1 The fallacy that there is only one correct solution to a problem.
2 The fallacy that logic is important in creativity.
3 The tendency to be practical.
4 The tendency to follow established rules unquestioningly.
5 The tendency to avoid ambiguity in viewing a situation.
6 The tendency to assign blame for failure.
7 The unwillingness to recognise the creative power of play.
8 The tendency to think too narrowly and with too much focus.
9 The unwillingness to think unconventionally because of the fear of appearing foolish.
10 The lack of belief that you can be creative.

Realising these blocks may exist in yourself can be the first step to dismantling them. It is never easy to change an inherent tendency, but it can be done and the techniques in the next section can help.

Techniques for generating new ideas

There are many techniques designed to help encourage the generation of new ideas. Most are directed at generating a higher quality of idea rather than a greater volume. People with different thinking styles will respond differently to each of them. Here are just a few of the more widely used ones.

Brainstorming

This is one of the most widely used techniques. It is practised in a group. In the session you do not question or criticise ideas. You suspend disbelief. The aim is to encourage the free flow of ideas – divergent thinking – and as many ideas as possible. Everyone has thousands of good ideas within them just waiting to come out. But people inherently fear making mistakes or looking foolish in front of others. Here making 'mistakes' and putting forward ideas which don't work is not only acceptable, it is also encouraged.

You might start with a problem to be solved or an opportunity to be exploited. You encourage and write down ideas as they come by facilitating all the dimensions of

Case insight

Who invented the World Wide Web (www)?

The first electronic mail transfer took place in July 1970 in the laboratories of consultants Bolt, Baranek and Newman. Building on the work of **Paul Baran** of the RAND Corporation, it was the result of a contract placed by the US Advanced Research Projects Agency (ARPA) to build a distributive network that enabled researchers at one site to log onto and run programs at another. **Roy Tomlinson**, who wrote the program, initiated the use of the symbol '@' to separate the name of the sender from the mailbox ID. He chose it because it was the only symbol that was unlikely to form part of a name or an ID.

Computer networks were also being built elsewhere and ARPA brought researchers from Britain, France, Italy and Sweden to form an international Network Working Group to investigate how the various networks could be connected. In 1973 there was a breakthrough as researchers realised that instead of trying to create a common specification, all they had to do was use dedicated computers as gateways between each network, thus creating a 'network-of-networks'. In 1977 the concept was made a reality as a message was sent on a 94 000 mile round trip from San Francisco to University College, London and back to the University of Southern California. An international network – or 'internet' – was created. The system continued to be used but only by scientists and specialists for many years.

In 1990 an Englishman, **Tim Berners-Lee**, working at CERN, the European Particles Physics Laboratories in Geneva, proposed a solution to the problem of capturing and coordinating the work of the scientists and then locating it in such a way that this accumulating knowledge was easily available. He devised a 'hypertext' system that would give access across the internet, allowing users to access the same information from different computer systems and add their own links to information. It also enabled links to be made to live data that kept changing. The system was called the World Wide Web. Shortly after this he devised a 'browser' that linked the resources on the internet in a uniform way. He also devised a protocol to specify the location of the information – the Unique Resource Locator (URL) – and one to specify how information exchanges between computers should be handled – the HyperText Transport Protocol (HTTP). Finally, he invented a uniform way to structure documents, proposing the use of HyperText Mark-up Language (HTML). In 1992 the browser was made publicly available to anyone with an internet connection to download.

In 1993 a University of Illinois team working at the National Center for Supercomputer Applications (NCSA) developed the CERN system, which used high powered workstations and the Unix operating system, to operate on PCs and Macintosh. In the same year one of the team, **Marc Andreesen**, posted a message on some specialist Usenet conferences. It read: 'By the power vested in me by nobody in particular, alpha/beta version 0.5 of NCSA's Motif-based networked information systems and World Wide Web browser, X Mosaic, is hereby released. Cheers, Marc.' The World Wide Web, as we know it, had been born.

With the help of Jim Clark, the wealthy founder of Silicon Graphics, Marc Andreesen and others in the team went on to set up **Netscape**. When the company went public it was valued at $3 billion, a valuation that in those days was huge.

●

Case insight

Alex Tew, a Nottingham Trent University student from Cricklade, Wiltshire may be only 21 years old but he might be about to become a dollar millionaire – just six months after having a very bright idea. His website, milliondollarhomepage.com has caught the attention of internet surfers worldwide. It consists of a single page divided into 10,000 boxes, each 100 pixels in size. Alex sells the space to advertisers at $1 for each pixel, with a minimum of 100 pixels. The result is a montage of company logos which have hyperlinks to the advertiser's website.

The site took just two days to set up and cost £50. He sold the fist blocks of pixels to his brothers and some friends and used that money to advertise the site. The site address began appearing in internet blogs and chat rooms. As the site caught on, more and more advertisers signed up – after all $100 was not a lot to pay. By December 2005 he had sold 900 000 pixels. He expects to reach the 1 million mark by January 2006, at which point he will close the site to new entrants and leave it on the internet.

The idea for the website came from brainstorming whilst Alex lay on his bed at home in August 2005:

'I have always been an ideas person and I have a brainstorming session every night before I go to bed and write things down on a note pad.'

Sunday Times 18 December 2005

creative thinking in Figure 4.1. There are no 'bad' ideas. All ideas are, at the very least, springboards for other ideas. You allow the right side of the brain full rein and only engage the left brain to analyse the ideas you come up with at a later date. It is often best undertaken with a multidisciplinary team so that the issue can be approached from many different perspectives, encouraging the cross-fertilisation of ideas.

Negative brainstorming, thinking about the negative aspects of problem or situation, can often be used initially to unblock more creative and positive brainstorming. It is particularly useful in getting people to think about what might happen if they do not think more creatively and can be used to help change motivations and behaviour.

A variant on brainstorming is called *brainwriting*, whereby ideas are written down anonymously and then communicated to the group (computer technologies, like those used in the Royal Mail's Creativity Centre, can help with this), thus avoiding the influence of dominant individuals.

Analogy

This is a product centred technique that attempts to join together apparently unconnected or unrelated combinations of features of a product or service and benefits to the customer to come up with innovative solutions to problems. Analogies are proposed once the initial problem is stated. The analogies are then related to opportunities in the market place. Operated in a similar way to brainstorming, it is probably best explained with an example. Georges de Mestral noticed that burdock seed heads stuck to his clothing. On closer examination he discovered the seed heads

How to run a brainstorming session

1 Describe the outcome you are trying to achieve – the problem or opportunity – BUT NOT THE SOLUTION. This could be a broad area of investigation – new ideas and new markets can be discovered if you don't follow conventional paths.

2 Decide how you will run the session and who will take part. You need an impartial facilitator who will introduce things, keep to the rules and watch the time. They will restate the creative process if it slows down. The group can be anything from 4 to 30. The larger the number the more diverse the inputs but the slower (and more frustrating) the process – so something around 12 is probably ideal.

3 Set out the room in a participative (i.e. circular) and informal style. Comfortable chairs are important. Refreshments should be available continuously. Make certain there are flip charts, coloured pens etc. or, if you want to be high tech, you can use some of the specialist software that is available (e.g. Brainstorming Toolbox). Each person should also have a note pad so they can write down ideas.

4 Relax participants as much as possible. The style is informal. The rules of engagement should be posted clearly for all to see and run through so that everybody understands:

- Quantity counts, not quality – postpone judgement on all ideas.
- Encourage wild, exaggerated ideas – all ideas are of equal value.
- Build on ideas rather than demolish them.

5 Open the session by asking for as many ideas as possible. Get people to shout out. Write every one down on the flip chart and post the sheets on the wall. Encourage and engage with people. Close down criticism. Try to create group engagement.

6 When the ideas have dried up – it might take a little time for it finally to do so – close the session, thanking participants and keeping the door open for them should they have any ideas later.

7 Analyse the ideas posted. Brainstorming helps generate ideas, not analyse them. What happens from here is up to you. Sometimes the people who generated the ideas can also help sort them, but remember to separate out the sessions clearly. Perhaps excellent ideas can be implemented immediately, but do not forget to investigate the interesting one – no matter how 'off-the-wall'.

For more information on the technique visit www.brainstorming.co.uk.

contained tiny hooks. His analogy was to apply this principle to the problem of sticking and unsticking things and to develop what we recognise today as Velcro.

In this way, the first steps to building an analogy are to ask some basic questions:

- What does the situation or problem remind you of?
- What other areas of life or work experience similar situations?
- Who does these similar things and can the principles be adapted?

Often the analogy contains the words 'is like' So you might ask why one thing 'is like' another? For example, why is advertising like cooking? The answer is because there is so much preamble to eating. Anticipation from presentation and smell, even the ambience of the restaurant you eat in, are just as important as the taste and nutritional value of the food itself.

Attribute analysis

This is another product centred technique designed to evolve product improvements and line extensions – used as the product reaches the mature phase of its life cycle. It uses the basic marketing technique of looking at the features of a product or service which in turn perform a series of functions but, most importantly, deliver benefits to the customers. An existing product or service is stripped down to its component parts and the group then explores how these features might be altered but then focuses on whether those changes might bring valuable benefits to the customer.

So, for example, you might focus on a domestic lock. This secures a door from opening by an unwelcome intruder. The benefit is security and reduction/elimination of theft from the house. But you can lose keys or forget to lock doors and some locks are difficult or inconvenient to open from the inside. A potential solution is to have doors that sense people approaching from the outside and lock themselves. You could have a reverse sensor on the inside that unlocks the door when someone approaches (which could be activated or deactivated centrally). The exterior sensor could recognise 'friendly' people approaching the door because of sensors they carry in the form of 'credit cards' or they could be overridden by a combination lock.

The 'why? why?' technique, explained in the last chapter, can also be used to question why an existing product or service is designed in a particular way. The technique could have been used to question why the domestic lock was designed in a particular way, taking nothing for granted. In this way the technique should uncover the prime attributes that users are seeking. An alternative solution to the problem can then be constructed.

Gap analysis

This is a market-based approach that attempts to produce a 'map' of product/market attributes based on dimensions that are perceived as important to customers, analysing where competing products might lie and then spotting gaps where there is little or no competition. Because of the complexity involved, the attributes are normally shown in only two dimensions. There are a number of approaches to this task.

Perceptual mapping places the attributes of a product within specific categories. So for example, the dessert market might be characterised as hot vs cold and sophisticated vs unsophisticated. Various desserts would then be mapped onto these two dimensions. This could be shown graphically (see alongside). The issue is whether the 'gap' identified is one that customers would value being filled – and means understanding whether they value the dimensions being measured. That is a question for market research to attempt to answer.

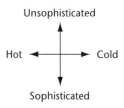

Non-metric mapping maps products in groups that customers find similar and then tries to explain why these groupings exist. A classic example would be in the soft drinks market where products might be clustered and then described simply in terms of still vs carbonated and flavoured vs non-flavoured. The key here is also finding the appropriate dimensions that create opportunities for differentiating the product and creating competitive advantage. The mapping of soft drinks on the two dimensions above is unlikely to reveal any gaps in the market.

Repertory grid is a more systematic extension of this technique. Customers are asked to group similar and dissimilar products within a market, normally again in pairs. They are then asked to explain the similarities and dissimilarities. The sequence is repeated for all groups of similar and dissimilar products. The explanations are then used to derive 'constructs' which describe the way in which customers relate and evaluate the products. These constructs form a grid that can be used to map the products, applying the words used by the customers themselves.

Personal Construct Theory and the Repertory Grid

George Kelly was an American engineer who became a highly respected clinical psychologist, best known for the development in 1955 of his own theory of personality known as Personal Construct Theory and a tool to explore people's personalities in terms of the theory, called the Repertory Grid. Kelly believed that the personality theories of the day suffered from three things: an inherent observer bias, a lack of precision and prediction and an over-reliance on the expert.

Kelly believed that we all have our own 'constructs' – views of the world or biases – that help us navigate our way around the world quickly. Certain words will trigger certain preconceptions, be they logical or otherwise. When you walk through a door you do so without consciously thinking what you are doing but you are preconditioned to act in a way that has opened a similar door before. The fact that it is locked can often come as quite a sharp surprise. Construct systems influence our expectations and perceptions subconsciously – and introduce bias. This means that one person's constructs are not those of another – and sometimes they can even be internally inconsistent because we never question them.

The Repertory Grid attempts to get rid of this bias. The technique identifies a small set of *elements* (objects, entities) and the user is asked to define some *constructs* (attributes, slots) which characterise those elements. All these terms are identified in terms of the user's own language. So, for example, 'good' can only exist in contrast to the concept of 'bad'. Any construct can reasonably be measured by answering the question 'compared to what?' Construct values are given for each element on a limited scale between extreme polar points. The process of taking three elements and asking for two of them to be paired in contrast with the third is the most effective way in which the poles of the construct can be discovered and articulated.

It is beyond this book to explain, in detail, how this technique should be deployed. However, one of the most accessible and short books on the topic is by Devi Jankovicz (2003). It really is 'the easy guide to Repertory Grids'.

Encouraging creativity

So, there are a number of skills and defined techniques that can help develop the skill of creativity in the individual. And ultimately creativity comes from an individual or group of individuals. But in an organisational context creativity needs to be encouraged. That means valuing and rewarding it. It is most likely to flourish in a trusting environment that does not over-control and has open internal and external channels of communication. The ultimate issue is the degree of *freedom* given to individuals (Sinetar, 1985). Creative people need freedom in the way they work, and slack in the resources they control – and this applies at whatever level they operate.

Encouraging creativity means tolerating the unconventional and encouraging people to challenge the conventional way things are done. It means encouraging curiosity and seeing problems as challenges. It means providing support for creativity. It means expecting and tolerating mistakes. It means developing a culture where dreaming is encouraged and being creative is fun. But unfettered creativity can be dangerous. This sort of exciting place to work may all too easily turn out to be anarchic. Entrepreneurship can focus creativity towards exploiting a commercial opportunity – developing imaginative and original solutions to problems or opportunities that customers face. But even then there needs to be a disciplined approach to exploiting the opportunities generated.

> 'To encourage people to innovate more, you have to make it safe for them to fail.'
> **Michael Dell** (1999)
> ➜

Case with questions

Lastminute.com offers last minute deals on theatre tickets, flights, holidays and even restaurants. It was set up in 1998 by **Brent Hoberman** (then 30 years old) and **Martha Lane Fox** (then 26) after raising £600 000 in venture capital. In 1999 it had a turnover of £195 000 and did not make a profit. By early 2000 the company was operating in the UK, France, Germany and Sweden, had 162 employees and 800 000 registered subscribers and sales of £30 million. In the same year it was floated on the Stock Market at a valuation of more than £400 million. Lastminute has been one of the dot.com survivors, indeed successes, and by 2004 had a turnover of almost £400 million producing operating profits of £7.5 million.

Back in 2000, apart from the general dot.com frenzy of the time, there were four main reasons for the high float valuation of Lastminute.com, which together led commentators at the time to think the company would be a success:

1 *Brand* Lastminute.com claimed early on to be the most recognised e-retailer in the UK after Amazon. This is partly as a result of a very 'old-media' advertising and promotion campaign. Branding recognition is vital to dot.coms, without it nobody visits their sites. Even today its aim is to be the Number 1 independent online travel and leisure group in Europe.

2 *Timing* It was first in the market place and, only by 2000, were there signs of real competition. First movers have a distinct advantage in e-commerce – as the success of other dot.coms such as eBay and Amazon has proved. But the company decided that, whilst it had first-mover advantage, economies of scale were important in this market and it needed to continue to grow quickly simply to survive as competition started to emerge. It therefore decided on a policy of aggressive acquisition to help it achieve scale in either a product category or in a relevant geographic market. Early on it purchased Dégrif-tour, France's biggest online travel company, followed by the Destination Holdings Group, a direct-selling international tour operator. Even by 2005, Lastminute.com continued to have an aggressive acquisition strategy, taking over potential competition and consolidating its brand across

➜

Europe for example with the acquisition of Med Hotels, First Option, Gemstone and, most importantly, Lastminute.de in Germany, which created the largest online travel company in Germany. Market share was important, and timing – when the market share was acquired – was vital.

3 *Innovation*   The products/services it offers are tailor-made for the internet. Not only are its partners eager to sell off their products at a discount to customers who have forgotten to buy them in the first place, it is also attempting to create a last minute market place in its own right, when people can leave decisions about holidays etc. until a time that suits them. It is not just selling on cheapness, it is about getting its partners to provide a sufficient supply to make buying at the last minute a viable and reliable option. Hotel chains and airlines were generally receptive to the idea as it was a low-risk venture for them. No investment was required by Lastminute.com, all they had to do was allocate a certain amount of their product. As a result Lastminute.com developed an established supply chain very quickly. By 2004 it could start to expand down its supply chain through strategic acquisitions.

4 *Track record*   Although young, the founders grew the company with determination and a clear vision. Both had worked for Spectrum Strategy, a company that wrote business plans for technology firms, which gave them the opportunity to study the sector and understand what was needed for a successful dot.com start-up. They also recruited a strong, experienced management and directorial team from the very beginning. At various times the Board included Peter Bouw, former chairman and chief executive of KLM, Bob Colliers, vice president of Intercontinental Hotels, Linda Fayne Levinson, who ran Amex Travel, and Allan Leighton, former CEO of Wal-Mart and Chairman of Royal Mail Group. All have enormous experience and credibility with funding institutions. The finance director is David Howell who was formerly at First Choice Holidays. How did they attract such a strong management team? Martha Lane Fox explains:

'We decided not to be greedy about equity but to recruit a highly talented and experienced management team by selling them a dream – a stake in lastminute.com.' (*The Times* 24 March 2000)

'You try to attract the best person for the job, usually far too qualified for the stage that the company is at, but you hope it will grow to accommodate them. If as founders you think you can do better than everyone else, you are in big trouble, because you never can.' (*Sunday Times* 28 July 2002)

The success of Lastminute.com's business model depends on the number of site 'hits' it receives, how many convert into registrations for regular e-mail newsletters and how many then actually buy something. In 2004 it handled transactions to a value of more than £990 million.

'We knew that if we had special offers we would get people onto the site, sign up for the e-mail, and forward it to someone who would take up the offer to go to New York for £100. The idea is to convert lookers into bookers. Our customer conversion rate is 19 per cent and we want to get it even higher. Small percentage points have a huge impact on sales. That is critical to the business. It's all about the cost of attracting customers and how much we have to spend to attract them balanced by what they're spending. We still need to build our customer base.'

Questions
1 Why has this company been successful when most dot.coms have not?
2 In what direction would you take the firm now?

Different people have different thinking styles that need to be respected and encouraged. Indeed if these different styles are encouraged they can generate different ideas, assumptions, approaches, frames of references and even solutions to problems. However, in the context of a team working together this can lead to conflict that has to be managed and resolved. What needs to be encouraged, ultimately, is for a whole brain solution to a problem or opportunity to be formulated, perhaps using left and right sides more dominantly at different stages in the process. That in itself may be demanding for an individual. What is more, although creativity may be an important – perhaps the most important – element of entrepreneurship, it is only one. To be successful the entrepreneur also needs to be good at the basics of starting, running and growing a business. Who said entrepreneurship was easy?

Summary

Creativity is the soul of entrepreneurship. It underpins innovation and, as such, many business concepts such as that of **Monorail Corporation** and **Lastminute.com**.

Creativity is a right brain activity that involves lateral as opposed to vertical thinking. It is intuitive, imaginative and rule breaking. It requires interpersonal and emotional skills and is people focused. Creative types do exhibit certain common characteristics and there are tests that purport to detect them.

The creative process involves four steps:

1 Generating knowledge and awareness.
2 Incubation.
3 Generating ideas.
4 Evaluation and implementation.

There are blocks to creativity. Realising they exist can be the first step to dismantling them. What is more, there are also techniques, such as brainstorming – the technique used by **Alex Tew**, analogy, attribute analysis and gap analysis that can

---

Creativity Resources

To find what must be the world largest resource of creativity and innovation resources go to *www.creax.com/portal.aspx*. The website contains hyperlinks to around 1000 other sites around the world. These include: authors, articles, books, basic research, creative environments, creative thinking pioneers, design, e-learning and creativity, education, creativity tools, ideas factory, ideas markets, imagination tools, innovation tools, internet assisted creativity, mind mapping, online techniques, ideas management, tests and puzzles and many, many more.

All the techniques discussed here – and more – are covered in more detail somewhere on this website. There are also tools and resources to help you try them.

help in the process. A key element is the ability to spot relationships and then replicate them in a different context. Appropriate facilities and environments can help with the process.

The thread that binds this all together is the entrepreneurial firm that links creativity and ideas to a commercial opportunity and, like **Lastminute.com**, offers an effective business model with good management that allows the idea to be exploited successfully. Entrepreneurs may have to be creative, but they also have to be good at business.

Essays and discussion topics

1 What do you think is involved in being creative? Give examples.
2 Compare and contrast creative vs logical thinking.
3 Creativity is a more difficult skill than entrepreneurship to develop. Discuss.
4 Why is creativity the soul of entrepreneurship?
5 Can you think of an entrepreneur who was not creative?
6 Do you believe any of the blocks to creativity apply to you?
7 Are you a left or a right brain person?
8 Are you comfortable being creative? If not, why?
9 Why do many people believe the creative process is best handled in small, entrepreneurial firms or units?
10 Can one individual undertake the whole creative process without help?
11 Do you see yourself more as an explorer, artist, judge or warrior? Why?
12 Can you learn to be creative? How might creativity be encouraged?
13 Is creativity good in all individuals and organisations? Give examples to support your argument.
14 Can you make a living out of being creative without being entrepreneurial?
15 What lessons do you learn from how the World Wide Web has developed?

Exercises and assignments

1 Try assessing your creative potential. You can find many resources by undertaking an internet search on 'creativity'. Tests can be found on:

   ● www.creax.com/csa
   ● www.web-us.com
   ● www.angelfire.com/wi/2brains

2 List the barriers that you feel inhibit you from being creative at home and at your college or university. How might they be removed or circumvented?
3 List the sources for awareness and new ideas you have at your disposal. What do you need to do to capitalise on them in a systematic way?
4 Like **Alex Tew**, try applying brainstorming in a group to the generation of new ideas. Try thinking of a new product/service application. Define an area for review, for example by looking at a problem you face in your everyday life and trying to find a solution to it. If you have problems with the technique, go to *www.brainstorming.co.uk* for further explanation.
5 Trying to use analogy in a group to come up with innovative solutions to problems can be more difficult – even with a group of friends. Start with a problem to be solved and find the way similar problems might be solved in a different context. Alternatively find a natural solution to a problem and consider whether it can be applied to a different circumstance.
6 Try using attribute analysis in a group. Again, this can be difficult. Focus the group on an everyday product or service. Select one feature or aspect and ask 'why does it have to be that

way – what benefit does it bring to the customer?' Try it a few times with different product/ service features.

7   Try using gap analysis. Select an everyday product or service. Characterise the product or service in two dimensions and use perceptual mapping to plot where competing products lie on these dimensions. Is there a gap in the market? Repeat the exercise for another product/ service.

8   Try applying some of the creativity techniques to generate new ideas. Try thinking of a new product/service application. Define an area for review, for example by looking at a problem you face in your everyday life and trying to find a solution to it.

References

de Bono, E. (1971) *Lateral Thinking for Management*, Harmondsworth: Penguin.

de Bono, E. (1995) 'Serious Creativity', *The Journal for Quality and Participation*, 18(5).

Dell, M. (1999) *Direct from Dell: Strategies that Revolutionized an Industry*, New York: Harper Business.

Jankowicz, D. (2003) *The Easy Guide to Repertory Grids*, New York: John Wiley & Sons.

Kirby, D. (2003) *Entrepreneurship*, London: McGraw Hill.

Majaro, S. (1992) 'Managing Ideas for Profit', *Journal of Marketing Management*, 8.

Mintzberg, H. (1976) 'Planning on the Left Side and Managing on the Right', *Harvard Business Review*, 54, July/August.

Page, A.L. (1993) 'Assessing New Product Development Practices and Performance: Establishing Crucial Norms', *Journal of Product Innovation Management*, 10.

Parkhurst, H.B. (1999), 'Confusion, Lack of Consensus and the Definition of Creativity as a Construct', *Journal of Creative Behaviour*, 33.

Sinetar M. (1985), 'Entrepreneurs, Chaos and Creativity: Can Creative People Really Survive Large Company Structures?', *Sloan Management Review*, 65(5).

von Oech R. (1986) *A Kick in the Seat of the Pants*, New York: Harper & Row.

von Oech R. (1998) *A Whack on the Side of the Head*, New York: Warner Books.

Part 2

Start-up

5

The Decision

Contents

LEARNING OUTCOMES

By the end of this chapter you should be able to:

- Describe the motivations of people who start up their own business, what prevents them from doing so and what influences this process;

- Explain what is needed to successfully launch your own firm;

- Generate new business ideas, linked to customer need;

- Describe the personal attributes needed to run your own business;

- Evaluate competitors in a sector or industry and how a firm might be differentiated from them;

- Explain Porter's generic marketing strategies;

- Explain the basis for economies of scale and economies of small scale;

- Explain the wide range of resources needed to start up a business and the phrase 'bootstrapping';

- Describe the importance of using informal and formal networks to marshal resources and gain credibility.

The start-up decision

Why does anybody want to take the risk of starting up their own business? It is hard work without guaranteed results. But millions do so every year around the world. The start-up is the bedrock of modern-day commercial wealth, the foundation of free market economics upon which competition is based. So can economists shed light on the process?

Economists would tell us that new entrants into an industry can be expected when there is a rise in expected post-entry profitability for those entrants. In other words, new entrants expect to make extra profits. They tell us that the rate of entry is related to the growth of that industry. They also tell us that entry is deterred by barriers such as high capital requirements, the existence of economies of scale, product differentiation, restricted access to necessary inputs and so on. What is more, the rate of entry is lower in industries with high degrees of concentration where it may be assumed that firms combine to deter entry. However, research also tells us that, whereas the rate of small firm start-up in these concentrated industries is lower, the rate of start-up for large firms is higher (Acs and Audretsch, 1989).

'Many people talk about business ideas but don't get on and do them. Starting up a business is like taking part in an amateur boxing match. You don't know how good either guy is – but unless you get in there and have a go, you never will.'

Gary Redman
founder of **Now Recruitment**
Sunday Times 8 August 2004
➡

These seem useful, but perhaps obvious, statements about start-ups. But do they really explain what happens and why? Somehow economists fail to explain convincingly the rationale for, and the process of, start-up. They seem to assume that there is a continuous flow of entrants into an industry just waiting for the possibility of extra profits. But people are not like that. They need to earn money to live; they have families who depend on them. Leaving a secure job to start up a business, for example, needs more of a rationale than just 'extra profits'. Certainly the personal characteristics of owner-managers and entrepreneurs and their antecedents are factors that economists are both unfamiliar and uncomfortable with. Economists are not really interested in individuals who are likely to set up their own firm – and their motivations for doing so. Economists are just interested in explaining how many might consider doing so and into which

Case insight

Steve Hulme retired from teaching on health grounds in 1997. For two-and-a-half years he got by on his pension and the salary earned by his wife. However, he became restless and decided to write a textbook for teenagers about problem-solving and lateral thinking. Based on this he decided to become self-employed and run courses for the young unemployed to introduce them to the kind of 'joined up' thinking skills he believed industry was looking for.

He set up his training business, aged 52, with the help of the Prince's Initiative for Mature Enterprise (Prime). It is a scheme, set up in 1999, to provide advice, support and loans for those over-45s who are jobless.

sectors they might be expected to go. What is more, economists are generally not altogether happy with the idea that the number of start-ups can be influenced by non-economic factors like antecedence and culture; but most people believe they are.

Figure 5.1 seeks to explain how start-ups happen and why, sometimes, they do not. Most people, at some time in their life, have an idea that could form the basis for establishing their own business. But few people choose to do so. What is needed is a trigger to spur them into action, to turn the idea into reality. These triggers can take the form of 'push' or 'pull' factors. Push factors are those that push you into self-employment – unemployment or forced redundancy, disagreement with your boss, being a 'misfit' and not feeling comfortable in an organisation for some reason, or simply having no alternative because, for example, you have a physical disability or illness. These are very strong motivations for self-employment, but not necessarily to

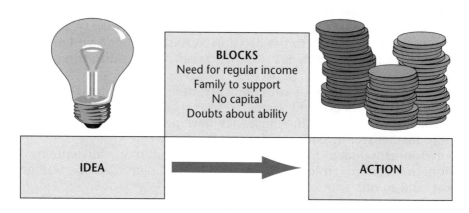

TRIGGER

PUSH FACTORS	PULL FACTORS
Unemployment	Independence
Disagreement with management	Achievement/Recognition
Does not 'fit in' to company	Personal development
No other alternatives	Personal wealth

Figure 5.1 Reasons for setting up in business

grow your business. Worse still, unemployment as a strong push factor may indicate a higher probability that the business will have a short life span. A growth business is far more likely to be established because of the positive motivation or pull factors – the need for independence, achievement and recognition, personal development and wealth. Sometimes the factors combine and an entrepreneur emerges with a positive motivation, for example, to make a success of an innovative idea, having felt a 'misfit' in their old organisation.

All too often these triggers are blocked by other factors – the need for regular income, a family to support, no capital or a doubt about your own ability. These all boil down to two things – insufficient self-confidence and an inability to cope with high risk and uncertainty. Without these key ingredients the business will not get past the ideas stage.

It is no coincidence that many people try to start up their own businesses either at an early age or in their late thirties and forties. The blocks are fewer. This is particularly the case later in life when children will probably have grown up and left home and there might be some capital saved that can be used in the start-up. At the same time the prospective entrepreneur will have gained experience and confidence and, very possibly, be seeking new challenges for self development.

Motivations can be difficult to disentangle and, although growth businesses are more likely to be set up as a result of pull factors, often people face a combination of push and pull factors. What is more, size of business may not feature in their vision at start-up. Indeed motivations change over time. Many owner-managers may start out with no wish to grow their company to be a future Microsoft or Virgin. However, if a business shows potential for being successful, few owners will hinder growth until their personal resources are really stretched. At this point the owner reaches a watershed.

Another perspective on the start-up influences on the entrepreneurial character has been developed by Cooper (1981). He provides a framework for explaining the various factors that contribute to the decision to start-up your own business, and these factors are set out in Table 5.1. Cooper classified them into three groups:

1 The antecedent influences on entrepreneurs: their background, family, age, education, job experience and so on.
2 The incubator organisation in which they have previously been working: its location, market sector, skills required and so forth.
3 The environmental factors external to the individual that contribute to the decision: the economy, role models, availability of finance, advice, staff and other support, and so on.

But more is needed than just an idea and a trigger to establish a successful business. As we saw from the failure statistics, too many start-ups fail within the first three years. For the idea to be translated into a reality with a chance of success you need to have the personal skills and personal qualities needed to run the business. You need to find customers and understand the market. You need to know who your competitors are and how you might be certain you will attract the customers to you rather than them. You need to think through how you are going to market the product or service. Finally, you need to ensure that you have sufficient resources. And that usually means raising finance. All of these factors are summarised in Figure 5.2.

Table 5.1 Influences on the start-up decision

Antecedent influences	Incubator organisation	Environmental influences
Genetic factors	Geographic location	Economic conditions
Family influences	Nature of skills and knowledge	Accessibility of finance
Education	Contact with other start-ups	Entrepreneurial role models
Previous career experience	Motivation to stay or leave organisation	Opportunities for interim consulting
	Experience in a small business setting	Availability of staff and supporting services
		Accessibility of customers

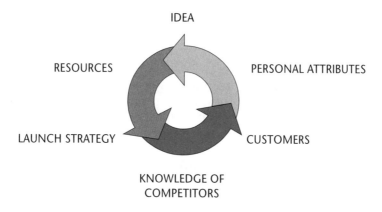

Figure 5.2 What you need to start your own business

The idea

Many business ideas are not good commercial opportunities. To be so they must be linked to market demand. And often the first attempt at putting that product or service together in a marketable way fails, so what may be necessary is a series of trial-and-error iterations. Howard Head, the inventor of the steel ski, made some 40 different metal skis before he finally made one that would work consistently. Most people usually base their business upon skills, experience or qualifications that they have already gained from a previous job, or through a hobby. Often they think that their employer is not making the most of some opportunity. Sometimes they have an idea but cannot persuade their employer to take it up, so they decide to try it themselves. Often they have contacts in the industry they believe they can exploit to their own advantage.

Other people spot gaps in the market: opportunities that are not being taken by existing businesses such as goods or services that are sold in one part of the world but not another. The entrepreneur has been distinguished from the owner-manager as being a person who is likely to spot these opportunities and be innovative in the way they take them up. Motivations may appear little different at start-up but how entrepreneurs spot opportunities and find ways of exploiting them starts to set them apart even at this early stage.

Gaps in markets come from change. Think of changes that are taking place and the implications they may have, for example:

- Products or services that you have seen but are not available in your area can mean there are opportunities. Experience of overseas countries and markets is always valuable.
- Changes in customer demands or fashions can mean needs are not being met.
- Changes in markets can lead to opportunities; for example, the opening up of new retail outlets, shopping areas or sales channels such as the internet.
- Changes in legislation can create opportunities; for example, changes in Health and Safety regulations and Food Hygiene regulations have created opportunities in the past.

As we saw in Chapter 3, you can create your own change and your own opportunity through innovation; for example, innovation could mean:

Invention: Although, as we saw in the previous chapter, this is not necessarily the same thing as innovation. Often inventors are best advised to sell on their idea rather than to try to exploit it themselves.

Ways of doing things better or cheaper: Better is good; cheaper, as we shall see, can lead to problems.

New developments in technology: Computing, telephonics and the internet are at the forefront of technological change at the moment.

New ways of getting goods or services to markets: Direct selling of certain types of goods or services firstly over the telephone and now the internet have created many millionaires in the last couple of decades.

As we have already noted, Bolton and Thompson (2000) suggest that there are three basic approaches to innovation in this context which are not mutually exclusive. Firstly, *have a problem and seek a solution*. They cite as an example Edwin Land's invention of the Polaroid camera because his young daughter could not understand why she had to wait to have pictures of herself printed. Secondly, *have a solution and seek a problem*. They cite 3M's Post-It notes as an example of a product with loosely-sticking qualities that was applied to the need to mark pages in a manuscript. Finally, *identify a need and develop a solution*. The example they cite is James Dyson's dual cyclone cleaner that he developed because of his frustration with the inadequate suction provided by his existing vacuum cleaner when he was converting an old property.

There are many sources of potential new business ideas. They come from an exposure to business and commerce around the world – an inquisitiveness and a constant searching for commercial opportunity. They come, not so much from asking the question 'why?', but rather from asking the question 'why not?' And many of the techniques discussed in the previous chapter can be used to generate them. They could come from:

- Existing businesses around the world – either what they *are* offering or what they are *not* offering;
- Existing franchises not offered in certain countries;
- Innovations – your own or those belonging to other people;
- Patents and licences – your own or those belonging to others that are not yet fully exploited;
- Research institutes – where new products may have commercial potential;
- Industry and trade contacts yielding insights into gaps in markets;
- Industry and trade shows where new products and services are seeking new markets;
- Newspapers and trade journals – where new products, services or markets around the world are reviewed and, most importantly, gaps in markets might be exposed;
- Business networks and contacts – which might provide the blinding insight that a market opportunity exists;
- Television and radio.

One significant factor, of course, will be the sectors and markets in which small firms are currently growing most quickly. It is here that opportunities currently exist. But will you be able to capitalise on these developments as quickly as existing firms? And will those opportunities still exist in five years time? A good business idea has a window of commercial opportunity. Too early or too late and it is unlikely to be successful. Cecil Duckworth set up his engineering firm to manufacture self-service petrol pumps, but when petrol in the UK was still being served by attendants. He did not sell a single one and the business nearly failed. However, within 18 months he started manufacturing central heating boilers and laid the foundations for the highly successful Worcester Engineering Group that he subsequently sold for over £30 million.

Case insight

Business Ideas

Harry Cragoe visited California in the early 1990s. 'When I arrived in Los Angeles, I rented an apartment near the beach and found myself in the body-beautiful epicentre of the world. It was very English, very white and overweight. Everybody was focused on looking good and being healthy. There were juice bars churning out things called smoothies and I got hooked on them.' But when Harry returned to the UK he could not find his favourite drink. 'I couldn't believe they weren't available here. All you could find were vac-packed cartons of apple or orange juice. I could see there was a real opportunity' (*Sunday Times*, 23 May 2004). Ten years later his firm, **PJ Smoothies**, had become the market leader in the UK fresh drinks sector with a turnover of £12 million in 2004.

In 1978 **David Arculus** came up with the simple idea of printing the words to pop songs in a magazine. The magazine was called *Smash Hits* and it was an instant success. The cash flow was ploughed back into a string of magazines that came to form the **Emap** publishing group: 'It was a really simple idea. We noticed all these girls dancing round in discos trying to sing the words of pop songs. We thought, 'Why don't we produce a magazine that prints the words of the songs? We went from 10 000 copies of the first issue up to one million within a year.'

David Vanrenen thought he had an angle on e-commerce with his company, **EarthPort.com**. The company acts as a kind of global internet 'wallet' – a secure electronic payment system. You obtain an account with the company by logging your personal and credit card details with it. You can then use your account to buy goods and services from other internet suppliers without having to repeatedly fill out forms and give out your credit card details. This 'locks' subscribers into the site and there is the added advantage of having a ready-made customer base and valuable personal information. Today EarthPort.com is listed on the Alternative Investment Market.

Inventors of board games are usually best advised to sell their idea on to companies with an existing range of games. However, there are exceptions. **Abalone** is a game invented by two Frenchmen, **Michel Lalet** and **Laurent Levi**. With a hexagonal board and 15 black and 15 white marbles, the idea is to position your marbles in a way that pushes the opponent off the side of the board. Lalet and Levi could not raise the finance to produce and market the game from either banks or publishers and after eight months were about to give up when they happened to discuss the idea with a neighbour. He wanted a business plan – no more than 20 pages long – and then agreed to put in about £50 000. Unfortunately, this was only one-third of what they originally thought they needed. Whilst it was enough to pay for an initial production run, it left precious little for marketing. Their reaction was novel. They took the game around bars and clubs giving demonstration games and creating their own PR and hype over the game. They sold the game to shops themselves. The approach worked, in the first three months they sold 9000 copies and the pair have now become quite famous in France.

The game became a craze spawning a jazz record label and other merchandising. Over two years they sold 130 000 copies. Lalet and Levi then sold their share of the business to their neighbour in exchange for a royalty on sales. Abalone is now sold world-wide.

Personal attributes

It goes without saying that, if certain operating skills are needed to run a business, somebody in the firm must have them. Normally that person will be the founder. You cannot be a carpenter without having the skills of a carpenter. However, if you have six carpenters working for you, the primary skills you might need could be those of a salesperson. In fact a self-employed carpenter probably needs to be a salesperson too, as well as an administrator and bookkeeper. The smaller the business the more the owner-manager needs to be a jack-of-all-trades, an all-rounder. Only as the business grows can she afford the luxury of buying in specialist help.

However, it is not just relevant operational skills that you need. You are likely to have the characteristics of owner-managers and entrepreneurs that we have already discussed. But you also need certain personal qualities:

- *Stamina*: In your own firm you work long hours with few holidays, so you need the stamina for hard work. Robert Wright, who set up a small airline company called Connectair in the 1980s after leaving Cranfield University, called it '90% perspiration, 10% inspiration'. Running your own business really is a 24/7 activity.
- *Commitment and dedication*: In order to be motivated to put in that hard work you need to be committed and dedicated. And that can put a strain on relationships. You need to be tenacious and disciplined, willing to make personal sacrifices.
- *Opportunism*: This means taking opportunities almost before they appear. You need to be in the right place at the right time, almost making your own luck by playing the odds.
- *Ability to bounce back*: It is often said that the most common word in business is 'no' and this can be very dispiriting. All the more so if you are self-employed. So you need to be able to bounce back and ask the question again and again. You need to be persistent.
- *Motivation to excel*: You need to be results orientated, with high but realistic goals and a drive to achieve them. One thing is for certain; it can be very lonely running your own firm, so you need to be self-motivated.
- *Tolerance of risk, ambiguity and uncertainty*: If you crave certainty, regular routine and clear job definitions, do not go into business on your own.

Running your own business is not an easy option. It needs people with outstanding qualities and they deserve our admiration.

> **Case insight**
>
> **Gary Frank** started **Delicious Doughnut Company** in 1989 with £15 000 borrowed from his family.
>
> 'In those days I employed a girl to help me make the doughnuts. We started making them at midnight and this lasted four or five hours. Then I would load up the van and make the deliveries. After that I had to do the paperwork and snatch a few hours sleep before starting again.'
>
> **Gary Frank**, founder of the **Delicious Doughnut Company**
> *Sunday Times* 5 September 1999
> ➜

Customers

Ralf Waldo Emerson once said: 'If a man can make a better mousetrap than his neighbour, though he builds his house in the wood, the world will make a beaten path to his door'. He was wrong. Two further things are essential. Firstly, the world must *need* the mousetrap. There must be a market demand for a business idea for it to be capable of being transformed into a viable business. Customers will buy a product or service because it solves a problem for them, meets a need they have or adds value to them. Secondly, the world must *know about* the mousetrap and be persuaded to buy it. Customers must know about a new product or service and be persuaded that it will perform as promised before they will buy it. That can also mean understanding their motives for buying and tailoring the product or service better to meet those needs.

Inventors are particularly prone to mousetrap myopia; they tend to focus on the product and not on the market. But market demand is the key to commercial viability, and you need to start with basics:

- Who is going to buy the product or service? Name names and describe the customers.
- Why will they buy it?
- What needs do they want the product or service to meet?
- Is the customer reachable? If so, how?
- What are the channels of distribution?
- Is the market for the product or service new or mature?
- Is the market growing or declining?
- How big is the market?
- Does it have boundaries (for example, geographic location)?
- Are there competitors? If so, why should customers buy your product or service rather than that of the competitor?
- Is the product or service unique in any way?
- Is the market highly concentrated or fragmented?

Many of these things are difficult to assess at start-up, but some market research really is vital. One of the things you are trying to estimate is the sales potential of your product or service. This will, amongst other things, determine the scale and nature of the resources you need. Estimating the size of a completely new market for a completely new product or service can be a daunting task. For example, the market for PCs was completely underestimated when they were first introduced. However, where there are existing markets for similar products or services the task will be easier. Nevertheless, sometimes the quickest and cheapest way of finding out these things is by starting the business, limiting the costs and risks, and closely monitoring the outcomes. This approach is attractive to owner-managers because they are action orientated and learn by doing. However, all too often it is just an excuse for not undertaking any market research at all.

Competitors

It is particularly important that a start-up business understands the nature of the competition it faces. This involves undertaking market research to develop a detailed knowledge of competitors and how your product or service compares to theirs.

Research indicates that low growth firms have the least understanding of their competitors (Storey *et al.*, 1987). Ultimately you will have to find some form of competitive advantage over them if you are to be successful. A major survey of over 2500 small firms concluded that there was an inverse relationship between the number of competitors and growth performance (Cosh and Hughes, 1998). In other words, as you might expect, the fewer competitors the better.

However, few competitors can also be a bad thing, in some circumstances. If you are entering a market where there is high concentration, then it may be that these competitors will combine to deter entry. High concentration can also mean bigger, more powerful companies as competitors. You need to think carefully before entering a market dominated by big companies because they will have well established market positions and the resources to fight off new entrants.

Location can be an important factor dictating competition. In the UK, as in other countries, there can be marked variations in the sectoral, size and age structure of firms in different regions of the country and at different points in time. Whilst in the past surveys have found that small firms in the UK have tended to grow more quickly in rural rather than urban areas (ESRC, 1992), the survey noted earlier, which is more recent, found the opposite. Of course, some of this may be due to factors other than competition. So for example, whilst firms in the south east of England face fiercer competition than firms in other parts of Britain, the survey also noted that they tended to enjoy higher growth rates. One reason for this might be that the market for their goods or services was growing faster and therefore greater competition could be sustained.

The structure of the market – the customers, suppliers, competitors – and the potential substitutes and barriers to entry determine the degree of competition and therefore the profitability you are likely to achieve. Michael Porter (1985) developed a useful structural analysis of industries which he claims goes some way towards explaining the profitability of firms within it. The aim of any competitive strategy, he says, 'is to cope with and, if possible, change the rules in favour of the company'. Unfortunately, a small firm is unlikely to be able to change those rules, so it pays to understand them. Porter claims that five forces determine competitiveness in any industry. These are shown in Figure 5.3.

1 *The power of buyers*   This is determined by the relative size of buyers and their concentration. It is also influenced by the volumes they purchase, the information they have about competitors or substitutes, switch costs and their ability to backward integrate. Switch costs are the costs of switching to another product. The extent to which the product they are buying is differentiated in some way also affects relative buying power. The greater the power of the buyer, the weaker the bargaining position of the firm selling to them. So if buyers are large firms, in concentrated industries, buying large volumes with good price information about a relatively undifferentiated product with low switch costs they will be in a strong position to keep prices low.

2 *The power of suppliers*   This is also determined by the relative size of firms and the other factors mentioned above. So, if suppliers are large firms in concentrated industries, with well differentiated products that are relatively important to the small firms buying them, then those small firms are in a weak position to keep prices, and therefore their costs, low.

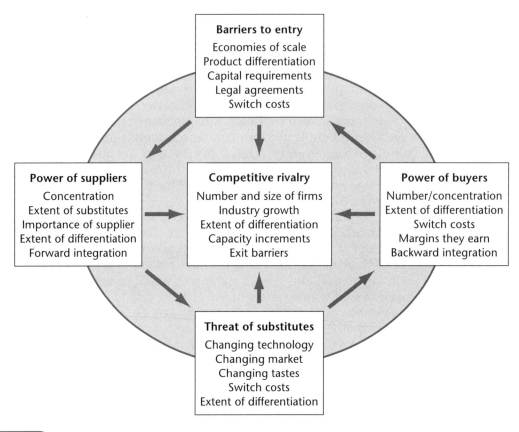

Figure 5.3 Porter's Five Forces

3 *The threat of new entrants* Barriers to entry keep out new entrants to an industry. These can arise because of legal protection (patents and so on), economies of scale, proprietary product differences, brand identity, access to distribution, government policy, switch costs, capital costs and so forth. For example, a firm whose product is protected by patent or copyright may feel that it is relatively safe from competition. The greater the possible threat of new entry to a market, the lower the bargaining power and control over price of the small firm within it.

4 *The threat of substitutes* This revolves around their relative price performance, switch costs and the propensity of the customer to switch, for example because of changes in tastes or fashion. The greater the threat of substitutes, the less the ability of the firm to charge a high price. So, a small firm selling a poorly differentiated product in a price sensitive, fashion market should find it difficult to charge a high price.

5 *Competitive rivalry in the industry* The competitive rivalry of an industry will depend on the number and size of firms within it and their concentration, its newness and growth and therefore its attractiveness in terms of profit and value added together with intermittent over-capacity. Crucially important is the extent of product differentiation, brand identity and switch costs. The greater the competitive rivalry, the less the ability of the firm to charge a high price.

These five forces determine industry profitability and, in turn, are a function of industry structure – the underlying economic and technical characteristics of the industry. These can change over time but the analysis does emphasise the need to select industries carefully in the first place. It also provides a framework for predicting, *a priori*, the success or otherwise of the small firm. For example, a small firm competing with many other small firms to sell a relatively undifferentiated product to a few large customers in an industry with few barriers to entry is unlikely to do well without some radical shifts in its marketing strategies. How many small firms face just such a situation?

Generic marketing strategies

There have only ever been three ways of selling products or services and at the launch of your business you need to decide which one applies to you. You see two of them being used every day in any street market. At one end of the market there is a street trader offering the cheapest goods in the market – fruit, vegetables or whatever; at the other end there is another offering something different – freshest or organically-grown fruit, vegetables or whatever. The more different you are, the higher the price you can charge. But there is also a third way to charge a higher price – not to go to the market, but rather to take the product to the customer. This is focusing on the customer and their needs.

Michael Porter (1985) gave this piece of common-sense the catchy title of 'generic marketing strategies' and argued that there are only three fundamental ways of achieving sustainable competitive advantage:

- Low price;
- High differentiation;
- Customer focus.

These lead to the four market positions, or 'generic marketing strategies', shown in Figure 5.4.

Figure 5.4 Generic marketing strategies

Commodity supplier

This is where the firm sets out to be the lowest priced producer in the industry appealing to a very broad market with a relatively undifferentiated product. To have the lowest price means you must have the lowest costs. This assumes that costs can be reduced, for example through economies of scale, and that this is important to the customer. If a firm sets up in a market where economies of scale are achievable and are important to customers it must grow quickly, just to survive. A firm can find itself in this situation when the market or product may be new and economies of scale have yet to be developed. Firms may not yet have grown to their optimal size to achieve these economies and the battle is on to see who can get there first – it will be a risky battle with many casualties along the way. This is shown in Figure 5.5. Technological change can cause a step change downward in this curve at any time. Minimum cost on this curve is at output A with average cost per unit A1.

This strategy is an inherently unattractive alternative for most smaller firms as they can rarely achieve the economies of scale of large firms and seldom have the capital to invest constantly in new technology. What is more, it is likely that sustainable cost leadership can only be achieved by means of 'substantial relative market share advantage' because this provides the firm with cost advantage through economies of scale, market power and experience curve effects. This means that any firm pursuing this strategy will have to fight competitors hard to sustain its advantage. It will also try to set up as many barriers to entry into the industry as possible. A start-up coming into this established industry will have its work cut out just to survive.

The average size of businesses varies from industry to industry. For example, the average size of a chemical firm is very large, whereas the average size of a retail firm is relatively small. One of the reasons for this is the extent to which economies of scale affect an industry; that is, how total cost per unit produces changes as more units are produced. Generally this can be expected to decline up to some point, for example, as an expensive piece of machinery is used more fully. However beyond this point unit costs may start to increase, for example, as economies of scale of production become increasingly offset by rising distribution costs. The potential for economies of scale is often greatest in capital-intensive industries like chemicals. This is shown in

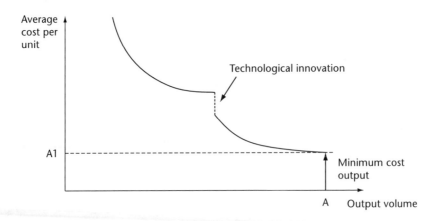

Figure 5.5 Economies of scale

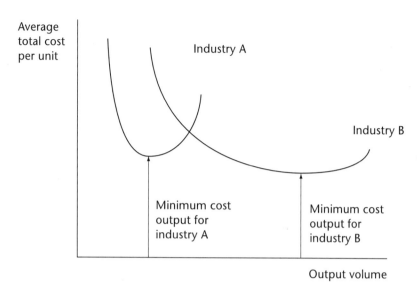

Figure 5.6   Economies of scale in two industries

Figure 5.6. Total costs include production, selling and distribution costs and are therefore dependent upon the state of technology, the size of the market and the location of potential customers. The unit cost for industry A turns up at a relatively low level of output, implying the optimal size of firm is relatively small, in contrast to industry B where there are considerable economies of scale. Porter calls these 'fragmented' industries where economies of scale just do not exist and large firms cannot, therefore, dominate the industry. These are clearly easier industries for a small business start-up. Where economies of scale are considerable, and they are valued by the customer, this is an industry that a small business start-up should avoid.

An example of the effects of economies of scale is the microcomputer industry. Born in the late 1970s with unknown demand for its products and no established producers, it has grown rapidly. However, the industry offers substantial economies of scale, particularly in R&D for hardware and software. Consequently the market has consolidated, with many small firms going out of business. The survivors have been one of two types of firm. First, there are firms like Microsoft for software and Apple Corporation for hardware which recognised that the industry would eventually be dominated by a few large firms offering low cost or premium quality products. Microsoft's big break came when IBM chose its operating system for its first PC in 1981 and the company was then able to ride to market dominance on the back of IBM's entry into the PC market. Secondly there were firms like Sun Microsystems which specialised in CAD/CAM equipment and aimed at even smaller specific market segments. Sun Microsystems established an effective market niche for itself and headed off any direct competition with big companies. Customers valued their expertise and economies of scale were less important. As often happens, it has been the middle-sized firm which has pursued neither strategy which has suffered in this industry.

Case insight

The **Apple Corporation** realised that economies of scale were achievable and would become increasingly important to customers as the basic microcomputer became more and more a commodity. Based upon an excellent product range, Apple grew rapidly, grabbing market share worldwide, so that it was in a good position to compete with big company entrants to the hardware industry such as IBM.

However, even Apple made mistakes, and the worst was keeping control of its operating systems so that the PC, using the ubiquitous Microsoft operating system, came to dominate the market. With market dominance came greater economies of scale. Companies like Dell have become expert at keeping their cost base as low as possible by using the internet to help manage their supply chain and direct marketing. Now Apple is trying hard to compete on things such as capability and design rather than price, particularly with new products – which is where the iPod came in.

●

Market traders

And yet, we do see very small businesses surviving in highly price-competitive markets where economies of scale exist. Just visit your local Saturday market to see some examples. How do they do it? The answer lies in businesses that are classified as market traders.

When an economist draws a production cost curve like Figure 5.7 it is almost assumed that there will be economies of scale and that minimum cost output will be at some point A yielding a unit cost of A1. But have you ever noticed that the curve economists draw never touches the vertical axis? So what happens to the left of the curve? The truth is not something economists discuss. In many industries it is possible to start up with an absolute minimum of overheads enabling you to compete

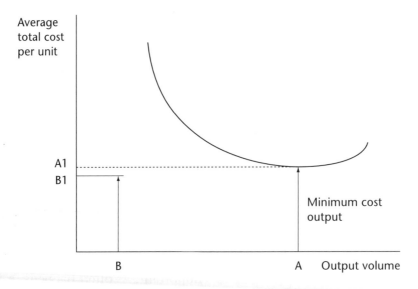

Figure 5.7 Economies of small scale

with bigger companies who achieve the economies of scale. For example, consider the consultant working from home or the 'metal-basher' operating from a low-cost workshop under the railway arches. The average cost of production might then actually be lower than that of the big firm, for example B1. The problem is that that will only hold true of production levels up to a certain level, say B. To grow the business beyond this size means that the firm must increase its overheads and then it starts to move down the cost curve. In order to increase volume and cross the 'no-man's-land' between B and A the firm will need high investment and it will need to move quickly. The chances of making this dash successfully are relatively low. Businesses in this category are therefore unlikely to see growth.

Small firms, therefore, can compete on price as market traders. They may also compete in industries where economies of scale exist but are either unimportant to the customer or cannot be achieved because of limitations in the size of the market, either in total or geographically. This happens particularly in highly specialist industries. The problem for market traders is that they are unlikely to see growth.

Niche player

Differentiation means setting out to be unique in the industry along some dimensions that are widely valued by customers. This is called developing a unique selling proposition (USP). The firm sets out to establish itself as unique and different from its competitors in some way. It can then charge a premium price.

Where the firm combines this with a focus on a narrow target market segment it is said to be following a strategy of 'focused differentiation', better known as a niche strategy. Economists call this occupying the 'interstices' of the economy. Clear differentiation often goes with well-aimed segmentation as it is easier to differentiate yourself in a small, clearly identified market. The key to segmentation is the ability to identify the unique benefits that a product or service offers to potential customers. Thus, for example, there may be two electrical engineers producing similar products but, whereas one is a jobbing engineer producing a range of products for many customers with no particular competitive advantage, the other might differentiate itself on the basis of its market – that it sells to a few large companies with whom it has long-term relationships, being integrated into their supply chains.

Being a niche player involves four things:

1 Finding out what elements in the marketing mix are 'unique' to the business. That means understanding what the customers really want when they buy the product or service and why they buy it from you rather than a competitor. Uniquenesses can be product- or market-based.
2 Specialising in customers and/or products rather than methods of production, which is important when competing on price. You must understand your customers thoroughly and ensure that your product or service precisely meets their needs. Ongoing, thorough market research is essential.
3 Stressing the inherent strengths of the firm and the USPs of the product or service, such as innovation, flexibility or personalised service, over its competitors.
4 Emphasising in your marketing the non-price elements of the marketing mix (see page 127) that differentiate you from the competition. Niche players should be able to charge a premium price and sustain a high margin, clearly a very attractive option for smaller firms.

It is vital that any firm understands the basis of its competitive advantage. For a firm pursuing a differentiation strategy this means understanding the basis for its differential advantage. This can be based in law (a licence, copyright, patent and so on), upon elements of the product (quality, design and so on), the service offered or intangible things like image. For a shop it may be based on location (the only shop on the estate). The more elements that the firm can claim to set it apart from the competition the better. However, these elements must be a real benefit and add value to the customer. If the firm has elements of differentiation then it should aggressively promote them, usually through a strong brand identity.

Case insight

One Huntingdon-based family company that has been very successful in differentiating its products and selling to a small but lucrative market segment is **Quad Electroacoustics**. Originally founded in 1936 by **Peter Walker** as an 'acoustical manufacturing company' to produce 'public address' systems, today its silvery grey, bizarrely sculptured audio equipment looks like no others. It sounds superb as well. When Japanese 'competitors' bring out new models every year, Quad's stay the same and last forever. Its original electrostatic loudspeaker was in production for 28 years. Quads are a byword for quality, reliability and design originality – but they are not cheap. Current models sell for over £3000 and still 70 per cent of Quad's sales are exported, especially to Europe, USA and Japan.

Establishing a market niche is most effective when aimed at a narrowly defined market segment. Sometimes this can involve concentrating on gaps in the market place left by larger companies. One problem of a niche market is its very narrowness, which limits it, but what might be limited for larger companies offers smaller firms a range of opportunities. Entrepreneurs often run businesses in different niches, finding growth through diversification. However the environment can change; markets grow or shrink, technology changes and customers move around. As the picture changes, so do opportunities, and what might offer a good niche in one decade may turn into a free-for-all in another.

The general thrust of research strongly suggests that market positioning is a key contributor to growth and that developing a market niche by differentiating a business from its competitors is a strategy that offers smaller firms the best chance of success and possibly sustainable growth. For example, in a survey of some

Case insight

One company, that arguably could make even higher margins by charging a higher price for its products, is the **Morgan Motor Company**. Founded in 1909, it is the world's oldest privately owned car manufacturer, making a quintessentially British sports car.

Every Morgan is hand-built and looks like it came from the 1930s. Each car is different, with a choice of 35 000 body colours and leather upholstery to match. It takes seven weeks to build a car and customers are invited to the factory to see the process. Morgan sells only about 500 cars a year, half overseas, and demand exceeds supply, cushioning the company from the vagaries of demand. Morgan is, arguably, a unique car manufacturer and certainly a niche player.

1500 smaller companies across Europe, it was found that those companies that had seen their sales and/or profit grow in the 1990s were those who had 'better or different products or services', and this led to weak-to-normal levels of competition (Burns and Whitehouse, 1994). Those that had seen sales, but particularly profits, decline competed on price and encountered fierce competition. Another survey into 3500 of Britain's 'Superleague Companies' concluded that most of these high-growth companies served niche markets (3i, 1993). Storey *et al.* (1989) concluded that the owner-managers of the fast-growing firms were much more likely to emphasise competitive advantage as being in areas such as innovation and product or service quality. By way of contrast, the owner-managers of the slow-growing firms emphasised price.

Case insight

Back in the 1970s **Alan Pound** was making sound-mixing equipment in his garage and selling it through trade magazines. But in 1988 he moved into the computer-telephony market and started making hardware and software that is used in voice mail systems. Today **Aculab** has sales of over £20 million with 185 employees based in five countries. Alan Pound's view of the reasons for his success is simple, to the point and a lesson to us all:

'The company's success stems from picking a profitable niche in an area where there is little competition, high margins and huge barriers to entry.'

There are, of course, risks with any marketing strategy. The risks associated with a policy of differentiation are that the basis for differentiation cannot be sustained as competitors imitate or if the USP becomes less important to customers. If the premium charged for the product or service is too high, customers may decide not to purchase. The risks associated with a policy of focus are that the segment becomes unattractive for some reason, or that smaller segments start to appear, chipping away at what is already a small customer base, or that the basis for segmentation disappears as the differences between segments disappear. Despite these risks, the niche player stands the best chance of launching and then growing a successful start-up.

Outstanding success

Sometimes firms that differentiate themselves effectively turn out to have a very broad market appeal, and what may have started as a niche business turns out to be an outstanding success and experiences rapid and considerable growth. However, it is unlikely that many businesses will start life here, except perhaps in areas of real innovation. Commodity suppliers try desperately to differentiate themselves, with varying degrees of success. Those companies that succeed in differentiating themselves do so through the effective use of branding.

Eventually even the big company can feel threatened by a large number of extremely effective niche companies. The computer industry as a whole has now fragmented into many different segments and no company now tries to compete in every segment, including Japan's Fujitsu, Hitachi and NEC. Every firm concentrates on the area where it can be best. Apple, Sun Microsystems, Intel, Compaq and

Microsoft have all thrived in recent years despite brutal price wars. Companies with broader product lines based on large machines, such as DEC, Bull, Siemens-Nixdorf and Japan's computer makers have seen their profits collapse. This process is nowhere more evident than in IBM. Its profits evaporated and it had to completely reorganise to face the competition from effective niche marketers.

Based upon these generic marketing strategies, a specific launch strategy for the business needs to be developed and that needs resources and careful planning.

Resources

The next consideration is resources. The resources needed will depend ultimately upon the size of the business and this is difficult to predict at start-up. Most start-ups need money, but sometimes this can be minimised by borrowing resources or obtaining assets on lease or hire purchase. Certainly in the early days it does not pay to be burdened by high-interest payments and flexibility is crucial. A golden rule in start-ups is to keep your fixed costs as low as possible, thus keeping that all important break-even point low. This will be explained in the next chapter.

However, there are other less obvious resource needs. The business needs customers, suppliers, perhaps employees and a landlord. Even if it is to borrow the money, it will need a banker. The process of assembling these resources is a difficult one and is crucially dependent on one factor – credibility. The whole process has been likened to the credibility merry-go-round, shown in Figure 5.8, that can be mounted at any point (Birley and Norburn, 1984).

If you go to a banker with an ill-thought-through proposal, not knowing how much money you need, your credibility in terms of whether you are likely to manage the start-up effectively will be very low. The banker is looking for you to persuade him that your start-up will succeed. He might suggest you go out and get your first customer. But if you go to potential customers and ask them to place an order for your product or service they might ask about reliability or after-sales service. They might also reasonably expect to see the product. They might even ask for evidence of previous satisfied customers. The same problem happens when you approach suppliers or a landlord. They will ask for a bank reference, or look to a trading track record – none of which you have. So how do you get off the merry-go-round?

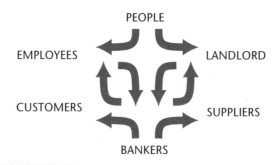

Figure 5.8 The credibility merry-go-round

Credibility can be established in a number of ways. Education and track record are important. If you can demonstrate achievements, particularly in the industry that you want to start up in, it counts for a lot. Personal contact is the key to any relationship and networks of friends and commercial contacts can be important. A strong personal relationship can bring with it credibility. Your network of contacts might provide you with your first customer, or provide you with low cost or free office space. They might even provide you with the cash that the banker is so reluctant to provide. Networks can also provide you with professional advice and opinion, often without charge. Formal networks such as Chambers of Commerce, Business Links in the UK, Small Business Development Centers in the USA and Trade Associations can be invaluable for this.

> **Case insight**
>
> **Richard Branson** may have been lucky to find someone willing to let him have the premises for his first Oxford Street record shop rent free, but when he launched **Virgin Atlantic** he showed that he understood that high capital costs lead to high risks. He minimised these risks by leasing everything and then being able to offer a good quality service at attractive prices.
>
> Richard Branson's main skills are said to be networking, finding opportunities and securing the resources necessary for their exploitation.
>
> ➜

Deciding what resources are needed, when and how to acquire them are important strategic decisions for a start-up. Entrepreneurs typically seek to use the minimum amount of resources at each stage of the business. The important thing to remember is that you do not have to own a resource to be able to use and control it. Owning a resource normally means buying it and that ties up capital which increases the risk that the business faces. It has even been suggested that entrepreneurs who do not own a resource are in a better position to commit and de-commit quickly, giving them greater flexibility and reducing the risks they face (Stevenson *et al.*, 1985). In the USA, minimising the resources that you own but still use and control is called 'bootstrapping', more formally defined as a 'multistage commitment of resources with a minimum commitment at each stage or decision point' (Bhidé, 1992). Clearly, to bootstrap you need to tap into as wide a network of contacts as possible.

> **Case insight**
>
> In the early 1990s **Robbie Cowling** started **Jobserve** in his spare time from his bedroom by finding out what contract work was available locally and sending the list to subscribers. A year later he had some 3000 subscribers and his job as an IT consultant with the Ministry of Defence was relegated to four days a week. Soon the business started spilling out of the bedroom. This was the point at which he decided to dedicate himself to it full-time. He also decided that he needed to move to a bigger house, which he also used as an office. Only one year later did he decide that the business had grown sufficiently to warrant taking the risk of moving to a dedicated office of its own. By 2004 the Jobserve recruitment service had a turnover of some £9 million and Robbie Cowling was a millionaire – at least on paper.
>
> ●

Planning

Assembling the resources needed to start up a new business needs careful planning. Writing down what you intend to do and what you need helps ensure that you do things systematically, in a coordinated fashion. It means others can comment upon and help improve your plans. For many people it also adds a touch of certainty to an otherwise highly uncertain activity. For them, the plan represents the vision of what they want the business to become and how they will go about achieving it. It can become a symbol of what they are striving for. Self-employment creates uncertainty about income generation and small firms face greater market uncertainty than large firms. As we saw in a preceding chapter, the ability to deal with uncertainty is a central feature of entrepreneurship. Planning helps address this issue.

What is needed is a business plan, and what goes into that we address in later chapters. However, it means that we need to address three issues:

1 **Viability** – customers, competition and marketing strategy, but also the profitability of the business. These are the bare bones of the business plan.
2 **Resources** – people and other resources, but most important of all the money needed to finance the start-up, over what period and how it will be repaid. This requires a cash flow forecast.
3 **Credibility** – track record and experience. This is important if you are to use the plan to assemble the resources you need.

Of course, a plan will not make uncertainty go away or even diminish it. It is simply that planning is the best way man knows of preparing for uncertainty, both practically and psychologically. It is also the best way we have of convincing others that we are prepared and addressing the issue of credibility. It is not that there is any simplistic formula for successfully starting a business. It is just that by planning you give yourself a better chance of avoiding at least some of the pitfalls.

In many ways it is the planning process that is more valuable than the plan itself, unless, perhaps, you are seeking finance. So the plan itself needs to be fit for purpose. A plan which seeks to convince others to lend to or invest in a business will be something of a selling document. The more money being sought, the more it needs to convince and, therefore, the longer that plan. A plan which is for your own purposes can be a brief working document. Whatever its purpose, it needs to be flexible because the only thing that is certain in life is that the future is not. So it is quite likely that plans will have to adapt or even change completely.

> **Case insight**
>
> Advice to start-ups:
>
> 1 Network – find out who your mentors are.
> 2 Find out what you want to do and look at the competition and decide on how you can improve on the competition.
> 3 What is your USP? What is it about your business that makes you different from anyone else. And once you have found those little uniquenesses state them time and time again because those little uniquenesses are the things the competition will find difficult to duplicate.
>
> **Anita Roddick** founder of
> **Body Shop**
> Personal interview
> ➡

Networks of friends and colleagues can be an invaluable source of advice and opinion about your business plan. What is more, advice is available from a myriad of more formal sources. Many banks produce free booklets detailing what is needed to set up your own business and how to go about developing a business plan. There are government agencies in many countries that give start-up advice, usually without charge. Further details about sources of help and advice in the UK are given in the section at the end of the book. The more rapid the growth your business will face, the more likely you are to need advice. Indeed, evidence shows that fast-growth firms are more likely to seek out and use advice than average-growth businesses (Cosh and Hughes, 1998). However, it cannot be proved directly that the advice they received led to their growth.

Case with question

Richard Thompson is a serial entrepreneur. He was entrepreneurial even at school. He got his mother to make more packed lunch than he needed and then sold it in the playground. He even bought stationery from liquidating companies and then sold it to family and friends. He left school at 16 to join a company called Copycat which sold peripherals in the rapidly growing computer market of the 1980s. He quickly decided that there were more lucrative opportunities selling the actual computers but the company refused to move into an area that it felt it did not know enough about. Richard investigated the market and developed industry contacts whilst working for Copycat.

Because of his frustration at the unwillingness of the company to move into the personal computer area he decided to set up his own business. He drew up a business plan for a business that would make door step sales, delivering the computers by mail order. The company was called **First Stop Solutions** and was set up in 1986. On the back of his business plan he secured a £15 000 loan and, at first in his spare time, started buying and selling computers in Croydon, just outside London.

Richard Thompson quickly decided to leave Copycat and concentrate on his business full-time. First Stop Solutions first rented an office in a shared workspace. But Richard wanted to sell premier brand computers such as IBM or Compaq to blue-chip customers. His first problems came with trying to persuade IBM to give him a dealership. Part of the process was a visit to his offices by IBM. Convinced that he would have a credibility problem with IBM if they realised how small his business was and that he shared office space, he persuaded the owner of the workspace to let him take down their sign and put up one saying First Stop Solutions. He also persuaded the other businesses sharing the space to pretend to be part of the business for the day. He introduced a company specialising in importing car parts as his administration department and another selling office supplies as his accounts department. The trick worked. He got the dealership and within two years the company was voted 'IBM Quality Dealer of the Year'. It soon dominated the local area and then went national, supplying computers to companies like McDonald's. By 1994 it was making profits of £400 000 on sales of £4 million.

In 1994 Richard Thompson set up a second business called **EMS**, which placed trained staff into computer stores to represent manufacturers. By 1996 this had grown so large that Richard decided to sell the old business to his employees for a few hundred thousand pounds. By 1998 EMS had grown to employ 500 staff on sales of £4.9 million and profit of £700 000. He then sold it to the US-based Mosaic Group for some £5 million.

Question: From the evidence here, what do you think motivates Richard Thompson? Which entrepreneurial character traits do you recognise in Richard?

The motivation to set up your own business can come from deep inside and wait a long time to find the best opportunity. The process is not linear or necessarily sequential – and many might say luck is involved. **Stephen Waring**'s entrepreneurial instinct kicked in at the age of 14 when he started framing old prints and selling them at local fetes around his home town in North Wales in his spare time. Stephen's father was the sales director for a loft insulation firm and by the age of 16 he was helping canvass potential customers by knocking on doors. He was good at selling, and so when he left school at 17 he set up his own loft insulation firm – it came naturally. He was so successful he even persuaded his older brother to come and help him. When his brother married an American girl in 1985, Stephen went to the USA for the wedding. There he met his new sister-in-law's uncle who owned a lawn treatment company. He found out that 24 per cent of homes in the USA hired someone to treat their lawns in some way.

Despite the scepticism of his parents, Stephen researched the idea. First he set out to find competitors by looking through the Yellow Pages telephone directories, but he could not find anybody offering the same service in the UK. The question was whether nobody else had thought about this idea or whether there was no demand for this sort of service. Stephen could not believe that a service that sold to millions of people in the USA would not sell in the UK so he decided to persevere. Next he set out to find the best mix of fertiliser ingredients for the UK. He experimented on his parents' lawn, turning it orange and black in the process. Having perfected a suitable mix, Stephen next spent £64 on printing 1000 leaflets and hand-delivered them around housing estates near his home. Then he went around doing what he did best – knocking on doors and selling. In this way he secured 70 customers.

Thus, **Green Thumb** was born. Stephen quickly developed a routine of visiting customers four or five times a year to treat their lawns, as in the USA. The treatment worked and word-of-mouth brought in more customers, so Stephen brought in his younger brother to help him. By 1995, Green Thumb had several thousand regular customers and that was when the next stage in the business's development came about. A customer asked him to sell him a Green Thumb franchise. By 1996 Stephen was selling franchises around the UK. By 2005 there were some 113 franchises servicing over seven million customers, each spending about £26 per year on lawn treatment. Franchisees had sales of £25 million a year, giving the company royalties of £5 million. Green Thumb is growing at 5 per cent per year.

'When people ask me if I ever imagined that my business would be as successful as it has turned out to be, I have to say yes. And we are still embryonic in our growth … The challenge was developing an industry from scratch as opposed to jumping on the bandwagon of somebody else who was already doing it … It helps to have a strong belief in your abilities and not to feel insecure.'

Sunday Times 2 October 2005

Questions
1 In what ways did Stephen minimise his start-up and growth costs?
2 How much of Stephen's success was down to luck?
3 Would Stephen have succeeded in any business?

Summary

Many people have business ideas but few, as **Gary Redman** of **Now Recruitment** points out, have the confidence to start up their own business. The blocks to doing so include the need for regular income to support a family, the lack of capital and self-doubt. What is needed is a trigger. This can be a push factor such as unemployment or a pull factor such as a desire to make money. As we saw with **Steve Hulme**, it can be a combination of these factors. **Jessica Hatfield** set up **The Media Vehicle** to prove that an idea her employers had turned down would work. Generally businesses set up for positive motives or pull factors are most likely to grow.

Influences upon this decision can be antecedents such as family, the incubator organisation in which they have worked or other environmental factors, such as general economic conditions. Often seeds of entrepreneurship can be seen at an early age, as in the case of **Richard Thompson** who went on to set up **First Stop Solutions** and **EMS**, and the motivation to start businesses, almost for the thrill of it, is high.

To start a business, not only do you need an idea, you also need certain personal attributes, customers, an ability to deal with competitors, a launch strategy and finally resources. The motivation to set up your own business can come from deep inside and wait a long time to find the best opportunity. As we saw with **Stephen Waring** and his business, **Green Thumb**, the process is not linear or necessarily sequential – and many might say luck is involved.

Business ideas can come from many sources. They are based upon bold, different ideas. These ideas can come from an individual's skills and experiences – **Harry Cragoe** came back from the USA to start **PJ Smoothies**, having seen similar products sold there. They can come from spotting gaps in the market – like **Anita Roddick** and **Body Shop**. They can come from innovation and invention – as with **Abalone**, who invented and successfully marketed a new board game, and **EarthPort.com**, who found a new angle on e-commerce. Unless you are content to simply let ideas 'come to you' as they did to **David Arculus** for his business **Emap**, you need to approach the problem of creative idea generation more systematically, in the ways outlined in the previous chapter.

To run your own firm you must be willing to work hard for long hours like **Gary Frank** and his **Delicious Doughnut Company** You must be committed and dedicated. You must be opportunistic, able to bounce back in adversity, motivated to excel and tolerant of risk.

An idea is of no use unless it is linked to market demand. There must be a need for the product or service in the market place that is capable of being exploited. You need to know who your customers will be and why they will buy from you rather than competitors. Careful research needs to be undertaken into the sector or industry into which you are launching the business. You are most likely to succeed where there is little direct competition. However, even if there are few competitors, if they are large firms you might still face an uphill struggle. Porter's Five Forces is a useful way of making judgements about the degree of competition in a market. It looks at the power of buyers and suppliers, the threat of new entrants and substitutes and the competitive rivalry within the industry.

You need a launch strategy for your business, but you first need to understand that there are only three fundamental ways of achieving sustainable competitive advantage:

- Low price;
- High differentiation;
- Customer focus.

These combine to provide four generic marketing strategies that have been around since markets began:

- *Commodity supplier*, where you are selling a commodity on price alone. You therefore need to be the lowest-cost producer, making the most of any economies of scale that are available.
- *Market trader*, where you are still selling on price but using economies of small scale, in particular low overheads, to keep costs low. However, in these circumstances you must be aware of the limitations to the size of your market and the risks you face in trying to grow the business.
- *Niche player*, selling a differentiated product or service to a targeted, narrow market segment, like **Quad Electroacoustics** or **Morgan Motor Company**. This strategy offers the best chance of success for a small firm, as **Alan Pound** and **Aculab** have proved.
- *Outstanding success*. Sometimes niche firms become outstanding successes as the market they originally sold to expands beyond their expectations.

Apple Corporation realised that they had to grow fast in their early years to achieve economies of scale that would become important to customers. More recently, however, they have started to differentiate themselves in terms of machine capabilities and design and, of course, developed their technology into new areas with iPods.

Most business start-ups require a broad range of resources and acquiring them can be a problem because of the lack of credibility of the entrepreneur. What is more, it is important for most businesses that overheads and the break-even point are kept as low as possible. **Robbie Cowling** understood this when he started **Jobserve** from his bedroom. **Stephen Waring** understood this when he set up **Green Thumb**. Even if you need assets to set up your business you do not always have to own them. You can beg and/or borrow them – called 'bootstrapping'. Using informal and formal networks of contacts can be vital in helping you do this. What is more, even if you need to own them you do not always need to purchase them outright, thus at least saving on the capital cost – which is how **Richard Branson** started his **Virgin Atlantic** airline.

Finally, the start-up needs to be thought through and the business plan is a vital tool in allowing you to do this. It can be no more than a brief, working document that allows you to marshal your ideas in a systematic way. However, if you need it to raise finance it will have to be more comprehensive and much more of a 'selling document'.

Essays and discussion topics

1 What are the blocks you personally face in starting up your own business? Against each block consider the changes that would be needed for it to be removed.
2 Can people be trained to be creative and generate business ideas?
3 How can government persuade more people to set up their own business? Should they attempt to do so?
4 Do you think you have the personal attributes needed to run your own business?
5 Why do you need to undertake market research before setting up in business? What sort of market research do you need to undertake?
6 Can a lifestyle business still cater for customers' needs?
7 If a business idea is good, is it not the case that there is bound to be competition?
8 Is it better to have big company or small company competitors?
9 Why might many small firms perceive themselves as having no competition?
10 Are there really only three ways to sell a product or service?
11 How might you go about driving down costs if you were a commodity supplier?
12 What are the risks that a market trader faces in growing a business? How might they be overcome?
13 Do you know of any small firms that compete successfully on price? How do they do it? Can they grow?
14 Do you know of any niche players? How do they differentiate themselves? What market segment(s) do they sell to?
15 Can a niche player grow? If so, how and what are the dangers they face in doing so?
16 How important is a brand in communicating differential advantage?
17 Can differential advantage be sustained indefinitely?
18 Why are networks important?
19 How do you generate a network of contacts in a systematic way?
20 How important is 'good luck' in setting up your own business?
21 If the future is uncertain, what is the point of planning?
22 What is meant by 'flexibility' with regard to the business plan? Why is this important?

Exercises and assignments

1 Write a mini case study on the motivations of and other influences on an entrepreneur you know who set up their own business.
2 Select a market or industry and, using library data, evaluate the competitive forces within it using Porter's Five Forces.
3 List 10 ways a product or service can be differentiated from competitors. Against each, list how that differential advantage might be sustained.
4 Consider the market for a commodity, for example petrol. List the different market segments this sells to, whether the segments offer the opportunity to develop a differential advantage and if so what these are. Note whether there are pricing differences between the segments.
5 Select a product or service that is clearly differentiated. List the ways it is differentiated, the value to the customer and how these differential advantages are communicated to the customer.
6 Write a mini case study about how an entrepreneur you know who set up their own business managed to assemble all the resources they needed.
7 List the friends, relatives and contacts that might be useful to you were you to set up your own business. Against each name jot down why they might be useful.

References

Acs, Z. and Audretsch, D.B. (1989) 'Births and Firm Size', *Southern Economic Journal*, 55.

Bhidé, A. (1992) 'Bootstrap Finance: The Art of Start-Ups', *Harvard Business Review*, November/December.

Birley, S. and Norburn, D. (1984) 'Small versus Large Companies: The Entrepreneurial Conundrum', *Journal of Business Strategy*, 6(1), Summer.

Bolton, B. and Thompson, J. (2000) *Entrepreneurs: Talent, Temperament, Technique*, Oxford: Butterworth-Heinemann.

Burns, P. and Whitehouse, O. (1994) *Winners and Losers in the 1990s*, 3i European Enterprise Centre, Report no. 12.

Cooper, A.C. (1981) 'Strategic Management: New Ventures and Small Business', *Long Range Planning*, 14(5).

Cosh, A. and Hughes, A. (eds) (1998) *Enterprise Britain: Growth Innovation and Public Policy in the Small and Medium Sized Enterprise Sector 1994–97*, Cambridge: ESRC Centre for Business Research.

ESRC Centre for Business Research (1992) *The State of British Enterprise: Growth, Innovation and Competitive Advantage in Small and Medium-Sized Firms*, Cambridge: ESRC.

Porter, M.E. (1985) *Competitive Advantage, Creating and Sustaining Superior Performance*, New York: Free Press.

Stevenson, H.H., Roberts, M.J. and Grousebeck, H.I. (1985) *New Business Ventures and the Entrepreneur*, Homewood, IL: Irwin.

Storey, D.J., Keasey, K., Watson, R. and Wynarczyk, P. (1987) *The Performance of Small Firms: Profits, Jobs and Failures*, London: Croom Helm.

Storey, D.J., Watson, R. and Wynarcyzk, P. (1989) *Fast Growth Small Business: Case Studies of 40 Small Firms in North East England*, Department of Employment, Research Paper No. 67, London: HMSO.

3i European Enterprise Centre (1993) *Britain's Superleague Companies*, Report no. 9.

6

Making the Start-up Happen

Contents

- Marketing strategies
- Pricing
- Differentiation
- Developing customer focus
- Entrepreneurial marketing
- Undertaking market research
- Developing selling skills
- Using the internet
- Legal forms of business
- Summary

LEARNING OUTCOMES

By the end of this chapter you should be able to:

- Explain why customers buy products or services and the difference between features and benefits;
- Explain what is meant by the term 'marketing mix' and how it can be used to describe elements of the marketing strategy;
- Recognise the influences on pricing decisions and explain how the price of a product or service might be set;
- Calculate the break-even point for a business;
- Explain what is needed to differentiate a product or service;
- Explain how markets can be segmented and what is meant by market focus;

- Construct an appropriate marketing mix for different market segments;
- Describe the different forms of market research and how to go about collecting information;
- Develop a market research questionnaire and a market research plan;
- Explain what is needed to sell effectively and how selling skills might be developed;
- Explain how the internet can be used to help sell a product or service;
- Decide on the appropriate legal form for a business start-up.

Marketing strategies

How do you decide which of the generic marketing strategies to adopt? This depends upon a thorough understanding of customers (what they want), competitors (how their product or service compares) and the degree of competition in the market (Porter's Five Forces). The fiercer the competition in the industry, the better the product or service competitors have to offer, then the more a start-up will have to compete on price.

However, the first thing is to understand why customers buy a product or service. Take, as an example, why people might buy a mundane item like a drill bit. They do not buy it for its aesthetic qualities, they buy it because they want to drill a hole, perhaps to fix something to a wall. The drill solves the problem of creating a hole or fixing something to a wall. If there happens to be a more efficient or easier way of making holes or fixing things to walls, the drill manufacturer is in trouble. A founder of a successful cosmetics firm once said that in the factory he made perfume but in the shops he sold dreams.

In marketing terms, this is called understanding the *benefits* the customer is looking for. They do not buy the *features* that describe the product or service, they buy the benefits it brings to them. You do not buy oil for your car because of its colour or viscosity as such, you buy it because it makes the engine run smoothly, extends its life and reduces repair bills. The features might convince you of the benefits, but it is the benefits you really want. So, different people buying a pen might be looking for different benefits. Of course it must write, but if that were the only benefit they were looking for, why would anybody buy anything but the cheapest pen available? An expensive pen is rarely bought just as a writing implement (for the *consumer*), but more usually as a gift that reflects warmly on the giver (the *customer*). If the customer is not the consumer then a product or service must offer benefits to both. The customer is buying intangible benefits such as status or esteem for the recipient. The consumer will derive benefit from a writing implement that is aesthetically pleasing and the fact that the donor held him in such esteem that she went to the trouble and expense of buying the gift. There is a market for both cheap and expensive pens, but to different customers.

Understanding the difference between features and benefits is the cornerstone of marketing. It is important in tailoring the marketing offered to customers, deciding on your competitive advantage and building a growth strategy to sustain it. It is real tangible benefits to the customer that differentiate a product or service and allow a premium price to be charged. Unfortunately, many owner-managers like to define their products in physical terms and therefore think they are selling one thing, only to find customers are buying something else.

Features can be turned into benefits, for example:

Feature		Benefit
Our shop takes credit cards	⇨	You can budget to suit your pocket
Our shop stays open later than others	⇨	You get more choice when to shop
Our shop is an approved dealer	⇨	You can be guaranteed that we know and understand all technical aspects of the product
Our shop is a family business	⇨	You get individual, personal attention from somebody who cares

So, listing the features of a product or service can be the start of the process of understanding the benefits that the customer is seeking from them. However, it is more convincing to start with the benefits that customers are looking for and then construct features that provide those benefits. Which actually comes first is a little like the chicken and the egg.

One technique that is widely used to describe the features of a product or service is called the marketing mix or The Five Ps, a convenient short-hand for a range of sub-elements consisting of product (or service), price, promotion, place and people. This is shown in Figure 6.1.

The customer buys the marketing mix as a package, and the mix must be consistent to reinforce the benefits that the customer is looking for. The marketing mix is only as strong as its weakest link. As we saw in the last chapter, there is a trade-off between price and the other elements of the mix. The stronger or more distinctive and different these elements, the higher the price you are normally able to command. Too many small firms compete primarily on price because they believe the other elements of their marketing mix are insufficiently different from their competitors. However, price is more usually a barrier to sale rather than a positive inducement.

Central to the whole marketing mix are entrepreneurs and their personal approach which will probably, of necessity, involve a very much hands-on, face-to-face way of

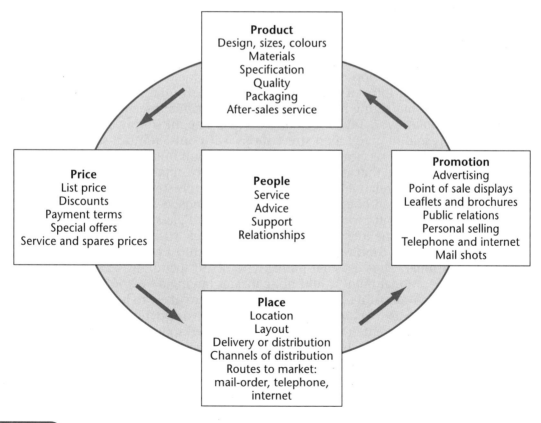

Figure 6.1 Marketing mix: the five Ps

Adrian Wood set up **GTI**, a publishing company, in 1988 whilst at university. Adrian and two friends, Mark Blythe and Wayne Collins, were thinking about their futures and realised they did not know much about the jobs they were thinking about going into. The idea was to explain to students what was involved in various occupations. Adrian first thought of the idea in his second year studying economics at Reading University. He decided that he needed to 'sell' the idea to students – and more importantly to advertisers – by attracting some well-known business names to contribute articles to the magazine. So he wrote to dozens of well-known people and some, including Sir John Harvey-Jones, agreed to contribute.

Initially, Adrian and his two friends each put £200 into the business and used the university careers adviser as a consultant. Their first publication tackled quantity surveying and property. They took a week off studying and interviewed lecturers in different departments. They even got the backing of the head of education of the Royal Institute of Chartered Surveyors. About half of the publication was devoted to advertising and they personally delivered copies of it around the country. It made £6000 profit.

And so the company was born – 'to produce careers publications and an honest view of life'. The following year five magazines were published and sales came to £120 000. In 1990 GTI bought a barn in Wallingford, Oxfordshire and converted it into offices. Today GTI employs some 100 people, publishes over 70 titles in three languages, including the TARGET family of career publications, doctorjob magazines and the gradireland directory together with related websites.

marketing. They will develop relationships with customers in this way and this in itself can be a distinct form of competitive advantage over large firms.

The appropriate marketing mix depends on the benefits the customer, and consumer, are looking for. Take for example a pen, bought simply as a writing implement. It is sold in many high street shops, with only point-of-sale display materials (probably self-service), with no promotion and minimum service at a very low price. The benefit is that it writes and can be easily obtained. Other elements of the marketing mix are relatively unimportant, so there is strong price competition. On the other hand, a pen bought as a gift has an expensive looking exterior, is also sold in the high street but probably from behind locked glass display stands that can be accessed only with the help of an assistant. It comes with a guarantee and is promoted at Christmas time with the realisation that most pens are bought as gifts, not by the consumer. The customer probably wants to spend, say, £25 on a gift and even a so-called 'rational man' would not consider buying a box of 250 cheap, disposable pens as a substitute gift, even though they are likely to last longer than the expensive pen. The way to go about marketing these two apparently similar products is therefore totally different. The point is that you need to know what the customer and consumer are buying – which may not be the same as you think you are selling.

Customers do not usually sit and wait for a new business to open its doors. They need to be informed of what it has to offer and convinced to try it, and word-of-mouth recommendations can take time. Advertising is only one, very expensive, form of promotion. Many small firms cannot afford it and indeed prefer more personal forms of communication with customers. More recently, large firms have started calling this relationship marketing. Once established, small firms have an advantage in this because the relationship is usually sincere and built on the trust that owner-managers will deliver the product or service they promise. If they do not, they face the risk of going out of business.

Many firms do not advertise because of its expense and because all too often it is not targeted at specific customers. Body Shop does not advertise, relying instead on its window displays in the high street, because it feels that it is inconsistent with its ethical stand and general brand image. J. Barbour & Sons, the manufacturer of upper-class but utilitarian waterproof jackets, spend very little on advertising, preferring to sponsor outdoor events such as horse trials.

Stokes (1998) makes the point that owner-managers typically prefer 'interactive marketing' – interacting on a one-to-one basis with customers – because they have strong preferences for personal contact with customers rather than impersonal marketing through mass promotions. He points out that this extends to their preference in terms of market research. They prefer to talk to and observe customers, rather than undertake desk or other more formal research. Promotion is often by word of mouth and recommendation – something that can be crucial to purchasing decisions in some consumer and business-to-business markets (Bayus, 1985). One reason for this preference is, of course, cost but the other is that this is something that large firms are not as good at. This preference for interactive marketing also underlines the importance of networking. In small firm marketing the most important P is probably the personality of the entrepreneur.

The term 'place' in the marketing mix encompasses channels of distribution. Not all businesses sell direct to the end users. Many sell through intermediaries – agents, wholesalers, mail order companies, retailers, specialist outlets or other routes. Often these are established routes to particular markets offering the advantage of loyal customers and local knowledge as well as possible savings in terms of distribution costs or reduced stock holding. For a start-up it might be difficult and risky to ignore these established distribution channels, although that is precisely what many e-commerce start-ups are doing – a topic we shall return to later in this chapter. For example, a designer and producer of novel greeting cards had little practical alternative but to sell his cards through high street shops. However, he decided to sell directly to selected shops rather than go through wholesalers, selling to small shops rather than chains. Doing things differently can be risky, but the rewards of success can be high. The decision about channels revolves around matching the product or service to the customer and their needs in a way that provides an adequate return. However, the evidence points towards small firms rarely being adventurous in their choice of distribution channels.

The elements of the marketing mix, related to the customers they are targeted at, together make up the marketing strategy of the firm. The strategy is just a series of related tasks that, taken together, have a coherence and give direction to the firm. The strategy adopted at the launch of a new business may change as it becomes more established. For example, special price offers may be appropriate at launch, in order to get customers to try the product or service and then repeat buy. On the other hand, if the product or service is sufficiently unique and different, then it may be possible to premium price at launch, particularly if the product or service is unlikely to be repeat purchased quickly. Similarly, some advertising or a mail-shot might be appropriate at launch to inform customers of the new business, whereas, because of expense, word-of-mouth recommendation might be relied on more later on.

Case insight

It is often the case for a start-up that a potential mass market is better ignored in favour of a niche opportunity – at least in the short term. It means that the high fixed costs often associated with mass markets and all too unaffordable by the typical start-up are avoided. It means a premium price can be charged, albeit on a smaller volume. And often that niche is bigger than the founder ever imagined.

Jemella Group, which trades as **GHD** (Good Hair Day), was started by **Martin Penny** in 2001. Based in West Yorkshire, the company revolutionised the hair industry with an iron that straightened hair between two heated ceramic plates. But when Martin took the idea to his bank, asking for a £50 000 loan, the bank manager was sceptical, seeing the product as 'just another set of hair tongs'. The only way Martin got the money was on the strength of his track record running an environmental consultancy. But Martin decided on two important strategies that were to underpin the subsequent success of his business. The first strategy was not to manufacture the product himself, indeed the product was manufactured in Korea where costs were lower. In this way he could focus on sales and keep his fixed costs to a minimum. The second was not to sell through the high street but instead to target firstly up-market London West End hair salons and then salons across the UK. The 'hair styling irons' were sold both for salon use and through the salons themselves. Despite keeping costs low the product itself was priced high and, partly in this way, differentiated from 'just another set of hair tongs'. It was seen as professional, special and up-market.

Largely because of these strategies sales have increased 365 per cent a year, from an annualised £459 000 in 2001 to £24.1 million in 2004. In 2005 turnover jumped again to £46 million. The company claims that the iron is now used in more than 10 000 UK salons – 85 per cent of the market. But celebrities such as Madonna, Victoria Beckham, Jennifer Aniston and Gwyneth Paltrow are also happy to pay the high price for the product – which helps to give it a certain exclusive cachet that helps sell the product to the general public. Based on this success the company is now diversifying into other hair-care products such as shampoo, conditioner and styling gel, and has launched a new brand called 'Nu:U', aimed at the mid-price, mass salon market.

Let us return to the three fundamental ways of achieving sustainable competitive advantage shown in Figure 6.2 – low price, high differentiation and customer focus – and explore what this means for a start-up.

Pricing

Many start-ups are uncertain about how to set prices. They often feel that they must be cheap to attract customers and feel insecure about charging a premium price compared to the competition. To sustain a low-price strategy you must be a low-cost provider and do whatever is needed to drive costs down. However, there are other approaches to pricing.

The price charged for a product or service ought to reflect the value of the package of benefits to the customer. The value can be different to different customers and in different circumstances. Take, for example, the price charged for emergency, compared to routine, plumbing work. A premium price reflects the benefit to the customer of preventing the house being flooded. However, the features of that

Broad market

COMMODITY
SUPPLIER

OUTSTANDING
SUCCESS

Low price

High price

Low differentiation

High differentiation

MARKET
TRADER

NICHE
PLAYER

Focused market

Figure 6.2 Generic marketing strategies

emergency service, as reflected in the marketing mix, must reflect the benefits the customer is looking for; for example, ease of telephone call-out, 24-hour fast, efficient service, clear-up, facilitation of insurance claims and so on. Similarly, a railway company is able to charge a range of different prices for what is essentially the same service, transportation from one place to another. Given these things, there is often a 'going rate' for a similar product or service.

One factor in the pricing decision is the costs you face in doing business. There are many cost concepts and this book does not intend to go into them in detail. The conventional profit maximising model developed by economists tends to indicate that price should be set at a point where *marginal cost* – the cost of producing and marketing one extra unit – is equal to *marginal revenue* – the income generated by the sale of the additional unit. In practice this is difficult, if not impossible, to apply. This is because the economists' model assumes that price is also determined by demand, whereas in reality this is not always the case.

Many people use what is called *cost-plus* pricing. This takes the total cost of producing a product or delivering a service and divides it by the number of units produced to arrive at the *average cost* of production, to which a target mark-up is then added. As well as the notorious difficulties in allocating cost there is the problem of reconciling price with demand. What happens if volumes are not as predicted? Some costs, often called *overhead costs*, are *fixed* – they do not change with volume, for example, rent and insurance. So if volumes are less than predicted, the same costs have to be spread over smaller volumes – which means that you would have to charge a higher price to recover the overheads and the decrease in volume, a strategy that itself is likely to lead to falling sales. The reverse is true if volumes are greater than predicted.

This is shown in Figure 6.3. Fixed costs are the horizontal line AB. Producing the product or delivering the service will mean incurring additional *variable costs* – costs that vary with volume like materials and piece-work labour. Every time an additional unit is produced and sold, an additional cost is incurred. Line AC therefore represents the total cost of producing the product or delivering the service – the fixed cost plus the variable cost. Over large volumes, this line may curve downwards as the effects of economies of scale are felt. Line LM represents the revenue generated by sales – sales

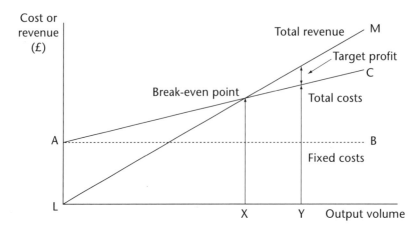

Figure 6.3 Costs, volume and revenue

volume multiplied by unit price. At volume X all costs are covered by revenue. This is called the *break-even point*. At volume Y a certain target profit is reached. Obviously the problem with this sort of approach to pricing is that it tends to assume that at a given price, a given number of products will be sold, whereas in reality the quantity sold will be linked in some way to the price charged. The break-even point can be easily calculated. To do so requires two further terms to be defined. *Contribution* is the difference between sales price and variable cost. *Total contribution* is the difference between total sales (or turnover) and total variable costs for a specified period. *Contribution margin* expresses this as a percentage of sales price or total sales. For example (assuming sales of 100 units per week):

Sales price	£10	Total sales	£1000
Variable cost	£ 6	Total variable costs	£ 600
Contribution	£ 4	Total contribution	£ 400
Contribution margin	0.40 or 40%	Contribution margin	0.40 or 40%

Break-even (expressed in £ turnover) is defined as:

$$\frac{\text{Total fixed costs}}{\text{Contribution margin}}$$

If total fixed costs are £200 per week, the break-even point is:

$$\frac{£200}{0.40} = £500 = 50 \text{ units}$$

Verifying:

Break-even sales 50 units @ £10	£500
Variable costs 50 units @ £6	£300
Total contribution	£200
Total fixed costs	£200
Profit	–

Once above the break-even point, each £1 of sales contributes £0.40 or 40 per cent to profits. So, if the target profit is £400 per week then sales would have to be:

$$\frac{£400}{0.40} = £1000 \; above \; the \; break\text{-}even \; point = £1500$$

Verifying:

On sales of £1500:

Total contribution @ 40%	£ 600
Total fixed costs	£ 200
Profit	£ 400

As we shall see in the next chapter, break-even is an important concept for many reasons. However, whilst competitors may know about costs, customers rarely do and, just sometimes, as in the case of prestige pens bought as gifts, they may want to pay a high price. How demand holds up to changes in price is determined by the cross elasticity of demand (see definition on page 58). The more differentiated the product or service, the more price inelastic is demand – it does not vary greatly with changes in price. The more the product or service is a commodity, the more price will be elastic – it will be affected by price changes. Price elasticity may sound a highly theoretical concept, but the practical applications of it are important.

Case insight

When **Jean Young** set up as a sole trader offering training to the healthcare sector she estimated her sales in the first year to be a modest £17 200. Deciding on a *per diem* charge was easy, the market would pay in the range of £300 to £1200 per day. Whilst she was experienced, Jean was a start-up so she reckoned that a safe rate would be £400. At this rate she already had some days booked and she estimated that she could sell 43 days in her first year.

With no variable costs she had a contribution margin of 100%. Her fixed costs were reasonable as well since she worked from home. The main element was depreciation on her car and computer equipment. Her fixed costs for the year were estimated at:

Depreciation	£2667
Secretarial wages	330
Transport	430
Telephone	450
Stationery	570
Repairs	350
Other	285
Insurance	100
Total	£5182

She therefore worked out her break-even point as £5182 of turnover, and that included the depreciation on her car that she would keep with or without the business. Since she already had firm commitments for training work totalling £17 200, she felt certain the business was viable. What is more, she only needed 13 days' work before she started making a contribution – a salary she could 'take home'.

●

Table 6.1 Price cuts – percentage increase in sales volume required to generate the same level of profit after a price cut

Price reduction	Contribution margin		
	20%	30%	40%
−5%	33%	20%	14%
−10%	100%	50%	33%
−15%	300%	100%	60%

Table 6.1 shows the increase in sales volume required to maintain the same level of profitability as a result of a price reduction. This depends on the contribution margin before the price cut. If the contribution margin is only 20 per cent and you were tempted to cut prices by 15 per cent, you would have to increase sales volume by a massive 300 per cent, or quadruple sales, just to make the same amount of profit as before. The higher the margin, the less the effect. But even at 40 per cent margin, you would still have to increase sales by 27 per cent. In the face of static or declining sales many owner-managers would be tempted to cut prices. The table makes you think twice about that strategy. Of course there may be other important factors influencing the decision such as reducing stocks or bringing in some much-needed cash. However, seeking to increase profits by increasing sales at low prices is fraught with dangers.

The arithmetic of pricing is even more persuasive when it comes to price increases. Table 6.2 shows the decrease in sales volume that could sustain the same level of profitability in the face of a price increase. The same 20 per cent margin could see a reduction in sales volume of 43 per cent in the face of a 15 per cent price increase and would still achieve the same level of profitability. Of course the effect is less the higher the margin. Nevertheless such deep reductions in volume may see profits actually increase as overheads are cut (why maintain the same level of staff with less work?). Alternatively you might decide to improve the level of service offered so as to justify the higher price. What is more, the lower volumes mean that stock holdings and other capital costs are likely to come down, an important consideration if capital is scarce.

Table 6.2 Price increases – percentage decrease in sales volume required to generate the same level of profit after a price increase

Price increase	Contribution margin		
	20%	30%	40%
5%	−20%	−14%	−11%
10%	−33%	−25%	−20%
15%	−43%	−33%	−27%

The actual effect of price on volumes sold depends on the cross elasticity of demand and a small firm can decrease it by attempting to differentiate itself from the competition as much as possible and, in so doing, charging as high a price for its goods or services as the market will bear. This price must, however, be consistent with the other elements of the marketing mix. Tables 6.1 and 6.2 give you some indication of the price–volume–profit effects – so long as you know the contribution margin.

Case insight

In 1988 **Neil Summers** was discharged from the Royal Marines because of an agonising and potentially crippling back disorder. Never one to give in, he came up with an idea for relieving pressure on the back which involved stretching backwards over a wooden stool. This became the now famous **Back Stretcher** – a curved wooden block in which are placed rolling slats. He started selling it at dinner parties and within months was producing dozens. In 1995 he won Britain's Inventor of the Year award. Now he produces hundreds of thousands each year and there are many imitators.

However, all did not go smoothly. It was a painful discovery that it would cost over £120 to produce the device in Britain when he knew that he could only sell it for about £80. The answer was to set up the factory in Posnan in Poland with a partner, which is where the device is now manufactured. What continues to be even more painful are his attempts at selling the device in Britain. Whilst the Back Stretcher is now as well-known in Japan as a Dyson vacuum cleaner is in Britain, the paucity of specialist outlets makes the British market a difficult nut to crack.

Pricing, therefore, is a question of judgement. It is certainly not a science. The range of prices that a business can charge is shown in Figure 6.4. At the bottom of the range is variable cost – the cost of producing one additional unit, normally the same as marginal cost (except when additional fixed costs will be incurred by increasing production). If the price charged falls below this then any additional sale costs more to produce than the revenue it generates. However, variable cost is likely to be too low a price to charge since, by definition, it does not include any fixed costs. These are only covered when average cost is reached.

The top end of the range depends totally on the differential advantage the firm enjoys – and how well the firm can capitalise upon it. However, no business can afford to ignore competition. Even products or services that are unique face price resistance and ultimately there will be a price that is 'too high' for the customer. At the other extreme there will be a price that is so low that customers will not believe the product or service can deliver the claims that it makes. Indeed for some products,

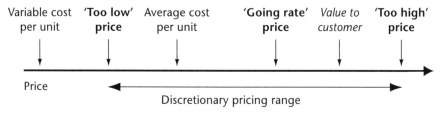

Figure 6.4 The pricing range

like the exclusive pen bought as a gift, a high price can be very much part of what the customer is expecting to buy.

Whilst you may have a longer-term pricing policy, in relation to this there are two further pricing options to be considered at start-up stage as part of a well-thought-through launch strategy, consistent with other elements of the marketing mix:

1 *Skimming* – charging a high initial price at launch. This tends to work best when demand is relatively price inelastic, or there are likely to be a number of different groups of customers and you can appeal to those who will pay a higher price first and move on to the rest later, or little is known about the costs of producing and marketing the product or service. So, for example, when large LCD, flat screen TVs were first offered for sale the initial price was high and it was sold very much as an innovative, exclusive product. Prices rapidly fell as they became more of an everyday product. Skimming generates high profits and, as the volume sold is usually low, the capital needed for the business is reduced.

2 *Penetration* – charging a lower price at launch. This tends to work best when demand is relatively price elastic or competitors are likely to enter the market quickly, or there are no distinct price-customer groupings or there is the possibility of achieving economies of scale if volume sales can be achieved. It builds sales quickly where no regular customers exist. So, for example, when a new washing powder is launched there may be special 'two for the price of one' offers to get customers to try it. Special offers of this sort are particularly useful as they benchmark the price at a higher level and creates the expectation that the price will rise at some future date. Without that there might be resistance to any subsequent price rise.

Differentiation

Differentiation is about being different and distinctive. It can come from being innovative in some way. However, many firms might not be described as innovative but are still clearly differentiated from the competition. For both a product or a service differentiation can come about through function, design, quality, performance, technology or other tangible characteristics. So, for example, Mercedes Benz and Bang & Olufsen aim to differentiate themselves through quality in their respective sectors. McDonald's does it, in part, through quality of service (speed, cleanliness and so on). Differentiation might come from the other elements of the marketing mix, for example, the channels of distribution. When Direct Line started selling motor insurance over the telephone it was so radically different that it was seen as an innovation in financial service delivery that had applications in other sectors. And yet the innovation was simply the use of another, much cheaper, channel of distribution.

Differentiation can, however, prove costly if the basis that is chosen subsequently proves inappropriate. So, for example, Sony devised the Betamax format for its video recorders but ultimately had to adopt JVC's VHS system. Companies try to protect the basis for differentiation in any way possible. It might be that a product can be patented, the design registered or, for written material, copyrighted.

Differentiation is helped by clear branding. A brand should be the embodiment of the product or service offering to customers. So, for example, the Mercedes Benz,

Case insight

In the ubiquitous mobile phone market you might think it hard to differentiate yourself. When **Charles Dunstone** set up **Carphone Warehouse** in 1986 with his savings of £6000 he was only 24 years old. His original vision was to sell mobile phones from shops so that people could browse before they bought. Nobody else was selling mobile phones in this way at the time.

Whilst making the most of a high-growth market, the real opportunity to differentiate the firm came when Vodafone and Cellnet started offering packages with different combinations of rental and call charges. Customers had to decide which tariff was best for them and many were confused about the packages on offer. Carphone Warehouse set itself up to provide independent, reliable advice, something few other retailers offered. In a highly competitive market place the firm was able to claim some element of differentiation, a claim that it used extensively in its advertising.

Part of the success of the company comes from the emotional and personal involvement of Charles Dunstone – he still cannot let go. He has been described as a 'monofocused, workaholic . . . a retail-detail obsessive with a calm exterior . . . in love with the great Carphone Warehouse: its shops, its products, its people, its advertising and, above all, its customers and its sales' (*Sunday Times*, 28 July 2002). Although he enjoys sailing – he owns two big boats – he is quite likely to spend a weekend as a duty manager in one of the shops and will serve at counters if he finds customers waiting on one of his frequent store visits. Not unexpectedly he was still unmarried in 2006 at the age of 42. The *Sunday Times* described him as 'driven by anxiety and a tough competitive streak. That way he remains always alert to rivals and constantly worried about strategy' (16 April 2006). Pierre Danon, former Chief Executive of BT Retail and now advisor at JP Morgan says: 'Charles is clever, he is customer focused, he has very good strategy allied with a down-to-earth management style' (*Sunday Times*, 16 April 2006).

By 2006 Carphone had some 1771 stores across Europe (669 in Britain) and is considered one of the country's great retail successes. Charles Dunstone is now a millionaire, estimated to be worth over £300 million. He sold £56 million worth of shares when Carphone floated in July 2000 but still holds 34% of the equity. However, like most telecom shares, the share price has dropped since its float price of 200p and with mobile phone ownership across Europe now averaging 70–75 per cent it looks unlikely to ever return to these levels. However, the arrival of 3G networks which allow music and pictures to be downloaded and sent to other phones has rejuvenated this market to some extent. Dunstone's response to this has been to reposition the company to be less dependent on new phone sales. Over 45 per cent of revenues now come from 'recurring revenues', generated from managing customers for the networks. Consistent with this strategy, in 2006 he launched his latest venture – 'free' broadband connections in Britain. Actually it was only 'free' if purchased as part of his fixed-line service, called *Talk Talk*, which also offered unlimited landline calls, all for a fixed line rental. Dunstone's rationale for 'selling cheap' comes from his belief that phones, television and internet are all converging, so it is important to build market share as quickly as possible, since economies of scale will become increasingly important.

Jaguar and BMW brands all convey quality. Virgin is the embodiment of Richard Branson; brash, entrepreneurial, different, anti-establishment. Body Shop is environmentally friendly. The Co-op bank is ethical whereas Coutts Bank is for the wealthy. Many so-called brands, however, fall far short of this instant recognition of values and virtues, being little more than expensive logos. What do the Barclays, Shell or BT brands convey, other than a knowledge of what the firm sells?

In a world where products and services are often all too homogeneous, a good brand is a powerful marketing tool that must be the cornerstone of any strategy of differentiation. Not only can it help turn prospects into customers, if everything else is right it can turn them into regular customers. What is more, as shown in Figure 6.5, it can help turn them into supporters – regular customers who think positively about the brand – or even advocates – who are willing to recommend the product and bring in new customers. This is an approach far more in tune with interactive marketing, one that is easier to achieve with the personal touch.

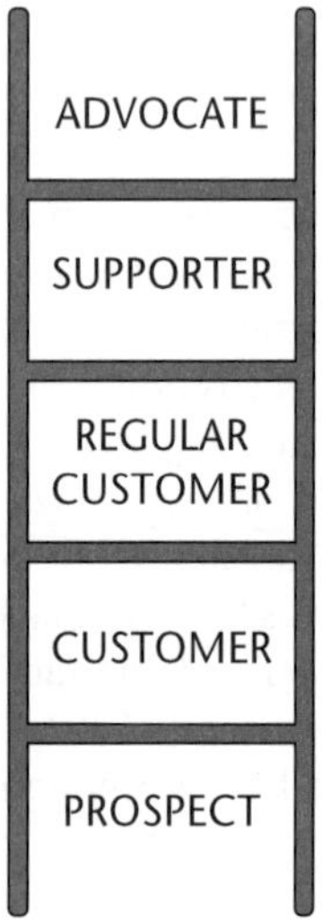

Branding and things like patents and copyrights are about securing differential advantage for as long as possible and creating barriers to entry into the market. The bigger the market, the more difficult and expensive this is to achieve. That is why differentiation is most successful when combined with a strategy of customer focus.

Figure 6.5   The customer loyalty ladder

Case insight

Cobra was set up in 1990 by **Karan Bilimoria** to sell a different type of beer to Indian restaurants. The company now has a turnover in excess of £57 million, sells to 30 countries, and has a very recognisable brand.

'I entered the most competitive beer market in the world against long established brands. The product itself was innovative – an extra smooth, less gassy lager that compliments all cuisine and appeals to ale drinkers and lager drinkers alike … Deciding to import the beer in a 650ml bottle was important in positioning the product within the market and raising the profile among restaurant owners. It also promoted a new, shared way of drinking … The brand's point-of-sale items, such as unique and different glasses, were another effective way of establishing brand awareness … Also [the packaging] is embossed with six icons telling the story of Cobra beer, from concept and production to growth and development, and this is the first time in the world that, to our knowledge, the brand has incorporated its story directly into its packaging.'

The Times 23 May 2004

Developing customer focus

Focus involves breaking down markets into different groups of customers; these are called *segments* – groups of customers who have similar characteristics or needs. The key for most start-ups is to focus their attention and resources on just three or four clearly defined market segments, tailoring the marketing mix to the needs of customers in those segments and communicating the benefits to them in an appropriate way and through an appropriate medium. This is the starting point of niche marketing referred to in the last chapter. Studies show that there is a relationship between profitability and gaining a high market share of a particular segment.

There are many ways of segmenting markets. You are looking for groups of customers with similar needs that can be identified and described in some meaningful and useful way. For consumer markets these include personal characteristics (demographics) such as age, gender, socio-economic group, occupation, location of home, stage in family life cycle, and so on. If the group can be identified in this way information on their buying habits is relatively easy to obtain and it is also possible to find out the best media through which to reach them. For example, ACORN (A Classification of Regional Neighbourhoods) breaks down the whole of the UK into about 40 different neighbourhoods, each identified by postcode. So, for example, large inner-city Victorian houses near universities may, reasonably, be assumed to house a lot of university students, which could be important if that is your target market.

For business markets, segments might include type of business, size, location, nature of technology, creditworthiness and so on. The most commonly used classification is the official standard industrial classification (SIC), which breaks down all businesses into broad groups and sub-groups according to activity.

Market segments can be any one – or a combination of – descriptive factors associated with the product or service, the customer, channels of distribution, sales territories and so forth. As shown in Figure 6.6, it is also possible to vary the degree of aggregation of segments. There are no prescriptive approaches to segmentation. It requires creative insight into customers' buying habits as well as an understanding of the unique benefits offered by the product or service to these groups. This means understanding the market and competitors, but most of all the customers.

The slimmer the market segment that the product or service is tailored to suit, the higher customer satisfaction is likely to be. We all like personal service and the ultimate market segment comprises just one customer. However, this might not be a viable segment economically. The trend is towards slimmer and slimmer market

---

Mini case

Radio Spirits Inc. is certainly a niche business. Based in Illinois, USA, it sells old-time radio shows such as 'The Lone Ranger', 'Dragnet', 'The Jack Benny Show' and 'The Burns and Allen Show'. Collecting these shows started as a hobby for its founder, **Carl Amari**. It now has a catalogue of over 4000 shows that it mails to 350 000 potential customers across the USA. It also has a pay-per-listen website. Despite being a niche business the company still manages sales that run into the millions of dollars.

●

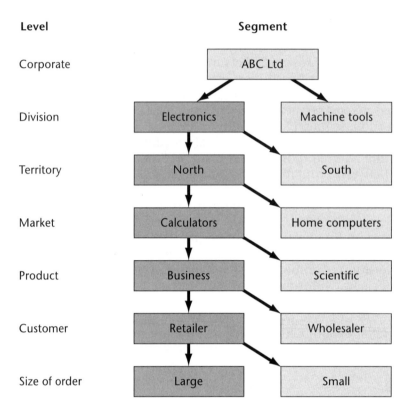

Level	Segment
Corporate	ABC Ltd
Division	Electronics / Machine tools
Territory	North / South
Market	Calculators / Home computers
Product	Business / Scientific
Customer	Retailer / Wholesaler
Size of order	Large / Small

Source: Adapted from Ratnatunga (1983).

Figure 6.6 Segmentation levels

segments. The danger facing firms selling to slim market segments is their over reliance on a small customer base. If tastes change the segment might disappear. It is vital therefore that niche businesses keep in close touch with the changing needs of their customers.

One small firm producing motor components found itself competing unsuccessfully against a large multinational that undercut it on price. It decided to rethink its whole marketing strategy and found there were many opportunities for products manufactured to a high technical specification in which quality and supplier reputation were more important than the price charged. By focusing its marketing strategy on these segments, the company was able to establish itself as a niche player in what was otherwise a highly competitive industry.

Once you understand what your customers or market segments are looking for, you can start to tailor the product or service that you offer. Once you understand your competition, you will start to understand the strength or otherwise of your competitive advantage. With this in mind you can decide which of Porter's generic marketing strategies is most appropriate to each product/market offering. From that you start to understand the imperatives you face and what tasks need to be addressed in your marketing plan. The advantages of developing a market niche can be

Case with questions

When **Chris Hutt** set up **Unicorn Inns** he did not think he would sell it ten years later in 1996 to Moorland for over £13 million. But it was not until 1991 that he analysed and started to understand the successful *Newt & Cucumber* formula.

Newt & Cucumber is a prime-sited town or city-centre free house close to offices, shopping centres and focal points of entertainment, feeding off continuous pedestrian flow. It has a 'traditional but trendy' atmosphere and serves regional real ales alongside national lagers and premium bottled beers. It is open all day and offers food. It is designed to appeal to a wide and varying target market according to the time of day and time of week. It has a large floor space which allows it to have different areas with an informal, basic and unpretentious décor. These areas combine hard-floored, stand-up drinking areas and soft-carpeted, sit-down eating sections. There are large open vistas but there are also intimate corners. It is meant to display 'traditional' pub values – the primacy of beer over any elaborate and frivolous decoration. In this way it is meant to appeal to a wide range of drinkers. It feeds off heavy pedestrian flows. A Newt & Cucumber free house offers:

- A wide range of premium liquor brands;
- Tasty, filling, value-for-money lunch-time meals, served fast;
- Competitive pricing;
- A warm, traditional and lively atmosphere;
- Efficient, friendly service by motivated staff;
- A safe, secure environment with no games of pool or juke boxes.

It is a formula very similar to the Wetherspoon chain of pubs. An extract from the firm's original business plan, showing their target markets and marketing mix is shown in Table 6.3.

Questions

1 Why is Table 6.3 so informative? If the plan works, what will it achieve?
2 What other factors are essential for the plan to work?
3 What reservations might you have if you were purchasing a pub-chain of this sort?

→

considerable. If done properly it is profitable and avoids confrontation and competition.

Research indicates that small firms often go about the process of niche positioning in a 'bottom-up' sort of way (Dalgic and Leeuw, 1994). Often they start by pursuing an opportunity through matching innovative ideas to their resources, testing it by trial and error in the market place. The entrepreneur does not always use formal research at this stage, relying perhaps more on intuition. If the idea attracts customers (whether or not they conform to an expected profile), the entrepreneur gets to know them through regular contact. Expansion then comes by looking for more customers with the same profile. Often this is, again, a gradual process of self-selection with some encouragement from the entrepreneur rather than a process involving formal research and deliberate choice.

Table 6.3 Newt & Cucumber's business plan

SEGMENTS:	Shoppers	Office/ professionals	Pensioners/ low paid
Time	12–5	12–2	12–2
Male/female split	10/90	40/60	90/10
Marketing Mix:			
Product:	Coffee/tea, soft drinks	Choice of good food	Cheap beer
Service:	Friendly	Fast	Low priority consideration
Price:	Competitive	Food up to £3.50	Worthington Bitter £1.04
Place:			
– environment	Safe, sit down, clean toilets	Clean, comfortable	Warm
– convenience in choice of pub	90%	80%	50%
Critical Sucess Factors	Safe, clean environment	Rapid delivery of tasty, filling, good value meals	Cheap beer

Entrepreneurial marketing

One dimension in which entrepreneurial marketing differs from conventional marketing is its heavy reliance on relationships. More recently this has been recognised and christened 'relationship marketing', which can be contrasted to the more traditional transaction marketing. Supporters of this 'new' approach – in fact, long used by small firms – believe that it can deliver sustainable customer loyalty (Webster, 1992). The two approaches are contrasted in Table 6.4. This approach may not be viable with all products or services, but it does add yet a further dimension to Porter's generic marketing strategies. Relationship marketing can be mixed with any of the four strategies to create a relationship hybrid that implies a different set of strategic imperatives from those implied by a transaction marketing approach.

However, a reliance on relationships may not in itself be sufficient to mark out the entrepreneurial firm. Chaston (2000) says that truly entrepreneurial firms have a distinctively different approach to marketing which he defines as 'the philosophy of challenging established market conventions during the process of developing new solutions'. The entrepreneurial marketing process is essentially simple, involving understanding conventional competitors and then challenging the approach they adopt. The process of 'rational entrepreneurship' is shown in Figure 6.7. In essence, he is suggesting that marketing is judged to be entrepreneurial by its degree of innovation. Since this is the essence of entrepreneurship, this is difficult to dispute.

As Chaston points out, even relationship marketing can be copied, although larger firms may find it more difficult to sustain than smaller firms. Here again he

Unemployed	Office/ professionals	Students	Regulars	Pre-clubbers
2–5 90/10	5–7 60/40	any time 50/50	7–11 60/40	7–11, Fri/Sat 60/40
Cheap beer	Wide range of quality drinks	Wide range of quality drinks	Wide range of quality drinks	Fashionable brand leaders
Low priority consideration	Friendly	Low priority consideration	Friendly	Fast
Worthington Bitter £1.04	20% discount	Competitive	Competitive	Low priority consideration
Music/TVs	Upbeat atmosphere	Relaxed, safe	Home from home	Lively, 'in place'
50%	80%	70%	50%	80%
Cheap beer	Cheap drinks and upbeat atmosphere after work	Relaxed atmosphere and used by other students	Good service and atmosphere	'In place' reputation

encourages the entrepreneur to do things differently. For example, many internet businesses foster relationships with their customers by generating a sense of community on their website. Chaston's approach is deceptively simple as he points out that there are many conventions that can be challenged. He suggests three categories:

1 Sectoral conventions are the strategic rules that guide the marketing operations of the majority of firms in a sector such as efficiency of plants, economies of scale, methods of distribution and so on. So, for example, insurance used to be delivered through insurance brokers until Direct Line came along, challenged the conventional wisdom, and began to sell direct, over the telephone.
2 Performance conventions set by other firms in the sector such as profit, cost of production, quality and so forth. In the 1960s Japanese firms ignored Western performance conventions en-masse and managed to enter and succeed in these markets.
3 Customer conventions which make certain assumptions about what customers are looking for from their purchases, for example price, size, design and so on. Anita Roddick redefined the cosmetic industry's 'feel-good factor' to include environmental factors.

In most sectors there are factors that managers believe are critical to the success of their business. Chaston encourages entrepreneurs to ask 'why?' These conventions are all worth questioning and doing things differently is what entrepreneurship is about, but doing things differently is risky and Chaston is the first to say it takes

Table 6.4   Relationship vs transactional marketing

Relationship marketing	Transactional marketing
• Encourages close, frequent customer contact.	• Limited contact.
• Encourages repeat sales.	• Orientated towards single purchase.
• Focus on customer service.	• Limited customer service.
• Focus on value to the customer.	• Focus on product/service benefits.
• Focus on quality of total offering.	• Focus on quality of product.
• Focus on long-term performance.	• Focus on short-term performance.

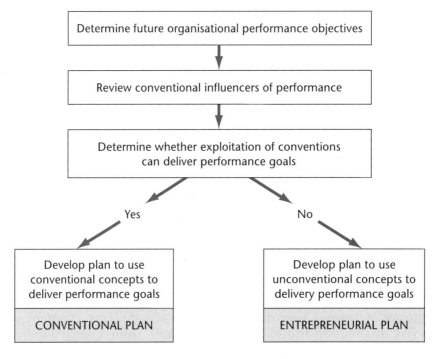

Source: Chaston (2000).

Figure 6.7   Entrepreneurial vs non-entrepreneurial planning parthway

careful research and analysis, matching opportunities to the firm's capabilities. He proposes a somewhat different approach to marketing planning which he calls 'mapping the future'. This eight-stage process is shown in Figure 6.8. Although shown as linear and sequential, the process is interrupted as new market information is discovered and earlier decisions are revisited. The process also includes small-scale market entry and trial to gain further information.

The process starts with the development of a detailed understanding of sector conventions. Stage two involves assessing the performance gap between aspirations of future performance and the level of performance currently being delivered. If the size is sufficient to attract an entrepreneurial approach (that is, an incremental

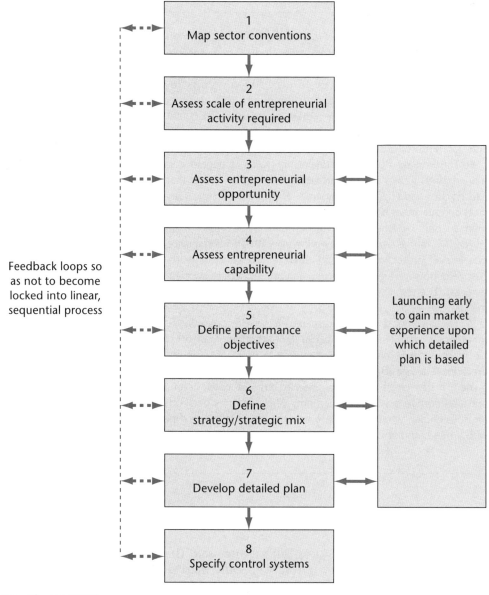

Source: Chaston (2000).

Figure 6.8 The entrepreneurial marketing planning process

approach is not warranted), then the opportunity is investigated using an innovative approach that questions all current assumptions about delivery. Whatever that approach is, it must next be matched to the ability to deliver. If the firm has the capability, then the remaining processes are more straightforward; defining performance objectives, defining strategy, developing a detailed plan and specifying control systems. All these will be considered in greater detail in subsequent chapters and pulled together into a detailed business plan in Chapter 14.

Case insight

The Korean car company **Daewoo** entered the UK car market based upon an innovative, mould-breaking marketing strategy – and in its first six months sold 14 000 cars. It decided to sell directly to customers rather than through a franchised distributor network, thus eliminating commission payments. However, to persuade customers to try their offering they had to persuade them that it was safe to buy from them. They also set out to reduce the stress and risks involved in buying a car. Their market research revealed that car buyers disliked dealers on commission, hard-sell, aggressive sales techniques, over exaggerated promotional campaigns and poor after-sales service.

So Daewoo set up its own dealerships with staff paid a salary rather than commission – trained, helpful sales advisors providing information rather than pressing for sales. Showrooms had crèches and children's play areas and offered coffee. Cars were not serviced at the same location, but rather by the well known retailer Halfords in their out-of-town service centres. The themes used by Daewoo to further differentiate itself included good value, reliable cars (3-year warranties, AA breakdown cover) with additional safety features (e.g. ABS brakes and side impact protection) and additional features and benefits that would otherwise be extra cost (e.g. power steering, no-fuss guarantees, courtesy cars or pick up and collection for services). The result was that in the first six months Daewoo sold a remarkable 14 000 cars in the UK.

When Daewoo set up their second-hand car operation they had to set about putting together a similarly impressive package of additional benefits to augment the product offering 12 months comprehensive warranty; 116-point AA-approved inspection; 12 months AA breakdown assistance; independent mileage check; free MOT tests for as long as the car is owned; a free check to ensure the car has not been stolen or written off and there is no outstanding hire purchase agreement; 30-day money back guarantee; direct contact with the previous owner, where possible; 6 months road tax; a free mobile phone; fixed price servicing with a free courtesy car anywhere in mainland UK.

Undertaking market research

The President of Harvard Business School once said that if you thought knowledge was expensive, you should try ignorance. Some market research is essential before a business is started. It helps minimise risk and uncertainty and provides some basis on which to make the decisions about marketing strategy. Collecting information and making judgements on it are key entrepreneurial competencies (Carson *et al.*, 1995). Market research is about getting information about customers and competitors. For a start-up any information is probably of value, but the key question that needs to be answered is – why should anyone buy from you rather than from competitors? To answer this question break it down into four elements:

1 Who will buy?
2 What are they buying?
3 Who are your competitors?
4 Why do people buy from them?

'If you ask me how we find new markets, the answer is research, research, research For us research is critical when it comes to opening new outlets. We put a lot of work into demographics and social indicators and really know our business. But they can fail: we put a store in Dewsbury, West Yorkshire, four years ago, everything looked good, we did the groundwork, but what the figures didn't show was that our site was in the middle of the town's devoutly Muslim centre. They ate only halal meat, and they certainly weren't eating pizza. We got it wrong and we had to shut the store.'

Stephen Hemsley, Chief Executive,
Domino's Pizza
Sunday Times 23 May 2004
●

Clarifying who the customers are likely to be will enable the firm to focus on those that will give it most business. Knowing as much as possible about them and why they might buy will enable the firm to fine-tune its marketing better to suit their needs and help it to identify both new customers and, eventually, new products or services.

Knowing who the competitors are is just as important. A pizza restaurant may face competition from a whole range of other local restaurants, not just those offering pizza. Understanding why customers buy from competitors gives a further insight into the needs of customers and ideas about how you may combat competition.

Market research, therefore, might involve estimating the size and nature of the market including profiling of consumer or industrial customers. A consumer profile might include age, sex, income, occupation, social status, geographic location and so on. An industrial profile might include sector, size, geographic location and so forth. It might involve understanding why, where and when customers buy, the nature of distribution channels and the nature of economic and other environmental trends that might affect the business. It might involve analysing competitors in terms of their product/ service offering, size, profitability, operating methods. If a new product or service is involved, it might involve some testing so as to get customers' reaction. The important thing is to start by specifying what market information is needed.

There are two ways to research a market (Table 6.5):

1 Field research;
2 Desk research.

Field research can involve conducting face-to-face individual or group interviews, telephone surveys or administering postal questionnaires. Simple observation and discussion will go a long way without costing much other than time. Asking questions of potential customers face to face, by mail shot or by telephone will provide a lot of valuable information. Visiting competitors at their place of business, perhaps buying their product or service and talking to other customers will give an insight into how they operate.

Research based on interviewing has to ensure that a representative sample of respondents is seen and that, where a structured interview is used, the subject areas are covered comprehensively. When questionnaires are used, the questions must be clear and unambiguous. They should not 'lead' respondents by implying an answer to the question. Their design should facilitate interpretation and possible data processing.

Case insight

Mark Dorman was an advertising executive who had worked for 20 years in the business. In 1995 he was sitting in a hotel bar in the USA feeling jet-lagged. The barman offered him a vodka or a coffee, black or white, to help him come round. Something registered in his mind – what a brilliant idea if you could really have black vodka. It would be completely unique and instantly branded as it was poured into the glass.

When he got back to the UK he decided to investigate the idea. He asked for help from a friend, Christopher Hayman, who worked for Beefeater Gin. After some experimentation they found that it could be done by colouring the vodka with black catechu, a Burmese herb. There was also the added advantage that if you put a mixer in first, as the Americans do, the vodka floats to the top, giving a distinctive cocktail. He also found out that there was a lucrative market in the USA with more than 350 million cases of vodka sold annually.

By 1997 Mark had invested some £750 000 of his own money in the idea, a third of which was simply the legal costs of registering the product in different countries. He had a company, imaginatively called the **Black Vodka Company**. However, he had run out of money and was still unable to produce the vodka in volume.

The story has a happy ending. Mark was able to find a private backer who shared his faith in the product and bought a share of the company. In 1998 black vodka went on sale in Britain and the USA. It was a success. In 1999 Francarep, the capital development arm of the Rothschild family, bought a 27 per cent stake in the company. The company went on to be listed on AIM and then obtained a full listing ahead of merging with a US drinks company to become known as Blavod Extreme Spirits. Although Mark no longer has anything to do with the company, it wasn't a bad idea from a barman!

Table 6.5   Advantages and disadvantages of field vs desk research

	Field research	Desk research
Advantages	• Reflects your needs • You control quality • Up to date	• Cheap • Quick • Good for background information
Disadvantages	• Expensive • Takes time • Can tell competitors what you are up to	• Not specific to your business • Can be incomplete or inaccurate • Can be out of date

For retailers, location is obviously very important. Once prospective premises have been identified, local trade needs to be checked out. Find out how many and what type of customers pass by the location. Are shops in the immediate vicinity an advantage or disadvantage? Location can be important for other businesses, for example proximity to customers or a workforce. Many start-ups locate where the owner-manager happens to live. It is not a positive decision. Some lifestyle businesses also locate where the owner-managers want to live. The advantages of different types of field research are shown in Table 6.6.

Table 6.6   Advantages and disadvantages of different types of field research

	Personal interview	Telephone interview	Postal questionnaire
Quality of data	Very good	Good	Good
Quantity of data	Very good	Fair	Poor
Speed	Good	Very good	Poor
Response rate	Good	Good	Poor
Cost	High (your time)	Fair	Fair

Desk research can provide information quickly and cheaply. Information on markets, sectors and industries is published in newspapers, trade magazines, industry surveys and reports, trade journals or directories, many of which will be available at the local business library. There will be websites that provide information. Desk research can provide information on product developments, customer needs or characteristics, competitors and market trends. However, for many start-ups local information is of far more importance than regional or national information and that might come from local Chambers of Commerce and other local sources of help and advice.

For many start-ups the easiest and cheapest way to undertake market research is to test-market and launch the business in a low-cost way, constantly reviewing what is happening and how customers react and refining the product or service offered to them. However, this can be a very expensive way of doing market research if things go wrong and some basic market research is essential for just about any start-up. The bigger the start-up, the more important is proper market research.

Case insight

Euravia Engineering is a Lancashire-based company that repairs and overhauls aircraft engines. It was started in 1988 by **Dennis Mendoros**, a Greek who originally came to Britain to study aeronautical engineering but returned to Greece to work in the aero-industry.

When he decided to set up the business he also had to decide where to locate it. He decided on Britain rather than the USA or other European locations because of lifestyle reasons but also because of the UK's established markets, engineering standards that were almost universally recognised and the international reputation of its aero-industry. He decided on Lancashire because of its concentration of aeronautical companies.

Initially he located near to Manchester airport, but that proved to be a mistake because it was expensive and he could not get suitably qualified staff. He quickly moved 40 miles to Barnoldswick where Rolls-Royce Aero-engines had recently closed a factory leaving a pool of highly skilled and experienced engineers. His staffing problems were solved. He also set the business up in an old textile mill so as to keep down costs.

In 1994, with 15 employees, the company moved to a new factory in Kelbrook, Lancashire, a few miles south, where it now remains. Euravia Engineering is thriving and now has a three facilities on the same site.

Whilst any and all information is probably worth having, we need to know what we are looking for. The vital need is to understand why customers buy and how they might be influenced. We need to understand how to go about matching what the firm is capable of producing with what the customer needs – and that is called marketing. Marketing is first and foremost an attitude of mind about always putting the customer first. Understanding customer needs and motivations is central to marketing.

Developing selling skills

Whatever the 'theory' of marketing might be, the practical reality is that most owner-managers will have to do at least some of their own selling at start-up. The first thing to do is to identify the customer. It sounds obvious but, particularly for business-to-business products or services, the consumer or user of the product or service is not always the buyer. Indeed to get a sale you might have to persuade a range of people – called the 'decision-making unit' (DMU) – each with different interests. The DMU tends to increase with the size of firm you are selling to. The DMU might involve, say, two engineers, a buyer and somebody from the finance department, each looking for different things. Each one has to be satisfied.

It is important to plan a sales interview so as not to waste time or create a bad impression. This starts with knowing as much as you can about the prospective customer and being clear about what you want from the interview. It is important to be able to evaluate the business potential from each customer so as to make the most of your time. The other variable here is their attitude towards you, but whilst you can affect attitude, you are unlikely to be able to affect business potential. Figure 6.9 shows a selling potential matrix that salesmen can use to improve their use of time. Most time should be spent with friendly customers with high potential. Salesmen tend to spend time with any and all friendly customers. In fact they must husband their time between these and the high business potential customers, so as to move these from less friendly to more friendly over time.

		Business potential of customer		
		High	Medium	Low
	Friendly	Most time	Increasing time	Some time
Attitude	Indifferent	Increasing time	Some time	Perhaps
	Unfriendly	Some time	Perhaps	Opportunistic

Figure 6.9   The selling potential matrix

It is important to gain the customer's attention, arouse their interest and build confidence. All the time you are trying to find out three important things:

1 What they want.
2 How to match this to the product or service you have to sell.
3 How to build up agreement that it does indeed meet their requirements.
4 How then to close the sale.

The sales interview is the ideal opportunity to bridge the gap between a customer's needs and the benefits offered by a product or service. If you can do that, and convince the customer that the product or service does indeed meet their requirements, you have a sale. Sales interviews can be started in a number of ways:

- *Question*: You might ask a question that ascertains that the customer buys these sorts of products or services.
- *Statement*: You might state the benefits of the product or service directly, for example 'our service will save the average household 20% on their phone bills'.
- *Reference*: You might give a personal reference like 'Mr Smith in your other factory was impressed with our service and said you might be interested ...' You can equally use impersonal references like an article in the trade or national press.
- *Sales aids*: You might launch straight into looking at photographs, brochures and so on.
- *Demonstration*: If you have the product with you, a demonstration may be the best way to get going.
- *Link to earlier contact*: You may have phoned or made contact earlier and agreed to the meeting.

Once you have opened, your aim should be to state the features and benefits of the product and start matching them to the needs of the customer. There are various techniques to help get your message across. Visual stimuli like support materials, demonstrations or presentation all help. Building the relationship is vital. Small things can be important to help achieve this in the short space of time available. For example, dressing appropriately, being punctual, keeping eye contact, being confident and enthusiastic about the product or service, listening to the customer and trying to see things from their point of view, being courteous and polite, and avoiding negative body language like looking bored. The most important advice of all, particularly if the interview goes wrong, is to let the customer talk and to really listen to what he is saying. All the time he is giving you information which should enable you to match the benefits of your product or service to his needs. This entails understanding how to turn features into benefits, as discussed earlier. Relationships are built on over time and networks of contacts can be developed through good customer relationships, so pressurising a customer is unlikely to pay off in the long run.

Selling benefits means understanding both the product or service and the needs of the customer, being able to match the two and then convince the customer that he should buy. That often means avoiding jargon and talking the customer's language.

As the sales interview progresses the customer may show a lack of interest. If this is the case, then the opening was probably not sufficiently interesting and you need to discover what other areas of need – if any – the product or service might meet. In other words you need to ask questions. If the customer raises an objection – which is more than likely at some point in the interview – then at least he is showing an interest and in raising the objection he is providing additional information. If the customer has a fundamental objection, for example, you are trying to sell double glazing and it turns out to be a new house, then it may be time to move on. But just sometimes this is not the case and it may be worth asking why he does not see the need for the product or service. It may just be worth trying to convince him of the benefits it offers over what he already uses, even if the time to change is some way in the future. There are six other types of objection, some of which can be dealt with. They are:

- *Feature objection*: Where some of the features do not meet the customer's approval. This can be dealt with by emphasising the positive reasons for these features.
- *Information seeking objections*: Where the customer is not fully convinced by some aspect of the presentation. This provides the opportunity to give relevant information and tailor it to the customer's requirements.
- *Price objections*: This may be fundamental but often can be made in the hope of negotiating a lower price. Benefits should be restated compared to the price difference in competing products. Value for money needs to be stressed and a discount only offered as a last resort, perhaps using it to secure a larger order.
- *Delay objection*: The customer wants to put off making a decision. This is difficult if the delay is genuine. Arranging a return visit when the time is right may be all you can achieve.
- *Loyalty objection*: There may be an established relationship with a competitor. Stress the benefits of the product or service and never 'knock' the competitor. Try to find reasons why they should change supplier, for example, are they being taken for granted in terms of the service they receive? Always keep contact as it may just take time to convince them to try you.
- *Hidden objection*: The buyer prevaricates for no obvious reason. This is another difficult situation. It is important to get to the unstated objection and deal with it, so ask questions.

Some people actually have problems recognising buying signals and can continue relentlessly through their presentation long after the customer actually wanted to buy the product or service. Buying signals can be many and various; the customer becoming interested and animated, positive body language such as leaning forward or wanting pick up or try the product. If interest is confirmed by asking a few questions, the whole process can be short-circuited and you can go to the most important stage of all – closing the sale.

There are six well-known techniques used for closing the sale:

- *The trial close*: You can try this one immediately you see a buying signal. This close uses the opportunity of an expression of interest to ask a further question which implicitly assumes a sale. For example, 'You will want to take our extended credit, won't you?' or 'It is the quality of the product that has convinced you, hasn't it?' Notice the trial close ends with a question and if the answer is positive then you can proceed straight to close the sale.
- *The alternative close*: This forces the customer to a decision between options. For example, 'Do you want 1000 or 5000?' or 'Can we deliver next month or would you prefer next week?'
- *The summary close*: This is useful if the buyer is uncertain about the next step. It summarises what has been said and sets out the next steps. For example, 'So those are the advantages our service offers over the one you are using at the moment and I think you would agree we are better in every respect. Do you agree?'
- *The concession close*: Concessions are usually on price. They may secure orders but should not be given away too soon, only at the end of the interview when you judge it necessary to tip the balance in your favour. For example, 'And if you place an order in December, there is a special 5% discount.'
- *The quotation close*: Often you have to provide a formal quote at the end of the sales interview. If this is the case, then it should be followed up with another visit to the customer to clarify the main points, answer any queries and secure the sale.
- *The direct close*: Just sometimes it is actually necessary to ask for the order directly – and then remain silent and listen to the answer. If the answer is 'no' at least it should provide some objections that you might be able to overcome.

Successful selling means knowing your product or service inside out and understanding the needs of your customers. It is not just about winning orders, it is about building relationships – vital for a small firm that does not have the advertising and promotion budget that a large firm might have. Relationships are built on trust and respect and, if you cannot get these from the customer, then you are simply an order-taker and the business could easily disappear at any time.

Using the internet

The internet was probably the most important innovation affecting business at the end of the twentieth century. It created major opportunities for new and small firms. Firstly there was the opportunity to establish new innovative trading businesses that exploited the unique characteristics of the internet. Certainly the internet service providers came out of the boom. Firms like eBay, arguably the most successful of the internet-based firms, did not exist 15 years ago. Its success comes from its innovative business model – a model that could not exist without the internet. The internet encouraged the development of community sites, many of which started as hobbies but developed into money-making ventures. Friendsreunited.com could not have existed without the internet and started in just this way.

But the internet did more than just allow innovative businesses to be established. It allowed small firms to compete in a global market place on price, the differentiated qualities of the products or service or by being able to focus even more effectively on market segments – niche marketing. The lasting legacy that the internet gave us was the new routes to market that change the balance of power in the small versus large firm equation of competition. Almost any market on the planet is now accessible by the smallest of firms. With barriers down, competition is likely to intensify.

Business-to-business trading has seen particular growth. Large companies such as Dell Computers show the way forward with their 'information partnership' and 'fully integrated value chain' linking customer, Dell and their suppliers which allows stock to be delivered on a just-in-time basis and costs to be minimised. However, the increasingly symbiotic relationships between large assemblers and small suppliers carry many dangers for the supplier.

Business-to-consumer retailing has expanded dramatically as broadband networks have expanded. There are many opportunities for small firms on the internet that allow them to tap large markets without the overheads associated with the high street. Firms like Amazon, Lastminute.com in the UK, Dangdang.com in China and NCsoft in Korea are all examples of this. However, the big high-street names are increasingly looking to establish themselves on the internet and they will capitalise on their established brand and a loyal customer base.

Selling on the web offers the opportunity to do business 24 hours a day, seven days a week and the chance to build relationships and develop an understanding of individual customer's buying patterns. It does not necessarily require the major fixed costs of a retail business like the site and the shop-floor staff – something called a pure internet firm – but many traditional bricks-and-mortar business are also trading on the internet. At the moment internet-based retail is most successful for branded products where the features are already understood, or for 'low touch' products or services such as books, CDs, airline or theatre tickets where, once again, customers understand precisely what they are buying. However, even here the nature of trading is changing as media is increasingly downloaded directly rather than being delivered through the post.

Brady (1999) argues that success for a purely internet start-up depends on several factors, although, interestingly, all but the last factor could apply to any business:

- Providing something different.
- The business must be clearly focused but be sufficiently flexible to change quickly to sustain growth.
- The management must be good with a good plan, a grasp of critical issues and credibility in the eyes of financiers.
- The business must develop a strong brand and, on the back of this, create and maintain very high levels of service.
- Delivery must be on time.
- The site must be readily accessible, orders must be simple to place and easily tracked whilst they are in the system.

Case insight

Crucial to success for dot.com firms is the 'business model' – how income will be generated. Arguably the most successful model is that of the online auctioneer **eBay**. eBay was founded by **Pierre M. Omidyar** in 1995. It now has 69 million registered users worldwide and hosts over 12 million items on its website. It is the largest site for used car sales in the USA. Someone buys a computer game every 8 seconds on it. By 2005 it had over 8000 employees and sales topped $4 billion.

eBay's success comes from being nothing more than an intermediary – software running on a web server. Its customers, both buyers and sellers, do all the work. Sellers pay to set up their own auction, buyers use eBay's software to place their bids, shipping and payment are arranged between the seller and buyer and eBay takes between 7 and 18 per cent of the selling price as commission for letting them use their software. eBay is simply the trading platform. It holds no stocks and its involvement in the trade in minimal. After each transaction each buyer and seller rate the other. Next to each user's identification is a figure in brackets recording the number of positive comments – thus encouraging honesty and trust. It is a truly virtual business which also sells advertising space.

eBay developed a 'virtuous circle' in which more buyers attracted more sellers, who attracted yet more buyers and sellers – called 'network effects'. At the core of eBay's business is software rather than people. The company has bought software companies to gain exclusive use of their technologies and make the auction process more efficient. It therefore faces enormous economies of scale in attracting as many auction transactions as possible and, with that in mind, has moved into new areas such as used cars and even plans to host storefronts for small merchants. It has also started to sell private-label versions of its service to companies, for a fee.

In 2002 eBay purchased **PayPal**, the dominant provider of internet payments in the USA with over 12 million customers, of whom 3.2 million are fee-paying business customers. The two companies are complementary but depend on each other. Indeed, auctions account for 61 per cent of PayPal's business. PayPal allows customers to register details of their credit card or bank account with it so that when they buy something on the internet they just enter an e-mail account and an amount. Like eBay, it is fully automated, relying on software rather than people. Like eBay, it also relies on 'network effects'. It initially paid users $10 to sign up their friends to enable it to reach its critical mass, but now the firm is signing up 28 000 new users a day without this incentive.

The key to successful trading on the internet is a good website. A good site is one that gets people to visit and then revisit it. It must be easy to navigate. Registration with the internet service providers of both the firm and key words associated with the products or services it sells is important. This brings recognition on the search engines that people use to find out what is available on the web. Firms might also decide to advertise on related sites or in traditional print media. The site must also be secure if it is to take credit card transactions. Many sites try to build community interests. This generates web loyalty and customer trust. Whilst you can always build your own site, if you are setting one up for commercial purposes you are best advised to seek professional advice.

E-business is not just a new element to be added into the marketing mix. It is a fundamental and dramatic change in the way we do business which increases the degree of competition and makes us reinterpret some of the fundamentals of marketing.

Legal forms of business

Nothing, in the overregulated world of today, is ever simple. Before a new business is launched some thought should be given to the legal problems that need to be dealt with. There is a checklist at the end of this book setting out the regulations to be met in starting up a business in the UK. The first issue is the legal form for the business. The three most popular are: the sole trader (almost 60 per cent of businesses), partnership and limited liability company.

Sole traders

This is the business owned by one individual. The individual is the business, and the business is the individual. The two are inseparable. A sole trader is the simplest form of business to start – all that is needed is the first customer. It faces fewer regulations than a limited company and there are no major requirements about accounts and audits, although the individual will pay personal taxes which are based upon the profits made by the business.

There are two important limitations, however. The first is that a sole trader will find it more difficult to borrow large amounts of money than a limited company. Lending institutions prefer the assets of the business to be placed within the legal framework of a company because of the restrictions then placed upon the business. It is, however, quite common for a business to start life as a sole trader and incorporate later in life as more capital is needed.

The second disadvantage is that the sole trader is personally liable for all the debts of the business, no matter how large. That means creditors may look both to the business assets and the proprietor's assets to satisfy their debts. However, this disadvantage should not be over emphasised because of the widely adopted practice of placing some family assets in the name of the spouse or another relative and because, even as a limited company, a bank is likely to ask for a personal guarantee from the proprietor before giving a loan.

Partnerships

Some professions, such as doctors and accountants, are required by law to conduct business as partnerships. Partnerships are just groups of sole traders who come together, formally or informally, to do business. As such it allows them to pool their resources, some to contribute capital, others their skills. Partnerships, therefore, face all the advantages of sole traders plus some additional disadvantages.

The first of these disadvantages is that each partner has unlimited liability for the debts of the partnership, whether they incurred them personally or not. Clearly partnerships require a lot of trust. The second disadvantage is that the partnership is held to cease every time one partner leaves or a new one joins, which means dividing up the assets and liabilities in some way, even if other partners end up buying them and the business never actually ceases trading.

Generally, if you are considering a partnership you would be well-advised to draw up a formal partnership agreement. It is very easy to get into an informal partnership with a friend, but if you cannot work together, or times get hard, you may regret it. If there is no formal agreement, then in the UK the terms of the Partnership Act 1890 are held to apply. Partnership agreements cover such issues as capital contributions, division of profit and interest on capital, power to draw money or take remuneration from the business, preparation of accounts and procedures when the partnership is held to 'cease'. Solicitors can provide a model agreement which can be adapted to suit particular circumstances.

Limited companies

A company (registered in accordance with the provisions of the Companies Acts in the UK) is a separate legal entity distinct from its owners or shareholders, and its directors or managers. It can enter into contracts and sue or be sued in its own right. It is taxed separately through Corporation Tax. There is a divorce between management and ownership, with a board of directors elected by the shareholders to control the day-to-day running of the business. There need be only two shareholders and one director, and shareholders can also be directors.

The advantage of this form of business is that the liability of the shareholders is limited by the amount of capital they put into the business. What is more, a company has unlimited life and can be sold on to other shareholders. Indeed there is no limit to the number of shareholders. Therefore a limited company can attract additional risk capital from backers who may not wish to be involved in the day-to-day running of the business. Also, because of the regulation they face, bankers prefer to lend to companies rather than sole traders, although they may still require personal guarantees. Clearly this is the best form for a growth business that will require capital and will face risks as it grows.

Table 6.7 Advantages and disadvantages of different forms of business

	Sole trader	Partnership	Limited company
Advantages	• Easy to form • Minimum of regulation	• Easy to form • Minimum of regulation	• Limited liability • Easier to borrow money • Can raise risk capital through additional shareholders • Can be sold on • Pays Corporation Tax
Disadvantages	• Unlimited personal liability • More difficult to borrow money • Pay personal tax	• Unlimited personal liability for debts of whole partnership • More difficult to borrow money • 'Cease trading' whenever partners change • Pay personal tax	• Must comply with Companies Acts • Greater regulation • Greater disclosure of information

Nevertheless there are some disadvantages to this form of business. In the UK under the Companies Acts, a company must keep certain books of account and appoint an auditor. It must file an annual return with Companies House which includes accounts and details of directors and shareholders. This takes time and money and means that competitors might have access to information that they would not otherwise see. Advantages and disadvantages of different forms of business are summarised in Table 6.7.

The easiest way to set up a company is to buy one 'off the shelf' from a Company Registration Agent. In the UK this costs as little as £200. This avoids all the tedious form-filling that is otherwise required. It also saves time. Agents will also show you how to go about changing the company's name if you want to.

Franchises

These are not so much a legal form of business as a way of doing business. They are increasingly popular, particularly with individuals who are less entrepreneurial but wish to run their own business. A franchise is a business in which the owner of the name or method of doing business (the franchisor) allows a local operator (the franchisee) to set up a business under that name. The local operator may be a sole trader or a limited company.

Table 6.8 Advantages and disadvantages of being a franchisee or franchisor

	Franchisee	Franchisor
Advantages	• Business format proved. Less risk of failure • Easier to obtain finance than own start-up • Established format. Start-up should be quicker • Training and support available from franchisor • National branding should help sales • Economies of scale may apply	• Way of expanding business quickly • Financing costs shared with franchisees • Franchisees usually highly motivated since their livelihood depends on success
Disadvantages	• Not really your own idea and creation • Lack of real independence Franchisor makes the rules. • Buying into franchise can be expensive • Royalties can be high • Goodwill you build up dependent upon continuing franchise agreement. This may cause problems if you wish to sell • Franchisor can damage brand	• British Franchise Association rules take time and money to comply with • Loss of some control to franchisees • Franchisees can influence the business • Failure of franchisee can reflect on franchise • May be obligations to franchisee in the franchise agreement

In exchange for an initial fee (anything from a few thousand to hundreds of thousands of pounds) and a royalty on sales, the franchisor lays down a blueprint of how the business is to be run; content and nature of product or service, price and performance standards, type, size and layout of shop or business, training and other support or controls. Since the franchise is usually a tried and tested idea, well-known by potential customers, the franchisee should have a ready market and a better chance of a successful start-up. Indeed only about 10 per cent of franchises fail.

There are hundreds of franchises in the UK as well as tens of thousands of franchisees. Most established franchisors are members of the British Franchise Association, which has a code of conduct and accreditation rules, based on codes developed by the European Franchise Association. One key principle is that the franchisor shall have operated the business concept with success for a reasonable time, and in at least one pilot unit before starting the franchise network. Table 6.8 summarises the advantages and disadvantages of being a franchisee and a franchisor.

Summary

Customers buy products or services to obtain benefits. Sometimes there are separate customers and consumers for the product or service, both looking for benefits. It is important to understand what benefits they are looking for. All too often owner-managers focus just on the features of the product or service.

One way of describing the features is the marketing mix, or 5 Ps:

- *Product*: the tangible characteristics of the product or service;
- *Price*: the price, including discounts or special offers;
- *Promotion*: advertising, point of sale displays, PR, selling and so on;
- *Place*: location, layout, channels of distribution and so on;
- *People*: the service, advice, support and relationships, particularly important to owner-managed businesses.

The marketing mix must be consistent, reinforcing the benefits the customer is looking for. It is only as strong as its weakest link. The stronger, more distinctive and different the other elements of the marketing mix, the higher the price that can be charged. Like **GTI**, it is essential to understand what your customers are looking for in order to build a strong marketing mix. The elements of the marketing mix, related to the customers they are targeted at, together make up the marketing strategy of the firm.

Owner-managers prefer 'interactive marketing' – doing things themselves and using one-to-one contact with customers for anything from market research to promotion. For them the fifth P in the marketing mix is their personality.

Too many small firms sell on price because they fear competition. The price charged ought to reflect the benefits customers obtain from a product or service. Therefore similar products or services might be able to command different prices with different target markets. There is a pricing range available to most firms with a number of other benchmarks: variable cost, average total cost and, important for **Jean Young**, the going rate. Also important is the break-even point. Many firms 'cost-plus' price based upon break-even and a target level of profitability.

Case with questions

Anita Lucia Roddick, née Perilla, was born in Littlehampton, England in 1942, one of four children of Italian immigrants. Her parents settled in Littlehampton to run the Clifton Cafe. Her father died when she was ten and the children then helped to run the cafe. From school Anita went to Bath College of Education where she took a teacher training course. She started teaching, but wanted to live abroad so she got a job with the United Nations in Geneva. She had never had a holiday as a child and so, with the tax-free money she earned in Geneva, she decided to spend a year travelling around the world. She visited Polynesia, New Caledonia, Australia and Africa where her interest in the use of natural ingredients for cosmetic purposes was aroused. In Tahiti she saw local women plastering themselves with cocoa butter. Half the bean was used for chocolate and the other half was used as a cosmetic. In Morocco she saw women washing their hair in mud.

Returning to England, she met Gordon Roddick, a graduate of the Royal Agricultural College at Cirencester. He had farmed overseas and in the UK before settling in Littlehampton. They married in 1970. Originally they planned to travel overland to Australia and buy a pineapple plantation, but the arrival of first one and then two children made them change their plans. Instead they bought and ran a restaurant and later a small hotel in Littlehampton.

In 1976 Anita opened the first **Body Shop** in a back street in Brighton. It sold only about a dozen inexpensive 'natural' cosmetics, all herbal creams and shampoos, all in simple packaging. She thought it would only appeal to a small number of customers that shared her values. Gordon even went off to ride a horse across the Americas about a month after it opened. But Anita was wrong. It proved to be a huge success. However, whilst this idea was novel at the time it was easily copiable. The firm's initial roll-out owes much to Anita and Gordon Roddick's clear focus on where their competitive advantage lay. They realised that their idea could be easily copied and success would only come from developing the brand and a rapid expansion. Unfortunately they had little cash to do either. It was Gordon who had the idea of a franchise, which meant that franchisees paid to become part of Body Shop and managed the shop themselves. The Roddicks initially decided not to manufacture their products or even invest in a distribution system, but rather to concentrate on getting the franchise formula right, developing the brand and protecting it from imitators. The franchisees generated sufficient cash to finance early expansion until 1984 when the company went to the stock market.

In the 1980s Body Shop reversed its decision and started its own warehousing and distribution network, based upon a sophisticated stock control system, and built up a substantial fleet of lorries. Products could typically be delivered within 24 hours. It also started manufacturing many of its cosmetics mainly in the UK, although many of the ingredients came from overseas under its 'trade-not-aid' policy. These two elements of strategy initially worked well and generated substantial sales and profit growth, but the manufacturing policy was reviewed in the late 1990s.

Body Shop remains an international franchise chain of shops. Body Shop International Ltd is the franchisor. Franchisees pay an initial fee plus an annual operating charge for a fixed term, renewable franchise. Franchisees buy a 'turn-key' system with a tightly controlled retail format providing shop fitting and layout, staff training, financial and stock control systems and even help with site identification. Body Shop can also help arrange finance to purchase the franchise. Body Shop, of course, makes a margin on the products it sells to the franchisees.

→

Franchisees receive regular visits from company representatives who provide assistance with display, sales promotion and training. Information packs, newsletters, videos and free promotional material are made available and franchisees have to return a monthly report on their sales. This enables the company to monitor both trading results and the local sales performance of individual products. The company closely monitors the use of the Body Shop trade mark in all franchisees' literature, advertising and other uses.

In the early years Body Shop could not afford to advertise. Developing the brand was heavily reliant upon Anita's personality and her ability to get free PR for the environmental causes associated with the firm. Indeed, advertising would have been very much against the firm's image. In those early days her outspoken, controversial views – concerning just about anything – guaranteed her media coverage and helped her win the Businesswoman of the Year award just before the stock market launch. Even today the Body Shop brand is inexorably linked with its culture, which in turn is grounded firmly in its ethical and environmental beliefs and values. Based very much around the charismatic Anita Roddick's views that business can be a vehicle for social and environmental change, the firm has championed numerous causes. These not only show themselves in window displays and PR activities, they also underscore everything the company does. Franchisees are selected partly upon their 'fit' with her ideas. Employees receive regular newsletters and videos concentrating on Body Shop campaigns. Employees are given time off to work on local social projects. In 1995 the firm introduced in-store satellite transmitted radio. Body Shop takes every opportunity to put forward its values and beliefs which it sees as setting it apart as distinctive and different from its high street competition.

Body Shop is now a global brand, but what does it stand for and what are customers buying? Even Anita Roddick admitted they were not just buying cosmetics – 'oil and water will not make their hearts sing'. The marketing mix comprises cosmetics made from high quality, natural ingredients which do not involve cruelty to animals. They can be bought in a range of refillable containers, including trial sizes, that are plain and simple with clear factual statements about their ingredients. Tester bottles are freely available in shops and staff are trained not to sell products 'hard' and to respond to questions honestly, if necessary going to the product information manual. The company does not advertise, relying instead on PR and their prime-site shop windows that often promote environmental issues rather than products. The green shop decor with its ambience of a sweet shop reinforces the environmental, no-frills image. Staff receive regular training, not only on business but also on environmental issues. They are encouraged to work in the community, on company time.

Unlike other cosmetics companies, Body Shop is selling a feel-good factor with a strong ethical dimension. It campaigns on behalf of many environmental causes such as the destruction of the Brazilian rain forests, 'trade not aid', recycling and, famously, animal testing of cosmetics. The Body Shop brand is deeply emotional, based upon a marketing mix that reinforces the 'save the planet' image and really does 'make the heart sing'.

Questions
1 Why has Body Shop been so successful?
2 Which strategic decisions contributed most to the successful initial roll-out of Body Shop? Why were they correct?
3 Why did the company make the decision to stop distribution and manufacturing?
4 What are the dangers of having the brand so linked to the entrepreneur?

Whether it is possible to charge a higher price like **GHD** depends on the elasticity of demand which in turn depends, in part, on the uniqueness of the product or service. There are considerable benefits to being able to charge a higher price and, for many firms, small increases can more than compensate for relatively large reductions in the volume of sales. In setting price, information on the variable and average cost of production is relevant, but there will be a going rate that is influenced by the value to the customer and the price charged by competitors. Ultimately however, for any product or service, there will be a price that is too low for credibility and one that is too high. **Back Stretcher** had to engineer its costs so as to be able to pitch the product at a price customers were willing to pay, no matter how unique it was. Variations in pricing strategy at start-up might include skimming or penetration, depending on product-market characteristics.

Differentiation is about being different or distinctive in some way. As with **Carphone Warehouse**, it does not necessarily involve innovation but can be made up from a myriad of small distinguishing features. Differentiation is helped by clear, effective branding – like **Cobra Beer** and **Body Shop**. Differentiation can be safeguarded by patents, design registrations and copyrights. A brand should be the embodiment of the product or service offering to the customer. A good brand can help turn prospects into customers and move customers up the loyalty ladder. It helps a business secure differential advantage.

Customer focus involves breaking markets down into segments that have similar characteristics or needs. For a start-up this allows resources to be focused on segments where there is the highest possibility of making a sale. It can also lead to niche positioning, which can be very profitable. The slimmer the market segment, the easier it is to defend against competition, but slim segments carry the danger that customers' tastes might change and the market disappears. **Unicorn Inns** demonstrates how a slightly different marketing mix can be applied to each market segment.

As we saw with **Radio Spirits Inc**, there are many different market segments and there is no prescriptive way of segmenting a market. It requires creative insight into customers' buying habits as well as an understanding of the unique benefits offered by the product or service. If you want to be entrepreneurial in your approach to marketing you need to understand what the conventions are in your market place and try do things differently if you have the capabilities, an approach that helped **Daewoo** despite an undistinguished product.

Market research is important for a start-up. It minimises risk and uncertainty and provides information on which to build a marketing strategy. The key question to be answered is why someone should buy from you rather than from competitors. As we saw with **Blavod**, the range of information needed can vary enormously. There are two approaches to getting information; field research and desk research. Field research involves discussions and interviews. It might use postal questionnaires or telephone surveys. It might involve simple observation. Desk research involves getting published information from a variety of sources. It is quick and cheap and can provide invaluable background information. It helped **Euravia Engineering** decide on the location for the business.

Many start-ups do not undertake formal market research – a risk that **Stephen Hemsley**, founder of **Domino's Pizza**, is unwilling to take. They treat the launch as market research, constantly reviewing customer reaction. However, if things go wrong this can be an expensive form of research.

The ability to sell is important at start-up. Selling is about matching the benefits of the product or service to the needs of customers and then convincing them to buy. As with **Goldsmith's Fine Foods**, the benefits customers are looking for are not always obvious, but the sales role is important in finding out what they are. Over time the salesperson can build a relationship of trust and respect that can lead to new customer networks being developed. Selling skills can be developed with practice. There are ways to start a sales interview; there are sales aids that can be used in the interview itself. There are techniques to handle objections and to help close a sale.

The internet offers new opportunities for innovative businesses – such as **eBay** – and new routes to a global market for small firms generally. It increases competitive pressures and emphasises the need to understand what you are selling, to whom and why your customers continue to buy from you.

There are sole traders, partnerships and limited liability companies. Sole traders are easy and quick to set up but, if the business is to grow, it is probably best to form it into a limited company sooner rather than later. Franchise is a popular, low-risk way of setting up in business using the ideas, expertise and systems of an established organisation like **Body Shop**.

Essays and discussion topics

1 Are customers logical?
2 Why are people willing to pay quite high prices for bottled water?
3 Why do owner-managers prefer interactive or personal marketing?
4 Why is it said that the three most important elements of the marketing mix for a retail business are location, location and location?
5 Advertising is the most expensive way of one person talking to another. Discuss.
6 What is marketing?
7 What is the difference between marketing and selling?
8 Why is marketing important?
9 Costs determine prices. Discuss.
10 Is there really a limit to the price you can charge for a product or service?
11 Can you really sell less and make more profit?
12 How can you charge different prices for the same product or service?
13 How different does a product or service have to be to mean that you are following a strategy of differentiation?
14 Every product or service is different. Discuss.
15 Why is branding so important?
16 Is creating a brand easier or more difficult for a small firm?
17 What makes a good brand?
18 Is Carphone Warehouse really different from other shops selling mobile phones? If so, how? If not, why not? Does it matter?
19 We spent most of the twentieth century creating mass markets and will spend most of the twenty-first breaking them down. Discuss.
20 Is market segmentation an art or a science?
21 Is market research worthwhile?
22 Do most small firms set about market positioning in a haphazard sort of way with the result that success or failure is really just luck?

23 Business is 90% perspiration and 10% inspiration. Discuss.

24 If you think knowledge is expensive, try ignorance. Discuss.

25 How do you go about undertaking market research prior to starting a business?

26 How do you find out who your customers might actually be?

27 Describe some sorts of customers that might not be interested in the service that Goldsmith's Fine Foods provides. What elements of the marketing mix might they be more interested in?

28 Selling is not an honourable profession. Discuss.

29 What are the advantages and disadvantages of being a small supplier to a large assembler linked through a fully integrated supply chain?

30 What are the particular problems facing a small firm wanting to sell on the internet and how might they be overcome?

31 What are the particular problems facing a purely internet start-up and how might they be overcome?

32 Are there any good business opportunities left using the internet?

33 Why are franchises an attractive business opportunity?

34 What is the best legal form of business?

Exercises and assignments

1 Select five products or services. List their features and translate these into benefits for the customer. Alongside this list any proof that might be needed to convince the customer that the benefit is real.

2 Place the five products or services in each of the four boxes of Porter's Generic Marketing Strategies. Explain why you place them where you do.

3 Select one product or service and write up its history – how it got to be where it is, what strategies the firm followed and how competitors reacted.

4 If a company has fixed costs of £160 000 and sells only one product at £25, with a variable cost of £17, calculate its break-even point. If the same company introduces a second product to increase sales above the break-even point and achieves total sales in this year of £960 000 against total variable costs of £720 000, calculate the new break-even point. Fixed costs remain unchanged. Calculate the profits it makes at this level of sales. Why has the break-even point changed? Is the change good or bad?

5 List as many generic ways to differentiate a product or service as you can think of. Alongside them jot down what you need to do to sustain these differences.

6 Develop a market research questionnaire to find out what benefits existing customers of a health club are looking for from their membership.

7 Develop a market research plan to evaluate the commercial potential of opening a shop selling sportswear in a small market town.

8 Select a product or service from Exercise 1. Team up with two other students, one as a customer, another as an observer. Conduct a role-playing sales interview with the customer lasting 15 minutes. Make certain each of you understands the role you are playing. Plan your interview using the outline contained in this chapter. When it is finished, get the observer to give you feedback on how you performed.

References

Bayus, B.L. (1985) 'Word-of-Mouth: The Indirect Effects of Marketing Efforts', *Journal of Advertising Research*, 25(3), June/July.

Brady, G. (1999) 'New Rules for Start-ups', *e-business*, December.

Carson, D., Cromie, S., McGowan, P. and Hill, J. (1995) *Marketing and Entrepreneurship in SMEs*, London: Prentice Hall.

Chaston, I. (2000) *Entrepreneurial Marketing: Competing by Challenging Convention*, Basingstoke: Macmillan – now Palgrave-Macmillan.

Dalgic, T. and Leeuw, M. (1994) 'Niche Marketing Revisited: Concept, Applications and Some European Cases', *European Journal of Marketing*, 20(1).

Ratnatunga, J.T.D. (1983) *Financial Controls in Marketing: The Accounting–Marketing Interface*, Canberra College of Advanced Education, Canberra.

Stokes, D. (1998) *Small Business Management: A Case Study Approach*, London: Letts Educational.

Stokes, D., Blackburn, R. and Fitchew, S. (1997) *Marketing for Small Firms: Towards a Conceptual Framework*, Report to Royal Mail Consulting, Small Business Research Centre, Kingston University, July.

Webster, J.E. (1992) 'The Changing Role of Marketing in the Corporation', *Journal of Marketing*, 56, October.

Answers to exercises and assignments

$$4 \quad \text{Contribution margin 1} \quad = \frac{£(25-17)}{£25} \quad = 0.32$$

$$\text{Break-even 1} \quad = \frac{£160\,000}{0.32} \quad = £500\,000$$

$$\text{Contribution margin 2} \quad = \frac{£(960\,000 - £720\,000)}{£960\,000} \quad = 0.25$$

$$\text{Break-even 2} \quad = \frac{£160\,000}{0.25} \quad = £640\,000$$

$$\text{Profit 2} \quad = £(960\,000 - 640\,000) \times 0.25 = £80\,000$$

Break-even point has moved up, which makes the firm more risky. On the other hand it is now making a profit of £80 000 which it was not before. If it could have made sales of £960 000 from the original product alone, it would have been better off.

7

Control and Decision-making

Contents

LEARNING OUTCOMES

By the end of this chapter you should be able to:

- Explain the difference between profit and cash flow;

- Draw up a cash flow forecast;

- Describe the information conveyed in a profit statement and balance sheet;

- Draw up a profit statement;

- Identify and explain why the key financial drivers of a business are important;

- Record the financial information needed to effectively control a small firm;

- Use profit–cost–volume information for decision-making;

- Recognise the need for a start-up to minimise its fixed overhead costs and maximise its contribution margin.

Cash flow and Death Valley

Cash flow is the lifeblood of a business; it pays the bills and the wages, but most small firms are short of it. A start-up may spend cash on premises, equipment, stock and so on even before the first customer walks through the door. Even that first sale might be on credit and it can take time before debts are collected. During this time the business will have a negative cash flow. It is called the Death Valley Curve and is shown in Figure 7.1. The depth of Death Valley depends on how much you need to invest in premises, equipment and stocks. The length and depth of Death Valley varies from firm to firm and industry to industry. The length can be affected by the trading cycle – how long it takes to turn £1 of investment into £1 (hopefully more) of cash from sales. It is affected by the time it takes to get a product or service to the market place – a long time for a new drug, less than 24 hours for some market traders.

Be warned – many firms do survive to come through to the other end of Death Valley, so you need to plot its course. Just about every firm that fails runs out of cash but to do so at the *start* of a new venture – one that might be very successful – just because you have not planned for this very predictable challenge is just plain stupid.

Death Valley may not be a problem if you have sufficient capital – your own or borrowed – so that you can trade all that time when no cash is coming in. But you need to map out Death Valley to see what you face. Work out its depth – how much cash is needed – and its length – how long you will need the cash. Death Valley might be deeper and longer than you expect. Indeed if you get some unexpected orders and sales really take off, Death Valley could get longer or deeper, or both because you need to buy and pay for extra stocks, perhaps even hire extra staff to cope with the demand – all before the cash starts rolling in.

The way to chart a path through Death Valley is by preparing a *cash flow forecast* which lists the estimated cash receipts and payments of the business. This can be done on a daily, a weekly or, more normally, a monthly basis. The total cash receipts minus the cash payments in any period is called cash flow. In Death Valley cash flow is negative. Cash flow is added to (or, if negative, subtracted from) the balance at the end of the previous period to show the balance at the end of this period. If the balance

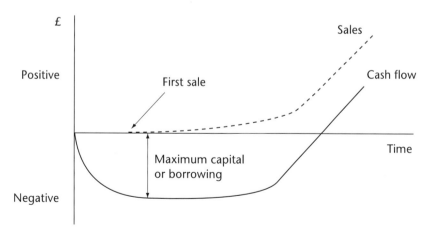

Figure 7.1 The Death Valley curve

is negative, you will need to seek external funds, possibly from a bank – and we shall explain how that can be done in a later chapter. For now, we shall concentrate on generating that vital piece of information – the cash flow forecast.

An example of a cash flow forecast is shown in Figure 7.2 using a pro forma cash flow worksheet. Jean Young is a start-up sole trader offering consultancy and training to the health sector. She is working from home, so her overheads are low. She also has a working husband so they have agreed that she does not have to withdraw cash from the business until March. Below are her best estimates of what the business will face during its first year of trading.

1 Sales estimates are the key to any business plan. In most cases sales at start-up are overestimated. It takes longer for a start-up to gain customers than the owner-manager usually appreciates. In this case, however, Jean Young plans a modest build-up of her training days, selling only one day at £400 in November. This she will invoice (+ VAT) immediately and she assumes the invoice will be paid one month later, which are her normal terms of trade.
2 £2000 is the capital introduced to pay for the capital purchases (see below).
3 The VAT reclaim of £299 relates to the capital expenditure on computer equipment (£1701 plus VAT @ 17.5%).
4 Expenditures are estimated cash payments in appropriate months. Capital purchases are a printer, software and other expenditure (including £299 VAT).
5 In the UK VAT is usually payable on invoiced sales only. It is paid to HM Revenue and Customs on a quarterly basis in the month indicated. VAT reclaimable has not been estimated (except for capital purchases) as it is unlikely to be large and would be complicated to calculate. *In fact, Jean Young's turnover is sufficiently low to mean that she does not have to register for VAT.*

Because of the low level of overheads, Jean Young only has a negative cash flow in November and then in March as a result of her starting to take drawings out of the business. If she were to take an economic wage from the business from start-up, Death Valley would be much longer. A comprehensive and more complex example of a cash flow and profit forecast for an existing business is included in the appendix to Chapter 11.

The profit statement

It is important to realise that profit is not the same as cash. Profit is the difference between sales and costs or unit selling price and unit cost. It tells you how all the assets of a business have grown (or shrunk) through trading. You can make a profit but have no cash, for example because the person who has bought the good or service has not yet paid for it. It is true that eventually the profit should turn into cash, but meanwhile bills and wages need to be paid, and if you do not have the cash to pay them you may go out of business. Figure 7.3 shows how profit is made and, at the same time, money flows around the business. Start at the top, at 1, and work through the diagram in the sequence detailed below.

1 A business starting up needs to find capital in the form of cash. This could be a sole trader's own money or, for a company, shareholders contributing share capital, both perhaps supplemented by bank borrowings.

Month:	Nov	Dec	Jan	Feb	Mar	April	May	June	July	Aug	Sept	Oct	Total
SALES													
Volume: days	1	1	2	2	3	4	5	5	5	5	5	5	43
Value:	400	400	800	800	1200	1600	2000	2000	2000	2000	2000	2000	17200
RECEIPTS													
Sales – cash													
Sales -debtors +VAT		470	470	940	940	1410	1880	2350	2350	2350	2350	2350	17860
Capital introduced	2000												2000
Grants, loans and so on.													
VAT on cap.ex		299											299
TOTAL (A)	2000	769	470	940	940	1410	1880	2350	2350	2350	2350	2350	20159
PAYMENTS													
Materials													
Wages/salaries Sec	10	120	20	20	20	20	20	20	20	20	20	20	330
Rent													
Heat/light/power													
Advertising													
Insurance		100											100
Travel – Petrol	10	10	20	20	30	40	50	50	50	50	50	50	430
Telephone	120			100			100			100			420
Stationery/postage	130	40	40	40	40	40	40	40	40	40	40	40	570
Repairs/renewals		200						150					350
Local taxes													
Other Prof. fees	50										125		175
Other		10	10	10	10	10	10	10	10	10	10	10	110
Capital purchases	2000												2000
Loan repayments													
Drawings/dividends					820	850	970	860	730	770	875	785	6660
VAT on purchases													
VAT paid to C&E		70			350			840			1050		2310
TOTAL (B)	2320	550	90	190	1270	960	1190	1970	850	990	2045	1030	13455
CASH BALANCES													
Cash flow (A) – (B)	(320)	219	380	750	(330)	450	690	380	1500	1360	305	1320	
Opening balance	–	(320)	(101)	279	1029	699	1149	1839	2219	3719	5079	5384	
Closing balance	(320)	(101)	279	1029	699	1149	1839	2219	3719	5079	5384	6704	6704

Figure 7.2 Cash flow forecast for Jean Young

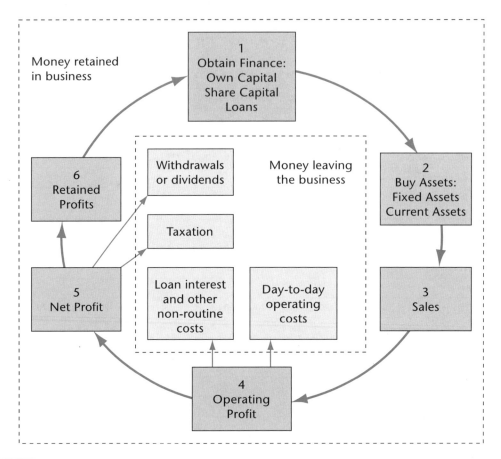

Figure 7.3   The flow of money

2   This is now invested in assets to be used in the business. The assets will comprise long-term or fixed assets such as plant and machinery, office equipment, computers, vehicle and so on, and assets for use on a day-to-day basis. These will also include stocks of goods for resale, stocks of consumables to be used in the office, and, of course, cash to pay the bills. These are usually called current assets. The cash has now turned into other assets, but all these funds are still retained in the business.

3   The assets are then used to generate sales. Goods are resold, services are rendered. This is the first stage on the way to making profits.

4   Of course, making sales is not enough to guarantee profits. Sales might be high, but if day-to-day business costs are higher, then a loss rather than a profit will emerge. So there is a need for management to control day-to-day costs and produce an operating profit. Other non-operating costs, such as loan interest, might also have to be deducted.

5   The result is net profit. This is still not, necessarily, cash since customers might owe you money or you might not have paid all your bills. However, it does represent an increase in the total assets – or funds – of the business. If the business

is established as a sole trader, money may now be withdrawn. If the business is a limited company, corporation tax is deducted, and then dividends may be paid to shareholders. Sole traders pay income tax on the profits of the business and shareholders pay income tax on their dividends.

6 The balance of retained profits represents another injection of capital into the business. However, this capital is not, necessarily, cash. This is important as any business will need a constant flow of capital to replace existing assets which are used up and/or to expand or grow. As we know, many small firms prefer to finance their expansion using their own money rather than borrowing or giving equity away.

Successful businesses sell their goods or services for more than they cost to produce, so this flow of finance will continually increase. However, the hidden ingredient in this is time. By speeding up the flow of funds you can decrease the amount of capital you need – or simply take more out of the business.

The key to this is debtors and creditors. Debtors are those customers that owe you money because they have not paid immediately and creditors are those suppliers that you owe money to. By getting debtors to pay quickly you speed up the flow of funds. You can speed up the collection of debts by:

• Choosing customers carefully to start with and invoicing them immediately upon sale. In choosing credit customers always ask for, and check up on, trade references, ask for a bank reference, make credit checks with other suppliers, check any published information (such as accounts) about the customer and, if possible, visit their premises.

• Setting appropriate credit limits and making payment terms clear. Once the customer's references are checked they can be set a credit ceiling that must be kept. This minimises exposure to any bad debts. Bad debts are expensive. If you are making a 20 per cent margin, you need to increase sales by £4 to recover each £1 of bad debt.

• Taking the right measures to speed up payments. These include sending statements, following up outstanding debts by telephone – it could be there is a problem with the delivery or the cheque has gone astray, offering discounts for prompt payment or charging interest on overdue accounts, withholding supplies, threatening to reclaim your goods, taking legal action or using debt collectors when all else fails.

By getting creditors to wait for payment you also speed up the flow because you have the use of their money. But you must always handle creditors carefully because, if you get a reputation for late payment, you may find it difficult to get credit at all. If you make an arrangement, then stick to it. Always try to agree good terms at the beginning, try for part payment of large orders or buy in small quantities, do not pay early and, if in trouble, keep talking to your creditors – silence is often taken as a sure sign of bad news.

It is one thing to realise that profit is not the same as cash flow, but it is altogether more difficult to reconcile the two figures. Let us go back to the example of Jean Young. At the end of October she projected a healthy £6804 would be in her bank account. Her projected profit statement, reproduced from the previous chapter, looked like this:

Sales		£17 200
Overheads:		
Depreciation	£2667	
Secretarial wage	330	
Transport	430	
Telephone	450	
Stationery	570	
Repairs	350	
Other	285	
Insurance	100	£ 5 182
Net Profit		£12 018
Drawings		£ 6 660
Profit retained in business		£ 5 358

The question therefore is, what this profit retained in the business represents and how it reconciles to the increase in cash of £6704. The reconciliation is shown below.

Profit statement		Cash flow		Reconciling items		Note
INCOME:		RECEIPTS:				
Sales	£17 200	Paid	£15 200	Debtor outstanding	£2 000	1
		+ VAT	£2 660	+ VAT outstanding	£350	
		Total	£17 860	Total	£2 350	
		Capital	£2 000	Capital	£2 000	2
		VAT reclaim	£299	VAT reclaim	£299	5
		Total	£20 159			
EXPENSES:		PAYMENTS:				
Sec. wage	£330	Sec. wage	£330			
Transport	£430	Transport	£430			
Telephone	£450	Telephone	£420	Tel. bill outstanding	£30	4
Stationery	£570	Stationery	£570			
Repairs	£350	Repairs	£350			
Other	£285	Other	£285			
Insurance	£100	Insurance	£100			
Depreciation	£2 667			Depreciation	£2 667	3
		Capital purch.	£2 000	Capital purchase	£2 000	3
		VAT paid	£2 310	VAT paid	£2 310	5
Drawings	£6 660	Drawings	£6 660			
Total	£11 842	Total	£13 455			
Retained	£5 358	Cash	£6 704			

Notes:

1 Jean has not received payment for all the work she has done. The outstanding debtor – a current asset of the business – is the sale invoiced in October but not expected to be paid until November. The invoice is for £2000 + £350 VAT.

2 Jean introduced capital in the form of cash of £2000. This is not part of the trading profit of the business.

3 The fixed assets of a business wear out over time and lose their value. Depreciation is a way of showing this in the profit statement. The simplest way of doing this is called 'straight-line depreciation' which writes off the asset in equal amounts over its life. For example, if there was an asset that cost £5000 and would have a working life of 5 years, at which time it could be sold off for £1000, the annual depreciation would be:

$$\frac{\text{Initial cost} - \text{final or residual value}}{\text{Working life}}$$
$$= \frac{£(5000 - 1000)}{5}$$
$$= £800$$

The value of the asset would go down each year by £800. At the end of year one it would have a value of £4200, year two £3400 and so on, until year five when it would be £1000. Depreciation does not represent any cash expenditure. That takes place when the asset is purchased. In Jean's case the depreciation is on her car and computer equipment and the actual calculation is not shown. However, the computer equipment was purchased with the £2000 she put into the business (£1701 + £299 VAT).

4 The telephone charges outstanding are an estimate of the call charges for September and October that have not yet been invoiced or paid, but are nevertheless a liability of the business. These are called accrued liabilities.

5 VAT can be complicated. A business collects it on behalf of HM Revenue and Customs and it is therefore not part of the trading income of the business. However, it may deduct from the amount collected any VAT that it pays to suppliers, paying over only the net amount. VAT does therefore affect cash flows. Jean Young can reclaim £299 of VAT on the capital purchases. VAT is charged to customers on her sales of £17 200 is £3010 (£17 200 × 17.5%). It is, if you like, her problem that she has so far only collected £2660 leaving £350 owing still from customers. Since she has only paid £2310 to the Customs and Excise Authorities, she still owes them £700 (£3010 − £2310).

The profit statement, therefore, can tell you how the assets of the business are growing through trading. As we have seen it does not tell you about cash. It is not an exact figure since it involves elements of judgement, for example in the calculation of depreciation or an accrued liability. However, there are some other things it does not do. It does not tell you about the profitability of individual product lines. Nor does it tell you, on its own, how well you are doing. If you make a profit of £50 000 from a capital investment of £2.5 million you are making a return of only 2 per cent (£50 000 ÷ £2 500 000) and would be better off putting your money in a building society. It does not tell you about capital investment – for that you have to go to the balance sheet.

The balance sheet

The balance sheet is a snapshot at a point in time that shows two things:

- Where the money in a business is invested;
- Where this money came from.

Money initially comes from the capital the owner puts in (called share capital, if it is a limited company) and loans. It is increased by the profits that are retained in the business. This money is invested in the assets of the business – fixed assets; things the business means to keep such as vehicles, machinery and so on, and working capital; things the business means to sell or turn over. Working capital comprises current assets such as stock, debtors or cash less current liabilities such as creditors and accrued expenses. In other words, the balance sheet gives details of all the money retained in the business as shown in Figure 7.3.

There are two sides to a balance sheet and they always balance. If £1000 were put into a business as cash the balance sheet would balance:

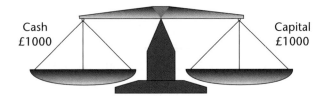

This would be shown as:

Where money is invested:	Cash	£1000
Where it came from:	Capital introduced	£1000

If £500 of this is spent on machinery and £500 on stock the balance sheet would not change much:

Machinery	£ 500
Stock	£ 500
	£1000
Capital introduced	£1000

Only when the business starts trading do additional funds start to be generated in the form of profit as you can see from Figure 7.3; if the stock were to be sold for cash of £1000, a profit of £500 would be made and the balance sheet would still balance:

Machinery	£500
Cash	£1000
	£1500
Capital introduced	£1000
Retained profit	£ 500
	£1500

If the balance sheet does not balance then either assets are missing or there is an arithmetical mistake.

To see how a balance sheet is constructed let us turn back to the case of Jean Young. If we were told that her car was valued at £12 130 (excluding VAT) and the computer equipment £1504 at the start of the year (both of which she introduced to the business), and that together with the other equipment she purchased for £1701 these were expected to last five years at which point only the car would have a residual value of £2000, then her depreciation charge would be:

$$\frac{(£12\,130 + £1504 + £1701) - £2000}{5} = £2667$$

And these fixed assets at the end of the year would have a value of:

$$(£12\,130 + £1504 + £1701) - £2667 = £12\,668$$

From this and the information in the previous section we could draw up her balance sheet as a sole trader at the end of October:

Fixed assets			
Car			£12 130
Computer and other equipment			3 205
			£15 335
less: Depreciation			2 667
			£12 668
Current assets			
Debtors		£2 350	
Cash		6 704	
		£9 054	
less: **Current liabilities**			
VAT	£700		
Telephone	30		
	£730		
Net current assets			£ 8 324
Total assets			£20 992
Represented by:			
Capital introduced			
Cash			£ 2 000
Other assets			£13 634
			£15 634
Net profit for year			£12 018
less: Drawings			£ 6 660
Total capital			£20 992

As with profit statements, you can have projected balance sheets or historic balance sheets – ones that explain what actually happened. A start-up will prepare projected cash flows and profit statements, possibly balance sheets. Once the business starts running it needs to monitor how it is doing against these projections to make certain things are going as planned. Historic profit statements and balance sheets are derived from the books of account that are used to control a business. The appendix to this chapter explains what information a business needs to keep and shows how it can be recorded.

Financial drivers

Accounting systems can provide enormous amounts of information, including full profit statements, balance sheets and details of outstanding debtors, creditors and stock-holding levels. Sometimes they produce so much information that owner-managers cannot cope and prefer to ignore it. In fact, most small firms can be controlled by monitoring, on a timely basis, just six pieces of information that tell the owner-manager different, but vital information on the performance of the business. These are called the financial drivers of small firms. They are like the instruments on a car dashboard. They tell you different things about the engine and different pieces of information are important at different times and in different circumstances. On a road with a speed restriction you watch your speedometer. When changing gear at speed you watch your rev-meter. When low on petrol your eye never strays from the petrol gauge. The financial drivers tell you all you need to know about driving the business. The six financial drivers are:

1 Cash

As we have already seen, it is vital to monitor cash. Without cash the bills cannot be paid. For a start-up or when it is in short supply cash may have to be monitored on a daily basis, but most small firms need to keep an eye on it at least on a weekly basis. Actual balances need to be compared to forecasts.

2 Sales

This tells the firm about the volume of activity it is experiencing. This should also be compared to forecasts. If sales are running ahead of forecasts, does the firm have the resources to meet these demands? Current sales may be a good indicator of future sales, but if not, then order books may also have to be monitored. It is sales that always drive cash flow and profitability. It should be monitored on a daily or weekly basis for most start-ups and at least monthly even for an established business.

3 Profit margins

In the process of setting prices in line with projected costs, the owner-manager will also be setting profit targets. These can only be achieved if the sales volume targets are met, at the appropriate prices, and costs are controlled. Profit margins give the owner manager this information. They should be compared to original forecasts and kept as high as possible. Margins probably need only be monitored on a monthly basis. It might be that it is sufficient simply to monitor contribution margin. This would be the case if fixed overheads are unlikely to change dramatically or quickly. In the example of Jean Young, there are no variable costs and in this case it is therefore more appropriate to monitor net profit margins. The net profit margin is net profit expressed as a percentage of total sales. In the previous example of Jean Young this is:

$$\frac{\text{Net profit} \times 100}{\text{Sales}} : \quad \frac{12\,018 \times 100}{17\,200} = 70\%$$

4 Margin of safety or break-even

Break-even is an important reference point and we shall be looking at this important concept in more detail in the next section. However, as a business grows the break-even point is likely to increase. That is a fact of business. In order to grow most businesses must, at some point, take on more fixed overheads. This increases the break-even point. What is important is not so much the absolute level, but rather how much above it the firm is operating. The margin of safety is a measure of how far sales are above break-even, expressed as a percentage of total sales. In the example of Jean Young, because she has no variable costs, this happens to be the same as the net profit margin and is:

$$\frac{(\text{Total sales} - \text{Break-even sales}) \times 100}{\text{Total sales}} : \quad \frac{(17\,200 - 5182) \times 100}{17\,200} = 70\%$$

The higher the margin of safety the better, because the safer the firm is in terms of maintaining its profitability should sales suddenly decline. Margin of safety is therefore a measure of operating risk. However, it reflects a number of factors; level of sales, ability to maintain contribution margins and ability to control fixed overheads. It is therefore a powerful piece of information and needs to be checked monthly.

The margin of safety is of great interest to bank managers. If you started up in business manufacturing, say, umbrellas and anticipate sales reaching 2000 per month shortly after the factory opens, at this level of sales your margin of safety will be 10 per cent. A bank would be worried about granting a loan with such a small margin of safety. They know from bitter experience that sales forecasts, particularly for new ventures, are notoriously unreliable. On a risky lending proposition most bank managers would be looking for a margin of safety of at least 50 per cent. However, be aware that if sales were actually to start falling and the company approached its break-even point, prudent businessmen would try to cut their fixed costs – particularly discretionary ones that they control – and thus reduce the break-even point and perhaps restore the margin of safety. In other words the break-even point, and therefore the margin of safety, are not set in concrete, they can be engineered to minimise the risks.

5 Productivity

For most firms the single largest and most important expense they face is their wage costs. It therefore needs to be controlled carefully. However, as with break-even, as a firm grows its wage costs are likely to increase. Wages are therefore best measured in relation to the productivity that they generate. For many firms this is most easily measured by the simple percentage of wages to sales. Often there are industry norms that can be used to measure productivity. For example, in the licensed trade the benchmark for this is 20 per cent. Wages of bar staff should be about 20 per cent of sales. If higher, the pub is over-staffed, if lower, it is under-staffed – a crude but simple and effective measure that needs to be checked weekly or monthly.

6 Debtor or stock turnover

Similarly most firms will have one important current asset on their balance sheet that represents over 50 per cent of their total assets. For a service business this will be debtors. For a retail business it will be stocks. For a manufacturing business it could be both. This asset needs to be monitored on a monthly basis. However, as with previous figures, as the firm grows it is likely to increase, so what is important is not its absolute size but rather its relationship to the level of activity or sales of a business. Two statistics are widely used:

1 Debtor turnover: $\dfrac{\text{Sales}}{\text{Debtors}}$

If sales were £120 000 per year and debtors stood at £20 000, debtor turnover would be 6. This means debtors turnover six times a year. In other words, debtors pay after every 2 months. This can be compared to the plan, the terms of trade and the industry norm to judge whether debtors are being controlled effectively. If they are not, the firm will be having problems with its cash flow.

Case insight

Chris Hutt believed that rigorous, centrally applied financial controls were the key to profitable operation at **Unicorn Inns**. He appointed Geoff Jones, aged 30, as Finance Director in 1993 on a part-time basis to provide the Board with in-house financial management skills. As part of Chris's emphasis on control, the company ensures:

- Daily checks on cash takings and bankings, carried out by telephone and direct computer input to the company's bank account.
- Weekly sales and profit performance measured within 16 hours of each week ending. Results are reviewed immediately by management and priorities for action identified.
- Weekly stocktaking to ensure there were no stock losses and gross margin targets were attained.
- Labour costs, as a percentage of sales, monitored through monthly management accounts, mailed to all affected parties no later than 10 working days after each period.

All of these factors were linked to targets set for each pub manager and tied into their bonus scheme.

Chris believed that two of the key pieces of financial information any growing business needs to monitor are the break-even point and the margin of safety. He monitored this data monthly and above his desk he kept a graph showing sales against break-even point. (The difference between the two is the margin of safety.) It makes interesting reading, showing the gradual improvement in the margin of safety because of the high margins and low fixed costs as Unicorn Inns rolled out the Newt & Cucumber concept.

→

2 Stock turnover: $\dfrac{\text{Sales}}{\text{Stocks}}$

If sales were £120 000 and stocks stood at £30 000, stock turnover would be 4, meaning that stock turns over four times a year, equivalent to every 3 months. This can be compared to the plan and the industry norm to judge whether stock is being controlled effectively. If not, the firm is likely to be having problems with its cash flow.

It is important for a growing firm to have appropriate and relevant financial information that can be produced promptly and on a timely basis, at an acceptable cost. The financial drivers give the owner-manager simple, understandable information. They can be reproduced on a single piece of paper. They provide the headline information on how the business is doing. If they disclose a problem then more information might be needed to decide on the appropriate course of action. For example, if debtors are not being controlled effectively only a detailed list of debtors and when the amounts owing were due for payment (called an *aged listing of debtors*) will provide the information needed so that action can be taken.

Break-even

Figure 7.4 reproduces the familiar **cost–profit–volume** chart introduced in the last chapter. However, the simplified **profit–volume** chart in Figure 7.5 is far easier to interpret and use and emphasises the two most important financial principles of start-up:

1 **Keep fixed overheads as low as possible**. The lower the fixed cost AB, the lower the break-even point and therefore the lower the risk. If fixed costs AB can be reduced, line AC moves parallel and to the left in Figure 7.5 – and therefore the risk is lower. High fixed operating costs are called high *operating gearing* or *leverage*. One way of measuring this is as the proportion of total costs represented by fixed

Case insight

David Speakman is a serial entrepreneur. But when his second business, a restaurant, failed losing him £500 000 he decided to list the prime attributes of the ideal business. He wrote: 'no fixed labour costs, commission only sales, large volume and low overheads'.

He was already running a small travel agency with a turnover of £548 000, but the experience of failure decided him to re-jig it. The result was **Travel Counsellors**, started in 1994. The firm has a small head office handling marketing, billing and supplies. However, it relies mainly on some travelling counsellors equipped with portable computers and mobile phones who visit customers' homes mapping out itineraries, online counsellors working from their own homes, fielding telephone and Teletext enquiries and arranging visits to customers.

The idea proved to be both successful and profitable. By 2004 turnover topped £128 million. But with 540 counsellors and only 100 staff in the head office in Bolton, Lancashire, the emphasis was still very much on keeping fixed costs as low as possible.

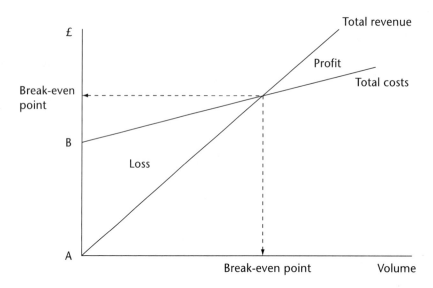

Figure 7.4 Cost–profit–volume chart

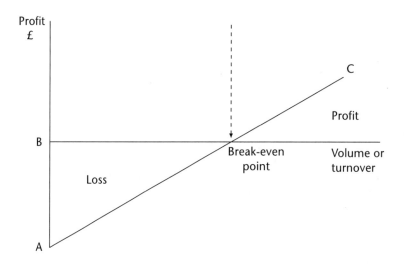

Figure 7.5 Profit–volume chart

overhead costs. This percentage should be kept as low as possible, particularly at start-up. Remember, higher fixed assets also mean higher depreciation charges and therefore higher fixed overheads. Investment in fixed assets can therefore increase a business's break-even point.

High borrowings – perhaps to finance investment in fixed assets – mean high interest costs, which are fixed and over which there is little discretion. If turnover goes down, interest payments stay the same. Indeed, sometimes interest rates, and therefore interest payments, can go up when turnover and therefore profit goes down. This is the classic situation that happens when interest rates go up in order

Case insight

Flitwick Manor Hotel is a country house hotel in Bedfordshire. With a turnover of £922 000 per annum, it has high fixed costs of £426 000, of which 34 per cent represents permanent staff and 20 per cent loan interest; 82 per cent of its variable costs represents consumables such as food and wine. It lets out rooms and sells food and drink and therefore the average contribution margin can be used to calculate its break-even point:

Turnover (ex VAT)	£922 000	
Total variable cost	£326 000	
Contribution	£596 000	64%
Fixed costs	£426 000	
Profit	£170 000	

$$\text{Break-even} \quad \frac{£426\,000}{0.64} = £666\,000$$

Margin of safety = 27.8%

With the high fixed costs and high contribution margin it is important that Flitwick keeps its beds and restaurant full. It therefore spends heavily on promotion. It also has a luncheon club, offering cheap lunches to regular customers, who also receive regular promotions from the hotel.

●

to decrease overall demand in the economy. The small firm faces a squeeze with higher costs and lower turnover. High financing costs are called high *financial gearing* or *leverage*.

Businesses with high operating or financial gearing (or both) need to make certain they achieve their sales targets. They have very little day-to-day influence over their fixed costs so their business imperative is to attract a sufficient volume of customers – and that is about marketing and sales. They can afford to offer special price deals if their margins are high, so as to attract different market segments at different prices. For example, running a train from London to Manchester incurs mainly fixed costs and the train operator must fill the train as full as possible. The company does this by offering a range of fares with all sorts of different terms and conditions or facilities to a range of different customers. In that way a business man might pay eight times as much as the off-peak student traveller on the same train and yet not feel that he is getting a bad deal.

As we saw in the previous chapter, the lowest price at which a product or service can be offered is its variable cost. Above this every £1 is extra contribution to fixed costs or, if the business is operating above its break-even point, extra profit. If, in addition to high fixed costs, a firm faces low variable costs, then it is able to offer its product or service at a very low price in order to attract marginal business – extra business it would not otherwise have. So, for example, our railway company may offer a £1 special offer fare, possibly linked to other conditions or purchases, and would still make £1 extra profit. The only problem with this is that, unless you are able to make this product or service sufficiently different from the normal product or service you offer, all your regular customers might be attracted to it and sales might never be high enough to meet fixed costs.

Marginal business can be very attractive, particularly to businesses with high fixed costs, such as railways, airlines and hotels. The railway has to run its trains to a predetermined timetable and so the marginal cost of an extra passenger is very, very low – hence all the special schemes and discounts to encourage people to travel on the off-peak services. Standby tickets for air flights are a similar case, as are weekend bargain breaks in hotels. The danger, of course, is that all the customers end up wanting cut-price fares and you end up not making a profit at all.

Case insight

As its name implies, **Penforth Sofa Beds** makes sofa beds. Selling to large retail outlets, its margins are squeezed and, despite low fixed costs of £102 000, it makes a contribution margin of only 17 per cent on a typical sofa bed.

Selling price (ex VAT)	£200	
Variable cost	£166	
Contribution	£ 34	17%
Break-even	$\dfrac{£102\,000}{0.17} = £600\,000$	

78 per cent of the variable costs represent materials and 12 per cent represent piecework labour. With this cost structure and because Penforth cannot influence the price it charges, it is vital that all variable costs are tightly controlled. Materials must be sourced from the lowest cost provider and labour costs kept down to a minimum.

➡

2 **Keep contribution margins as high as possible**. Do not sell just on price, find a differential advantage. Higher margins increase the angle of line AC, pivoting it in an anticlockwise direction about A, and lowering the break-even point. Once past the break-even point every £1 of sales revenue yields even higher profits. However, high contribution margins generally mean high differential advantage.

Businesses with low contribution margins cannot afford to cut their prices. What is more, their business imperative must be to control these high variable costs. For them, a 1 per cent reduction in the contribution margin can have disastrous effects on their profitability, so cost control and cost minimisation is a vital day-to-day activity for the owner-manager.

Decision-making

Break-even analysis is a powerful tool. As we have seen, it gives you the tools you need to make decisions about pricing and how the finances of a business should be structured. These are basic, important principles. However, it also gives you the tools to answer four other sorts of important business questions:

1 'How well is the business doing?' questions;
2 'What if?' questions;
3 'Which product or service is more profitable?' questions;
4 'Where should I focus limited resources?' questions.

How well is the business doing?

The break-even point is a benchmark above which the business starts to make a profit. But if you know the break-even point and the contribution margin, it is very easy to *estimate* the level of profitability – given the level of sales – without needing to resort to an accounting system. The formula to use is:

$$\text{Profit} = \frac{(\text{Sales} - \text{Break-even sales})}{\text{Contribution margin}}$$

So, we saw in the last chapter that, when Jean Young had sales of £17 200, her profit was £12 018. This can be calculated simply and quickly using the formula above:

$$\frac{(£17\,200 - £5182)}{1} = £12\,018$$

Similarly, if break-even were £500 a week and contribution margin were 40 per cent, at sales of £1500 the profit would be:

$$\frac{(£1500 - £500)}{0.40} = £400$$

What if?

The most asked question in business, particularly for a start-up, is 'what if?' What if I invest in a van? What if I place that expensive advertisement in the newspaper? Contribution analysis can help answer the question by giving information about the additional sales needed to make sufficient profit to recoup the cost. This may not make the decision about what to do, but it does provide invaluable information on which to base it. So, for example, if the advertisement costs £1000 and the contribution margin is 40 per cent, the extra sales needed would be £2500. This can be calculated using a simple formula:

$$\begin{aligned}
\text{Extra sales needed} &= \frac{\text{Increase in fixed costs}}{\text{Contribution margin}} \\
&= \frac{£1000}{0.40} \\
&= £2500
\end{aligned}$$

Contribution analysis can also be used to answer 'what if' questions about price. Suppose that a competitor to a business selling skateboards at £20 each starts price-cutting, selling equivalent boards at just £16. The problem is to decide whether to match the price reduction, or to seek a more profitable alternative strategy. Look at the calculation overleaf.

Case insight

Penforth Sofa Beds sold between 4000 and 5000 sofas a year, giving it a turnover of £800 000–£1 million and a profit of £34 000–£68 000. **John Douglas**, the owner-manager, was also the company salesman. He often thought about hiring another salesman. If he paid a basic salary of £15 000 with a 5% commission, to justify hiring he would have to increase sales by:

$$\frac{£15\,000}{(0.17 - 0.05)} = £125\,000$$

$$= 625 \text{ sofas}$$

Since he was far from certain he could get a good salesman for this salary package, and because in a good year the company was pretty near to full capacity, so far he had decided against trying to recruit anybody.

Column 2 shows the effect on profits if prices are maintained with the result that there is a one-third fall in sales. Column 3 shows the effect on profits if prices are reduced in order to maintain the level of sales.

	1 Current position	2 Competitor lowers price & we hold price	3 Competitor lowers price & we lower price
Price	£20	£20	£16
Variable cost	£12	£12	£12
Contribution	£8	£8	£4
Sales volume	£ 3 000	£ 2 000	£3000
Total contribution	£24 000	£16 000	£12 000
Fixed costs	£16 000	£16 000	£16 000
Profit	£ 8 000	£ –	£(4000)

As we see from column 3, the business will actually lose money (£4000 per month) if it follows the price lead of the competitor. If it maintains its prices, the position is rather better, although it will still not make a profit (column 2). However, there may also be the opportunity in this situation to reduce overheads to reflect the lower sales, or even to spend more on advertising to persuade customers that the board is better and worth £20. Despite the evidence that an analysis of this kind often reveals, many companies automatically cut prices as a 'knee-jerk' reaction to competitive pressures, without appreciating the real costs or evaluating the alternatives.

Which product or service is more profitable?

For any business producing more than one product or service the question as to which is the more profitable, and therefore the one which is to have its sales 'pushed' hardest, is an interesting one, the answer to which is not as straightforward as you might think. However, it is a fundamental question in deciding upon the mix of sales.

Suppose the skateboard company can produce three versions; 'Standard', 'All-terrain' and 'Freestyle', and the costs and margins are as follows:

	Standard	All-terrain	Freestyle
Price	£25	£32	£50
Variable cost	£10	£16	£30
Contribution	£15	£16	£20
Contribution margin	60%	50%	40%

This shows that Freestyle gives the highest £ contribution per board, but that Standard has the best contribution margin. So which is the one that the firm should encourage the sales of most? The answer depends on the market that the different products are selling to.

Let us say that the total market for skateboards is limited and selling more of one reduces demand for the others. In this case, as can be seen below, for every £500 spent the company can make a bigger profit from selling the Standard board, with its higher contribution margin.

	Standard	All-terrain	Freestyle
Price	£25	£32	£50
Variable cost	£10	£16	£30
Contribution	£15	£16	£20
Contribution margin	60%	50%	40%
Contribution from £500 sales	£300	£250	£200

However, where the products or markets are independent, that is if the Freestyle board sold to one customer, the Standard to another and the All-terrain to a third, then selling one does not reduce the budget available for the others. In which case, sell as much as you can of the Freestyle board first, moving onto the All-terrain board and finally the Standard board.

The general rule therefore is, where you are selling products or services which compete with each other in the same market, push the sales of those products which have the highest contribution margin. Where you are selling independent products which do not compete against each other, first sell the items that give the highest £ per unit contribution.

In the case of the customer with a limited budget, the firm has to take account of a limiting factor, the amount of money available to buy their products. This is a special case of the situation considered next.

Where should I focus limited resources?

All businesses face some form of limiting factor. For example, think about possible constraints which might limit the launch of a new product or service. Apart from the obvious constraint of demand, there can be several other factors that limit an organisation's ability to expand, such as a lack of skilled labour, limited machine capacity, shortage of raw materials, lack of management expertise, or shortage of money. Retailers often regard available shelf space as being their main limiting factor, while for a fast-growing manufacturing business the limiting factor may well be the availability of cash to finance their working capital needs.

Where a limiting factor exists, then a business will maximise its profits by making the best use of the limiting resource. For example, retailers need to make the best use of their available shelf space.

Assume that the skateboard company has a shortage of machinery which reflects itself in availability of machine hours. It needs to decide how to use the machine hours available to maximise its profits. This is done by looking at the contribution per machine hour:

	Standard	All-terrain	Freestyle
Price	£25	£32	£50
Variable cost	£10	£16	£30
Contribution	£15	£16	£20
Machine hours needed per 100 boards	1	0.5	2
Contribution per machine hour	£1500	£3200	£1000

As we see, the contribution per machine hour is greatest from the All-terrain boards. Every 1 hour of machine work produces 200 boards and yields £3200 contribution. Therefore, if machine hours really is the key limiting resource, they should produce All-terrain boards first, until demand is satisfied, followed by Standard boards, until demand is satisfied, and make up any unfilled capacity finally with the Freestyle board.

The general rule, where a limiting factor exists, is that the business should give priority to those products or services (or to those customers and markets) which generate the highest contribution per unit of limiting factor.

As always, the real world doesn't behave quite like a mathematical formula. If a supermarket filled its shelves entirely with small, high margin items it might find it had a lot of dissatisfied customers unable to find the bread, sugar and washing powder. Similarly, a manufacturer may prefer to sell to reliable large customers rather than to take greater risks selling to small traders, even though the contribution per sale may be higher in the latter case.

Another practical problem when a company has a range of products, each with different contribution margins is interpreting just what the break-even point means. The calculation is easy. It does not change. But what does this mean in terms of the sales mix? The answer is that the mix of sales at break-even is identical to the mix of sales that yields the average contribution margin. The problem is that if the sales mix changes, so too does the break-even point.

If the fixed costs for our skateboard company were £190 000 and the sales were as detailed below, producing an average contribution margin of 50 per cent, we could go on to calculate the break-even point using the usual formula:

	Standard	All-terrain	Freestyle		Total
Volume	8000	2000	4000		
Price	£25	£32	£50	Turnover	£464 000
Variable cost	£10	£16	£30	Variable cost	£232 000
Contribution	£15	£16	£20		
Contribution	£120 000	£32 000	£80 000		£232 000
Margin	60%	50%	40%		(50%)
				Fixed costs	£190 000
				Profit	£42 000

$$\text{Break-even} = \frac{£190\,000}{0.50} = £380\,000$$

The problem is that this break-even point only holds if the mix of sales always remains the same, that is for every eight Standard boards sold we always sell two All-terrain boards and four Freestyle boards. Should the mix change, then the break-even point will change.

Notwithstanding this, an understanding of which products, customers or markets generate the best contributions, and of the optimal way to utilise limited resources, can make a significant difference to the overall profitability of the business. You will be in a much better position to optimise the sales mix if you know which products are most profitable. It is also essential to know the break-even point, together with its limitations and manage it in the appropriate way.

---

10 PRACTICAL TIPS FOR A SUCCESSFUL START-UP

1 **Don't run out of cash** – plan your cash flow so that you can chart the length and depth of Death Valley and find the funds you need to start up.

2 **Understand the mechanics of the business** – what it takes to make the product or service, and make certain you can deliver.

3 **Understand yourself** – what your strengths and weaknesses are, and make sure you play to your strengths and avoid (or compensate for) your weaknesses.

4 **Understand your customers** – who they are (name names), and why they should buy from you.

5 **Understand your competitors** – who they are (name names), and why customers will buy from you and not them.

6 **Don't be afraid to be different** – but understand why customers value it.

7 **Don't be afraid to charge as high a price as possible** – but be able to justify doing so and make certain customers agree.

8 **Keep your fixed costs as low as possible** – and for as long as possible.

9 **Plan ahead** – but any plan should not constrain you, it should allow you to think through and plan for contingencies, and don't be afraid to change it if circumstances change.

AND

10 **Don't run out of cash.**

Summary

Cash flow is the lifeblood of a business. You can be making a profit and still run out of cash which means that bills go unpaid. Start-ups face the danger of Death Valley; they need to chart its length and depth by producing a cash flow forecast like **Jean Young** and using it to plan to meet their financing needs.

Money flows around the business and it is important to make sure it keeps flowing as quickly as possible. That means making sure debtors pay as quickly as possible – choosing credit customers carefully, invoicing promptly, setting credit limits and following up promptly on late payment. Stocks should be kept to a minimum, buying only the minimum needed, and all available supplier credit should be taken.

Profit represents the growth in the assets of a business that comes about through trading. Profit can be represented in any asset, not just cash. The balance sheet is a snap shot at a point in time that tells you where the money in a business comes from and where it is invested. Fixed assets, such as equipment and vehicles, are things the business means to keep. Working capital, which comprises current assets such as stocks and debtors and current liabilities such as creditors, is the thing the business means to sell or turn over.

Most businesses, like **Unicorn Inns**, can be controlled by monitoring six important financial drivers on a regular and timely basis. These drivers are:

1 Cash;
2 Sales;
3 Profit margins;
4 Margin of safety;
5 Productivity;
6 Debtor or stock turnover.

Companies like **Travel Counsellors** understand that it is vital to keep fixed overhead costs as low as possible, particularly at start-up. It is also important to keep contribution margins as high as possible. Whilst **Flitwick Manor Hotel** had high operating and financial gearing, it also had high contribution margins. When operating gearing is high it is important that sales targets are met. A high contribution margin gives some discretion on pricing, allowing very low prices to be charged based upon the low marginal cost involved. However, this should only be tried when differential pricing – charging different prices to different customers – is practical. **Penforth Sofa Beds** had low fixed costs but also low contribution margins. Low contribution margins make it imperative that variable costs are closely monitored. They also make it impossible to drop prices any further.

Contribution and break-even analysis are powerful tools. They tell you about the risk the business faces and the imperatives for management. Break-even is a benchmark above which a business starts to make profit. If you know how much above your break-even you are operating at, and your contribution margin, then it is easy to estimate your profitability.

Contribution analysis can also be used to answer 'what if?' type questions such as the question for **Penforth Sofa Beds** as to whether to recruit a new salesman or not. It tells you the value of extra sales needed to cover the increased fixed costs. Contribution analysis tells you which products or services are most profitable and, when some critical resource is limited, which to push the sales of. All in all, contribution analysis is a vital tool for the owner-manager.

Essays and discussion topics

1 Why is cash flow not the same as profit?
2 What would you do to ensure your start-up makes it through Death Valley?
3 There is no such thing as certainty, therefore there is no point in trying to forecast the future. Discuss.
4 The most important three pieces of advice for a start-up are:

- Think customer;
- Plan ahead;
- Don't run out of cash.

Discuss.
5 Profit is just something that an accountant constructs. The amount of profit depends on the assumptions the accountant decides to make. Therefore profit is not objective and means nothing. Discuss.
6 Why do you think owner-managers are not interested in accounting and control?
7 Do you think computer-based accounting systems make the task of controlling a small business easier?
8 What steps would you take in your start-up business to ensure debtors are kept to a minimum?
9 What steps would you take in your start-up business to ensure stocks are kept to a minimum?
10 Do you really think you can control a business by monitoring six financial drivers?
11 Entrepreneurs make decisions by instinct and not by using financial analysis. Discuss.
12 Cost–profit–volume analysis reflects the way owner-managers think. Discuss.
13 The margin of safety tells you about the long-term viability of a business, the risks it faces and the earning quality of each £ of turnover. Discuss.
14 Behind every successful entrepreneur there is an accountant. Discuss.

Exercises and assignments

1 Put a tick in the appropriate box (sometimes more than one) for the direct effects of each of these transactions:

		Increase cash	Increase profit	Decrease cash	Decrease profit
(1)	Sales of stock on credit				
(2)	Sale of old fixed assets				
(3)	Purchase of fixed assets				
(4)	Purchase of stock for cash				
(5)	Payment of creditors				
(6)	Payment of wages				
(7)	Payment of dividends				
(8)	Receipts from debtors				
(9)	Issue of new shares				
(10)	Receipt of loan				
(11)	Repayment of loan				
(12)	Payment of interest				

2   Work out the straight-line depreciation plus the recorded value of the assets each year for an asset originally costing £4000 using the following assumptions:

	Life expectancy	**Residual value**
A	5 years	£1000
B	8 years	£400
C	10 years	nil

3   Check your understanding of how balance sheets are drawn up. Put a tick in the appropriate box (sometimes more than one) for the direct effects of each of these transactions.

	Increase cash	Decrease cash	Increase other assets	Decrease other assets	Increase profit	Decrease profit	Increase liabilities	Decrease liabilities
(1) Purchase of fixed asset for cash	☐	☐	☐	☐	☐	☐	☐	☐
(2) Sale of fixed asset at balance sheet value for cash	☐	☐	☐	☐	☐	☐	☐	☐
(3) Sale of fixed assets for more than balance sheet value for cash	☐	☐	☐	☐	☐	☐	☐	☐
(4) Sale of fixed asset for less than balance sheet value for cash	☐	☐	☐	☐	☐	☐	☐	☐
(5) Depreciation of fixed asset	☐	☐	☐	☐	☐	☐	☐	☐
(6) Increase in value of freehold land	☐	☐	☐	☐	☐	☐	☐	☐
(7) Advance payment of rates	☐	☐	☐	☐	☐	☐	☐	☐
(8) Receipt of advance payment of subscription	☐	☐	☐	☐	☐	☐	☐	☐
(9) Write off bad debt	☐	☐	☐	☐	☐	☐	☐	☐
(10) Estimate of telephone charges not yet received	☐	☐	☐	☐	☐	☐	☐	☐

4 To check your knowledge of accounting, complete the following short test. It is not comprehensive, but should give you an indication of your understanding. Tick the appropriate box to show that you agree or disagree with a statement; if you do not understand any of the technical terms, tick the 'Don't know' column.

	Agree	Don't know	Disagree
(1) The balance sheet tells you how much a business is worth.	☐	☐	☐
(2) All the fixed assets of a business are shown at their market value.	☐	☐	☐
(3) By depreciating the fixed assets of a business, you ensure that you have sufficient cash to replace them at the end of their life.	☐	☐	☐
(4) All capital is good; therefore you want as much working capital as possible.	☐	☐	☐
(5) It is always better to borrow money from the bank than to seek further equity, perhaps from other shareholders.	☐	☐	☐
(6) Loans are repaid out of accumulated profits.	☐	☐	☐
(7) Reserves represent the cash the business has accumulated over its life.	☐	☐	☐
(8) A company that is making profits can always pay its bills.	☐	☐	☐
(9) Any company making higher profits than another is doing better than that company.	☐	☐	☐
(10) To understand accounting you have to be able to do double-entry book-keeping	☐	☐	☐

5 An engineering company can produce an additional 1500 units of either valve A or valve B per year. The additional fixed costs to be invested to achieve this production would be £15 000 for A and £20 000 for B. A sells for £35 and variable costs per valve total £15 (contribution £20 per valve). Valve B sells for £36 and variable costs per valve total £11 (contribution £25 per valve). Which valve should it produce?

6 Given the data below, which products would you 'push' the sales of?

	A	B	C	D	E
Selling price per unit	£1.30	£1.00	£1.00	£1.00	£1.70
Variable costs per unit	£0.68	£0.49	£0.66	£0.68	£1.80
Contribution per unit	£0.62	£0.51	£0.34	£0.32	(0.10)
Contribution margin	48%	51%	34%	32%	NA

7 If you only had 2000 machine hours which product would you 'push' the sale of?

	A	B	C	D
Selling price per unit	£1.30	£1.00	£1.00	£1.00
Variable costs per unit	£0.68	£0.49	£0.66	£0.68
Contribution per unit	£0.62	£0.51	£0.34	£0.32
Contribution margin	48%	51%	34%	32%
Product time per 1000 units (hours)	2	1	4	2

8 If each line had limited sales potential how much of each would you actually produce?

	A	B	C	D
Contribution per unit	£0.62	£0.51	£0.34	£0.32
Contribution margin	48%	51%	34%	32%
Product time per 1000 units (hours)	2	1	4	2
Contribution per 1000 units per hr	£310	£510	£85	£160
Ranking	2	1	4	3
Sales potential (1000 units)	250	1000	750	500

9 How much profit would you make if fixed costs were £450 000?

10 Building on the previous exercises, what is the break-even point for the company, given the final outcome of your analysis?

£000s	A	B	D	Total
Sales	£325	£1000	£250	£1575
Variable costs	£170	£ 490	£170	£ 830
Contribution	£155	£ 510	£ 80	£ 745
Fixed costs				£ 450
Profit				£ 295

11 What does this mean in terms of the sales mix?

12 What happens if this mix changes?

13 A company has come to you for a £10 000 loan to finance its expansion. Currently its contribution margin is 60 per cent and this is expected to be maintained. Annual repayments of the loan, including interest, amount to £1200. How much extra sales turnover does the firm have to make to cover the annual loan repayments?

14 A company currently sells 200 000 units at a selling price of £25 and a variable cost of £15. Fixed costs are £1 400 000. It is currently considering three business strategies:

   (1) Halve the price and double the sales volume;
   (2) Drop price by £5 and increase sales by 20%;
   (3) Increase price by £5 and allow sales to fall by 20%.

   Which would you recommend?

15 ABC Co. produce plastic bottles. The company could fit another bottle-making machine in its factory without increasing existing overheads. However, it is not sure it can sell all of its production. The machine would cost £20 000 and last 5 years, and therefore depreciation would be £4000 per year. The machine operator would be paid £8500 per year. Materials and other variable costs would come to £0.15 per 100 bottles, and they could be sold at £0.65 per 100 bottles.

   (1) Calculate the breakdown point;
   (2) Calculate the profit on sales of:
       (a) 3 million bottles.
       (b) 4 million bottles.

16 Irene runs a hair salon and is considering opening late to offer 'half-price' hair cuts, perms and so on, to pensioners. The additional 28 hours opening time will be staffed using three girls working for £3.00 an hour. Each girl will handle 2 customers an hour and each customer will pay £10.00. Other additional variable costs come to £9.00 per hour. Is the idea worth doing?

17 A special Mediterranean Sea Cruise for a liner costs £250 000 to undertake in terms of staff, fuel, depreciation and so on. Each passenger has additional variable costs (food, linen and so on) of £200. The price for a ticket is £700 and one week before departure 500 tickets have been sold, 200 tickets remain unsold. What price can be charged for them?

18 When you have read it, check your understanding of the appendix to this chapter. Using the Accounting Worksheet below, record the following transactions and draw up the balance sheet and profit statement.
   A £1000 cash from share capital received. £500 cash from bank loan received;
   B Fixed assets purchased on credit for £1100;
   C Stock purchased on credit for £550;
   D Some stock sold on credit for £500;
   E Pay creditors £1250;
   F Receive £1250 from debtors;
   G Pay cash expenses (no invoices) of £30;
   H Depreciation of fixed assets charged at £110;
   I Stock at the end of the period is £350;
   J Repair work to the value of £40 undertaken, still awaiting invoice.

19 Arrange for a presentation of the Sage accounting system. Visit the company's website on www.sage.com and investigate the range of packages available.

Accounting worksheet

	Assets £				=	Capital £		Liabilities £	
	Cash	Debtors	Stocks	Fixed Assets		Shares	Profit	Bank Loan	Creditors
A					=				
A					=				
B					=				
C					=				
D					=				
E					=				
F					=				
G					=				
H					=				
I					=				
J					=				
					=				

Start-up exercise

Undertake steps 10 and 11 of the start-up exercise at the back of the book.

Appendix: Information for control

The Companies Acts require that all companies keep certain accounting records to show and explain the company's transactions. This involves keeping the following:

1 A record of day-to-day cash receipts and expenditures;
2 A record of assets and liabilities;
3 A statement of stock at the end of each financial year, and a statement of stocktaking from which it was prepared;
4 Except for ordinary retail trade, statements of all goods sold and purchased showing the goods and the buyers and sellers.

Whilst sole traders and partnerships are not required formally to keep all these records, they would be well advised to do so. After all, without adequate accounting information it is impossible to monitor the performance of the business.

It is reckless to run a business without any accounting records and yet many smaller firms do just that. The simplest accounting system can be very cheap and relatively easy to operate. It can provide regular and timely financial information. As the size of a business grows, so too does the complexity of the task of controlling it. However, computers have come to the rescue providing an increasingly cheap way of processing a lot of data. Nevertheless, any system, manual or computerised, is only as good as the information entered into it. If you put garbage in, then you will get garbage out.

Let's start with the simplest accounting system, where the only accounting record is a cash book showing receipts and payments. This is the barest essential for any business since it needs cash to pay the bills and, without a record of it, there might be nothing in the bank account to pay them. Cash books take many forms. The simplest comprise four columns:

One column to describe the transaction;
One column to record amounts deposited;
One column to record amounts spent;
The final column recording the resulting balance in the account.

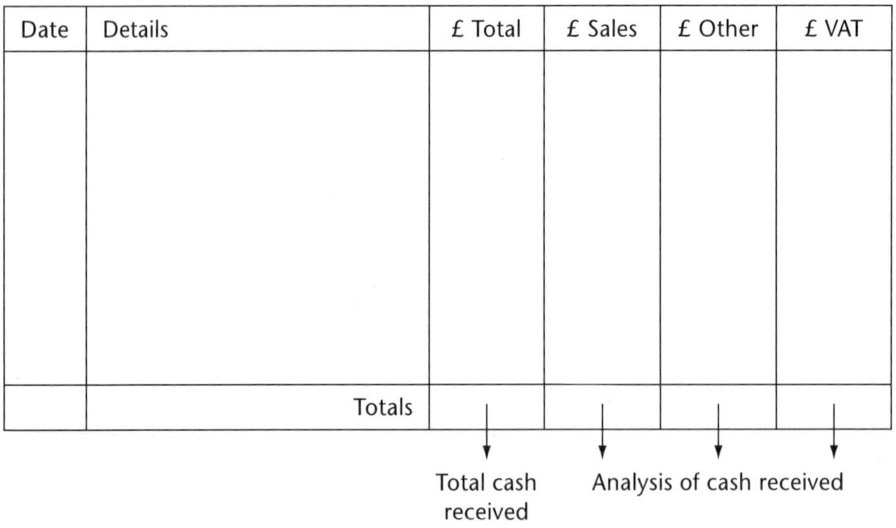

Figure 7.6   Cash receipts book

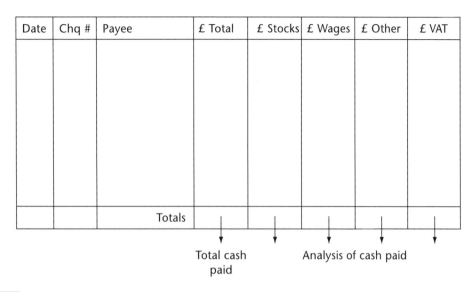

Date	Chq #	Payee	£ Total	£ Stocks	£ Wages	£ Other	£ VAT
		Totals					

Total cash paid   Analysis of cash paid

Figure 7.7   Cash payments book

Only slightly more complicated are the ones that separate out receipts and payments and provide some detailed analysis of where the cash came from and where it is going. An example of this given in Figure 7.6 and 7.7. Typically, the cash book records the cash held in the bank rather than actual cash on hand in the business. The balance in the bank is the difference between total receipts and total payments, plus or minus any amounts brought forward in the account. As you might expect, this does not always agree to the balance shown on your bank statement as being in your account. This is because transactions may be recorded in your accounting system at different times to the bank's. These are called 'timing differences'. However, other differences could arise because of recording errors, bank errors – or theft! Because of these differences, it is important that any cash book is reconciled with the bank statement regularly.

Most firms will also have some cash, however small an amount, actually on hand. This is normally called 'petty cash'. The easiest way to control and account for this if it is a small amount is through what is called an 'imprest system'. You start with a cash file with, say, £100 in it. Every time cash is needed to purchase something the cash is replaced with either an invoice or a properly authorised petty cash voucher describing what was purchased. At any time that total value of cash plus invoices plus vouchers will always be £100. At the end of every week or month, or simply when the cash runs out, the vouchers are replaced with cash from the bank account and the invoices and vouchers written up in the normal way. If the volume of cash transactions is too great for this system then a separate cash book for the cash on hand will have to be kept.

Cash books can form part of accounting systems and all accounting systems are based on the idea of double entry book-keeping. You will recall the earlier comment that the balance sheet should balance. This means that the idea of liabilities and assets balancing may be viewed as being an equation. If one part of such a balancing equation were to change, so another corresponding change should be recorded to ensure that the equation, and thus the balance sheet, remains in balance. For example, if the asset cash decreases because a bill is paid, so the liability of creditors should also be reduced. This leads to the idea of double entry book-keeping. Double entry is a system of book-keeping which ensures that the accounting equation shown below is always kept in balance:

Capital = Assets – Liabilities

or

Assets   = Capital + Liabilities

Capital comprises the capital introduced – in a limited company this is by way of share capital – and retained profit. The process of recording is simple: every time an additional asset is created or purchased for the organisation, recognition of where it came from must also be made. For example, if you put £1000 in cash into the business, recognition of its source must be made, let us say, by showing £1000 increase in capital. If for any reason the accounts do not 'balance', then some aspect of the transaction has not been properly recorded.

The illustration below shows how the process of double entry works. The transactions below relate to a fictitious business, ACE Computers Ltd, which buys and resells software. The details relate to its first year of operations.

A   The owners contributed £25 000 in cash as share capital. A bank loan for £10 000 was obtained, repayable in five years with an interest rate of 10% per annum.
B   Fixed assets costing £20 000 were purchased for cash.
C   Sales totalled £60 000, being 50% for cash and 50% to account customers on credit.
D   Depreciation on fixed assets amounted to £5000.
E   Sundry operating expenses totalled £10 000 of which £1000 remained unpaid at the year end.
F   Loan interest of £1000 was paid.
G   Stock costing £25 000 was purchased on account.
H   Trade creditors were paid £20 000 in cash.
I   Debtors paid £25 000 in cash.
J   Stocks at the end of the year had cost £10 000.

The details above are to be used to construct an accounting worksheet for ACE Computers, shown in Figure 7.8.

Explanation of ACE Computers worksheet

A   Cash of £25 000 is obtained as capital from the owners. Cash increases by £25 000 on the assets side; on the liabilities side capital increases by £25 000 and the accounting equation remains in balance. A bank loan of £10 000 is obtained. Cash increases by £10 000 on the assets side with the bank loan, a liability, increasing by the same amount.
B   Fixed assets are purchased for £20 000. Cash decreases on the assets side by £20 000. This is one asset being exchanged for another so fixed assets increase by £20 000
C   Here, the sales figures are recorded. On the assets side, cash goes up by £30 000 (50 per cent of the sales for the year) with debtors also increasing by £30 000 (the other 50 per cent). All of the £60 000 is recognised as a sale even though some of the cash from debtors may not have been received. This is an important accounting idea – sales can be recorded as sales and thus increase profits whether or not the cash inflow has taken place. In this case the increase of £60 000 on the assets side of the accounting equation is balanced by an addition to profits of £60 000 on the liabilities side.
D   Depreciation is calculated as being £5000 for the year. This results in, on the assets side, fixed assets being reduced by £5000, with profits on the liabilities side being decreased by the same amount.
E   Here, the sundry operating expenses are recorded. As with the accounting idea of cash not having to be received to be recognised as a sale, so we see an illustration of cash not having to

	Assets £				=	Capital £		Liabilities £	
	Cash	Debtors	Stocks	Fixed Assets		Shares	Profit	Bank Loan	Creditors
A	+25 000				=	+25 000			
A	+10 000				=			+10 000	
B	−20 000			+20 000	=				
C	+30 000	+30 000			=		+60 000		
D				−5 000	=		−5 000		
E	−9 000				=		−10 000		+1 000
F	−1 000				=		−1 000		
G			+25 000		=				+25 000
H	−20 000				=				−20 000
I	+25 000	−25 000			=				
J			−15 000		=		−15 000		
	+40 000	+5 000	+10 000	+15 000	=	+25 000	+29 000	+10 000	+6 000

Figure 7.8 Accounting worksheet for ACE Computers Ltd

be paid to be recognised as a charge against profits. Although only £9000 of the £10 000 sundry operating charges has been paid, accountants charge all of the £10 000 against profits, recognising the unpaid £1000 as an accrued charge – a liability. Thus on the assets side cash goes down by £9000; on the liabilities side profit decreases by all of the £10 000 with sundry accruals being increased by £1000. The entries recorded keep both sides of the accounting equation in balance – a decrease of £9000 on the assets side and a net increase of £9000 on the liabilities side. It's worth noting that the £1000 increase against sundry accruals could have been shown as an increase against Trade creditors as an acceptable alternative.

F   The loan interest paid results in cash on the assets side going down by £1000 with profits going down by £1000 on the liabilities side.

G   Stocks being purchased on credit for £25 000 is reflected in stocks on the assets side increasing by £25 000, with the same increase in creditors on the liabilities side.

H   The payment of £20 000 to creditors results in both cash and creditors decreasing by that amount.

I   Here the payment of some of the sums owed by debtors is recorded. Cash increases by £25 000 and debtors decreases by £25 000. Note that although this sum is associated with sales there is no impact upon profit. This is because we recorded the debtors' impact upon sales earlier (the £30 000 in line D)

J   This line relates to the fact that stocks costing £10 000 are left at the year end. We know (from line H) that stocks costing £25 000 were purchased. If stocks costing £10 000 are left then stocks costing £15 000 must have been sold (hopefully not stolen). Thus on the assets side stocks decreases by £15 000 with a corresponding decrease against profits on the liabilities side.

The final row shows the totals for each column. We see that, at the end of the year:

There is £40 000 in the form of cash and in the bank;
Debtors owe £5000;
There are unsold stocks to hand which had cost £10 000;
Fixed assets, having originally cost £20 000, are now valued at £15 000;
£5000 is owed to trade creditors and £1000 to other creditors in respect of accrued sundry operating expenses, whilst £10 000 is still owed to the bank in respect of the bank loan;
No further capital has been introduced BUT, as a result of operations, profits of £29 000 have been made. This amount is shown as capital as it is held on behalf of the owners by the organisation, owed back to them. Until such time as the owners take back some or all of the profits, the profits are retained and shown on the balance sheet as capital.

A simple accounting worksheet like this can be used to record the transactions of a very small business but proper books of account will soon be needed. Indeed, these days computer-based accounting systems such as Sage are so cheap that more and more start-ups are using them from day one. Computers are excellent at dealing with large volumes of repetitive tasks quickly and accurately. However, they often do not reduce the time taken to keep the records, rather they improve the information generated by them. Most small firms still need a book-keeper to run the computerised system. However, one option is to out-source the book-keeping function and either have a professional come in to undertake the accounting work, say one day a week, or take details of the transactions to them on a regular basis.

The worksheet in Figure 7.8 contains all the information needed to construct the financial statements. The profit statement details are contained in the profits column. These are represented in the form of a profit statement below:

ACE Computers: profit statement for the year

		£000s	£000s
Sales	for cash	30	
	on account	30	60
less:			
cost of stock sold			15
Gross profit			45
less:			
operating expenses		10	
depreciation		5	15
Operating profit			30
less:			
bank loan interest		1	1
Net profit			29

The profit statement is divided into sections. The first section determines the gross profit. This is the profit ACE Computers makes on buying and reselling stock. It is important as it is this gross profit figure from which other expenses are deducted. If the gross profit is low but other expenses are high a loss will result. In Jean Young's profit statement she did not have a gross profit line because she did not buy and sell goods.

For ACE the remaining expenses and charges are sundry operating expenses (£10 000), depreciation (£5000) and bank loan interest (£1000). Not all of these other items are charged in one section – the bank loan interest is kept apart from the operating expenses and the depreciation charge. By grouping these latter items together and deducting them from the gross profit we arrive at a profit figure which reflects the surplus – the operating profit – of £30 000 made on day-to-day activities. The bank loan interest is not an operations expense; rather it is a cost of financing. Although the loan interest (£1000) is deducted from the operating profit to give the net profit of £29 000, the day-to-day performance of management teams is normally related to the generation of operating profits.

Since ACE Computers is a limited company, the final net profit figure is the figure from which dividends can be paid. In their case there are no dividends so this is also the profit retained in the business. Compare this to Jean Young's profit statement. She also had net profit from which her drawings as a sole trader were deducted to arrive at the profit retained in the business. The balance sheet at the end of the first year for ACE Computers is shown below. It comes directly from the worksheet.

ACE Computers: balance sheet at end of first year

	£000s	£000s
Fixed assets		
at cost	20	
less: depreciation to date	5	15
Current assets		
cash/bank	40	
debtors	5	
stocks	10	55
less:		
Current liabilities		
creditors	(5)	
accruals	(1)	(6)
Net current assets		49
Total assets		64
less:		
creditors falling due after one year		
bank loan	(10)	(10)
Net assets		54
Represented by:		
Shareholders funds		
share capital	25	
retained profit	29	54

This balance sheet shows the company's assets and liabilities at the year end. However, the balance sheet also reveals whether shareholders' funds have increased or decreased over the year with a resulting change in the net worth of the organisation. In this case the shareholders' funds (and so the net assets) has increased from the original investment of £25 000 to £54 000 as a result of the profit made and retained of £29 000. Notice, however that cash increased only by £15 000 from £25 000 to £40 000. The difference is represented in the other assets shown in the balance sheet which increased by £14 000, net of liabilities.

Answers to exercises and assignments

1

		Increase cash	Increase profit	Decrease cash	Decrease profit
(1)	Sales of stock on credit		✓		
(2)	Sale of old fixed assets	✓			
(3)	Purchase of fixed assets			✓	
(4)	Purchase of stock for cash			✓	
(5)	Payment of creditors			✓	
(6)	Payment of wages			✓	✓
(7)	Payment of dividends			✓	✓
(8)	Receipts from debtors	✓			
(9)	Issue of new shares	✓			
(10)	Receipt of loan	✓			
(11)	Repayment of loan			✓	
(12)	Payment of interest			✓	✓

Notes: Other balance sheet effects:
(1) Decrease stocks and increase debtors
(2) Decrease fixed assets
(3) Increase fixed assets
(4) Increase stocks
(5) Decrease creditors
(6) None
(7) Often called an 'appropriation' of profit
(8) Decrease debtors
(9) Increase share capital
(10) Increase loan capital
(11) Decrease loan capital
(12) None

2

	Straight line					
	A		B		C	
	Charge £	Asset value £	Charge £	Asset value £	Charge £	Asset value £
Original cost		4000		4000		4000
Year 1	600	3400	450	3550	400	3600
Year 2	600	2800	450	3100	400	3200
Year 3	600	2200	450	2650	400	2800
Year 4	600	1600	450	2200	400	2400
Year 5	600	1000	450	1750	400	2000
Year 6			450	1300	400	1600
Year 7			450	950	400	1200
Year 8			450	400	400	800
Year 9					400	400
Year 10					400	nil

3

	Increase cash	Decrease cash	Increase other assets	Decrease other assets	Increase profit	Decrease profit	Increase liabilities	Decrease liabilities
(1) Purchase of fixed asset for cash		✓	✓					
(2) Sale of fixed asset at balance sheet value for cash	✓			✓				
(3) Sale of fixed asset for more than balance sheet value for cash	✓			✓	✓			
(4) Sale of fixed asset for less than balance sheet value for cash	✓			✓		✓		
(5) Depreciation of fixed asset				✓		✓		
(6) Increase in value of freehold land			✓		✓			
(7) Advance payment of rates		✓	✓					
(8) Receipt of advance payment of subscription	✓						✓	
(9) Write off bad debt				✓		✓		
(10) Estimate of telephone charges not yet received						✓	✓	

4 Answers to this question are given below. In fact, all the statements are false; your ticks should all be in the 'disagree' column.

  (1) What a business is worth depends entirely on what a buyer will pay for that business. It may depend upon the use to which they are put. Anyway, the assets shown in the balance sheet are generally valued at their historic cost, not what they are worth today.
  (2) Only land and buildings may be shown at market value. All other assets are shown at depreciated historic cost.
  (3) Depreciation is an accounting transaction that reflects how the costs of an asset are allocated as charges against profit. A proportion of cost is charged against each over the asset's life. Depreciation does not represent any cash flow. Equally, profit (even after depreciation) does not represent availability of cash to replace the asset.

(4) Capital is the funds invested in the business. The best companies get the highest returns from the smallest capital. These achieve high rates of return on their net assets (or capital). Working capital is particularly large for most companies and can be decreased by good control.

(5) If you borrow money you have to pay the interest, whether or not the business is making profit. Dividends paid to shareholders need only be paid when the company is making a profit. Loans will normally be repaid at some predetermined point in the future. Shareholders may liquidate their investment but normally only by selling their investment to another shareholder. Also the amount that you can borrow normally depends upon the amount of money shareholders have put in. In other words, there are many circumstances when further equity investment could be preferable to borrowing money.

(6) Loans are repaid out of cash, not profit.

(7) Reserves represent growth in all the assets of a business, not just cash. Indeed the other assets of a business could have grown to such an extent that cash might actually have decreased.

(8) Profit is not the same as cash. A profitable company can still have insufficient cash to pay its bills, because it has over-expanded its other assets.

(9) It is the profit obtained in relation to the net assets that is important, not just profit. For example, a business may make a profit of £200 on net assets of £1000, compared to another business making a profit of only £30 but on net assets of £100. The first business has a return of 20 per cent, the second 30 per cent. The second is making better use of the assets it controls. Given £1000 it might be able to make profits of £300.

5 The break-even point for A is 750 valves (£15 000/£20) and for B is 800 valves (£20 000/£25). If the company can sell its production of 1500 valves, valve A would generate a profit of £15 000 ((£35 – £15) × 1500 – £15 000)) and valve B a profit of £17 500 ((£36 – £11) × 1500 – £20 000)). The profit-volume charts for A and B are shown below.

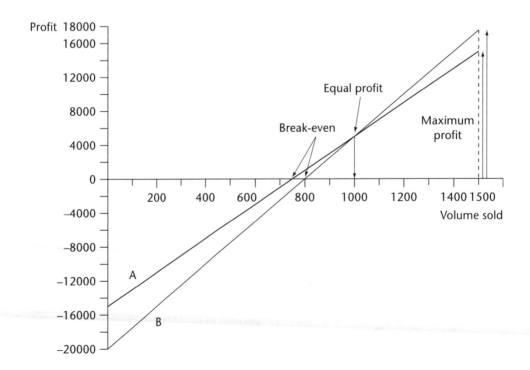

Since the business can invest in either valve A or valve B, but not both, the decision depends critically upon the estimate of sales. If sales are above 1000 per year, A yields a higher profit (or a lower loss). In other words valve B offers the chance of a higher return, but this has to be set against the risk of a greater loss, and losses occurring when sales fall below only 800 valves.

6 Drop product E and push the sales of all other products, but particularly B since it has the highest contribution margin.

7 From the analysis below, you should push products B, A, D and C, in that order, since this is the ranking of the products with the highest contribution per machine hour. Machine hours are the limiting factor for this product.

	A	B	C	D
Contribution per unit	0.62	0.51	0.34	0.32
Contribution margin	48%	51%	34%	32%
Product time per 1000 units (hrs)	2	1	4	2
Contribution per 1000 units per hr	310	510	85	160
Ranking	2	1	4	3

8 Actual sales and profit:

	A	B	C	D	Total
Sales potential (1000 units)	250	1000	750	500	
Ranking	2	1	4	3	
Actual production (1000 units)	250	1000	Nil	250	
Productive hours taken	500	1000	Nil	500	2000
Contribution per 1000 units	620	510	NA	320	
Actual production (1000 units)	250	1000		250	
Contribution per 1000 unit	620	510		320	
Total contribution (£000)	155	510		80	745
Fixed costs (£000)					450
Profit (£000)					295

9 Profit calculation:

£000	A	B	D	Total
Sales	325	1000	250	1575
Variable costs	170	490	170	830
Contribution				745
Fixed costs				450
Profit				295

10 Break-even point:

Average contribution margin: $\dfrac{745}{1575} = 47.3\%$

Break-even point: $\dfrac{450\,000}{0.473} = £951\,350$

11 Sales mix:

	A	B	D
Actual production (1000) units	250	1000	250
Sales mix	1:	4:	1

The sales mix is assumed to stay the same at the break-even point. Therefore:

$\dfrac{\text{Break-even}}{\text{Actual sales}} = \dfrac{951\,350}{£1\,575\,000} = 60.4\%$

Break-even sales = Actual × 60.4%. Therefore:

	A	B	D
Actual production (1000) units	250	1000	250
Break-even production (1000) units	151	604	151

12 The break-even point will change and will have to be recalculated. This is a major shortcoming with the technique if the products sold have widely different margins.

13 Extra sales needed to cover loan repayments:

$$\frac{£1200}{0.60} = £2000$$

14 The answer is C.

At this price contribution rises to £15. A 20% drop in sales means 160 000 units and a contribution of £2.4 million (160 000 × £15). Definitely the best option.

For the others:

A: This does not make sense at all. Each unit currently makes a contribution of £10 (£25 − £15). At £12.50 each unit would actually make a loss of £2.50 (£12.50 − £15). The more you sell, the higher the loss. If you sold 400 000 units, the loss would be £1 million.

B: At this price contribution drops to £5. A 20% increase in sales means 240 000 units and a contribution of (240 000 × £5) £1.2 million. Unfortunately previously it was (200 000 × £10) £2 million. So this is not a good idea either.

15(1) Contribution = £0.65 − £0.15 = £0.50 per 100 bottles

Contribution margin = 77%

$$\text{Break-even point} = \frac{£4000 + £8500}{0.77} = £16\,250$$

(This is equivalent to 2.5 million bottles at £0.65 per 100)

15(2)

	3 million	4 million
	£	£
Total sales	19 500	26 000
Break-even sales	16 250	16 250
Sales above break-even	3 250	9 750
Contribution margin	77%	77%
Profit	2500	7500

16 Irene's Hair Salon:

Incremental revenue per week:
£10.00 2 per hour 3 staff 28 hours   = £1680.00

Incremental costs:
(£5.00 per hour 28 hours) + (£9.00 per hour 28 hours)
= £420.00 + £252.00   = £ 672.00

Surplus   = £1008.00

Answer, therefore, is 'yes'

However, might some customers transfer to take up the half-price offer?

17 The liner:

$$\text{Break-even point} = \frac{£250\,000}{£(700 - 200)} = 500 \text{ passengers}$$

The liner is therefore covering its fixed costs at the moment and therefore any price above the variable cost per passenger (£200) makes an additional contribution to the profit of the cruise.

However, thought must be given to how other passengers feel about some passengers paying only, say, £201. If next time all the passengers waited until the last week and paid only £201 the cruise would make a loss:

Contribution = (£201 − £200) × 700 passengers	=	£	700
Fixed costs	=	£250 000	
Loss		£249 300	

For this reason, the cruise liner might decide not to drop its price at all.

18 The Accounting Worksheet is shown on the next page. The balance sheet at the end of the period will be:

Fixed assets		£ 990
Current assets:		
stock	£350	
debtors	£300	
cash	£420	£1070
Current liabilities:		
creditors		£ 440
Total assets		£1620
Liabilities due over 1 year:		
bank loan		£ 500
Net assets		£1120
Represented by:		
share capital		£1000
retained profit		£ 120
		£1120

The profit statement will be:

Sales	£500
Cost of sales	£200
Gross profit	£300
Overheads	£180
Net profit	£120

Accounting worksheet

	Assets £				=	Capital £		Liabilities £	
	Cash	Debtors	Stocks	Fixed Assets		Shares	Profit	Bank Loan	Creditors
A	+1000				=	+1000			
A	+500				=			+500	
B				+1100	=				+1100
C			+550		=				+550
D		+500			=		+500		
E	−1250				=				−1250
F	+200	−200			=				
G	−30				=		−30		
H				−110	=		−110		
I			−200		=		−200		
J					=		−40		+40
	+420	+300	+350	+990	=	+1000	+120	+500	+440

Part 3

Growth and Decline

8

From Entrepreneur to Leader

Contents

- Change or die
- Entrepreneurial organisations
- Changing skills
- Coping with crises
- The role of leader
- Vision and mission
- Values

- Creating culture
- Leadership style
- Building the management team
- The board of directors
- Entrepreneurial leadership skills
- Summary

LEARNING OUTCOMES

By the end of this chapter you should be able to:

- Describe how the entrepreneur must change as the business grows;
- Explain the implications of growth models of business development for the entrepreneur, their style of management, the organisation of the firm and the practical application of the functional aspects of management;
- Explain how an entrepreneurial organisation is likely to be structured, the advantages and disadvantages of this structure and appreciate how it might have to change as the firm grows;
- Explain what the job of a leader entails;
- Explain what is meant by vision and values – what they entail and how they can be communicated effectively;

- Write a vision or mission statement;
- Recognise the importance of culture for the success of a firm and describe the elements of culture that go towards making a successful entrepreneurial firm;
- Evaluate your preferred leadership style and recognise what is appropriate for a growing firm;
- Evaluate how you and other people handle conflict;
- Evaluate your preferred team role;
- Explain why some teams work and others do not;
- Describe the role and importance of the board of directors and the skills they need to undertake their job effectively;
- Explain what is required to become an entrepreneurial leader.

Change or die

As the business grows the entrepreneur needs to change and adapt. The more rapid the growth, the more difficult this is. It is not just that the role of the founder and the qualities and skills needed to manage the business successfully change, it is also that the application of the functional disciplines of marketing, accounting and people management change. The entrepreneur super-hero needs to metamorphosise into a leader. The business needs to change the way it operates and become more formal without becoming more bureaucratic. And all of these changes need to be properly managed if the firm is to grow successfully. It is little wonder that so few firms grow to any size.

Chapter 2 gave some clues about the background of the entrepreneurs who make this metamorphosis successfully. Research shows what their antecedent influences generally are:

- They were well-educated;
- They start the business for positive motivations;
- They leave a managerial job in an established company to start the business;
- Historically they tend to be middle-aged but there is some evidence that there is a new generation of very young entrepreneurs, particularly in the e-business sector;
- They are willing to share ownership of the business with other key managers.

These qualities impact upon the process of change and how the entrepreneur handles them. There are a number of growth models that seek to describe the changes that the entrepreneur faces and, by inference, how the changes need to be managed. One of the most widely used models was developed by Greiner (1972). This is shown in Figure 8.1; it offers a five-stage framework for considering the development of a business, but more particularly the managerial changes facing the founder. Each phase of growth is followed by a crisis that necessitates a change in the way the founder manages the business if it is to move on and continue to grow. If the crisis cannot be overcome then it is possible that the business might fail. The length of time it takes to go through each phase depends on the industry in which the company operates. In fast-growing industries, growth periods are relatively short; in slower-growth industries they tend to be longer. Each evolutionary phase requires a particular management style or emphasis to achieve growth. Each revolutionary period presents a management problem to overcome. Only phases one to four really apply to smaller firms.

'You start the business as a dream, you make it your passion for a while and then you get experienced managers to run it because it's not as much fun as starting. I think there's a lot to be said about starting a business and lot to be said about running a business when its mature. I think I'm capable of making the distinction and coping with both.'
Stelios Haji-Ioannou
founder, **easyJet**
Sunday Times 29 Octobber 2000
➜

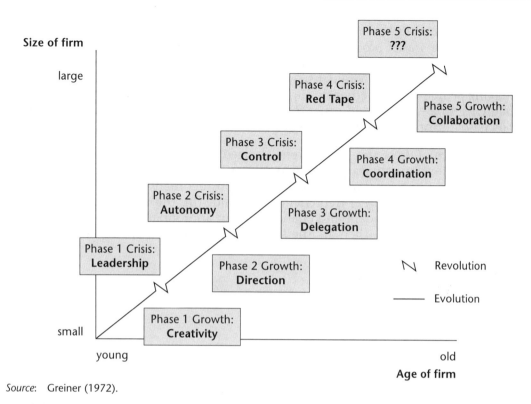

Size of firm

large

Phase 5 Crisis:
???

Phase 4 Crisis:
Red Tape

Phase 5 Growth:
Collaboration

Phase 3 Crisis:
Control

Phase 4 Growth:
Coordination

Phase 2 Crisis:
Autonomy

Phase 3 Growth:
Delegation

Phase 1 Crisis:
Leadership

Phase 2 Growth:
Direction

Revolution

Evolution

Phase 1 Growth:
Creativity

small

young

old

Age of firm

Source: Greiner (1972).

Figure 8.1 The Greiner growth model

- **Phase 1** Growth comes through entrepreneurial creativity. However, this constant seeking out of new opportunities and the development of innovative ways of doing things leads to a crisis of leadership. Staff, financiers and even customers increasingly fail to understand the focus of the business – where it is going, what it is selling – and resources become spread too thinly to follow through effectively on any single commercial opportunity.
- **Phase 2** Growth comes from the direction given by effective leadership in this phase. The entrepreneur must become more of a leader and give the business the direction it needs. However, entrepreneurs have a strong internal locus of control, which means that there is a danger that they will be unable to delegate responsibility to their management team. The leader then faces a crisis of autonomy that will only be addressed by putting that management team in place and delegating work to it.
- **Phase 3** Growth in this phase comes because the team is in place and effective delegation is taking place. The business is no longer a one-man-band. However, there is always the danger that delegation becomes abdication of responsibility and, as the firm continues to grow, there is a loss of proper control. Entrepreneurs are notorious for not being interested in the detail of controlling a business.
- **Phase 4** Growth now comes from effective coordination of management and its work force. Controls are in place and are working effectively. By this stage the firm

will have ceased to have many of the characteristics of an owner-managed firm because there are set procedures and policies for doing things. The danger now is that it might lose its entrepreneurial drive and the next crisis it might face is one of red tape or bureaucracy. Greiner says this can only be overcome by collaboration – making people work together through a sense of mission or purpose rather than by reference to a rule book. In other words, creating an appropriate culture in the business – a topic we return to in Chapter 18.

To address each of these crises entrepreneurs need to adapt and change. In particular, they need to develop into leaders. They need to put in place a management team and work as part of this team – difficult when you consider many of the strong personal characteristics exhibited by entrepreneurs. Alongside this the organisational structure of the firm will need to adapt and change, and an appropriate business culture will need to be created. These then are the four challenges entrepreneurs face as the business grows:

- Leadership;
- Team-working;
- Organisation structure;
- Culture.

Entrepreneurial organisations

Entrepreneurial organisation structures, seen most clearly at the start-up phase, have been likened to the spider's web shown in Figure 8.2a. The entrepreneur sits at the centre of the web with each new member of staff reporting to them. The management style tends to be informal, one of direct supervision. Just as entrepreneurs prefer informal marketing techniques, building on relationships, they prefer informal organisation structures and influences rather than rigid rules and job definitions. They persuade and cajole employees, showing them how to do things on a one-to-one basis, rather than having prescribed tasks. They rely on building personal

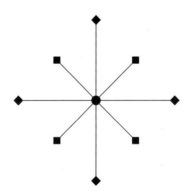

Formal reporting lines ————

Figure 8.2a The entrepreneurial spider's web

relationships. After all, the business is growing rapidly and there are no precedents to go by. The future is uncertain, so flexibility is the key. The pace of change probably means that rigid structures would be out of date quickly. What is more, in a small firm everybody has to be prepared to do other people's jobs because there is no cover, no slack in the system if, for example, someone goes off sick. It is also perfectly flat and therefore efficient – overheads are reduced – and it is responsive – communication times are minimised. This is the typical small, entrepreneurial structure with the entrepreneur leading by example and communicating directly.

The entrepreneurial structure works quite well up to a couple of dozen employees. However, around this point it starts creaking at the seams as entrepreneurs try to do everything themselves. Even when they try to delegate and introduce new staff who report to existing members of staff, entrepreneurs tend to meddle and the new employees soon find an informal reporting line to the entrepreneur, short circuiting the manager or supervisor they are supposed to report to, as in Figure 8.2b. It is no wonder that this creates frustration, resentment and an unwillingness to accept responsibility in the manager. Why should they take responsibility when their decisions are likely to be questioned or reversed, or when staff supposedly reporting to them are constantly being checked up on by the entrepreneur?

The root cause of these problems lie in the entrepreneurial character and, in particular, the strong need for control that can exhibit itself in some entrepreneurs. Derek du Toit (1980), an entrepreneur himself, said that 'an entrepreneur who starts his own business generally does so because he is a difficult employee'. He probably finds it difficult to be in the alternating dominant and then submissive role so often asked of middle management. He hates being told what to do and wants to tell everybody what to do. He also believes he can do the job better than others, which may be true, but he must find a way of working through others if the business is to grow successfully.

Kets de Vries (1985) was probably the first to argue that these traits can lead to entrepreneurs wanting to over-control their business – becoming 'control freaks'. This is not such a problem in a micro business, where the owner-manager does everything

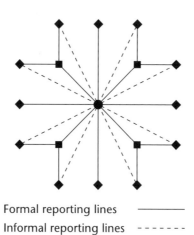

Formal reporting lines ————
Informal reporting lines - - - - - -

Figure 8.2b The entrepreneurial spider's web grows

themselves anyway, where their business is their life and their life is the business. Indeed it can be a virtue – making certain everything gets done properly. However, as the business grows this characteristic starts to be a problem. For example, in a fruit juice bottling plant with about 200 employees the owner-manager could not bear to relinquish any control to senior managers and insisted that copies of all external correspondence came to him. In this way he believed he still had some control. De Vries says employees in these situations become 'infantilised', expected to behave as incompetent idiots, taking few decisions and circulating little information. The better ones just do not stay.

There is no single 'correct' organisation structure, but the entrepreneurial structure must evolve to become more formal, although not bureaucratic. Whilst keeping levels of management to a minimum, there needs to be a hierarchy of some sort that gives managers confidence that they have the authority to manage. The traditional hierarchical structures of the kind shown in Figure 8.3a are most suited to organisations that require security and stability. The matrix or task structure shown in Figure 8.3b is often seen in organisations undertaking project work, for example consultancies. It can be combined very effectively with the hierarchical structure.

Traditional hierarchical structures as in Figure 8.3a are most appropriate where firms are tackling simple tasks with extensive standardisation, in stable environments, where security is important. As the environment becomes more liable to change, standardisation becomes less viable and responsibility for coping with unexpected changes needs to be pushed down the hierarchy. Complex tasks in stable environments mean that it becomes worthwhile developing standard skills to tackle the complexities. The matrix organisation shown in Figure 8.3b is appropriate here with teams working within set protocols – as they do, for example, in a surgical operation.

The appropriate organisation structure therefore depends upon the complexity of the task and the degree of change in the environment. The main characteristic of the entrepreneurial environment is change. In a changing environment where there is high task complexity an innovative, flexible, decentralised structure is needed. Authority for decision-making needs to be delegated. Team-working is likely to be the norm with matrix structures involved somehow in the organisation. Decentralisation often involves having structures within structures. As the entrepreneurial organisation becomes larger this is likely to evolve into the organic structure explained further in Chapter 18.

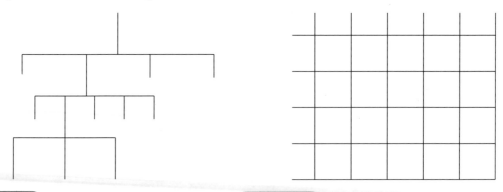

Figure 8.3a The hierarchical structure   **Figure 8.3b** The matrix structure

Where there is low task complexity in a changing environment there is scope for greater centralisation but the structure needs to be responsive to change, probably through central direction and supervision from the entrepreneur. The structure, although hierarchical, should be relatively flat with few middle management positions. However, culture is still important because the workforce still need to be motivated to make these frequent changes to their work practices. A business is a little like a house. If people are the bricks that are used to build it, the organisation structure is the plan for the house and the culture is the cement that holds the bricks together. Ignore any one element at your peril.

Changing skills

As the business grows and the scale of activities increases, the entrepreneur has to learn to delegate. The business will need to take on a more formal hierarchical structure and the structure will need to be adhered to, by everybody. The entrepreneur has to learn to control the business by monitoring information rather than by direct physical intervention – which is their preferred approach. They have to rely on collecting information in different ways, at appropriate times. This information comes in different forms but it generally relates to the business functions

Case with questions

David Poole set up his direct-marketing agency **DP&A** in 1995. By 1999 turnover was £25.1 million, profit £349 000 and cash reserves totalled £1.2 million. Although it ranks 15th in its industry, it is still a small player compared with the top five. Dan Douglas, creative director, and Tony Appi, commercial director, each own 20 per cent but David Poole maintains 60 per cent. He wants to expand rapidly but a newspaper article on the firm highlighted the issue of control. Here are some quotes from David Poole:

> I have got to do things my way and prove I've got what it takes ... I love my business and find it massively stimulating, but I guess it all boils down to ego.

> I haven't spent a lot of time on strategic planning ... I have an open and honest relationship with my fellow directors, but they haven't yet been involved in strategic planning. I don't want to distract them from their core work. I'm capable of taking the decisions myself ... A venture capitalist will have a strategy that is not necessarily in line with the best interests of the company and will always be looking towards a profitable exit, so effectively I would not be in charge.

> [Going to the stock market] would give access to funding for development and provided I continued to perform well then I would keep control [but] quite simply we are too small.

Sunday Times 20 February 2000

Question
What insights do David Poole's comments give you into his views, priorities and personality?

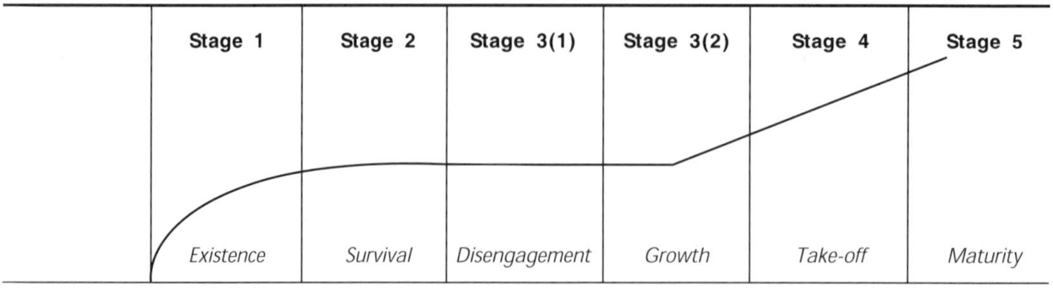

	Stage 1	Stage 2	Stage 3(1)	Stage 3(2)	Stage 4	Stage 5
	Existence	*Survival*	*Disengagement*	*Growth*	*Take-off*	*Maturity*
Management style	Direct supervision	Supervised supervision	Functional	Functional	Divisional	Line and staff
Organisation	Simple	Growing	Growing	Growing	Growing	Sophisticated
Extent of formal systems	Minimal to non-existent	Minimal	Basic	Developing	Maturing	Extensive
Major strategic imperative	Existence	Survival	Maintaining profitable status quo	Obtain resources for growth	Growth	Return on investment

Figure 8.4   The Churchill and Lewis growth model

of people management, marketing and financial control. Information then has to be translated into action, and again the processes have to become more formalised. In other words, at the same time as the role of the founder is changing, so too are the skills they require.

The Churchill and Lewis (1983) model, shown in Figure 8.4, is often used to link marketing, people and financial management issues. The five stages are identified as follows:

1 *Existence*   The business strategy is to stay alive, and the company needs to find customers and deliver products/services. Everything has a short-term time horizon. The organisation is simple, typically the spider's web in Figure 8.2a, with one-to-one relationship management and direct supervision. The owner does everything, or at least is involved in doing everything. Planning is minimal, sometimes non-existent.

2 *Survival*   The business imperative is to establish the customer base and product portfolio. The company has to demonstrate that it has sufficient products and customers to be a viable business. It has to control its revenues and expenses to maintain cash flow. The organisation is still simple and planning is, at best, short-term involving cash flow forecasting. The owner is still 'the business'. The spider's web still exists, with one-to-one relationship management and direct supervision.

3 *Success*   By this stage the company is big enough and has sufficient customers and sales to establish itself with confidence. The owner has supervisors or managers in place and basic marketing, financial and operations systems are operating.

Planning is in the form of operational budgets. This company has two strategic options:

- Option 1 is disengagement. If it can maintain its market niche or adapt to changing circumstances, it can stay like this for a long time. If not, it will either cease to exist or drop back to the survival stage. This is what we described in an earlier chapter as a lifestyle business.
- Option 2 is growth. If this is a viable and desirable option then the entrepreneur must consolidate, clarify the vision and ensure that resources are diverted into growth. This is where they must start to give clear leadership, based upon the vision they have for the firm and a clear strategy as to how the vision might be achieved. However, throughout all this the business must remain profitable.

4 *Take-off* This stage is dangerous and therefore critical. The entrepreneur must ensure that satisfactory financial resources and good management are in place to take the company through it. If this stage is handled properly the company can become very successful and large.
5 *Maturity* The business now begins to develop the characteristics of a stable, larger company with professional management and formal information systems, and will have established strategic planning.

Churchill and Lewis also developed a simple summary of the key factors which affect the success or failure of a business in the different stages of its life. These are split between the attributes of the owner-manager and resources. Table 8.1 shows the factors and their relative importance. The important point is the move from the owner's operational ability to their strategic ability as the business grows. This is one of the key qualities of leadership. Lifestyle businesses can survive on high levels of operational ability and relatively lower levels of managerial and strategic ability. This changes at the take-off stage. Even when the business is mature, in the final stage, the

Table 8.1 Churchill and Lewis's growth stage imperatives

	Stage 1 Existence	Stage 2 Survival	Stage 3 Success	Stage 4 Take-off	Stage 5 Maturity
Owner's attributes					
Own goals	☆☆☆	☆	☆☆☆	☆☆☆	☆☆
Operational ability	☆☆☆	☆☆☆	☆☆	☆☆	☆
Management ability	☆	☆☆	☆☆	☆☆☆	☆☆
Strategic ability	☆	☆☆	☆☆☆	☆☆☆	☆☆☆
Resources					
Financial	☆☆☆	☆☆☆	☆☆	☆☆☆	☆☆
Personnel	☆	☆	☆☆	☆☆☆	☆☆
Systems	☆	☆☆	☆☆☆	☆☆☆	☆☆
Business	☆☆☆	☆☆☆	☆☆	☆☆	☆

Critical ☆☆☆   Important but manageable ☆☆   Not very important ☆

Table 8.2 The Scott and Bruce growth model

	Top management role	Management style	Organisational structure
Inception	Direct supervision	Entrepreneurial and individualistic	Unstructured
Survival	Supervised supervision	Entrepreneurial and administrative	Simple
Growth	Delegation and coordination	Entrepreneurial and coordination	Functional and centralised
Expansion	Decentralisation	Professional and administrative	Functional and decentralised
Maturity	Decentralisation	Watchdog	Decentralised and functional/product

ability of the owner to think strategically is still critical to its development. The other point to notice is the increasing importance of personnel and systems resources at the take-off stage. In lifestyle businesses these are less important, although some lifestyle businesses do have strong systems that allow them to 'tick over' with the minimum intervention of the owner-manager.

Drawing heavily upon the work of Greiner and Churchill and Lewis, there have been a number of other growth models. Scott and Bruce (1987) proposed a five-stage model, summarised in Table 8.2. This shows the appropriate management role, style and organisational structure at different stages. As can be seen, once into the expansion phase the firm loses many of the characteristics of the entrepreneurial firm.

A four-stage model proposed by Burns (1996) summarises the main business imperatives as a firm grows in terms of the orientation of the firm and then the main functional disciplines of management, marketing, accounting and finance. This is shown in Table 8.3. It also emphasises the drift from informal to more formal structures. In this model, lifestyle businesses that never go beyond the survival stage can exist using an informal, tactical orientation on a day-to-day basis. Once they go into the success phase they need to take on a far more strategic orientation, with more formalised procedures and structures. At this phase they also start to recruit managers to the business. Managers coming from other, often larger, firms is associated with successful growth. Perhaps this is related to the changes in culture that are taking place in the firm at this stage.

An interesting feature of this model is the way it describes the changes in the functional disciplines. For example, marketing changes from simply getting customers, developing relationships and finding out why they buy from you into developing a unique selling proposition (USP) based upon what is working (called 'emergent strategy formulation'), and then using relationships and networks to get repeat sales. In the growth phase this becomes the basis of defining and developing some form of competitive advantage which will allow the firm to attack the competition.

Table 8.3 The Burns growth model

	Existence	Survival	Success	Take-off
Orientation	• Tactical	• Tactical	• Strategic	• Strategic
Management	• Owner is the business and is 'jack of all trades' • Spider's-web organisation • Informal, flexible systems • Opportunity driven	• Owner is still the business • Still spider's web organisation • Some delegation, supervision and control	• Staff start to be recruited • Organisation starts to become formalised • Staff encouraged and motivated to grow into job • Delegation, supervision and control • Strategic planning	• Staff roles clearly defined • Decentralisation starts • Greater coordination and control of staff • Emergence of professional management • Operational and strategic planning
Marketing	• Get customers • Undertake market research • Develop relationships and networks	• Generate repeat sales • Develop unique selling proposition (USP) and select market segmentation • Use relationships and networks	• Generate repeat sales and find new customers • Develop competitive advantage based upon USP and target markets • Use relationships and networks	• Select new customers and generate repeat sales • Aggressively attack competition • Use relationships and networks
Accounting	• Cash flow	• Cash flow • Accounting controls • Break-even and margin of safety	• Cash flow • Accounting controls • Break-even and margin of safety • Balance sheet engineering	• Cash flow • Accounting controls • Break-even and margin of safety • Balance sheet engineering
Finance	• Own funds • Creditors, HP, leasing • Bank loans	• Own funds • Creditors, HP, leasing, factoring • Bank loans	• First phase venture capital • Creditors, HP, leasing, factoring • Bank loans	• Venture capital • Creditors, HP, leasing, factoring • Bank loans

These models are often used as predictors of the problems that the firm is likely to face as it grows. However, they have four problems associated with them:

1 Most firms do not experience growth and never get beyond the first stage, many dying shortly after start-up.
2 If they do experience growth, it is not quite in the way or sequence as the models predict. There are so many variables that it is unlikely all will come together at the same time. For example, the owner-manager's managerial style might be inherited from their previous employment and be out of phase with the organisational structure.
3 Often firms reach a plateau in their development at certain stages of the model – particularly survival – and do not progress beyond that phase, preferring to remain a lifestyle business. Indeed most firms do not survive the recurrent crises they face.
4 The actual sequence of issues or imperatives predicted by the models is not supported by empirical research. This is particularly true of Greiner's model.

Because of these issues the models are probably best used as checklists of the imperatives that an entrepreneur and a firm ought to face up to if they wish to grow through the different stages of development. The models should not be applied mechanistically, but rather with judgement and discretion, particularly in relation to sequence and timing. However, they provide an invaluable description of the changing role of the entrepreneur and the skills they need. Whatever you may think of these models, there is a well documented process of growth to crisis to consolidation that many surviving firms follow (shown in Figure 8.5).

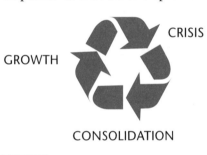

GROWTH

CRISIS

CONSOLIDATION

Figure 8.5 The growth process

Coping with crises

Figure 8.5 glosses over the considerable problem of coping with successive crises. As the company passes through each crisis, the entrepreneur faces a rollercoaster of human emotions as they find themselves facing a different role with new demands. The classic change/denial curve shown in Figure 8.6 illustrates these changes very well and can offer insights into the attitude of the entrepreneur at each stage (Kakabadse, 1983). At each stage in the growth curve the entrepreneurs must learn to become more effective in their new roles and to adopt new attitudes and skills. As with any change, this can take time.

- *Phase 1* The unfamiliarity of entrepreneurs with their new roles makes them feel anxious about their contribution and so their effectiveness drops slightly. They need to get used to the new circumstances. Within a short time, having become used to the role using previously successful skills, and finding support to help

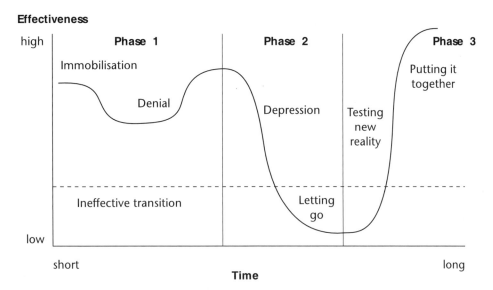

Effectiveness

Phase 1

Immobilisation

Denial

Ineffective transition

Phase 2

Depression

Testing new reality

Letting go

Phase 3

Putting it together

high

low

short

long

Time

Figure 8.6 Work effectiveness through change

them, their effectiveness improves and they start to believe that they do not have to change. This is the denial phase.

- *Phase 2* Real demands are now being made and entrepreneurs experience real stress as they realise that they do have to develop new skills to keep up with the job. They need to relearn their role. Although they may eventually learn how to do their new job, a period of anxiety makes them less effective because they can no longer rely on their old skills and they may believe that they can no longer cope. In fact this 'low' indicates that the person is realising that they have to change and then, at some point, they abandon the past and accept the future. However, it is the most dangerous point in the change cycle as the entrepreneur feels really stressed and may be tempted to give up.

- *Phase 3* This testing period can be as frustrating as it can be rewarding. Mistakes can recreate the 'low', but, as the newly learnt skills are brought into play effectively, the entrepreneurs' performance improves and they achieve a higher level of effectiveness than at the beginning of the stage. They now have a set of new skills alongside their old ones. However, this transition is not inevitable and some people fail to acquire new skills or cannot pull themselves out of the 'low'. The risk is that entrepreneurs may give up.

The role of leader

The challenge for the entrepreneur as the firm grows is to become an effective leader of a cohesive management team. Timmons (1999) says that successful entrepreneurs are 'patient leaders, capable of instilling tangible visions and managing for the long haul. The entrepreneur is at once a learner and a teacher, a doer and a visionary.' He talks about six dominant themes for successful entrepreneurs:

1 Leadership;
2 Commitment and determination;
3 Opportunity obsession;
4 Tolerance of risk, ambiguity and uncertainty;
5 Creativity, self-reliance and ability to adapt;
6 Motivation to excel.

Case insight

Born in 1965, **Michael Dell** is the ninth richest man in the world with a fortune in excess of £12.5 billion. He started **Dell Computers** in 1984 with just £620. Today the company is worth billions and employs some 37 000 people, globally.

His entrepreneurial career started early. At the age of 12 he made £1200 by selling his stamp collection. At the age of 14 he devised a marketing scheme to sell newspapers which earned him over £11 000. From the age of 15 his interest in calculators and then computers started to grow. He started buying microchips and other bits of computer hardware in order to build systems because he realised that he could buy, say, a disk drive for £500 which would sell in the shops for £1800. In 1983 he began a pre-med degree at the University of Texas but dropped out fairly quickly to set up his own business selling computers direct to end-users.

From the start Michael Dell knew what was the critical success factor for his business. He used an expert to build prototype computers whilst he concentrated on finding cheap components. The firm grew at an incredible pace, notching up sales of £3.7 million in the first nine months. The company has gone on to pioneer direct marketing in the industry and, more lately, integrated supply chain management. At all times it has focused clearly on a low-cost/low-price marketing strategy.

Michael Dell has moved from being an entrepreneur, wheeling and dealing in cheap components, then innovating in direct marketing techniques, to being a visionary leader, understanding where his competitive advantage lies and then putting into place the systems and processes to keep his company two steps ahead of the competition.

➡

If ever the job definition for a leader were written it would probably include five elements:

1 *Having vision and ideas* It is this that gives people a clear focus on the key issues and concerns facing the firm, the values it stands for, where it is going and how it will get there. Entrepreneurs, typically, find this part of the job definition easiest. They have vision and ideas in abundance, indeed often too many ideas and the problem is persuading them to focus on any one at a time.
2 *Being able to undertake long-term, strategic planning* It is one thing to know where you want to go, it is quite another to know how you get there. The heart of leadership is about being able to chart a course for future development that steers the firm towards the leader's business aims. Most textbooks talk about strategies being deliberate, consciously intended courses of action. Entrepreneurs often

believe they are bad at this. However, strategies can also emerge as consistent patterns that lead to success over a period of time or course of events. They 'emerge' without advance deliberation. The trick for entrepreneurs is to spot the successful patterns, capitalise upon them and use them as part of future strategy. Body Shop's characteristic green-painted pine decor was as much born out of lack of cash as anything else, yet it came to symbolise its 'no-frills' approach to retailing. Any start-up needs some luck to survive, but the skill for the entrepreneur is to recognise what works and what is needed to build upon that success. Subsequent chapters deal with this process.

3 *Being able to communicate effectively* Even if entrepreneurs have a vision and a strategy, they still have to communicate it to the stakeholders in the business. This is about inspiring and motivating staff, customers and financiers so that they understand where the business is going, how it is going to get there and motivating them to make it happen. It is about persuading them that the firm can deal with an uncertain environment and manage that most difficult thing of all, rapid change.

4 *Creating an appropriate culture within the firm* We defined culture in Chapter 2 as 'the collective programming of the mind which distinguishes one group of people from another.' At a firm level we might simply call it 'how it is around here' – that pattern of taken for granted assumptions. Creating an appropriate culture in the firm is the single most important thing a leader has to do.

5 *Monitoring and controlling performance* This is the routine task that entrepreneurs like least and are probably worst at doing. Typically, entrepreneurs prefer informal systems which involve direct, personal supervision and control, rather than formal systems which involve checking information and dealing with paperwork. However, as the firm grows the informal systems start to break down and need to be replaced by regular, routine procedures and some elements of a hierarchical organisation structure are bound to appear.

Nevertheless control information can be tailored so as to be the minimum needed to manage the firm on an exception basis. For example, rather than poring over detailed financial statements every month the entrepreneur could monitor the six financial drivers covered in Chapter 7. Only when these are out of line with the budgets will further investigation be necessary. In a later chapter we shall look at how larger firms are controlled and how budgets can be used to help entrepreneurs delegate.

Vision and mission

Vision is a key element of both entrepreneurship and leadership. A vision is a shared mental image of a desired future state – an ideal of what the enterprise can become – a new and better world. It must be a realistic, credible and attractive future and one that engages and energises people (Nanus, 1992). It is usually *qualitative* rather than quantitative (that is the role of the objectives). Vision is seen as inspiring and motivating, transcending logic and contractual relationships. It is more emotional than analytic, something that touches the heart. It gives existence within an organisation to that most fundamental of human cravings – a sense of meaning and purpose. As Bartlett and Ghoshal (1994) explain:

Traditionally top-level managers have tried to engage employees intellectually through the persuasive logic of strategic analysis. But clinically framed and contractually based relationships do not inspire the extraordinary effort and sustained commitment required to deliver consistently superior performance ... Senior managers must convert the contractual employees of an economic entity into committed members of a purposeful organisation.

Visions, then, are aspirational but they can take many forms. They can be intrinsic, directing the organisation to do things better in some way, such as improving customer satisfaction or increasing product innovation. They can be extrinsic, for example beating the competition. But what do you do when you have beaten the competition? Vision is formally communicated through the vision or mission statement. This often includes reference to the product or service (basis for competitive advantage, quality, innovation and so on), customer groups and the benefits they derive or competitors. Often it encompasses the *values* upheld by the company. Any vision or mission statement should be short, snappy and as memorable as possible. Some examples are given in the box below. Wickham (2001) suggests a generic format:

(*The company*) aims to use its (*competitive advantage*) to achieve/maintain (*aspirations*) in providing (*product scope*) which offers (*benefits*) to satisfy the (*needs*) of (*customer scope*). In doing this the company will at all times strive to uphold (*values*).

Dell Mission

Dell's mission is to be the most successful computer company in the world at delivering the best computer experience in markets we serve. In doing so, Dell will meet customer expectations of:

- Highest quality;
- Leading technology;
- Competitive pricing;
- Individual and company accountability;
- Best-in-class service and support;
- Flexible customisation capability;
- Superior corporate citizenship;
- Financial stability.

easyJet Mission

To provide our customers with safe, good value, point-to-point air services. To effect and to offer a consistent and reliable product and fares appealing to leisure and business markets on a range of European routes. To achieve this we will develop our people and establish lasting relationships with our suppliers.

> 'Entrepreneurs have to make their own decisions and follow their vision. They must motivate their team, get them to ignore shaky markets and a possible war and look positively to the future, to keep exploring uncharted territory. To do that they have to subscribe to the entrepreneur's vision – but they don't necessarily have to agree with it.'
>
> **Derrick Collin** founder and managing director of **Brulines Ltd**
> *The Times* 10 October 2001
> ●

Having your own individual vision is relatively easy. Building a shared vision in an organisation is no easy task – it is not about simply going off and writing a 'vision statement'. Visions are living things that evolve over time. Developing the vision is a continuous process. It involves continually checking with staff to ensure that the vision has a resonance with them – modifying it little by little, if appropriate. Entrepreneurs can find this difficult and frustrating as they are more used to setting goals and seeking compliance. But to survive in a larger organisation they need to develop their political skills.

Good visions motivate. Two strong motivations for people are fear and aspiration. Fear is probably the strongest motivation that helps galvanise action and force people to change, but probably lasts only a short time. This motivation worked well for Winston Churchill in the Second World War. However, aspiration – what we might become – has a greater longevity and is altogether a more positive motivator. It is the one that underpins most entrepreneurial organisations. It emphasises striving – a continuous journey of improvement.

It is not sufficient simply to have a vision, that vision must also be communicated. In this respect the leader is often held out as being a storyteller. Gardner (1995) maintains this is *the* key leadership skill. This storytelling skill can be either verbal or written, however, leaders must 'walk-the-talk' – practise what they preach – otherwise they have no credibility and are not believed. Gardner maintains that the most successful stories are simple ones that hit an emotional resonance with the audience, addressing questions of identity and providing answers to questions concerning personal, social and moral choices. Is it any wonder that entrepreneurs skilled at developing personal relationships can also become powerful leaders?

> 'Where any three people within an organisation will give the same answer to a question on the company's mission statement. That reflects total coherency and a focused workforce.'
>
> **Gururaj Deshpande** serial entrepreneur and founder of **Sycamore Networks**
> *Financial Times* 21 February 2000
> ●

Senge (1992) highlights the creative tension this storytelling must create:

The leader's story, sense of purpose, values and vision establish the direction and target. His relentless commitment to the truth and to inquiry into the forces underlying current reality continually highlight the gaps between reality and the vision. Leaders generate and manage this creative tension – not just themselves but in an entire organisation. This is how they energise an organisation. That is their basic job. That is why they exist.

John Kotter's Seven Principles for Successfully Communicating a Vision

1 *Keep it simple*: Focused and jargon free.
2 *Use metaphors, analogies and examples*: Engage the imagination.
3 *Use many different forums*: The same message should come from as many different directions as possible.
4 *Repeat the message*: The same message should be repeated again, and again, and again.
5 *Lead by example*: Walk the talk.
6 *Address small inconsistencies*: Small changes can have big effects if their symbolism is important to staff.
7 *Listen and be listened to*: Work hard to listen, it pays dividends.

Source Adapted from Kotter, P. (1996) *Leading Change*, Boston: Harvard Business School Press.

He goes on to underline how this can create within an entire organisation the sense of internal locus of control – emphasising the belief in control over destiny – that is an essential part of the entrepreneurial character: 'Mastering creative tension throughout an organisation leads to a profoundly different view of reality. People literally start to see more and more aspects of reality as something that they, collectively, can influence.' And this is one important psychological way that individuals within the entrepreneurial organisation deal with the uncertainty they face. You might recognise it as one aspect of 'empowerment'.

Bennis and Nanus (1985) talk about a 'spark of genius' in the act of leadership which 'operates on the emotional and spiritual resources of the organisation.' For them the genius of the leader lies in 'this transcending ability, a kind of magic, to assemble – out of a variety of images, signals, forecasts and alternatives – a clearly articulated vision of the future that is at once simple, easily understood, clearly desirable, and energising'. But entrepreneurial leadership that is to perpetuate itself is more than just charismatic leadership. Charismatic leaders deal in visions and crises, but little in between. Entrepreneurial leadership is about systematic and purposeful development of leadership skills and techniques – which can take a long time. It is about developing relationships. It is about creating long-term sustainable competitive advantage based upon the 'architecture' of entrepreneurial leadership outlined in Chapter 18.

Values

Values are the core beliefs upon which the organisation is founded. They underpin vision and, as you can see with the case of Body Shop, they also underpin the mission of the organisation. They set expectations regarding how the organisation operates and how it treats people. The vision and mission of the organisation must be consistent with its values. All three go hand-in-hand, one reinforcing the other. In a start-up they reflect the values of the founder, but as the organisation grows they often reflect a wider community and face the risk of being diluted to the point where they are not clear. Organisations with strong values tend to recruit staff who are able

Body Shop

Values

- We consider testing products or ingredients on animals to be morally and scientifically indefensible;
- We support small producer communities around the world who supply us with accessories and natural ingredients;
- We know that you are unique, and we'll always treat you as an individual. We like you just the way you are;
- We believe that it is the responsibility of every individual to actively support those who have human rights denied to them;
- We believe that a business has the responsibility to protect the environment in which it operates, locally and globally.

Mission

- To dedicate our business to the pursuit of social and environmental change;
- To creatively balance the financial and human needs of our stakeholders, employees, customers, franchisees and shareholders;
- To courageously ensure that our business is ecologically sustainable: meeting the needs of the present without compromising the future;
- To meaningfully contribute to local, national and international communities in which we trade, by adopting a code of conduct which ensures care, honesty, fairness and respect;
- To passionately campaign for the protection of the environment, human and civil rights, and against animal testing within the cosmetics and toiletries industry;
- To tirelessly work to narrow the gap between principle and practice, whilst making fun, passion and care part of our daily lives.

to identify with those values and thus they become reinforced. Body Shop tends to recruit franchisees who identify with its moral and environmentally friendly values.

Values are important because they create a constant framework within which to operate in a turbulent, changing environment. As represented in Figure 8.7, whilst strategies and tactics might change rapidly in an entrepreneurial firm, vision and values are enduring. They form the 'road-map' that tells everyone in the organisation where it is going and how it will get there, even when one route is blocked. Values form part of the cognitive processes that help shape and develop the culture of the organisation. They guide strategy and help delegate authority – telling people what is the 'right' thing to do. Shared values form a bond that binds the organisation together – aligning and motivating people. They help develop a high-trust culture that cements long-term relationships.

Values need to be articulated and taught by leaders by 'walking-the-talk' or practising what they preach. They are not negotiable and need to be reinforced through recognition and reward. They need to be embedded in the systems and procedures of the organisation, so that everybody can see clearly that the

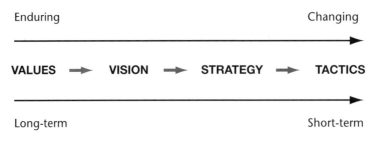

Figure 8.7 Values, vision, strategy and tactics

organisation means what it says. Nonaka (1991) recommends the use of language, metaphor and analogy in promoting values, which he sees as promoting the special capabilities of the organisation that enable resources to be leveraged internally, thereby creating competitive advantage.

Case insight

The **John Lewis Partnership**, the department-store group, is Britain's largest unquoted company. Its founder, **John Spedan Lewis**, had strong moral beliefs. He believed in ensuring the well-being of all his employees by giving them a stake in the business. Today they own 100 per cent of it. He opened his first drapers store in Oxford Street, London in 1864 with another pledge that is still kept today – never knowingly undersold.

Today the company has 26 department stores, with a flagship branch in London's Oxford Street, and 145 Waitrose supermarkets with 60 000 employees, all partners in the business sharing in its profits. It also owns 40 per cent of the online grocery retailer Ocado, which delivers Waitrose products. Profits in the year to January 2004 were £202 million on sales of £4.5 billion. Chairmen of the company still have to swear an oath that they will never investigate demutualising the business.

Creating culture

Edgar Schein (1990) says that the only important thing that leaders do may well be constructing culture. He says that an organisation's culture is grounded in the founder's basic beliefs, values and assumptions. So, how do you go about creating culture in an organisation? We have identified and explored the crucial role of values – what is worth having or doing – and vision – where we are going and how we will get there – and how it is communicated in creating culture. Having entrepreneurship at the core of these values is fundamental and essential for the success of the entrepreneneurial organisation. Values related to entrepreneurship include creativity, achievement, ownership, change and perseverance.

This is the first step, a necessary but not a sufficient condition. It underpins everything else. Beyond this, Bowman and Faulkner (1997) talk about organisational culture being formed or embedded in an organisation from three influences; organisational processes, cognitive processes and behaviours. All these influences are represented in Figure 8.8.

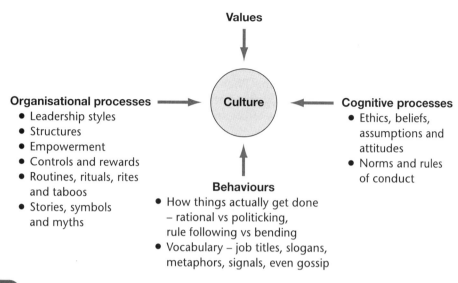

Figure 8.8 Constructing culture

- *Organisational processes* These can be deliberate or emergent, evolving organically from within the organisation and may not be intended. There are many influences on this:

  - The organisational structure can influence culture. Hierarchical organisations can discourage initiative. Functional specialisation can create parochial attitudes and sends signals about which skills might be valued.
  - The power to make decisions is an important dimension for entrepreneurial organisations. Flat, decentralised structures send signals about encouraging decision-making, although sometimes informal power can lie outside formal hierarchies.
  - Controls and rewards send important signals about what the firm values. People take notice of what behaviour gets rewarded – as well as what gets punished – and behave accordingly. Status, praise and public recognition are powerful motivators.
  - Management and leadership styles, as we shall see later in the chapter, are an important influence. They send signals about appropriate behaviour. How managers allocate time sends signals about priorities.
  - Routines and rituals can have a strong subconscious influence. They form the unquestioned fabric of everyday life, but they say a lot about the organisation. 'Guarded' or 'open' management offices, reserved or unreserved parking spaces, dress codes, normal methods of communication all influence the culture of the organisation.
  - Stories and symbols have a part to play in preserving and perpetuating culture. Who are the heroes, villains and mavericks in the firm? What do staff talk about at lunch? Are there symbols of status that are important such as car or office size? How do staff talk about customers? How do staff talk about the entrepreneur and other senior managers?

- *Cognitive processes* These are the beliefs, assumptions, values and attitudes staff hold in common and take for granted. They are embedded and emanate from the organisation's philosophy, values, morality and creed. They are likely to be strongest in firms that have a long history and where staff join young and stay on in the firm for most of their careers. Therefore in a new, entrepreneurial firm they can be moulded and developed by the enthusiasm and personality of the entrepreneur. Even in larger firms this can be developed through training processes.
- *Behaviour* This is what actually happens in an organisation. Behaviour in organisations normally reflects and reinforces culture. However behaviour can also be influenced by a wide variety of external influences, within society as a whole, within a profession or within a sector or industry. Behaviour that becomes routine can be difficult to change. However, attitudes can be influenced over time by getting people to behave in certain ways.

Most small firms start life with a 'task culture' – getting the job done. If the entrepreneur finds it difficult to delegate that may turn into a 'power culture' – where people vie to have power and influence over the entrepreneur. As this sort of firm grows, especially if the delegated authority is not genuine, there is a danger of developing a 'role culture' whereby job titles become too important. These cultures are not conducive to success and are to be avoided. Timmons (1999) says that a successful entrepreneurial culture can be described along six dimensions:

- The degree of organisational clarity in terms of goals, tasks, procedures and so on;
- The degree to which high standards are expected;
- The extent to which employees are committed to the firm's goals;
- The extent to which they feel responsible for these goals without being constantly monitored;
- The extent to which they feel they are recognised and rewarded for high performance;
- The extent to which there is a sense of cohesion and team working within the firm.

An entrepreneurial culture needs to motivate people to do the right things, in the right way, for the organisation as well as for themselves. Entrepreneurs are good at doing this by example – 'walking-the-talk' – but as the firm grows they need to find different ways of communicating with more people. Body Shop now sends out a monthly video to all employees giving news of what has been happening, new business initiatives as well as reinforcing the values the firm stands for. Equally simple things can tell you a lot about the culture of the firm. What impression does a firm with reserved parking spaces and managers in offices 'guarded' by secretaries give you? If salaries are based mainly on sales bonuses and there is a monthly league table of the best sales people, what does this tell you about the firm, its values and its goals? The culture of a firm comes from the entrepreneur, it reflects their personal values, but it is made up of a lot of small items of detail. Cultures can come about by chance, but if entrepreneurs want to plan for success, they need to plan to achieve the culture they want. And, as we shall see in Chapter 18, it is a vital element in maintaining the entrepreneurial focus in a larger organisation.

Leadership style

The role of leader is normally based on some sort of authority. Authority can derive from role or status, tradition, legal position, expert skills or their charismatic personality. Timmons (1999) believes that in successful entrepreneurial ventures leadership is based on expertise rather than authority and this then means there is no competition for leadership. Many of the best known, successful entrepreneurs clearly also have charisma.

It is a myth to think that leaders are born, not made. Like entrepreneurship, leadership is a skill that can be developed. However, it is a complex thing. As represented in Figure 8.9, it depends upon the interactions and interconnections between the leader, the task, the group being led and the situation or context. A leader may prefer an informal, non-directional style, but faced with a young apprentice working a dangerous lathe he might be forgiven for reverting to a fairly formal, directive style with heavy supervision. In that situation the change in style is appropriate. Try the same style with a group of senior creative marketing consultants and there would be problems. Many different styles may be effective, with different tasks, different groups and in different contexts. What is more, there is no evidence of any single leadership style characterising successful businesses.

Figure 8.9 Leadership style

Leader and task

The leadership grid shown in Figure 8.10 was developed by Blake and Mouton (1978). It shows style as dependent upon the leader's concern for task compared to their concern for people. Entrepreneurs are usually more concerned with completing the task but, as the firm grows, must become more concerned with people if the tasks are to be accomplished. Task leadership may be appropriate in certain situations, for example emergencies, but concern for people must surface at some point if effective,

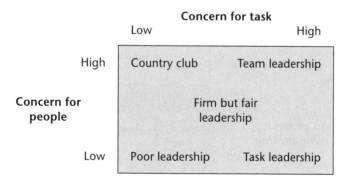

Figure 8.10 Leader and task

trusting relationships are to develop. Low concern for both people and task is hardly leadership at all. High concern for people – the country-club style – is rare in business but can be appropriate in community groups, small charities or social clubs where good relationships and high morale might be the dominant objectives.

Timmons (1999) believes that the emphasis in successful entrepreneurial ventures is more on performing task orientated roles although 'someone inevitably provides for maintenance and group cohesion by good humour and wit'. If this is the case then it is even more important to ensure that there is an appropriate and effective management team in place.

Leader and group

Leadership style also depends on the relationship of the leader with the group they are leading. Figure 8.11 shows this in relation to the leader's degree of authority and the group's autonomy in decision-making. If a leader has high authority but the group has low autonomy, they will tend to adopt an autocratic style, simply instructing people what to do. If they have low authority, for whatever reason, they will tend to adopt a paternalistic style, cajoling the group into doing things, picking off individuals and offering grace and favour in exchange for performance. If the leader has low authority and the group has high autonomy, then they will tend to adopt a participative style, involving all the group in decision-making and moving forward with consensus. If the leader has high authority then they will seek opinions but make the decision themselves using a consultative style.

A survey of small-business managers in Britain, France, Germany, Spain and Italy showed that most used a consultative style (Burns and Whitehouse, 1996). However, 20–30 per cent of managers in all countries other than Germany used an autocratic style. It has been said that growth orientated companies are initially characterised by an autocratic or dictatorial style, but as the company grows, a more consultative style develops (Ray and Hutchinson, 1983). The survey confirmed this. Leadership styles also seem to be influenced by national culture. The survey revealed that a significant (35 per cent) proportion of German managers use a participative style, despite the fact that none of them thought their subordinates liked it. This probably reflects cultural differences at a national level, where consultative or participative decision-making is the norm, particularly when unions are involved. However, this mismatch between actual style, dictated by cultural norms, and desired style must create tension for German entrepreneurs.

	Leader's authority	
	Low	High
High	Participative	Consultative
Low	Paternalistic	Autocratic

Group autonomy in decision-making

Figure 8.11 Leader and group

Leader and situation

John Adair (1984) put forward the view that the weight the leader should put on these different influences depends on the situation or context they find themselves in. In an entrepreneurial firm that situation can be characterised as one of uncertainty, ambiguity and rapid change. What does that tell us about the context? Timmons (1999) observed that:

> There is among successful entrepreneurs a well-developed capacity to exert influence without formal power. These people are adept at conflict resolution. They know when to use logic and when to persuade, when to make a concession, and when to exact one. To run a successful venture, an entrepreneur learns to get along with different constituencies, often with conflicting aims – the customer, the supplier, the financial backer, the creditor, as well as the partners and others on the inside. Success comes when the entrepreneur is a mediator, a negotiator, rather than a dictator.

How good entrepreneurial leaders approach any task, with any group, therefore depends on the situation they face. But entrepreneurial firms face an environment that is constantly changing, which can often lead to conflict as they try to get people to do different things or things differently. The Thomas-Kilman Conflict Modes instrument (p. 234) gives us an insight into how conflict might be handled. Whilst each style has its advantages in certain situations, generally compromise or better still collaboration is generally thought to be the best way for a team to work.

Entrepreneurial leaders face uncertainty and ambiguity, trying to manage people who often have unclear job definitions because they are having to cope with change. This can create conflict that has to be resolved on an every-day basis. The implications of the entrepreneurial situation are:

- Entrepreneurial leaders must move away from using an autocratic or dictatorial leadership style, especially with their senior management team, if they want staff to take more control over their actions and develop an entrepreneurial organisation.
- Entrepreneurial leaders must be adept at using informal influence. Their powers of persuasion and motivation are important. They should meet and influence people. Relationships and organisational culture are important.
- Entrepreneurial leaders must be adept at conflict resolution. In these situations Timmons (*op. cit.*) observes: 'Successful entrepreneurs are interpersonally supporting and nurturing – not interpersonally competitive.' In terms of the Thomas–Kilman Conflict Modes this is the 'collaborating' or 'compromising' mode.

This means that entrepreneurial leaders have to be flexible and adapt their leadership style to suit different and changing circumstances. These changes are a lot to ask of anybody and many entrepreneurs cannot make the transition. Some learn that they are best at start-ups and sell the business at the point where proper controls and procedures need to be put in place and management teams developed, recognising their strengths but equally their weaknesses.

How do you behave in situations involving conflict?

Often in business you find yourself at odds with others who hold seemingly incompatible views. For leaders to be effective they need to understand how they handle these conflict situations and be able to modify their behaviour to obtain the best results from others. Based on research by Kenneth Thomas and Ralph Kilman, the Thomas–Kilman Conflict Modes questionnaire published by Xicom shows how a person's behaviour can be classified under two dimensions:

- Assertiveness – the extent to which individuals attempt to satisfy their own needs;
- Cooperativeness – the extent to which they attempt to satisfy the needs of others.

These two dimensions lead the authors to identify five behavioural classifications which the questionnaire can identify in individuals:

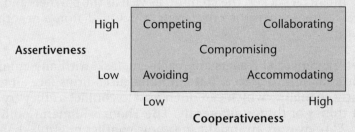

1 *Competing* is assertive and uncooperative. Individuals are concerned for themselves and pursue their own agenda forcefully, using power, rank or ability to argue to win the conflict. This can be seen as bullying with less forceful individuals or, when others use the same mode, it can lead to heated, possibly unresolved, arguments.

2 *Accommodating* is unassertive and cooperative, the opposite of competing. Individuals want to see the concerns of others satisfied. They might do so as an act of 'selfless generosity' or just because they are 'obeying orders', either way they run the risk of not making their own views heard.

3 *Avoiding* is both unassertive and uncooperative. It may involve side-stepping an issue or withdrawing from the conflict altogether. In this mode any conflict may not even be addressed.

4 *Collaborating* is both assertive and cooperative, the opposite of avoiding. Issues get addressed but individuals are willing to work with others to resolve the conflict, perhaps finding alternatives that meet everybody's concerns. This is the most constructive approach to conflict for a group as a whole.

5 *Compromising* is the 'in between' route, the diplomatic, expedient solution to conflict which partially satisfies everyone. It may involve making concessions.

Each style of handling conflict has its advantages and disadvantages and can be effective in certain situations. However, management teams or Boards of Directors, if they are to get the most from each member over a longer period of time, work best when all members adopt the collaborating or compromising modes. A team made up of just competers would find it difficult to get on and, indeed, to survive. A team made up of just accommodaters would lack assertiveness and drive.

Jim Clark is worth about $3 billion. He is now a cross between a serial entrepreneur and a venture capitalist because he realised that he is better at start-ups than running the business in the longer term. He discovered this with his first company, **Silicon Graphics (SGI)**, which he built around a graphic chip called the Geometry Engine that he invented in the 1970s. He spent 13, mainly unhappy, years at SGI where he found he just did not like the discipline of running a successful growing business.

He left in 1994 and invested $3 million of his own money in a primitive web browser called Mosaic and a 22-year-old who helped develop it called Marc Andreesen. **Netscape** went public 18 months later and made Jim Clark a billionaire.

In 1995 he moved on and founded another company called **Healtheon**, which uses the internet to share patient and administrative information between doctors, hospitals, insurance companies and the patients themselves. Again the business was run by somebody else, Mike Long.

Jim Clark has now started up another company, **MYCFO**, this time using the internet to help the wealthy manage their financial affairs. It also satisfies a necessary condition for success: Jim Clark is not planning to run it.

Building the management team

Entrepreneurs will only succeed in growing their company if they get a good management team to work with. Attracting good staff is always difficult for small firms because of perceived lack of job security, uncertainty about promotion prospects and the fact that it is often difficult for new people to fit into an existing team. Hence the need, often, to offer shares in the company.

'Once you have a business up and running the best way to keep in touch is to employ great people and empower them. This brings with it trust, communication and team spirit. When you work as a team you are in touch. My business style is non-aggressive, non-confrontational – it's who I am. It's important to be yourself. It comes from a background where you have to get on with people to get on. I believe that if you treat people like dirt on the way up it will come to haunt you as you find yourself on the way down.'

Jonathan Elvidge
founder of **Gadget Shop**
The Times 6 August 2002

Selecting a team will depend upon the mix of functional skills and market or industry experience required in the firm, as well as the personal chemistry between its members. For a team to be effective individuals need to have the right mix of a certain set of personal characteristics. Dr Meredith Belbin (1981) identified nine clusters of personal characteristics or attributes which translate into 'team roles'. Individuals are unlikely to have more than two or three of them, yet all nine clusters of characteristics need to be present in a team for it to work effectively.

The leader's role is to select the team and then to build cohesion and motivation. In most cases this involves

'Management is about communication and listening to people. I believe the people on the ground have the answer. If you can find what the answer is you'll get a much better solution for the business ... Leadership to me is picking good teams and putting them together. And also putting yourself out for those people in terms of helping them when they're stuck, finding out what their concerns are, navigating them through problems. That, to me, is what leadership is about – not doing it yourself, but putting in place people who can do it for you.'

David Arculus, former MD, **Emap** group;
chief operating officer, United News and Media; and chairman, IPC
The Times 3 May 2004

building consensus towards the goals of the firm, balancing multiple viewpoints and demands. However, too great a reliance on achieving consensus can lead to slow decision-making, so a balance is needed that will strain the interpersonal skills of the leader. However, in the best entrepreneurial firms leadership seems to work almost by infection. The management team seem to be infected by the philosophies and

'I can't remember a single day when I didn't want to go to work. I had such a good team. There was an incredible feeling of trust. None of the boys would let me down.'

Tom Farmer
founder of **Kwik-Fit**
Daily Mail 11 May 1999

attitudes of the entrepreneur and readily buy into the goals set for the firm, something that is helped if they share in its success.

All personal relationships are based upon trust and this is the cornerstone of a good team. It is imperative that the management team trust the entrepreneurial leader. For the leader this involves being firm but fair, flexible but consistent in values and in dealings with individuals and always placing the interests of the firm first, also being supportive for individuals and having their interests at heart. Trust also has to be built up between other members of the management team. It takes time to build and needs to be demonstrated with real outcomes.

Effective teams, therefore, do not just happen, they have to be developed, and that can take time. It is said that teams go through a four-stage development process:

1 The group tests relationships. Individuals are polite, impersonal, watchful and guarded.
2 Infighting starts in the group and controlling the conflict is important. However, whilst some individuals might be confrontational, others might opt out and avoid the conflict altogether. Neither approach is good. Collaboration is best. This is a dangerous phase from which some groups never emerge.
3 The group starts to get organised, developing skills, establishing procedures, giving feedback, confronting issues.
4 The group becomes mature and effective, working flexibly and closely, making the most of resources and being close-knit and supportive.

The whole process of team formation and development has been likened to courtship and marriage, involving decisions based partly on emotion rather than logic. For that

What sort of team player are you?

Developing a successful team depends not just on the range of professional skills it has, but also on the range of personal characteristics – the chemistry of the team. Based upon research into how teams work, Dr Meredith Belbin (1981) identified nine clusters of personal characteristics or attributes which translate into 'team roles'. The roles are:

The Shaper: This is usually the self-elected task leader with lots of nervous energy. They are extrovert, dynamic, outgoing, highly strung, argumentative, a pressuriser seeking ways around obstacles. They do have a tendency to bully and are not always liked. However, they generate action and thrive under pressure.

The Plant: This the team's vital spark and chief source of new ideas. They are creative, imaginative and often unorthodox. However, they can be distant and uncommunicative and sometimes their ideas can seem a little impractical.

The Coordinator: This is the team's natural chairman. They are mature, confident and trusting. They clarify goals and promote decision-making. They are calm with strong interpersonal skills. However, they can be perceived as a little manipulative.

The Resource Investigator: This is 'the fixer' – extrovert, amiable, six phones on the go, with a wealth of contacts. They pick other people's brains and explore opportunities. However, they can be a bit undisciplined and can lose interest quickly once initial enthusiasm has passed.

The Monitor-Evaluator: This is the team's rock. They are introvert, sober, strategic, discerning. They explore all options and are capable of deep analysis of huge amounts of data. They are rarely wrong. However, they can lack drive and are unlikely to inspire or excite others.

The Team-Worker: This is the team's counsellor or conciliator. They are mild mannered and social, perceptive and aware of problems or undercurrents, accommodating and good listeners. They promote harmony and are particularly valuable at times of crisis. However, they can be indecisive.

The Implementer: This is the team's workhorse. They turn ideas into practical actions and get on with the job logically and loyally. They are disciplined, reliable and conservative. However, they can be inflexible and slow to change.

The Completer-Finisher: This is the team's worry-guts, making sure things get finished. They are sticklers for detail, deadlines and schedules and have relentless follow-through, picking up any errors or omissions as they go. However, they sometimes just cannot let go and are reluctant to delegate.

The Specialist: This is the team's chief source of technical knowledge or skill. They are single-minded, self-starting and dedicated. However, they tend to contribute on a narrow front.

Most individuals are naturally suited to two or three roles. However, to work effectively a team must comprise elements of all nine roles. If a team lacks certain 'team roles' it tends to exhibit weaknesses in these areas.

reason it is important that the team shares the same values and is committed to the same goals. They may disagree on tactics but they all agree on the destination and how they are going to get there. It is also important that team roles are clearly defined, although given the uncertainty involved with rapid growth, it is also important that flexibility is maintained.

The board of directors

In many firms the management team will also function as the legal board of directors of the company. The legal duties and responsibilities of directors arise out of common law and statute. Directors have a fiduciary duty to act honestly and in good faith, exercise skill and care and undertake their statutory duty. The broad functions of the board are summarised in Figure 8.12 along the dimensions of inward/outward looking and past/future orientation. The prime function of the board is to establish corporate strategy and policy:

- Overall strategic planning;
- Approval of strategies in key areas;
- Changes in the scope or nature of operations;
- Changes in organisational structure;
- Major company decisions.

The other responsibilities include:

1 Monitoring and supervising management performance;
2 Planning for management succession;
3 Setting remuneration levels;
4 Providing proper accountability to other stakeholders in the firm, for example, by appointing auditors and approving the annual financial statements, as well as ensuring that the company complies with all aspects of the law.

Whilst establishing corporate strategy and policy is the most important job for the board, it is unlikely that it will be given the appropriate weighting in terms of time allocation. Most boards spend too much time on the other functions, particularly monitoring management performance.

	Past and present orientation	Future orientation
Outward looking	Provide accountability	Strategy formulation
Inward looking	Monitoring and supervision	Policy-making

Figure 8.12 The role of the board of directors

Whilst corporate governance and business ethics are high on the agenda of many high-profile public companies, that is not necessarily the case for smaller firms. There are, of course, exceptions. 'Green' issues were always high on the agenda of Body Shop, even as a start-up. Research shows that business ethics for smaller firms tends to take the form of informal codes of practice and an understanding of acceptable and unacceptable behaviour rather than standardised, formal procedures, which are a feature of the larger firm (Spence, 2000).

A strong management team and board of directors is invaluable and their worth is no more evident than in the criteria venture capitalists use for investment; management, management and management. To help boards develop and operate more effectively, the Institute of Management has published a useful set of best practice checklists based upon a model of board-level competencies (Allday, 1997). Twenty-three board-level skills were identified grouped together under the four key headings shown in Figure 8.13. These generic competencies need to be balanced and tailored to particular circumstances and specific functional board roles.

More than 90 per cent of the *Financial Times* Stock Exchange (FTSE) companies comply with the recommendation that they have non-executive directors. However, in small unquoted companies the proportion is much, much smaller. Often non-executive directors are imposed by financial backers to oversee their investment. However, non-executive directors have a valuable role bringing different skills, an independent and objective perspective and a new network of contacts. They should act as an early warning system for potential future difficulties, and as we shall see, their role can be particularly valuable in family firms.

Strategy: Guiding strategic direction	People: Practising 'human' skills
Strategic thinking Systems thinking Awareness of external environment Entrepreneurial thinking Developing the vision Initiating change Championing causes	Communicating Creating a personal impact Giving leadership Promoting development of others Networking
Culture: Developing organisation culture	Operations: Exercising executive control
Customer focus Quality focus Teamwork focus People resource focus Organisational learning focus	Governance Decision-making Contributing specialist knowledge Managing performance Analysing situations Awareness of organisational structure

Figure 8.13 The Institute of Management model of board-level competencies

Entrepreneurial leadership skills

Kirby (2003) likens entrepreneurial leaders to the leaders of jazz bands. They decide on the musicians to play in the band and the music to be played but then allow the band to improvise and use their creativity to create the required sounds. In the process they have fun as the leader brings out the best in them. The leader's authority comes from their expertise and values rather than their position. They lead by example – playing themselves. They empower their teams and nurture leaders at all levels – encouraging solo performances.

An entrepreneurial leader must combine many of the traditional skills of management with those of the entrepreneur. They must also reconcile the conflict between the impatience of the entrepreneur with the constraints imposed by an organisation in its desire to control events. That is where different structures can be important as well as the role of change agents such as intrapreneurs. The leader's role, however, is more than that of the change agent, championing individual initiatives. Pursuing innovative ideas may be exciting but the leader needs to give the firm a sense of direction and purpose by aligning these developments to the vision and direction of the organisation. That means standing back from the developments and providing a measure of impartial and objective evaluation. The leader must take an overview; reconciling differing perspectives – which may involve conflict resolution, creating a climate of cooperation – which will involve coordination, but also exercising authority when needed to bring forward some initiative whilst pushing back others.

However, on the spectrum of traditional management to entrepreneurship, context is everything. What might be appropriate in one context can be inappropriate in another. And should innovation come from the bottom or be led from the top? Lessem (1987) identified a number of roles or archetypes other than that of '*leader*' needed to move innovation along in different business contexts:

Adventurers These are major risk-takers who go in search of opportunity into new and difficult markets. They forge ahead and make things happen, but can rub people up the wrong way and can be difficult to control.

Innovators These are the first users of new ideas. They link creativity and research with commercial reality, but can be too obsessed with the project they see as owning and may lack objectivity in evaluating its commercial potential.

Animators These are essentially the 'team workers' needed to get cooperation and good team working.

Change agents These are the people who are not bound by convention and change the status quo. They launch new products, implement new systems, reorganise working arrangements. To make all this happen they require enormous political skills.

Enablers These are people who use their behavioural skills to encourage appropriate behaviour – to challenge convention and, through collaboration with others, to come up with new ideas.

Table 8.4 Entrepreneurial leadership skills

- Visionary
- Ability to communicate
- Ability to influence, informally
- Ability to motivate
- Ability to think strategically
- Ability to manage change
- Ability to resolve or reconcile conflict
- Ability to build confidence

- Ability to work as a team
- Ability to form deep relationships
- Ability to generate trust
- Ability to delegate
- Ability to build cohesion and a sense of belonging
- Ability to clarify ambiguity and uncertainty
- Ability to be firm but fair
- Ability to be flexible but consistent

This chapter has highlighted the need for an entrepreneurial leader to have good interpersonal and team working skills. It has emphasised the need for strong influencing skills alongside good conflict resolution skills. Indeed entrepreneurial leaders need a wide range of interpersonal skills – all focused towards taking the organisation with them by consensus and agreement, rather than dictate. These skills are summarised in Table 8.4. Lessem's approach reminds us that the appropriate approach and use of these skills depends on the context. It also emphasises the need for an effective team comprising individuals who possess the qualities appropriate for the task they face.

All the skills in Table 8.4 can be developed and improved over time. But this can be a painful way to manage, necessitating considerable dedication and commitment by the leader. However, in the long term the gains from a motivated and dedicated workforce, acting as an effective team, can be considerable.

Case insight

Now Recruitment is a successful recruitment agency with 100 staff in seven offices across Britain and an eighth recently opened in Sydney, Australia. In 2004 its turnover was £28 million. It is 90 per cent owned by **Gary Redman**, who readily admits that his management style has had to change dramatically to accommodate the growth. The company stalled when turnover reached £6 million as staff turnover shot through the roof. Gary brought in a management consultant:

'He told me that the biggest problem in the business was me. He explained that staff were saying they were not clear where the business was going, they didn't know what I wanted and they didn't get a chance to voice their opinions ... The way I operated was to shout at people ... I thought you got results out of people by putting them under pressure. It was a ruthless kind of culture where if you performed well you were in, and if you didn't perform well you were out.'

Addressing another personal problem, Gary also went on a management development course which taught him how to delegate responsibility rather than try to control everything himself. Changing his style of management worked. Staff retention improved and the business started to grow again.

Sunday Times 8 August 2004

Summary

As firms grow the role of the founder needs to change. Like **Michael Dell**, founder of **Dell Computers**, the founder needs to metamorphosise into a leader; this change is not easy. Some, like **Stelios Haji-Ioannou**, founder of **easyJet**, can make the change, others cannot. Some, like **Jim Clark**, founder of **Silicon Graphics**, **Netscape**, **Healtheon** and **MYCFO**, choose to only do what they enjoy and are good at – start-ups.

As they develop, firms typically go through a period of growth, followed by crisis and then a period of consolidation. In going through each crisis the entrepreneur faces a roller coaster of human emotion that they may not be able to handle. The classic change/denial curve seeks to describe their emotions at each stage. This range of feelings was expressed by **David Poole** of DP&A.

Greiner's growth model predicts the crises a firm will face as it grows and the associated causes of growth. These are:

Growth through creativity	⇨ Crisis of leadership	⇨
Growth through direction	⇨ Crisis of autonomy	⇨
Growth through delegation	⇨ Crisis of control	⇨
Growth through coordination	⇨ Crisis of red tape	⇨

Richard Branson has realised that as a business grows the entrepreneur needs to change and adapt. However, some entrepreneurs, like **Jim Clark**, prefer not to change and become serial entrepreneurs. The four main challenges entrepreneurs face as the business grows are:

- Leadership;
- Team-working;
- Organisation structures;
- Culture.

An entrepreneurial organisation structure is a spider's web, with the entrepreneur at the centre. Entrepreneurs prefer informal structures and management styles relying on building personal relationships and influence. They lead by example. However, this can lead to over-control and, whilst it may be flat and efficient, it only works up to a certain size. What is more, managers can find that it undermines their authority and that leads to frustration, even 'infantilisation'. Whilst avoiding bureaucracy, more formal structures need to be introduced as a business grows. The entrepreneur needs to recruit managers from outside and learn to delegate

The Churchill and Lewis growth model summarises management style, organisational characteristics, formality of systems and major strategies at different stages of the firm's life. It distinguishes between lifestyle and growth firms at the 'success' stage and highlights the changes that take place at this point for the different types of firm. It emphasises the importance of the entrepreneur's strategic abilities, compared to their operating abilities, as the firm grows. The changes in the entrepreneur's role and style as well as the organisational structures are emphasised by the Scott and Bruce model. The Burns model emphasises the drift from informal to formal structures in many aspects of how the firm is managed, including the main functional disciplines.

A job definition for a leader would include five elements:

1 Vision and ideas;
2 Strategic planning;
3 Effective communication;
4 Creation of culture;
5 Monitoring and controlling performance.

Entrepreneurs are defined by Timmons (1999) as 'patient leaders, capable of instilling tangible visions and managing for the long haul ... a learner and a teacher, a doer and a visionary.' Having and communicating a vision is a key skill of both entrepreneurship and leadership. Developing the vision is a continuous process, checking with staff that it resonates with them, modifying it to suit changing circumstances.

A vision is a desired future state. It is best communicated as a 'story' that, in some way, appeals to the emotions of staff and, as **Derrick Collins** founder of **Brulines** says, motivates them to achieve. It communicates the values and sense of purpose of the leader and, as **Gururaj Deshpande** founder of **Sycamore Networks** says, helps focus the workforce. It must be credible – acknowledging the tension created by a realistic appraisal of the current situation. The vision for an organisation is formally communicated through the vision or mission statement.

Underpinning vision are the values of the organisation – the core beliefs upon which it is founded. **Body Shop** and the **John Lewis Partnership** are examples of organisations with strong values. Values are enduring and long-term. They influence culture and strategy and bind the organisation together. Visions and values are best articulated by leaders as 'stories' that have an emotional resonance. However, the leader must behave as they talk – walk-the-talk.

Creating an appropriate culture in the firm is the most important, and probably the most difficult, task. Culture is influenced by organisational and cognitive processes and behaviour. As in the case of **Body Shop**, it can be based upon the entrepreneur's strongly held beliefs and values. It can be deliberate or emerge organically. Entrepreneurs 'infect' staff with a culture that motivates them to do the right things, in the right way. They create culture by example. However, as the firm grows culture can be influenced through training. Most firms start with a 'task culture' which can easily evolve into a 'power' or 'role' culture if care is not taken. An effective entrepreneurial culture involves:

- Clear goals;
- High standards;
- Commitment;
- Recognition;
- Team cohesion.

Leadership stems from authority. Entrepreneurial authority, in the main, comes from expertise. There is no single best leadership style. The appropriate style depends upon the leader, the group, the task and the situation or context they are in. **Jonathan Elvidge**, founder of **Gadget Shop**, believes it is important to be yourself. In the context of a growing firm, an autocratic or dictatorial style is unlikely to be appropriate. Entrepreneurial leaders must be adept at using informal influence to get their way. Entrepreneurs must also be adept at resolving conflict, through a collaborative or compromising approach.

David Arculus believes is about picking good teams but building the team is not just about appropriate skills. It is about assembling a mix of different personalities. Belbin identified nine characteristics that need to be present to form an effective team: shaper, plant, coordinator, resource investigator, monitor-evaluator, team-worker, implementer, completer-finisher and specialist. Teams have strong interpersonal relationships and, as **Tom Farmer** founder of **Kwik-Fit** points out, all relationships are based upon trust. Building this up takes time and the team is likely to go through a four-stage process in its development:

1 Testing;
2 Infighting;
3 Getting organised;
4 Mature effectiveness.

The board of directors becomes an increasingly important team as a company grows. Its most important functions are strategy and policy formulation. It also has to monitor the performance of management and provide accountability to stakeholders. Members therefore need to be able to give that strategic direction, develop organisational culture, practice 'human' skills and exercise effective executive control. Non-executive directors are valuable in providing different skills, objectivity and a new network of contacts. They can be particularly valuable for family firms.

As **Gary Redman** of **Now Recruitment** found, leaders of entrepreneurial organisations need the range of skills listed in Table 8.4, including the skill of managing and facilitating change, although they do not always control that change. They need to use all the levers available to them to shape the organisation. Above all, however, they need good interpersonal skills.

Essays and discussion topics

1 How do the role of and skills required by the founder change as the business grows?
2 Is the Greiner growth model an accurate predictor of the growth process?
3 How are the antecedent influences on an entrepreneur likely to improve their chances of successfully growing the firm?
4 What are the advantages and disadvantages of an entrepreneurial organisation?
5 What are the possible negative consequences of the internal locus of control that is characteristic of so many entrepreneurs.
6 Discuss how the typical entrepreneur's preference for physical intervention and informal, personal controls shows itself. Is this a good thing?
7 Critically evaluate the three growth models by Churchill and Lewis, Scott and Bruce, and Burns.
8 Is operational capability more important than strategic capability at start-up?
9 How is the marketing function likely to change as the firm grows?
10 As long as small firms are not homogeneous, growth models will not work. Discuss.
11 How are the recurrent crises facing the growing firm likely to affect the entrepreneur and how do they react to them?
12 How does the role of leader differ from that of entrepreneur?
13 What is vision? How can it it be developed? How can it be communicated?
14 Compare and contrast the mission statements of Dell and easyJet. Do they fit the format suggested by Wickham? Are they effective?
15 Why are values important? Are they dangerous?
16 Are the values of Body Shop reflected in their mission statement? What do you think of the mission statement?
17 What is culture and how can it be developed?
18 What is an entrepreneurial culture? Do Timmons' six dimensions adequately describe it?
19 What is the relationship between an entrepreneurial culture within a firm and an entrepreneurial national culture? Can one exist without the other?
20 Is there such a thing as an effective leadership style for a growing business?

Leadership Style Questionnaire

For each of the following statements, tick the 'Yes' box if you tend to agree or the 'No' box if you disagree. Try to relate the answers to your actual recent behaviour as a manager. There are no right and wrong answers. Scoring is given on p. 247.

		Yes	No
1	I encourage overtime work	☐	☐
2	I allow staff complete freedom in their work	☐	☐
3	I encourage the use of standard procedures	☐	☐
4	I allow staff to use their own judgement in solving problems	☐	☐
5	I stress being better than other firms	☐	☐
6	I urge staff to greater effort	☐	☐
7	I try out my ideas with others in the firm	☐	☐
8	I let my staff work in the way they think best	☐	☐
9	I keep work moving at a rapid pace	☐	☐
10	I turn staff loose on a job and let them get on with it	☐	☐
11	I settle conflicts when they happen	☐	☐
12	I get swamped by detail	☐	☐
13	I always represent the 'firm view' at meetings with outsiders	☐	☐
14	I am reluctant to allow staff freedom of action	☐	☐
15	I decide what should be done and who should do it	☐	☐
16	I push for improved quality	☐	☐
17	I let some staff have authority I could keep	☐	☐
18	Things usually turn out as I predict	☐	☐
19	I allow staff a high degree of initiative	☐	☐
20	I assign staff to particular tasks	☐	☐
21	I am willing to make changes	☐	☐
22	I ask staff to work harder	☐	☐
23	I trust staff to exercise good judgement	☐	☐
24	I schedule the work to be done	☐	☐
25	I refuse to explain my actions	☐	☐
26	I persuade others that my ideas are to their advantage	☐	☐
27	I permit the staff to set their own pace for change	☐	☐
28	I urge staff to beat previous targets	☐	☐
29	I act without consulting staff	☐	☐
30	I ask staff to follow standard rules and procedures	☐	☐

Adapted from J. Pfeiffer and J. Jones, (eds) (1974) *A Handbook of Structured Experiences from Human Relations Training*, Vol. 1 (rev.), University Associates, San Diego, California.

21   Why is an ability to handle conflict important in the growing firm?
22   How do you build an effective team?
23   How do you generate trust?
24   What is the role of the non-executive director? How important are they for the growing firm?
25   Leaders are born not made. Discuss.
26   In what contexts might Lessem's five entrepreneurial archetypes succeed?

Exercises and assignments

1   List the questions you would ask an entrepreneur who has successfully grown their business to try to assess how they and the skills they have needed have changed as the firm grew.
2   Based upon these questions, interview a successful entrepreneur and write an essay describing the changes they have faced and how they coped.
3   Based upon a small firm with about a dozen employees, draw the formal organisation chart and then, based upon interviews with employees, draw the informal organisation.
4   Answer the Leadership Styles Questionnaire and plot your score on the Leadership Grid at the end of this chapter.
5   Obtain the Thomas–Kilman Conflict Mode questionnaire from Xicom and evaluate how you handle conflict.
6   Using the questionnaire in Meredith Belbin's book, evaluate your preferred team roles.

References

Adair, J. (1984) *The Skills of Leadership*, London: Gower.

Allday, D. (1997) *Check-a-Board: Helping Boards and Directors become More Effective*, London: Institute of Management.

Bartlett, C.A. and Ghoshal, S. (1994) 'Changing the Role of Top Management: Beyond Strategy to Purpose', *Harvard Business Review*, November/December.

Belbin, R.M. (1981) *Management Teams – Why They Succeed and Fail*, London: Heinemann Professional Publishing.

Bennis, W. and Nanus, B. (1985) *Leaders: The Strategies for Taking Charge*, New York: Harper & Row.

Blake, R. and Mouton, J. (1978) *The New Managerial Grid*, London: Gulf.

Bowman, C. and Faulkner, D.O. (1997) *Competitive and Corporate Strategy*, London: Irwin.

Burns, P. (1996) 'Growth', in P. Burns and J. Dewhurst (eds), *Small Business and Entrepreneurship*, London: Macmillan – now Basingstoke: Palgrave Macmillan.

Burns, P. and Whitehouse, O. (1996) 'Managers in Europe', *European Venture Capital Journal*, 45, April/May.

Churchill, N.C. and Lewis, V.L. (1983) 'The Five Stages of Small Business Growth', *Harvard Business Review*, May/June.

du Toit, D.E. (1980) 'Confessions of a Successful Entrepreneur', *Harvard Business Review*, November/December.

Gardner, H. (1995) *Leading Minds: An Anatomy of Leadership*, New York: John Wiley & Sons.

Greiner, L.E. (1972) 'Evolution and Revolution as Organisations Grow', *Harvard Business Review*, July/August.

Kakabadse, A. (1983) *The Politics of Management*, London: Gower.

Kets de Vries, M.F.R. (1985) 'The Dark Side of Entrepreneurship', *Harvard Business Review*, November/December.

Kirby, D. (2003) *Entrepreneurship*, London: McGraw Hill.

Lessem, R. (1987) *Intrapreneurship*, Aldershot: Gower.

Nanus, B. (1992) *Visionary Leadership: Creating a Compelling Sense of Direction for your Organization*, San Francisco: Jossey-Bass

Nonaka, I. (1991) 'The Knowledge-Creating Company', *Harvard Business Review*, November/December.

Ray, G.H. and Hutchinson, P.J. (1983) *The Financing and Financial Control of Small Enterprise Development*, London: Gower.

Schein, E.H. (1990) 'Organisational Culture', *American Psychologist*, February.

Scott, M. and Bruce, R. (1987) 'Five Stages of Growth in Small Businesses', *Long Range Planning*, 20(3).

Senge, P. M. (1992) *The Fifth Discipline*, London: Century Business.

Spence, L.J. (2000) *Priorities, Practice and Ethics in Small Firms*, London: The Institute of Business Ethics.

Timmons, J.A. (1999) *New Venture Creation: Entrepreneurship for the 21st Century*, Singapore: Irwin/McGraw Hill.

Wickham, P.A. (2001) *Strategic Entrepreneurship: A Decision-Making Approach to New Venture Creation and Management*, Harlow: Pearson Education.

Leadership Style Questionnaire Scoring

To obtain your leadership orientation rating, score 1 point for the appropriate response under each heading, then total your scores. If your response is inappropriate you do not score. As a guide, a score of 5 or less is low, and 12 or more is high.

PEOPLE SCORE (maximum score 15)
'Yes' for questions 2, 4, 8, 10, 17, 19, 21, 23, 27.
'No' for questions 6, 13, 14, 25, 29, 30.

TASK SCORE (maximum score 15)
'Yes' for questions 1, 3, 5, 7, 9, 11, 15, 16, 18, 20, 22, 24, 26, 28.
'No' for questions 12.

Next plot your position on the Leadership Grid below.

9

Strategies for Success

Contents

- Ingredients of success
- Barriers to growth
- Developing strategy
- The SWOT analysis
- Financial performance analysis
- Value chains
- SLEPT analysis
- Strategy misfit
- Securing competitive advantage
- Successful entrepreneurial strategies
- Summary

LEARNING OUTCOMES

By the end of this chapter you should be able to:

- Describe the ingredients of success for a growing firm;

- Describe what small firms consider to be barriers to their growth;

- Undertake a financial appraisal of a small firm using ratio analysis;

- Explain the concept of a value chain and describe how it can be used;

- Undertake a SLEPT analysis and explain how it can be used;

- Undertake a SWOT analysis on a small firm;

- Explain which strategies are most likely to lead to successful growth.

Ingredients of success

In the turbulent world of business, survival – over a longer period – is a badge of success. The growth models we looked at in the last chapter indicated that this was something of a watershed. Should the business continue as it is or grow even further? This is the critical point where the entrepreneur makes some important decisions. Do they want the firm to grow? Can they make the personal changes needed to make the firm successful in the next phase? Notwithstanding these questions, the basis for a successful transition through this phase is an understanding of why the firm has actually been successful. Often the business starts out trying to do one thing and, just a few years later, the things that made it successful can look more like luck than good judgement.

Entrepreneurs like Bill Gates and Richard Branson managed to do more than just survive, they managed to grow their businesses and grow them extremely quickly and with enormous success. Despite being few in number, high-growth businesses – companies that go on to the take-off phase in our growth models – are important to national economies. Harrison and Taylor (1996) claim that in the USA it has been estimated that, whilst 15 000 medium-sized businesses represent just 1 per cent of all businesses, they generate a quarter of all sales and they employ a fifth of all private sector labour. For the UK, Storey *et al.* (1987) have asserted that 'out of every 100 small firms, the fastest growing four firms will create half the jobs in the group over a decade.'

So, is there such a thing as a recipe for success? The answer is that we know the ingredients, but the precise recipe can vary from situation to situation. The ingredients of success are shown in Figure 9.1; they comprise:

- *The entrepreneurial character* This is the vital ingredient. Growth rarely happens by chance. The owner-manager must want it and possess all the characteristics of the entrepreneur. Previous chapters have shown how this needs to adapt and change over time, as the business grows.
- *The business culture* The previous chapter showed how this is an important tool for effective leadership of an entrepreneurial firm. Having the right culture is probably more important than the right structure. What is more, part of the culture must be

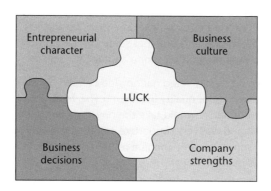

Figure 9.1 The ingredients of success

the ambition to grow. Companies which have risen to positions of global leadership over the last 20 years invariably began with ambitions that were out of proportion to their size or resources. They maintained an obsession with winning long enough to succeed.

- *Company strengths* For successful growth a company needs a good management team and good financial control systems. It needs to understand who its customers are and why they buy from them rather than competitors. This chapter will show you some frameworks that help you evaluate both the strengths and weaknesses of the company. It will show you how to undertake the SWOT analysis so beloved by most Business Schools – an analysis of the Strengths and Weaknesses of an organisation and the Opportunities and Threats it faces – and introduces some tools to help with this process.
- *Business strategies* Having no business strategies can be just as disastrous as having bad strategies. We've already introduced you to the concept of strategy, But which strategies are more likely to lead to success and growth and how might they be developed? This chapter will outline some of the strategies that research has shown are most likely to lead to success.

All of which leaves the question of luck. Whether success was due to luck or good judgement or good timing is a difficult question to answer. Timing is everything and a good product or service, launched before its time, with insufficient demand is likely

---

Case insight

Perween Warsi's parents arranged for her to marry a doctor at the age of 16 in India. The couple moved to Britain in 1975 with their two sons. Bored, with time on her hands, Perween decided to try producing high quality, authentic Indian food and set up **S&A Foods** (named after her sons Sadiq and Abid), working from her kitchen with six staff, selling to neighbourhood takeaways. Within six months she had moved to a unit on a local industrial estate and within a year was selling to Asda, followed by Safeway, Waitrose, Budgen, Morrisons and even Welcome Break and Scottish & Newcastle. S&A now has four factories in Derby, a workforce of 1100 and an annual turnover of £100 million. Warsi is the second richest Asian businesswoman in Britain and her husband, Talib, gave up being a GP in 1995 to become S&A's marketing manager.

The target market for the food is 'cash-rich, time-poor' consumers. The firm has to keep on top of a rapidly developing market and launches some 300 new products each year, developing thousands more. S&A is expanding into Europe and already sells to supermarkets in France.

I knew my products could be marketed nationwide before I had sold a single samosa. There was a huge gap in the market for quality Indian and Thai food . . . When the business started I was very busy. In the mornings I would take the boys to school, then come home and make food all day . . . My husband was very supportive, but I still feel very guilty that I wasn't always there for my beautiful sons . . . I can't imagine retiring. What would I do? Our future is bright and we are always looking to innovate.

Boss Women, BBC1 24 July 2000

Case insight

Specialist cereals producer **Jordans** is a family company tracing its origins back to 1855 with milling and the supply of animal feed. In the 1960s the company switched from producing white to wholemeal flour in the face of fierce price competition from big conglomerates. It also started producing small quantities of oat-based cereals, which it sold to health food stores.

By the 1970s health foods had really caught on and Jordans was selling to the supermarkets. Two keys to their growth since then have been product quality and innovation. Quality, backed with a respected brand identity, have allowed them not to be drawn too far into the vicious food price wars. Innovation has kept them one step ahead of the big-company competition. They were among the first to introduce 'food on the run' cereal bars. They were also amongst the first to introduce freeze-dried fruits to their breakfast cereals, even innovating in the packaging by introducing cellophane bags. They pioneered the introduction of 'conservation grade' ingredients which are cheaper than organically grown but contain few pesticides.

However, Jordans has also entered the own-brand market and 20 per cent of its £50 million turnover comes from this source. Even here it trades on its 'brand integrity' – its ability to produce tasty and nutritious cereals in an environmentally-friendly way. But it has had to control costs. It is also entering the adult savoury market with its low-fat cereal-based oven-crisped chips. It now plans a major expansion into Europe. Bill Jordan explains the key to his strategy:

> The company needs to differentiate its products rather than slog it out on price. We need to sustain advertising support to develop customer demand, which is the key to getting our goods placed on the supermarket shelf.

Sunday Times 12 March 2000

---

to fail, as we saw with Cecil Duckworth and his self-service petrol pumps. How many of the factors that made for Body Shop's success – the ethical and environmentally friendly emphasis, the cheap, green painted pine decor, the plastic reusable bottles – were luck?

Barriers to growth

Another approach to the issue of growth in small firms is the so-called 'barriers to growth' literature. Table 9.1 shows the barriers to growth reported in a survey of some 2500 UK small firms in 1997 by the ESRC Centre for Business Research at Cambridge University, probably the most authoritative recent survey. Only a factor score of over 2.5 indicates any real problem, therefore only the top three factors are significant. It is interesting that the top two are both external factors, increased competition reflecting the intensification of competitive pressures in the 1990s. The issue of raising capital is a perennial problem for small firms and is dealt with in a subsequent chapter, but the barrier is likely to reflect cost and issues of collateral rather than general availability. Even in the 1990 survey, when Britain was in recession, availability and cost of finance and market conditions – although this time growth of market demand – were the two most important barriers.

Table 9.1 Barriers to growth

Barrier	Nature	1997	1990
Increased competition	External	2.67	2.40
Availability and cost of finance for expansion	External	2.63	2.75
Marketing and sales skills	Internal	2.53	2.29
Availability and cost of overdraft finance	External	2.38	2.72
Growth of market demand	External	2.35	2.59
Management skills	Internal	2.31	2.14
Skilled labour	Internal	2.25	1.90
Acquisition of new technology	?	1.95	1.29
Difficulty implementing new technology	Internal	1.89	1.20
Availability of appropriate premises	External	1.75	1.16
Access to overseas markets	?	1.60	1.05

Key: 1 = insignificant, 5 = crucial.
Sources: For 1997, A. Cosh and A. Hughes (eds) (1998), *Enterprising Britain: Growth, Innovation and Public Policy in the Small and Medium-Sized Enterprise Sector 1994–1997*, ESRC Centre for Business Research, Cambridge. For 1990, Small Business Research Centre (1992), *The State of British Enterprise: Growth, Innovation and Competitive Advantage in Small and Medium-Sized Firms*, Cambridge.

The survey also showed that manufacturing small firms faced greater constraints in more areas than did service firms, larger (that is, medium-sized) firms faced greater constraints than did micro-firms and innovating small firms faced higher levels of constraints than did non-innovating firms. Medium-sized firms tended to rate inadequate management skills, and to a lesser extent marketing and sales skills, more highly as a constraint. Newer and fast-growing firms rated financial constraints more highly and faster-growing ones also rated management skills and skills shortages more highly.

Much has also been said by lobby groups and in the press of government regulation and general 'red tape'. However, this is probably a greater burden for the smallest companies rather than medium-sized ones. The survey of supergrowth companies by Harrison and Taylor (*op. cit.*) cited 'barriers to entry' when penetrating new markets as the biggest obstacle to growth, followed by 'establishing a reputation' and 'intense competition and monopoly practices'. The reality seems to be that, whilst competition and finance are general problems, many of the others are specific to the firm and need to be overcome in different ways, which comes down to understanding the business through reworking the SWOT analysis.

Developing strategy

The SWOT analysis is the first step in developing strategy. You need to understand where you are (the SWOT) and where you want to go (your vision) before you can start to plan how to get there (your strategy). Figure 9.2 sets out a process for how strategy might be developed in a systematic way. In Chapter 11 we shall reconsider how strategy is actually developed by most entrepreneurs. Strategy should be more than a wish list driven by a leader's vision. A vision must be realistic and credible and

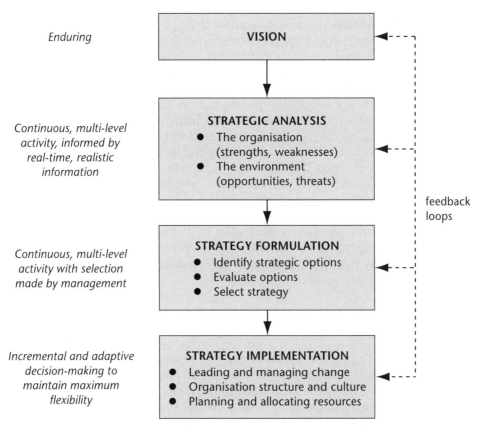

Enduring

Continuous, multi-level activity, informed by real-time, realistic information

Continuous, multi-level activity with selection made by management

Incremental and adaptive decision-making to maintain maximum flexibility

feedback loops

Source: P. Burns (2005) *Corporate Entrepreneurship: Building an Entrepreneurial Organisation*, Basingstoke: Palgrave Macmillan.

Figure 9.2 The strategic planning process

the leader's job involves developing 'creative tension' by contrasting the vision to the reality of the current situation. So, too, with strategy. Effective strategy must be rooted in the distinctive capabilities of the business. It starts with a thorough understanding of its strengths and weaknesses. It then goes on to contrast this with the opportunities and threats it faces in the environment. This is the classic SWOT analysis (strength, weaknesses, opportunities and threats). What is more, other tools have been developed to help this analysis be undertaken in a systematic and rational way.

The second element in the strategic process is strategy formulation. A strategy is just a linked pattern of actions. First you identify the strategic options, evaluating each one in terms of fit with the strengths and weaknesses of the organisation and finally selecting the most appropriate option. As we saw in an earlier chapter, there are some common or *generic* marketing strategies that a business might consider, and we shall return to these later. In an entrepreneurial organisation strategy formulation should be a continuous process undertaken at many different levels with varying degrees of formality. The 'right' strategy will emerge as part of consultative process but it will never be sufficiently rigid to inhibit the pursuit of opportunity – and that means generating strategic options and evaluating them.

The final element is strategy implementation. This involves leading and managing the process, developing the organisational structure and culture to sustain it and planning and allocating resources to make it happen. In fact, in the hands of a skilled strategist, strategy formulation and implementation are inextricably linked, because the likelihood of the strategy being successfully implemented, given the organisational capabilities, is part of the formulation process. What is more, the process of implementation will feed back on both the analysis and formulation stages, particularly in an entrepreneurial organisation. The success or otherwise of implementation will even affect the vision. The whole process is, therefore, an inextricably interlinked and a never-ending process.

We can break the planning process down into further detail and show how it leads to the development of, first, a marketing plan and then a financial plan which together form a coherent and consistent business plan. This explains where the business is going, how it will get there and the resources it needs to make it happen. This process is shown in Figure 9.3.

The SWOT analysis

As you can see from Figure 9.3, the basic tool of strategic analysis is the SWOT analysis. This is just a shorthand way of looking at you and the business – strengths and weaknesses – and the market environment in which it operates – opportunities and threats. This is partly to do with your personal strengths and weaknesses, in relation to the business idea, but it is also to do with the business idea and its fit with the market place. Because of their subjective nature, it is easy to under or over-estimate the importance of elements of the SWOT and it is often a good idea to ask the opinion of a friend or colleague. But it is equally important to remember always to challenge the conventions of the market place, to find ways of turning a weakness into a strength, of finding opportunities by being unconventional.

What the SWOT process is seeking to achieve is an overlap between the business environment and the firm's resources. In other words, a match between the firm's strategic or core competencies and a market opportunity. This match, as such, may not create *sustainable* competitive advantage – it may be copied – and may change over time. The secret to success, therefore, starts with identifying this unique set of competencies and capabilities. This portfolio of resources can be combined in various ways to meet opportunities or threats. They could, for example, allow a firm to diversify into new markets by reapplying and reconfiguring what it does best. But, what is more, it is the continuing process of analysis, positioning and repositioning that is important. In other words, the value of planning is really as a continuing process, repeated regularly in either a formal or informal way. Indeed if you talk to successful entrepreneurs you get the feeling that they are continually reviewing their strategies – often called strategising – and reviewing the options generated in the continually changing market and environment they thrive in.

Two of the chief proponents of this approach are Prahalad and Hamel (1990). They see core competency as the 'collective learning of the organisation, especially how to coordinate diverse production skills and integrate multiple streams of technology ...

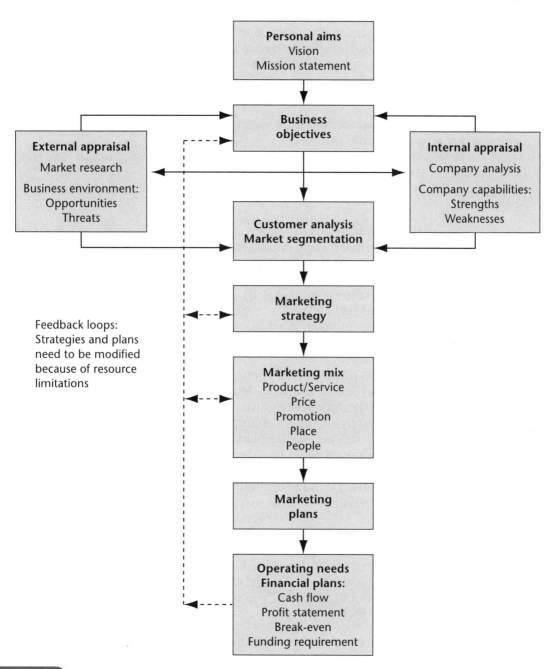

Figure 9.3 The business planning process

[through] ... communication, involvement, and a deep commitment to work across organisational boundaries ... Competencies are the glue that binds existing businesses. They are also the engine for new business development.' Prahalad and Hamel suggest that there are three tests, which can be applied to identify core competencies:

1 They provide potential access to a wide variety of markets rather than generating competitive advantage only in one.
2 They make 'a significant contribution to the perceived customer benefits of the end-product' – they add value.
3 They are difficult for competitors to copy. Products are easier to copy than processes.

The SWOT analysis is also the basis for undertaking customer analysis and deciding on market segmentation. It informs marketing strategy but equally must be interpreted in the context of a particular market, taking into account both customers and competitors. Strengths can be transformed into weaknesses in a different market and vice versa. The market context is crucial. Thus a SWOT analysis on the fast-food chain McDonald's in the context of the US market would yield completely different results to one undertaken in the context of the Russian market. In the USA it is a mature product, facing declining sales amidst severe competition. In Russia it is still a novel product in high demand.

The whole process is an art rather than a science. There is no prescriptive approach. Successfully pursuing opportunities is about identifying attractive business opportunities which, given the firm's capabilities, have a high probability of success. This probability is influenced by the firm's strengths, in particular how its distinctive competencies match the key success requirements to operate in the market, given the existing competition. Most opportunities also carry associated threats. Threats may be classified according to their seriousness and probability of occurrence. A view of the overall attractiveness of a market is based upon the opportunities it offers balanced by the threats that it poses. In making this judgement it is often useful to list the factors – whether you control them or not – that are critical to the success of the venture.

To undertake a SWOT you have to be brutally honest about yourself and your business. That means not pretending that something is a core competency when really it is not. As Gary Hamel urges, it means listening to people with different opinions and judging what is the prevailing wisdom in the company. Treacy and Wiersema (1995) pose five questions about the status quo that need to be answered honestly:

- What are the dimensions of value that customers care about? They claim there are only three value disciplines:
  - *Operational excellence* A good product/market offering (e.g. McDonald's or Dell);
  - *Product leadership* The best quality, most innovative product (e.g. Dyson or Rolls Royce);
  - *Customer intimacy* Understanding and developing relationships with customers (eg. Body Shop).
- For each dimension, what proportion of customers focus on it as their primary or dominant decision criterion?

Case insight

Rachel Elnaugh was only 24 when she set up **Red Letter Days** in 1989, working from the living room of her home. It was set up with £25 000 of her own money plus £7000 invested by family and friends. Since then it has been a self-financing operation that has grown organically by reinvesting profits in the business. Today it is has a turnover of £20 million and employs 150 people. The company sells 'experiences' – like driving a racing car, or taking a helicopter ride, or white-water rafting, or a day at a health spa. It does not provide the service or experience itself, it just packages and sells it, effectively taking a commission on the sale.

But it has not all been easy for the business. The very first problem was getting people to understand the 'product'. In 1989 it was completely unique. Trying to sign up the providers of the 'experiences' proved a problem. They thought Rachel was just trying to sell advertising space. And even when they agreed things went wrong. The first brochure advertised only 25 'experiences' but was expensive and unwieldy. It was not until a designer produced a slimmed-down leaflet that could be inserted into Sunday newspapers that the business really took off. Sales are particularly high around the Christmas period.

In 2002, however, there was a fundamental rethink. By then the company was selling all sorts of different 'products' through different outlets, using different brands. They decided to focus on the Red Letter Days brand and pull out of outlets such as the supermarket Tesco, where they sold gift ranges. They became leaner, more focused and more profitable. Before this decision, in 2000, sales had been £14 million. They dipped but by 2004 they had recovered to £17.4 million.

'The temptation, when you are hungry, is to just grab everything. So you end up with hundreds of different projects, without any kind of focus or strategy. That happened to us.'

Sunday Times 23 May 2004

- Which competitors provide the best value in each of these value dimensions?
- How does the firm compare to the competition on each dimension?
- Why does the firm fall short of the value leaders in each dimension of value?

From the answers to these questions realistic options can be listed and choices made. But, once again, honesty is essential because this means being realistic about the options even if some of them are not very pleasant.

A number of techniques can help in a SWOT analysis. These are summarised in Table 9.2. We have covered some tools and techniques already. For example, the generic marketing strategies are relevant to the internal appraisal and market research, knowledge of economies of scale and Porter's Five Forces analysis of industry competitiveness are relevant to the appraisal of the external environment.

Central to a SWOT analysis are the concepts of benchmarking and market research. Benchmarking performance has been around in one form or another since the 1960s. It usually involves developing performance ratios. These can be compared over time, measuring improvement or deterioration, or compared to other companies in the same industry or used as absolute measures of performance. Financial ratios are important. These can be judged against budgets, trends over time or against industry norms, based on published financial data produced by organisations like the Centre for Interfirm Comparison or ICC Business Ratios.

Table 9.2 Tools of the SWOT analysis

Internal appraisal (strengths, weaknesses)	External appraisal (opportunities, threats)
• Benchmarking; • Financial ratio analysis; • Value chains; • Generic marketing strategies (see Chapter 5); • Life cycle analysis (see Chapter 10); • Portfolio analysis (see Chapter 10).	• Market research (see Chapter 6); • Economies of scale (see Chapter 5); • Porter's Five Forces industry analysis (see Chapter 5); • SLEPT analysis.

However, performance ratios need not always be financial; benchmarking performance has been around in one form or another since the 1960s and in 1996 the DTI launched the UK Benchmark Index aimed at smaller firms. The index gathers data on a wide range of performance indicators including customer satisfaction rates, profitability, earnings per worker, productivity and stock turnover. It can be accessed via local Business Links or via www.benchmark/index.com. It has now gathered data on thousands of companies. *Closing the Gap*, a report based on this data shows that companies in the top quartile achieve profit margins five times higher than those in the bottom quartile. They achieve 98 per cent supplier accuracy and delivery reliability against 60 per cent accuracy and 85 per cent reliability for companies in the bottom quartile. Also, in these companies spending on training is ten times higher and staff absenteeism 75 per cent lower. The initiative is now being extended to the continent and the EC is funding its use in middle-sized firms across a number of European countries. It is also now being used in the USA, Singapore, South Africa and Australia.

Case insight

J. J. Cash, a Coventry-based textile manufacturer with 138 staff, put the company in for the UK Benchmarking Index and got some surprising results. They knew they had good product quality and thought they had excellent labour relations. However, the Index showed that the customer satisfaction rate was not good. Despite good product quality, the speed of response, vital in the fashion-led clothing industry, was not fast enough. Where they had lead times of four to six weeks, other firms could manage two. What is more, a set of key indicators such as accident rates, absenteeism and staff turnover revealed that the workers were suffering a lack of motivation.

What followed was nothing short of a complete culture change in the company. The old assembly-line production methods were dropped and new team-working structures were implemented across the entire organisation, underpinned with a generous training budget. Teams were given more authority and new 'two-way' communications procedures were put in place. As a result delivery-on-time rates increased from 60 per cent to 90 per cent, prototypes leave the factory in 48 hours, stock waste has fallen from 6.5 per cent to 2 per cent, stock turnover has increased and staff absenteeism and turnover rates have gone down.

Financial performance analysis

No SWOT analysis would be complete without an analysis of the company's financial position. Chapter 7 set out many of the elements of this – break-even and margin of safety remain important measures of risk. However, once established, investors and other backers of a firm start to look for other things and make use of a technique called 'ratio analysis'.

This starts by assuming that owners (shareholders) of the firm want to maximise their investment. Whatever they invest in, investors are ultimately interested in the final return they receive, after all expenses, in relation to their investment. If they invest £10 and receive £1, after all expenses, they receive a 10 per cent return which can then be compared to other investment opportunities. Shareholders, who own all the profits of the firm, want to maximise the return they receive on the shareholders' funds they have invested (share capital + retained profit). The critical performance ratio, that must be kept as high as possible, is therefore:

$$\text{Return to shareholders (\%)} = \frac{\text{Profit after interest (and all other costs)}}{\text{Shareholders' funds}}$$

This is expressed as a percentage. To maximise it means operating profit should be as high as possible, interest should be as low as possible and shareholders' funds should also be as low as possible. And here lies the dilemma. One way of keeping shareholders' funds low is to borrow (shareholders' funds = total assets – loans), but this increases interest payments. So the question is, how much to borrow? The following example should provide the answer. The business makes a return on all the money invested in it, both shareholders' funds and loans. Let us say that the shareholder puts £50 into the business and then obtains a bank loan of £50 on which interest of 10 per cent is payable. The business makes a return of 25 per cent on the total £100 invested in it. The situation is set out below:

Investment:		Return:	
Total assets	£100	Business @ 25%	= £25
comprising:		less:	
Loans	£ 50	Interest @ 10%	= £ 5
Shareholders' funds	£ 50	Balance for shareholder	= £20

The shareholder therefore gets to keep £20 – a 40 per cent return on investment. This is above the 25 per cent return the business is making because the shareholders are willing to take the risk of borrowing money on which they only pay a 10 per cent rate of interest. They get to keep the additional 15 per cent. However, this is a risk. If the business were only able to make a 5 per cent return (return = £5) then all the money would go to pay interest, leaving nothing for the shareholders. Similarly, in the unlikely event of interest rates rising above 25 per cent, the return to the shareholders would suffer.

As long as the return the business is making is above the rate of interest charged, the shareholders' return will be increased by maximising borrowing. However, in doing this the riskiness of the business increases because fixed interest costs increase. The appropriate level of borrowing, called gearing or leverage, is the classic risk/return trade-off decision – it is a question of judgement. However, bankers do have some benchmark ratios to inform their lending decisions, as we shall see in a later chapter.

Therefore, as far as the business is concerned, the critical performance ratio, that must be kept as high as possible, is:

$$\text{Return on total assets (\%)} = \frac{\text{Operating profit (before interest)}}{\text{Total assets}}$$

This is also expressed as a percentage. It is a measure of the operating efficiency of the business, the return operations make as opposed to the way the business is financed. It should be as high as possible, but be aware that the owner will also be taking a salary out of the business which is deducted in arriving at operating income. The measure can therefore be distorted if salaries are unrealistically low or high. The ratio, in turn, depends on two further ratios that when multiplied together yield the above ratio:

↓

$$\text{Profit margin (\%)} = \frac{\text{Net profit}}{\text{Sales}}$$

This measures the profit margin the firm is able to command and is expressed as a percentage. The ratio should be as high as possible.

↓

This ratio in turn depends upon how its constituent parts perform:

Gross profit margin (%)

$$= \frac{\text{Gross profit}}{\text{Sales}}$$

Gross profit is the difference between sales or turnover and the costs to produce the goods sold. The ratio should be as high as possible.

In addition, there are some key cost ratios, also expressed as percentages, that should be kept as low as possible:

$$\frac{\text{Cost of materials}}{\text{Sales}}, \frac{\text{Cost of labour}}{\text{Sales}},$$

$$\frac{\text{Overhead costs}}{\text{Sales}}$$

There may be other costs that are high and sensitive to changes in the market place that can be usefully measured against sales in this format.

↓

$$\text{Asset efficiency} = \frac{\text{Sales}}{\text{Net assets}}$$

This measures how efficiently the assets are being used in relation to the level of activity, measured by sales, and is expressed as a number. It should be as high as possible.

↓

This ratio in turn depends upon how its constituent parts perform:

$$\text{Debtor turnover} = \frac{\text{Sales}}{\text{Debtors}}$$

This number tells you how many times debtors turn over each year. If sales are £3.0 million and debtors are £0.6 million, they turn over 5 times a year, equivalent to every 1.2 months. You can compare this to the credit terms offered to customers.

$$\text{Stock turnover} = \frac{\text{Sales}}{\text{Stock}}$$

$$\text{Fixed asset turnover} = \frac{\text{Sales}}{\text{Fixed assets}}$$

These ratios are expressed as numbers and should be as high as possible.

Ratios are useful because they measure one number against another – they therefore allow for growth. So, for example, debtors are bound to increase as the business grows and sales increase, but what is important is not the absolute value of debtors but rather its relationship to sales, measured by debtor turnover. Similarly, there is no way of knowing whether a £2 million profit in one company is better than a £1 million profit in another unless you know how much was invested in each to achieve it.

To obtain a high return to the shareholder, a firm needs effective profit management and efficient asset management. Put crudely, margins need to be as high as possible and assets should be kept as low as possible. Systematic calculation of these ratios can give you clues about how profit might be increased and where assets might be reduced. Of course to do this you need some benchmarks. One fundamental benchmark is the rate of interest. The return on total assets should never fall below this, otherwise you are better off closing the company and putting the money in the bank. Another benchmark is your payment terms against which debtor turnover can be judged. All the others are a question of judgement, but you can judge them against:

- *Projected budgets*: ratios can be based on projected as well as actual financial information. Comparing actual to budgeted financial performance is part of effective financial control.
- *Trends over time*: ratios do change over time and trends can give both good and bad news.
- *Industry norms*: industry-based ratios, often based on published financial statements, are produced by organisations like the Centre for Interfirm Comparison and ICC Business Ratios.

There are also two ratios that measure the liquidity of a business. These are of particular interest to people offering credit to the business as they measure the firm's ability to repay them. These ratios are all expressed as numbers:

$$\text{Current ratio} = \frac{\text{Current assets}}{\text{Current liabilities}}$$

This is expected to be greater than 1, indicating that current assets exceed current liabilities.

Quick ratio

$$= \frac{\text{Current assets excluding stock}}{\text{Current liabilities}}$$

This is expected to be near to 1, perhaps as low as 0.8.

The level of borrowing is called gearing or leverage. High gearing or leverage is risky. It is measured by a number of ratios that are of particular interest to bankers:

Gearing (%)

$$= \frac{\text{All loans} + \text{overdraft}}{\text{Shareholders' funds}}$$

Bankers like this ratio to be under 100 per cent, indicating that shareholders have put in more money than the banks. Frequently for growing firms this is not the case. Above 400 per cent is considered very high risk and the business likely to fail. However, some management buy-outs can have gearing above this level.

Performance

Return on shareholders funds (%):

$$\frac{\text{Net profit (after interest)}}{\text{Shareholders funds}}$$

Return on total assets (%):

$$\frac{\text{Operating profit (before interest)}}{\text{Total assets}}$$

Profitability

Net margin (%):

$$\frac{\text{Net profit}}{\text{Sales}}$$

Gross margin (%):

$$\frac{\text{Gross profit}}{\text{Sales}}$$

Cost of materials (%):

$$\frac{\text{Cost of materials}}{\text{Sales}}$$

Cost of labour (%):

$$\frac{\text{Cost of labour}}{\text{Sales}}$$

Overhead cost (%):

$$\frac{\text{Overhead costs}}{\text{Sales}}$$

Asset efficiency

Capital/Net asset turnover:

$$\frac{\text{Sales}}{\text{Net assets}}$$

Debtor turnover:

$$\frac{\text{Sales}}{\text{Debtors}}$$

Stock turnover:

$$\frac{\text{Sales}}{\text{Stock}}$$

Fixed asset turnover:

$$\frac{\text{Sales}}{\text{Fixed assets}}$$

Liquidity

Current ratio:

$$\frac{\text{Current assets}}{\text{Current liabilities}}$$

Quick ratio:

$$\frac{\text{Current assets excluding stock}}{\text{Current liabilities}}$$

Gearing

Gearing ratio (%):

$$\frac{\text{All loans + overdrafts}}{\text{Shareholders funds}}$$

Short-term debt ratio (%):

$$\frac{\text{Short-term loans + overdrafts}}{\text{All loans + overdraft}}$$

Interest cover:

$$\frac{\text{Trading profit}}{\text{Interest}}$$

Risk

Margin of safety

$$\frac{\text{Sales} - \text{Break-even sales}}{\text{Sales}}$$

Figure 9.4 Financial ratio checklist

Short-term borrowing (%)

$$= \frac{\text{Short-term loans} + \text{overdraft}}{\text{All loans} + \text{overdraft}}$$

Long-term loans give greater security than short-term loans. Therefore the higher this ratio, the riskier the firm. The ratio must be read alongside gearing. Low gearing means the percentage short-term borrowing can be higher.

$$\text{Interest cover} = \frac{\text{Operating profit}}{\text{Interest}}$$

This measures how secure interest payments are. The higher the number the better.

The margin of safety remains an important ratio measuring the riskiness of the business due to its level of fixed costs. A financial ratio checklist which includes the margin of safety is shown as Figure 9.4. You may wish to revisit Chapter 7 where many of these terms and some of these ratios were explained.

Value chains

Real advantages in cost or differentiation need to be found in the chain of activities that a firm performs to deliver value to its customers. Michael Porter (1985) says that the value chain, shown in Figure 9.5, should be the start of any strategic analysis. He identified five primary activities:

1 Inbound logistics (receiving, storing, disseminating inputs)
2 Operations (transforming inputs into a final product)
3 Outbound logistics (collecting, storing and distributing products to customers)
4 Marketing and sales
5 After-sales and service

and four secondary or support activities:

1 Procurement (purchasing consumable and capital items)
2 Human resource management
3 Technology development (R&D and so on)
4 Firm infrastructure (general management, accounting and so on).

Porter argues that each generic category can be broken down into discrete activities unique to a particular firm. The firm can then look at the costs associated with each activity and then try to compare it to the value obtained by customers from the particular activity. By identifying the cost or value drivers – the factors that determine cost or value for each activity – and the linkages which reduce cost or add value or discourage imitation, the firm can develop the strategies that lead to competitive advantage.

This is a way of focusing on the drivers of value in a business that ought to influence the strategy of the firm. For example, the low cost supply situation may be linked to being close to a key supplier and could therefore disappear if the firm decides, as part of its expansion plans, to move to another location. The value chain is also a useful way of thinking about how differentiation might be achieved. For example, a high-quality product might be let down by low quality after-sales service – the value to the customer not being matched by the investment. In other words,

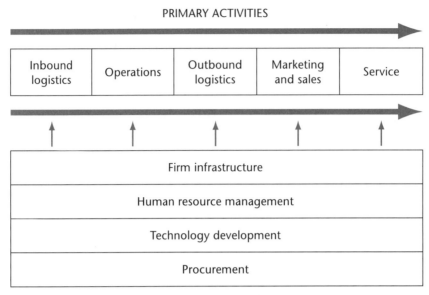

Figure 9.5 The value chain

differentiation is likely to be achieved by multiple linkages in the value chain – a consistent marketing mix. If multiple compatible linkages can be established, they are more difficult to imitate than single linkages. Similarly, building switch costs into the value chain can also enhance competitive position. However, the advent of e-commerce has generally made it easier to disaggregate the value chain, establishing markets at different points along it, allowing firms to radically rethink or 're-engineer' the way their product/market offering is put together.

Entrepreneurs can add value to customers in a number of ways, not least by developing the close relationships they are so good at. A particularly effective entrepreneurial strategy is to identify a sector in which relationships are weak and create value by tightening them up.

SLEPT analysis

SLEPT analysis can be useful in thinking about future developments in the environment and how they might affect the business, but not necessarily the firm's possition in the environment. The analysis looks at the changes that are likely to occur in the areas spelt out by the acronym SLEPT:

Social   Social changes such as an ageing population, increasing work participation often from home, 24-hour shopping, increasing crime, increasing participation in higher education, changing employment patterns, increasing number of one-parent families and so on.

Legal	Legal changes such as Health and Safety, changes in employment laws, food hygiene regulations, patent laws and so on.
Economic	Economic changes such as entry into the Euro currency area, changes in interest rates, growth, inflation, employment and so on.
Political	Political changes like local or central government elections; political initiatives, for example on competitiveness in car prices or at supermarkets, new or changed taxes, merger and take-over policy and so on.
Technological	Technological developments such as the internet, increasing use of computers and chip technology, increasing use of mobile phones, increasing use of surveillance cameras and so on.

The trick is to brainstorm and think outside the square about how these developments might affect the business. For example, the development of the internet and broadband networks might be thought to dramatically bring into question the future viability of shops selling CDs or videos. The development of teleconferencing might be seen as a threat to those firms providing business travel over long distances, such as airlines. The development of internet shopping might cause developers to rethink the purpose and structure of our town centres as well as individual shops to re-engineer the way they meet customer needs. The future may be uncertain, but it cannot be ignored.

Another technique used sometimes to help think about the future in a structured way is called 'futures thinking'. Futures thinking tries to take a holistic perspective, avoiding a rigid approach to strategic planning. With it a vision about a desired future state is developed and planning then takes place, backwards, from that state to where the firm is at the moment. Current constraints to action are ignored and in this way the barriers to change are identified. Some barriers may be permanent, but some might not be.

Similar to this is 'scenario planning' which can be a valuable tool for assessing a firm's environment in conditions of high uncertainty over a longer term, say five years or more. With this technique, views of possible future situations that might impact on the firm are constructed. Often major trends in the environment are identified from the SLEPT analysis and built into scenarios. These situations must be logically consistent possible futures, usually an optimistic, a pessimistic and a 'most likely' future, based around key factors influencing the firm. Optional courses of action or strategies are then matched to these scenarios. In effect, the scenarios are being used to test the sensitivity of possible strategies. They also allow assumptions about the status quo of the environment in which a firm operates to be challenged. So, for example, a company planning overseas expansion may be uncertain about factors like exchange rate fluctuations or tariff barriers and might construct possible futures that help it decide whether to manufacture in the UK and export or to set up a manufacturing base in the country.

Scenario planning takes the firm away from the short-term, day to day imperatives and helps it think about long-term trends and changes in its environment. Most entrepreneurs, however, prefer to learn by doing and take a short-term, incremental approach to decision-making, reacting to events as they occur. However, in a risky environment, or one where high capital costs are involved, scenario planning has a lot to recommend it – and it is a lot cheaper than making mistakes.

Strategy misfit

Of course the SWOT analysis may lead the firm to conclude that their strengths and resources do not match their high aspirations. Based upon a study of firms that have challenged established big companies in a range of industries, Hamel and Prahalad (1994) say that, in reconciling the misfit, successful firms use something they call 'strategic intent', which is about developing a common vision about the future, aligning staff behaviour with a common purpose and delegating and decentralising decision-making. They argued that 'the challengers had succeeded in creating entirely new forms of competitive advantage and dramatically rewriting the rules of engagement'. Managers in these firms could imagine new products, services and even entire industries that did not exist and then went on to create them. They were not just benchmarking and analysing competition, they were creating new market places that they could dominate because it was a market place of their own making. Hamel and Prahalad claim that the trick is to answer three key questions:

- What new types of customer benefits should we seek to provide in 5, 10 or 15 years?
- What new competencies will we need to build or acquire in order to offer these benefits?
- How will we need to reconfigure our customer interface over the next few years.

Whilst these managers may be revolutionaries, they have their feet firmly on the ground because they understand very clearly the firm's core competencies – that is, the skills and technologies that enable the company to provide benefits to customers. Which brings us back to understanding our marketing strategies and reworking our SWOT analysis.

Securing competitive advantage

The distinguishing feature of entrepreneurs is that they recognise what works and replicate it quickly before competitors can react. So, the first thing that a growing firm needs to understand is why it has been successful so far. It needs to revisit the generic marketing strategies in relation to the SWOT analysis in order to be certain it can answer four key questions that enable it to understand the basis of its competitive advantage and capitalise on the relevant factors:

1 Who are our customers?
2 What benefits are they looking for when they buy or products or services?
3 Why do they buy from us rather than our competitors?
4 What strengths do we have and how can they be used to build advantage?

Each of the generic marketing strategies (reproduced in Figure 9.6) has certain strategic decision-making implications. These are actions that you would expect the firm to be undertaking in order to secure its competitive advantage for as long as possible. After the initial success of a start-up it is good to just pause to consider how this will be achieved.

Figure 9.6 Generic marketing strategies

A company that is selling on price needs to maintain cost leadership. This means imposing tight cost controls and being aware of how cost savings might be achieved, for example through economies of scale, the introduction of more efficient ways of working or the introduction of new technology. To be market leader implies being the lowest cost provider and doing whatever it takes to achieve this. This means constantly moving down the cost curve and keeping all costs as low as possible, for example by moving production to countries with low cost labour, changing the materials used in manufacture or minimising sales and distribution costs. To sustain cost leadership can be a constant struggle and to help in this, wherever possible, companies develop patents and copyrights on their processes and procedures. Accountants play an important part in running this sort of company. The commodity supplier needs to have a strategy for doing all these things.

As we discussed in previous chapters, it is vital for a company following a policy of differentiation that it understands the basis of its differential advantage very clearly and then does whatever is needed to reinforce and build it. Differentiation involves

Case insight

Dell Computers' market place is highly competitive. Dell prides itself on good marketing of quality products but, most important, speedy delivery of customised products. Nevertheless, whilst it might not sell the cheapest computers in the market place, the price it asks must always be competitive and that means costs must be kept as low as possible.

Dell decided early on that its competitive advantage lay in the computer-based processes it used to keep costs low and to build to order, quickly. In the 1990s, in order to sustain these competitive advantages, Dell started applying for patents, not for its products, but for different parts of its ordering, building and testing processes. It now holds about 80 such patents. However good, the machines it sells have become commodities using homogenous components from hard disk drives to microprocessors – mostly from Intel – but the processes Dell uses to build them allow the company to achieve competitive advantage and to sustain it.

➡

'Basically any brand is an assurance to customers. It is an assurance of quality, an assurance of consistency. There is an immediate recognition, when you see the Cadbury signature on the front of the chocolate bar or box of Milk Tray, all those things are guaranteed.'

Sir Adrian Cadbury
The Times 8 July 2000
➡

being different and distinctive in some way. It often involves innovation. Branding has a vital role to play for a company trying to differentiate itself. A brand should be the embodiment of the product or service offering to customers. It takes time to build as it is based upon trust that the product or service will consistently deliver what it promises. A good brand is a valuable business asset and a firm following a differentiation strategy will need to invest time and money in developing it.

If a firm is focusing on a narrow market, then it needs to be undertaking regular market research to monitor changes in that market segment. Are tastes changing? Should the firm be adapting its offering to reflect these tastes, after all, the strength of the business should be its knowledge and close relationship with the narrow market segment that it sells to. One danger is that the smaller the number of customers in a segment, the greater the risk that the changing buying patterns of just a few will have a dramatic impact on the firm. However, these days focusing on a narrow market segment can go hand in hand with having a global market of millions of customers.

Case insight

Gary Frank understands the importance of image and branding, particularly for a small firm trying to carve a niche in the market for itself. The company he set up in 1989, the **Delicious Doughnut Company**, was turning in lacklustre performance. It did not even produce doughnuts any more. So in 1997 he decided to create a new image and re-brand the company with the name **Fabulous Bakin' Boys**. He invested £300 000 in the name change and recruited a marketing manager.

Sales increased instantly by 6 per cent. They have now become one of Europe's leading muffin makers and their eye-catching products can now be seen on the shelves of Tesco, Sainsbury and Safeway. Profits have grown to £400 000 on sales of £7 million.

●

Successful entrepreneurial strategies

So, Porter wants you to select one of his generic strategies – cost leadership, differentiation or focus. Hamel and Prahalad want you to focus on core competencies. On the other hand, Treacy and Wiersema want you to select operational excellence, product leadership or customer intimacy. Which theory do you choose? *The key theme is that strategy should emphasise something that makes the firm as unique as possible and delivers as much value to the customer as possible today, and more importantly, tomorrow.* And we might add that, whatever you do, you must do it quickly so as to seize the market opportunity and that means, inevitably, that your strategy cannot be spelt out in detail. You need a firm idea of your general direction – your vision – and the rest of the firm will have to deal with the detail on a day-to-day basis.

And what does research tell us are the specific strategies that are most likely to ensure growth? In their survey of 179 supergrowth companies, Harrison and Taylor's (*op. cit.*) entrepreneurs identified five 'winning performance factors', most of which can be supported by other research:

1 *Compete on quality rather than price.* Competing on the quality of a product or service rather than price is an important element of success for entrepreneurial firms across Europe (Ray and Hutchinson, 1983, Storey *et al.*, 1989; Burns, 1994). By way of contrast, slow growing firms tend to emphasise price (Burns, *op. cit.*).
2 *Dominate a market niche.* Many surveys support this conclusion about niche marketing (Solem and Steiner, 1989; Storey *et al.*, 1989; Birley and Westhead, 1990; Macrae, 1991; Siegel *et al.*, 1993 and 3i, 1993). There is also a strong relationship between market share and financial return (Boston Consulting Group, 1968, 1972 and Buzell *et al.*, 1974, Buzell and Gale, 1987 and Yelle, 1979).
3 *Compete in areas of strength.* This relates particularly to the previous point since the ability to differentiate effectively is a considerable strength.
4 *Have tight financial and operating controls.* Researchers often link strong financial control with planning (3i, 1991).
5 *Frequent product or service innovation (particularly important in manufacturing).* Innovation and new product introduction are also seen as important by many researchers (Dunkelberg *et al.*, 1987; Solem and Steiner, 1989; Storey *et al.*, 1989; Woo *et al.*, 1989 and Wynarczyk *et al.*, 1993).

'We learned to identify our core strengths . . . The idea of building a business solely on cost or price was not a sustainable advantage. There would always be someone with something that was lower in price or cheaper to produce. What was really important was sustaining loyalty among customers and employees, and that could only be derived from having the highest level of service and very high performing products.'

Michael Dell (1999)
➡

The conclusion is obvious. If you want to play the odds, *the strategy with the best chance of generating the highest profits is to differentiate with the aim of dominating that market and do it effectively and quickly, then continue to innovate based on your differential advantage.* And one important element of differentiation in our entrepreneurial firm is the entrepreneurial architecture that will allow it to pursue this strategy successfully and, more importantly, sustain it.

However, one final word of caution, but also reinforcement. Nohria and Joyce (2003) report the results of a ten-year study of 160 companies and their use of some 200 different management techniques. They conclude what we all suspect; that it does not matter so much which technique(s) you apply but it matters very much that you execute it flawlessly. They claim flawless execution is something too many management theorists have forgotten. Attention to detail is important. They also highlight three other things that distinguish successful companies over time:

1 A company culture that aims high.
2 A structure that is flexible and responsive.
3 A strategy that is clear and focused.

Case with questions

One firm that has successfully followed the low-price strategy is **easyJet**. It was founded by **Stelios Haji-Ioannou**, a graduate of London Business School, in 1995 with £5 million borrowed from his father, a Greek shipping tycoon. Copying similar operations in the USA and Ryanair flying out of Ireland, easyJet was one of the first 'low-cost' airlines in the UK, flying from Luton to Scotland. He then launched similar low-cost, no-frills services to continental Europe. The company has transformed the European air travel market and has beaten off many rival imitators. easyJet was floated on the Stock Market in 2000 at 310p a share, making Stelios £280 million profit.

> 'You start the business as a dream, you make it your passion for a while and then you get experienced managers to run it because it's not as much fun as starting. I think there's a lot to be said about starting a business and a lot to be said about running a business when its mature.' (*Sunday Times*, 29 October 2000)

A central strategy of being low-price is being low-cost and that has a number of implications for the way easyJet and its rivals are run. Low costs come from two driving principles – 'sweating' the assets and high operating efficiency. easyJet flies its Boeing 737s for 11 hours a day, 4 hours longer than BA. Their pilots fly 900 hours a year, 50 per cent more than BA pilots. In terms of operating efficiency, it means:

- Aircraft fly out of low-cost airports. These are normally not the major airport serving any destination and can be some distance from them;
- Aircraft are tightly scheduled. They are allowed only 25 minutes to off-load one set of passengers and load another, less than half the time of its scheduled full-fare rivals;
- Aircraft must leave and arrive on time (they will not wait for passengers), and if there are delays they can have horrendous knock-on consequences for the timetable. Nevertheless punctuality is varied, with the low-cost carriers just as good as full-fare airlines on some routes;
- There are is no 'slack' in the system. easyJet admits to having 'one and a half planes' worth' of spare capacity compared with the dozen planes BA has on stand-by at Gatwick and Heathrow. If something goes wrong with a plane it can lead to cancellations and long delays;
- There are fewer cabin crew than full-fare rivals and staff rostering is a major logistical problem.

In terms of customer service, it means:

- No 'frills' such as free drinks, meals or assigned seats;
- There is no compensation for delays or lost baggage;
- The low-cost airlines do not guarantee transfers as the planes could be late:
- The low-cost airlines concentrate on point-to-point flights, whereas the full-fare airlines tend to concentrate on hub-and-spoke traffic.

easyJet is aggressive in promoting its brand and running advertising promotions to get more 'bums on seats'. It realises that its planes must have a high seat occupancy to be economic. To this end it is particularly inventive with pricing, encouraging real bargain hunters onto the less popular flights during the day and promoting early bookings with cheaper fares.

easyJet has been at the forefront of the use of the internet for virtual ticketing, to the point where it now sells most of its tickets over the web. This means it does not have to pay commission to travel agents and check-in can be quicker and more efficient. Its website has been held up as a model for the industry and many have copied it.

→

However, easyJet does have competition and some airlines are cheaper. Whilst easyJet claim an average price of £45 per 600 kilometres, Ryanair claim £34. This compares to British Airways' price of £110. Interestingly Ryanair has so little faith in its timetable that it advises passengers not to book connecting flights.

One of the fears about low-cost airlines is that they will be tempted to compromise on safety for the sake of cutting costs. The British Airline Pilots Association has claimed that pilots of low-cost airlines can be tempted to cut corners to achieve flight timetables. Stelios himself has fuelled the safety debate by expressing doubts about Ryanair's use of 20-year-old planes on some of its routes, pointing out that though they might improve profits in the short term, they put the future of the whole airline at risk in the event of an accident. Ryanair is phasing these planes out and does have an unblemished safety record. But the industry is all too aware that the low-cost US airline, Valuejet, went bankrupt after one of its planes crashed in 1996, killing all 110 people on board. As the *Economist* says (17 August 2002): 'the low cost airline business is not for the faint-hearted'.

Only seven years after founding the company, in 2002, and still owning 29 per cent of easyJet Stelios realised that he was not suited to managing an established public company and was better suited to being a serial entrepreneur, so he resigned as Chairman, aged only 35. He was to be replaced by Sir Colin Chandler, aged 62, part of London's financial establishment as chairman of Vickers Defence Systems, deputy chairman of Smiths Group and director of Thales.

> 'Running a company that is listed on the Stock Exchange is different from building up and running a private company. The history of the City is littered with entrepreneurs who hold onto their creations for too long, failing to recognise the changing needs of the company. I am a serial entrepreneur . . . It is all part of growing up. I've built something and now it is time to move on.' (*The Times*, 19 April 2002)

Shortly after Stelios' departure easyJet took over Go, the low-cost airline set up by British Airways and sold off to its management. Newspaper comment at the time suggested Stelios had been blocking such a deal and this might have been one reason for his departure.

Go had been in fierce price competition with easyJet on certain routes, to the point where tickets were being given away with only airport tax to pay. One of the first things easyJet did was to close the Go flights on these routes and restore prices. As well as eliminating competition, the purchase of Go had other strategic reasoning behind it. easyJet were purchasing market share in a fast-growing market (in 2002 it grew 60 per cent) where there are economies of scale. They were also buying new routes and landing rights, which can be difficult to secure.

Stelios still has many other 'easy' ventures to grow. These include **easyRental** – a car rental business, **easyEverything** – a chain of internet cafes and cinemas, and **easyValue** – which provides impartial comparisons for online shopping. He still has everything to play for, doing something he enjoys more and possibly does better.

Questions
1 Based upon this information, undertake a SWOT analysis on easyJet
2 Compared to Ryanair and British Airways, where would you place easyJet in terms of Porter's generic marketing strategies? Is this sustainable?
3 What is the underlying strategy behind all of Stelios' 'easy' ventures? Can this strategy be replicated in any market? What is required for it to work?

Summary

The ingredients of successful growth, as shown by the experience of **S&A Foods**, are:

1 An owner-manager who is an entrepreneur;
2 The right business culture;
3 A strong company;
4 Deciding on the right business strategies;
5 Luck.

Barriers to growth vary according to the economic conditions of the time and many company-specific factors. However, consistent general barriers are market conditions and cost or availability of finance.

A strategic framework is useful but a good framework is minimalist. Effective strategy must be rooted in the distinctive capabilities of the firm. The strategic process involves four stages:

1 Developing vision.
2 Strategic analysis, which involves undertaking a SWOT analysis and highlighting the core competencies of the organisation.
3 Strategy formulation, which involves identifying, evaluating and selecting strategic options.
4 Strategy implementation, which involves leading and managing a change process, putting in place the appropriate organisation structure and culture and planning and allocating resources.

The basic tool of strategic analysis is the SWOT analysis. However, there are a number of other strategic tools that can also help. The main ones are summarised in Table 9.2. They seek to highlight the core competencies of the organisation and match them to the opportunities in the market place to create sustainable competitive advantage. Core competencies can be used in a variety of markets, add value and are difficult to copy.

Financial ratio analysis is an important part of a SWOT analysis. Based on the premise that shareholders want to maximise the return they make on their investment, it provides information on how profit might be increased and assets reduced. It also provides information about liquidity and gearing or leverage. As **J.J. Cash** found, other non-financial performance ratios can also be calculated and used to benchmark performance via local Business Links.

Securing competitive advantage involves understanding who customers are, what benefits they are looking for and why they buy from you rather than competitors. What are your core competencies? How do you add value to customers? Which strategies have worked in the past? Future strategy should build upon these strengths. A basic review of these elements caused **Red Letter Day** to rethink its strategies and refocus, pulling out of some markets. An understanding of the generic marketing strategies and the value chain can inform these judgements. **Dell** understands where its competitive advantage lies and uses patents to secure it. **The Fabulous Bakin' Boys** use image and branding to secure their competitive advantage.

When there is a strategic misfit between aspirations and resources, strategic intent is the one binding force that allows managers to change the face of the markets they enter. SLEPT analysis, scenario planning and futures thinking are techniques that can help develop that vision.

Whilst Porter emphasises cost leadership (a strategy followed by **easyJet**), differentiation or focus, Hamel and Prahalad highlight core competencies and Treacy and Wiersema emphasise operational excellence, product leadership or customer intimacy. The unifying theme to come from these theorists is that strategy should emphasise something that makes the firm as *unique* as possible and delivers as much *value* to the customer as possible today and, more importantly, tomorrow.

Research tells us that the strategy with the best chance of generating the highest profits is to *differentiate* with the aim of *dominating that market niche,* compete in areas of strength, and do this effectively and *quickly*, and continue to *innovate based on your differential advantage*. **Jordans** is a good example of a firm that fits this profile.

Essays and discussion topics

1 Most small firms will not grow to any size. It is therefore not worthwhile trying to 'pick winners'. Discuss.
2 How much luck is involved in successfully growing a business?
3 Are there any real barriers to growth or are there only excuses?
4 In different contexts, strengths can be weaknesses and opportunities all too easily turn into threats. Discuss.
5 How can you go about making a SWOT analysis as objective as possible?
6 Planning frameworks are good in theory but in the real world entrepreneurs do not plan. Discuss.
7 Porter wants you to select cost leadership, differentiation or focus, Hamel and Prahalad want you to focus on core competencies and Treacy and Wiersema want you to select operational excellence, product leadership or customer intimacy. All these strategies are just fad and fancy. Nobody really knows how to generate competitive advantage. Discuss.
8 How important is speed of action – 'first-mover advantage' – to the entrepreneurial firm?
9 Everything can be copied, therefore competitive advantage can never be sustained. Discuss.
10 Value chains are an elegant concept but cannot be operationalised. Discuss.
11 You cannot determine profit in a small firm because there are too many ways for the entrepreneur to manipulate it. Any form of financial analysis will therefore not work. Discuss.
12 How might you go about determining the profitability of a small firm so that financial analysis can be undertaken?
13 Death Valley just goes on and on for the growing firm. Explain why.
14 What should a small firm do to ensure that debtors pay promptly?
15 We can only guess what the future might hold, so there is no point in trying to predict it. Discuss.
16 If you are being really innovative – revolutionary – you are venturing into the unknown and you cannot plan for that. What form might planning take in these circumstances?
17 How can futures thinking and scenario planning help you think about the future?
18 How do you think music will be sold in the future? How can firms make a profit?
19 A firm needs two plans – one for the provider of capital that 'sells' the business idea to them and a second that is a true evaluation of how the firm might perform. Discuss.
20 How would you go about undertaking a SWOT on an established small firm?

Exercises and assignments

1   Select a successful entrepreneur such as Bill Gates or Richard Branson and research their backgrounds showing how their business developed and analyse why they have been so successful.
2   For a selected set of published financial statements, undertake a financial analysis using the Financial Audit Checklist in Figure 9.4.
3   Undertake a SLEPT analysis on your university, college or department. Based upon this, try scenario planning on one major trend that you identify.
4   Undertake a SLEPT analysis on a selected firm. Based upon this, try scenario planning on one major trend that you identify.
5   Undertake a SWOT analysis on your university, college or department. Draw up a list of action points that follow from your analysis.
6   Undertake a comprehensive SWOT analysis on your course. Draw up a list of action points that follow from your analysis.

References

Birley, S. and Westhead, P. (1990) 'Growth and Performance Contrasts Between "Types" of Small Firms', *Strategic Management Journal*, II.

Boston Consulting Group (1968) *Perspectives on Experience*, Boston, MA: Boston Consulting Group.

Boston Consulting Group (1972) *Perspectives on Experience*, Boston, MA: Boston Consulting Group.

Burns, P. (1994) *Winners and Losers in the 1990s*, 3i European Enterprise Centre, Report no. 12, April.

Buzell, R.D. and Gale, B.T. (1987) *The PIMS Principles – Linking Strategy to Performance*, New York: Free Press.

Buzell, R.D., Heany, D.F. and Schoeffer, S. (1974) 'Impact of Strategic Planning on Profit Performance', *Harvard Business Review*, 52(2).

Dunkelberg, W.G., Cooper, A.C., Woo, C. and Dennis, W.J. (1987) 'New Firm Growth and Performance', in N.C. Churchill, J.A. Hornday, B.A. Kirchhoff, C.J. Krasner and K.H. Vesper (eds), *Frontiers of Entrepreneurship Research*, Boston, MA: Babson College Press.

Hamel, G. and Prahalad, C.K. (1994) *Competing For the Future: Breakthrough Strategies for Seizing Control of your Industry and Creating the Markets of Tomorrow*, Boston, MA: Harvard Business School Press.

Harrison, J. and Taylor, B. (1996) *Supergrowth Companies: Entrepreneurs in Action*, Oxford: Butterworth-Heinemann.

Macrae, D.J.R. (1991) 'Characteristics of High and Low Growth Small and Medium-Sized Businesses', paper presented at 21st European Small Business Seminar, Barcelona, Spain.

Nohria, N. and Joyce, W. (2003) 'What Really Works', *Harvard Business Review*, July/August.

Porter, M.E. (1985) *Competitive Advantage: Creating and Sustaining Superior Performance*, New York: Free Press.

Prahalad, C.K. and Hamel, G. (1990) 'The Core Competence of the Corporation', *Harvard Business Review*, 68(3), May/June.

Ray, G.H. and Hutchinson, P.J. (1983) *The Financing and Financial Control of Small Enterprise Development*, London: Gower.

Rogers, E.M. (1962) *Diffusion of Innovation*, New York: Free Press.

Siegel, R., Siegel, E. and MacMillan, I.C. (1993) 'Characteristics Distinguishing High Growth Ventures, *Journal of Business Venturing*, 8.

Solem, O. and Steiner, M.P. (1989) 'Factors for Success in Small Manufacturing Firms – and with Special Emphasis on Growing Firms', paper presented at Conference on SMEs and the Challenges of 1992, Mikkeli, Finland.

Storey, D.J., Keasey, K., Watson, R. and Wynarczyk, P. (1987) *The Performance of Small Firms: Profits, Jobs and Failures*, London: Croom Helm.

Storey D.J., Watson R. and Wynarczyk, P. (1989) *Fast Growth Small Business: Case Studies of 40 Small Firms in Northern Ireland*, Department of Employment, research paper no. 67.

3i European Enterprise Centre (1991) *High Performance SMEs: A Two Country Study*, Report no. 1, September.

3i European Enterprise Centre (1993) *Britain's Superleague Companies*, Report no. 9, August.

Treacy, M. and Wiersema, F. (1995) *The Discipline of Market Leaders*, Reading, MA: Addison-Wesley.

Woo, C.Y., Cooper, A.C., Dunkelberg, W.C., Daellenbach, U. and Dennis, W.J. (1989) 'Determinants of Growth for Small and Large Entrepreneurial Start-Ups', paper presented to Babson Entrepreneurship Conference.

Wynarczyk, P., Watson, R., Storey, D.J., Short, H. and Keasey, K. (1993) *The Managerial Labour Market in Small and Medium-Sized Enterprises*, London: Routledge.

Yelle, L.E. (1979) 'The Learning Curve: Historical Review and Comprehensive Survey', *Decision Sciences*, 10.

10

Life Cycles and Portfolios

Contents

- Life cycles
- Product portfolios
- Portfolio strategies
- Managing the product life cycle
- Financial implications of the product portfolio
- Implications for the entrepreneur
- Summary

LEARNING OUTCOMES

By the end of this chapter you should be able to:

- Explain the effect of product life cycles on marketing strategy;

- Explain how the life cycle can be lengthened through product expansion and extension;

- Use the Boston matrix to present marketing strategies for a portfolio of products;

- Describe the effects of the product portfolio on cash flow and profitability;

- Describe the implications of the product portfolio on management styles and the problems this creates for the entrepreneur;

- Explain how the concept of life cycle can be extended to companies and industries and what the implications of this are for management.

Life cycles

As they grow most firms become more complex organisations selling a range of different products or services into a range of different markets, each with a different strategy. These are called different 'product/market offerings'. The same product can even be sold to different market segments with a slightly different strategy. Slightly different products might also be developed to better meet the needs of different market segments. The permutations are endless.

One important influence on strategy is the point the product or service is at in its life cycle. This can be used to identify the different market segments attracted to the product and the degree and nature of competition it faces. From this comes another set of 'routine patterns, based on experience', which can be used either as a strategy checklist or as a benchmark to assess how different you dare to be – but remember the odds! This concept can, in turn, be used to better understand the complexity of the portfolio of different product/market offerings and how that portfolio can be managed. It also raises issues about how corporate entrepreneurship can be managed across a large, complex organisation.

The concept of the product life cycle is based on the idea that all products or services have a finite life cycle and that, to some extent, the appropriate marketing strategy is dictated by the stage it is at in this life cycle. Life cycles can vary in length from short for fashion products, such as clothing and other consumables, to long for durable products like cars. Often the life cycle can be extended by a variety of marketing initiatives. Figure 10.1 shows a four-stage product life cycle with the implications for marketing strategy at the different stages. The simplicity of the model has much to recommend it. However, these broad generalisations must be treated with caution because all products are different, as are different market segments and the customers that comprise them.

At the introductory phase the objective should be to make potential customers aware of the product and to get them to try it. The benefits need to be explained and the relevance to the customer needs to be underlined. Early customers are likely to be 'innovators', that is people who think for themselves and try things. Rogers (1962) estimated they make up some 2.5 per cent of the population. Entrepreneurial firms launching innovative new products are particularly interested in this phase.

At the growth phase the objective should be to grab market share as quickly as possible because competitors will be entering the market. This means that prices will have to be competitive, depending on the uniqueness of the product and how well it can be differentiated. The promotion emphasis should shift to one of promoting the brand and why it is better than that of competitors. 'Early adopters' will now be buying the product. These tend to be people with status in their market segment and opinion leaders. They adopt successful products, making them acceptable and respectable. These are estimated to represent some 13.5 per cent of the population. The product range should start to be developed at this stage so as to give customers more choice and gain advantage over competitors.

The 'middle and late majority' now start buying the product and take it into the mature phase of its life cycle. The middle majority (comprising some 34 per cent) are more conservative, with slightly higher status and are more deliberate purchasers. They only adopt the product after it has become acceptable. The late majority (also comprising some 34 per cent) are typically below average status, are sceptical and

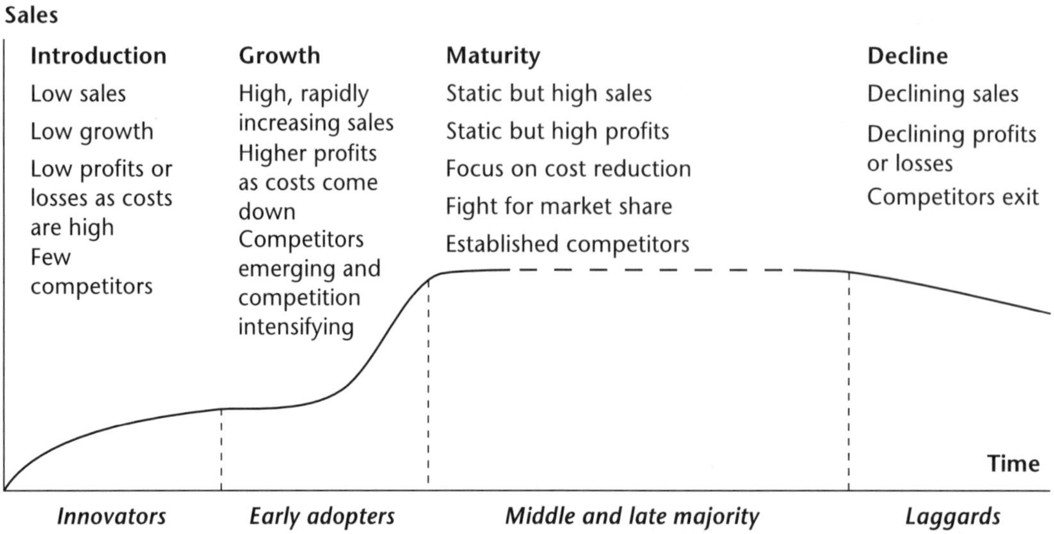

Sales

Introduction	Growth	Maturity	Decline
Low sales	High, rapidly increasing sales	Static but high sales	Declining sales
Low growth	Higher profits as costs come down	Static but high profits	Declining profits or losses
Low profits or losses as costs are high	Competitors emerging and competition intensifying	Focus on cost reduction	Competitors exit
Few competitors		Fight for market share	
		Established competitors	

Time

Innovators | *Early adopters* | *Middle and late majority* | *Laggards*

Elements of marketing strategy

Basic product	Develop product extensions and service levels	Wide range in place but expansion slows down or eventually ceases	Range narrows
Price low for repeat purchase products where trial is important	Price competitively to combat competition and penetrate market	Modify and differentiate	Weak products are dropped
Price high where novelty or uniqueness is valued, particularly if purchases are infrequent	Promote actively and aggressively	Develop next generation	Price high if reducing number of competitors means demand still high
	Build brand	Price defensively – meeting or beating competitors – to ensure maximum return	
Promote actively and aggressively	Intensive push on distribution	Emphasise brand	Price low to dispose of stocks at end of life, in line with declining demand
Explain product benefits	Limited trade discounts	Differentiate	
Build awareness, encourage early adoption		Selective marketing, based around special offers or promotions	Minimum promotion required to maintain loyalty
Selective distribution		Intensive push on distribution	Emphasis on low price
		Trade discounts offered	Distribute selectively
			Phase out weak outlets

Figure 10.1 The product/service life cycle

adopt the product much later. In this phase competitors are becoming established as some companies fall by the wayside. In order to maintain market share, pricing tends to be defensive at, or around, the level of competitors. There should be an emphasis on cost reduction so that profits are as high as possible. The accountant's influence should be evident at this stage in the life cycle. It is at this point that products tend to get revamped – by changing designs, colours, packaging and so on – in order to extend their life cycle. Toward the end of this period, price reductions may be hidden by offering extra elements to the product for the same price. Cars, for example, often get this treatment with limited edition models offering many extras for the same price.

'Laggards' (comprising some 16 per cent) tend to view life through the rear view mirror and will continue buying products because of habit. The interesting thing about the decline phase of the life cycle is that there may still be the opportunity to charge high prices and make good profits, at least in the short term, because competitors may be exiting the market quicker than demand is tailing off. Exactly when to exit is therefore a matter of careful judgement.

The problem with this concept is one of trying to establish where a product might actually be. Firms plotting their own product sales are not recording the product's life but their ability to manage it. Bad management can lead to an early downturn in sales which is not necessarily the mature phase of the life cycle, and vice versa. What is more, products can be in the mature phase of their life cycle in one market but at the introductory phase in another. You only have to see the queues and check the prices for McDonald's hamburgers in Russia to realise that the product has a long way to go in that market. Entrepreneurial management is most effective in the early phases of the life cycle.

Not only can the length of the life cycle vary from country to country and product to product, but the length of each phase can also vary. The take-off phase comes when slow initial sales accelerate towards a mass market. This introductory phase averages six years after launch in both the USA and Europe. White goods – refrigerators, washing machines, freezers and so on – have generally taken longer. Brown goods – TVs, CD players, VCRs and so on – have generally taken less time. But the average 'time-to-take-off' also varies from country to country. Tellis *et al.* (2003) studied 137 new product launches across 10 consumer durable categories in 16 European countries and found that, despite the Common Market, there were considerable differences, summarised in Table 10.1.

Scandinavian countries tended to have the shortest 'time-to-take-off' – for example 3.3 years in Denmark. This was well ahead of the largest EU economies of France, Germany, Italy, Spain and the UK. The average time in Scandinavian countries was 4 years compared to 7.4 years in Mediterranean countries. They concluded that cultural factors partly explain the differences. In particular, the probability of take-off increases in countries that are placed high in an index of achievement and industriousness and low in uncertainty avoidance. Economic factors were found not to be strong or robust explanatory variables. They also found that the probability of a new product's take-off in one country increased with prior take-offs in other countries. The authors therefore recommend that managers adopt a 'waterfall' strategy for product introduction in Europe, putting them first into the countries that are likely to have the shortest 'time-to-take-off'.

Table 10.1 New products: Average time-to-take-off in Europe

Upper quartile: 8 to 10 years	Greece Britain
Upper-middle quartile: 6 to 8 years	France Spain Italy Germany
Average: 6 years	
Lower-middle quartile: 4 to 6 years	Finland Sweden
Lower quartile: up to 4 years	Norway Denmark

Life cycle stage

Competitive position	Start-up	Growth	Maturity	Decline
Dominant	Grow fast	Grow fast Attain cost leadership	Defend position Attain cost leadership Review	Defend position Renew Grow with industry
Strong	Differentiate Grow fast	Grow fast Catch up Differentiate	Reduce costs Differentiate Grow with industry	Find and hold niche Grow with industry Harvest profit
Satisfactory	Differentiate Focus Grow fast	Differentiate Focus Grow with industry	Harvest profit Find niche Grow with industry	Consolidate Cut costs
Weak	Focus Grow with industry	Harvest, catch up Find and hold niche Turn around	Harvest profit Turn around Find niche Consolidate	Divest
Very weak	Find niche Grow with industry	Turn around Consolidate	Withdraw Divest	Withdraw

Figure 10.2 The life cycle and competitive position

The consulting firm Arthur D. Little linked the life cycle to competitive position within a product/market sector to produce the resulting implications for strategy based upon Porter's generic strategies. Figure 10.2 summarises their analysis. In many ways it is an over-simplified version of Figure 10.1, but it does, once more, act as a checklist that allows you to focus on the imperatives for the business. At the two extremes it emphasises that if you dominate a market at start-up, it pays to grow fast, whilst if you are in a very weak position with a product at the end of its life cycle you might as well cut your losses and get out of the market as quickly as possible.

Product portfolios

As already mentioned, if a company has more than one product or service, then it might be following different strategies for each of the different product/market offerings it has and one important reason for this is that each of these offerings might be at a different stage of its life cycle in the particular market. So, for example, McDonald's may have a different marketing mix for its products in Russia, where it is at the introductory or take-off phase of its life cycle, compared to the USA, where it a mature product – although the length of the life cycle in Russia is likely to be a lot shorter than it was in the USA.

This added complexity of having a portfolio of product/market offerings can be handled using a technique adapted from the 'Boston Matrix', which derives its name from the Boston Consulting Group that developed it. The original matrix was adapted by McKinsey so as to have more realistic multi-dimensional axes. Figure 10.3 shows the adapted matrix. Market attractiveness – the strengths and resources that relate to the market – is measured on the vertical axis. The strength of product or service offering in the market – sales, relative market share and so on – is measured on the horizontal axis. When a product or service offering is first developed it will be launched into an attractive market (otherwise why do it?), but the firm is unlikely to have a great deal of strength. This is called a Problem Child and is equivalent to the introduction phase of the life cycle. Sometimes the market proves to be unattractive – then the life cycle is very short. This is called a Dog. More often, if the market is attractive, sales will grow and the product or service offering will become more established and will strengthen in the market. This is called a Star. Eventually, however, the market will mature and the product or service will become a Cash Cow. These are market leaders with a lot of stability but little additional growth because they are at the end of their life cycle.

There are many problems with the framework at an operational level, centring around measurement of the elements on the two axes. For example, defining the market a firm is in so that you can measure market share or market growth. You can use just one factor on each axis or, indeed, a number of them weighted appropriately using some sort of simple scale. Nevertheless the problem of measurement remains. The Boston matrix is therefore probably best used as a loose conceptual framework that helps clarify complexity. Treated with caution, as we shall see, it can be extremely valuable. In a complex world, anything that simplifies complexity and therefore helps our understanding must be of value.

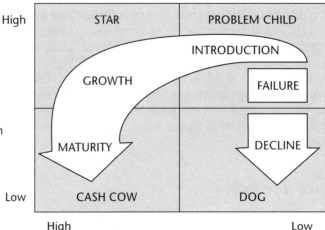

Market attractiveness
Measures:
● Size
● Growth
● Profitability
● Level of price
● Degree of competition
● Customer loyalty
● Reliability

Market strength
Measures:
● Market share
● Reputation and image
● Base of loyal customers
● Technical expertise
● Production or delivery expertise

Figure 10.3 The Boston matrix

Case with question

Heineken is Europe's largest brewer and is second only to the US brewer Anheuser-Busch world-wide. The brand is recognised around the world. However, its dominant market position, particularly in Europe where 40 per cent of the world's beers are consumed, is maintained by actually having a portfolio of brands that allow it to adjust its marketing mix to suit the tastes and needs of local markets. It also allows it to create the necessary distribution network and achieve high levels of economies of scale in production. Heineken typically has three core brands in each European country:

● A local brand aimed at the largest market segment, offered at a competitive price. In France it has '33', in Spain it has Aguila Pilsner and in Italy it has Dreher.
● A brand aimed at the upper end of the market such as Amstel or the locally produced Aguila Master in Spain.
● The premium Heineken brand itself where every effort is made to maintain quality and brand integrity. In the UK the product itself has been developed (called product expansion) into Heineken Export Strength, a stronger version more like the usual Heineken found throughout the rest of Europe.

Question
Why does Heineken opt for a mix of internationally known brands alongside local beers?

Portfolio strategies

One of the things the Boston matrix does is to allow us to make some broad generalisations about marketing strategy for product/service offerings in the different quadrants. These are shown in Figure 10.4. If you can place the product/market offering within its life cycle on the matrix, these would be the elements of marketing strategy you would, a priori, expect to see. But remember that, whilst this framework reflects product life cycles, it does not reflect Porter's generic marketing strategies, which need to be superimposed on them. However, as a product nears the end of its life cycle, and becomes a cash cow, it is more likely to be on its way to becoming a commodity and therefore having to sell on price.

The Boston matrix also allows us to present complex information more understandably, particularly when linked to forecasting future market positions and strategies involved in getting there. For example, Figure 10.5 represents a hypothetical three-product portfolio for a company. The size of each circle is proportionate to the turnover each achieves. The lighter circles represent the present product positions, the darker circles represent the positions projected in five years time. The portfolio looks balanced and the diagram can be used to explain the strategies that are in place to move the products to where they are planned to be. Again, one essential added complexity is the generic marketing strategies. If products A and B are commodities, selling mainly on price, with low margin under intense pressure, it has implications not only for strategy but also for the cash flow available to invest in product C. This is particularly applicable if this is a niche market product needing heavy investment.

	Market strength	
High	STAR	PROBLEM CHILD
Market attractiveness	*Objective:* Invest for growth ● Penetrate market ● Expand geographically ● Sell and promote aggressively ● Differentiate ● Promote brand, if possible ● Accept moderate short-term profits ● Extend product range	*Objective:* Develop opportunities ● Be critical of prospects ● Invest selectively in products or services ● Specialise in strengths ● Shore up weaknesses
	Objective: Maintain market position and manage for earnings ● Maintain market position with successful products or services ● Prune less successful products in range ● Differentiate ● Promote brand, if possible ● Stabilise prices, except where temporary aggressive pricing is required in the face of competition	*Objective:* Either kill off or maintain and monitor carefully ● Minimise expenditure ● Improve productivity ● Maximise cash flow ● Live with declining sales until the best time to kill off product
Low	CASH COW	DOG
	High	Low

Figure 10.4 The Boston matrix – strategy implications

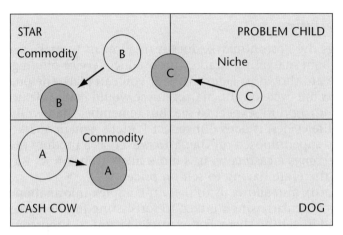

Figure 10.5 Boston matrix for hypothetical company

Case with questions

In 1969 Cadbury merged with Schweppes to form the international confectioner and fizzy drinks giant **Cadbury Schweppes**. Both companies have a long history. Cadbury has come a long way from its days as a chocolate manufacturing family firm with Quaker values and ideals. The original shop was opened in 1824 selling chocolate as a virtuous alternative to alcohol. However, the company went on to become a large-scale manufacturer of chocolate based at the now legendary Bournville factory, built in 1879, and its picturesque village with red-brick terraces, cottages, duck ponds and wide open parks. Over the next 100 years it developed the products that have become so familiar: *Dairy Milk* in 1905, *Milk Tray* in 1915, *Flake* in 1920, *Creme Egg* in 1923 and *Roses* in 1938. Jean Jacob Schweppe, a German, invented a system for making carbonated water in 1783 and opened a factory in London in 1790. Ownership changed in 1834 and the company started making flavoured soda drinks like lemonade. It produced Ginger Ale and the famous Tonic Water in 1870, popular in India because the quinine helped prevent malaria.

Most of Cadbury Schweppes' core products are at the mature stage of their life cycle and sales are therefore stagnant, so it must search for ever more inventive ways of achieving the ambitious growth targets it sets itself. However, these core areas are also hugely cash generative, giving the company between £300 and £400 million a year. The company is constantly looking for new markets for its products, but since most of these products already sell around the world, it has now developed a two-pronged growth strategy, with both approaches reliant upon the company's strong cash flow.

Firstly, because about 70% of its products are bought on impulse, it is looking for new channels of distribution so as to encourage sales, or 'indulgence opportunities' as they are called. Chocolate bars and drinks are now sold anywhere from petrol stations to off licences. Vending machines selling them can be found anywhere from factory floors to tube stations. The company wants more products to be sold in restaurants and pubs.

The company's portfolio of products are sold around the world and many are international brands, such as *Dr Pepper* and *7 UP*. In the late 1990s the company decided to focus on strong

➡

regional beverages – in particular in the Americas and Australia. In 1999 it sold off its beverage businesses in about 160 countries to focus on these regions. In 2006 it concluded the sale of its European beverages business.

North America is the largest market for its drinks. But distribution here is complex and problematic. Coca-Cola (40% of the market), Pepsi (30%) and Cadbury (20%) all use franchises to manufacture, bottle and distribute their products within geographic areas. However, Cadbury had no dedicated distribution system of its own and channelled 20% of its product through those of Coca-Cola, 30% through those of Pepsi and 50% through independent bottlers. The relationships eventually broke down to such an extent that Cadbury sued Pepsi, alleging that the company tried to block the distribution of its product to a large US restaurant chain. As a result the company decided to distribute all of its product through the independent bottlers. At the same time it took shareholdings in five of them and merged them to form the Dr Pepper/Seven UP Bottling Group, in which it has a 40% stake. In this way it now has more control over its distribution in the USA and is able to present more consumers with 'indulgence opportunities'. In Australia the company bought the Pepsi Lion Nation joint venture to secure its distribution channels.

The second strand to the company's strategy is buying into other related high growth segments, where the company can capitalise on its existing distribution chains. The company has followed an acquisitions strategy for many years. In 1986 it bought *Typhoo Tea*, *Kenco Coffee*, and *Canada Dry* and *Sunkist* soft drinks. In 1989 it bought *Crush* soft drink and *Bassett* and *Trebor* in the UK. The best selling US brands, *Dr Pepper* and *7 UP*, were purchased in 1995. The company has also diversified out of fizzy drinks, which in 1998 accounted for 85% of the important US market, with the acquisition of brands like *Snapple*, *Hawaiian Punch* and *Nantucket Juices*. By 2002 fizzy drinks accounted for only 50% of sales. The next target for acquisitions was the fast growing chewing gum market. In 2000 it bought *Hollywood*, the French gum maker, and *Dandy*, the Danish gum maker. In 2002 it purchased the US company Adams from Pfizer. Adams' brands include *Halls*, *Trident*, *Dentyne*, *Bubbas*, *Clorets*, *Chiclets* and *Certs*. But there have been other acquisitions such as Green & Black's in 2005. These acquisitions make Cadbury the market leader in non-chocolate confectionery including gum and 'functional' products such as sore throat remedies, and will give it a foothold in markets such as Japan and Latin America.

Cadbury Schweppes' growth exceeds market trends, despite its ageing portfolio of products. In 2005 sales increased 7% to £6.5 billion and profits from operations rose 8% to £1033 million. This continuing growth comes from three sources: organic growth, mainly though finding new channels of distribution; accquisition of new brands; efficiency saving (profit only) as ageing products are produced at a lower cost.

Questions
1 List, in broad terms, the product/market offerings mentioned in the case.
2 With its ageing portfolio of products, what are the main strands of Cadbury Schweppes' strategy for continued growth? Do you think this strategy is sound?
3 What do you consider to be the main challenges facing the company?
4 Is the company just good at sales and marketing or is there any evidence to suggest that it is 'entrepreneurial'? What is the difference?
5 Is there a limit to this growth? If so, when might it be reached? What external factors or events might affect this?

Managing the product life cycle

Product innovation is not just about entirely new product/market offerings. Every product has a life cycle and that cycle can be managed in a way that expands and extends it and grows the market. Early adopters are the customers characterised as buying products in the growth phase of the life cycle. This is the point when the company can start *expanding* the product offering and start meeting the needs of selected market segments in order to counter the threat of competition moving in. Expanding the offering means developing product variations. So, for example, a car manufacturer might start offering sports or estate variants or a soft drink

Barbie
'I'm a blonde bimbo girl, in a fantasy world . . . Life in plastic, it's fantastic.' (Aqua)

Barbie was born in 1959 but she has never aged because she is a doll. To date over 1 billion Barbies have been sold by the US company that own her – **Mattel Corporation**. Ruth Handler, who founded the company along with her husband, Elliot, modelled the doll on an 11½ inch plastic German toy called Lilli sold to adult men. She named the adapted doll after her daughter, Barbara. It is estimated that the average girl aged between 3 and 11 in the US owns ten Barbies, in Britain or Italy she owns seven and in France or Germany she owns five. With annual sales of over $1.6 billion, it is little wonder that the Barbie brand is valued at some $2 billion – making it the most valuable toy brand in the world. But how has this plastic doll endured for so long in an industry notorious for its susceptibility to fickleness and fashion? Surely it must have come to the end of its life cycle? The answer lies in innovative marketing and product extension.

When originally introduced into the market Barbie was competing with dolls that were based on babies and designed to be cradled and cared for. By way of contrast, Barbie, with her adult looks – exaggerated female figure normally with blonde hair and pouting lips – was seen as adult and independent – a child of 'liberated' times, one that could become anything or anyone the child wanted. But Mattel describe Barbie as a 'lifestyle, not just a toy . . . a fashion statement, a way of life'. Barbie was not only innovative, it was intended to be more than just a doll.

Every year Mattel devises some 150 different Barbie dolls and 120 new outfits. She has always been trendy and continues to reinvent herself. She was a 'mod' in the 1960s and a hippie in the 1970s. Her hair style has changed from ponytail, bubble-cut, page boy, swirl to side-part flip. She has various roles in life – from holidaying in Malibu to being an astronaut, soldier, air force pilot, surgeon, vet, doctor, dentist, engineer, fire fighter, diplomat, fashion model, Olympic athlete, skier, scuba diver, ball player, TV news reporter, aerobics instructor, rock star, rap musician and presidential candidate. Each role has numerous accessories to go with it – from cars to horse and carriage, from jewellery box to lunch box – and including a partner called Ken. You can even buy a 'Make-me-pretty talking styling head' play set.

Dressing and undressing, grooming and making-up is what Barbie is made for. And Mattel has worked hard to generate brand extension – more add-ons to the basic Barbie doll. The 2002/03 Rapunzel Barbie came with a handsome prince not to mention a computer animated video and 14 product tie-ins. A previous video based on Barbie in the Nutcracker grossed

→

manufacturer might start to offer new flavours of a successful brand. The original product might also be modified in terms of quality, function or style so as to address any weaknesses or omissions in it. In many cases service levels will be improved.

At the same time the company might want to try to find new distribution channels so that more customers gain exposure to the product. Sometimes they move from a selective distribution network to a more intensive network. Associated with this is a more aggressive promotion and pricing strategy that encourages further market penetration ahead of the rapidly emerging competition. Building the brand is important and this will be a vital part of the advertising message.

$150 million in sales, including associated products. By 2006 the company had produced the sixth Barbie movie, *The 12 Dancing Princesses*, each accompanied by special dolls. By wearing a motion-sensor bracelet and shoe clip, the latest *Let's Dance Barbie!* allows the doll to follow the child's dance steps. In addition, Mattel license production of hundreds of different Barbie products: including make-up, pyjamas, bed clothes, furniture and wall papers.

Mattel also continue to segment the market – trying to find new markets to sell the doll and its accessories to. The product extensions attempt this. But selling beyond the basic market, for example to older girls, is problematic. The main problem is that 'age compression' – girls getting older sooner – means that it is increasingly hard to hang on to the basic market, let alone try to extend it. By 2002 sales were down 3% from a peak of $1.8 billion in 1997. One variation launched in 2002 called *My Scene* attempts to sell three Barbie variants, with an older, more 'hip' look, together with perfume, cosmetics and music to this older group. This doll has a moveable face feature that allows girls to create expressions on the doll's face like frowns, pouts, smirks and smiles.

Over the years Barbie has become a cult. There are Barbie conventions, fan clubs, magazines, websites and exhibitions. She is seen by many as the ideal vision of an American woman. In 1976 the USA included Barbie in the bicentennial time capsule. There are sociology courses in the USA based upon her, speculating on this image and what it implies. Mattel has cultivated these images. They have also worked hard to defend Barbie's image (or reputation). In 1997 they prosecuted (unsuccessfully) the pop group *Aqua* who produced the satirical song 'Barbie Girl', some of whose lyrics are reproduced at the head of this case. Nevertheless, Barbie seems now to have become something of a gay icon. Whether gay or not, collectors have been known to pay up to $10,000 for a vintage model. The question is whether young girls will continue to want the Barbie fantasy world.

The problem remains that Barbie is getting old and must be nearing the end of her product life cycle. Sales peaked at $1.8 million in 1997. Since then they have fallen continuously every year. Compared to 2004 sales fell 7% worldwide and a massive 21% in the USA in 2005. So the question is, how long can innovations sustain Barbie? And how much longer can life stay fantastic?

Questions
1 Why has Barbie been so successful?
2 Barbie is hardly a high-tech product, but has it been innovative?
3 What are the lessons for product innovation?

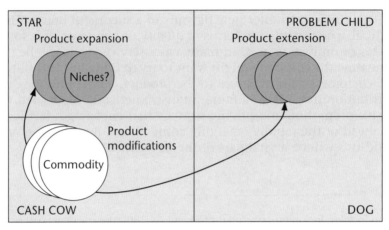

Figure 10.6 Product life cycle management

Further growth may even be possible in the mature phase of the life cycle. In many cases a mature market presents opportunities to start segmenting the market and tailoring the product range that was expanded in the previous phase through product *modification*, so as to better meet the different needs of the different market segments that purchase them. This might lead to further expansion of the range and further product modification in terms of quality, function or style. In this way, using the terminology of the Boston matrix, the cash cow product can be 'reinvented' to become a series of smaller star products, all of which are highly profitable. Another technique is called product *extension*. In this way a successful brand can be extended to similar but different products that might be purchased by the same customers. In this way a number of chocolate bars, such as Mars, successfully extended their brand into ice cream. The key to success here is having a strong brand – one that actually means something to customers – with values that can be extended onto the other products. Thus Timberland, a company well known for producing durable outdoor footwear, extended its product range to include durable outdoor clothing. Many so-called new products are in fact line extensions. This strategy is generally a less expensive and lower risk alternative for firms seeking to increase sales. The cash cow product can therefore also be 'reinvented' to become a series of smaller problem children. However, these will face all the challenges of a problem child and may face stiff competition from existing companies in the market. Risk is, however, mitigated compared to a completely new product launch because of customer loyalty to the brand.

Product modification, extension and expansion opportunities can be represented in the Boston matrix. Again this is a useful visual aid to understanding strategy options. An example of this is shown in Figure 10.6.

Financial implications of the product portfolio

The concept of product portfolios and the need to manage each product/market offering differently has a number of implications for corporate entrepreneurship. The

STAR		PROBLEM CHILD	
Revenue	+ + +	Revenue	+
Expenditure	– – –	Expenditure	– – –
Cash flow	neutral	Cash flow	negative
Revenue	+ + +	Revenue	+
Expenditure	–	Expenditure	–
Cash flow	positive	Cash flow	neutral
CASH COW			DOG

Figure 10.7 Cash flow implications of the Boston matrix

first relates to the cash flow likely to be generated by product/market offerings in each of the different quadrants of the Boston matrix (Guiltinan and Paul, 1982). This is shown in Figure 10.7.

The problem child consumes cash for development and promotional costs at a rate of knots, without generating much cash by way of revenues. The star might start to generate revenues but will still be facing high costs, particularly in marketing to establish its market position against new entry competitors. It is therefore likely to be cash neutral. Only as a cash cow are revenues likely to outstrip costs and cash flow likely to be positive. There are two kinds of dogs. One is a cash dog that covers its costs and might be worth keeping, for example if it brings in customers for other products or services or it shares overheads. The other is the genuine dog which is losing money – both in cash flow and profit terms – and should be scrapped. It is from this model that phrases like 'shoot the dog', 'invest in stars' and 'milk the cow' came.

Ideally entrepreneurial companies need a balanced portfolio of product/service offerings so that the surplus cash from cash cows can be used to invest in the problem children. These funds can be used almost as venture capital to invest, selectively, in new products and services. This ideal firm is self-financing. The problem arises with an unbalanced portfolio. If the entrepreneurial firm has too many problem children and stars in its portfolio (too many good, new ideas) then it will require cash flow injections which will only be forthcoming if it can either borrow the capital – and that largely depends on the strength of the balance sheet – or raise more equity finance. The challenge is to develop and then effectively manage a balanced portfolio using the different structures available.

Remember, however, that cash flow is not the same as profit. Whilst the analysis above refers to cash flow, the following technique uses profitability. The ABC Sales/Contribution analysis measures success in terms of the profitability of a product in relationship to its sales within the overall product portfolio. High sales and high contribution are the ideal combination. It helps identify those products that are of longer-term value to the company – really successful products. An example is shown in Figure 10.8. Sales are measured on the vertical axis and contribution on the horizontal axis. The 45° diagonal line from bottom left to top right is the optimum,

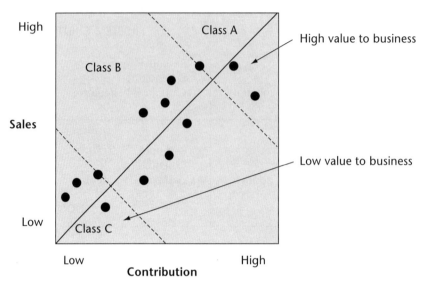

Figure 10.8 ABC analysis contribution chart

but of course most products will fall either side. Class 'A' products are the ideal. They have high sales and make a large contribution to the firm. Class 'B' are less attractive and class 'C' least attractive.

This analysis highlights attractive products – where contribution and sales are high – but it can also be used to identify attractive customers or markets. If sales are low but contribution is high, it shows where a sales push, even if margins are eroded, would yield the greatest reward. Similarly it identifies products, customers or markets where sales are high but contribution is low. Cash flow may be good, but contribution and hence profitability are not helped. Cash flow and profitability measure different things – like a rev meter and speedometer on a car. Ideally, but rarely, they go hand in hand. How the portfolio is managed when they are out of phase is a question of judgement. You need profit for long-term return and growth, but you need sufficient cash flow for survival. If cash flow is insufficient you need to be able to borrow to tide you over the short-term problem.

Implications for the entrepreneur

The product life cycle has some important implications for the entrepreneur. Entrepreneurial skills are most valued in the problem child phase – the start-up. Once the product is in its mature phase it needs to be managed as a cash cow – milked for all the cash flow it can generate. That means high levels of efficiency are needed, probably achieved through a high degree of control and direction. If the problem child is best managed by an entrepreneur, the cash cow is probably best managed by an accountant. And, if we are to characterise the management discipline needed to manage the star, it would probably be marketing. In other words, as the product works its way through its life cycle the approach to management needs to change from entrepreneurial to a more marketing orientation to one of greater emphasis on control and efficiency.

In a one-product company this presents a challenging but manageable problem. In a multi-product firm the problem is more complex. Do you separate out problem children into different, discrete organisations? Do you set them up as individual organisations? Perhaps you should group them together to make the most of entrepreneurial expertise? And what happens as they progress through their life cycle? Do you transfer them to different organisations, delineated not by their product specification but by the stage they are at in their life cycle and the managerial style therefore required? And at what point do you make the transfer? All of these issues are dealt with in Chapter 18 with the topic of 'corporate entrepreneurship'.

What is clear is that, with a portfolio of different products or services, management is more complex and entrepreneurs may well find it very difficult to span the different range of skills and temperaments required. In other words they are certain to need an effective team to help them undertake this task – a management team with complementary skills to their own, and one to which they have to provide overall leadership (Chapter 8). They may also have to look to more complex organisational structures. These are reasons why many entrepreneurs prefer to sell a successful business before it grows too large and too complex – they do not have the skills to manage this complexity and do not want to develop them, perhaps preferring instead to start up another business. How they can exit their business is dealt with in Chapter 12.

Summary

Products and services face a predictable life cycle that has implications for marketing strategy at different phases. Most firms, like **Heineken** and **Cadbury Schweppes**, have a range of products and services at different stages of their life cycle. These can be represented in a Boston matrix – a loose conceptual framework that helps clarify the complexity of the portfolio. The two axes of the matrix represent market attractiveness and market strength. Products at different points in the matrix have different strategic imperatives and different marketing strategies.

You can manage the product life cycle through product modification, expansion and extension. By using these strategies, the **Barbie** doll has been around for over 40 years but is now at the end of its life cycle.

The Boston matrix has cash flow implications; problem children use cash, stars are cash neutral, generating but also using large amounts, and cash cows generate cash. Only when the portfolio is balanced will cash flow be stable. However, cash flow is not the same as profitability. The ABC analysis allows you to analyse product in terms of sales and contribution – those with high levels of both are very attractive (class A products). But equally it can be used to adjust other elements of the marketing mix, such as price, so as to maximise sales.

Problem children are best managed by entrepreneurs – or entrepreneurial firms – and cash cows by accountants – or administrative firms. Where a business has a balanced portfolio of products, the challenge is to find a form of organisation that allows them all to flourish. There are many different approaches to this.

Essays and discussion topics

1 Some products – basic necessities such as food and water – do not have a life cycle. Discuss.
2 How useful are the labels of 'innovators', 'early adopters', late adopters' and 'laggards' to customers at different stages of the life cycle?
3 In practical terms it is impossible to find out where a product is at in its life cycle. Discuss.
4 What is the relationship between marketing mix and the product life cycle?
5 How useful is the Boston matrix?
6 How would you go about creating a scale for each axis of the Boston matrix that reflects a range of factors? Give a practical example.
7 In what circumstances might you not want to 'shoot a dog'?
8 Give some examples of product expansions and extensions.
9 Can a problem child be profitable? How and why?
10 Is a star always likely to be a 'class A' product? Explain.
11 In what circumstances might you have a cash cow that is unprofitable? What would you do with it?
12 If management is an art, there is no point in studying it. Discuss.
13 What is the relationship between life cycles and leadership style?
14 How can a company become a dominant market force by the mature stage of its product life cycle, other than through mergers and acquisitions?

Exercises and assignments

1 Select a well known product that is now in the mature phase of its life cycle and chart how the marketing strategy has changed over that life cycle.
2 For a selected company, analyse their product portfolio using the Boston matrix. What are your conclusions?
3 Select a mature industry. Research the three major companies in this industry and find out how they gained their market dominance.

References

Guiltinan, J.P. and Paul, G.W. (1982) *Marketing Management: Strategies and Programmes*, New York: McGraw Hill.
Rogers, E.M. (1962) *Diffusion of Innovation*, New York: Free Press.
Tellis, G.J., Stremersch, S. and Yin, E. (2003), 'The International Take-off of New Products: The Role of Economics, Culture, and Country Innovativeness', *Marketing Science*, 22(2).

11

Making Growth Happen

Contents

- Growth options
- Market penetration
- Product/service development
- Market development
- Diversification
- Risk
- Mergers and acquisitions
- Strategy development
- Planning and control
- Summary
- Appendix: Forecasts and budgets – a comprehensive example

LEARNING OUTCOMES

By the end of this chapter you should be able to:

- Describe the growth options facing a firm, the reasons for pursuing them and the advantages and risks associated with each;

- Explain the consequences of selecting particular strategies and the factors that are important to make each strategy work;

- Describe the different types of diversification and explain the degree of risk faced in pursuing each one;

- Describe the different types of mergers and acquisitions, the reasons for following this strategy and the risks involved;

- Pick out the strategies that are most likely to lead to successful and sustained growth;

- Prepare a detailed budget for a medium-sized business.

Growth options

The move from the success to take-off stage in the growth models outlined in Chapter 8 is dangerous. It can take, well, as long as it takes. Without a clear understanding of what has made the business successful, there is no sound foundation for the move forward. Some entrepreneurs understand what they are doing, what works and what does not, as they do it, sometimes almost instinctively. Others are more reflective and need time to analyse the situation. Getting the right people and putting the right systems in place can take time. Some situations are more complex than others. Once entrepreneurs understand the basis for their successful survival, so far, they can start to plan their take-off, the growth that will eventually make them leaders of the very small number of high-growth businesses upon which whole economies are so dependent for their growth. This is the point where the small business caterpillar, having become a butterfly, will try to fly.

In general terms, to achieve growth a company should build on its strengths and core competencies, shore up its weaknesses and develop a marketing strategy for each product/market offering that reflects:

- the appropriate generic marketing strategy;
- the stage a product/market offering is at in its life cycle;
- all placed in the context of its portfolio of product/market offerings.

In that context, research tells us that product/service innovation leading into a niche marketing strategy, involving selling a differentiated product or service not selling primarily on price, that allows the company to dominate its market niche, is the strategy that is most likely to lead to success. The unique elements of the differentiation strategy are likely to be based on distinctive capabilities that, applied to a relevant market, become a competitive advantage. This will become the firm's core market, the one in which it has a distinct advantage by adding the greatest value for its customers. A focus on core business was emphasised in the 1980s (Abell, 1980) and popularised by Peters and Waterman (1982) as 'sticking to the knitting'. However, core competencies may be relevant to other markets and, even if they are not directly relevant, can often be leveraged by entering other markets in which, although the firm may not have the same distinctive competitive advantage, it can

		Product or service	
		Existing	New
Market	Existing	1 Market penetration Other options: consolidation or withdrawal	2 Product development
	New	3 Market development	4 Diversification – related – unrelated

Figure 11.1 The product/market matrix

use economies of scale or its channels of distribution to gain market share. Although firms following other strategies do, of course, succeed, the importance of this research-based finding cannot be over-emphasised. Business, like life, is about playing the odds. You ignore these odds at your peril.

Whilst the objective of entrepreneurial strategy is growth, its essence is that it is opportunity driven. Stevenson and Gumperter (1985) describe the entrepreneur as 'constantly attuned to the environmental changes that may suggest a favourable chance.' However, in order to start planning the take-off phase, there is one further tool that we need. It helps analyse how growth can be achieved in a systematic fashion. It is called the Product/Market Matrix, was originally devised by Igor Ansoff (1968), and is shown in Figure 11.1. This simple conceptual framework uses existing/new products on one axis and existing/new markets on the other. It then goes on to explore the options within the four quadrants of the matrix and how the options might be achieved. Like all useful business frameworks it is attractively simple and intuitively logical. To achieve growth a company has four options:

1 Market penetration – staying with existing products/services and existing markets and customers;
2 Product development;
3 Market development;
4 Diversification.

To use this framework we need to explore each option systematically in greater detail, find out what it entails and weigh up the risks and returns associated with each one. Empirical research tells us a lot about which are likely to work and which are not.

Market penetration (quadrant 1)

Market penetration involves selling more of the same product/service to the same market – just selling more to existing customers. If the firm has strong relationships with its existing customers this may be possible. It can also involve finding new customers from the same market segment. In the last chapter we saw that Cadbury Schweppes achieve this by constantly improving their channels of distribution and giving customers more 'indulgence opportunities' for their impulse buy products. Using the Boston matrix, this is how you move from 'problem child' to 'star'. The best way of finding new customers is to understand existing customers – assuming that they are happy with the product/service offering – and try to find more of the same. This involves understanding why they buy and being able to describe the customers' common characteristics – effectively describing the market segment(s) buying the product or service. In a growth market there may be ample opportunity to achieve further growth in this way. Figures 10.1 and 10.4 detailed some ways this can be achieved. Chapter 10 underlined the importance of gaining market dominance as quickly as possible in these circumstances (hence the strategy currently adopted by Carphone Warehouse – see page 137). However, the ease with which a business can pursue this policy will depend on the nature of the market and the position of competitors. In a static or declining market it is much more difficult to pursue this option, unless competitors are complacent or are leaving the market. To attract customers from an established competitor, they must be convinced that the alternative product or service offers greater perceived value, and that might involve price reductions – not always an attractive strategy.

Market penetration is an essential part of gaining market dominance. However, once the market is mature there is unlikely to be significant sales growth. Consolidation should generate profit growth, but this strategy inherently starts to go against the entrepreneurial grain and is not one that an entrepreneurial firm is designed or inclined to follow. Inevitably the entrepreneurial firm will start to look at the other quadrants of the matrix to achieve its aims.

There are also a couple of other options in this quadrant. Firstly, the entrepreneur might decide to withdraw, perhaps selling the business to capitalise on the growth so far. Richard Branson did this in 1982 when he sold his original business, Virgin Records, to concentrate on the airline business. It might also be just the right time to get a very good deal, for example because of consolidation in the industry. Alternatively the entrepreneur might not see themselves as being able to change and develop in the way that is needed to lead a growing firm. They might prefer to go into another start-up.

Secondly, there is the option to consolidate, that is keeping products/services and markets the same, but changing the way the firm operates. Often this is not a sensible option in a growing market as it leaves competitors free to take market share, which might then affect the firm's competitive cost base. In a mature market it is common for companies to place increasing emphasis on quality, marketing activity or reducing their cost base so as to create barriers to entry for new competitors. In a declining market, consolidation may involve cost reduction, volume reduction and ultimately selling off part or all of the business.

Staying in this quadrant can be attractive for a number of reasons particularly for the 'lifestyle' owner-manager. Essentially it involves staying very much the same so there are none of the risks associated with developing new products or markets. It allows the firm to focus on what it is doing and to do it better, rather than always having to run in order to stand still. Customers may appreciate better service and may even be willing to pay for it. Staying the same also allows the firm to develop its reputation. It might allow the firm to do what it is doing more efficiently and therefore cut costs. It is said that it costs five times less to sell to existing customers than it does to new ones. However, there are also dangers with this approach. As we have seen, the strategy is operationally difficult in a static or declining market where there is the additional question of how much life is left in the product/service. Similarly, it may be risky in a growing market when it may be important to grab market share as quickly as possible. There is also the danger of complacency in just doing the same thing and perhaps ignoring changes in the market.

Product/service development (quadrant 2)

We have already seen that product/service innovation is one of the key characteristics of successful growth companies. In Ansoff's framework the first option is to do this for existing markets. It may be that completely new products are introduced into the portfolio because market opportunities are spotted. These might be completely new, innovative products to either replace or sell alongside the existing product range. It might involve product development or extension of existing products where the

Case insight

Established in 1900, the family bakery business of **Wilson & Son** has had to adapt to some radical market changes in order to stay in business. A hundred years ago families would buy two or three crusty loaves each day from one of a dozen bakers in close proximity to their shop. **Charles Wilson** introduced doorstep delivery to combat that competition. The First World War saw bread rationing, which at least made demand very predictable, and government subsidies to cushion prices. But it was the arrival of low-priced, factory-produced bread that did most to threaten the business.

Today, families often shop only once a week and prefer soft bread. Competition comes from supermarkets who offer loaves for as little as 20 pence. And the economics of breadmaking have changed. Today's loaf costs 94p, equivalent to 10 minutes work in the bakery. In the 1950s the loaf cost 6 pence, equivalent to 15 minutes work, and in the 1920s the loaf cost only 2 pence, but this was equivalent to 30 minutes work.

Today **Andrew Wilson** runs the bakery helped by his sister, brother and wife. They offer a wide variety of bread including sunflower, seeded and wholemeal, all baked in the traditional way, free of chemical additives. However, they rely far more for their profits on cakes, fresh sandwiches, pizzas and other take-away food.

changes are small and evolutionary, or it might entail developing 'me-too', copied products where another firm has successfully pioneered the product in the market. This may be necessary when a product is in its growth phase – through product extension. It may also be necessary at the mature phase when the product is nearing the end of its life cycle – product replacement. It may also be necessary as other firms produce a 'better' product and the firm is forced to react. This can be a particular problem for small firms pioneering a product in a market with low barriers to entry, especially if the product develops into a commodity.

One justification for following this growth path is that the company's existing customers are loyal and demand is growing. However, probably the most important reason for following this path is that the firm has a close relationship with customers – a customer focus – and a good reputation for quality or delivery that can be built upon. If there is a relationship of trust, customers are more likely to try the new product, provided of course they perceive a need for it and that means the company must also be good at communicating with customers in whatever way is most appropriate. In developing new products the customer focused firm will have an advantage because, if it understands how its customers' needs are changing, it ought to be able to develop new products that meet them. The key to this strategy, therefore, is building good customer relationships, often associated with effective branding.

One advantage of this approach is that is often far more cost-effective to increase the volume of business with existing customers than it is to go out looking for new ones. What is more, good relationships often result in customers bringing in new customers through word of mouth or referral. However, developing new products, even for existing customers, can be expensive and risky. Development must be grounded firmly in the needs of the existing market. And even then, if done too rapidly, it can mean resources are spread too thinly across an unbalanced portfolio.

Virgin and Saga are good examples of brands that have been applied to a wide range of diverse products, mainly successfully, linking customers and their lifestyle aspirations. Virgin, however, rarely undertake 'production', relying instead on partners with developed expertise. On the other hand Mercedes Benz is a brand that has a strong association with quality and the company has capitalised on this by producing an ever wider range of vehicles, always being able to charge a premium price for its product. This has allowed it to move into new and different segments of the vehicle market.

Case insight

Virgin is one of the best-known brands in Britain with 96 per cent recognition and is well-known worldwide. It is strongly associated with its founder, **Sir Richard Branson** – 95 per cent can name him as the founder. The company has pioneered the concept of a branded venture capitalist, mirroring a Japanese management structure called 'keiretsu', where different businesses act as a family under one brand. The Virgin Group is made up of more than 20 separate umbrella companies, operating some 200 companies worldwide with a global turnover of over £3 billion in 1999.

Virgin now uses its brand as a capital asset in joint ventures. Virgin contributes the brand and Richard Branson's PR profile, whilst the partner provides the capital input – in some ways like a franchise operation.

The brand has been largely built through the personal PR efforts of its founder. However, between January 1997 and November 1999 the Group spent £137 million on advertising. According to Richard Branson,

> Brands must be built around reputation, quality and price . . . People should not be asking 'is this one product too far?' but rather, 'what are the qualities of my company's name? How can I develop them?'

According to Will Whitehorn, director of corporate affairs at Virgin Management:

> At Virgin, we know what the brand name means, and when we put our brand name on something, we're making a promise. It's a promise we've always kept and always will. It's harder work keeping promises than making them, but there is no secret formula. Virgin sticks to its principles and keeps its promises.

→

Case with questions

Sidney De Haan died in 2002. Two years later the business he had founded, **Saga Group**, was sold by his son Roger who had taken over as chairman and was controlling shareholder with the remaining shares held in a family trust. None of the family was involved in the business. At that point Saga Group employed 3000 people, had a turnover of £340 million and made profits of £51 million. Over the five years between 1998 and 2003 the company enjoyed a compound annual growth rate of 20 per cent.

Saga is best known for providing holidays for the over-50s, claiming 60 per cent of those who holiday with the company will have done so before. But in fact 80 per cent of its profits now come from insurance – home, car, travel, medical, pet, boat and caravan. And its range of

→

businesses extends to publishing, financial services, share trading, internet services, telecoms and radio – all targeted at the same over-50s market. With nearly 44 per cent of Britain's adults now over 50 years old, this is the fastest growing and wealthiest consumer sector in the UK and one in which Saga has a strong brand image. This older generation has the time, money and inclination to take holidays. It now accounts for about 22 per cent of domestic holidays and 26 per cent of holidays abroad. And the market is similarly skewed in other countries. This older generation accounts for 40 per cent of tourism in Germany and 17 per cent in Ireland.

Born in the East End of London in 1919, one of 11 children of a shoe factory foreman, Sidney De Haan left school at 14 to work as a chef at the Waldorf Hotel before joining the Royal Medical Corp at the start of the Second World War. After the war he bought the 12-bedroom Rhodesia Hotel in Folkestone, Kent which he ran with his wife Margaret. It was in the winter of 1949 that he came up with the original Saga business concept. He was sitting on a park bench worrying about how to fill his empty hotel when he realised that he was surrounded by pensioners who had plenty of time on their hands. So he came up with the idea of selling low-priced, out-of-season, all-inclusive full-board holidays at his hotel, complete with travel by coach to his door. He was forced to market it himself because travel agents refused to believe that pensioners had spare money to spend on holidays. The idea was a resounding success and he soon bought a second hotel. It did not take long for Saga to start marketing similar holidays in other hotels along the south coast and then overseas. It was Saga that first spotted the potential of Romania, Yugoslavia and the Algarve as holiday destinations. The profile of customer has changed and got younger. Saga now offer short and long breaks, long-haul travel, cruises, safaris and even activity holidays.

However, it was the attention to its target market and the resulting attention to service detail that gained Saga the loyal customer base that it enjoys. Taxis can still pick you up from your door and representatives are always at hand to meet customers when they change their form of transport or arrive at their destinations. In the early days they even checked out the number of steps into the hotel and specified it in their reservation system. Their hotel contract would even specify a minimum and maximum temperature in the hotel rooms.

Saga was floated on the stock market in 1978 and bought back by the family in 1990, although only a minority of the shares were ever traded. It was in this period that the Saga Group started to sell new products to its target market, building on the trusted reputation that the brand enjoyed. Just about everything has worked from credit cards to magazines. For example, with a readership of 2.5 million, *Saga Magazine* is now Britain's second largest subscription magazine after *Reader's Digest*. Even its radio reaches 600 000 listeners a week.

Sidney De Haan retired in 1984. His son, Peter, stood down as a director in 1999 to pursue other business interests, leaving Roger in control. But in 2003 Roger reached the age of 55 and decided he wanted to spend more time with his family and travel. He had spent much of the previous few years steadily delegating his responsibilities to a new management team, led by Andrew Goodsell, Saga's deputy chief executive, and getting less involved with the day-to-day running, preferring instead to spend more time on his charitable interests. In 2004 he sold Saga to Charterhouse, the private-equity firm, in a £1.35 billion management buy-out led by Andrew Goodsell.

Questions
1 Why has Saga been so successful?
2 Is there any limit to the range of products or services Saga can sell?

Market development (quadrant 3)

Market development is the natural extension of market penetration. Instead of selling more of the same to your existing customers, you find new customers for those products or services. Any growing firm will have to find new customers and the key to doing so is to understand the customers you have – who they are and why they buy – and then try to find more customers with similar profiles. Many firms start out by selling locally and gradually expand their geographic base by selling regionally and then nationally.

However, it is one thing to find new customers in a market that you are familiar with, but it is quite another to enter completely new markets, even when you are selling existing products or services that you are familiar with. Nevertheless, if a firm wants to grow it will have to do so. These new markets might be new market segments or new geographical areas. In seeking new overseas markets the lowest risk option is to seek out segments similar to the ones the firm already sells to. The issues associated with 'going international' are covered in Chapter 16. Trying to sell the same product or service to new market segments usually involves reconfiguring the marketing mix in some way. Simply lowering the price will always attract new customers who would not otherwise buy. However, as we have seen, this is not always a sensible way to maximise profits. More likely to be successful is finding new or different channels of distribution, or altering the promotional strategy in some way. However, there is always the danger that by seeking to attract

---

Case insight

Noto Catering was set up in 1991 to offer Japanese lunches to a largely Japanese customer base. However, with the mushrooming popularity of sushi, its fortunes have been transformed largely because it was a pioneer in the UK market.

The company was founded by Japanese, including Mr Shimo, a well known sushi chef. The company takes its name from the Noto region on Japan's West Coast, which is noted for its sushi. The company originally set up a number of sushi bars in London including one in Harrods but it went on to develop new wholesale markets and now also supplies a number of supermarkets. The Prêt à Manger chain now also buys sushi from Noto and this accounts for one-third of Noto's turnover.

●

Case insight

Tim Slade and **Julian Leaver** started out selling their own printed T-shirts in the ski resort of Meribel in France. They originally set up the clothes manufacturer and retailer **Fat Face** in 1993 in order to finance their lives as 'ski bums'. It has now become a cult brand for sports enthusiasts and the company has over 50 shops and a turnover of over £25 million. Julian Leaver explains how they got there:

> When you buy a Fat Face product, you are not just buying the fleece, you are buying the experience – the chat in the shop about the snow in Val d'Isère – or surfing in Cowes. Staff are selected because they are passionate about the lifestyle.

➡

In 2000 the company raised £5 million expansion capital from Friends Ivory & Sime Private Equity to finance their expansion but they were careful to manage the brand as they did so. Julian Leaver explains:

> We could easily wholesale the hell out of it and be in every ski and surf shop and department store inside a year. Within two years, we would have trashed the brand.

Slow, planned expansion came through increasing the number of shops in Britain and Europe and eventually the rest of the world, making certain that the right sort of staff, with the right sort of personality, were recruited. Initially Fat Face entered new markets based upon intuition and on a experimental basis, later they undertook more professional market research. Their typical customer is a well-off professional in their mid-30s who enjoys skiing or water sports. And they try to keep close to their customers by getting feedback by email and face-to-face and regular panel meetings. Julian Leaver believes the Fat Face brand, like Virgin, is transferable to drinks, surfboards or even four-wheel drive vehicles and therefore expansion is ultimately about brand management.

Sunday Times 27 February 2000

different market segments you will lose market focus and lose your grip on existing customers – particularly if you are following a niche marketing strategy.

Of course, market development and product development might go hand-in-hand, since the move into a new market segment may involve the development of variants to the existing product offering by altering the marketing mix or even minor changes to the product range. However, we are talking about incremental and minor changes rather than brand-new products. Any major change of product or service accompanied by a move into a completely new market is called diversification.

Diversification (quadrant 4)

The final growth option is to sell new products into new markets – called diversification. The rationale for this is normally one of 'balancing' the risk in a firm's business portfolio by going into new products and new markets. However, since this strategy involves unfamiliar products and unfamiliar markets, it is actually a high-risk strategy, with too many unknowns in the equation. Nevertheless, it is worth distinguishing between two types of diversification, each with different degrees of risk.

1 **Related diversification** where development is beyond the present product and market, but within the confines of the 'industry' or 'sector' that the firm operates in. There are three variants of this:

   ● *Backward vertical integration*, where the firm becomes its own supplier of some basic raw materials or services or provides transport or financing. When Anita Roddick first set up Body Shop is was purely as a retail business. After a few years the firm started manufacturing its own products, but more recently it has started to move away from this and concentrate on its core retailing activity.

- *Forward vertical integration*, where the firm becomes its own distributor or retailer, or perhaps services its own products in some way. In this way Timberland, the boot and shoe maker, has opened a number of prominently sited retail outlets selling Timberland branded products.
- *Horizontal integration*, where there is development into activities which are either directly complimentary or competitive with the firm's current activities, for example, where a video rental shop starts to rent out video games. In this way Ford now earn more from financial services related to car purchase than from the manufacture of the vehicles themselves.

All strategies entailing new product or service technologies and new customers or markets are relatively risky but not as risky as the second form of diversification.

2 **Unrelated diversification** where the firm develops beyond its present industry or sector into products and markets that, on the face of it, bear little relationship to the one they are in. This tends to work better for service rather than manufacturing business where there is strong brand association. Some of Virgin's ventures into new product areas might be described as diversification.

'Synergy' is often used as a justification for both related and unrelated diversification, particularly when it involves acquisition or merger. Synergy is concerned with assessing how much extra benefit can be obtained from providing linkages between activities or processes which have been previously unconnected, or where the connection has been of a different type, so that the combined effect is greater than the sum of the parts. It is often described as 'one plus one equals three'. Synergy in related diversification is mainly based upon core product or market characteristics. The claimed synergy in unrelated diversification is normally based on financing – the positive cash flows in one business being used for the funding requirements of another. Another often claimed synergy is based on the managerial skills of the head office.

Whilst Johnson and Scholes (1993) claim that attempts to demonstrate the effects of diversification on performance are inconclusive, they also admit that successful

---

(Case insight)

Wing Yip came to Britain from Hong Kong in 1958 with only £10 in his pocket and got a job as a waiter in a Chinese restaurant. Within a few years he had his own small chain of Chinese restaurants but he had trouble getting the food supplies he needed. Nobody stocked everything and he had to spend valuable time travelling to a number of different suppliers. This led him to realise that other Chinese restaurants were facing the same problem. And so, in 1970, he decided to set up a cash-and-carry business for Chinese restaurants with his brother Sammy, based in Birmingham.

By 1998 **W. Wing Yip & Brothers** supplied more than 2000 outlets and made profits of £2.9 million on sales of £65 million. Based in Nechells, Birmingham, their main site now houses the head office, a Chinese medical practice, a travel agency, a law firm serving the Chinese community and a 250-seater restaurant called Wing Wah. The company acts as agents for Hong Kong suppliers and sells to other cash-and-carries such as Booker. They also make their own range of Chinese sauces which they sell to most of the big supermarket chains.

●

Case with question

David Sanger set up his first business in 1991 at the age of 25. Since then he has made enough mistakes to last many people a life-time but has learnt from them and managed, not only to survive, but prosper.

Using savings of £50 000 and a £50 000 bank loan he opened what he hoped would be the first of a chain of sandwich bars in west London in 1991. Called **Rollover**, it was initially a dismal flop, partly because he had no experience of the industry. David worked in the sandwich bar 16 hours a day, but after three months it was still losing money, so he decided to change tack. If the customers would not come to him, he would go to the customers. He hired a manager to run the shop and went out himself looking for wholesale customers for his sandwiches such as hotels and hospitals. Within two months sales had tripled. By 1995 David had eight sandwich bars, using the same business model.

It was whilst on a holiday in Copenhagen that the next stage in Rollover's development came. David kept coming across street traders selling hot dogs. He tried one and thought they were delicious – far better quality than those available in England – and he was also taken by the special machine that inserted the sausage inside the bread roll, completely enclosing it and making it easy to hold and eat whilst on the move. Indeed he was so intrigued that he bought one and took it home where he had it modified so that customers could see what was going on inside, installed it in one of his shops and started importing the high-quality German sausages to go in it. Sales went so well that he installed a machine in each of his sandwich bars. They became known as 'Rollovers with ketchup' by accident because they were wrapped in a napkin with the Rollover name on it. Then his local pub asked if it could borrow a machine to make hot dogs for customers watching an international rugby match. It was so successful that within two weeks the pub chain's area manager hired six machines for pubs in the area and Rollover's wholesale hot-dog business was born.

This new business went so well that in 1995 David sold the sandwich bars for £350 000 to concentrate on the hot-dog business. But then he made his second big mistake. Rather than concentrating on wholesale, he borrowed £750 000 and opened 18 hot-dog retail outlets in the space of 18 months. Without proper controls in place the rapid roll-out was a disaster. There were thefts and staff irregularities, which all resulted in mounting losses. David spent the next 18 months closing the worst outlets and franchising the rest. He lost some £1 million. Fortunately the wholesale operation survived – indeed prospered. Rollover™ now sells some 25 million branded hot-dogs a year – 'the best hot dog in the world' – and can be seen at most Premiership football clubs, theme parks and concert halls in England, giving the company a turnover of £7 million in 2004.

Question
What are the lessons you learn from David's experience?

diversification is difficult to achieve in practice. However, many researchers have found that more focused firms perform better than diversified ones (Wernerfelt and Montgomery, 1986). This is reflected in their low share price. Diversified conglomerate manufacturing companies are valued at some 20 per cent less on average, than the sum of their parts (*Economist*, 7 July 2001). What is more, it has been demonstrated that smaller firms that diversify by building on their core business – related diversification – do better than those who diversify in an unrelated way

(Ansoff, 1968). This was established for a broader range of firms in the 1970s (Rumelt, 1974) and used as part of Porter's (1987) argument for firms that build on their core business doing better than those who diversify in an unrelated way. The conclusion must be that diversification generally is risky and therefore requires careful justification. Nevertheless one of the companies that has adopted a strategy of diversification most successfully is Lonrho, and its strategy has been one of unrelated diversification. Its interests range from hotels in Mexico to freight forwarders in Canada, from motor distribution in Africa to oil and gas production in the USA.

Risk

Ansoff's analysis gives us a valuable insight into the risks associated with growth. Bowman and Faulkner (1997) added an extra dimension to Ansoff's analysis by considering core competency and method of implementation. They pointed out that any move into new markets or new products/services becomes riskier, the further the firm strays from its core competencies. Combining these approaches we can see that:

- The lowest risk strategy of all is market penetration, but in growth markets, where gaining market share as quickly as possible is important, security might be short-lived.
- Market development is most successful for firms whose core competencies lie in the efficiency of their existing production methods, for example in the capital goods industries, and are seeking economies of scale, or for firms adept at sales, marketing and developing close customer relationships – the very qualities of an entrepreneurial firm.
- Product and process development are most successful for those firms whose competencies lie in building good customer relationships, often associated with effective branding. However, of equal importance could be the ability to innovate. Innovation is a core characteristic of an entrepreneur.
- The highest risk strategy of all is diversification, with unrelated diversification being extremely high risk. This can be likened to the introduction of new-to-the-world products. Related diversification is safest for companies who are adept at both innovation and developing close customer relations. Thus it was just as well that the Mini – truly a mould-breaking innovation in car design – was produced by a car manufacturer.

At the extreme, entrepreneurial innovation – introducing new products or services to a new market – is radical and risky. But whilst this may be risky, the returns can be equally large. As Cannon (1985) points out: 'The ability of the entrepreneurial mould-maker to break free from bureaucratic rigidities, fan the flames of innovation and create new situations has been the basis of the growth of many of today's great corporations. Ford, Durant, Kellogg, Singer, Krupp, Eastman, Courtauld, Daimler, Biro, Siemens and Daussault all built giant enterprises which are virtually synonymous with their industries'. Building on the Ansoff matrix, this is the equivalent of diversification. These developments are represented in Figure 11.2.

With the exception of the 'no innovation' option where risks are minimal in the short term but high in the long term, risk gets progressively higher as the firm moves

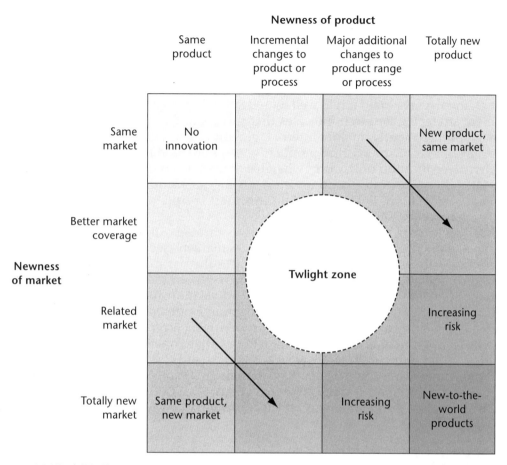

Source: A.J. Ward (1968) *Measuring, Directing and Controlling New Product Development*, London: In Com Tec, London.

Figure 11.2 Growth and risk

to the bottom right hand corner of Figure 11.2 in terms of its strategy. This is indicated by the increasingly darker shading. However, risk is not a linear relationship. In the 'twilight zone' – marked by the dotted circle at the centre of the matrix – risk can be lowered. This is the zone where continuous, small incremental changes in product and market can greatly expand the product/service offering and its market place and this is where risk can be lowest. It is the zone where the entrepreneurial firm may have the greatest competitive advantage and therefore face lower risk than other firms in related diversification or develop new products for slightly different markets.

The riskiest strategy of all is to introduce a new product or service into a completely unknown market – 'new to the world', with a completely new invention. For example when PCs were introduced in the late 1970s, IBM refused to enter the market, partly because market research could not identify a demand for the product. Potential domestic customers could not understand the product, or more particularly, what it would do for them – how it would add value. Existing applications were commercial.

Why would families want a machine to 'do sums'? Why was it better than a typewriter? Of course the PC took off when the domestic applications were identified such as games and the internet, and now most homes in the Western world have (at least) one. But investment in the early-stage development of PCs was a leap of faith.

Of course this is not to say that a company should not take risks, but rather that growth involves risks and it is as well to understand the degrees of risk associated with different strategies. Research indicates that successful entrepreneurial firms follow a strategy of incremental, mainly internal, growth (Burns, 1994). They move carefully into new markets with existing products or sell new products to existing customers. Related diversification only works when based on core competencies. The strategy of unrelated diversification – or innovation – is high-risk and only to be adopted after careful consideration. Entrepreneurial firms must consider carefully whether this is really appropriate to their needs.

One way of mitigating the marketing risk is through joint ventures or strategic alliances, particularly in marketing to overseas markets (see Chapter 16). Both can be set up relatively quickly. In these circumstances the partner may possess much needed competencies or expertise, such as market knowledge. It even works with product development. This was the basis of the relationship Mercedes had with Swatch when the Smart cars were developed. Swatch offered fashion design. Mercedes offered engineering and production quality. With such relationships the risks can then be compartmentalised and failure will not therefore endanger either core business. What is more, the strategy avoids high set-up costs. And it relies on what an entrepreneurial firm should be good at – building relationships. On the down side, it does mean that the profits must be shared and control is lost to some extent – which is why firms also consider mergers and acquisitions as a way of diversifying or indeed

---

Case insight

In 1934 Reg Bott, a German chemist, fled the Nazis and set up **Standard Photographic** in Leamington Spa. It is now a fourth generation family firm run by **Gordon Bott**. Standard stopped making photographic film in 1967 and instead now buys film from the big producers and repackages it as 'own-brand' film for firms such as Boots, Dixons, Tesco and Truprint. But Standard has diversified beyond this, always in small incremental moves. It also converts photographic paper by cutting it to the size used by mini-laboratories, publishing houses and X-ray laboratories. It has also diversified into film processing, handling mail-order processing for Fujifilm, Agfa, Boots and Jessops slide products, making it one of the largest operations of its kind in the UK.

But perhaps the most unlikely diversification was into general warehousing and logistics. Because the film elements of the business require good logistics – a 36-hour nationwide delivery of replacement film stock is guaranteed – the firm diversified into delivering similarly high value products such as floppy disks and printing and publishing products. Based on this success, the firm diversified into more general warehousing and logistics handling goods for cosmetics customers and high street stores across the UK and Ireland. It offers same- or next-day delivery and is competing against firms like Exel, Business Express, Securicor Omega and many others. It also offers distribution services to e-businesses for orders taken over the internet. All of this is a long way from making photographic film.

buying a foothold in a new market. As we saw with Dell, because of their nature, entrepreneurial firms can have some advantage in developing these relationships.

One further important point; for a small firm with limited resources, pursuing all four strategies within any one time frame is likely to be extremely risky. Assuming market penetration will always continue, it is best advised to follow only one other strategy at a time, perhaps alternating the strategy over time. Making the right choice is an important decision, but one that has to be made by a conscious choice rather than by drift or force of circumstance.

One very practical application of these techniques is to help evaluate sales projections or targets. The projections can be broken down into the constituent elements of the product/market matrix (Figure 11.1) or the growth and risk matrix (Figure 11.2). Probabilities of achieving these projections or targets can then be attributed to each constituent element of the matrix. Any projection based largely on market penetration, *a priori* unless the market is saturated, has a high probability of being achieved. Any projection heavily dependent on diversification is, *a priori*, not only highly risky, but also has a low probability of being achieved. Sales people can also use these matrices to have sales targets set with commission rates in the various elements of the matrix reflecting the different levels of risk, for example, basic commission for sales of existing products to existing customers, higher rates for further market penetration and higher rates still for sales of new products. As the probability of achieving sales targets decreases, sales commissions can be increased.

Mergers and acquisitions

Mergers and acquisitions are frequently used by entrepreneurs as a tool for achieving rapid growth and also as a short-cut to diversification. The compelling reason for this tactic is the speed at which it allows the entrepreneur to enter a new product/market area. Another reason might be that the firm lacks a resource, such as R&D or a customer base, to develop a strategy unaided. Often, particularly when a market is static, it is seen as the easiest way to enter a new market, for example overseas. Sometimes the reason for buying out a competitor is to buy their order book, perhaps related to shutting down their capacity, cutting costs and gaining economies of scale.

However, this tactic can be time-consuming, expensive and risky. By distracting the entrepreneur, it can also damage short term business performance. In fact there is no evidence that commercial acquisitions or take-overs (other than in a distress sale) add value to the firm. Many studies show that mergers and acquisitions suffer a higher failure rate than marriages, and business history is littered with stories of failed mergers of titanic proportions such as AT&T's purchase of NCR in 1991, the second largest acquisition in the history of the computer industry. The evidence seems to be that the great conglomerate-merger wave of the 1960s did not generally lead to improvements in performance for those firms involved, and was reversed by the large-scale selling of unrelated businesses in the 1980s. Porter (1987), in his study of 33 major corporations between 1950 and 1986, concludes that 75 per cent of unrelated acquisitions were subsequently sold off rather than retained, and the net result was dissipation of shareholder value. And yet companies of all sizes persist in following this strategy. In 1999 the global value of mergers and acquisitions rose by over a third to more than $3.4 trillion.

All too often acquisitions have too much of the entrepreneur's ego tied up in the deal and that can lead to a loss of business logic. It is important that there is a clear logic to the acquisition, related to the product/market matrix; for example:

- As a defensive acquisition to maintain market position, perhaps to gain economies of scale, or as a result of aggressive competitive reaction from rivals;
- As part of a strategy to develop new products when the firm does not have the capability to do so, for example because of R&D or technology;
- As part of a strategy to develop new markets, for example overseas;
- As part of a strategy of diversification, although this must be seen as the highest of high-risk growth strategies.

In searching for companies to acquire, it is first necessary to decide on the industry. Related diversification will normally be into the same industry. If it is unrelated diversification, then the industry should be one where the acquiring company has the core competencies required for success in the sector and, where there is a deficiency, they should be addressed by being present in the target company. The attractiveness of the industry will depend to some extent on the strategic direction of the company, informed by an analysis of the industry (perhaps using Porter's Five Forces and a SLEPT analysis). The acquisitions that are most likely to succeed are those where an attractive market presents itself to a company with a good 'mesh' between the acquiring company's core competencies and the sector's required key competencies.

Of course, some acquisitions are simply opportunistic. For example, when a rival firm or a firm in a related area goes into receivership, the temptation to buy it out cheaply and quickly from the receiver might be irresistible and might also make sound commercial sense. Most acquisitions take three to nine months to complete but a sale from a receiver can be completed in as little as three weeks. Whether buying a trading company or one in receivership, it is always important to take professional advice although fees can amount to 5–7 per cent of the value of the business. Accountants undertake what is called 'due diligence' work, which ensures that the assets on the balance sheet are as stated, there are no undisclosed liabilities and that profit projections are put together in a logical and consistent way, based upon reasonable and explicit assumptions. Accountants can also undertake searches for acquisition prospects and most of the major firms keep informal 'books' of companies that they believe might be available for purchase.

The major reason mergers and acquisitions fail is because of failure of implementation. Claimed synergies may not be achieved, perhaps rationalisation is insufficiently ruthless, possibly because clear management lines and responsibilities are not being laid down. However, one of the major reasons for this failing boils down to the clash of organisational cultures that does not get resolved. This can arise because of many factors, but it results in the merged organisations being unable to work together effectively. That was the major reason for the seemingly logical, but ultimately disastrous, take-over of NCR by AT&T in 1991, which nearly brought down both companies. Ten years later America Online (AOL), the world's largest internet service provider merged with Time Warner, the media conglomerate. Not only could the staff not work together – by 2003 all of AOL's top management had left – but the claimed synergies never materialised. For whatever reason, one common outcome of mergers or acquisitions is that many managers in the acquired company will leave within a short space of time. They may, of course, be 'pushed' rather than leave of their own volition, but nevertheless this means that the time scale for proactive management of change can be very short.

Company valuation in mergers and take-overs is crucial but problematic for smaller firms, especially if they operate in new areas of business such as e-commerce. A company with a high value placed on its current level of earnings can use this to its advantage in buying out a company with a low valuation, particularly if the deal is based upon shares rather than cash. This is dealt with in Chapter 12.

Strategy development

The last two chapters have talked very much as if strategy can be developed in a systematic, logical way. To a large extent strategy can be developed in this way. However, many entrepreneurs develop strategy instinctively – often they call it 'gut feel'. They do not know the jargon, do not use the frameworks we have developed – and justified with empirical evidence – but instinctively they arrive at the right decision. There is nothing wrong with this. These words and frameworks give meaning and logic to what they do. Many excellent musicians or athletes were not taught what they do. They picked up the skills instinctively. Explaining why they do what they do can give confidence to replicate their successes and even improve.

Strategic frameworks replicate what is good practice. They ought to be logical, common sense. They are not in the nature of a scientific discovery. They are, to quote a colleague, 'a glimpse of the blindingly obvious', something you knew all along but were never quite able to express it in that simple way. As John Kay (1998) explained:

> An organisational framework can never be right, or wrong, only helpful or unhelpful. A good organisational framework is minimalist – it is as simple as is consistent with illuminating the issues under discussion – and is memorable ... The organisational framework provides the link from judgement through experience to learning. A valid framework is one which focuses sharply on what the skilled manager, at least instinctively, already knows. He is constantly alive to strengths, weaknesses, opportunities, threats which confront him ... A successful framework formalises and extends their existing knowledge. For the less practised, an effective framework is one which organises and develops what would otherwise be disjointed experience.

Some entrepreneurs may claim to have achieved their success through luck. Never underestimate luck, we all need it, but remember that entrepreneurs have a strong internal locus of control which means that they may believe in luck, but they do not believe in fate. They believe they can, and will, shape their own destiny and that may mean working to create more opportunities than most people. By creating more strategic options and opportunities, they improve their chances of successfully pursuing at least one. Make no mistake, entrepreneurs to a large extent create their own luck.

And yet there is always the nagging doubt that perhaps entrepreneurs are more opportunistic and adaptive, rather than calculating and planning in the way strategy

'You just need to look at where Virgin is now to see that business is a fluid, changing substance. As far as I'm concerned, the company will never stand still. It has always been a mutating, indefinable thing and the past few years have demonstrated that.'

Richard Branson

is laid out in books. In fact this view is as old as strategy itself and was called by Lindbolm (1959) 'the science of muddling through'. The implications of this for strategy were developed by Mintzberg (1978) who contrasted deliberate with emergent strategy. As he put it: 'The strategy-making process is characterised by reactive solution to existing problems ... The adaptive organisation makes its decisions in incremental, serial steps.' And here we do catch reflections of how the entrepreneur, in their spider's web of influence, approaches decision-making in a risky, uncertain and rapidly changing environment. But then there is nothing wrong with strategy that is incremental and adaptive, and that does not mean that strategy cannot be analysed, managed and controlled. The frameworks are just as useful. And successful entrepreneurs are constantly strategising – thinking about the future and analysing their options. Indeed, Sir George Mathewson, Executive Deputy Chairman of the very entrepreneurial Royal Bank of Scotland Group (which includes NatWest, Direct Line and even Coutts Bank) has gone so far as to propose that formalised strategic planning is inappropriate in today's changing environment. What is needed instead is more strategising and the development of strategic options – options that lead the firm in the general direction it wants to go – with decisions on which option to select depend upon market conditions and opportunities (Mathewson, 2000). The greater the number of strategic options open to the firm, the safer it is in an uncertain environment.

So, for some firms, strategy development may be systematic and deliberate but for many entrepreneurial firms it is likely to be emergent. It is likely to be incremental and adaptive. 'Strategic intent' is still needed to give the firm clear direction, only the path to achieve these goals is not always clear. In these circumstances the process of strategising or strategy development is vital. The development of multiple strategic options is the key to success, with decision-making based upon opportunistic circumstances at the time.

'If you set yourself goals that are really high and keep working to achieve them, then success should be possible. Just look back and say I gave it my best shot.'

David Darling
founder **Codemaster**
The Times 10 October 2002

What holds this all together is a strong vision of where the organisation is going. Thus entrepreneurs need to know the goal they are ultimately seeking and need to have the frameworks to make those incremental, adaptive decisions. There is nothing wrong with having a map with a planned route, but it makes sense to find a way around any road blocks you encounter rather than going headlong into them.

One interesting research study indicates that these stages might lead, not only to changes in strategy, but also to changes in the strategy development process itself, causing shifts from the emergent to the deliberate style, at least for a period (McCarthy and Leavy, 2000). The study suggests that the strategy development

Figure 11.3 The strategy formulation cycle

process in small firms is *both* deliberate and emergent in nature and the degree of deliberateness in the early phase of development is influenced most by the personality of the entrepreneur and the nature of the business context. Over time strategy formulation follows a phase pattern, moving from an early fluid phase to a more defined phase, usually triggered by a crisis or defining episode, so that the degree of deliberateness is also a function of history, with firms oscillating between emergent strategy development, when learning is taking place, and deliberate planning modes over time. Rather than entrepreneurs having only one style, they would seem to adopt both, depending on circumstances. In this way the well documented process of growth to crisis to consolidation parallels a process of emergent to deliberate to emergent strategy formulation, represented in Figure 11.3.

Planning and control

Rapid growth can be every bit as dangerous as start-up. It can lead to the danger of over-trading – the Death Valley curve getting longer and deeper. Proper planning and management of cash flow is therefore vital. If cash is needed to finance growth, bankers like to be forewarned so that facilities can be made available in advance. It also makes sense to negotiate from a position of strength rather than weakness. Planning and good management might also allow a firm to minimise its cash flow requirements. Just as the preparation of financial plans was important at start-up, it is important for a growing firm.

Plans and budgets are an invaluable tool to control and monitor performance of the business. By comparing actual financial results to budget on a timely basis, the entrepreneur can 'manage by exception', only intervening when performance deviates from plan. This can free up time to concentrate on strategy or dealing with real problems. The budget provides a framework against which the performance of the firm can be judged. For a larger firm, the detail involved in pulling together a complicated budget can be time-consuming, but by this stage it is certain that the firm will have its own accountant who can undertake the task. Nevertheless the appendix to this chapter contains a detailed example of how to go about drawing up a budget for a medium-sized firm – cash flow forecast, profit statement and balance sheet.

As the firm grows, budgets can be prepared at the department and division level, rather than just at the company level. This has the advantage of encouraging the entrepreneur to delegate responsibility for planning and decision-making to other managers, whilst at the same time providing them with sufficient information to satisfy themselves that everything is running as planned. The budgeting process can then be used as a tool for communicating and coordinating the activities of responsible managers. It can become a systematic tool for establishing standards of performance, providing motivation and assessing the results managers achieve. An essential element in this process of making managers accountable is that each knows exactly what they are held responsible for, and each does indeed control this aspect of the firm's operations. Responsibility cannot be assigned without authority. A fundamental necessity is to have a clear management structure. The principle is to make every manager responsible for the costs and revenues they control, even if they, in turn, delegate responsibility down the line.

Of course, if managers are going to be held responsible for the costs and revenues they control, they are going to want to be involved in the budgeting process. The advantage of this is that often they know more about certain aspects of the business than the owner. Also, if budgets are to motivate staff, they have to 'buy into' them and believe that they are realistic and achievable. Once they accept the standards of performance against which they are to be judged, they will normally try hard to achieve them. Imposing budgets from above normally causes resentment and leads to a lack of commitment.

The basics of sound financial control remain the same as outlined in Chapter 7. Financial drivers are just as useful for a medium-sized firm as for a start-up. Perhaps the difference is one of scale. But also, all medium-sized firms now operate computerised accounting and budgeting systems. The most popular is produced by Sage. These speed the processing of transactions and the production of financial information. They also help with the management of trade credit. Almost all business transactions are on credit terms and it has been estimated that trade debtors represent 28 per cent of total assets in small firms whilst trade creditors are equivalent to 11 per cent, and yet managing trade debtors seems to be the Achilles heel of most small firms – they are just bad at it (Chittenden *et al.*, 1998).

Before embarking on a growth path a company needs to have in place robust financial planning and control mechanisms. It needs to have a strategy and to plan how it will grow, not just in terms of the product/market matrix, but also by producing detailed budgets that reflect the consequences of the growth and indicate any financing needs. In other words, it probably needs to prepare another business plan.

Summary

To achieve growth, a company should build on its strengths and core competencies, shore up its weaknesses and develop a marketing strategy for each product/market offering that reflects:

- the appropriate generic marketing strategy;
- the stage the product/market offering is at in its life cycle;
- all placed in the context of its portfolio of product/market offerings.

It has four options:

1 Stay with existing products/services and existing markets and customers;
2 Product development;
3 Market development;
4 Diversification.

Any start-up must focus initially on market penetration – selling more to existing customers. If a company wants growth, staying with the existing products/services and existing customers usually means further market penetration, rather than just selling more to existing customers and the best way of finding new customers is to understand your existing ones and then try to find more of the same. This can be difficult in a static or declining market but also, if the market is growing, you run the risk of being left behind.

Product/service development involves developing new products or services and selling to your existing market, like **Wilson & Son** have done. This is often a successful strategy for firms that have a strong relationship with their customers – a customer focus – and a strong reputation. The firm can develop products that customers want and their loyalty means they will try them. Getting existing customers to buy more is also often very cost-effective. Often associated with this strategy is a strong brand identity. **Virgin** is probably the best-known brand in Britain today, but the company has evolved into a branded venture capitalist, using its brand as a capital asset in joint ventures. Similarly **Saga** has developed its brand and applied it to a range of different products and services, but always targeting the same market segment.

Market development is about finding new markets for existing products or services – like **Noto Catering** – thus benefiting from economies of scale or capitalising on the firm's product knowledge competency. In deciding on which markets to enter, consideration should be given to entry and exit barriers. The classic example of market development is into overseas markets, either opening overseas ventures like **Fat Face** are doing or by exporting. However, exporting is risky and most small firms do not try it.

Diversification is the riskiest of the four options – as **David Sanger** discovered with his firm **Rollover**. Related diversification is about staying within the confines of the industry through either backward vertical integration – becoming your own supplier; forward vertical integration – becoming a distributor or retailer; or horizontal integration – moving into related activities. Unrelated diversification is the riskiest strategy of all and involves developing beyond the firm's present industry, normally because of the claimed benefits of synergy. **W. Wing Yip & Brothers** and **Standard Photographic** may be seen as doing this, but in fact their growth into new markets and new products is more incremental.

The product/market matrix is a useful tool to help evaluate the risks associated with a growth strategy and the probabilities attached to the related sales estimates. For small firms with limited resources pursuing all four strategies within any one time frame is likely to be extremely risky. Assuming market penetration will continue, they should select only one other strategy within any time frame, otherwise they risk spreading themselves too thinly.

Mergers and acquisitions are frequently used as a means of achieving rapid expansion. However, the tactic can be time-consuming, expensive and risky. The frequent failure of mergers arises because of failure of implementation, with claimed synergies not being realised.

Strategy development in most growing small firms is likely to be incremental and adaptive – emergent rather than deliberate – with strategic intent giving direction. The process of strategising and the generation of strategic options are therefore important. However, small firms do adopt both types of strategy development, depending upon circumstances, with shifts from one mode to another precipitated by some form of crisis.

Effective planning and control is essential for the risky take-off stage of growth. Growth eats into cash and the financing needs of the firm during its growth need to be anticipated and planned. Comprehensive budgets need to be prepared – cash flow, income and balance sheet. These help in the management of the firm and can be a useful tool to encourage the entrepreneur to delegate control to the managers they have recruited. Increasingly from here the firm will start to look more professional with formal organisation and control systems. It is about to stop being a 'small firm' – by any definition.

Essays and discussion topics

1 Penetrating the market is just about selling more. Discuss.
2 Penetrating the market is a low-risk option and therefore always the most attractive option. Discuss.
3 In what circumstances might product development be a lower-risk strategy than market development, and vice versa?
4 How might a small firm go about exporting so as to minimise the risks that it faces?
5 Exporting is expensive and risky. It is therefore not an attractive growth option. Discuss.
6 How do you go about minimising your exposure to currency fluctuations?
7 What business is Virgin in?
8 Diversification is the 'Wally Box' of the product/market matrix. Discuss.
9 Under what circumstances might diversification be an attractive option?
10 Diversified companies underperform 'focused' companies. Discuss.
11 Why might a small firm be looking for another to acquire?
12 Under what circumstances might an acquisition or merger be attractive?
13 What is synergy and how might it be achieved?
14 Why do so many mergers or acquisitions fail? Give examples.
15 What advice would you give to a company taking over another?
16 In an uncertain world, planning is a waste of time and developing strategy a meaningless activity. Discuss.
17 How do entrepreneurs develop strategy? Explain and give examples.
18 Are entrepreneurs lucky?
19 Why is budgeting so important at the take-off stage?
20 Budgeting helps entrepreneurs to delegate effectively. Discuss.

Exercises and assignments

1 For your own department in your university or college, use the product/market matrix to list the growth options that it faces for the courses on offer.
2 Select a country and find out what help there is available in order to export to it.

3   Research the history of a merger or acquisition such as AT&T and NCR or Daimler Benz and Chrysler and analyse the reasons for its success or failure.
4   Interview an entrepreneur and find out how they develop strategy.
5   Work through the budget setting process for the PC Modem company in the Appendix to this chapter. Make certain you understand the calculations and processes.
6   Analyse the projected performance of PC Modem using the financial ratio checklist on page 262.

Appendix: Forecasts and budgets – a comprehensive example

Preparing forecasts or budgets can be complicated, particularly for a manufacturing company. This is a comprehensive example for just such a company. This company is already in business, producing two specialist computer modems (A and B). The year-end (31 December 2010) balance sheet for the company is shown as Table A1. We shall prepare the budget for 2011 only. The budgeting process would be easier for a start-up company, since there would be no balance sheet at the beginning of the period, and easier for a service business, since there would not be a manufacturing process to complicate the costing. This business is also registered for Value Added Tax (VAT) and accounting for that is an added complication.

Table A1   Balance sheet, 31 December 2010

	£	£	£
FIXED ASSETS			484 000
CURRENT ASSETS:			
Stock			
– Finished goods: modem A (400)	30 400		
modem B (360)	19 800		
	50 200		
– Raw materials base stock	10 000		60 200
Debtors		VAT	
– estimated payment January	66 000	11 550	
– estimated payment February	78 000	13 650	169 200
			229 400
CREDITORS DUE WITHIN ONE YEAR:			
Overdraft			(30 000)
Creditors		VAT	
– due for payment January	20 880	3654	
– due for payment February	20 880	3654	(49 068)
Corporation tax (due September)			(27 500)
			(106 568)
NEW CURRENT ASSETS (WORKING CAPITAL)			122 832
NET ASSETS (FIXED ASSETS *less* NET CURRENT ASSETS)			606 832
CREDITORS DUE AFTER MORE THAN ONE YEAR:			
Long-term loan			(100 000)
			506 832
CAPITAL AND RESERVES:			
– Share capital			10 000
– Profit-and-loss account			492 832
			506 832

The company has been fairly successful so far and the owner is looking for a return (profit before interest and tax) on his net assets of 15 per cent per annum. So far it has funded its fairly rapid expansion by a long-term loan of £100 000, which is not due for repayment until 2018, and an overdraft which, this year, reached its maximum permissible level of £30 000. Because of the highly cyclical nature of demand, the company has experienced difficulty with supplies of modems at certain times of the year. Since the modems are always required for immediate delivery, if an order cannot be met within a few days, it will be lost. The company would like to rectify this problem by increasing its stock of finished modems.

Sales budget

The sales manager sees the 2011 market as continuing to be extremely good for the company. He is aware that this is an expanding market but equally aware that costs are going up ahead of inflation. He feels that a 5 per cent increase in selling price can easily be accommodated and sales volume would still increase by an estimated 20 per cent. Looking at the pattern of last year's sales and noting the requirements of existing major customers, he arrives at his first estimate of sales, broken down by month, as shown in Table A2. Since he knows that his budget exceeds the productive capacity of existing plant, before proceeding further he passes it on to the managing director and the production manager for consideration.

Table A2 Preliminary sales budget

Units	Jan	Feb	Mar	Apr	May	June	July	Aug	Sep	Oct	Nov	Dec	Total
Modem A	400	400	440	280	100	100	80	80	200	360	360	440	3 240
Modem B	600	660	520	320	160	160	120	120	360	660	780	780	5 240

Production budget

The company would like to be able to meet the tentative sales budget and to build up finished modem stocks. However, demand is cyclical, whereas production needs to be kept fairly stable throughout the year, since skilled labour cannot be hired and fired at will. Also, even if new machinery were to be purchased in January, it could not be installed and working effectively until March. An added problem is works holidays: one week in December and January and two weeks in August. In those months production is always down, *pro rata*.

Based upon the production schedule, the production manager decides how many new machines to purchase. These machines will cost £120 000 (+ VAT @ 17½% = £21 000) and can be installed in January. Like all creditors, payment can be delayed by two months. These machines will increase production of modem A from the normal 240 to 320 per month and of modem B from 400 to 520 per month from March onwards.

The budgeted production schedule is shown in Table A3. Opening stocks of value A were 400 and of value B 360. The new production schedule will indeed result in higher year-end stocks of 640 and 830 respectively. The lower production in January, August and December reflects the works holidays. Monthly stock levels were computed to compare with the provisional sales budgets to ascertain whether demand will be met. Unfortunately this is not always so, and it is estimated that sales of 100 A modems and 200 B modems will be lost in March and February

Table A3   Production budget

Units	Jan	Feb[1]	Mar[1]	Apr	May	June	July	Aug[2]	Sep	Oct	Nov	Dec[3]	Total
Modem A													
Start stocks	400	180	20	0	40	260	480	720	800	920	880	840	
+ production	180	240	320	320	320	320	320	160	320	320	320	240	3380
− sales	400	400	340	280	100	100	80	80	200	360	360	440	3140
= End stock	180	20	0	40	260	480	720	800	920	880	840	640	
Modem B													
Start stocks	360	60	0	0	200	560	920	1320	1460	1620	1480	1220	
+ production	300	400	520	520	520	520	520	260	520	520	520	390	5510
− sales	600	460	520	320	160	160	120	120	360	660	780	780	5040
= End stock	60	0	0	200	560	920	1320	1460	1620	1480	1220	830	

[1] sales = lower of budgeted sales (Table A2) or stock in hand.
[2] $\frac{1}{2}$ production.
[3] $\frac{3}{4}$ production.

respectively. However, our investment appraisal tells us it is not worth installing extra productive capacity to satisfy demand in these months. Thus budgeted annual production, sales and stock figures are agreed:

	Units	Modem A	Modem B
	Stock 31 Dec 2010	400	360
plus	Production	3380	5510
minus	Sales	−3140	−5040
	Stock 31 Dec 2011	640	830

The costs of production, after taking into account inflation in material prices and wage increases, are shown below. These are derived from the company's detailed costing record.

Cost per unit (£)	Modem A	Modem B
Direct labour (fixed cost)	24	15
Direct materials (variable cost)	22	18
Variable factory overheads	15	12
Fixed factory overheads (depreciation)	15	10
	76	55

Workers are on fixed weekly wages. The current wage bill is £10 290 per month. With wage increases due in March and the new operatives needed in that month, this will jump to £14 319 per month (a total of £163 770 for the year). This level of direct labour will be sufficient to meet the planned range of production. Direct material and variable overheads are paid under normal trade terms, on average delaying payments by two months. Fixed factory overheads is depreciation of plant and equipment. This totals £105 800 (£15 × 3380 + £10 × 5510). These unit costs give the following estimates of production costs, cost of sales and stock costs:

		Modem A		Modem B	
		Units	£	Units	£
	Stock 31 Dec 2010	400	30 400	360	19 800
plus	Production (costs)	3380	256 880	5510	303 050
minus	Sales (costs)	−3140	−238 640	−5040	−277 200
	Stock 31 Dec 2011	640	48 640	830	45 650

The company keeps a tight control over raw material stocks, and the current base stock of £10 000 will be maintained in value terms.

Purchasing budget

The next task for the company is to prepare the monthly purchasing budget. This is shown in Table A4. The unit variable costs of direct material and overheads and fixed direct labour costs are applied to the production schedule shown in Table A3 to arrive at estimated purchases each month.

Table A4 Budgeted purchases, overheads and wage payments

	Jan	Feb	Mar	Apr	May	June	July	Aug	Sept	Oct	Nov	Dec	
Modem A													
Production (units)	180	240	320	320	320	320	320	160	320	320	320	240	
Direct materials @ £22 £	3960	5280	7040	7040	7040	7040	7040	3520	7040	7040	7040	5280	
Variable overheads @ £15 £	2700	3600	4800	4800	4800	4800	4800	2400	4800	4800	4800	3600	
Labour @ £24 £	4320	5760	7680	7680	7680	7680	7680	3840	7680	7680	7680	5670	
Modem B													
Production (units)	300	400	520	520	520	520	520	260	520	520	520	390	
Direct materials @ £18 £	5400	7200	9360	9360	9360	9360	9360	4680	9360	9360	9360	7020	
Variable overheads @ £12 £	3600	4800	6240	6240	6240	6240	6240	3120	6240	6240	6240	4680	
Labour @ £15 £	4500	6000	7800	7800	7800	7800	7800	3900	7800	7800	7800	5850	
Totals													**Totals**
Direct materials & variable overheads £	15 660	20 880	27 440	27 440	27 440	27 440	27 440	13 720	27 440	27 440	27 440	20 580	290 360
Related VAT @ 17½% £	2241	3654	4802	4802	4802	4802	4802	2401	4802	4802	4802	3602	50 814
Quarterly VAT totals £		11 197			14 406			12 005			13 206		
Labour £	10 290	10 290	14 319	14 319	14 319	14 319	14 319	14 319	14 319	14 319	14 319	14 319	163 770

Notice that VAT at 17½ per cent has been added to purchases of materials and overheads, assuming all purchases are chargeable. A company acts as a collector of VAT for HM Revenue and Customs. Although it will have to pay VAT on purchases and charge VAT on most sales, it can reclaim the VAT paid and must repay the VAT it collects to the Customs and Excise on a quarterly basis. Therefore, while VAT does not affect a business's profitability (except in so far as it may deter customers), it can cause cash flow problems, as the business pays and collects VAT at different times from its payments to HM Revenue and Customs.

Revised sales budget

The original sales budget could not be met and therefore it will have to be revised, in line with Table A3. The revised sales budget is shown in Table A5. Modem A is priced at £90, and modem B at £75, excluding VAT. Notice that, once more, VAT chargeable is shown separately. This will only affect the cash flow budget.

To achieve this level of sales it is estimated that selling, distribution and general costs will have to rise to £24 000. Let us assume, for simplicity, that these costs incur VAT at 17½ per cent (£4200), they accrue evenly over the year, and that they are paid monthly.

Table A5 Final sales budget

		Jan	Feb	Mar	Apr	May	June	July	Aug	Sep	Oct	Nov	Dec	Total
Modem A units		400	400	340	280	100	100	80	80	200	360	360	440	3140
@ £90 each	£	36 000	36 000	30 600	25 200	9000	9000	7200	7200	18 000	32 400	32 400	39 600	282 600
Modem B units		600	460	520	320	160	160	120	120	360	660	780	780	5040
@ £75 each	£	45 000	34 500	39 000	24 000	12 000	12 000	9000	9000	27 000	49 500	58 500	58 500	378 000
Total	£	81 000	70 500	69 600	49 200	21 000	21 000	16 200	16 200	45 000	81 900	90 900	98 100	660 600
Related VAT @ 17½%	£	14 175	12 338	12 180	8610	3675	3675	2835	2835	7875	14 333	15 908	17 168	115 607
Quarterly VAT totals				38 693			15 960			13 545			47 409	

Budgeted income statement

The budgeted income statement is shown in Table A6. Sales are as shown in Table A5 and cost of sales was calculated from the costing records detailed previously. The budgeted profit before interest and tax payments is £120 760: a margin of 18 per cent on sales. Notice that this calculation excludes VAT.

Cash flow forecast

The cash flow forecast is shown in Table A7. This shows the cash flow surplus or deficit each month and the resulting effect on the cash balance or overdraft of the business. Sales receipts and related VAT are lagged by two months. In other words, sales in January (see Table A5) do not generate cash receipts until March. Obviously this means sales in November and December will not have been collected by the year-end. Similarly, purchases and related VAT are lagged by two months. January purchases (see Table A4) are not paid until March, and November and December

Table A6 Budgeted income statement, 2011

	Modem A	Modem B	Total
Sales	£282 600	£378 000	£660 600
Cost of sales	238 640	277 200	515 840
GROSS PROFIT	£43 960	£100 800	£144 760
Selling, distribution and general costs			24 000
PROFIT BEFORE INTEREST AND TAX			£120 760
Estimated corporation tax			18 000
Profit before interest but after tax			£102 760

purchases are not paid by the year end. Selling, distribution and general costs and related VAT are paid in the month incurred, as are direct labour costs. The capital expenditure and related VAT is paid in March, and the corporation tax bill shown in last year's balance-sheet is paid in September.

VAT payments to HM Revenue and Customs are quarterly, at the end of March, June, September and December. There are various schemes for VAT, including cash accounting which is based simply on VAT received *less* VAT paid. However, once turnover exceeds a certain limit, as in this case, the company must apply invoice accounting which is based upon the VAT you have

Table A7 Cash flow forecast 2011

£	Jan	Feb	Mar	Apr	May	June	July	Aug	Sept	Oct	Nov	Dec	Total
RECEIPTS													
Sales receipts	66 000	78 000	81 000	70 500	69 600	49 200	21 000	21 000	16 200	16 200	45 000	81 900	615 600
Related VAT	11 550	13 650	14 175	12 338	12 318	8 610	3 675	3 675	2 835	2 835	7 875	14 333	107 731
Total receipts A	77 550	91 650	95 175	82 838	81 780	57 810	24 675	24 675	19 035	19 035	52 875	96 233	723 331
PAYMENTS													
Direct materials and overheads	20 880	20 880	15 660	20 880	27 440	27 440	27 440	27 440	27 440	13 720	27 440	27 440	284 100
Related VAT	3 654	3 654	2 741	3 654	4 802	4 802	4 802	4 802	4 802	2 401	4 802	4 802	49 718
Selling, general etc.	2 000	2 000	2 000	2 000	2 000	2 000	2 000	2 000	2 000	2 000	2 000	2 000	24 000
Related VAT	350	350	350	350	350	350	350	350	350	350	350	350	4 200
Direct labour	10 290	10 290	14 319	14 319	14 319	14 319	14 319	14 319	14 319	14 319	14 319	14 319	163 770
Capital expenditure			120 000										120 000
Related VAT			21 000										21 000
VAT payments			5 446			504			490			3 315	339 593
Corporation tax										27 500			27 500
Total payments B	37 174	37 174	181 516	41 203	48 911	49 415	48 911	48 911	76 901	32 790	48 911	82 064	733 881
CASH FLOW A–B	40 376	54 476	−86 341	41 635	32 869	8 395	−24 236	−24 236	−57 866	−13 755	3 964	14 169	−10 550
Brought forward	−30 000	10 376	64 854	−21 489	20 146	53 015	61 410	37 174	12 938	−44 928	−58 683	−54 719	−30 000
CASH BALANCE	10 376	64 854	−21 489	20 146	53 015	61 410	37 174	12 938	−44 928	−58 683	−54 719	−40 550	−40 550

Table A8 VAT quarterly returns summary

	Mar	June	Sep	Dec	Total
VAT receivable	£38 693	£15 960	£13 545	£47 409	£115 607
minus					
VAT payable					
Materials and overheads	−11 197	−14 406	−12 005	−13 206	−50 814
Selling and general	−1050	−1050	−1050	−1050	−4200
Capital expenditure	−21 000	—	—	—	−21 000
Quarterly payments	£5446	£504	£490	£33 153	£39 593

charged *less* the VAT charged to you during the period, irrespective of whether or not you have received or paid it. Budgeted VAT payments have been calculated in Table A8. VAT receivable is taken from Table A5 and VAT payable on materials and variable overheads from Table A4. Selling and general costs and capital expenditures are as detailed. This complication is unfortunate, but essential, since VAT can make an enormous difference to the cash flows of any business and often a small business can experience difficulty meeting these quarterly bills.

The budgeted cash flow statement is essential for short-term planning. The business started the year with an overdraft of £30 000, which was the maximum facility offered by the bank. This overdraft limit will not be exceeded until September, when an overdraft of £44 928 will be required. This will increase to £58 683 in October, and even at the end of the year will be £40 550. Obviously the business must either arrange to increase its overdraft facility in advance for these months or arrange for a term loan to inject the necessary cash. But would the banks lend to the business? To find this out, we need to look at the business's profit and its balance sheet.

Budgeted balance sheet

The budgeted balance sheet is shown in Table A9. Debtors and related VAT represent November and December sales, and creditors and related VAT represent November and December purchases of materials and overheads. Finished goods stock was calculated in the production schedule and the raw materials base stock is maintained at £10 000. The overdraft was calculated from the budgeted cash flow statement. Corporation tax is estimated at £18 000.

Fixed assets are calculated below:

	brought forward 31 Dec 2010 (net)	£484 000
plus	purchases	120 000
minus	depreciation	−105 800
	carried forward 31 Dec 2011 (net)	£498 200

Depreciation is calculated by writing off assets over an estimated 10-year life. The company does this by charging depreciation of 10 per cent on the gross cost of the asset over a 10-year period.

Net assets for the company total £709 592, an increase of £102 760 over last year, which represents the profit the business has made this year since our budget shows no increase in share or loan capital. For those readers with a more detailed knowledge of accounts, Tables A9 and A10 analyse the movement on key balance sheet accounts.

The business is making a return on net assets of:

$$\frac{120\,760}{709\,592} \times 100 = 17\%$$

This is well above the target set by the owner, and above current interest rates. However, this return does exclude interest and taxation. The capital gearing is

$$\frac{(40\,550 + 100\,000)}{609\,592} \times 100 = 23\%$$

This is well below the maximum level of security that many lenders require. That maximum gearing level of 10 per cent would be reached with outside loans of £609 592 on the same capital base. In other words, the business would probably be able to support more loan capital to enable it to meet the cash flow deficit. The owner now has all the information he requires either to approach the bank manager or another source of funds.

Table A9   Budgeted balance sheet, 31 December 2011

	£	£	£
FIXED ASSETS (NET)			498 200
CURRENT ASSETS:			
Finished goods: modem A (640)	48 640		
modem B (830)	45 650		
	94 290		
Raw material base stock	10 000		104 290
Debtors		VAT	
– November sales	90 900	15 908	
– December sales	98 100	17 168	222 076
			326 366
CREDITORS DUE WITHIN ONE YEAR:		VAT	
Overdraft			(40 550)
Creditors			
– November materials and overhead purchases	(27 440)	(4 802)	
– December materials and overhead purchases	(20 580)	(3 602)	(56 424)
Corporation tax (estimate)			(18 000)
			(114 974)
NET CURRENT ASSETS			211 392
NET ASSETS			709 592
CREDITORS DUE AFTER MORE THAN ONE YEAR:			
Long term loan			(100 000)
			609 592
CAPITAL AND RESERVES:			
Share capital			10 000
Profit-and-loss account			
– brought forward 2010	496 832		
– 2011 profit	102 760		599 592
			609 592

Table A10 Analysis of accounts

Debtors		**Stock**	
brought forward 2010	£144 000		
+ sales	660 600		
− cash received	− 615 600		
carried forward 2011	£189 000		
Creditors		**Stock**	
brought forward 2010	£ 41 760	brought forward 2010	£ 60 200
+ purchases	290 360 →	+ purchases	290 360
− cash paid	− 284 100	+ depreciation allocation	105 800
carried forward 2011	£ 48 020	+ labour costs	163 770
		− cost of sales	− 515 840
		carried forward 2011	£ 104 290

VAT		
Brought forward 2010: debtors (Nov & Dec)	£25 200	
− creditors (Nov & Dec)	− 7 308	£ 17 892
− collected from sales		−107 731
+ paid on purchases (materials and overheads)		49 718
+ paid on selling and general costs		4 200
+ paid on capital expenditure		21 000
+ VAT paid quarterly to C & E		39 593
Carried forward 2011: debtors (Nov & Dec)	£ 33 076	
− creditors (Nov & Dec)	− 8 404	£ 24 672

References

Abell, D.F. (1980) *Defining the Business*, Hemel Hempstead: Prentice Hall.

Ansoff, H.I. (1968) *Corporate Strategy*, London: Penguin.

Bowman, C. and Faulkner, D. (1997) *Competitive and Corporate Strategy*, London: Irwin.

Burns, P. (1994) *Winners and Losers in the 1990s*, 3i European Enterprise Centre, Report no. 12, April.

Cannon, T (1985) 'Innovation, Creativity and Small Firm Organiation', *International Small Business Journal*, 4(1).

Chittenden, F., Poutziouris, P. and Michaelas, N. (1998) *Financial Management and Working Capital Practices in UK SMEs*, Manchester Business School.

Johnson, G. and Scholes, K. (1993) *Exploring Corporate Strategy*, Hemel Hempstead: Prentice-Hall International.

Kay, J. (1998) *Foundations of Corporate Success*, Oxford: Oxford University Press.

Lindblom, L.E. (1959) 'The Science of Muddling Through', *Public Administration Review*, 19, Spring.

Mathewson, Sir G., (2000) Keynote address, British Academy of Management Annual Conference, Edinburgh.

McCarthy, B. and Leavy, B. (2000) 'Strategy Formation in Irish SMEs: A Phase Model of Process', British Academy of Management Annual Conference, Edinburgh.

Mintzberg, H. (1978) 'Patterns in Strategy Formation', *Management Science*, 934–48.

Peters, T.J. and Waterman, R.H. (1982) *In Search of Excellence*, London: Harper & Row.

Porter, M.E. (1987) 'From Competitive Advantage to Competitive Strategy', *Harvard Business Review*, 65(3).

Rumelt, R.P. (1974) *Strategy, Structure and Economic Performance*, Boston, MA: Harvard University Press.

Stevenson, H.H. and Gumperter, D.E. (1985) 'The Heart of Entrepreneurship', *Harvard Business Review*, March/April.

Wernerfelt, B. and Montgomery, C.A. (1986) 'What is an Attractive Industry?', *Management Science*, 32, 1223–9.

12

The Exit

Contents

LEARNING OUTCOMES

By the end of this chapter you should be able to:

- List the ways an owner-manager can exit their business;

- Explain what constitutes business failure;

- Recognise when a small firm is most at risk of failure and explain what contributes to it;

- List the options open to owner-managers in order to harvest their investment in their business and explain what needs to be done to get the best deal;

- Explain how company valuations are arrived at.

Stagnate and die

Most small firms are born to stagnate or die. As we saw in Chapter 1, in the UK most do not grow to any size – almost two-thirds of businesses comprise only one or two people, and often the second person is the spouse. Some 95 per cent of firms employ fewer than 10 employees and 99 per cent fewer than 50 employees. Half of businesses cease trading within three years of being set up, although, as pointed out, this does not necessarily mean that the closure has left creditors unpaid and it can be viewed in a positive light as part of the dynamism of the sector as it responds to changing opportunities in the market place. What is more, when the number of start-ups increases, the number of businesses ceasing to trade tends to do so as well. The pattern is broadly similar internationally, although the USA has an even higher closure rate (Bannock and Daley, 1994). A cynical observer might conclude that, in such a turbulent environment, mere survival is a badge of success.

The exit of an owner-manager can be a thing of sadness or joy, depending on how it is achieved. Ceasing to trade can be a sadness if creditors are left unpaid. For a sole trader this might lead to their personal bankruptcy (which can only be discharged by a court of law) as creditors pursue their debts by claiming their personal assets. Only a tiny number of business exits involve bankruptcy. For a limited company an inability to pay creditors can lead to insolvency and then liquidation, when a liquidator is appointed to dispose of the assets of the business, with their value going to the creditors. Statistically, total insolvencies are defined as all liquidations of insolvent companies plus all personal bankruptcies. These are what most people would agree to call business failures.

However, even with this definition there are problems of interpretation. It is not uncommon for a bank to foreclose on its debt, forcing a company into liquidation, knowing that it will secure repayment of its preferential debt at the expense of other creditors, and then to provide support for a 'new' company set up by the owner-manager undertaking exactly the same type of business. Is this a business failure?

The liquidation of a company, in itself, may be a natural way of bringing the business to an end. This is called a voluntary liquidation. If there are surplus assets then the company is not insolvent and the owner-manager may make a capital gain after creditors are paid. But perhaps the most attractive exit for owner-managers is to sell the firm as a going concern. If they can achieve this they will reap the harvest of

---

Case insight

The Iron Bed Company achieved a turnover of £12 million before becoming Feather and Black in 2004. However, things were not always so successful. The founders, **Anne** and **Simon Notley** were unable to raise finance for the start-up because of their business track record. This included a failed pine shop and a business importing classic cars from the USA that collapsed in the early 1990s. The couple then ran a windsurfing school for three years before setting up the company. But they had to invest £70 000 from the sale of their home because they could not raise a bank loan. Consequently, they spent their money very carefully, operating from disused chicken sheds and preferring to invest in promotion and marketing, including risqué newspaper advertisements. Eventually they started opening their own stores, but their past failures taught them always to be prudent with cash.

their years of investment in the business. But, even with a sale, definitions are not straightforward because it could be that the sale was prompted by the business making continuing losses which could ultimately have led to failure. Nevertheless, even this form of 'distress sale' may still yield a capital gain for the owner-manager.

Whilst in the USA business failure can be seen as a worthwhile experience for entrepreneurs, provided they are seen to learn from it, in the UK there is still a stigma attached to it. Being associated with a failed company can lead to problems when it comes to raising cash for another start-up. Bankers, in particular, need some convincing to persuade them to give an entrepreneur a second chance – particularly if they lost money on the first attempt.

Failure

Notwithstanding these definitional problems, in his review of the literature Storey (1998) identified a number of factors that influence the probability of business failure. These are not necessarily independent of each other. The factors he identified as having the strongest influence were:

- *Age of business*: simply reviewing the statistics tells you that young firms are more likely to fail than older firms. Half of firms cease trading within their first three years of existence. The longer a firm survives, the less likely it is to fail. One study estimated that a 1 per cent change in age leads to a 13 per cent improvement in the probability of survival (Evans, 1987).
- *Size of business*: similarly, the likelihood of failure is greater the smaller the firm. Size is, of course, related to age but it is easier to close a small firm than a large one. Also, as we saw in a previous chapter, large firms have more assets than smaller firms and are therefore better able to weather adversity in the short term. The survey cited above estimated that a 1 per cent change in firm size leads to a 7 per cent improvement in the probability of survival.
- *Past growth*: firms that grow within a short period after start-up are less likely to fail than those that do not.
- *Sector*: failure rates vary from sector to sector with the construction and retail sectors showing the highest level of failures. Storey concludes, however, that the influence of sector is not as great as the first three factors above.

Storey also considered a number of factors which he concluded had a less certain influence on failure. These were:

- *Management*: most people would accept that the character and skills of the owner-manager as well as the team they draw around them influence the probability of either success or failure. Storey reviewed studies that tried to gauge the influence of work history (for example prior business ownership, management experience, unemployment), family background, personal characteristics (age, gender and ethnic background) and education but found the influences 'complex and difficult to predict' and failed to detect any patterns.
- *Economic conditions*: small firms are traditionally thought to be vulnerable to changes in economic activity with business failures expected to increase in times of recession. However, studies have failed to establish a clear relationship because of the influence of other factors such as previous levels of start-up.

- *Type of firm*: there is evidence that, unsurprisingly, franchises have a lower chance of failure than other businesses. More surprising, Storey concluded that limited companies are somewhat more risky than either self-proprietorships or partnerships, presumably due to the potential for unlimited personal liability.
- *Location*: there are clear regional variations in failure rates, however, these tend to correspond, with high rates of start-up going hand in hand with high levels of failure. The influence is therefore unclear.
- *Ownership*: the influence of ownership is less clear but it is suggested that larger firms with more than one plant are more likely to close a plant when facing difficult trading conditions than single-plant firms.
- *Business in receipt of state subsidies*: because state subsidy is often given to the weakest businesses, this influence is also difficult to verify.

Storey's review tells us little about the process of failure and therefore how it might be avoided. It implies that failure is mainly influenced by factors outside the owner-manager's control, many being the inevitable consequences of start-up. He points out that failure is endemic in the small business sector and that it has probably always been characterised by high levels. His overall conclusion – that 'the young are more likely to fail than the old, the very small are more likely to fail than their larger counterparts, and that, for young firms, probably the most powerful influence on their survival is whether or not they grow within a short period after start-up' – may be statistically accurate, but it is of hardly any use to owner-managers.

In an extensive review of some 50 articles and five books on the subject of small business failure, Berryman (1983) focused more on the managerial causes of failure. He listed some 25 causes and categorised them under six headings:

1 *Accounting*: accounting problems such as debtor and stock control or inadequate records were cited most frequently in this review of the literature.
2 *Marketing*: marketing problems came a close second. These can be many and various, from a lack of understanding of customer needs or identification of target customers to poor selling skills.
3 *Finance*: financing a firm that is failing is bound to be a problem. Cash flow will be poor and further finance may be unavailable. However, this is simply an obvious symptom of the problem rather than a root cause. Nevertheless, as many firms have found, undercapitalisation at start-up can be a significant factor in subsequent failure. Firms that are highly successful almost from start-up can face the danger of overtrading if they are undercapitalised.
4 *Other internal factors*: for example excessive drawings, nepotism or negligence.
5 *Behaviour of owner-manager*: Berryman lists such personal problems as inability to delegate, reluctance to seek help, excessive optimism, unawareness of the environment, inability to adapt to change and thinness of management talent as reasons for failure.
6 *External factors*: the effects of the economic environment or changes in the industry or market. Personal problems can also be significant.

Berryman notes that conclusions are difficult because of the lack of homogeneity of small firms. He also notes that many of the items in his list, particularly in categories 1 to 4, are symptoms rather than causes of failure. He categorised them simply as 'poor management' and concluded that this combines with the personality traits of the owner-manager and external factors to cause failure. However, his review still fails to help us understand the process of failure and, therefore, how it might be avoided.

The ingredients of failure

Figure 12.1 shows the ingredients of business failure and can be used to understand how the process happens. It builds on the work of Berryman and uses the model developed for business success depicted in Figure 9.1. Just as with business success, there is a recipe for business failure. Whilst the precise recipe varies from situation to situation, we know the ingredients of failure. It is a coincidence of a number of factors that is likely to lead to failure, as in a complex chemical reaction. The ingredients of failure comprise entrepreneurial character, business decisions, company weaknesses and the external environment.

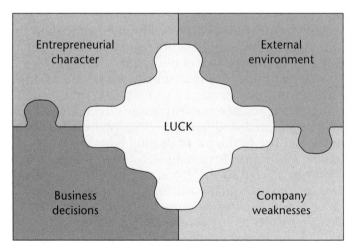

Figure 12.1 The ingredients of business failure

Entrepreneurial character

Referring back to Chapter 2, we recall that certain of the character traits of owner-managers and entrepreneurs can have very negative effects. For example, the strong internal locus of control can lead to 'control freak' behaviour such as meddling, an inability to delegate, a mistrust of subordinates or an unwillingness to part with equity in the business. Similarly, the strong need for public achievement might lead to unwise overspending on the trappings of corporate life, or the 'big project' that is too risky. The strong self-confidence can, *in extremis*, become 'delusional' behaviour evidenced by an excessive optimism, an exaggerated opinion of their business competence and an unwillingness to listen to advice or seek help. On top of this can be layered the problems associated with family firms. These combine to produce a potent set of behavioural ingredients which might become underlying causes of failure.

In their empirical research of business failure, Larson and Clute (1979) listed eight personal characteristics to be found in owner-managers of failed firms. It is interesting how many of these factors are the negative sides of the character traits of entrepreneurs that we have already noted. The characteristics were:

- Exaggerated opinion of business competency based upon knowledge of some skill;
- Limited formal education;
- Inflexible to change and not innovative;
- Use of own personal tastes and opinions as the standard to follow;
- Decisions based upon intuition, emotion and non-objective factors;
- Past- not future-orientation;
- Limited reading in literature associated with the business;
- Resistant to advice from qualified sources but, paradoxically, accepts it from less-qualified.

Business decisions

By definition, bad business decisions are the opposite of good ones. They often stem from a lack of reliable information or an unwillingness or inability to understand it. For example, bad marketing decisions feature regularly in the literature on causes of failure and these often stem from a lack of understanding of what customers are really buying (benefits), who customers are (market segmentation) and why they do not buy from competitors (competitive advantage). This is basic marketing.

Some of the points when an entrepreneur is most likely to make bad management or personnel decisions are predicted by Greiner's growth model (Chapter 8). These crises are predictable and the problems of dealing with them are anchored in the entrepreneurial character. Hence, for example, an unwillingness to bring in an outside manager may be related to the entrepreneur's unwillingness to delegate, or their unwillingness to give up equity (control) to attract a suitably experienced manager, or because of the mistrust of non-family managers. Many bad decisions stem from the character traits of entrepreneurs. For example, the decision to undertake the risky 'big project' that eventually brings the company down may have been influenced by the entrepreneur's need to demonstrate achievement and receive public applause and recognition.

One study analysed the events that threatened the survival of small firms and found that 38 per cent were marketing-related, 32 per cent finance-related, 14 per cent management-related, 13 per cent personnel-related, 10 per cent were 'acts of God' and 18 per cent had no associated crisis (Watkins, 1982).

Larson and Clute (*op. cit.*) listed nine 'managerial defects' of failed firms. Many of these we would call bad decisions, but some we would classify under 'weaknesses'. They were:

● Inability to identify target market or customers;
● Inability to delineate trading area;
● Inability to delegate;
● Belief that advertising is an expense, not an investment;
● Only rudimentary knowledge of pricing strategy;
● Immature understanding of distribution channels;
● No planning;
● Inability to motivate;
● Belief that the problem is somebody else's fault and a loan would solve everything.

Company weaknesses

Weaknesses and bad decisions are closely related, like chicken and egg. Many weaknesses stem from bad decisions in the past. For example, high gearing may be due to a decision not to dilute the equity of the firm by going to a venture capitalist. In this case the decision may again have stemmed from the character of the entrepreneur and their wish to retain control of the business. On the other hand, many bad decisions stem from poor information caused by inadequate systems.

A frequently cited weakness that is a contributory cause of failure is poor financial control – poor, infrequent information, lax debtor control and/or high stock holding. Poor financial control inevitably leads to the reappearance of Death Valley and a cash flow crisis. If you couple that with poor planning, then you have the potential for failure.

A major weakness cited by a number of studies is the typical overdependence of small firms on a small number of customers for too high a proportion of their sales (Cosh and Hughes, 1998). Another angle on this is the size of the product range. Some studies have shown that the wider the range, the lower the likelihood of failure (Reid, 1991).

Case insight

Tech Board, a hard-board maker in Ebbw Vale, South Wales, was Britain's biggest venture capital backed start-up when it began trading in 1995. It was a £40 million project with £25 million of funding from a consortium of private equity houses, led by 3i. Its history in many ways reflects what has been happening to UK manufacturing since then. In 1998 it went into receivership and was rescued by Enron, the American energy and power firm that itself failed. The new company, called **Imperial Board Products**, was sold in April 1999 to a management buy-out team. The purchase was funded by a combination of a loan from Enron, invoice discounting and some state aid. The management buy-out was very highly geared and probably undercapitalised from the start. In August 2000 the firm went into liquidation.

External environment

Firms must cope with an ever-changing market place. Although direct effects cannot be proved statistically, small firms appear particularly vulnerable to macroeconomic variables – after all, they have less financial 'fat' than larger firms. Changes in overall consumer demand, interest rates and inflation can have a disproportionate effect on smaller firms. Many dot.com start-ups that received first-round finance in 1999 failed to obtain second-round finance in 2000 because the market had changed so dramatically, forcing them to cease trading. There are also the 'acts of God' – the strike, the fire, the loss of the major customer – which a larger company might weather but the smaller firm cannot. Some external influences are clearly due to bad luck but some are due to bad judgement – the wrong place at the wrong time – and luck can have a disproportionate effect on smaller firms.

Case insight

ZedZed.com

'This is a story with an unhappy ending about my dot.com company **ZedZed.com**, a site for independent travellers, which went into liquidation in 2000. ZedZed.com was meant to be called ZigZag.com but that name had already gone. We raised £800 000, which was no mean achievement, but it wasn't enough. In February we encountered dot.com envy from our friends. In March we were winning awards and being asked to speak at conferences in Paris. In June we achieved 1800 user reviews per week. In August we were calling in the liquidators.

Mistakes are always easier to see with the benefit of hindsight, and our worst error was to believe that internet businesses should be valued by the number of subscribers rather than the transactions that they make ... Today you have to be profitable or else you are not going to get funded again. They say that internet speed is fast but three months is a short period of time to reverse your whole *raison d'être*.

I think we did a lot right too. We built a site in six weeks on a very complicated back-end platform. We chose a content management system that would make us a serious force in the market, and we successfully leveraged that asset with larger organisations who might otherwise have ignored us. We devised a very successful low-cost user subscription campaign without the help of an expensive marketing agency like so many dot.coms. We kept our non-essential expenditure to a minimum, which allowed us to return 20 per cent of the initial subscription to investors. We employed 19 people on low salaries who genuinely loved their daily work. Being a chartered accountant, I knew where our financial position was on a daily basis and knew when the time had come to close the door.

Setting up a dot.com business has been the most exciting, rewarding experience of my life, and of the lives of the team that I had around me. We did something new, different and useful to other people. Sadly for us and our investors, the capital markets have changed to such a degree that we have had to end our quest early. In doing so we are showing that there is sanity amid the madness. Don't pity the pioneers – envy us for our experience. Oh, and pay us well for them too!'

Edward Johnstone
Co-founder of **ZedZed.com**
Daily Telegraph 17 August 2000

In reality the effect of the environment depends upon the time period, geographic area, and market sector in which the firm operates. Perhaps the most significant effect on smaller firms is the degree of competition within its industry and therefore Porter's Five Forces influence not only profitability, but, *in extremis*, the likelihood of failure. A small firm operating in a highly competitive market is more likely to fail than one operating in a market with low levels of competition.

This model gives us an insight into the process of failure. It also reinforces many of the lessons of success. These four ingredients of failure interact together. Individually they are present in many firms, but it is only when they combine that the potential for failure is created. What makes the small firm different to the large one is the disproportionate importance of the influence of the owner-manager. Many bad business decisions stem from the entrepreneurial character. Many weaknesses stem from bad business decisions, which in turn may stem from the entrepreneurial character. However, the crisis that triggers the decline into failure is often brought about by some outside factor such as an unexpected change in the market place, customer tastes, competition or distribution channels. This may lead to further bad decisions being made by the owner-manager, for example a decision to overtrade or borrow too much. These, in turn, result in symptoms of failure such as running short of cash or declining profitability. The paradox is that the asset of the entrepreneurial character can become a liability in certain circumstances.

Predicting failure

It is one thing to understand the process of failure, but it is quite another to try to predict it. Nevertheless many academics both in the UK and USA such as Beaver (1966), Altman (1968) and Taffler (1982) have tried to do this, mainly using financial ratios as relevant variables. Most studies have looked at large public companies because of the ready availability of this information. Financial information in smaller businesses tends to be less reliable, with the profit figure more easy to manipulate, less complete, since they do not have to disclose the same the amount of information as public companies, and less timely, since they do not face stock market pressures. However, it has been argued (Keasey and Watson, 1991) that, because of these factors, if predictive models could be developed they would be extremely valuable, not only in terms of their predictive ability but also in terms of their information value or usefulness. This is not surprising given the problems of information asymmetry facing bankers in particular (this term is explained in Chapter 13). For this reason trying to predict failure in small firms using models that employ publicly available information has attracted just as much interest as trying to pick winners.

Most of these studies use multiple discriminant analysis on a sample of failed and non-failed firms to select financial ratios that best discriminate between the two groups and then combine them into a simple number, or 'Z score', which indicates the likelihood of failure. Companies are matched by industry and size. Most studies then go on to test the predictive ability of the 'Z score' on a hold-out sample which includes failed and non-failed firms. Studies have used the full range of ratios discussed in Chapter 9 – performance, profitability, asset efficiency, liquidity, gearing and risk – in an attempt to see which best predict failure. For example, one study looked at small firms in the construction and civil engineering sector (Love and D'Silva, 2001). It tested 25 ratios and the final 'Z score' was calculated as shown below, with companies scoring below 0.36 having a high probability of failure:

$$Z = -0.143 + 1.608a + 0.001b + 0.461c + 0.352d - 0.007e$$

where: a = net profit margin
b = debtor days
c = profit before tax divided by shareholder funds
d = profit before tax divided by current liabilities from the previous year
e = total sales over working capital from the previous year

In this study 72.9 per cent of the predictive ability came from the simple net profit margin ratio.

Studies like these have been criticised on many counts, not least because they look at symptoms rather than root causes of failure. In this respect the major practical problem with them is their timeliness. It is quite probable that by the time these symptoms manifest themselves in published accounts, the company will already have filed for bankruptcy. What is more, the effect of the external environment, particularly for smaller firms, is likely to be very high. For example, profit margins are likely to decline in most firms at times of recession and therefore any bank using this as a predictive tool might be tempted to foreclose on a large number of loans thus creating a self-fulfilling prophesy. One major UK clearing bank tested 'Z scores' extensively in the 1980s and decided not to use them.

Banks, of course, have a major piece of information at their fingertips that gives them an immediate insight into what is happening within the firm. This is the firm's bank account. From this banks can monitor cash inflows and outflows as well as balances and this can give them invaluable information about current performance long before it finds itself into published financial information. Notwithstanding this two major UK clearing banks started using an expert system called Lending Advisor in the 1990s to help them make lending decisions and monitor loans. This computer-based system combines 'hard' financial data with 'soft' judgmental data using weightings that can be adjusted to produce a lending 'recommendation'. The 'hard' financial data includes a range of historic as well as projected financial ratios. The 'soft' data includes a range of judgements about the management of the firm as well as its competitive advantage within its industry. In many ways the system simply attempts to make lending decisions more rational and consistent. The danger with it is that it masks the areas of judgement that are inevitably involved and focuses attention on the simple, final lending recommendation.

Harvest

For the entrepreneur to be able to harvest the investment he/she has made in a business, it must it must be of value to somebody else – demonstrated by a good financial track record – and must be able to function effectively without the entrepreneur – that means it must have good control systems and a good management team. The most attractive harvest option is probably to find a trade

> **Case insight**
>
> **Chris Hutt** planned his exit strategy almost from the first day he started rolling out the Newt &
> Cucumber chain. In 1996 he sold **Unicorn Inns** to the brewer Moorlands for £13.2 million. This
> was the culmination of almost five years work perfecting the Newt & Cucumber market
> offering, but always with an eye to the ultimate objective – an exit either through a trade sale or
> a stock market floatation. With this in mind Chris had developed the marketing plan we looked
> at earlier. But his experience of the trade told him that there were four critical success factors
> that would maximise its value so that when he exited from Unicorn the business would
> continue to prosper without him in what is a highly competitive industry:
>
> - Finding suitable sites to roll out the Newt & Cucumber pub formula so that they could get to
>   an appropriate size to benefit from bulk purchase discounts and to be sufficiently attractive to
>   potential buyers.
> - Recruiting and motivating good pub management. To this end he put in place training
>   programmes, appraisal systems and an attractive bonus package that rewarded managers
>   who achieved targets in sales, margins, stockholdings and staffing costs (as percentage of
>   sales) – four of the six key financial drivers.
> - Putting in place strong financial controls – daily checks on cash takings and bankings (the
>   fifth driver), weekly stocktaking and performance measurement against budget and the
>   production of monthly management accounts.
> - Promoting the brand, not only to customers, but also to the trade. To this end he started
>   writing articles for the trade press and made every effort to get PR. For example, in 1992
>   Unicorn won the Multiple Operator of the year award.

buyer, another company in the industry that understands the business. They are
likely to place a higher value on the business than others because they can see ways of
'adding value' through the purchase, perhaps by synergy. In many cases they might
be willing to pay cash, so the entrepreneur can walk away from the firm on the day of
sale. David Bruce founded the Firkin chain of pubs in 1979 but sold it to Midsummer
Leisure for £6.6 million nine years later when there were only nine pubs. Since then it
has been sold and resold. David went on to do the same thing with the Hedgehog and
Hogshead chain of pubs.

Another option may be a management buy-out (MBO) – managers in the firm
buying it from the founder. Although managers are unlikely to have the necessary
capital, many venture capitalists look very favourably on management buy-outs and
are keen to provide funds for them, provided the terms are right. However, managers
are likely to know as much about the firm as the founder and can negotiate a tough
deal. Indeed some management buy-outs fail because managers know the business
too well and are unwilling to meet the asking price. What is more, it is possible that
the owner might have to wait several years before the full balance of the sale price is
paid.

A similar option is a management buy-in – a team of managers, often with
experience in the industry buying the business. It is difficult to know where to turn to
find managers interested in this sort of option, however, some accountants keep
confidential registers of just such managers.

'There are plenty of divisions of large companies that are just not viable in terms of a MBO. You need quality of management because you are asking people to back you as a team, and a private equity house will be buying into your ability to add value. You need to make sure you have all the key positions covered by competent people who are either already in place or lined up to come in. Then the division has to show it has some quality earnings. If the business has just one contract with one large customer, and it is up for renewal in eight months, that is probably not a very attractive play. You also need a business that is cash generative, because if you are going to attach debt to it as part of the MBO, it has to be throwing off some cash to service the debt.'

Richard Hall partner **Ernst & Young**
Sunday Times 22 February 2004

Finding a buyer, valuing the business and negotiating its sale are a daunting series of tasks that really should not be undertaken without professional advice and help. Many larger firms of accountants can help find buyers, just as they can help find companies to purchase, and they can act as a confidential 'front' in the search process. They are also likely to take a more objective view on company valuation than the entrepreneur and are essential in sorting out the detail of the deal, including the inevitable warranties and indemnities that will be requested by the purchaser. Finally there is the important consideration of taxation, where planning can considerably increase the money actually pocketed by the entrepreneur.

Owner-managers of sizeable companies can achieve personal liquidity and raise additional capital by 'going public' – floating the company on a stock exchange and selling shares in it. This is the route Anita and Gordon Roddick took with Body Shop, floating it first on the smaller Unlisted Securities Market (equivalent to AIM) and then obtaining a full stock market quotation. However, this option is problematic if the entrepreneur wishes to retire because the stock market's assessment of public share issues centres on the future potential of

Case insight

Vivid Imaginations is now Britain's biggest toy company with annual sales of £130 million. It specialises in producing toys related to TV or cinema series by purchasing the franchise rights, and produced the official Spider-Man toys to coincide with the launch of Spider-Man 2 in the UK. It was set up by **Nick Austin** and **Alan Bennie** in the 1960s with £250 000 obtained by pooling their severance pay from their old jobs and remortgaging their houses. After some time a bank offered a rolling overdraft for the same amount.

In 1998 the pair decided to realise their investment and sell off the business to an American venture capital company for £27 million – a deal that generated almost £10 million each for them. The deal included an agreement for the pair to stay with the company for the next five years. But when the time to go arrived they could not bring themselves to leave the business they had set up. Instead, with the help of a British venture capital firm, they staged a management buy-out, buying back the company for £62 million, sharing ownership with employees and retaining 4 per cent each for themselves.

Case insight

Body Shop has come a long way from being set up by **Anita Roddick** in 1976 to becoming a multinational public company. It obtained a listing on the Unlisted Securities Market in the UK in 1984, offering shares at 95 pence, and it obtained a full listing in 1986. By the year ending 28 February 1991, turnover exceeded £100 million, profits £22 million and the share price 350 pence. Between 1984 and that date, against a *Financial Times* All Share Index of 100, its shares had risen from an index of 100 to 550. However, by mid-1995 the share price had fallen to 150 pence.

Increasingly the Roddicks were taking a back seat. Body Shop was attracting more competition from both newcomers and established retailers introducing 'natural' products. Because of the emergence of an aggressive US competitor called Bath and Body Works, it was forced into even more rapid expansion with a unfortunate effect on costs and profitability. It also faced criticism about the reality behind its ethical stance. In 1996 an attempted re-privatisation was abandoned because of the gearing implications. In 1998 a new Chief Executive was recruited with the Roddicks becoming co-chairmen. In 1999 the company withdrew from manufacturing. Profits and the share price have recovered. In 2000 **Anita** and **Gordon Roddick** resigned from Body Shop, multimillionaires, but retained a majority shareholding.

In March 2006 it was announced that Body Shop was to be sold to L'Oreal for £652 million. With the Roddick's stake in the company estimated at 18 per cent, they were expected to make £130 million. This was the final exit. L'Oreal assures the public it will take a 'hands-off' approach to managing the business, but with its very different image from Body Shop's, many analysts wonder whether the Body Shop values and ethos will really survive. Indeed, there are doubts over whether the brand can survive, not only without the Roddicks, but now as part of a larger multinational company – the very thing they hated so much. So can a company like Body Shop, linked so closely to the values and vision of its founders, survive after their exit? Only time will tell.

→

the firm, and if the float is simply intended to provide an exit for the entrepreneur, it is unlikely to be popular.

Most entrepreneurs want to sell on their firm rather than to pass it on within their family (Burns and Whitehouse, 1996). However, few plan how to do it. Most rely instead on their instincts for sorting out an opportunistic deal at the last minute. And yet they are far more likely to achieve the best price for their business by planning ahead and building in to the business plan any steps that are needed to help with the harvest.

Company valuation

In practice, there are two basic ways of valuing a business:

1 *Market value of assets*: businesses that are asset-rich, such as a farm or a freehold retail premises, are often valued in this way. Tangible assets such as debtors, stocks, equipment, fixtures and fittings and particularly property are valued at their market rate. This might give a higher value than the second approach.

2   *Multiple of profits*: many firms, particularly those with few tangible assets, are valued based upon some multiple of annual profit. For example, if an appropriate multiple of profits were 5, a company making £100 000 per year would be valued at £0.5 million. If you look in the *Financial Times*, every public company has its price–earnings ratio quoted – that is, how many times the price of its shares is a multiple of its earnings – the equivalent of a multiple of profits.

Companies can also be valued using a mix of both methods. Where there are tangible assets, such as property, these might be valued at market rates and then an element of 'goodwill' added based upon a multiple of profits.

The key question, of course, is what multiple of profits to use. Essentially buyers are interested in the future profits the business will make and they are using current profits as a proxy measure. So, one factor to influence the multiple is the 'quality' of earnings. The longer the firm's track record of profitable trading, the higher the multiple. Another factor may be the quality of the management the owner will be leaving behind to continue running the firm. Can they do it without him? Different industry sectors tend to have different multiples that reflect the risk they are perceived as facing. The higher the perceived risk, the lower the multiple. Small, privately-held firms typically command a lower multiple than public companies in the same industry because there is a market for shares in a public company. Multiples in single figures are usual for small firms but at the end of the day it depends how much the buyer wants the firm. If it has strategic importance, for example enabling it to get into a key overseas market, it can easily pay well over any normal market valuation.

One outside factor is the rate of interest. Higher interest rates usually mean lower multiples. Since the purchase of a business often necessitates a buyer borrowing funds, the gearing of the purchased firm, in its final form, can be a factor. If borrowings are high, as they often are in management buy-outs, the company is vulnerable to changes in profitability as it will have high, fixed interest charges. If the return on total assets falls below the rate of interest, it can be in trouble and the higher the borrowing, the greater the trouble. This is what happened to the heavily borrowed small firms in the early 1990s when interest rates soared at the same time as profits tumbled.

Planning is the key to a successful harvest. Selling at the right time can have a significant impact on the value of the business. The business will be worth most when profits are at their highest and can be seen to be growing. You need to consider the impact of the business cycle upon sales, profits

> **Case insight**
>
> **Julian Harley** and **Ian West** bought a seven-employee IT training firm in 1991 for £55 000. **Harley West Training** grew rapidly and by 1997 it had 200 employees and was valued in a trade sale at £8.5 million. Julian Harley gives some advice:
>
> 'You need to allow plenty of time, not just to find the right buyer, but to consider the implications of the sale ... Do your research and plan to sell in a market that's rising but hasn't yet peaked ... Get professional advice, but compare quotes carefully and remember you know more about your business than anybody else'.
>
> (www.businesslink.gov.uk)

and the order book. The general state of the economy – and in particular the sector the business is in – can have an effect on valuation. It is easier to find a trade buyer when a sector is doing well and interest rates are low with bankers willing to lend. Other factors – like strong internal controls and an effective management team – need to be in place. And finally, consideration needs to be given to the legal, tax and pension consequences of the sale. Most entrepreneurs will need advice on this and help finding buyers, so these need to be in place. All this means the harvest needs to be planned between three and five years ahead.

The never-ending cycle

The never-ending cycle of start-up and exit is part of the dynamic of the small firm sector as firms respond to the ever-changing market place. It is one of the reasons why governments all over the world now recognise that small firms have a vital and increasingly important part to play in the economy of the twenty-first century. In this environment survival is a badge of success. And behind every success, and indeed failure, there is a person and a human interest story to tell. Successfully managing growth is a Herculean task. Is it any wonder that so few owner-managers decide to try it? Those who do and succeed really are the super-heroes of the modern world.

Which brings us back to where we started this book – the entrepreneurs themselves. These individuals and their values, beliefs and actions really are the distinguishing feature of small firms, not size *per se*. They shape how the firm develops and the decisions it makes. They are influenced by a whole range of factors – they are both born and made, shaped by their background and experiences. And they are not always rational. Their spider's-web approach to management, using informal influence to get their way, has parallels in the business networks they develop and their relationship approach to marketing. For them the job of doing business is a social affair, a core part of their life. They are adept at resolving the conflict that is a constant part of their life. They have a particular hands-on approach to management – they like to manage by doing – and a short-term, incremental approach to decision-making. Strategy often emerges as they assess how they are doing – a reactive, adaptive and ultimately flexible approach to the uncertainty of the entrepreneurial environment. And the risk of failure and the implications for them and their family is a key factor influencing business decisions. Nevertheless they find ways of creating and making the most of the opportunities created by change. They innovate, albeit not in the classical Schumpeterian way. Table 12.1 tries to summarise the main distinguishing characteristics of the entrepreneurial small firm.

Because of these factors, small firms really are fundamentally different to large ones, where the interests of shareholders are normally assumed to be of major importance and the influence of any one individual is far less. What is more, just as every individual in the world is different, so too is every small firm. Not only are small firms a heterogeneous group, individual firms adapt and change as they grow and develop to meet the changing needs of the market place. And, although the stage models of growth help us towards an understanding of the dynamics of growth, this makes it difficult to generalise about the distinguishing characteristics of small firms. Table 12.1, therefore, contains many very broad generalisations that must be treated with caution. However, it does explain why small firms and entrepreneurs are worthy

Table 12.1 Distinguishing characteristics of entrepreneurial small firms

Distinguishing characteristics	• Influence of entrepreneur dominates
	• Influence of family can be important
	• Operates in a highly uncertain, risky environment
Approach to environment	• Sees opportunities and pursues them
	• Uses innovation to create competitive advantage
	• Short-term, incremental approach to decision-making
	• Flexible, adaptive, emergent approach to strategy
	• Personal implications of failure important influence
Approach to management	• Relationship-based approach to all aspects of business
	• Adept at handling risk, uncertainty and ambiguity
	• Good at resolving conflict
	• Action-orientated – a hands-on approach
	• Uses informal influence in managing people
	• Prefers informal, spider's-web organisation
	• Develops personal business networks
	• Personal relationship approach to marketing
	• Strongly intuitive, but self-reliant and confident
	• Evolves as business grows

of separate study. Small firms are not just scaled-down versions of large ones, they are interesting, exciting and unpredictable. And the entrepreneurs that run them really are the super-heroes of the twenty-first century.

Summary

Most firms are born to stagnate or die – not to grow to any size. There are three sorts of exit:

- *Cessation of trade* – where the business just winds up without creditors being owed any money. Most exits are of this form.
- *Failure* – which involves liquidation of insolvent companies and personal bankruptcy.
- *Harvest* – which involves selling the business on as a going concern.

In the USA investors see failure as part of the entrepreneurial learning process. However, in the UK, as **Anne** and **Simon Notley** found when they started up **The Iron Bed Company**, it is not always viewed in the same way and can cause entrepreneurs problems when it comes to raising cash for future ventures. The main factors influencing the statistical likelihood of failure are age and size of business, past growth and sector. The main managerial causes of failure involve poor management (accounting, marketing, financing and other factors), behavioural characteristics of the owner-manager and external factors.

The recipe for failure involves a coincidence of four factors which interact like a complex chemical reaction. These are:

- *Entrepreneurial character* – particularly 'control freak' behaviour, delusional behaviour and the need for achievement;
- *Business decisions* – such as inability to delegate or the 'big project';
- *Company weaknesses* – accounting controls and overdependence on a small number of customers are common. As with **Imperial Board Products**, lack of adequate finance is another common problem;
- *External environment* – for example, Porter's Five Forces measures the degree of competition in the industry.

Many weaknesses stem from bad business decisions, which in turn may stem from some inherent character traits of the entrepreneur. Often events in the external environment trigger the chemical reaction that causes the decline into failure. Luck plays a part but, as with **ZedZed.com**, it is not always clear what is luck or bad judgement.

The harvest involves selling the business as a going concern either to a trade buyer, a management buy-out or management buy-in. As with **Unicorn Inns**, this needs careful planning and professional advice. Sometimes, as with **Vivid Imaginations**, entrepreneurs can decide to buy back the company they have sold. Another option to raise liquidity may be 'going public', but the entrepreneur will find it difficult to exit in the short term. What is more, as Anita Roddick and **Body Shop** found, the Stock Market can exert strong short-term pressures that constrain the actions of management.

Company valuation is not a science. It depends on what a buyer is willing to pay, and therefore how important the purchase is to them. There are two commonly used methods of valuation – market value of assets and a multiple of profit. Multiples depend on the quality of earnings, the quality of management, the industry sector and the general economic climate. Few private companies command a multiple into double figures.

Timing of the sale is important and therefore careful planning is essential, as **Harvey West Training** found. To maximise the value of the business profits need to be high and rising, the sector needs to be booming with interest rates low, and good controls and an effective management team need to be in place.

The never ending cycle of start-up and exit is part of the dynamic of the small firm sector that shows it is responding to the changing demands of the market place. However, behind every exit there is a personal story, as we saw with **ZedZed.com**.

Small firms have three distinguishing characteristics – the uncertain, risky environment they operate in and the central influence of the entrepreneurs. Their approach to this environment is opportunity-driven, innovative, involving short-term incremental decisions and strategies that are flexible, adaptive and emerge from previous action. Ultimately they are concerned about the personal implications of failure. Their approach to management is hands-on, informal and relationship-based. They are adept at handling risk, uncertainty and ambiguity and good at resolving conflict. They develop networks and are good at relationship marketing.

Useful websites

www.businesslink.gov.uk: A succinct summary of the issues faced in selling a business, including UK tax issues, can be found on this site which offers practical advice to business.

Essays and discussion topics

1 Why do most small firms stagnate or die?
2 Is it good that so many small firms cease trading?
3 What constitutes failure in business?
4 What do you think of Storey's conclusion about failure; that 'the young are more likely to fail than the old, the very small are more likely to fail than their larger counterparts, and that, for young firms, probably the most powerful influence on their survival is whether or not they grow within a short period after start-up'?
5 How do you distinguish between causes and symptoms in business failure?
6 If you are trying to predict failure does it matter if you measure symptoms rather than causes?
7 Do entrepreneurs make their own luck?
8 The entrepreneurial character is as much a liability as an asset. Discuss.
9 You cannot distinguish between bad business decisions and business weaknesses. Discuss.
10 Running a growing small firm is one perpetual crisis. Discuss.
11 What do you think of Edward Johnstone's comments about ZedZed.com going into receivership?
12 What are the pros and cons of selling a business rather than passing it on within the family?
13 There is no such thing as company valuation, only a willing buyer and a willing seller negotiating a price. Discuss.
14 Are there any lessons from product/service pricing (Chapter 6) for company valuation?
15 Dot.com business valuations are just fantastical. Discuss.
16 How are small firms different from large ones?

Exercises and assignments

1 Find a business that has recently failed and try to fit the circumstances of its failure into the framework of the failure model shown in Figure 12.1.
2 Using desk research, write a case study of a failed business.

References

Altman, E.I. (1968) *Financial Ratio's Discriminant Analysis and the Prediction of Corporate Bankruptcy*, 23(24), September.
Bannock, G. and Daley, M. (1994) *Small Business Statistics*, London: PCP.
Beaver, W.H. (1966) *Financial Ratios as Predictors of Failure*, Journal of Accounting Research, Supplement on Empirical Research in Accounting, pp. 71–111.
Berryman, J. (1983) 'Small Business Failure and Bankruptcy: A Survey of the Literature', *European Small Business Journal*, 1(4).
Burns, P. and Whitehouse, O. (1996) *Family Ties*, 3i European Enterprise Centre, Special Report no. 10.
Cosh, A. and Hughes, A. (eds) (1998) *Enterprise Britain: Growth Innovation and Public Policy in the Small and Medium Sized Enterprise Sector 1994–97*, Cambridge: ESRC Centre for Business Research.

Evans, D. (1987) 'The Relationship between Firm Growth, Size and Age', *Journal of Industrial Economics*: 567–82.

Keasey, K. and Watson, R. (1991) 'The State of the Art of Small Firm Failure Prediction: Achievements and Prognosis', *International Small Business Journal*, 9.

Larson, C. and Clute, R. (1979) 'The Failure Syndrome', *American Journal of Small Business*, iv(2), October.

Love, N. and D'Silva, K. (2001) *A Model for Predicting Business Performance in SMEs: Theory and Empirical Evidence*, Paper presented at the British Accounting Association Conference, March 26–27, University of Exeter, England.

Reid, G.C. (1991) 'Staying in Business', *International Journal of Industrial Organisation*, 9.

Storey, D.J. (1998) U*nderstanding the Small Business Sector*, London: International Thomson Business Press.

Taffler, R.J. (1982) 'Forecasting Company Failure in the UK using Discriminant Analysis and Failure Ratio Data', *Journal of Royal Statistical Society*, 145, part 3.

Watkins, D. (1982) 'Management Development and the Owner-manager', in T. Webb, T. Quince and D. Watkins (eds), *Small Business Research*, Aldershot: Gower.

Part 4

Finance and Planning

13

Financing Small Firms

Contents

- Money
- Bank finance
- The banker's perspective
- Banking relationships
- Venture capital institutions and business angels
- The venture capitalist's perspective
- Stock market floatation
- Is there a financing gap?
- Summary

LEARNING OUTCOMES

By the end of this chapter you should be able to:

- List the principles of prudent financing;

- Describe the sources of finance available to small firms and their appropriate uses;

- Explain how small firms in the UK actually are financed;

- Recognise the perspective of bankers in assessing lending opportunities and monitoring a firm's performance;

- Recognise the perspective and priorities of venture capitalists in assessing an investment opportunity;

- Describe the options available when floating a company;

- Explain what is meant by the 'financing gap' and form an opinion as to whether it really exists for small firms.

Money

We saw in Chapter 9 that the availability and cost of finance is often cited by owner-managers as a barrier to growth. This is not new. Back in 1931 the Macmillan Committee believed it was extremely difficult for smaller firms to obtain long-term capital in amounts of less than £200 000 (a figure probably equivalent to about £5 million today; Macmillan, 1931). Since then there has been much debate about whether a 'financing gap' really does exist.

The adequate provision of finance is vital if small firms are to grow and make the most of their potential, but the topic raises paradoxes resulting from the ambiguous attitudes owner-managers have towards its provision. On the one hand they want outside finance in order to grow but, on the other hand, they do not want to lose independence or control. At the same time they want both maximum flexibility and maximum security – objectives that are not easily reconciled – at the lowest price.

The first thing to realise is that not all money is the same. Different sorts of money ought to be used for different purposes and not all types of money are available to all small firms. In fact many owner-managers, particularly at start-up, try to avoid using money at all by borrowing or using other people's resources wherever possible. Where this fails, they might borrow money from friends or relatives. Friends and relatives can be flexible, perhaps agreeing to lend at a low or zero interest rate and without any guarantees because they know and trust the person they are lending to. They might even help with running the firm and bring valuable experience with them. However, rather than relying on informal agreements, most advisors would recommend that more formal loan agreements are drawn up so as to avoid misunderstandings and arguments later. Many owner-managers make extensive use of personal credit cards, particularly at start-up, because of the problems they face in securing other sources of finance. Inevitably, however, most firms will need to obtain some form of external finance at some point in their life.

> **Case insight**
>
> **David Moulsade** trained as a dispensing optician through a correspondence course. In 1993, aged 24, he opened his first shop in Glasgow. Soon after he opened his third store in Edinburgh cash flow problems hit and he had to borrow from his parents to pay the wages. They re-mortgaged their home. **Optical Express** is now one of Britain's fastest growing companies, having taken over the Specialeyes chain in 1997.
>
> ●

Table 13.1 summarises the major forms of finance and how they ought to be used, in theory. The principle is that the term-duration of the source of finance should be matched to the term-duration of the use to which it is put. Fixed or permanent assets should be financed by long-term sources of finance and only working capital should be financed by short-term finance.

The owner-manager is likely to have to put some personal equity into the business, whatever its size. For a limited company this takes the form of share capital. Over time these funds grow as profits are retained in the business. The majority of small firms rely on internal funds to finance their business; 79 per cent use retained profits and 72 per cent cash flow to fund activities according to one survey (Bank of England, 1998). According to another, one-third of small firms across Europe do not borrow at all from banks with most preferring to use internal funds to finance growth and

Table 13.1 Sources and uses of finance

	Source of finance	Use of finance

Long-term	• Equity
	  – personal investment
	  – other people's money
	• Medium and long-term bank loans
	• Leasing
	• Hire purchase
		Fixed or permanent assets (land, buildings, furniture, equipment, plant, vehicles and so on)

Short-term	• Factoring • Short-term bank loans and overdraft	Working capital (debtors and stocks)

development; another third move into and out of overdraft regularly; and the final third are consistent borrowers (Burns and Whitehouse, 1995b).

For a growing company, there may also be the opportunity to get a venture capital institution or a private individual (called 'business angels') to invest equity in the business. Business angels invest smaller amounts of money (£10 000–£1 000 000) and operate in less formal ways than venture capitalists. This is also the permanent capital of the firm which can be used to finance long-term, permanent assets. These shareholders expect dividends and stand to see the value of their shares increase if the firm does well. They might also expect to exercise some degree of directorial control over the business. They will expect to realise their investment at some time in the future (normally 5–10 years) by selling on their shares in the business.

> 'You have to hang on to that initial money like its gold. Look after every pound because it will allow you to get your idea right and prove it. Nobody will give you money until you can prove your idea is a winner ... There's lots of money out there but only for proven concepts.'
> **Martyn Dowes**, founder **Coffee Nation**
> *Sunday Times* 23 May 2004
> ➜

Alongside this, a firm is likely to be able to borrow medium- or long-term funds from a bank which again can be used to finance medium- or long-term assets. The principle is to try to match the term of the loan to the life of the asset. Loans are serviced by regular interest payments and the capital will, ultimately, have to be repaid. Interest may vary with base rate or be fixed for the term of the loan. Agreeing to a fixed rate may involve a certain amount of crystal-ball gazing, but it does ensure that a small firm knows what its financing costs will be for some time to come. As we shall see in the next section, bankers are likely to look for the security of assets to act as collateral against the loan and, if they cannot get this, they may ask for personal guarantees from the owner-manager.

In the UK, where a small firm cannot provide a bank with the required security or does not have the track record to convince the bank to lend, then the Small Firms Loan Guarantee Scheme might be another way of getting finance. With this the government provides a guarantee to the bank against default by the borrowers. First

---

Case insight

Drive Assist UK may have been the fastest growing company in the *Sunday Times* 1999 Fast Track 100 companies but its growth was constrained by lack of capital in its early years. It was founded in 1992 by **Steve Binch** and **John Sherwood** after the car rental firm they worked for went into receivership. With £30 000 gathered from family and friends, they took no salary for the first 18 months, relying on their working wives to cover living costs. Eventually they secured two Small Firms Guarantee Scheme loans totalling £100 000.

The company provides replacement cars on a credit hire basis for drivers whose cars have been in an accident that was not their fault. From humble beginnings with only four employees it has diversified into accident-related activities like repairs and maintenance as well as car leasing and sales. It now has an annual turnover of over £150 million.

---

introduced in 1981, terms and conditions have varied over the years. In December 2005 the scheme was modified to reflect the recommendations of the Graham Review and as a result the scheme currently focuses on newer businesses. The scheme is administered through the banks, who continue to make all commercial decisions, however there are terms and restrictions. Information on the scheme can be obtained from the Business Link website or from most commercial banks. Many other countries have similar schemes.

There are two other ways of financing the purchase of equipment:

- Lease – which allows the firm to use the asset without owning it by making regular lease payments;
- Hire purchase – which allows the firm to purchase the asset over a period of time, again, by making regular payments with the asset acting as security in the case of default.

The main practical difference between the two methods is their tax treatment. The DTI (1998) produces a free booklet on this source of finance. Interest rates on lease and hire purchase schemes may be higher than on loans, but for a firm with little security to offer a banker they might be the only way to secure finance.

Short-term loans and overdrafts are most prudently used to finance working capital, like debtors and stock. However, most UK small firms make extensive use of overdraft finance. Most firms will use overdraft finance at some point in their life, but small firms in the UK have a far greater dependence on it as a source of finance than other firms in other European countries – 42 per cent of debt for UK small firms is overdraft compared to 17 per cent in Germany (Burns and Whitehouse, 1995b). What is more, they often imprudently use the overdraft to finance long-term investment. Overdrafts are ultimately flexible – once arranged with the bank they are available on demand – and cheap – although a higher interest rate is usually charged than for loans, you only pay interest on the outstanding amount. However, firms relying on this run the risk of the bank calling in the overdraft at any time and the high level of dependence seen in the UK may be linked to short-time horizons and pay-back periods for investment (Burns and Whitehouse, 1995a).

Factoring is a form of finance particularly suited to undercapitalised, growing firms, where the major asset on their balance sheet is debtors. The factoring company advances 75–80 per cent of the invoice when it is issued and the balance, less charges, when the invoice is settled. Interest is charged on the funds advanced at a rate of 2–4 per cent above base rate with a further administrative charge depending on the service required (they can take complete control of the debtors ledger and cover bad debts, if required), turnover and average size of invoice. It is therefore expensive, but for a firm growing rapidly it may, again, be the only way to raise funds. Factors do impose certain conditions such as minimum turnover, invoice value and maximum concentration of debt with a single customer. They will also insist on certain credit checks being undertaken on new customers. Where the firm retains control of its debtors ledger, this is more correctly called invoice discounting.

Finally there may be grants and other forms of 'soft loans' available to small firms. Grants are free, and therefore should always be taken if available. They vary enormously from country to country and region to region as well as changing frequently to reflect national and regional imperatives. In the UK the main groups that award grants are:

- The UK government. These currently fall into seven areas: research, development and innovation, access to knowledge, training, 'New Deal' (employment of the unemployed), young entrepreneurs (this is administered through the Prince's Youth Business Trust), economic regeneration and best business practice.
- The European Commission. In the UK much of this is distributed through the Regional Development Agency or the local Learning and Skills Council or local colleges;
- Regional Development Agencies.
- Local Authorities.
- Chambers of Commerce.
- County Enterprise Boards.

Business Link produces an interactive Grants and Support Directory for the UK which had some 2675 listings in 2005. The Directory allows firms to search for grants that might fit their requirements. This can be found on the finance and grants section of the Business Link website (www.businesslink.gov.uk).

Most firms use a range of financing to suit their differing needs and circumstances. The flowchart in Figure 13.1 attempts to guide the small firm through the process of deciding upon a suitable financing package. It is taken from the free DTI booklet on sources of finance (DTI, 1997). The advantages and disadvantages of these different forms of financing a business are summarised in Table 13.2.

Bank finance

Bank finance is the main source of external finance for the vast majority of small firms in the UK. What is more, it is a constant cause for complaint about unwillingness to lend, high charges and poor service. The 2000 survey by the Federation of Small Business of 22 000 of its UK members found that more than 70 per cent were dissatisfied with the charges levied by banks. Earlier in the year, the Cruickshank Report (Cruickshank, 2000) had found that more than a million small businesses were being overcharged by their banks to the extent of £500 million a year.

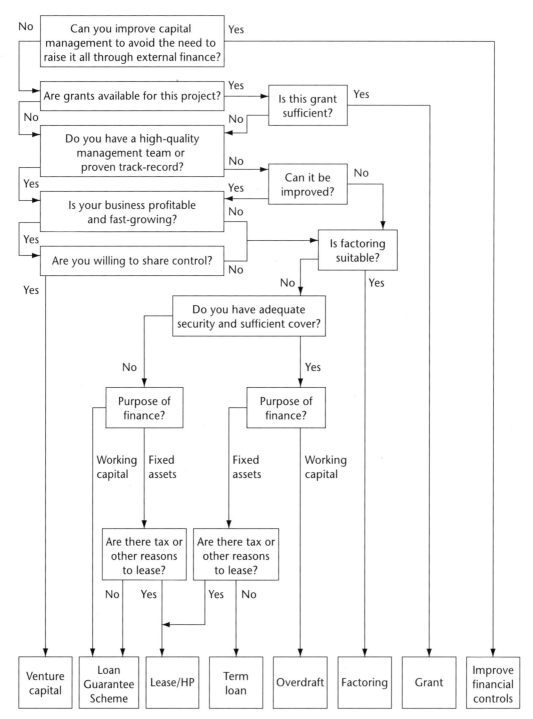

MAIN ELEMENTS OF THE FINANCING PACKAGE

Source: Adapted from DTI (1997) *Financing Your Business: A Guide to Sources of Finance and Advice.*

Figure 13.1 How to finance the entrepreneurial business

Table 13.2 Advantages and disadvantages of different forms of finance

Source	Advantages	Disadvantages
Family Loans	• Security unlikely to be required • Profit stays in the family	• Can strain family relationships if repayments are not made as expected • If business fails, all the family suffers • Family members may interfere in the business
Bank Overdraft	• Flexible – once agreed, available on demand • Cheap in that you only pay interest when you use it • Good solution to short-term financing needs	• Repayable on demand • Usually secured against business assets • Can be refused because of lack of security • Rate of interest charged is usually higher than loans
Bank Loans	• Term of loan is fixed – not repayable on demand • Interest and capital repayments fixed and known in advance • Rate of interest usually lower than for an overdraft	• Usually secured against business or personal assets • Can be refused because of lack of security • Requires good cash flow to pay interest and meet capital repayments
Factoring/ invoice discounting	• Security is on debts generated by sales – as sales grow, so too does available finance • Interest and charges deducted from balances paid to firm – no chance of non-payment	• Expensive compared to rates of interest charged on loans • Certain conditions imposed, including checks on new customers
Lease/HP	• Security is on assets purchased	• Expensive compared to rates of interest charged on loans • Requires adequate cash flow to meet regular payments
Equity/shares	• Good, secure long-term finance • No interest or capital repayments	• Dividends may be expected • Selling shares to outsiders dilutes your stake in the business and may lead to loss of control • Outsiders providing equity may want to interfere in the business
Business Angels (equity)	• Smaller amounts of equity available • Investment based on business plan rather than security • Investment usually made for 5 to 10 years • Often offers hands-on expertise • No interest or capital repayments	• Only really available to businesses with growth prospects • A significant proportion of the profits of the business will go to the investors • Dividends may be expected • Investors will want to sell on their stake in the business at some point in the future to realise their profit • Hands-on expertise may be seen as interference in the business
Venture Capital (equity)	• Investment based on business plan rather than security • Investment usually made for 5 to 10 years • Can offer longer-term strategic advice • Not normally involved in day-to-day running of business • Should be able to arrange loans to go with equity investment, if required • No interest or capital repayments, unless loans are part of the package	• Only really available to businesses with significant growth prospects • A significant proportion of the profits of the business will go to the investor • Dividends may be expected • Investors will want to sell on their stake in the business at some point in the future to realise their profit • Will require very detailed information about the company • Takes time to arrange

Despite this, few customers actually change banks (perhaps as few as 5 per cent each year), although this might be because they do not perceive another bank as being any better than the one they are at or because of the high switch costs associated with changing banks. All of which begs the question of the degree of competition between banks in the UK.

However, banks face significant problems in lending to small firms. Banks lend a sum of money in return for agreed interest payments and the repayment of the sum borrowed. They do not share in the profits of a highly successful firm. And if a firm fails, the bad debt is expensive to recoup. So, if banks make a 4 per cent margin on a loan (the difference between the rate they can borrow at and the rate they can lend at), then every £100 lost as a bad debt will need a further £2500 to be lent for the margin to cover it $(100 \div 0.04)$. Put another way, the bank has to make a further 25 loans to cover this one bad debt. Not unsurprisingly therefore bankers are risk averse and will do all they can to avoid a bad debt. What is more, they are all too aware of the failure statistics for business start-ups, which explains why it is often difficult to obtain start-up finance.

Even existing firms seem a risky lending proposition to a banker looking for security against their loan. Table 13.3 summarises the balance sheets of small and large companies in the UK. As pointed out by Burns (1985), comparison of the two would lead you to conclude that small firms, compared to large firms:

1 Overinvest in debtors and stock;
2 Underinvest in fixed assets;
3 Are overreliant on creditor finance – money that is probably due for payment in the very near future;
4 Are overreliant on short-term, particularly overdraft, finance;
5 Have insufficient capital and reserves and are undercapitalised.

As a banker you would see the small firm as the riskier lending proposition – higher, mainly short-term, gearing (particularly if creditors are taken into account) and fewer fixed assets to offer you security in the event of a bad debt. What is more, there is evidence of wide variability in gearing. Putting this in a European context, one survey in 1995 found that 56 per cent of small firms in Britain, France, Germany, Spain and Italy (52 per cent in Britain) had gearing levels of 50 per cent or less (gearing defined here as all loans divided by shareholders' funds) but 21 per cent had levels over 100 per cent (21 per cent also in Britain) (Bank of England, 1998). This had changed little since a previous survey in 1992 (Burns, 1992). Gearing levels tended to be lowest in Germany and highest in Spain, with Britain about average, although Britain was notable for its heavy reliance on overdraft finance – 42 per cent of debt compared to 17 per cent in Germany.

However, banks do not just lend on the strength of the balance sheet, they are interested in the general prospects of the business they are lending to and here the issue of information asymmetry – one party having better information than the other – arises. Where asymmetric information favours the small firm – the owner-manager having more or better information than the bank – the bank is likely to be more wary about lending because of greater uncertainty. This is less of a problem with larger firms because there is so much more public information about them and many independent analysts reviewing it for investment purposes. For the owner-manager it

Table 13.3 Balance sheet structures – small and large companies

	Small companies	Large companies
Fixed assets	32	57
Stock	20	14
Debtors	39	19
Cash	9	10
	100	100
Overdraft	13	8
Creditors	47	24
Long-term loans	9	15
Shares and reserves	31	53
	100	100

Sources: *Business Monitor MA3 Company Finance*, various issues, and Burns (1985).

means that they have an uphill task convincing the bank manager of the viability of their project. It underlines the importance of effective communication. For the bank, it means that they are likely to incur extra costs in getting the information they need to make and then monitor a loan, and it is worth noting that these costs do not rise or fall pro rata with the size of the loan. This is one reason why banks so often ask for collateral against a loan. Where sufficient collateral can be made available, the bank may feel that less information is required because the debt is more likely to be recovered in the event of default. What is more, bankers may also feel that the provision of collateral gives the owner-manager a strong incentive to see the business succeed. If the firm's balance sheet cannot provide it, the owner-manager may be asked to guarantee the loan, secured on their personal assets.

Interestingly, it has been argued that information asymmetry favours the bank for a start-up (Jovanovic, 1982). The bank manager may have a broader experience on which to base a judgement of whether a start-up will succeed or not than the owner-manager, who will probably learn mainly from the experience of trading. It is only by surviving that successful owner-managers distinguish themselves from the less successful ones.

One of the things that banks do to deal with the problem of information asymmetry is to create a portfolio of loans, combining a spectrum of different risk–return lendings across all the sectors of industry. The portfolio will always have firms that will fail but they will be more than balanced by those that survive and the risks the portfolio faces reflect those facing the whole economy.

The natural response of banks to the problem of information asymmetry is likely to be to charge higher rates of interest and to ask for collateral. However, it can be shown that charging higher rates of interest may not be to a bank's advantage because this discourages low-return but low-risk businesses (Stiglitz and Weiss, 1981). High-return but high-risk firms may continue to borrow but the banks do not share in their success – only their failure. The rational response to information asymmetry should therefore be to ration credit in some way rather than to raise interest rates, indeed

Table 13.4 Asset security values

Asset	% value that can be borrowed	
Freehold land and buildings	70	
Long leasehold	60	
Specialist plant and machinery	5–10	100% can be obtained by leasing but APR may be more
Non-specialist plant and machinery	30	100% can be obtained by leasing but APR may be more
Debtors	30–50	Depends on age and quality
Stock	25	Depends on age and quality and the significance of any retention of title clauses. Raw materials will be worth more than part processed stock.

Source: DTI (1997) *Financing Your Business: A Guide to Sources of Finance and Advice.*

whilst small firms typically do pay higher interest rates than larger firms, the difference is typically only a couple of points. If credit rationing is indeed taking place, then it leads to the question whether some borrowers are being excluded from access to credit, even though they might be willing to pay higher rates of interest. It therefore raises the question once more of the existence of a financing gap for riskier, growing firms.

In valuing collateral the bank assumes that the assets will be sold on a second-hand market and this typically leads to far lower prices being put on assets than many owner-managers would expect. Table 13.4 gives a guide to what to expect. Given these asset security values, it is clear that growing firms wishing to purchase new plant and equipment will have to spend more than the assets add to their collateral base. Because the business collateral base is insufficient for their needs they may well turn to lease, hire-purchase and factoring as ways of financing their growth and, if all else fails, the owner-manager may have to provide personal guarantees, perhaps using their house as collateral. However, this once more raises the question of debt gaps,

Case insight

Peter Kelly started **Software Catalogue,** his mail-order software business, in 1993. It is now called Softcat Limited and is one of the main suppliers of Microsoft products in Britain as well as providing a range of other IT products and services aimed at the SME market. However, success brought unexpected problems early in its life. Initially Peter drew up a business plan, put in £35 000 of his own money and found two external investors willing to each put in a further £10 000. The market of mail-order software was virtually untapped at the time and it was the firm's success that caused the problem. Within a year the firm had run out of cash and had reached the end of its ever-increasing overdraft limit as debtors were increasing at an alarming rate. The firm was overtrading – the classic example of success causing Death Valley to go on and on. Peter's response was to factor his debts – relying on the one asset in his balance sheet for security. It might have been more expensive than overdraft finance, but it helped the company survive, grow and become the success it is today.

particularly for growing firms, as it has been argued that a heavy reliance on collateral, particularly personal collateral, may effectively create such a gap because of the resultant erosion of limited liability status (Binks *et al.*, 1990). Many owner-managers observe that this frequent requirement to give personal guarantees means that the separation between a limited liability company and their own finances is little more than theoretical.

One solution to this problem, widely used in Europe but little seen in the UK, is the mutual guarantee scheme. Hughes (1992) points to their extensive use in Europe in 'pooling their private information about project riskiness and entrepreneurial quality, and developing mutual schemes to guarantee individual loan applications to banks by members of the group, after group screening based upon pooled information'. The problem is that, whilst individuals may benefit by easier access to finance and lower rates of interest, they also face the possibility of having to make good the bad debts of others in the mutual guarantee scheme.

The banker's perspective

Banks are in business to make as much money as possible with the least risk. Above all they want to avoid bad debts; they do not share in the profits of a successful firm, so they do not want to share in the risks. Bank managers are employees, they work in a highly regulated environment, and they have limited discretion. Two high-street banks use a computer-based expert-system which produces a lending recommendation for existing firms based upon historic and projected financial data and evaluations of various measures of competitive advantage and management capabilities. Lending decisions are heavily influenced by bank lending policies and procedures, and this can also reflect general economic conditions and the balance of the bank's lending portfolio. One bank can turn down an applicant that another will accept.

Having said that, bankers are likely to be interested in similar things to the providers of equity finance, albeit with a very different emphasis. Although the banker's priority is ensuring that interest is paid and the loan is repayable on the due date, making a judgement about the ability of management is also important. To this end they will want to understand the fundamentals of the business and to ask for financial information to enable them to measure management performance. The business plan is an excellent vehicle for providing this. However, make no mistake, bankers are interested primarily in the ability of the business to generate sufficient cash to pay interest and, in due course, repay the capital sum. They are interested in minimising short-term risks and are very keen to see good financial controls in place – tight debtor and stock control should lead to strong cash flow. They also expect to come first when interest has to be paid and that can mean delaying capital expenditures and reducing or delaying drawings from the firm.

Bankers see lending to a small firm in very much the same way as lending to the owner-manager – it is a personal rather than corporate relationship that needs to be established. One acronym often used by bankers as a framework for making lending decisions is **CAMPARI** (the name of a spirit drink). This spells out the criteria on which the decision is based:

Character	What is the business track record of the owner-manager and their personal credit history? Honesty and integrity are difficult to judge, but most bankers still think lending is a very personal thing and making a judgement on the character of the owner-manager is vital.
Ability	How able is the owner-manager to make the plan happen? This is about their management ability and their financial and business acumen.
Management	Is the management team adequate? The quality of management can be judged by relevant business experience, education and training, and proven track record.
Purpose	What is the purpose of the loan? Is it consistent with bank policy? Is it legal? Is it in the best interest of the business?
Amount	Is the amount requested correct? Have all associated costs for the project been included? Has the borrower put money in themselves? Is there a contingency?
Repayment	Will the business generate sufficient cash to make the interest payments and repay the capital? Is the repayment term realistic?
Insurance	Is security necessary? Is the security properly valued? Is personal as well as business collateral required?

Bankers are keen to look at certain financial information and ratios – based both on projected and past financial data (Table 13.5). The cash flow forecast is a vital document for them because it shows whether interest payments can be made. They are particularly keen to look at the break-even point and the margin of safety – this tells them about the operating risk of the business in terms of the overheads it faces and the margin it is able to command. They will work out the range of gearing ratios discussed in Chapter 9, which tell them whether the lender is over-borrowed and the financial risk they face. They will also look at the asset management ratios to reassure themselves that debtors and stocks are being properly managed. This is not to say that they will not look at the performance and profitability ratios discussed in Chapter 9, just that they are less important. Even after the loan is granted they will continue to monitor these figures, expecting to see annual audited accounts and budgets for the next year. What is more they will also monitor the bank account itself, looking out for irregularities and checking that throughput is in line with turnover expectations.

Banking relationships

The owner-manager and the banker need to have a good working relationship. A close relationship has the potential to provide the banker with the information they need about the firm and thus avoid the problem of information asymmetry. Like any relationship, this must be based on two elements, both of which have been weak between the banker and owner-manager:

- *Trust* – that both the owner-manager and the banker will honour the terms of the loan;
- *Respect* – that both the owner-manager and the banker are good at what they do.

Table 13.5 Financial data of particular interest to bankers

Cash flow forecast

Risk

Break-even point (£)	$\dfrac{\text{Fixed costs}}{\text{Contribution margin}}$
Margin of safety (%)	$\dfrac{\text{Sales} - \text{Break-even sales}}{\text{Sales}}$

Gearing

Gearing ratio (%):	$\dfrac{\text{All loans} + \text{overdrafts}}{\text{Shareholders funds}}$
Short-term debt ratio (%):	$\dfrac{\text{Short-term loans} + \text{overdrafts}}{\text{All loans} + \text{overdraft}}$
Interest cover:	$\dfrac{\text{Trading profit}}{\text{Interest}}$

Asset efficiency

Debtor turnover:	$\dfrac{\text{Sales}}{\text{Debtors}}$
Stock turnover:	$\dfrac{\text{Sales}}{\text{Stock}}$

Liquidity

Current ratio:	$\dfrac{\text{Current assets}}{\text{Current liabilities}}$
Quick ratio:	$\dfrac{\text{Current assets excluding stock}}{\text{Current liabilities}}$

Like any relationship, it is a personal thing that is developed by keeping in regular contact. That means visits and the provision of information. These days bankers like to make regular visits to their clients. They like to feel they know the firm and the individuals in it. More than anything, bankers do not like surprises. These are some of the things that start to make them worry that all is not well in a firm:

- Frequent excesses on the bank account beyond the agreed overdraft facility. This makes the banker start to think cash flow is not being properly controlled.
- Development of hard-core borrowing on an overdraft facility. This makes the banker believe that a term-loan would be more appropriate.
- Lack of financial information. If the accounts and other information does not arrive regularly, they worry about the firm's ability to produce control information and, *in extremis*, can become suspicious that all is not well.
- Unavailability of the owner-manager. If the owner-manager is never available for a meeting or even a telephone conversation, bankers will start to believe something is wrong. Most people do not want to give bad news and avoiding is one way of not having to.
- Inability to meet forecasts. The banker will eventually start to question the credibility of the forecasts and the owner-manager's understanding of the market.

- Continuing losses, declining margins and rapidly diminishing or even increasing turnover. At the end of the day the banker is really only interested in the ability of the firm to service its loan.
- Overreliance on too few customers or suppliers. The loss of just one customer or supplier can then create a disproportionate problem for the firm.

The relationship between bank, or more particularly the bank manager, and small business owner-manager is an essential ingredient in addressing the problem of information asymmetry. Put succinctly, good relationships help the owner-manager obtain and maintain finance and bridge any financing gap. Also, as you might expect, there is evidence that the closer the relationship, the greater the owner-manager's perception of the quality of banking service and the less likely they are to want to change banks (Binks and Ennew, 1996). It would therefore appear that working to improve the banking relationship benefits both sides. In recent years the banks have invested enormous amounts in training managers about both the problems facing small firms and how to analyse them, but also how to approach the issue of developing relationships. There are grounds for believing that a better relationship would prevail if owner-managers showed a greater willingness to participate in it (Hughes, 1992).

Venture capital institutions and business angels

Venture capital institutions provide equity and loan finance to businesses with substantial growth potential. The British Venture Capital Association has claimed that the UK has the most developed venture capital industry in Europe and is second only to the USA in the world (BVCA, 1999/2000). Since the inception of the BVCA in 1983, its members have invested almost £25 billion in thousands of companies. About half of all investments goes to help established companies expand and about a third goes into management buy-outs (the management of a firm buying it) or buy-ins (external managers buying a firm and normally replacing the management). There are over 100 venture capital funds and investments range from as little as £5000 to over £100 000 million.

Venture capitalists provide risk finance and the annualised rate of return they expect on their investment is high – from 30 per cent to 60 per cent, depending on the risk involved (Murray and Lott, 1995). They are therefore looking primarily for high growth firms to invest in. They reject some 95 per cent of the approximately 5000 applications made to them each year (Bannock, 1991; Dixon, 1991). The financing structure they put together varies from deal to deal. Usually they do not want to take control of the business away from the entrepreneur, so the deal usually involves a mixture of equity (less than a 50 per cent stake), preference shares and loans. Preference shares are normally non-voting, allowing the venture capitalist to take equity without taking control of the business. They give a preferential claim over the profits and assets of the business over ordinary shareholders. The dividend on them is limited to a fixed percentage of the face value and there is no right to a dividend if the directors do not declare one, but they always have priority over ordinary shareholders if dividends are paid. Most preference shares are 'cumulative' which means that unpaid dividends must be accumulated and made good before ordinary shareholders are paid. They also have preference over ordinary shareholders in the event of a liquidation. Some preference shares are 'redeemable', normally at their face value at some specified future date. Others are 'convertible' into ordinary shares, normally at the shareholder's option.

A 'convertible preferred ordinary share' is a hybrid form of share capital much loved by some venture capitalists. They carry the right to either fixed or variable dividends and allow the company to pay dividends on them without obliging ordinary shareholders to take a dividend which might, for tax reasons, be unattractive to them. When converted into ordinary shares, the right to these fixed dividends is lost and the shares become 'ordinary'.

Some 85 per cent of venture capital investment is in amounts over £100 000 and the average size of financing is about £3 million. Start-up investments therefore usually involve an investment in excess of £100 000 in a business capable of generating profits in excess of £250 000 within four or five years. There are relatively few institutions that regularly invest less than £100 000. The BVCA produces a free *Directory of Members* (2005), which gives a full list of venture capital institutions and their investment criteria and is updated annually. It also produces a very useful *Guide to Private Equity* (2004) which explains and offers advice on the venture capital raising process and outlines what should be included in a business plan intended for venture capitalists.

Smaller amounts of equity, between about £10 000 and £100 000, are also available from individual investors – called 'business angels' – either on their own or as part of an informal syndicate. Often this investment helps take the investee business to a point at which it is attractive for a venture capital firm. The typical UK business angel makes only one or two investments a year. Many have preferences about sectors or stages (seed, start-up, early stage, expansion, management buy-out or buy-in) of investment. Most prefer local investments in companies within, say, 100 miles from where they live or work. Most also prefer to stay anonymous. However, over the past few years a number of business angel networks have been established which act as 'introduction services'. Some of the networks can also provide help in raising finance

---

Case insight

Andrew Barber and **Robin Hall** left Rover, where they were design engineers, to set up their own company producing a specialist sports car – but only after they had taken the advice of their local Business Link. Originally they thought the car would sell to a mass market at a competitive price, but advisors convinced them to pitch it to a specialist market niche and charge £30 000 for the vehicle. In this case lower volume also meant higher price and lower capital needs. The Business Link also advised them where to get finance – the pair did not even have equity in their houses to offer a bank – and helped them develop and present a business plan. The company, called **FBS Engineering**, secured £240 000 from a Business Angel which it invested in premises in Brackley, Northamptonshire and tooling for its first car, called Census.

However, nothing in business is certain. It took the company two-and-a-half years to build eleven vehicles – three prototypes and eight customer vehicles (which were all sold). By that time cash flow had run out. The company went into administrative receivership in August 2003.

●

from other sources and in preparing a business plan for a fee. Many business angels belong to the British Business Angel Association, backed by the DTI. It has a code of conduct for its members and a directory of members is available on its website. Local business angels can also be contacted through the local Business Link or Enterprise Agency, who also have their own Local Investment Network Company (LINC) that seeks to match small firms seeking funds with potential investors. Investors receive a monthly bulletin of opportunities available, submitted to LINC as business plans from small firms seeking finance.

Venture capital is a cyclical business. In the UK, the 1980s saw recession followed by several years of increased economic growth, only to be replaced by recession at the start of the 1990s. The increasing economic growth of the late 1990s led to the massive investment in technology and in particular dot.com businesses only to be followed by a shake-out in 2000. Specialist venture capitalist networks have also evolved, such as First Tuesday, which specialises in finding venture capital for high-technology firms. Whilst the overall provision of venture capital has grown more rapidly than the economy as a whole, its provision is highly cyclical. One effect of this is that the time at which a fund is raised and starts investing has a major impact on its profitability. Irrespective of this cyclicality, Murray (1996) has argued that the industry in the UK is reaching its maturity, which means that competition is intensifying and profitability will increasingly be squeezed, whilst the 'big players' will consolidate their position.

> **Case insight**
>
> **Julie Meyer** and **John Browning** set up **First Tuesday** in 1998. The company brings together entrepreneurs seeking funding and venture capitalists looking to invest on the first Tuesday of each month. It specialises in high technology ventures. Starting as an informal network based in London, it now spans 28 cities in 15 countries around the world with over 41 000 active members, and has helped raise more than £100 million in seed finance. The business was franchised around the world. First Tuesday charges a membership fee but the bulk of its income comes from a 'marriage fee' of 2 per cent of the capital raised. The average deal size is £2.5 million. In 2000 First Tuesday was bought by Yazan, an Israeli investment company, for £34.5 million. A year later it was purchased by its network of First Tuesday cities, comprising a majority of the city licensees and a group of private investors.
> ●

The venture capitalist's perspective

Whilst venture capital institutions and business angels may look at the same range of criteria as a banker, their perspective is very different since, unlike the banker, they are sharing in the risk of the business. If it fails, they stand to lose everything. Consequently they are interested in risk and return. In particular they are interested in the return they will make on their investment rather than the security they can obtain from the entrepreneur. Because of this, the business plan is far more important to them and they pay far greater attention to the quality of management and experience of the entrepreneur and management team. When looking at the business plan they will apply the full range of performance criteria and profitability ratios outlined in Chapter 9 and summarised in Figure 9.4. In assessing risk the margin of safety is particularly important, but so too is a detailed assessment of the business risks. They will also want to be assured that they can sell on their investment at some time in the future and realise their profit. We shall expand on the venture banker's and venture capitalist's different perspectives on a business plan in the next chapter.

Most venture capital institutions will want to appoint a non-executive director to the board. Some, particularly business angels, may also expect a more a 'hands-on', day-to-day involvement in the business. However, others take a far more 'hands-off' approach and will only intervene in the management of the firm in exceptional circumstances. This is because they take a portfolio approach to their investments, diversifying the risks they face across industries and sectors. The role of the venture capitalist has been described as (Sapienza and Timmons, 1989):

- Offering support;
- Providing a strategic overview;
- Providing access to a larger network of business contacts.

> 'They're backing you. You've got to convince your investors that you won't give up. You've got to create a vision for your backers.'
> **Martyn Dowes,**
> founder **Coffee Nation**
> *Sunday Times* 23 May 2004
> ➡

As with bank managers, it is important to develop a close personal relationship with a venture capitalist – particularly a business angel. Ultimately they invest in people rather than businesses and, since they face more risk than the banker, they need to be convinced that the entrepreneur and the management team can make the business plan actually happen. Since they only make money if the firm succeeds, they are highly committed to helping the growing firm through the inevitable problems it will face. Many have valuable business experience, sometimes in the same business sector, and they can bring with them a wealth of business contacts. In short, used properly they can be a real asset to the firm.

Stock market flotation

Venture capitalists may expect high returns but they realise that their main reward will come in the form of a capital gain, rather than dividend or interest payments. Consequently they normally seek to realise their investment within 10 years. Often this means going for a public listing on a stock exchange – called a stock market flotation. A stock market flotation involves selling a percentage of the business in the form of shares on one of the stock markets. To do so requires a track record of solid profitability and good growth potential. Different criteria are required for each stock market which means that this form of finance is unlikely to be suitable for most businesses – a trade sale is far easier and cheaper. A flotation can be expensive and may mean a loss of management control. It certainly means that the business will then have to comply with a whole range of new regulations and disclosure requirements designed to make trading in their shares fairer – and this in itself has led some entrepreneurs to 'delist' their companies by buying back their shares.

Case insight

Fred Turok was born in Cape Town, South Africa, in 1955. His father was a white African National Congress activist who was twice imprisoned by the apartheid regime and forced to flee to Britain. Fred's time at school was troubled. He was dyslexic – a characteristic shared with Richard Branson – and was shunted around different schools. Whilst he was branded as stupid, his two brothers were very bright and both went on to become professors. Fred retreated into sport. He became a PE teacher in London, but that did not work out so he took a job at a David Lloyd centre as a swimming coach. David Lloyd saw the potential in Fred and made him a manager. It was here that he learnt about the fitness business.

Fred decided there was a gap in the market for a smaller club, so in 1990 he remortgaged his house to buy a loss-making private gym in a basement in Victoria in London's West End for £150 000. In the first year he turned a £30 000 loss into a £150 000 profit. Two years later he bought his second club in Kingston-upon-Thames and then a third in the Minories on the fringes of the City. The fourth club that he bought in Isleworth gave him the name for his business – **LA Fitness**. He paid for that in cash, but it used up every penny he had. So far all the acquisitions had been paid for by cash flow or borrowings but the business was doing very well and the fifth gym, a new-build in Golders Green, was also funded from cash flow. Fred's formula remains the same today – medium-sized club, always with a gym and pool, costing about £37 a month to join.

At this point Fred saw an opportunity to raise some money for growth by going to the stock market but the £3 million float (valuing the firm at £8 million) was only 50 per cent subscribed because another firm, Fitness First, floated just two weeks before it. Fred pulled the float and instead went to the venture capitalists 3i who put in £1.5 million in exchange for 30 per cent of the equity. After this he just kept building the chain. By the time LA Fitness had secured a Main Listing on the stock market in October 1999, 3i had put in another £1.5 million enabling the firm to grow to 15 clubs. The float valued LA Fitness at £55 million, including £15 million of new money. In 2000 the firm made a £10 million rights issue with a view to increasing the number of clubs even further. It also secured new bank facilities of £15 million with a further £25 million promised. By 2005 LA Fitness had 67 clubs with over 200 000 members and 3500 employees. Fred Turok had become a paper millionaire, worth over £20 million.

In May 2005 it was announced that the company would exit the London stock market and return to being a private company through its sale to MidOcean Partners, a private equity fund, and top management – including Fred Turok. The deal was worth £90 million (£141 million including debt) and Fred is estimated to have made £14 million on it.

'Yes I have banked the money but I also have a percentage of the institutional investment in LA Fitness which invests *pari passu* with MidOcean. My equity component is realised only on the success of the business, which is typically how venture capital works.'

Sunday Times 21 August 2005

There are three stock markets on which a business can be floated; the OFEX market, the Alternative Investment Market (AIM) or a full listing on the Stock Exchange Main Market. OFEX is aimed at smaller companies seeking to raise up to £10 million. It is the most 'junior' of the markets and, whilst it is regulated, the regulations are not as stringent as AIM or the main market. Costs are also lower but the pool of investors is limited and it is seen mainly as a vehicle for private investors rather than the public.

AIM was launched in 1995 by the London Stock Exchange with the aim of giving smaller firms access to the stock market without imposing on them the rigorous reporting and control requirements demanded for a listing on the Main Market. An increasing number of companies are seeking a floatation on AIM and a recent survey claimed that it was now the most popular market for those considering floatation, with the main market suffering a significant drop in popularity (HLB Kidson, 2000). It now has more than 550 quoted firms with an average market value of £29 million. To obtain a listing a firm simply needs to be incorporated and have a broker and nominated advisor who must be available at all times. Typically it takes at least six months to obtain a listing. Brokers ideally want two non-executive directors on the board to ensure a system of checks and balances. They also want some evidence of a track record that can assure them of good corporate governance. They are looking for quality of earnings – assurance that earnings will continue in the future with some degree of predictability – and prefer firms that offer some unique selling proposition rather than 'me too' companies.

The costs of an AIM floatation vary widely. However, with lawyers, accountants and brokers fees plus commission together with AIM joining fee and annual charge, firms with a valuation below £1 million are likely to find membership costs prohibitive. The disadvantage of membership is the exposure to greater outside scrutiny and the dilution of control and decision-making. Any owner-manager looking for an AIM quotation simply as a badge of success must realise that there is a high price to pay for it.

The two key reasons cited in the survey for floating on AIM were to raise funds for growth and to give investors and the entrepreneur the opportunity to release personal equity. This underlines the fact that AIM – and also OFEX – can also act as the first stage in the exit route that an entrepreneur may put in place to harvest the return from their years of personal investment in their business. OFEX and AIM are also the first steps on the route to a listing on the Main Market and once that happens the firm probably will have become large by any criteria.

> **Case insight**
>
> **Mears Group** floated on AIM in 1996 when it raised £950 000 and had a market capitalisation of £3.6 million, based on profits of £400 000. **Bob Holt** is Chairman and Chief Executive of the firm which initially provided councils with a range of building maintenance services, such as window replacement and kitchen refurbishment. He drew up a prospectus with his advisor, appointed a non-executive director and, after unsuccessfully approaching a number of brokers, found a sponsoring broker. The money raised was used to fund organic growth and acquisitions. By 2005 the company was still listed on AIM but, because of a highly successful diversification into social housing, its profits have leapt to £7.4 million on turnover of £173.7 million.

Is there a financing gap?

The question remains as to whether there is a financing gap – defined as an unwillingness on the part of suppliers of finance to supply it on terms and conditions that owner-managers need. Owner-managers who are unsuccessful in obtaining finance will always say there is. Survey after survey of owner-managers will reveal this to be a major 'barrier to growth'. However, just because the owner-manager might want finance – on specific terms – does not necessarily mean that it should be provided – either for the good of the owner-manager, the financier or the economy as a whole.

Case with questions

NDT (Non-Destructive Testing) is located in Strood, Kent and undertakes inspection and testing for the engineering industry – welding and crack inspection, ultrasonic and radiography inspection as well as destructive tests, material analysis and hardness surveys. This involves both on-site and laboratory work. NDT operates in a very specialised market with only about a dozen competitors in the UK. Its clients include many blue-chip companies and about 80 per cent of its turnover comes from 20 per cent of its clients. It started life as a management buy-out from Royal Insurance, who decided it was not part of its core business. The 12 owner-directors each own 5000 £1 shares (total share capital £60 000). The buy-out was financed by a two-year, interest-free debenture loan of £50 000 from Royal Insurance, repayable in two annual instalments and secured by a floating charge on the assets of the company. One year after the buy-out the company made a profit of only £4327 on turnover of £352 516. The 12 directors were paid £182 622. NDT's balance sheet from that year is shown below.

FIXED ASSETS (incl. vehicles: £56 000 and building: £40 000)		116 032
CURRENT ASSETS		
Stocks	4 350	
Debtors	53 334	
Cash	9 348	67 032
CREDITORS DUE WITHIN ONE YEAR		
(incl. debenture loan: £37 700 and vehicle HP: £32 441)		(103 395)
NET CURRENT LIABILITIES		(36 363)
TOTAL ASSETS LESS CURRENT LIABILITIES		79 669
CREDITORS DUE IN MORE THAN ONE YEAR		(15 342)
		64 327
Share capital		60 000
Retained profit		4 327

At this point NDT was successful in securing a contract from Aiton, of Derby, to test pipework in a power station. The contract was initially only for 10 weeks and the managing director, **Roy Davenport**, expected to finance this by using NDT's overdraft facility. Aiton was a large engineering firm and typically paid creditors in about six weeks. However, the initial work ➡

Economists would criticise the use of the word 'gap' and prefer to use the term 'market failure' or 'credit rationing' because there may be a 'gap' even in a perfect market simply because, for example, an owner-manager is unwilling to pay higher rates of interest or investors judge a project to be too risky. The preceding analysis has shown that 'gaps' can easily arise, largely as a result of information asymmetry, the fixed costs of providing small amounts of capital, in terms of assessing the project and monitoring the investment, and the requirement of bankers for small firms or owner-managers to provide collateral. Also there is the inherent reluctance of the owner-manager to share equity in their business. The question is, however, whether there is evidence that the gap actually exists.

---

disclosed some major problems which resulted in the need to test all the pipework in the power station. Staff on site were doubled after the first week, doubled again in the third week and doubled again two weeks later. NDT realised that the contract value would be over £3 million – ten times their current level of turnover.

The problem for Roy was how to finance this extremely lucrative work. Initially he relied on overdraft but within three weeks he had exceeded his modest overdraft facility of £20 000. The bank were very supportive but insisted that it could not provide the necessary funds without personal guarantees from the directors and not all of the 12 directors would agree to this. Roy decided to factor NDT's debts. Initially with some 80 customers on their books this worked well but the factoring company started to notice the heavy concentration of debt with Aiton. They agreed to a 40 per cent concentration, then a 59 per cent concentration and finally a 70 per cent concentration, but still the size of Aiton's debts kept mounting. When the concentration came to an unagreed 99.8 per cent the factoring company refused to accept any more invoices to Aiton.

Roy now had a major problem since Aiton currently owed NDT over £200 000 and, despite this extremely lucrative contract, there were no funds to pay salaries this month. He decided that he would go to Aiton and request a £100 000 advance on the work being undertaken plus a revision to the payment terms, which would mean that NDT received weekly payments one month in arrears. Aiton agreed to the revised terms but not the advance. Looking at the cash flow projections Roy realised that there was no way that the firm could undertake the work and survive without the advance. He decided to forgo the extra profit and withdraw from the contract.

Within 24 hours of him taking his men off site Aiton agreed to make the advance to NDT. What had not been meant as a threat had the same effect. Aiton realised that NDT was willing to walk away from the highly profitable contract because it could not finance the large cash flow deficit it created. Profit is not the same as cash flow.

Questions
1 Was NDT right to take the contract?
2 Was the bank right to do what it did?
3 Was the factoring company right to do what it did?
4 Was NDT right to pull out of the contract?
5 Was there any other course of action open to NDT?

On the one hand there is the evidence of the numerous surveys which ask owner-managers what they perceive to be barriers to the growth of their firm. Almost inevitably lack of appropriately priced finance will be cited as a major constraint, particularly for fast-growing and newer firms. However, this proves nothing – perception is one thing and reality another. Even if accurate, the lack of appropriately priced finance for certain projects may actually indicate that the market is working perfectly well.

The fact is that numerous surveys have been unable objectively to establish that a 'gap' exists in any systematic way. A survey of 1095 small, albeit mainly innovative, and growing firms by Aston Business School (1991) into growth constraints concluded that 'small firms in Great Britain apparently face few difficulties in raising finance for their innovation and investment proposals in the private sector'. Most authors agree. For example, Cosh and Hughes (1994) conclude that it is 'difficult to argue that there were financial constraints on business formations as a whole in the 1980s or that there is a more pervasive market failure for small firms in the availability of funds at least in quantitative terms'. Similarly, in his review of the literature, Storey (1998) concludes that 'the major empirical studies of the UK small business sector do not suggest the existence either of market failure or credit rationing on a major scale'. He adds that 'although there are instances where small firms are unable to obtain finance in the quantities and at the price they would like, the financial institutions in the provision of both loan and equity capital have increased their involvement with the small firm sector over the last ten years'.

Summary

The basic principle of prudent financing is to match the term-duration of the source of finance with the term-duration of the use to which it is put. Fixed or permanent assets should be financed with equity, medium- and long-term bank finance, leasing or hire purchase. Working capital should be financed by short-term loans and factoring, with fluctuations financed by overdraft.

Start-ups and fast-growing firms have particular problems raising finance. To get round this, they often 'borrow' resources and, where all else fails, like **David Moulsade** and **Optical Express**, they borrow cash from family and friends. Where they do not have the track record or security to obtain bank finance they may, like **Drive Assist UK**, be eligible for the Small Firms Loan Guarantee Scheme. However, most small firms prefer to rely on their own internally generated funds to finance their growth and development rather than to seek outside finance.

Leasing can be a particularly effective way for growing firms to finance fixed assets, matching finance with the security of the asset it purchases. Similarly, as **Software Catalogue** found, factoring, although expensive, can sometimes be the only way a growing firm can finance its way through Death Valley. **NDT** realised that if there is insufficient finance available to undertake a contract, even with factoring, then the company may have to walk away from it, however lucrative.

Bankers are very risk-averse. They do not share in the success of the business but stand to lose all their capital if the business fails, and therefore they will do all they can to avoid a bad debt. Small firms present a riskier lending proposition than larger firms because they have higher, mainly short-term, gearing and fewer fixed assets to offer as security in the event of a bad debt.

Information asymmetry is where one party in the lending transaction has more information than the other. Where this exists, it can be expensive for banks to get the information they need to make the lending decision and then monitor the loan. Banks' reaction to this problem is to seek collateral from small firms so as to offer them security in the event of default. Since the asset base of a small, growing firm is unlikely to be able to provide this, bankers often ask for personal guarantees from the owner-manager. Financing gaps can arise as a result of information asymmetry, the fixed costs of providing small amounts of capital and the requirement of bankers for small firms or owner-managers to provide this collateral.

Bankers look at a range of financial indicators in arriving at their investment decisions but they are particularly interested in the cash flow forecast because this shows the ability of the firm to make its interest payments and repay capital. However they are also interested in a range of business and personal factors, summed up in the acronym **CAMPARI**. It is important to have a good working relationship with the banker – it helps the owner-manager obtain and maintain finance and bridge any financing gap that might exist.

Venture capital is a mix of equity and loan finance for businesses with growth potential. Whilst the UK industry is the largest after the USA, it mainly invests in established companies and management buy-outs and buy-ins. It rarely invests sums of less than £100 000 and is not keen on start-ups unless they are capable of generating profits in excess of £250 000 within four or five years. There are some venture capital organisations investing smaller sums, but most of these investments come from 'business angels'. There are also specialist technology investment firms such as **First Tuesday** – which was a successful entrepreneurial start-up in its own right.

Venture capitalists share in the success or failure of the firm. Consequently, they look at the full range of performance criteria outlined in Figure 9.4 (p. 262). They are particularly interested in the quality and experience of the entrepreneur and the management team. They rarely take a controlling interest in the firm but typically ask to place a director on the board, although some ask for a more 'hands-on' involvement in terms of day-to-day management than others.. Typically they are looking for a 30 per cent to 60 per cent annualised return on their investment, normally taken as a capital gain in about ten years' time. As in the case of **LA Fitness**, often their capital gain is realised by taking the business to a stock market such as AIM and then on to a full stock market float. However, sometimes the entrepreneur ends up buying back their company.

Despite numerous 'growth constraints' surveys, it has been impossible to objectively establish that a financing gap – indicating market failure or credit rationing – exists in any systematic way in the UK.

Companies like **LA Fitness** and **Mears Group** have used most of the sources of finance outlined in this chapter to finance their growth at different stages. The appropriate source depends on what it will be used for and the business that will use it.

Useful websites

www.businesslink.gov.uk	Provides a practical guide to all forms of business finance and useful hyperlinks to related sites.
www.fairinvestment.co.uk	Provides an independent comparison of business banking services.
www.bbaa.org.uk	The website of the British Business Angels Association.
www.growthbusiness.co.uk	Provides a guide to UK venture capital funds.
www.venturesite.co.uk	A virtual network of business angels on which investment opportunities can be posted.
www.bvca.co.uk	The website of the British Venture Capital Association.
www.evca.com	The website of the European Venture Capital Association.
www.money-off.co.uk	A search engine for different sources of finance.
www.firsttuesday.com	The website for First Tuesday.

Essays and discussion topics

1 Does the financing gap still exist? If so, why? What are the likely consequences? If not, explain why.
2 What can or should the government do to improve the provision of finance to small firms?
3 How can banks improve the service they offer small firms?
4 If there is a financing gap, it is more the fault of the owner-manager than the banker. Discuss.
5 How can banking relationships be enhanced and how can they be hindered?
6 It is not fair to ask the owner-manager for personal guarantees. Discuss.
7 There is no such thing as limited liability for the owner-manager. Discuss.
8 What are venture capitalists looking for from their investments?
9 Why are MBOs and MBIs such attractive investments for venture capitalists?
10 Why do venture capitalists not invest more in start-ups?
11 Is the venture capital industry in the mature phase of its life cycle in the UK?
12 Why do entrepreneurs take their companies off the stock market?

Exercises and assignments

1 Interview an owner-manager and find out how the growth and development of their firm was financed and the problems they faced in securing finance.
2 As a bank manager, list the things that you would be looking for in lending to a small firm.
3 Interview a bank manager and find out how they go about making lending decisions and monitoring outstanding loans.
4 As a venture capitalist, list the pros and cons of investing in a start-up, other early stage and expansion stage ventures.
5 Investigate the provision of bank finance for small firms in Germany. Why is the system so different from the UK? Should the UK system be changed? If so, how?
6 Investigate the provision of venture capital in the USA. Is the provision different from the UK? Should the UK system be changed? If so, how?
7 If you are not based in the UK, research the sources of finance available to small firms in your country.

References

Aston Business School (1991) *Constraints on Growth of Small Firms*, Department of Trade and Industry, London: HMSO.

Bank of England (1998) *Finance for Small Firms*, 5th Report, January.

Bannock, G. (1991) *Venture Capital and the Equity Gap*, National Westminster Bank.

Binks, M. and Ennew, C. (1996) 'Financing Small Firms', in P. Burns and J. Dewhurst (eds), *Small Business and Entrepreneurship*, Basingstoke: Macmillan – now Palgrave Macmillan.

Binks, M.R., Ennew, C.T. and Reed, G.V. (1990) 'Finance Gaps and Small Firms', Royal Economics Society Annual Conference, Nottingham.

BVCA (British Venture Capital Association) (1999/2000) *Directory*.

BVCA (British Venture Capital Association) (2004) *A Guide to Private Equity*.

BVCA (British Venture Capital Association) (2005) *Directory of Members*.

Burns, P. (1985) 'Financial Characteristics of Small Firms in the UK', 8th National Small Firms Policy and Research Conference, Belfast, November.

Burns, P. (1992) *Financing Enterprise in Europe*, 3i European Enterprise Centre, Report no. 5, September.

Burns, P. and Whitehouse, O. (1995a) *Investment Criteria in Europe*, 3i European Enterprise Centre, Report no. 16, July.

Burns, P. and Whitehouse, O. (1995b) *Financing Enterprise in Europe 2*, 3i European Enterprise Centre, Report no. 17, October.

Cosh, A. and Hughes, A. (1994) 'Size, Financial Structure and Profitability: UK Companies in the 1980s', in A. Hughes and D.J. Storey (eds), *Finance and the Small Firm*, London: Routledge.

Cruickshank, D. (2000) *Review of Banking Services in the UK*, London: HMSO.

Dixon, P. (1991) 'Venture Capital and the Appraisal of Investments', *Omega*, 19(5).

DTI (1997) *Financing Your Business: A Guide to Sources of Finance and Advice*, URN 98/805.

DTI (1998) *Hire Purchase and Leasing*, URN 98/547.

HLB Kidson (2000) *Taking AIM: 4th Annual Survey*.

Hughes, A. (1992) 'The Problems of Finance for Smaller Businesses', Working Paper no. 15, Small Business Research Centre, University of Cambridge.

Jovanovic, B. (1982) 'Selection and the Evolution of Industry', *Econometrica*, 50.

Macmillan, H. (1931) *Report of the Committee on Finance and Industry*, Cmd 3897, London: HMSO.

Murray, G. (1996) 'Venture Capital', in P. Burns and J. Dewhurst (eds), *Small Business and Entrepreneurship*, Basingstoke: Macmillan – now Palgrave Macmillan.

Murray, G. C. and Lott, J. (1995) 'Have UK Venture Capital Firms a Bias against Investment in New Technology Based Firms?', *Research Policy*, 24.

Sapienza, H. and Timmons, J.A. (1989) 'The Role of Venture Capitalists in New Ventures. What determines their Importance?', *Academy of Management Best Papers Proceedings*.

Stiglitz, J. and Weiss, A. (1981) 'Credit Rationing in Markets with Imperfect Information' *American Economic Review*, 71.

Storey, D.J. (1998) *Understanding the Small Business Sector*, London: International Thompson Business Press.

14

Developing a Business Plan

Contents

- Why you need a business plan
- The planning process
- What a business plan looks like
- Using the plan to obtain finance
- The banker's view
- The equity investor's view
- Presenting a case for finance
- Pro forma business plan
- Summary
- Appendix 1: Business plan for Sport Retail
- Appendix 2: Business plan for Jean Young
- Appendix 3: Business plan for Dewhurst Engineering

By the end of this chapter you should be able to:

- Explain the importance of the business plan;

- Describe the business planning process;

- Develop your own start-up business plan to suit different purposes;

- Recognise the information needs of bankers and the providers of equity finance;

- Use a plan to assess the need for appropriate finance;

- Critically analyse a business plan.

Why you need a business plan

One of the most important steps in setting up any new business is to develop a business plan. It allows the owner-manager to crystallise their business idea and to think through the problems they will face, before they have to cope with them. It allows them to set aims and objectives and thereby give themselves a yardstick against which to monitor performance. Perhaps of more immediate importance, it can also act as a vehicle to attract external finance.

Success, for businesses of all sizes, is positively correlated with planning. Timmons (1999) claims that the vast majority of *INC.* magazine's annually-produced 500 fastest growing companies had business plans at the outset. In a research study, Woo *et al.* (1989) found that those firms which claimed to spend time in planning activities were those that experienced rapid growth. Another study by Kinsella *et al.* (1993) concluded that 93 per cent of fast-growth firms in his study had written business plans, compared to 70 per cent of matched firms. At a more pragmatic level, just try raising finance for your business without a plan and you will realise how essential it is.

Business plans do not have to be long and elaborate. In many ways the process of thinking through how to go about setting up the business is far more important than the final document and for that reason internal plans can be informal, working documents. Only when they are used to obtain external finance do they need to become a more elaborate 'selling document'.

The planning process

Planning is a three-stage process:

1 Understanding where you are;
2 Deciding where you want to go;
3 Planning how to get there.

The business plan is just like a road map and the planning process is just like map reading; decide on where you are and the town you want to go to, and then you can start to plan your route. You might decide not go in a straight line because there are longer but faster routes; you might be forced to take diversions because unexpected road works upset your plans; you might not get to your destination as quickly as you expect because the car breaks down. Indeed it is just possible that you will never reach your destination at all because of an accident. If you cannot decide where you are or where you want to go, the map is of little use. If you know where you are and where you want to go, a good map increases the chance of getting there. And planning the route will also help you estimate the petrol you need and the money you will therefore need to buy it. The business planning process is simple but systematic.

1 *Understanding where you are*

- Understanding your product or service and how it is better and worse than that of your competitors – your competitive advantage:
    - How do you compete in terms of price, quality and so on?
    - Is the product or service differentiated in any way?
    - How can this be reinforced?
    - Can the product or service be easily copied?
    - Can you discern any patterns in successful or unsuccessful competitors?
- Understanding who your customers are and why and how they will buy from you:
    - Can you identify market segments and can you get to them?
    - Are your existing customers happy with the product or service?
    - What is good and bad about your marketing mix?
    - Can more customers be found who are similar to your existing customers?
    - Are you selling to a niche market?
- Understanding your own and your firm's strengths and weaknesses:
    - What are your own aims, your own strengths and weaknesses?
    - How good are your people and your facilities?
    - Are you good at leadership and communication?
    - What are the critical success factors – those things that it is crucial that you get right if you are to grow?
    - What will be the critical problem areas if you grow?
    - Do you have money of your own to put into the business?
- Understanding the opportunities and threats that the market might present you with:
    - Are market tastes changing?
    - Is the market growing?
    - Are there changes in the social, legal, economic, political or technological environment that are likely to affect you in the future (SLEPT analysis)?
    - How easy is it for competitors to come into your industry (Porter's Five Forces)? Do you have new product or service ideas?

2 *Decide where you want to go*

- Decide the general aims you have for your business and for you. Do you want a lifestyle or do you want to go for growth? For some firms, aims become 'mission statements' – statements of what the owner-manager wants the business to become. For example, a medical general practice came up with the mission 'to provide the best possible healthcare for patients at all times by responding to needs, providing accessible medical and anticipatory care of the highest quality and doing all that is possible to improve the social environment of the community'.
- Set some specific objectives that signal you have achieved your aims. Objectives must be quantified, bounded in time and realistically achievable. They can then serve as useful goals and yardsticks against which to judge your performance. For example, an objective might be to achieve profit growth of 10 per cent with a minimum return on capital of 15 per cent. Objectives are the milestones on your journey. They tell you where you are going and let you know when you have arrived.

3 *Planning how to get there*

- Strategies need to be developed to enable you to achieve your objectives. Strategies are 'how to' statements. They are not complicated, they are just 'joined-up' tasks. Their development involves coordination of the different management functions – marketing, operations, people and finance.
- In particular, you will need to develop a marketing plan that produces a consistent and coherent marketing mix to address how to sell the product or service to the different customers.
- You will need to draw up financial budgets – profit and cash flow forecasts – to see what financial resources are needed to undertake the plan. Do you need to attract investors? Can you? If not, your plans might have to be modified.

The whole business planning process is shown in Figure 9.3, reproduced overleaf as Figure 14.1. Chapters 9, 10 and 11 covered strategy formulation and previous chapters have covered all the detailed aspects of the process. Figure 14.1 directs you to relevant chapters. The process starts with the aims of the owner-manager reflected in the vision or mission for the business. This was covered in Chapter 8.

The next element is a SWOT analysis (strengths, weaknesses, opportunities and threats) which gives a realistic appraisal of the options open to the business. This was covered in Chapter 9. The SWOT analysis should be short, succinct and easy to read. However, it is by definition a summary of the key issues emanating from the marketing audit and should contain clear indicators of the key determinants of success rather than just being a smorgasbord of apparently unrelated points. A useful discipline in writing a SWOT is to continually ask yourself what each point means for the business.

The SWOT, in turn, feeds into the business objectives and informs the analysis of customers (market segmentation – covered in Chapter 6). Business objectives should be quantified, realistic and set within a time frame so that they can be measured in order to know when they are achieved. Whereas a mission statement may endure for a number of years, the objectives of a business will change every year in line with commercial conditions. Objectives plot the route towards the aspirations for the firm, which are encapsulated in its mission statement. So, for example, if you aim to be the fastest growing firm in a sector, your objectives need to reflect this.

The marketing strategy is then developed into a detailed marketing plan, which involves constructing a marketing mix to suit each of the different segments the firm is targeting. This was covered in Chapter 6. Underpinning this is an understanding of the generic marketing strategy you are following and how it is to be achieved (covered in Chapter 5). The plans for different segments are developed into detailed marketing plans for each product/market offering – who does what and when.

These plans are then costed and developed into a detailed set of budgets known as a financial plan. The financial plan should contain a cash flow forecast, a profit statement, calculations of break-even and a clear statement of funding requirement. This was covered in Chapter 7 and there is a comprehensive example of budgeting in the appendix to Chapter 11.

Notice the numerous feedback loops where plans, strategies or even business objectives have to be modified because of resource limitations or other constraints. The business plan must be realistic. It is worth spending a few minutes thinking

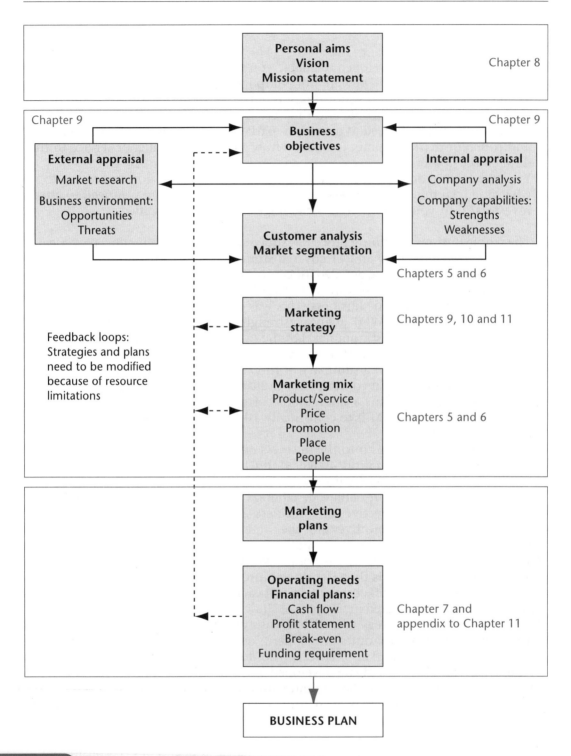

Figure 14.1 The business planning process

through how Figure 14.1 works and, if necessary, referring back to previous chapters to remind yourself of the component parts of this planning process.

Figure 14.1 sets out what Chaston (2000) would call a 'conventional plan' (see Figure 6.7). This is certainly what financial backers will be looking for. In the context of entrepreneurial marketing and the process Chaston proposed, this marketing plan can be described as the 'detailed map' (step 7 in Figure 6.8). The essential difference with Chaston's process is its emphasis on analysing the market, challenging conventional marketing approaches and trying to develop new approaches, within the capabilities of the business. This is a slightly different approach to the conventional SWOT analysis.

The great advantage of a business plan is that it forces you to think systematically and in detail about the future of the business. It forces you to think through the options that are open to you and justify the decisions you take, whilst thinking through the consequences of your actions. That is not to say you will anticipate all the problems you will face, but it will mean that you are better able to meet these challenges because you have a thorough understanding of the business and its market place. Remember, it is the process that is really important and a true entrepreneur is constantly refining or modifying their plan to meet changing opportunities and threats.

There are many sources of help and advice to assist in developing a business plan. Most banks provide free resource packs that include computer disks with pre-formatted cash flow forecasts. Once developed, it always pays to get feedback on your plan, particularly if you intend to use it to raise finance for the business. The more rapid the growth your business will face, the more likely you are to need advice. Indeed, evidence shows that fast-growth firms are more likely to seek out and use advice (Cosh and Hughes, 1998). However, it cannot be proved directly that the advice led to growth.

What a business plan looks like

There are no set rules that can be used to create a 'perfect business plan'. Each plan is particular to its business and will be different to others. Whilst later in the chapter we give a pro forma plan, even this will be adapted to say more or less about each heading, depending on the particular circumstances. One important point about the plan is that, as well as information about markets and finances, it must also convince the reader that you understand the operation of the business – how to do whatever needs to be done. If it is a retail business, do you understand retailing (for example, the importance of location)? If it is in manufacturing, do you understand the manufacturing process required? If a service business, how that service is delivered? Do you know what laws and regulations you need to comply with for your particular business? Some of the assurance needed will come through the track record of key people involved – their background in a particular industry – but usually it is a fine balance between including sufficient detail in the plan to convince the reader that you know what you are talking about, but not so much that they lose interest. Indeed, too much focus on the operations may convince investors that you are product- rather than market-focused – and that will definitely turn them off.

The seven-page pro forma at the end of this chapter covers the following areas:

- Business details – name, address, legal form, business activity;
- Business aims and objectives;
- Market information – size, growth, competitors;
- The firm's strengths and weaknesses as well as competitive advantage (who are your competitors and why are you different?);
- Details of customers perhaps with details of secured contracts – names, if selling to large industrial or commercial customers – or market segments, if selling to consumers. You need to assure the financier that you really know who will buy your product or service and why;
- Marketing strategy – advertising, promotion, pricing and so on;
- Premises and equipment needs. For a retail business location is vitally important. Remember also that a banker might be looking for security from these assets;
- Key people, their functions and background. Remember that investment is really in people, not bricks and mortar;
- Financial highlights – turnover, profit, break-even, funding details;
- Detailed profit forecast;
- Detailed monthly cash flow forecast.

This pro forma is intended for a relatively straightforward, small-scale start-up. For a large start-up, a proposal for development loans for an existing business or one seeking to attract equity finance would probably be longer, giving more detailed information and possibly covering forecasts for three years or more. A page showing key targets, with deadlines may be useful. Brochures and financial statements from past years might be appended. In these circumstances an executive summary at the front of the plan is essential – for a venture capitalist it may be all they ever read. The plan will also need a contents page.

Here are some further considerations:

1 When you write the plan have clear in your mind who it is intended for. If it is just for yourself, it can be brief, almost in checklist form. If you are trying to raise funds it may have to be longer. A proposal for venture capital funds may be 50 pages long, including appendices. *Have clear in your mind who your audience is and what they are looking for in the plan.*

2 Keep it as short and simple as possible. Do not pad it out. The plan should be sufficiently long to cover the subject adequately but short enough to maintain interest. To do this you need to be able to prioritise and focus on the important things for your business. Use appendices to provide necessary support information. Use Action Plans – which are not necessarily part of the Business Plan – to remind you of who has to do what, by when.

3 Do not exaggerate or overestimate the importance of your business idea. You do not need a great idea to start a business (but it does help); you need common sense, perseverance and time. Few businesses are based entirely on new ideas and a new idea is often harder to sell to financiers than an existing one, simply because they are unsure how it will work.

4 Ensure you are clear and specific. Are market segment clearly identified? Are objectives concrete and measurable? Are targets and deadlines clear?

5 Ensure the plan is realistic. Are sales targets, costs, milestone deadlines and so on realistic?

6 Check spelling, grammar, punctuation and, most important of all, financial accuracy. Errors damage your credibility and can throw you off when noticed as you present your plan. Word processors have grammar and spelling checks. A spreadsheet package can be used for the cash flow forecast and that will ensure arithmetic accuracy.

7 Ensure the plan is functional, clearly set out and easy to use. It does not have to be over elaborate or expensively produced. Modern word processing packages do an excellent job.

If you type 'business plan' into a Google search you will come up with, literally, millions of sites, most offering help, advice and products to help develop a business plan. There are books devoted solely to the topic and there is software to help you develop the plan. There are also a number of sites that offer you free specimen plans for a wide variety of different businesses. Try:

www.bplans.com
www.businessplanarchive.org
www.morebusiness.com
www.businessplans.org

Using the plan to obtain finance

Initially you need to decide who you are writing the plan for – bankers, equity investors or yourself. If you are writing the plan for bankers and investors, you need to decide whether you need equity or bank finance, or both. You need to decide how much and what sort of finance you need, so that you can decide who might provide it.

Start by working through Figure 13.1 (p. 352). This will give you guide to the main elements of the financial package you need. Next review your cash flow forecast for the planning horizon (say 3 to 5 years). Remember to show the money you take out of the business in this. The forecast will tell you how much cash you need – the maximum and the minimum. The cash flow forecast will also give you some clues about what sort of finance you need. For example, if the cash flow swings in and out of negative but shows no long-term negative trend, you may need only overdraft finance. If 'Death Valley' only lasts a year or so before cash flow becomes positive you may only require short-term bank finance. But if major initial investment is required in plant or buildings causing 'Death Valley' to be dramatic and long, you may require long-term finance such as a mortgage or a long-term loan or equity finance.

Finally, analyse your financial performance using the financial ratios outlined in Chapter 9, remembering to review contribution margins, break-even points and margins of safety. What do they tell you about the business? How profitable is the business? Venture capitalists are only interested in ventures that are very profitable, producing a return of at least 25 per cent per annum on their investment. Does the planned profitability meet this criteria? Remember also to look at the key ratios that interest bankers. How will the banker react to them? This financial ratio analysis will tell you how successful others will consider your venture and how attractive it is as an investment. It will also inform them about the riskiness of their investment.

The banker's view

Whether you want to borrow money from a bank or seek equity finance you will need to do two things:

1 You will need to establish a relationship of trust and respect;
2 You will need to present them with a business plan.

The reality is that both banks and equity investors ultimately invest in individuals, not in businesses or plans. The plan is just one way, albeit very important, of communicating with them. It must therefore reinforce the perceptions the banker or investor has of the individual(s) seeking finance. That perception must be that they know what they are talking about and that the business proposal has a good chance of success. However, banks and equity investors are looking for slightly different things and their approach to lending or investing was outlined in the previous chapter.

Banks are in the business of lending money; in that respect they are just like any other supplier of a commodity. However, about two-thirds of external finance for small firms comes from banks, which makes them an important supplier. The lending criteria banks adopt were set out in previous chapter. The thing to remember about them is that they are not in the risk business, they are looking to obtain a certain rate of interest over a specified period of time and see their capital repaid. They do not share in the extra profits a firm might make, so they do not expect to lose money if there are problems. What is more, the manager stands to lose a lot if he lends to a business that subsequently fails.

Bank managers represent a set of values and practices alien to many owner-managers. They are employees, not independent professionals. They often talk 'a different language' and are subject to numerous rules and regulations that an owner-manager would probably find very tedious. Since they trade in money, they often cannot make decisions on their own without getting approval from 'up the line'. In these circumstances the business plan is an essential weapon in helping them get authorisation for a loan. Any manager will only be able to lend within the bank's own policies, at acceptable levels of risk and with adequate security to cover the loan. However, each of these three constraints requires the exercise of judgement and can therefore be influenced, not least through the style and content of the business plan.

A business plan prepared for a bank needs to demonstrate how the interest on the loan can be paid, even in the worst possible set of circumstances, and the capital can be repaid on the due date. In this respect the cash flow forecast is something that the bank manager will be particularly interested in. As well as cash flow, they are also particularly interested in two important financial ratios:

- Break-even – which tells the banker about the operating risk the business faces;
- Gearing – which tells the banker about the financial risks the business faces from borrowing.

In an ideal world, they would like both of these to be as low as possible. Your business plan should address these issues head-on, by showing the calculations.

Bank managers are trained to examine business plans critically. So expect to be questioned. Make explicit any assumptions that the plan is based on. The plan should seek to identify and then reassure the bank manager about the risks the business faces. All businesses face risks, so the manager will expect them to see them identified. Bank managers tend to dislike plans that they see as over-ambitious, since they will not share in the success, so the plan needs to be conservative. Bank managers will always ask questions about some of the claims in the plan, so you must always be able to back them up. Avoid any tendency to generalise in order to disguise a weakness in your knowledge.

For a start-up it is particularly important to establish the credibility of the owner-manager and other key managers. Summarising skills and previous experience, particularly in a related field can do this. For an existing business the bank manager will be more interested in the firm's track record, particularly its financial performance, so previous financial statements will need to go with the plan. Where a long-term loan for R&D or capital expenditure is being sought, where there is little prospect of loan repayment in the short term, the plan must emphasise the cash-generating capacity of the business and take a perspective longer than one year.

However good the business plan, bankers are still likely to ask for a personal guarantee from the owner-manager. After all, if they don't ask, they certainly won't get it. And it does make any loan more secure, from their perspective. But be prepared to haggle and shop around. This is just a sales negotiation like any other and the banker is trying to 'sell' you a loan, albeit at a certain price and with certain conditions.

The equity investor's view

Individuals and institutions investing in unquoted companies are becoming increasingly sophisticated. Who these individuals and institutions are and their investing criteria are set out in the previous chapter. Most business people submit investment proposals to more than one institution for consideration. However, on the other side of the coin, most investment institutions are inundated with proposals. It has been estimated that less than one in 20 will ever reach negotiation stage. To a large extent, therefore, the decision whether to proceed beyond an initial reading of the plan will depend crucially on its quality. The business plan is the first and often the best chance that an entrepreneur has to impress prospective investors with the quality of their investment proposal. A good executive summary is, therefore, vital.

Because of this and the likelihood that the sums involved are higher than would be sought from a bank manager, business plans tend to be longer – more comprehensive and going into greater depth – and better presented. An equity investor, whether an individual or an institution, needs to be convinced of two things:

1 That a business opportunity exists which has the potential to earn investors the high return that they need, within a time frame that is acceptable. They are likely to be seeking a return in excess of 25 per cent per annum, including capital gains, and an exit route (sale of their investment) within five to ten years.
2 That the company proposing to exploit this opportunity can do so effectively. This depends on the firm's competitive advantage and the quality of management.

Any business plan must therefore address both issues. This requires a careful balance between making the proposal sufficiently attractive, on the one hand, while realistically addressing the many risks inherent in the proposal, in particular how rapid growth will be handled. To do this the plan needs to emphasise the strengths of the business, particularly compared to the competition. Behind all plans there are people, and equity investors, like bank managers, need to be convinced that the entrepreneur and key managers can deliver what they are promising. Venture capitalists often say that the single most important element in the decision whether or not to invest is the credibility and quality of the firm's management.

The most difficult aspect of any deal is deciding on the split of equity between the various partners. The simple answer is that there is no set of rules and the final result will depend on the attractiveness of the proposal and the negotiating skills of the individuals concerned. *Venture Capital Report* suggests the following rough starting point:

- 33 per cent for the idea;
- 33 per cent for the management;
- 33 per cent for the money.

It is also advisable to consider the objectives of the investing individual or institution. They will be interested in taking money out by way of dividends or interest and, over a longer period, through capital gains. What are they looking for and over what period? It may not be in the interests of the business to see cash going out in the first few years. Are there any tax implications to their preferred strategy? Are they looking to sell their investment? If so, when and to whom (their 'exit route')? This may be an opportunity for the entrepreneur to increase their share of the business by buying out the investor. It may also be an opportunity for the entrepreneur to dilute their share of the business or exit completely themselves, by encouraging a merger with, or

---

Case insight

Martyn Dowes set up **Coffee Nation** in 1996 with £50 000. The original idea was to sell ready-to-drink coffee from corner shops, but the idea only really worked when he switched from selling instant coffee to fresh espresso coffee and started securing contracts from national chains of shops, garages and hotels, rather than small retailers.

However by 1998 the concept still had not taken off and he was considering winding up the business because he had run out of money. Unexpectedly he met a contact from his previous job as a consultant who offered to invest £30 000 in the business. Buoyed by this, eventually he was put in touch with Great Eastern Investment Forum – a forum of business angels. He prepared a business plan and made a pitch to the forum offering members a 20 per cent equity stake in the business for £100 000 – effectively valuing the business he had previously thought of closing at £500 000. Martyn's plan was good, he was convincing and he got the money. Lloyds Bank matched the amount he raised with £90 000 in the form of a government-backed small-firm loan. Suddenly Coffee Nation was back on track.

In 2000 Martyn started looking for further expansion money, with guaranteed contracts from the petrol chain Texaco and the hotel chain Welcome Break. He found a firm of accountants to help him put together a further business plan and, after extended negotiations, secured £4 million from Primary Capital to roll out the business. On the back of this and with the track record of meeting every target set by Primary Capital, Martyn's next approach was to the banks, eventually securing loan capital for trials in Europe.

By 2004 Coffee Nation had a turnover of some £10 million from 170 coffee machines, with another 300 planned for 2005. A far cry from 1998.

buy-out by, another company. Exit routes and time scales need to be considered and agreed upon before any deal is done.

A related issue is how much control the entrepreneur is willing to surrender. Most want to part with as little as possible. Indeed few investors would want the entrepreneur's share to fall below 50 per cent, otherwise they might lose their sense of ownership and this might affect their motivation. Some equity investors prefer a 'hands-on' approach to managing their investment whereby they have a non-executive director on the Board, visit the firm monthly and keep in regular phone contact with the entrepreneur. Others have a 'hands-off' approach, preferring not to interfere once they have invested, perhaps meeting once a year to review the progress of the business. Finally, whereas a bank loan will probably take weeks to arrange, an equity investment will take months. It will involve numerous meetings, interviews and presentations. The investors, or their accountants, will undertake their own investigations into the business (called 'due diligence'). The development of the legal documentation will involve lengthy, detailed work. The sheer scale of the work is one reason for the continuing belief that it is difficult to raise equity sums below £100 000 from institutions, leaving the investment of sums less than this to 'business angels' who will either be willing to do much of the work themselves, or just 'take a risk'.

Presenting a case for finance

At some point the owner-manager can expect to be asked to 'present' their case for finance. Part of the reason for this will be to support and elaborate on details contained in the business plan but part of it will be to allow the potential backer to form judgements about the owner-manager, and possibly other managers in their team. They will be looking for motivation, enthusiasm and integrity but most of all the managerial ability to make the plan actually happen.

To get a business to grow successfully requires a genuine desire – amounting almost to a need – to succeed against all adversity. Owner-managers need to be able to motivate themselves and their team. They must be willing to take risks, but only moderate ones that can be overcome, and show to potential backers how this will be achieved. However, enthusiasm and drive must be tinged with a strong sense of realism in taking a market view of the business and its potential. Most successful companies are run by people who understand the market. The technician who has a good product idea but really only wants to build modified prototypes and is not interested in production, let alone selling and marketing, will not find anybody willing to back him without teaming up with others who have the qualities he lacks.

The presentation is an opportunity to demonstrate these personal qualities. First impressions are important, but an in-depth knowledge of the key areas in the business plan will go a long way towards generating the confidence that is needed. There are ways of enhancing a presentation. It is important to rehearse it thoroughly. Always stress the market and the firm's competitive advantage. Stress the competencies of all the managers. In terms of style, it is important to demonstrate the product and, in Western culture, to make frequent eye-to-eye contact. The owner-manager should manage the presentation with respect to any co-presenters. They should try to involve the investor and turn the presentation into a discussion or dialogue, responding to questions thoughtfully and honestly. Trying to weasel your way out of questions you do not know the answers to rarely works, so the best advice is to say you do not know but will get back with the answer in a few days.

A leading venture capitalist once admitted that, whilst discussions with the owner-manager centred on the business plan, the final decision whether or not to invest really was a result of 'gut feel' – a personal 'chemistry' between them and the owner-manager. At the end of the day, that chemistry must lay the foundation for a long-term relationship based, as with all relationships, on trust and respect.

Pro forma business plan

The business plan is a description of the business and what the owner-manager wants it to become over the next 12 months. It should contain targets, estimates and projections and describe how they will be achieved. It should help the owner-manager think ahead systematically and raise finance. It is an invaluable route map to help their business succeed.

The pro forma plan on the following pages is meant as a guide for how one should look. It is intended for a modest start-up. Notes are included in the relevant sections. A copy is available on the website accompanying this book (www.palgrave.com/business/burns). Specimen business plans based on this pro forma are shown in the Appendices. They are intended to be used for discussion only and not as examples of good or bad plans.

Business plan

Business name and address:

Proprietor's name and address:

Business form: [Sole trader/partnership/limited company]

Business activity:

[Enter here a description of the business, including product/service details. Obviously this is the core around which the plan revolves. It should describe it as thoroughly as possible, but can be supplemented with samples, photographs and so on. It should also give details of any intended future product/service developments.]

Aims:

[Aims for the business and the owner-manager should go here. For example, the aim might be to provide secure employment and an adequate income for the owner-manager and their spouse. The aims are broader than the objectives.]

Objectives:

[The objectives are the specific targets. For example, the objective might be to achieve sales of £150 000 in the first year and a gross profit margin of 40 per cent.]

Market size and growth:

[Market research information can go here. Try to estimate the size of the market the business is aiming for (either locally or nationally) and the share it hopes to capture, the growth in the last few years and any other characteristics. For example, it could be that there are many small competitors without the competitive advantage you have. A good product/service will sell only if a market for it exists or can be created.]

Competitors:

Names   *Strengths*   *Weaknesses*

[List major competitors together with their strengths and weaknesses. For example, there may be a major national competitor but they cannot deliver the personal service this firm offers. The aim is then to develop these advantages but also to counter any advantages competitors might have.]

Your business:

Strengths   *Weaknesses*

[In listing the strengths and weaknesses, the aim is to build on the strengths, particularly when they generate a competitive advantage. Weaknesses will need to be addressed in the marketing plan.]

Competitive advantages:

[Competitive advantage should come from the business strengths and weaknesses. This section also needs to address how the advantage will be maintained. For example, is there a patent or copyrights? Remember that if a new idea proves successful others will copy it.]

Proposed customers:

[This should describe the customers the business intends to sell to, if possible, naming names. For example, the business might intend selling to farmers in a particular geographic area. Try to quantify the number of customers.]

Advertising and promotions strategy:

[This should describe how the business will communicate with the proposed customers. For example, by telephone or mail shot. Will it be by advertising? If so what form might it take (for example, notice-board, newspapers, radio and so on).]

Pricing strategy:

[This should explain what the pricing policy is and why. Does the firm intend to be cheapest, most expensive or just take the 'going rate'. If relevant, it might describe how the price for a customer is arrived at.]

Premises:

[This should describe (size, location and any other special characteristics) the type of premises the business will operate from – private home, shop, workshop and so on. Note should be made of planning permissions required and cost – lease, rent or purchase.]

Equipment

[Any special equipment needed should be described here together with cost and proposed method of acquisition – lease, hire or purchase. Will more equipment be needed in the future?]

Key people and job functions:

[Key people, including the owner-manager, and their roles and responsibilities should be described here.]

Background details of key people:

[The background of the key people should be described here – qualifications, training, previous industry experience and personal strengths and weaknesses. If the plan is used to obtain finance, the owner-manager may need to give fuller background details. This helps establish credibility.]

Financial highlights

12 months to:

Turnover:

[This section summarises information from the profit and loss account.
Sales are the value of goods or services estimated to be sold in the year. It represents the value invoiced to customers and NOT the amount of cash received.]

Profit:

[Net profit (or loss) represents the difference between sales and direct variable and fixed costs. Out of this a sole trader would take drawings. On the other hand, the owner-manager of a limited company will pay themselves a wage or salary (shown in costs) but if they want to take more out of the business they might decide to do so by way of dividends.]

Break-even:

[The break-even calculation should be shown here. This is a measure of the operating risk facing the business. It should be as low as possible.]

Funding requirement:

[This should disclose any funding required and the months it is required, taken from the cash flow forecast. Remember, always to add something as a contingency against the plan going wrong. It should also describe where these funds are expected to come from.]

Source of funds:

[Here indicate the expected source and nature of funding (for example, overdraft for 8 months).]

Forecast profit and loss account

Business:

Period:

Sales:	£	(A)

Less direct (variable) costs:

materials	£
direct wages	£
other	£

Total direct (variable) costs:	£ _____	
Gross profit/contribution:	£	(B)

Fixed costs (overheads):

wages/salaries (including taxes)	£
rent	£
heat/light/power	£
advertising	£
insurance	£
transport/travel	£
telephone	£
stationery/postage	£
repairs/renewals	£
depreciation	£
local taxes	£
other _____	£
other _____	£

Direct (variable) costs are the costs of materials, labour and other expenditures that vary directly with sales activity. It represents the costs associated with the goods or services sold. It does not necessarily represent the total goods or services purchased, since some of these might have been purchased for stock. Nor does it represent the cash spent, as some goods might have been purchased on credit terms.

Fixed costs are the overhead costs of the business that do not vary with sales activity. For example, rent of premises. They do not represent the cash spent, as goods might be purchased on credit or services might be paid for in advance. Furthermore, items like depreciation represent an allocation of the cost of a fixed asset, not the cash spent on it.

Total fixed costs	£ _____	(C)
Net profit	£	
Less drawings or dividends	£ _____	
Profit retained in the business	£ _____	

$$\text{Break-even point} = \frac{(C) \times (A)}{(B)}$$

Cash flow forecast

Month:												

SALES

Volume:												
Value:												

RECEIPTS

Sales – cash												
Sales – debtors												
Capital introduced												
Grants, loans etc												
Total (A)												

PAYMENTS

Cash flow is the lifeblood of a business. The cash flow forecast shows where the cash will be coming from and where it will go. Each monthly column should show the actual amounts the business expects to receive and pay out. But remember, sales made in January may not generate cash until February or later if terms of trade are 30 days. Cash receipts, therefore, show cash coming in, including capital introduced and any loans or grants. Similarly, cash payments include loan repayments, withdrawals or dividends. They do not include depreciation, which is an allocation of the capital cost of an asset over its expected life.

The cash increase (or decrease) is the difference between total cash receipts and total cash payments. This is added to (or subtracted from) the opening balance to give the closing balance that month – that is, the surplus of cash in any month – which is carried forward into next month's column as the opening balance.

Materials												
Wages/salaries												
Rent												
Heat/light/power												
Advertising												
Insurance												
Transport/travel												
Telephone												
Stationery/postage												
Repairs/renewals												
Local taxes												
Other _____												
Other _____												
Capital purchases												
Loan repayments												
Drawings/dividends												
Total (B)												

CASH BALANCES

Cash flow (A)–(B)												
Opening balance												
Closing balance												

Summary

Developing a business plan is important to help you crystallise your business idea, think through the problems you might face and to develop a yardstick against which to measure your performance. It is also essential if you need to raise external finance, as in the case of **Coffee Nation**. The planning process is more important than the written business plan itself and a true entrepreneur is constantly refining the plan to meet changing opportunities and threats – even if this is not written down. Planning is a three-stage process:

1 Understanding where you are;
2 Deciding where you want to go;
3 Planning how to get there.

Starting with your personal aims and ambitions, you develop a business mission that leads business objectives that are quantifiable, realistic and bounded in time. These are based upon an internal appraisal of your business capabilities – the SWOT analysis. You go on to identify your customers and develop a marketing strategy based upon your marketing mix that will enable you to sell your product or service in the appropriate volumes to meet your business objectives. This is detailed in a marketing plan with can be translated into financial and operating budgets, called the financial plan

There is no standard format for a business plan; however, a typical one might contain the following:

- Business details – name, address, legal form, business activity;
- Business aims and objectives;
- Market information – size, growth, competitors;
- The firm's strengths and weaknesses as well as competitive advantage;
- Customers;
- Marketing strategy – advertising, promotion, pricing and so on;
- Premises and equipment needs;
- Key people, their functions and background;
- Financial highlights – turnover, profit, break-even, funding details;
- Detailed profit forecast;
- Detailed monthly cash flow forecast.

The business plan should only be as long as it needs to be. Keep it as short as possible, whilst delivering all relevant information.

A business plan presented to a bank needs to demonstrate how interest on the loan can be paid and the capital repaid on the due date. Particular attention, therefore, needs to be paid to the cash flow forecast. Bank managers are risk averse. To obtain a loan you need to gain their trust and develop their respect in your business ability. Credibility is vital.

A business plan developed for an equity investor needs to demonstrate that a business opportunity exists that can earn a high return (in excess of 25 per cent) in a five- to ten-year time frame and that the management team are capable of exploiting the opportunity. Issues of control and ownership need to be thought through.

Essays and discussion topics

1 List the contents of a business plan that is drawn up:

   (1)   For planning purposes within the firm;
   (2)   For raising external finance.

   How are they different?

2 Draw up a report for your superior in a bank outlining the criteria you recommend the bank to use in making a loan to:

   (1)   A start-up business;
   (2)   An established firm.

   How are they different? How much of the necessary information can come from the business plan?

3 How can computer-based systems help develop a business plan? What advantages do they offer? Are there any drawbacks?

4 What form do you think a business plan should take for your own, internal use?

5 In a rapidly changing world, is planning really of any use?

6 In a world 'turned upside down' and in chaos, full of uncertainty, how can you plan?

7 Are entrepreneurs congenitally incapable of planning?

8 Every business graduate can produce a good business plan, but not even one per cent can become entrepreneurs. Discuss.

9 The best business plan is a short business plan. Discuss.

Exercises and activities

1 Select one of the three specimen business plans in the Appendix to this chapter and review it. Critically evaluate the business proposition. Does the business require finance? If so, what form would you recommend?

2 Visit any of the websites that contain specimen business plans, select one and critically evaluate the business proposition.

3 Obtain another pro forma business plan by visiting the website of a major bank. Compare and contrast this to the one in the appendix to this chapter.

Appendix 1: Business plan for Sport Retail

Business name and address:

Sport Retail
14 Lower Street
Bedford

Proprietor's name and address:

John Bull
Address as above

Business form: Sole trader

Business activity:

The shop will sell general sportswear, clothing, footwear and sports accessories from a good secondary retail location close to the main shopping area of Bedford. Sports covered will include football, cricket, golf, tennis, archery, skiing and other sports, as appropriate to the season. In addition, the shop will sell general sports clothing and footwear such as track suits, trainers and so on. Suppliers will include major names such as Adidas, Nike, and so on.

Aims:

The aim of the business is to provide an adequate income for myself and my wife. We shall be living above the shop.

Objectives:

1. Sales of £250,000 in the first year
2. Gross profit margin of 40%
3. Net profit margin of 16%
4. Drawings at least £25,000

Market size and growth:

The last decade has seen a substantial increase in the popularity of sport and consequently the growth of the sportswear market. It is estimated that two-thirds of time spent on leisure pursuits is devoted to sport. The estimated size of the sport clothing and footwear market is some £1 billion. The market for sport equipment is about the same size and the market for swimwear and beachwear is over £200,000. These estimates are very approximate because the demarcation between sportswear and fashionwear is becoming increasingly blurred.

Competitors:

Names	Strengths	Weaknesses
Olympus Sports	Located in main shopping area	Lack of expert advice
Silver St.	Very price competitive	Lack of personal service
(400 yards away)	National promotion	Limited range
	Shop layout appeal to young	Lower end of market
2 Seasons	Skiing and tennis equipment	Poor location
Harpur St	Good service	Cramped shop, poor displays
	Well known brands	
Market stall	Cheap	No service
		Only open market day
		Poor quality low end of market

Your business:

Strengths	Weaknesses
Personal, expert service	Secondary location (better than 2 Seasons)
Wide range of equipment	Limited merchandising opportunities
Quality equipment	Cannot afford expensive promotions
Well-known brands	

Competitive advantages:

1. Personal, expert service
2. Football links – proprietor local football celebrity
3. Links with local sports clubs, schools and so on will enable equipment and sportswear to be purchased to meet their specific requirements
4. Wide range of quality merchandise

Proposed customers:

General public   Typical market segments: School age (male and female)*

Teenage and twenties

Middle age (mainly male)*

Impulse shopper

Dedicated buyer*

Sports clubs and schools*

* These are the groups we expect to attract

Advertising and promotions strategy:

1. Very limited advertising in local paper: shop opening and seasonal sales. It is proposed to get a well-known sportsman to open the shop.
2. Extensive promotion to sports clubs and schools offering special equipment and sportswear and 'discounts'. Displays may be mounted at Clubs and so on or special evenings could be arranged.
3. In-store seasonal promotions of particular sportswear or equipment. This could include special displays, promotional signs and, perhaps, a discounted 'loss-leader' to get customers into the shop.
4. Store displays would emphasise the professional football links.

Pricing strategy:

We cannot compete against Olympus on price and will not attempt to do so. We will offer good quality branded merchandise at recommended retail prices. We will attempt to stock alternative merchandise and brands to Olympus. We will offer good value for money but not lowest price.

Premises:

1000 square foot retail premises on Lower Street, Bedford. This is a prime secondary site close to the main shopping area of Bedford. Bedford itself offers a good location and is the main shopping centre for the north of the county. The premises are leasehold with 18 years to run, let on a full repairing and insuring basis with rent reviews every 5 years. There is a two-bedroom flat above the shop in which I intend to live with my wife.

Equipment

Shop display equipment only.

Key people and job functions:

Mr and Mrs Bull – Proprietors
There may be other part-time counter staff, as required for Saturday work and so on.

Background details of key people:

Mr Bull
Formerly professional footballer (joined from school). Retired 4 years ago. Worked as a salesman with Rank Xerox selling photocopiers to large companies. Made redundant 6 months ago.
Still maintains good links with local sports clubs and, in particular, old football club.

Mrs Bull
Housewife. No work experience since marriage.
Prior to marriage was employed as counter staff with Marks & Spencer.
Currently Parent Governor of Priory School and on organising committee for local Youth Club.

Financial highlights

12 months to: 30 April 2002

Turnover:

£250,000

Profit:

£40,000 before drawings

Break-even:

$$\frac{£60,000 \times 250,000}{100,000} = £150,000$$

Funding requirement:

Lease purchase	£20,000
Redecoration	5,000
Fixtures and fittings	15,000
Total	£40,000

+ Overdraft facility as required (see cash flow)

Source of funds:

Own funds	£25,000
Bank loan	15,000

We shall be seeking a 10 year, fixed interest rate loan.

Forecast profit and loss account

Business: Sport Retail

Period: Year to 30 April 2002

Sales:		£250,000	(A)
Less direct (variable) costs:			
materials	£150,000		
direct wages	£		
other	£		
Total direct (variable) costs:		£150,000	
Gross profit/contribution:		£100,000 (40%)	(B)
Fixed costs (overheads):			
wages/salaries (including taxes)	£ 12,000		
rent	£ 18,000		
heat/light/power	£ 3500		
advertising	£ 2500		
insurance	£ 1500		
transport/travel	£ 6000		
telephone	£ 3000		
stationery/postage	£ 2000		
repairs/renewals	£ 500		
depreciation	£ 4000		
local taxes	£		
other Professional fees	£ 5000		
other _____	£		
Total fixed costs		£ 60,000 (16%)	(C)
Net profit		£ 40,000	
Less drawings or dividends		£ 25,000	
Profit retained in the business		£ 15,000	

$$\text{Break-even point} = \frac{(C) \times (A)}{(B)}$$

Cash flow forecast

Month:	May	Jun	Jul	Aug	Sept	Oct	Nov	Dec	Jan	Feb	Mar	Apr	Total
SALES													
Volume:													
Value:	–	20.0	25.0	15.0	20.0	25.0	30.0	30.0	15.0	20.0	25.0	25.0	250.0
RECEIPTS													
Sales – cash		20.0	25.0	15.0	20.0	25.0	30.0	30.0	15.0	20.0	25.0	25.0	250.0
Sales – debtors													
Capital introduced	25.0												25.0
Grants, loans etc.	15.0												15.0
VAT on sales		3.5	4.4	2.6	3.5	4.4	5.3	5.3	2.6	3.5	4.4	4.4	43.9
Total (A)	40.0	23.5	29.4	17.6	23.5	29.4	35.3	35.3	17.6	23.5	29.4	29.4	333.9
PAYMENTS													
Materials	30.0	–	12.0	15.0	9.0	12.0	15.0	18.0	18.0	9.0	15.0	15.0	168.0
Wages/salaries	–	1.0	1.0	1.0	1.0	1.0	1.0	1.0	1.0	1.0	1.0	1.0	11.0
Rent	9.0	–	–	–	–	–	–	–	–	–	–	–	9.0
Heat/light/power	–	–	–	4.5	–	–	4.5	–	–	4.5	–	–	13.5
Advertising	–	0.5	–	0.2	0.2	0.2	0.3	0.2	0.2	0.3	0.2	0.2	2.5
Insurance	1.5	–	–	–	–	–	–	–	–	–	–	–	1.5
Transport/travel	0.5	0.5	0.5	0.5	0.5	0.5	0.5	0.5	0.5	0.5	0.5	0.5	6.0
Telephone		0.75	–	–	0.75	–	–	0.75	–	–	0.75		3.0
Stationery/postage	1.0				0.5						0.5		2.0
Repairs/renewals					0.25						0.25		0.5
Local taxes		0.5			0.5			1.0			1.5		3.5
Other _____													
Other _____	0.6	0.4	0.4	0.4	0.4	0.4	0.4	0.4	0.4	0.4	0.4	0.4	5.0
Capital purchases	20.0	20.0											40.0
Loan repayments													
Drawings/dividends													
VAT on purchases	5.3	–	2.1	2.6	1.6	2.1	2.6	3.2	3.2	1.6	2.6	2.6	29.5
VAT paid to C & E			0.5			4.2			4.2			5.5	14.4
Total (B)	67.9	22.4	17.75	24.2	12.7	22.4	24.3	23.3	29.25	17.3	19.7	28.2	309.4
CASH BALANCES													
Cash flow (A)–(B)	(27.9)	1.1	11.65	(6.6)	10.8	7.0	11.0	12.0	(11.65)	6.2	9.7	1.2	
Opening balance	–	(27.9)	(26.8)	(15.15)	(21.75)	(10.95)	(3.95)	7.05	19.05	7.4	13.6	23.3	
Closing balance	(27.9)	(26.8)	(15.15)	(21.75)	(10.95)	(3.95)	7.05	19.05	7.4	13.6	23.3	24.5	24.5

Appendix 2: Business plan for Jean Young (Consultancy)

Business name and address:

Ms. Jean Young
New House, West Street,
St Albans

Proprietor's name and address:

Ms. Jean Young
As above

Business form: Sole trader

Business activity

Management consultancy and training for the health care market.

Consultancy assistance with business planning, financial control and marketing will be offered. This will involve working with managers with responsibilities in these areas, to help them develop and use the necessary skills. Associated services will be the provision of standard or bespoke management training, developed to suit clients' needs and delivered at the clients' convenience. A range of standard training modules has already been assembled which can be used directly or tailored to suit client needs. The work will be carried out in association with one or more larger consultancy firms.

Aims:

To provide an independent income based upon my broad business skills and experience and to allow me to plan for the future.
My husband is also bringing in an income to the family that is sufficient to support us.

Objectives:

1. Income over £17 000
2. Profit over £12 000
3. To work with at least four separate organisations during the year
4. To obtain repeat work from them whenever it is available

Market size and growth:

The main market will be the four regions of the NHS in the south east of England: Oxford, North West Thames, North East Thames and East Anglia. Within these four regions there are 45 District Health Authorities, 29 Family Health Associations, approximately 100 NHS Units (mainly hospitals) and 81 NHS Trusts. In addition there are approximately 50 fundholding general practices. The regional and district structure of the NHS is undergoing massive change, with responsibilities being devolved to semi-independent organisations. All these organisations need to develop new management skills to cope with the changes and need help and advice to cope with the constant restructuring.

Competitors:

Names   *Strengths*   *Weaknesses*

Consultancy:

- Numerous small consultancies but the Directory of Management Consultancies in the UK lists only 14 in the relevant geographical area specialising in services for the health market.
- Large consultancies such as KPMG, PWC and Harvest usually take on major restructuring projects rather than work in the area I have targeted.

Training:

- Numerous sole traders, mainly ex-NHS employees with special connections. They tend to specialise in narrow, non-'business' fields and are often steeped in NHS tradition and practice. This is now often seen as inappropriate.
- Small consultancies are the greatest threat. They understand the NHS and are cheap. I can identify 10 small consultancies operating in the area.
- Large consultancies and education centres do not offer great competition in this area.

Your business:

Strengths   *Weaknesses*

NHS experience of training and consultancy   Small; could get overstretched
Small business experience   Possible perceived lack of credibility
Small, so flexible and responsive to customer needs
Low cost business to run
Only need to cover business expenses for first
    4 months

Competitive advantages:

The main success factor for consultants is good client relationships. Being small, these can be developed on a personal basis and services can be adapted to meet quite specific client needs. Some good relationships are already established and will be built on.

Also, I have worked in Trusts and hospitals applying for Trust status and am keenly aware of the issues they face. I have assisted business planning in a regional headquarters, worked with GPs and carried out training programmes for districts.

Proposed customers:

See section on 'Market size and growth'.

Buyers of my consultancy and training services will be at a number of levels within the NHS. There is no standard form of approach as each region, district, unit and Trust is different. However, there are a large number of discrete buyers, purchasing on an individual basis.

Advertising and promotions strategy:

1 Personal approaches, as appropriate, within the organisations. Brochures, advertising and so on are inappropriate.
2 Personal approaches will also be made to a number of the established small consultancies with a view to being taken on as an associate. This is an established mode of work, offering significant advantages to the firm and to the associate.

Pricing strategy:

Consultancy and training charges in the NHS range from £300 to £1200 per day (Health Service Journal).
I shall charge between £300 and £500, depending on circumstances.

Premises

Working from home as there will be no client visits. The local authority has confirmed that planning permission is not required. Consultancy will be at clients' premises and training at suitable venues.

Equipment

I already own a VW Golf and have an office at home with good quality PC, telephone and fax (value approximately £3600)
I need a laserjet printer, business software and overhead projector, flip charts and so on – cost approximately £2000.

Key people and job functions:

Background details of key people:

Ms Jean Young, BSc.(2i in computer science, Leicester University), MBA (South Bank University).
Age 34, married, one child
Work experience includes:
- 3 years as Senior Consultant with Talbot Hawkins, a small consultancy specialising in working for the NHS, including Trusts and GPs. Work undertaken included training and consultancy in the areas of business strategy, planning and marketing.
- 2 years as Business Development Manager with Saatchi & Saatchi, working with a range of public and private sector clients.
- 3 years as Business Development Manager with Medical IT, a small company providing software solutions to the NHS. My job was related to financial control and planning.

Financial highlights

12 months to: 31 October 1999:

Turnover:

£17,200

Profit:

£12,018 (before drawings of £6600)

Break-even:

$$\frac{5,182 \times 17,200}{17,200} = £5,182$$

$$= \text{approximately 13 days at a fee of £400 per day}$$

Funding requirement:

Printer	£1500	
Software	£300	
Other	£200	
Total	£2000	including VAT

Source of funds:

Own funds

Forecast profit and loss account

Business: J. Young, Consultant

Period: Year to 31 October, 1999

Sales:			£ 17,200	(A)
Less direct (variable) costs:				
materials	£			
direct wages	£			
other	£			
Total direct costs			£ –	
Gross profit/contribution:			£ 17,200	(B)
Fixed costs (overheads):				
wages/salaries (incl. taxes)	£	330		
rent	£			
heat/light/power	£			
advertising	£			
insurance	£	100		
transport/travel	£	430		
telephone	£	450		
stationery/postage	£	570		
repairs/renewals	£	350		
depreciation	£	2667		
local taxes	£			
other Prof. fees	£	175		
other Sundry	£	110		
Total fixed costs			£ 5182	(C)
Net profit			£ 12 018	
Less drawings or dividends			£ 6600	
Profit retained in the business			£ 5418	

$$\textbf{Break-even point} = \frac{(C) \times (A)}{(B)}$$

Cash flow forecast 1998/99

Month:	Nov	Dec	Jan	Feb	Mar	Apr	May	Jun	Jul	Aug	Sept	Oct	Total
SALES													
Volume: days	1	1	2	2	3	4	5	5	5	5	5	5	43
Value:	400	400	800	800	1200	1600	2000	2000	2000	2000	2000	2000	17200
RECEIPTS													
Sales – cash													
Sales – debtors		470	470	940	940	1410	1880	2350	2350	2350	2350	2350	17860
Capital introduced	2000												2000
Grants, loans etc.													
VAT on cap. expend.		299											299
Total (A)	2000	769	470	940	940	1410	1880	2350	2350	2350	2350	2350	20159
PAYMENTS													
Materials													
Wages/salaries Sec	10	120	20	20	20	20	20	20	20	20	20	20	330
Rent													
Heat/light/power													
Advertising													
Insurance		100											100
Travel Petrol	10	10	20	20	30	40	50	50	50	50	50	50	430
Telephone	120			100		100				100			420
Stationery/postage	130	40	40	40	40	40	40	40	40	40	40	40	570
Repairs/renewals		200						150					350
Local taxes													
Other Prof. fees	50											125	175
Other _____													
Capital purchases	2000												2000
Loan repayments													
Drawings/dividends					820	850	970	860	730	770	875	785	6660
VAT on purchases													
VAT paid to C & E		70			350			840			1050		2310
Total (B)	2320	550	90	190	1270	960	1190	1970	850	990	2045	1030	13455
CASH BALANCES													
Cash flow (A)–(B)	(320)	219	380	750	(330)	450	690	380	1500	1360	305	1320	
Opening balance	-	(320)	(101)	279	1029	699	1149	1839	2219	3719	5079	5384	
Closing balance	(320)	(101)	279	1029	699	1149	1839	2219	3719	5079	5384	6704	6704

Appendix 3: Business plan for Dewhurst Engineering Ltd

Business name and address:

Dewhurst Engineering Ltd.
Unit 7
Highgrove Industrial Estate
Coventry

Proprietor's name and address:

Nitin Shah
11 Prospect Place
Kineton
Warwickshire

Business form: Limited company

Business activity

The company specialises in undertaking high quality, high added value engineering work for local technology based companies. Such work is usually for prototypes, one-off projects or specialist requirements. The company was established in 1972 and is now offered for sale with its existing customer base by the owner who is retiring because of ill health. Excluding the owner, there are three full-time shop floor employees plus one part-time secretary/bookkeeper. The, as yet, unaudited accounts for the year ending 31 March 2000 show a turnover of £140,000 and a net profit of £10,000.
The company is offered for sale as a going concern for £50,000.

Aims:

To become a major supplier of specialist engineering services for technology based and other companies in the area (20 mile radius) within five years.

Objectives:

For year to March 2001:   Turnover £187,000, after tax profit £18,000.
For year to March 2002:   Turnover of £270,000, after tax profits of £30,000.

All of this to be financed through retained earnings and using the existing premises.

Market size and growth:

There are an estimated 250 technology based companies within a 20 mile radius of Coventry. The company currently sells to only about 30 of them. About 150 of the remaining companies are potential customers, judging from the Chamber of Commerce Directory of Companies.

Competitors:

Names   *Strengths*   *Weaknesses*

There are few direct competitors in the area who offer the same range of services. Most engineering firms concentrate on batch or production line engineering work in order to warrant the use of their expensive CNC machinery. The major competition comes from the potential use of in-house facilities by customers.

Your business:

Strengths
1. Good reputation for quality work
2. High level of repeat work
3. High level of service provision
4. Competent, loyal workforce

Weaknesses
1. Owner has let things drift during his illness

Competitive advantages:

No direct competition in the area.

Proposed customers:

The majority of existing customers are situated within 20 miles of Coventry. Typically, they are commercial companies or other organisations involved in R&D and/or design and manufacturing. They are technology based and include welding equipment, printing technology and new product R&D companies. Some work comes from motor manufacturers such as Jaguar. They value quality of work and service, including speed of delivery. A list of current customers is attached to this plan.

The marketing plan envisages doubling the customer base to approximately 60 companies within one year.

Initial orders, however, are likely to be relatively small.

Advertising and promotions strategy:

In the past, promotion has been mainly by personal selling. Over the last year, because of illness, the company has relied heavily on repeat business from existing customers.

Personal visits will be reinforced by direct mail to generate new customers. It is intended to mail 15 companies per month, which should result in 7 visits, from which it is hoped to generate 2 new customers.

Pricing strategy:

The component is usually a small part of the total product cost and therefore not subject to intensive price scrutiny. Currently pricing is based on 'cost +': a standard hourly labour charge + cost of materials + 40% mark-up. Sometimes the mark-up is increased when the job can stand it. However, sometimes jobs are taken on with a lower mark-up, to help contribute to overheads.

Premises

The company operates out of a 1000 sq foot unit leased from the City Council on the outskirts of the city. The lease runs to the end of 2002 at a cost of £6400 pa. This is very low. It is anticipated that the rent review will increase this by 50%.

Equipment

Existing: 2 × lathes   2 × milling machines   2 × gear shapers
1 × gear hob   1 × milling machine, horizontal   1 × surface grinder
Various other low value machines

All are fully paid for other than the milling machine on which payments finish this year.
No new machinery is needed this year.

Key people and job functions:

Nitin Shah	Managing Director
	Responsible for sales and organisation of production
Monty Young	Foreman
John Goody	Shop floor worker
Brian Johns	Shop floor worker
Sue Brown	Secretary/bookkeeper

Background details of key people:

Nitin Shah   Age 38
Formerly Production Manager at Hunting Engineering (a customer of Dewhurst).
17 years in the engineering industry, starting as a toolmaker and working up from the shop floor.
Experience and contacts in the industry.

Monty Young   Age 47
Foreman. Trained and qualified toolmaker. Been with the company 12 years.

John Goody   Age 38
Trained and qualified toolmaker. Been with the company 15 years.

Brian Jones   Age 43
Trained and qualified instrument maker. Been with the company 2 years.

Sue Brown   Age 27
Been with the company 4 years.

Financial highlights

12 months to: 31 March 2001

Turnover:

£187,380 (excluding VAT)

Profit:

£18,138, after tax
This represents a 48% per cent return on the £50 000 invested

Break-even:

$$\frac{118 \times 187.4}{143.8} = \text{Approximately £153,800 turnover}$$

This treats all wage costs (other than overtime) as fixed.
If wages were treated as variable, the break-even drops to £116,300.

Funding requirement:

The company is offered for sale as a going concern for £50,000.
This is not shown in the cash flow as it will be used to purchase the shares from the present owner.

Source of funds:

£3,000 own money
£20,000 loan for 10 years, plus overdraft facility of £15,000

Forecast profit and loss account

Business: Dewhurst Engineering

Period: 31 March 2001   £000

Sales: (excluding VAT)		£ 187.4	(A)
Less direct (variable) costs:			
materials	£ 28.4		
direct wages Overtime	£ 15.2		
other	£		
Total direct costs		£ 43.6	
Gross profit/contribution:		£ 143.8	(B)
Fixed costs (overheads):			
wages/salaries (including taxes)	£ 75.1		
rent	£ 8.0		
heat/light/power	£ 1.2		
advertising	£		
insurance	£ 0.9		
transport/travel	£ 9.4		
telephone	£ 1.8		
stationery/postage	£ 1.2		
repairs/renewals	£		
depreciation	£ 16.1		
local taxes	£		
other Professional fees	£ 1.9		
other	£ 2.4		
Total fixed costs		£ 118.0	(C)
Net profit		£ 25.8	
Less Interest		1.9	
Net profit after interest		23.9	
Less: Tax		5.7	
Profit retained in the business		£ 18.2	

Break-even point $= \dfrac{(C) \times (A)}{(B)}$

Cash flow forecast

2000/2001, £'000   *includes VAT   A schedule of debtor payments is attached

Month:	May	June	July	Aug	Sept	Oct	Nov	Dec	Jan	Feb	Mar	Apr	Total
SALES													
Volume:													
Value: *	16.4	15.3	16.5	16.5	21.5	16.5	16.5	22.6	11.8	23.7	20.4	20.4	218.1
RECEIPTS													
Sales – cash													
Sales -debtors *	8.0	13.2	16.4	15.5	16.3	17.4	19.9	16.9	17.6	19.8	15.1	21.8	197.9
Capital introduced													
Grants, loans etc													
VAT on sales													
TOTAL (A)	8.0	13.2	16.4	15.5	16.3	17.4	19.9	16.9	17.6	19.8	15.1	21.8	197.9
PAYMENTS													
Materials *	1.4	2.1	3.7	5.6	3.6	3.0	4.0	5.3	2.3	5.0	5.4	4.4	45.8
Wages/salaries	7.0	7.0	7.0	7.0	7.0	7.4	7.4	8.1	8.1	8.1	8.1	8.1	90.3
Rent			2.0			2.0			2.0			2.0	8.0
Heat/light/power													
Advertising													
Insurance					0.9								0.9
Transport/travel	0.7	0.7	0.8	0.8	0.8	0.8	0.8	0.8	0.8	0.8	0.8	0.8	9.4
Telephone			0.5			0.5			0.5			0.3	1.8
Stationery/postage	0.1	0.1	0.1	0.1	0.1	0.1	0.1	0.1	0.1	0.1	0.1	0.1	1.2
Repairs/renewals													
Local taxes												1.2	1.2
Other Prof. fees							1.9						1.9
Other	0.2	0.2	0.2	0.2	0.2	0.2	0.2	0.2	0.2	0.2	0.2	0.2	2.4
Capital purchases													
Loan repayments	0.1	0.2	0.2	0.2	0.2	0.2	0.2	0.2	0.1	0.1	0.1	0.1	1.9
Drawings/dividends													
VAT on purchases													
VAT paid to C&E	2.5			4.2			5.1			4.7			16.5
TOTAL (B)	12.0	10.3	14.5	19.0	11.9	14.2	19.7	14.7	14.1	19.0	14.7	17.2	181.3
CASH BALANCES													
Cash flow (A) - (B)	(4.0)	2.9	1.9	(3.5)	4.4	3.2	(0.2)	2.2	3.5	0.8	0.4	4.6	
Opening balance	(8.2)	(12.2)	(9.3)	7.4)	(10.9)	(6.5)	(3.3)	(3.1)	(0.9)	2.6	3.4	3.8	
Closing balance	(12.2)	(9.3)	(7.4)	(10.9)	(6.5)	(3.3)	(3.1)	(0.9)	2.6	3.4	3.8	8.4	8.4

References

Chaston, I. (2000) *Entrepreneurial Marketing: Competing by Challenging Convention*, Basingstoke: Macmillan – now Palgrave Macmillan.

Cosh, A. and Hughes, A. (1998) *Enterprise Britain: Growth, Innovation and Public Policy in the Small and Medium-Sized Enterprise Sector 1994–1997*, ESRC Centre for Business Research, University of Cambridge.

Kinsella, R.P., Clarke, W., Coyne, D., Mulvenna, D. and Storey, D.J. (1993) *Fast Growth Firms and Selectivity*, Dublin: Irish Management Institute.

Timmons, J. A. (1999) *New Venture Creation: Entrepreneurship for the 21st Century*, Singapore: McGraw-Hill International.

Wickham, P.A. (2001) *Strategic Entrepreneurship: A Decision-Making Approach to New Venture Creation and Management*, Harlow: Pearson Education.

Woo, C.Y., Cooper, A.C., Dunkelberg, W.C., Daellenbach, U. and Dennis, W.J., (1989) 'Determinants of Growth for Small and Large Entrepreneurial Start-ups', paper presented at Babson Entrepreneurship Conference.

Part 5

Topics in Entrepreneurship

15

The Family Firm

Contents

LEARNING OUTCOMES

By the end of this chapter you should be able to:

- Explain the significance of family firms in the business world;

- List the advantages and disadvantages of being part of a family firm;

- Describe and explain the conflict of cultures between family and business;

- Use a framework that helps identify points of conflict within the family firm and explain how they arise and how they might be resolved;

- Explain what is meant by an introvert firm and appreciate the dangers it faces;

- Use a framework that helps explain the problems of succession within family firms;

- Use a framework for planning succession;

- Describe what goes into a family strategic plan and how it might be developed;

- Describe what goes into a succession plan and explain how it might be developed.

The advantages of family

Starting up a business on your own can be a stressful, lonely way to make money. Many people start up a business with friends – they are known and trusted and may well possess complementary skills. So why not start up a business with the family? Trust is something that there is in abundance – particularly between husband and wife – and if all the family's income depends on the success of the venture then there is no doubting that the motivation to succeed will be strong, although this should be tempered with the recognition of the risk of having only one source of family income. There is the added advantage for husband and wife of giving each other support and friendship and working long hours may not be such a grind when with your partner. What is more, getting the whole family to help with the work brings an added resource to the firm – and one that may not have to be paid a wage.

Husband and wife teams, like Anita and Gordon Roddick of Body Shop, can work very successfully. For some couples being together all the time can help in their personal as well as business relationships; for others it might be a recipe for divorce and business failure. As with many issues relating to the family firm, there are few hard and fast rules. Conflict is most likely to arise in making decisions and here clear role definition and a separation between work and home are important. Based upon interviews with husband and wife teams in the USA, Nelton (1986) suggested that the successful teams shared the following characteristics:

- Marriage and children came first;
- The partners had enormous respect for each other;
- There was close communication between partners;
- Partners' talents and attitudes were complementary;
- Partners defined their individual responsibilities carefully;
- Partners competed with other companies, not each other;
- Partners kept their egos in check.

There is no theoretical justification for or clear evidence that family firms outperform non-family firms. Nevertheless, family firms have their advantages. Leach (1996) lists seven:

1 *Commitment*: family enthusiasm and family ties can develop added commitment and loyalty;
2 *Knowledge*: special ways of doing things in the business can be coveted and protected within the family;
3 *Flexibility in time, work and money*: putting work and time into the business when necessary and taking money out when the business can afford it rather than according to the dictate of a contract;
4 *Long-range planning*: because the firm is seen as the family's main store of value, something to be passed on to the next generation, family firms are better than others at taking a long-term view, although this may not involve formal planning processes;
5 *A stable culture*: relationships in family firms have had a long time to develop and the company's ethics and working practices are therefore stable and well established;

6 *Speedy decision-making*: like owner-managed companies, family firms can make decisions quickly because of the short lines of responsibility;

7 *Reliability and pride*: because of the commitment and the stability of their culture family firms can be very solid and reliable structures that, over time, build up good reputations with customers, reputations that the family guard with fierce pride;

Traditionally family businesses have been important in many primary sectors, such as farming. They also tend to thrive in areas such as hotels and restaurants, where high levels of personal service are required. The retail sector – butchers, bakers, florists, corner stores and so on – also boasts a large number of family firms. Family firms are also to be found in the cash generating food-processing industry. Finally there are many in the supply industries like transport and distributorships, especially in the motor sector.

> 'Inevitably when you are talking about family businesses there is a sense of generation. There has to be something to hand down, which is the greater shareholder argument of the long-term view. Other sorts of business may have different time horizons.'
> **Sir Adrian Cadbury**,
> *The Times* 8 July 2000
> ➡

> 'The continued strength of the Baxter's brand springs from the knowledge, involvement, passion and standards of the Baxter family. We determine the priorities and destiny of the company and so ensure that our family values are always reflected in all the products bearing the Baxter name.'
> **Audrey Baxter**, MD, **Baxter's Soups**
> *The Times* 8 July 2000
> ●

Family business is big business

It is estimated that as many as 70 per cent of all UK businesses are family owned and they employ 50 per cent of the country's workforce (Institute for Small Business Affairs, 1999). In the European Union the proportion of family firms is claimed to be 85 per cent, whilst in the USA the proportion is as high as 90 per cent (Poutziouris and Chittenden, 1996). What is more, the stereotypical image of family living above the shop does not do the sector credit. They are not all small, lifestyle firms. Family-owned companies account for a substantial proportion of the value of the stock market. In the USA, family firms – where a family own more than a quarter of the shares – represent more than a third of the Fortune 500 (Leach, 1996). In Europe the pattern is similar. But most family firms – of any size – are privately owned.

Family firms have some of the strongest brands in business today. Mars, Lego and Levi Strauss are global brands and remain private, family companies. In Britain many family firms are household names – R. Griggs Group (maker of the famous Doc Martens boots, founded 1901), J. Barbour & Sons (maker of the very British waxed jackets, founded in 1894), Wilkin & Sons (maker of the famous Tiptree jams founded in 1885), Morgan Motor Company (maker of Morgan sports cars, founded in 1909 and the world's oldest privately owned car manufacturer) and Quad Electroacoustics (maker of distinctive hi-fi equipment, founded in 1936). However, until it merged with Schweppes in 1969, probably the best-known family firm in Britain was the chocolate and cocoa manufacturer J. Cadbury & Sons, founded in 1924.

Timberland is a third generation family firm which started life as a small shoe company in south-east Boston, USA. Today **Jeff Swartz** leads the company and it has extended its product range from durable outdoor footwear to include durable outdoor clothing as well as opening a number of prominently-sited retail outlets selling its boots and other branded products. The company has an annual turnover of some £700 million ($1.3 billion) with profits in the first quarter of 2004 of some £16 million ($31 million).

Whilst Timberland is a strong retail brand, the business is also based on strong ethical foundations. Like his family, Jeff Swartz is an orthodox Jew and the values of the business reflect those of the family and its religion. It has a motto: 'Doing good by doing well.' And Timberland believes that these values reinforce the brand, because customers care about the same things as the company.

Timberland has a volunteering programme which allows employees to spend up to 40 hours paid-time a year on community projects. 95 per cent of employees use some portion of this time and in 2003 the Timberland workforce put in some 270 000 hours of community service. Alongside this Timberland has carved out a role as an industry leader in setting high working standards in its factories and in those of its suppliers. In part this stems from an accident Jeff's grandfather had when working late the night before his wedding in which his hand got caught in a machine and his fingers were severed. Timberland is also aiming to be free of toxins, carbon neutral and use 100% renewable resources.

'Investment in the community is important to me because this is a family company. It's not just because my grandfather and my father grew up on the factory floor but because I did too. Workers' health and safety, for instance, isn't just an ideal. It's as visceral to me as the missing fingers on my grandfather's hand.'

The Times 29 May 2004

Question
How important is ethical underpinning to the vision, values and culture of a business as well as its brand?

Not only have these firms been around a long time, but also the values and beliefs on which they were established are well-known and respected. Familial brands build consumer trust over long periods and can be very valuable assets.

Indeed, many of the best-known brands today started out as family firms before becoming public companies. For example, the H.J. Heinz company was in family hands until 1946, when it went public. It was founded in 1888, although Henry J. Heinz started producing bottled condiments from 1869. Many companies still have links with the founding family. For example, the Ford Motor Company was launched by Henry Ford in a converted wagon factory in Detroit in 1903. His great grandson, William Ford Jr was appointed chairman in 1998. The Disney Corporation is the largest entertainment conglomerate in the world. The vice-chairman, Roy E. Disney, is a descendant of the original Disney family and is the main principal shareholder.

The family firm has been the backbone of many continental European economies for decades. None more so than Italy where names like Agnelli, Pirelli and De Benedetti have long controlled large parts of Italy's industry. Because of the

Case insight

Cadbury merged with Schweppes in 1969, but the original family business was very much based on Quaker values and ideals. Founded by **John Cadbury** in 1824, the original shop sold drinking chocolate as a virtuous alternative to alcohol. In 1834 the firm started manufacturing drinking chocolate and cocoa.

John Cadbury's sons, George and Richard, saw the real expansion of the business. Whilst Richard concentrated on marketing, including the box designs for their chocolates, George concentrated on production. It was he who founded the now legendary Bournville factory and the picturesque village with its red-brick terraces, cottages, duck ponds and wide open park lands. Not only were workers given a fair day's pay, they were also rewarded with homes and education for their children.

Sir Adrian Cadbury, now sitting at the head of the chocolate-making family, has little to do with the company that was handed down from generation to generation for almost 200 years. He still believes that the closeness of family ties and the values that lie behind them are important. He even claims to sign his name in a strikingly similar way to the company's trademark name. However, today there is no longer a member of the family on the Board of Cadbury Schweppes and its values and ideals look more like those of a public company than a family business.

●

historically strong family networks, Italian owner-managers have been loath to surrender even part of the equity capital of their firms to investors and non-family managers have rarely received shares or share options.

But all this begs the question of what constitutes a family business. Essentially a family business is one that is owned or controlled by one family, although researchers have suggested many more precise definitions, for example:

1 An owner-managed enterprise with family members predominantly involved in its administration, operations and the determination of its destiny. Family members may include parents, children and grand-children; spouses; brothers, sisters and cousins (Poutziouris, 1994).
2 A company in which majority ownership (in terms of shares) or control lies in a single family and in which two or more family members are, or at some time were, directly involved in the business (Rosenblatt *et al.*, 1985).
3 For a quoted company, one in which 25 per cent of voting shares are controlled by the family (Nelton, 1986).

The search for a precise definition could be endless and rather fruitless. Probably the real answer is to ask the family. If family members are involved in the firm and feel a responsibility for it, then that is a good indication that it is a family business. They will probably say it is anyway. One of the overriding characteristics of the family business is the atmosphere of belonging and common purpose. Just as the small firm has the personality of the owner-manager imprinted on it, so the culture of the family is imprinted on the family firm. Rather than 'two arms, two legs and a giant ego', you have many arms, legs and egos. It is no wonder that the *Spectator* magazine once described the family business sector as 'an endless soap opera of patriarchs and matriarchs, black sheep and prodigal sons, hubris and nemesis'. And there you have the problem.

A conflict of cultures

At the heart of the family firm are its distinctive values and beliefs – its culture. Often the family culture can strengthen the business. For example, many successful family firms such as J. Cadbury & Sons and Wilkin & Sons were built around strong religious ethics whereby the success of the firm was shared with the workforce. In many ways the workforce becomes an extended family and relationships are cemented with trust and respect for the founding family. Families can display their values and beliefs in all sorts of quirky ways in the family firm. Sometimes these are good for the firm. They can bring clear values, beliefs and a focused direction. However, they can also bring a lack of professionalism, nepotism rather than meritocracy, rigidity and family conflict or feuding into the workplace. Any consultant who has worked with family firms realises how important it is to understand the family politics if they are to understand how the business operates.

Whilst family culture can be a tremendous asset for the firm, it can also create the potential for conflict. The problem arises when there are differences between the family and business cultures. Families exist primarily to take care and to nurture family members, whereas firms exist to profitably generate goods and services. Represented in Figure 15.1, the family culture is based on emotion emphasising loyalty, caring and sharing. It is inward-looking and lasts a lifetime. In contrast, business culture is unemotional, task-orientated and is based on self-interest. It is outward-looking, rewarding performance and penalising lack of performance. Conflict between the two cultures is unlikely at start-up but, as the firm grows and time passes, the potential for conflict increases.

The emotion-based family culture operates at a subconscious level. There are deep emotional ties that create love, trust and loyalty; but equally there can be disruptive influences like divorce, rivalry between brothers or conflict between son and father. Whilst families are based on permanence and stability, entrepreneurial firms are based on opportunity and change. Even the positive influences of the family may be bad for the business, for example, when parental pride and loyalty gets in the way of objectivity and a son or daughter is appointed to a management position they do not have the skills to undertake. If there is a conflict of interest between the family and

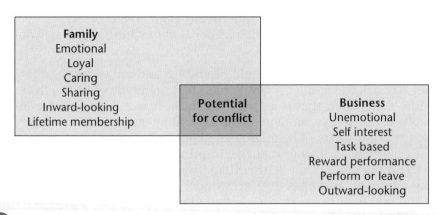

Figure 15.1 Family vs business cultures

Wilkin & Sons is a family-owned business founded in 1885 and best known for its luxury Tiptree jams which sell to over 50 countries. The more esoteric jams such as 'Little Scarlet Strawberry' have attained almost a cult status among jam lovers.

The company is committed to sharing success with its workforce. At the company's 450 hectare estate at Tiptree in Essex, managers and directors test products as well as man the production lines when required. More than 100 of the 180 workforce live in houses owned by the firm. It has operated a non-contributory pension scheme for over a century. The firm has also created a trust which will eventually leave employees with a 51 per cent shareholding in the firm.

There is another ethical dimension to the firm. It has never borrowed and does not want to.

the firm, for example in making the dividend payment that the family expects but the firm can ill afford, whose interest comes first? And the very closeness of the family can create an impenetrable barrier for the non-family manager who might feel 'passed-over' for promotion in favour of family or feel left out of the decision-making that seems to take place 'around the kitchen table'.

Family culture even influences the management style within a family firm. Research by Ram and Holliday (1993) suggests that family firms tend to adopt a style of 'negotiated paternalism'. Because of the relationships between family members, family businesses tend to use fewer formal management techniques. Family influence acts to dilute managerial power and discretion, with family members often able to negotiate their duties. In the researchers' opinion this can constrain operating efficiency and lead to management practices that are 'sub-optimal'.

What is more, business can influence the culture within the family. Indeed business can exact a toll on family life. The separation between the two can become very blurred in a family firm. Building a successful business can become an obsessive, single-minded occupation that drives family life into the shadows, creating tensions at home as well as at work. Married couples working together may feel unable ever to 'get away from the shop' and let the stress and tension of growing a business damage their personal relationship. Conflict at work – and there will be conflict in any growing business – may

Ferrero Rocher is a truly European family firm. It was founded by two brothers Piera and Pietro in the Italian Alba region in Piedmont in the immediate post war years. They produced a chocolate bar which included nougat and hazel nuts and called it passa giadujot. The same basic recipe is used today except the current head of the firm, 79-year-old **Michele Ferrero**, added liqueur.

The company is the fifth-largest sweet maker in the world with turnover of £2.4 billion. It is registered in Amsterdam but has 16 factories across Europe. The family has lived in Brussels for the past 30 years. They are obsessively secretive and Michele has been described as an autocrat with a paternalistic management style. Every 29 June, Ferrero executives must attend church in San Domenico to honour the day the company was founded. Each three years Ferrero organises a pilgrimage to Lourdes for all its 13 000 workers.

Case insight

Moss Bros became a public company in 1950 after 100 years as a family concern. Founded in 1850 by Moses Moss, the great-grandfather of **Monty Moss** the current President of the company.

Originally Moses bought second-hand clothes, job lots and bespoke suits that customers did not collect. He filled the gaps in his stock with suits made in Savile Row during the quiet season. He would then sell on his stocks throughout Britain. His two sons, George and Alfred, came into the business in 1897, when the Moss Bros name was formed. It was shortly after this that the brothers stumbled on a major element of their business – hiring clothes – when an eccentric stockbroker, turning to entertainment when his business failed, found he did not have a dress suit to wear because his own was in pawn and borrowed one from Alfred. Their reputation, initially was spread by word of mouth.

Alfred, the entrepreneurial one, built the business steadily until the 1930s when he began handing it over to George's son, Harry. Harry continued until the early 1970s with Alfred's son Basil and his own son, Monty eventually taking over as joint MDs.

There were always non-family members on the Board, but in 1970 the first of them, Harry Vanson, was appointed as joint MD and in 1976 became sole MD, with Basil as Chairman and Monty as Vice-Chairman. In 1988 they joined forces with Cecil Gee and Rowland Gee became MD. In effect, it became a two family business because Basil's son, Peter, also became Deputy Chairman and Monty's son, David, became Executive Director. Michael and Cecil Gee are also Board members.

●

---

continue at home, feeding on itself and intensifying. A husband and wife team that divorce will find it difficult to continue working together. To survive, a family must learn to separate family and business life. Business and family issues need to be addressed directly, but in an open and balanced way that allows the business to be run properly whilst not disrupting family harmony. This is not always easy.

Succession

The old adage 'from clogs to clogs in three generations' is definitely true in relation to family firms. With each successive generation the survival rate diminishes. Poutziouris and Chittenden (1996) observe that:

> Four out of five family businesses are managed by the first generation, which benefits from the entrepreneurial drive of the founder. However, less than one third of founders successfully pass ownership and management control of the family business to the second generation. Only 10 per cent of second generation family firms are transferred to third generation and less than 5 per cent ever reach beyond the third generation of family management.

However, not all owner-managers want to establish dynastic family firm A large scale survey by Burns and Whitehouse (1996) found that only 32 per cent of British owner-managers wanted to pass their business on within the family, most (68 per cent) preferring to sell the firm, most commonly to a trade buyer, in order to make a capital gain. This contrasted strongly with Germany (57 per cent), Italy (62 per cent) and Spain (74 per cent) where most owner-managers wanted to keep the firm in the family. The same study showed that most owner-managers who inherited their firm wanted to pass it on to their children.

Figure 15.2 shows a life cycle framework originally developed by Churchill and Hatten (1987) to aid the understanding of family business dynamics during the process of succession and transfer of power. The model suggests that changes in management, strategy and control can be planned and executed but are shaped by family relationships and driven by the inexorable human life cycle. In the model the life cycle of two generations is expressed as the level of influence a family member has on the strategic orientation and operations of the business, during the phases of family business development. Essentially it is a four-stage model that repeats, with increasing complexity as new generations join the firm.

> **Case insight**
>
> **Bharat Shah** has built up the family firm of **Sigma Pharmaceuticals** to a company making profits of £4.8 million on turnover of £190 million. Two of his brothers work in the business – Manish, as the accountant, and Kamel, in operations. His son Halul runs retail pharmacies.
>
> 'It's an Asian way of working. We are all focused on what we are doing and we are working for succession. It's all in the family. We are not growing the business for an exit route.'
>
> *Management Today* May 2004
> ●

Stage 1 *Owner-managed business* This is the early stage, beyond start-up, when the founder is in control but a son or daughter is introduced into the business on a permanent basis.

Stage 2 *Training and development of the new generation* This is the stage where decisions are made, although not always formally, about passing the business on to the son or daughter and a process of training and development should be taking place to groom them for their role.

Stage 3 *Partnership* This is the stage when the son or daughter shows sufficient business acumen and expertise that the founder starts to loosen the reins of control, delegates authority and starts to share responsibility with them.

Stage 4 *Power transfer* This is the phase when strategic planning, management control and operational responsibility shifts from one generation to another. The succession process accelerates as the founder begins to retire and reduces their active participation in the business.

Points of conflict

Would that succession were usually so systematic and trouble-free. It is not. The problems arise in the areas marked as 'anomalies' in Figure 15.2. Although daughters are being brought increasingly into the family business, the most common relationship revolves around father and son. Many father–son relationships can work extremely well but psychologists tell us that this relationship has a unique potential for conflict. If you revisit the personal qualities likely to be present in the entrepreneurial founder, detailed in Chapter 2, you will realise that he is likely to have a very close emotional link with the business. He is likely to see it as an extension of himself, a symbol of his achievement, even an extension of his masculinity. He may guard power jealously and have problems with delegation. He may want to facilitate his son's succession but he may also want to control it. Subconsciously he may feel the need to be stronger than, and in control of, his son and succession may be seen as a 'threat' to his masculinity. This can result in rivalry between father and son, each trying to be the dominant character.

From the son's perspective things are different. We are told that rebellion is natural in youth but, although it is tolerated and sometimes encouraged at home, at work it is something that is normally repressed. Even in its mildest form, this natural tendency will show itself in an increasing drive for independence from father. But if father is also the boss, there is potential for conflict, particularly if father is himself having problems delegating control. So the scene is set with a rebellious son, pressing for

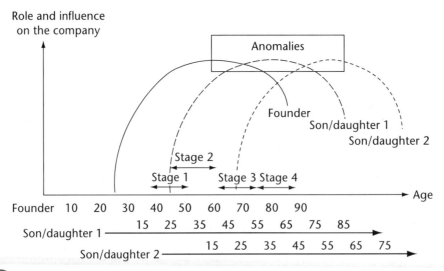

Figure 15.2 The family business life cycle

more power within the firm, seemingly opposed by a father who, at the same time, is saying that he wants to pass the business on to the son. To the son, the father may appear to be hanging on to power and he may begin to doubt whether father really will retire. In fact he may even begin to distrust his father, and that is the start of the end of the relationship. At the very least, the contradictory signals from the father are likely to lead to frustration in the son. What is more, for the son the option of leaving the business is problematic as it might be seen as disloyalty to the family.

With this high potential for conflict, it is a good idea to revisit Chapter 8 which gave us an insight into how conflict can be handled. Competing will simply intensify the conflict. Accommodating may result in the issues not being properly addressed. Worst of all is avoidance. Levingson (1983) describes how avoidance might show itself in the actions of the father. For example, the father may cultivate an atmosphere of ambiguity in decision-making where rules and boundaries are unclear and he can 'meddle', in this way avoiding any overt conflict. Alternatively he may defer decisions until the last possible moment. Avoidance is often the approach adopted because addressing the business issues may lead to conflict which might in turn damage the father–son relationship. As we saw in Chapter 8, conflict is rarely best handled through avoidance, but rather through collaboration or compromise.

Case insight

Noon Products was bought by W T Foods Group in 1999 but still remains a family business with four members of the board from the family business, four from the parent company and with one non-executive director. The firm produces Indian food for a range of customers including Birds Eye, Sainsbury's, Waitrose and Somerfield. It was founded by **Gulam Noon** and both his daughters, Zeenat and Zarmin, work in the firm as well as his brother, Akbar, and nephew, Nizar.

> You have to work with the family in a professional way. The most important thing … is to give them the job and resist interfering … If someone doesn't come up to expectation, then you get rid of them, don't allow it to drag on.

Zeenat is responsible for packaging of temperature-controlled food. She is the eldest daughter, has a management qualification and joined the firm at the start, having worked with a hotel chain in India and just had a baby. She is on the Board.

> You have to prove yourself more when its a family business. You have to show that you are serious about your job and about your career. You only get respect by working alongside people and not being just the boss's daughter.

Zarmin has a degree and worked for a travel firm before joining the business. She is director of Noon Restaurants, a separate enterprise.

> It was quite a culture shock coming into the family business. My father lets you get on with it, but he likes to see the figures. You're not expected to go to him with small problems … unless you come up against a brick wall. But even then he'd prefer you to break through it yourself.

Family Business, The Stoy Centre for Family Business, vol. 8, issue 1, 2000

Leach (1996) claims that father–daughter relationships are less problematic:

> Fathers seem more able to accept advice about the business and some criticism from daughters, and they often say that they would react to sons saying the same thing as if it were a personal attack.

He observes that fathers do not feel threatened by daughters, and daughters are more accommodating, being brought up to be more nurturing, attuned to emotional needs and giving priority to family harmony. Perhaps that is changing.

Nevertheless this may give us an insight into mother–son relationships in the family firm, about which there is little research. There is even less research into mother–daughter relationships. Indeed the assumed relationship in most of the literature is that of a patriarchal hierarchy within the family firm. We know next to nothing about the influences of an extended family, except in the context of ethnicity, or the development of new forms of families, such as those based upon gay relationships. Perhaps the future will see a redefinition of the term 'family firm'.

There can be yet another layer of complexity to the problems facing the family firm, this time caused by sibling rivalry. Sibling rivalry is normal, but some parents actively encourage it, particularly in the context of the family firm. If a number of sons and/or daughters work in the firm there may be rivalry between them as they vie for favour in the eyes of the father or mother. The custom of favouring elder sons with respect to inheritance, although in decline, still shows itself when it comes to succession in the family firm. Elder sons may be favoured at the expense of daughters or younger sons who may be more able. This can lead to the best talent leaving the family business or the brothers or sisters trying to carve out niches for themselves in the business to establish their independence. Even if the business is split equally between the children, there is the danger of sibling rivalry becoming institutionalised in the firm.

Case insight

In 1965 **Alex Ramsay** invited his three sons to work for the manufacturing firm he had set up in Sussex. He gave them and his three daughters large shareholdings in the business. But Alex did not find sharing control easy and the eldest son, William, left in frustration. Alex died in 1988. At this point William returned insisting that, as the eldest son, he should become managing director. The others, reluctantly, complied but his management style and free spending ways soon brought conflict. And when evidence of 'sharp business practice' came to light his brothers used their shareholdings to suspend him. One of the other brothers, Charles, explained what happened next:

> 'William decided that if he wasn't to run the company, then nobody would. My elder sister sided with William and they demanded to be bought out in cash – assuming that the business would have to be sold or split up as a result. But we remortgaged the company's property, sold some assets and managed to save the company ... It's sad. There were lots of things we could have done to stop the tensions becoming so damaging. We just got it badly wrong.'

Since then the business has recovered but the two sides of the family are still not speaking.

Sunday Times 25 May 2003

The introvert firm

All businesses must adapt and change to meet the demands of a changing market place, but there is a danger that family firms will become moribund and unable or unwilling to respond with each succeeding generation. Many firms do, of course, adapt. However some become increasingly introvert. They become inward-looking, unresponsive to messages from the market place and unreceptive to new ideas, they might even become unwilling to recruit managers from outside the firm or, worse still, from outside the family. How does this come about?

Families can become distracted from business for a number of reasons. Disagreement between family members might paralyse decision-making within the firm. Avoidance behaviour in the extreme might lead to important business issues not being addressed. Damage done to the firm and relationships within it by the traumatic succession from one generation to another might leave it weak and, like the rabbit caught in the headlights of the car, traumatised. The past success of the firm which has led to increased prosperity for the family might itself cause problems. The family might start to regard the firm as their main store of wealth demanding regular dividends when the firm can ill-afford them, imposing restrictions on commercial decisions that reflect their risk aversion or vetoing capital investment decisions because it would drain cash flow. The family might also start to view the firm as a milk cow draining the cash away through expense accounts, pensions, cars and other perks or 'jobs for the family'. Borrowings might be vetoed because the family do not want their main store of wealth and source of income to be exposed to any form of risk or the possibility that they might lose control. All of these things damage the business and can mean that it is not doing what it is supposed to do, that is, profitably generate goods and services.

This can be compounded by a sense of alienation felt by non-family members as they see cash being squandered, no decisions or bad decisions being made. The continuous conflict may make them feel uneasy and unsure about the future direction of the firm. They may feel forced to take sides when they do not wish to. They may feel that they are not part of the decision-making at all or that family considerations are always paramount. They may feel passed over for promotion in favour of less able family members. They might feel that there is no system for

> **Case insight**
>
> The family business of **J & B Wild** has had a stall in Manchester's New Smithfield Fish Market for 100 years. However, it has had to adapt and change in order to stay in business. Originally, it sold British white fish, made popular with the growth of fish and chip shops. Today British white fish is hard to find, fish and chip shops are in decline and the family has had to develop new products and find new customers just to survive.
>
> Many years ago it started selling chicken, mainly to Indian restaurants in the area. It still sells fish, but most fish is now foreign, flown in from around the world. Most fish is now sold filleted. J & B Wild has developed a reputation for stocking a wide variety of 'exotic' fish which are sold mainly to Chinese restaurants. Fish has now become a food that is susceptible to fashions and fads and the family have to keep on top of market trends.

adequately rewarding them for the good work they do, for example, by taking some equity in the firm, because the family would not countenance losing control. Indeed the family might actively discourage or prohibit the employment of non-family managers.

Many of these issues come down to the business no longer having clear leadership. Second-generation firms might have a board comprising three brothers or sisters each with equal shareholdings and none with clear control. None of them might possess the entrepreneurial spirit of the founder. To compound the problem, they may all hate each other and be unable to agree on anything. To avoid this catastrophe family firms need ways of resolving family conflict and managing succession. They also need to reward and promote family employees strictly in line with their contribution to the firm and regularly and objectively evaluate the performance of all staff. Delegation outside the family should be taking place and being a member of the family should not be part of the criteria for promotion or appointment. In other words, family business management needs to be seen to be objective for the good of the firm and its family and non-family employees alike.

Resolving conflict

Arguably, the only real way to resolve conflict in the family firm is to resolve conflict in the family – a very tall order indeed. However, confining ourselves to business, the key to conflict resolution is communication and the appropriate style is one of collaboration or compromise. Admitting and, most importantly, understanding the nature and cause of the problem is a good first step. Understanding that many of the problems come from our genetic make-up should help to defuse the situation and make it less personal. Understanding how individuals naturally react to conflict (remember Thomas–Kilman conflict modes) can help explain why arguments happen. With a will, behaviours can be modified. With particularly difficult situations a third-party facilitator – a friend or professional mediator or counsellor – might help. However, the British are known for avoiding sensitive personal and family issues and difficulties.

Leach (1996) advocates the development of a family strategic plan which should be articulated in a written constitution that sets out the family's values and policies in relation to the business. He advocates a four-stage process:

1 Addressing the critical issues relating to family involvement in the business. This involves looking critically at the business and the family and how they relate. How are conflicts between family and business interests to be resolved?
2 Establishing a family council to provide a forum in which members can air their views and participate in policy-making. The council should develop ground rules as to how it should operate.
3 Drawing up a family constitution which involves developing a written statement of the family's values and beliefs and going on to develop policies and objectives. Does the family have any shared values and beliefs in relation to the business? What does the family want from the business? What is the involvement of family to be? Does the family wish to retain control of the firm? What should be the criteria for family entry into the firm? What is the management succession policy? Should family members who are active in the business be treated differently from

Table 15.1 The family constitution checklist

- Family values, beliefs and philosophy
- Family objectives in relation to the business
- Family involvement in the business – share ownership and disposal, voting and control
- Family involvement in the business – board membership, voting
- Family involvement in the business – selection of chairman and managing director
- Family involvement in the business – jobs and remuneration
- Family council meetings
- Procedures for changing the constitution

those who are not? Who might own shares in the business and how might shares be disposed of? What should the dividend policy be? A checklist of what might go into a family constitution is shown in Table 15.1.

4 Monitoring the family's progress and maintaining communication within the family through regular council meetings.

Leach also advocates giving sons or daughters managerial autonomy within part of the business to help them grow and mature; separating out roles for other members of the family so as to minimise sibling rivalry. Many writers advocate the use of non-executive directors on the boards of family companies. They can be the insurance against companies becoming too introvert. They can bring balance to board-room discussions and should be relied on to put the firm, not the family, first. In that sense they bring independence to meetings and can help resolve family squabbles. Alongside this they bring their own particular expertise and a new network of contacts.

Case insight

Everard Breweries is a family company that was founded in Leicestershire in 1849. It brews beers such as Tiger Best Bitter, Beacon Bitter and Everard Original from its Castle Acre site near Leicester and has a pub and hotel estate of over 150 units.

The fifth generation chairman is **Richard Everard**. He sees himself as the 'custodian' of the family assets in the business. The family objectives are the driving force behind the philosophy and resulting strategy of the firm. When he became chairman he sat down with the family and outlined their objectives and set about changing the business strategy to reflect them. Now the emphasis is on property and brewing accounts for only 30 per cent of turnover.

We are fortunate in that we only ever had small families and only one surviving son per generation. After five generations, 90 per cent of the shares are held by only two family members ... There is a rule that only one family member can have an executive position on the board in any one generation ... We do not offer share options to attract senior people. That would be against our philosophy... I see my custodianship lasting another twenty years, but should anything happen to me I have left clear instructions on how the next generation should be trained for the position. This would include at least four years external training.

Family Business, The Stoy Centre for Family Business, vol. 7, issue 3, 1999

Managing succession

The usual approach to managing succession is to ignore the issue and do nothing. It is almost as if owner-managers, particularly founders, are in denial about ever leaving the firm. It is a blind spot that they do not wish to discuss – a little like death. They are reluctant to relinquish power and control, they fear that doing so will somehow reflect on them, diminishing their status, identity and masculinity. Sometimes planning involves making unwelcome decisions that might upset the family, particularly if it means selecting a successor from members of the family. Founders often fear retirement – the lack of activity, purpose, status, independence – and often typical entrepreneurs are so single-minded that they do not have other outside interests. However, if succession is not planned and managed it can be a traumatic and stressful event which might threaten the very existence of the firm.

Actually passing on the business within the family is just one of the options open to the founder. The other options are:

- *Trade sale.* Competitors may be interested in buying the business as a going concern, generating cash or shares for the founder and the family. This may be attractive if cash is needed for retirement or other family reasons. It might also be just the right time to get a very good deal, for example because of consolidation in the industry. It might simply be that the business has become less attractive or more risky than when the founder set it up and there are better new opportunities for children.
- *Management buy-out.* If there is a strong management team in the firm they might be interested in bidding for the firm if they can arrange funding.
- *Management buy-in.* An external management team might be persuaded to bid for the firm, again, as a going concern.

Case insight

Blackpool Pleasure Beach is a family business. **Geoffrey Thompson** has been Managing Director since 1976. Born in 1936 he is the grandson of the founder, William George Bean. His mother, Doris Thompson, born in 1903, is Chairman and still comes into the business every day, has lunch and signs cheques. All three children work in the business. The eldest is Amanda who is President of Stageworks Worldwide Productions, which presents stage and ice spectaculars at the Pleasure Beach.

Geoffrey is quite a workaholic but in 1997, at the age of 61, he had a stroke. Never daunted, he was soon back to work. Amanda says that her father has been a huge influence on her life and is concerned:

Daddy's working very hard again and he gets tired. Everyone asks him who's going to take over, but I know he wants to be in the company for ever . . . I've realised that nobody makes a decision without speaking to him first . . . I don't think daddy will ever come to terms with the fact that he might not be here for ever. But whatever happens, he's instilled his vision into all three of us that this will remain a family business.

(Sadly, Geoffrey Thompson died in 2004.)

Sunday Times Magazine 23 July 2000

- *Appoint a professional manager.* With this option the family remain as shareholders and probably non-executive directors, receiving dividends and hoping to see the value of the business grow,
- *Appoint a caretaker manager.* If the founder wishes to pass on the firm but the son or daughter is too young or inexperienced, they may appoint a caretaker manager to see the firm through until such time as the next generation is ready to take on the role.
- *Liquidate.* This is usually the least attractive option as the price for the assets will not reflect any goodwill.

If succession really is the chosen option it will need careful planning. Who should be the successor? Do they possess the necessary skills and temperament? If not, can they be developed through training and experience within the available time frame? What are the financial, tax and pension consequences? The issues that need to be addressed may seem endless. To help approach the task systematically, Leach (1996) proposes the following approach:

1 Start planning early. The most successful successions are those that involve the next generation early in the process so as to allow them to grow into the role rather than coming as an unexpected 'event'.
2 Encourage inter-generational teamwork. It is important that all issues surrounding the succession are addressed and agreed by all the next generation, not just the chosen successor.
3 Develop a written succession plan. This is an action plan setting down what has to be done, by whom and when. It will include details of the founder's reducing involvement and the successor's expanding role and responsibilities. It should also address the structure of the management team.
4 Involve the family and colleagues in your thinking and, when complete, show them the succession plan. This is about communication and getting commitment from everybody to the plan.
5 Take advantage of outside help. Succession has important financial, tax and pension consequences for the founder and the family. Consulting the firm's accountant and lawyer early in the process is vital.
6 Establish a training process. The plan should lay out how the successor is expected to develop the skills needed to take over the firm and over what time frame. This might involve education and training as well as job or work experience.
7 Plan for retirement. The owner-manager needs to be prepared financially and emotionally for retirement. Retirement will bring lots of free time and entrepreneurs, particularly, like to keep on the go.
8 Make retirement timely and unequivocal. When the timetable for succession is set, it is important to stick to it and not hang on in the job. Sonnenfield (1988) characterised the founder as typically having four exit styles, the last two having a more positive effect on the business:

  - *Monarchs*: who do not leave the business until they are forced out through ill-health, death or a palace revolt;
  - *Generals*: who leave the business, but plot a return and quickly do so 'to save the business';

- *Ambassadors*: who leave the business quickly and gracefully, frequently to serve as post-retirement mentors;
- *Governors*: who rule for a limited term and turn to other activities then to gain fulfilment.

It could be that the future will see a decline in the importance of family businesses. The break-down of family networks, increasing demands for capital that families cannot supply, a booming stock market which makes obtaining a listing attractive – all these factors may mean that more and more companies are sold on. Certainly the survey by Burns and Whitehouse (1996) indicates this trend is underway in Britain. However, the high proportion of owner-managers still wishing to pass businesses on to the next generation contrasts strongly with the proportion actually succeeding in doing so.

Case with questions

Mars Inc. is the seventh largest private company in the USA with income of over $15 billion a year from global food brands such as Mars, Milky Way, Snickers, Twix, M&Ms as well as Whiskas, Pedigree and Uncle Ben's. It is a second (arguably third) generation family firm – a family that is one of the richest in the world. Founded by **Forrest Mars Snr**, who died in 1999, it is now run by his sons Forrest Jr and John. Forrest Mars Snr was born into a confectionery-making family in 1904. His father, Frank, ran a modestly successful business in Minnesota where he made butter-cream candies overnight and his wife, Ethel, sold them from a trolley the next day. They had two main products, the Mar-O-Bar and Victoria Butter Creams, which became successful in 1923 when Woolworths started distributing them.

In Forrest Mars Snr claimed that the idea for the family's first really successful product, the Milky Way, came to him whilst sitting drinking a chocolate malt drink in a cafe and he suggested to his father that he should put it into a chocolate bar. Some time later, his father did just that, putting caramel on top of and chocolate around it. Milky Way was a huge success with sales of $800 000 in its first year. The family moved to Chicago and Frank built a mansion in Wisconsin. However, relations between father and son deteriorated as Forrest wanted further growth and expansion but Frank wanted to settle for an easy life.

In 1932 Forrest left to set up a one-room chocolate business in Slough, England. He quickly produced a similar product to Milky Way, calling it a Mars Bar, using creamier milk chocolate and a sweeter toffee filling. The Mars Bar is a very British product, unknown in the USA. The company returned to the USA in the late 1930s with the hugely successful M&Ms, the candy-coated chocolate 'that melts in your mouth, not in your hand'. Also in this period the company made the first moves into the European pet food industry by combining modern manufacturing techniques with nutritional science. In 1946 it applied modern manufacturing techniques to parboil rice and launched Uncle Ben's rice.

Mars Inc. is committed to remaining under private ownership. It is also a very secretive company. The founder, Forrest Mars Snr, was a recluse and his sons shun public life. They also live and work with a frugality that is in stark contrast to many modern firms. There are no company perks such as cars, reserved parking or executive toilets. Indeed, no one even has a

➡

Summary

Starting up as a family firm can be attractive because of the emotional support and helping hands that may not expect to be paid. As they grow, family firms can foster loyalty, responsibility, long-term commitment, not least to ethical standards, and a pride in 'the family tradition'. These virtues are often welded into a desire to transfer the firm from one generation to the next and to preserve it in difficult financial times, as in the case of **Sigma Pharmaceuticals**. Seventy per cent of UK business can be described as family firms, many with household names like **Mars** and **Cadbury**. Many of today's best-known public companies started life as family firms and still have relationships with the founding family. Familial brands like **Baxter's Soups** and **Timberland** build consumer loyalty over long periods and can be a very valuable asset.

private office. Memos are against company policy. Meetings take place 'as needed'. Elaborate presentations are seen as a waste of time. All employees must do their own photocopying, make their own telephone calls and travel economy class on planes. John and Forrest Jr even share a secretary with their sister, Jacqueline. All employees are known as 'associates' and are on first name terms. Everyone from the top to the bottom has to punch their time-cards daily and receives a 10 per cent bonus for punctuality.

A visit to the company website (www.mars.com) gives an impression of the strong culture within the organisation. Words like 'ethical', 'honest', 'trust', 'pride', 'passion', and 'support' abound as do phrases like 'we like being the best at what we do', 'we are passionate about how we do things and about quality' and 'I know that as a Mars associate I am ethical and have high standards'. The company is run according to a 24-page booklet which codifies Forrest Snr's management philosophy. These are called 'The five principles of Mars':

Quality – 'The consumer is our boss, quality is our work and value for money is our goal'.
Responsibility – 'As individuals, we demand total responsibility from ourselves; as associates we support the responsibility of others'.
Mutuality – 'A mutual benefit is a shared benefit; a shared benefit will endure'.
Efficiency – 'We use resources to the full, waste nothing and do only what we do best'.
Freedom. – 'We need freedom to shape our future; we need profit to remain free'.

Questions

1 What are the benefits of the Mars philosophy to both the company and to its employees?
2 In your opinion, does the Mars philosophy replicate itself in its retail brand? How does this compare to the Timberland brand?
3 Mars is a US company but its products are sold in over 100 countries. Does the Mars philosophy resonate in your country? Explain why or why not?
4 How important is the Mars family in generating this philosophy? If Mars were to move out of family control, would its philosophy have to change?

At the heart of the family firm is the family culture – its values and beliefs. These can be based upon ethical convictions, as in the case of **Timberland**, or they can be based on religious beliefs, as in the case of **Cadbury** and **Wilkin & Sons**, maker of Tiptree Jams. They can be quite quirky, as in the case of **Mars**. Sometimes they enhance the brand, sometimes these affect the terms and conditions of employment and the culture of the firm. That culture can mean that the firm is managed in an autocratic, paternalistic fashion like **Ferrero Rocher**.

There is, however, the potential for conflict because family culture is essentially based on emotion, emphasising loyalty, caring and sharing, whereas business culture is unemotional, task orientated and based on self-interest. The emotion-based family culture operates subconsciously and can get in the way of business, as it did in the case of **Littlewoods**. For example, family firms can suffer from nepotism and a lack of professionalism. Managers who are not family members can feel alienated and isolated, believing that important decisions are being made without their involvement, 'over the kitchen table' rather than in the office. Family conflict and politics can result in the firm being neglected or business decisions being made for other than commercial reasons – the introvert firm which tries to ignore commercial reality. It can also mean that the firm is used as a milk cow for the family and loses its commercial edge. As we saw with **J & B Wild**, all firms need to change and adapt, but introvert firms sometimes do not see the need to do so.

Succession in the family firm is often problematic and can itself lead to conflict, as was the case with **Littlewoods**. Like Geoffrey Thompson of **Blackpool Pleasure Beach**, founders tend to ignore it until the last minute. Many of the problems stem from the entrepreneurial characteristics of the founder that make him reluctant to relinquish control of the business. Added to this there may be father–son rivalry as the son rebels or strives for independence within the firm. If there are more sons or daughters, then sibling rivalry can intensify the problem, as in the case of **Alex Ramsay**. As we saw with **Noon Products**, introducing the founder's children into the business needs to be handled with care.

Resolving conflict in a family business is often difficult. It requires accommodation or compromise. It might help to understand the nature and underlying cause of the conflict. But ultimately the best approach is to develop a family strategic plan and a family council to monitor it. Setting family objectives led **Everard Breweries** to change their business strategy to emphasise property more.

Succession can be managed. Planning needs to start early and needs to be inter-generational, building in consultation with the firm's accountants and lawyers. A written succession plan should be developed which shows how the founder will exit and how the new generation will take over. It will detail any training and development needed and help the founder plan for retirement. Finally, when it is time to go, go!

Essays and discussion topics

1 What are the advantages and disadvantages of starting up a business with your partner or spouse?
2 What are the advantages and disadvantages of being part of a family firm?
3 Familial brands build consumer trust over long periods and can be very valuable assets. Discuss.

4 Family firms are more common on continental Europe than in Britain. Why do you think this might be?
5 In the future family firms will decline in importance. Discuss.
6 Does it matter how you define a family firm?
7 How might family and business cultures clash?
8 Why are there so many examples of successful family firms which are based on strong religious or ethical bases?
9 What are the problems you might face in being in charge of running a family firm?
10 What are some of the underlying causes of conflict in a family and how might these show themselves in a family firm?
11 The family business sector is an endless soap opera of patriarchs and matriarchs, black sheep and prodigal sons, hubris and nemesis. Discuss.
12 What are the advantages and disadvantages of being an non-family employee in a family business?
13 What are the problems you might face in being the son or daughter of the founder employed in their firm?
14 How would you get on if you were working for your mother or father?
15 What is an introvert firm? How might a business avoid becoming one?
16 How can succession be managed?
17 What do you think would be a good training programme for a son or daughter intending to take over the running of the family firm?
18 In what circumstances might it be wise not to pass on the firm to a member of the family?
19 What should go into a succession plan?
20 What problems might an entrepreneur encounter in facing retirement?

Exercises and assignments

1 List the questions you would ask members of the family working in a family firm in order to highlight the advantages and problems of working there.
2 Based upon these questions, interview members of the family and write an essay highlighting the advantages and problems of working in the family firm.
3 List the questions you would ask the manager of a second- or third-generation family firm in order to highlight the problems they encountered in taking over the firm.
4 Based upon these questions, interview the manager and write an essay highlighting the problems they encountered.
5 Research by Ram and Holliday (1993) suggests that a leadership style of 'negotiated paternalism' is to be found in many family firms. Referring back to Chapter 8, in what circumstances is this likely to be appropriate? In what circumstances is it likely to be ineffective?
6 Write a specimen family constitution.
7 Find out what are the tax consequences of succession in the family firm.

References

Burns, P. and Whitehouse, O. (1996) *Family Ties*, 3i European Enterprise Centre, Special Report no. 10.
Churchill, N. and Hatten, K. (1987) 'Non-Market Transfers of Wealth and Power: A Research Framework for Family Business', *American Journal of Small Business*, Winter.
Institute for Small Business Affairs (1999) *All in the Family*, Policy and Research Issues, no. 1, August.
Leach, P. (1996) *The BDO Stoy Hayward Guide to the Family Business*, London: Kogan Page.

Levingson, H. (1983) 'Consulting with Family Business: What to Look Out For', *Organizational Dynamics*, Summer.

Nelton, S. (1986) *In Love and in Business*, New York: John Wiley & Sons.

Poutziouris, P. (1994) 'The Development of the Familia Business', in A. Gibb and M. Rebernick (eds), *Small Business Management in New Europe*, and Proceedings of 24th ESBS – September, Slovenia, in *New Europe*.

Poutziouris, P. and Chittenden, F. (1996) *Family Businesses or Business Families*, Institute for Small Business Affairs and National Westminster Bank Monograph 1.

Ram, M. and Holliday, R. (1993) 'Relative Merits: Family Culture and Kinship in Small Firms', *Sociology*, 27(4).

Rosenblatt, P.C., de Mik, L., Anderson, R.M. and Johnson, P.A. (1985) *The Real World of the Small Business Owner*, San Francisco: Jossey-Bass.

Sonnenfield, J. (1988) *The Hero's Farewell: What Happens when CEOs Retire*, New York: Oxford University Press.

16

International Entrepreneurship

Contents

- Globalisation and international entrepreneurship
- The international start-up
- The stage model of internationalisation
- The influence of network and learning theory
- Export strategies
- The agency dilemma
- Summary

LEARNING OUTCOMES

By the end of this chapter you should be able to:

- Explain what is meant by the term 'international entrepreneurship':

- List the global influences and trends encouraging it and the factors that inhibit it;

- Explain the factors that encourage the international start-up;

- Explain the 'stage model' of internationalisation and the reasons why, although it may be logically appealing, it has been criticised;

- Describe the influence of network and learning theory on the process of internationalisation;

- List the practical problems related to exporting and explain how they might be overcome.

Globalisation and international entrepreneurship

The phrase 'international entrepreneurship' can mean different things. On the one hand it has been used to describe entrepreneurial behaviour in different countries and cultures. On the other it has been used to describe entrepreneurial behaviour across national boundaries. This chapter is concerned with the latter. Arguably the first articles on the internationalisation of small firms appeared in the 1970s (Johanson and Wiedershheim-Paul, 1975; Johanson and Vahlne, 1977; who popularised the stage model of internationalisation). Since then the field has broadened to include international start-ups, exporting, alliances and joint ventures, market entry modes, knowledge management and network theory.

In many ways it is surprising that the area took so long to develop. After all, entrepreneurship is about exploiting commercial opportunities and these are likely to exist where there are distant countries with different resources, different needs and different markets. Entrepreneurs are quick to realise that there is profit to be made from trading between different markets. Arguably European colonisation was just one example of international entrepreneurship. Indeed before that Columbus might be characterised as an international entrepreneur, financed by venture capitalists who happened to be Spanish royalty.

The area has become increasingly topical with the trend towards globalisation. Competition is becoming increasingly global as barriers to international trade are dismantled and international communication and information networks improve. The world's markets and economies are becoming increasingly integrated and this can affect the smallest of businesses. Accompanying this is a general loss of national sovereignty, a homogenisation of cultures and a democratisation of many aspects of life. All this has been hastened by ever-improving communication links through television, telephone and the internet. What happens on one side of the world can be seen on the other, instantly. What is available in one market can be communicated to another almost as quickly. Few national markets are now insulated from the effects of other national markets. Technology has therefore been a key element in the trend to globalisation. Technology and globalisation have become mutually reinforcing with the global market also enhancing the profitability of the new technologies (Aggarwal, 1999).

Global markets, products and brands have appeared. At the same time market niches have fragmented and become ever smaller in terms of product or service specification, making them economically viable only on a global basis. However, new technology and new forms of communication have enabled many of these niches to be exploited globally. The internet has made global sourcing a reality both for consumers and business customers. Dell is well known for its 'fully integrated value chain' – B2B2C – linking customers and their orders with suppliers around the world in real time via the company's extranet. Dell organises the supplies of components and assembles the computers. At the other extreme of size, Mansfield Motors, a small Land Rover garage set up in Essex, England in 1993, sells Land Rover parts around the world from its website, boasting a quicker delivery time than many local authorised Land Rover dealers.

The reality is that most small firms are not in any way international. One study (Carson, 1990) suggested that only 6 per cent of small firms in the UK, across all sectors, export. Most small firms still serve predominantly a local market – never mind a regional, national or international one. Indeed it is generally accepted that there continues to be a 'home country bias', with both personal and business consumers preferring to buy from their home country if at all possible. But actually setting up business in a foreign country can bring with it enormous risks. The roll of large British companies that have failed to establish themselves in foreign markets is as long as it is distinguished: Marks & Spencer, Sainsbury, Boots and the former Midland Bank. And that rings warning bells for the small firm. Bryan and Rafferty (1999) point out that, although it was changing, in the mid-1990s OECD production devoted to exports made up less than 10 per cent of total production; foreign direct investment only 5 per cent of world investment; multinational enterprises contributed just 6 per cent of world production and only 1.5 per cent of the world population worked outside their country of citizenship.

Case with question

Not all British retailers fail in overseas ventures. **B&Q**, the UK do-it-yourself (DIY) store chain, is hardly a small business but its experience in setting up in China is interesting. Up until 2005, when China joined the World Trade Organisation, foreign retailers were prevented from opening more than three stores in any one city and some towns were completely off limits. What is more they had to work with Chinese partners. B&Q opened its first store in China in 1999. By 2004 it had 18 stores with sales of £131 million. It had done deals with a number of Chinese organisations, normally giving them a 35 per cent stake in the business, but making it very clear that B&Q intended to buy them out as soon as it could.

The stores were a huge success and the Beijing store now boasts the highest average customer spend of any store in the world (over £50). But it is the cultural similarities and differences and how they affected the retailer that are really interesting. The stores look very similar to those in the UK, although they are usually considerably bigger. At 200 000 sq ft, the Beijing store is the largest of its kind in the world. Staff wear similar orange overalls. The products offered are also very similar, although the space devoted to garden products is considerably smaller and the Chinese B&Q also sells soft furnishings.

But the big difference is that Chinese customers do not want to 'do-it' themselves at all, they prefer to get others to do it for them. The Chinese customers are typically middle class and wealthy. They come to the store to select what they want and get it installed by a professional. The reasons for this are partly cultural and partly economic. Labour is significantly cheaper than in the West but also things like painting would be regarded as a major DIY job in China. What is more, if you buy one of the thousands of apartments being built in Beijing you buy a concrete shell – with no garden – and customers will then purchase everything else they need – plumbing, lighting, kitchens, bathrooms and furnishings – from one store. B&Q therefore started to offer more services to customers – designers and contractors to install its products. The Beijing store has a room full of designers working at computer terminals, ready to design the customer's living room, kitchen or bathroom. Teams of workers then deliver and install the products. 25 per cent of all B&Q sales in China now involve some kind of B&Q service.

At the moment B&Q is the only national DIY chain in China and is seen as the market leader. B&Q want to keep it that way. By 2008 they plan to have 75 stores.

Question
Why has B&Q been successful in China?

But the world is changing. And there are many positive reasons for SMEs to think international. They can increase sales and therefore profits. If theirs is a unique product or service, selling to a niche market, that niche could be very large internationally. And with increased volumes may come economies of scale. In fact this is even more important if the product is perceived as a commodity and cost leadership is dependent upon achieving those economies. Whether a niche or a commodity product, speed of market roll-out and 'first-mover advantage' can be important in new product development. Another reason for thinking international might be that a company's key competency lies with the product it produces, for example with capital goods like cars, and therefore the continued exploitation of the product through continual market development is the preferred and logical route for expansion. Most capital goods companies follow this strategy – opening up new overseas markets as existing markets become saturated – because of the high cost of developing new products.

There are also reactive reasons for internationalising. By way of contrast, many service businesses such as accounting, insurance, advertising and banking have been pulled into overseas markets because their clients operate there and their clients demand an international service. Some firms enter overseas markets because there is over-capacity or stiff competition at home. Indeed it might be that the product or service is nearing the end of its life cycle in the existing market and their home market is in terminal decline. This was the case with McDonald's and its entry into the East European markets in the 1990s. Hamburgers were a mature product in the West but an exciting new one in Eastern Europe.

So, there are many attractive advantages to internationalisation. But how do most SMEs do it and why do some do it at start-up?

The international start-up

Alfred Weber was probably the first economist to propose a location theory for the firm, based upon lowest cost. He argued that a firm would locate where transport and labour costs were lowest, and that these costs would be reduced where there was a concentration or *cluster* of several producers in a single location. Proximity of customers and suppliers are crucial. However this theory tried to explain specific location rather than lack of location implied by an international start-up.

The increasing number of new ventures that are established as international start-ups generally do so because they derive some other significant form of competitive advantage from going international (Oviatt and McDougall, 1994). These firms start with an international business strategy, for example at the outset making international product/market offering decisions or making use of international sourcing of components. They deploy their assets internationally. Typically they use alliances and networks to overcome resource deficiencies – a topic we shall return to later in this chapter.

One strand to the literature is the 'resource-based' perspective, with the firm seen as owning certain valuable assets that can be exploited in or transferred to a foreign location (Oviatt and McDougall, *op. cit.*). The new technology or innovation upon which the start-up is based is one example of this. However, it could also be the international experience and contacts possessed by the founding team (Oviatt and

McDougall, 1995). In this way they can capitalise on international market imperfections by linking resources from around the world. The systematic and effective exploitation of this key asset is seen as the prime reason for early internationalisation.

Aggarwal (*op. cit.*) observes that many of these international start-ups conduct business in high technology niche markets world-wide. Empirical studies indicate that they do this through necessity (Litvak, 1990; Coviello and Munro, 1995; Oakley, 1996). They need to internationalise early because the high cost of R&D precludes a purely domestic orientation if costs are to be recouped and profits made. Economies of scale are important. What is more, the ever accelerating pace of technological innovation means that product life cycles are shortening and first-mover advantage in all markets becomes vital. Rapid international expansion is designed to counter competitive reaction. High technology, in particular, seems to be a highly competitive, fast-moving, global market place, even for the start-up venture.

In a review of the literature and a study of twelve high technology international start-ups, Johnson (2004) found many factors influencing the decision to internationalise. These are summarised in Figure 16.1. However, he concluded that the principal factors influencing this decision were:

- The international vision of the founders;
- Their desire to be international market leaders;
- The identification of specific international opportunities;
- The possession of specific international contacts and sales leads.

These basic entrepreneurial qualities can be summarised as vision, drive, opportunity perception and relationship development. It is interesting to observe that they remain so important for high technology start-ups.

The stage model of internationalisation

The international start-up is a relatively modern, but still infrequent, phenomenon reflecting the increasingly global nature of all markets. It has been argued that most small firms progress through specific stages of export development. Vernon (1966) characterised the process of internationalisation using a product life cycle of domestic product development, followed by exporting as overseas demand grows, and finally foreign production as the home market matures and cost reduction becomes more important. Eventually the foreign producers may start to export themselves as cost becomes a driving force for competitiveness and production shifts to low-cost countries.

Dicken (1998) also envisaged a sequential process, starting with the firm serving its domestic market, and moving through stages, first starting to export as its home market is saturated and finally moving into overseas production. These stages are shown in Figure 16.2. In this model expansion into overseas markets may take a number of different forms. Exports may start by using the services of an agent. However, if this is successful, the firm may seek a more permanent presence by setting up its own sales outlets. It may also consider licensing other manufacturers in the country to produce the product particularly where it is able to safeguard its intellectual property right through patents, for inventions, or trademarks, through brands.

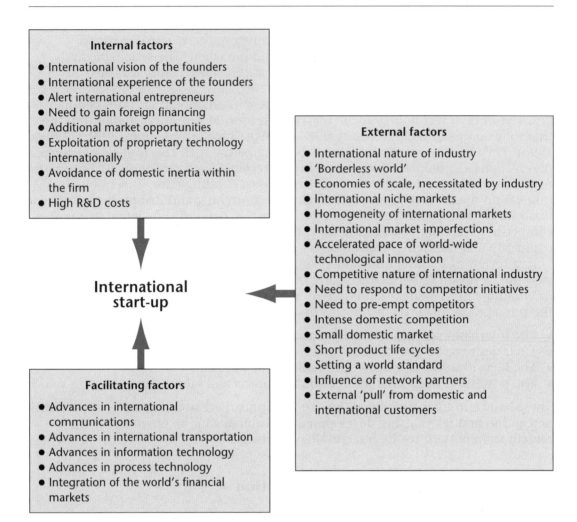

Internal factors

- International vision of the founders
- International experience of the founders
- Alert international entrepreneurs
- Need to gain foreign financing
- Additional market opportunities
- Exploitation of proprietary technology internationally
- Avoidance of domestic inertia within the firm
- High R&D costs

International start-up

External factors

- International nature of industry
- 'Borderless world'
- Economies of scale, necessitated by industry
- International niche markets
- Homogeneity of international markets
- International market imperfections
- Accelerated pace of world-wide technological innovation
- Competitive nature of international industry
- Need to respond to competitor initiatives
- Need to pre-empt competitors
- Intense domestic competition
- Small domestic market
- Short product life cycles
- Setting a world standard
- Influence of network partners
- External 'pull' from domestic and international customers

Facilitating factors

- Advances in international communications
- Advances in international transportation
- Advances in information technology
- Advances in process technology
- Integration of the world's financial markets

Source: J.E. Johnson (2004) 'Factors Influencing the Early Internationalisation of High Technology Start-ups: US and UK Evidence', *Journal of International Entrepreneurship*, no. 2.

Figure 16.1 Factors influencing the early internationalisation of international start-ups

However, it was Johanson and Vahlne (*op. cit.*) who looked in detail at this process, trying to explain where firms export to and how they extend their process of internationalisation beyond export. They popularised what has become known as the stage model of internationalisation, also called the Uppsala model because it was based upon studies of Swedish manufacturing firms in that region. The model proposes that small firms take an incremental stepwise approach to internationalisation over time. They target psychically close markets – ones that they feel mentally comfortable with – initially using market entry methods that require limited commitment, such as exporting. As they gain knowledge and experience from their market involvement over time, so they increase their commitment. This process is repeated from market to market. This form of creeping international

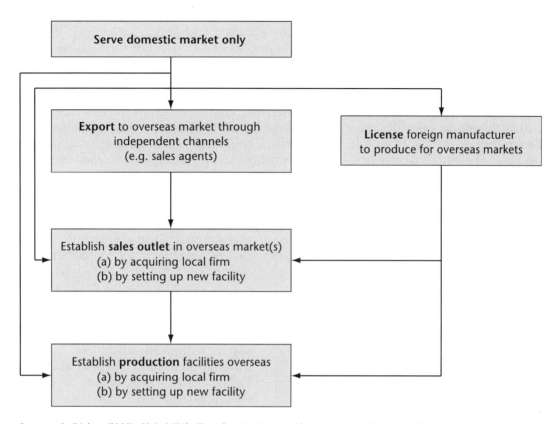

Source: P. Dicken (!998) *Global Shift: Transforming the World Economy,* London: Paul Chapman Publishing.

Figure 16.2 International development

incrementalism is called 'graduated entry'. Small firms start with low-cost, low-risk entry modes and then, if the experience is rewarded, they move to more complex, often higher-risk, modes.

Leonidou and Katsikeas (1996) characterise this as having three stages – pre-engagement, initial and advanced. The pre-engagement phase is when the firm is active in its domestic market but not in an export market. The initial phase is when it has sporadic or exploratory export activity. The advanced phase is when it is actively and consistently involved in exporting and internationalisation of its activities. If these phases are successful the firm builds confidence, eventually embedding internationalisation into the mainstream of its activities. However, should it experience failure then it can retrench and re-evaluate its growth options without endangering its core markets and activities.

The model is appealing, not least because of its inherent risk-minimising logic. It also mirrors the way entrepreneurs 'learn by doing'. In addition, the stepwise progression towards internationalisation mirrors the incremental approach entrepreneurs have towards business development and decision-making. It is also conditionally compatible with the 'resource-based' view of internationalisation. As the firm develops its resource base over time, so too will it develop its export capability.

However, the model has been criticised (Leonidou and Katsikeas, *op. cit.*). Whilst firms seem to fit into different stages of the model at any point of time (using cross-sectional data), there is no empirical evidence of dynamic progression based upon longitudinal studies over time. Indeed the existence of international start-ups suggests that this model is but one of a number of approaches to internationalisation and it has been suggested that firms may skip or compress different stages to the point where the model becomes meaningless (Welch and Loustarinen, 1988; Sullivan and Bauerschmidt, 1990). From a logic viewpoint, graduated entry can also be criticised because it fails to recognise first-mover advantage and the competitive reaction to the failure to exploit it. That is not to say that the model was not a meaningful generalisation when it was proposed. However, the world continues to change rapidly and once-distant markets now seem altogether closer – which may cause management attitudes to shift and first-mover advantage to take on a shorter time frame.

One important factor in the timing of internationalisation is management. Management with international experience seem to be a key ingredient in early internationalisation (Reuber and Fisher, 1997). This seems to be a key resource that allows small firms access to markets that they would otherwise avoid – which takes us back to the 'resource-based' strand of literature. But it may be useful to draw a distinction between type of resource and volume of resource. Type and quality of resource is probably more important than volume as volume can always be levered using external resources. Hence, very small firms need not feel resource-constrained because of size. The pattern of internationalisation they follow is likely to be far more determined by the type and quality of the resource they control, in particular the experience of the founders.

> **Case insight**
>
> The internet has made it easier for many small firms to sell their products overseas. **Michael Ross**, Chief Executive of **figleaves.com**, a UK online retailer of women's lingerie, has managed to penetrate one of the most difficult markets in the world – the USA. Launched in 1999 as easyshop.co.uk, the company changed its name the following year after it decided to focus on lingerie. But the secret for figleaves.com was that, when it launched in the USA, it was already its second largest market, because it sold on the internet and because American women were not concerned that the lingerie they ordered came from Britain.
>
> Now figleaves.com have set up a separate US website and all the online marketing deals are negotiated by somebody who flies out once a month from the UK. The company even has a concession within Amazon.com. Its 'Shock Absorber' bra was launched in the USA together with Amazon, by holding a tennis match between Amazon's founder, Jeff Bezos, and the tennis star Anna Kournikova. In 2004 turnover was £14 million.

The influence of network and learning theory

Networking is an important entrepreneurial skill and it gives us some insights into internationalisation. SMEs can use their networks to identify international opportunities, gain access to resources, improve their strategic position, learn new skills, gain market knowledge, establish credibility and control transaction costs. Both Johnson (*op. cit.*) and Oviatt and McDougall (1995) identified strong international business networks or contacts as one of the most important characteristics of successful international start-ups. McDougall *et al.* (1994) explained that networks helped international start-ups to identify international business opportunities and that the networks influenced country choices more than psychic distance. Coviello and Munro (*op. cit.*) added that these network contacts also influenced market entry initiatives in such a way that the resulting strategies appeared 'random and somewhat irrational, when in fact the span of activities can be linked to opportunities emerging from the network of relationships'. The conclusion is clear, that networks are a vital influence on small firm internationalisation. They produce the knowledge that helps identify opportunities and the community of resource that enables their exploitation.

Networks are based on personal relationships and reciprocity, and all relationships are based on trust and reputation (Dubini and Aldrich, 1991; Larson, 1992). However, organisational networks can develop based upon multiple networks of individuals. In these networks relationships may be multi-level rather than flat, formed by clusters of coalitions at different hierarchical levels. These complex networks can facilitate many forms of organisational relationships such as strategic alliances or joint ventures. The many links in these networks are strengthened by increased interaction and can be further strengthened by an entrepreneurial leader pulling the network together and giving it stability and direction. Since assets are owned by the constituent individuals or organisations, the financial resources needed and the risk associated with any joint venture are spread and flexibility increased. These organisational networks can create distinctive capabilities based on trust and mutual self-interest.

Learning theory also has a role to play in the literature on international entrepreneurship. The need to acquire local knowledge is important – it mitigates risk. Learning helps overcome the barrier of 'foreignness' and lack of local market knowledge (Lord and Ranft, 2000). Thus learning was central to Johanson and Vahlne's (*op. cit.*) stage model of internationalisation. Organisational learning is complex, particularly when taking place across national boundaries involving different languages, cultures and corporate governance structures and relevant to this is the concept of the learning organisation (see Chapter 18).

But knowledge can also form the basis of competitive advantage, particularly for the international start-up. To conduct business successfully in another country, a firm needs knowledge of:

- the needs and tastes of local customers;
- the general demand conditions in the local market;
- local competitors;
- how the marketing mix might be adapted to better suit local needs – product, price, promotion and distribution.

Related to this, Autio *et al.* (2000) put forward the interesting proposition that there is competitive advantage in newness because new organisations find it easier to learn than older ones and this helps them grow in new environments, including foreign markets. New firms therefore have an advantage over old, and by implication small over large firms. However, this is not borne out by statistical evidence that shows exporting to be most likely to be undertaken by large (and therefore older) organisations. Selassie *et al.* (2004) conclude that within small firms the proportion of firms engaged in exporting increases with firm size: 'The larger the firms the higher the export intensity and the more the experience in internationalisation.' Burns (2005) broadens the debate by placing learning and relational networks at the centre of the entrepreneurial architecture needed to develop larger entrepreneurial organisations. To him these are key entrepreneurial components in any context or arena, including age and size.

Export strategies

Exporting is one example of market development. Namiki (1988) suggests that small firms pursuing export markets adopt one of four competitive patterns of actions, and that stategies 3 and 4 better suit most small firms' resource capabilities:

1 *Competitive pricing; branding; control over distribution; advertising; and marketing innovation.*   This pattern requires a sophisticated understanding of marketing. Both brand development and control over distribution networks take time and an intimate knowledge of marketing. Innovation in marketing takes entrepreneurial flair. In that sense this pattern is more likely to be seen in a mature small firm that has had time to develop its resource base. However, remember always that type of resource is probably more important than volume.

2 *Capability to manufacture speciality products for customers, broad range of products; and new product development.*   This pattern requires significant capability and experience in tailoring products, to make broad product offerings available and to innovate. Again this pattern is more likely to be seen in a mature small firm that has had time to develop its resource base.

3 *Technological superiority and product innovation.*   This includes new-to-the-market products and innovations that can just as easily be marketed by start-ups based upon their uniqueness rather than their resource base.

4 *Customer service and high quality products.*   Again this uniqueness of product, possibly coupled with a narrow target (niche) market means it is a pattern that can be adopted by start-ups or very small firms.

But as we have observed, few small firms actually export. This may be because they do not want to – they are a lifestyle business – or because internationalisation may seem impractical to a 'market trader' such as a window cleaner.

Even if there is the potential and a will to internationalise, there can be disincentives. This may be because the owner-manager has a lack of knowledge and experience in the target market, coupled with a lack of information. Risk based upon ignorance is an important factor. We always know more about our own world rather than that of others and information asymmetry – a topic covered in Chapter 13 in respect of financing small firms – is a factor.

Owner-managers may fear lengthy payment terms or the possibility of bad debts. They face economic and financial risks such as currency fluctuations, cycles in economic activity and changing or punitive tax laws. They face political risks such as unstable governments, ideological differences and wars and other conflicts. They face social risks arising from religious or class differences, high disparities in wealth distribution, union militancy and riots or other forms of disorder.

Hop Back brewery was set up by **John** and **Julie Gilbert** in 1987 in the cellar of their pub near Salisbury in Wiltshire, England. In 2001 it started exporting its best known cask beer, *Summer Lightning*, to Italy where they now supply over 50 bars in Rome, Milan and Turin. Having sought advice initially from the government-backed organisation UK Trade and Investment, it now exports about 2700 gallons each year through Food from Britain in Italy, a marketing-development consultancy for British food and drink producers.

To some extent the decision not to internationalise reflects simple patriotism – a softer term than jingoistic nationalism – whereby both owner-manager and customers prefer to trade with local suppliers. Hence, given a straight choice, we will often buy the local product because we know how it was produced and, if it fails, we know where we can return it to obtain a refund. But cultural differences can also create significant barriers to trade in terms of taste, communication, lifestyles and values.

In the past the costs of international participation – such as transport, communication and taxes imposed as tariff barriers – were high, so prices of international products and services were also high, thus weakening demand. There was (and still is) exchange rate volatility. There is also political volatility. Who could have predicted the events of 9/11 and their effects on world trade?

Governments try to address these barriers by offering a range of support to firms wishing to export. However most of the literature is sceptical about generic programmes to motivate SMEs to export, pointing to certain behavioural characteristics that need to be addressed first (Karagozoglu and Lindell, 1996; Crick and Choudhry, 1997).

Help and Advice on Exporting in the UK

There are a number of schemes providing help and assistance for those firms wanting to follow this route in the UK. For example, UK Trade and Investment provides information on trading with most countries (over 200 countries across 34 market sectors) through their various country desks. Its Passport to Export programme was set up to help small firms do business overseas by providing training, planning, trade missions and support. They are able to put potential exporters in touch with the British embassy, high commission or consulate in their target country and help identify potential partners.

The British Chambers of Commerce issue export documentation and often, together with local Business Links, provide advice; the Central Office of Information offers export publicity information; and the Export Credits Guarantee Department of the DTI can arrange insurance against the possibility of non-payment. This can be assigned to a bank or other lending institution in order to obtain export finance.

For more information visit the following websites:

- UK Trade and Investment: www.uktradeinvest.gov.uk
- British Chambers of Commerce: www.britishchambers.org.uk
- Business Link: www.businesslink.gov.uk

Exit barriers

		Low	High
Entry barriers	Low	Low, stable returns	Low, risky returns
	High	High, stable returns	High, risky returns

Source: R.M.S. Wilson and C. Gilligan (1997) *Strategic Marketing Management: Planning, Implementation and Control*, Oxford, Butterworth-Heinemann.

Figure 16.3 Entry and exit barriers, profitability and risk

Two further factors affecting market attractiveness are entry and exit barriers. These are shown in Figure 16.3. The most attractive market from the point of view of profitability is likely to be one with high entry barriers and low exit barriers – few firms can enter but poor performers can easily exit. With high entry barriers but high exit barriers, poor performers are forced to stay on, making the returns more risky as they fight for market share. Unfortunately, a firm seeking to enter these markets has to overcome the high entry barriers, whatever they be. For example, this could involve overcoming legal barriers or high investment costs. If entry barriers are low, returns are likely to be low, but stable if exit barriers are low and unstable if exit barriers are high, and poor performers are forced to stay on if the market worsens.

Whilst, as we have seen, personal knowledge and the existence of personal relationships is likely to be a major element in selecting the overseas markets to try to exploit, underlying this must be sound commercial opportunities and legal realities. Exporting can be expensive and the margins in the export market must therefore be sufficient to justify it. All the risks and disincentives must be outweighed by the potential economic gain if the owner-manager is to internationalise.

The agency dilemma

For many small firms, exporting often means finding a distributor or sales agent in the country to which they wish to export that understands the local distribution channels and variations in customer needs (Dicken's model in Figure 16.2). In such situations the firm is very dependent upon the distributor. The distributor might influence changes in the product or other elements of the marketing mix to suit local needs. The firm might be expected to finance advertising and promotion themselves and with no certainty of a profitable return. Finding a distributor can be difficult enough but if, for whatever reason, the distributor does not push the firm's products (as in the case of P&M Products opposite) then there is little the firm can do other than seek to change distributors, unless they are willing to take on the job of setting up a sales outlet of their own in the country – and that can be both expensive and risky.

However, the relationship is not all one-sided. The sales agents – often themselves small firms – also face risks. Firstly, they are likely to be paid on a commission-only

Case with questions

P&M Products Ltd holds the world-wide licences to Blitzer and Blowpen, children's pens that create airbrush effects. It was set up in 1992 by Doug Eaton and now has sales of over £10 million, 80 per cent coming from exports to over 45 countries. This sales growth was derived from a simple strategy of selling the product into these countries through distributors, thus reducing the financial risk of expansion abroad. P&M simply exhibited and signed up distributors at overseas toy fairs.

In 1999 its own growth, the emergence of a global retail market influenced by mergers and the demand for consolidation of suppliers forced it to rethink its strategy. In particular a benchmarking exercise underlined the differing performance of distributors. Whilst a highly committed Finnish distributor achieved a 60 per cent penetration amongst its target market of 5- to 13-year-olds, its US distributor achieved only 3 per cent and its average was 20 per cent. Upon investigation it emerged that the US distributor had many other products in his portfolio and viewed P&M's products as marginal. After a six-month search P&M could not find a distributor that might be more committed to their products and decided to change strategy and set up its own subsidiary in this vital market. It adopted a strategy of direct response television promotions and spent some £650 000 on 'infomercials', which appeared at prime time on kids channels giving an 0800 telephone number and website address. The campaign was successful and big retailers like Toys 'R' Us and Wal-Mart started to take interest. US sales rose from $1 to $5.5 million in 1999.

The experience P&M Products Ltd had in the USA forced it to realise that, as large retailers rationalised their suppliers, they would continue to be squeezed as they did not offer a range of products that was large enough to be attractive. Consequently P&M decided to reposition itself as a pan-European supplier that could also sell products from other, smaller producers. Part of this strategy involved acquiring other, smaller firms so as to increase its product range. It now intends to get to a position where 25 per cent of sales are generated from new lines.

Questions
1 What do you think of this new strategy?
2 What are the advantages and disadvantages of it?
3 What risks does the company face in pursuing it?

basis – no sales, no commission. They may have an exclusive contract but it will relate to a specified geographic area, so they cannot expand without the agreement of the exporter. Nor are they likely to be able to sell competing products. What is more, the contract will be time-limited so that if they are too successful exporters may be tempted to distribute the product themselves and save paying the commission. Agents may be expected to finance advertising and promotion themselves but they are likely to be dependent on the exporter for a range of sales and promotional information and materials. All of these things will be set out in the contract and, when the contract comes to an end, its terms can be renegotiated. Finally, the agent is completely dependent on the exporter for product and product range development. If the exporter does not invest in this the agent may have difficulties no matter how good their sales skills.

A variation on the agency model is the franchise model. In this model the franchisee pays the franchisor to use the brand and sell the products or services.

Body Shop's rapid growth owes much to its successful global roll-out. Overseas expansion followed the same model as in the UK. In most countries a head franchisee was granted exclusive rights as user of the trademark, distributor and, after an initial trial of running a few shops themselves, the right to sub-franchise. In this way the firm built upon local market knowledge and minimised its risks. This model was not always followed because of the quality of the head franchisee. For example, the firm took back control of the franchise in France because the head franchisee was not delivering the volume of sales expected.

Franchisees may be appointed in any country, although a more usual model is to appoint a head franchisee in a country with the power to appoint sub franchisees. Commissions are then shared with the head franchisee. In this way local knowledge is used to roll out the franchise in the that country.

To be effective the agent, distributor or head franchisee must have a symbiotic relationship with the firm that appointed them, one based upon mutual trust and with effective incentives on both sides to ensure success. However, over time this relationship may well break down.

If, eventually, the firm decides to set up its own production facility, it may consider a *joint venture* with a local partner. Sometimes this is required by local law, sometimes it is simply a prudent way of gaining local knowledge of the business environment. The joint venture will probably involve setting up a new entity in which both partners acquire an ownership stake. However, it is the local firm that will typically control and manage the joint venture and that gives it the upper hand. As with distributors, a good deal of trust is required to make a success of a joint venture, especially given the likely cultural differences between partners (Hoon-Halbauer, 1999). And that is where personal relationships, rather that legal agreements, can be important for small firms.

Hightech Components started life as a representative agent for Inland Motors, a US manufacturer of high quality precision servo components for closed loop control systems. It was set up by **Roger Lacey**, who had initially worked for Precision Systems, the UK subsidiary of Inland Motors, as a salesman. However sales were disappointing and Inland decided to close its subsidiary, instead offering Roger an exclusive contract to operate as UK sales representative for Inland Motors on a commission-only basis.

A servo is a system in which the main mechanism is set in operation by a subsidiary mechanism and is able to develop a force greater than the force communicated to it. It is used in a wide variety of specialist applications such as radar systems and robotic arms where mechanisms need to rotate or move in different directions simultaneously. The servo components and systems Hightech sold were very high quality, precision instruments and the company quickly became an approved supplier for a large number of military, aerospace and industrial applications on land, sea and in the air. It also became an approved supplier to the Ministry of Defence in the UK.

Ten years later the company had seven employees and a turnover of £2 million. It had over 200 active accounts, mainly with blue-chip customers. Hightech now exclusively represented

→

five companies in the UK including three divisions of Inland Motors – Speciality Products, Defence Products and the Sierra Vista Division – as well as three other US companies – Inductosyn International, Sequential Electronic Systems Inc and Airflyte Electronics Company – and Thomson CSF of France. In acting for these companies Hightech was able to offer its customers a full range of servo products, including drives, controls, position and velocity transducers and amplifiers. Few UK competitors offered the comprehensive range of components that Hightech now offered. This meant that customers could obtain all the servo components that they needed to build systems without needing to go to other suppliers.

Hightech had a very professional approach to selling, following through on leads in a systematic manner, researching companies and their applications before approaching them and building close relationships once they became customers. It presented itself as a professional organisation helping engineers solve difficult technical problems. It offered seminars either in-house or at the premises of client companies. Rather than advertise, staff devoted time to writing technical articles for magazines, always mentioning the Hightech name. The only advertising space the company bought was in the trade reference manuals used by engineers looking for Hightech's type of equipment. The company only exhibited once or twice a year. It had high-quality sales literature, using bright colours which would stand out on an engineer's cluttered desk. In this way company achieved a conversion rate of enquiries to orders, of around 15 per cent compared to the industry average of about 5 per cent.

Hightech had found a comfortable market niche for itself, but growth prospects were limited. This incremental growth was mainly based on finding new customers, particularly as new applications for servo mechanisms emerged, but also based on making the most of the excellent relationships they already had with their existing customers to try to sell more to them. To help with this strategy Hightech continued to try to find new companies to represent in the UK. However, the problem was that these would have to be complementary products and be acceptable to the companies Hightech currently represented – particularly Inland Motors.

Hightech continued with this successful strategy. Five years later it had over 300 active accounts and turnover had topped £3 million. Hightech was also representing two new companies; Astro Instrument Corporation of the USA, which manufactured a unique brushless motor gearhead range that produced very high torque, and PMI Technologies of the USA, a sister company to Inland Motors producing low inertia printed circuit motors.

Relationships with the companies Hightech represented, particularly Inland Motors, were always good. Roger Lacey paid regular visits to them and Hightech made extensive use of the company's promotional material, suitably rebranded. However, Hightech's continuing success was not going unnoticed. Two year later, Kollmorgen Motion Technologies Group, owners of Inland Motors, purchased the assets and liabilities of Hightech and Roger Lacey became Director of European Business Development at Kollmorgen, responsible for improving the company's market penetration in Europe. Both parties were happy with the outcome.

Questions
1 Why was Hightech successful? How would you describe its marketing strategy?
2 What were the continuing business risks that Hightech faced as an agent during its seventeen years of independent life?
3 Was Hightech's approach to growth sensible? What other options did it have and why might they not have been pursued?

Summary

International entrepreneurship is a term used to describe entrepreneurial activities across national boundaries. The trend towards globalisation has encouraged interest in the area.

Most small firms are local in orientation, not international. The reasons for this may be simply that most small firms are lifestyle businesses that do not wish to internationalise. However there are real barriers to and risks associated with international trade. These range from cultural differences, legal, political and financial disincentives to lack of knowledge of the markets (information asymmetry). Having said that, some firms, like **B&Q**, can adapt and thrive in overseas markets.

A small but increasing number of start-ups are international from inception. These are often high-technology firms that need to exploit this advantage as quickly as possible. But a more important advantage is the international experience, networks and knowledge of the founders.

Figure 16.1 summarises the influences on the decision to internationalise but the principal factors are:

- The international vision of the founders;
- Their desire to be international market leaders;
- The identification of specific international opportunities;
- The possession of specific international contacts and sales leads.

The stage model of internationalisation sees small firms progressing through an incremental, sequential process of serving domestic markets, exporting, opening sales outlets and finally setting up production outlets – also called graduated entry. They target psychically close markets initially using market entry methods that require limited commitment, such as exporting. As they gain knowledge and experience from their market involvement over time, so they increase their commitment. This process is repeated from market to market. Although appealing, this model can not be proved using longitudinal research and ignores the increasing importance of 'first-mover advantage'.

As in the case of **figleaves.com**, the internet has made exporting easier for many small firms.

Networks produce the knowledge that helps identify opportunities and the community of resource that enables their exploitation. Learning underpins the stage theory of internationalisation but is key to the successful exploitation of any overseas market whether you agree with this model or not.

In most countries government agencies have been set up to help small firms, like **Hop Back** brewery, wishing to export. However most of the literature is sceptical about generic programmes.

Many firms use a commission-only agent to distribute their products in international markets. To be effective the firm and the agent or distributor must have a symbiotic relationship, one based upon mutual trust and with effective incentives on both sides to ensure success. However, over time this relationship may break down. Either, as **P&M Products** found, their products are not 'pushed' as hard as they would hope or, as **Hightech Components** found, the agents are too successful and are taken over by the exporter.

Useful websites

The International Monetary Fund (IMF) has a range of briefs on its website: *www.imf.org.*

The World Trade Organization website: *www.wto.org.*

The World Bank website: *www.worldbank.org.*

The United Nations Conference on Trade and Development publishes a World Investment Report annually. Highlights can be found on its website: *www.unctad.org.*

The International Chamber of Commerce has a world business organisation website: *www.icccwbo.org.*

The Institute of International Economics website contains numerous resources and links related to trade issues: *www.iie.com.*

The International Forum on Globalization has a website: *www.ifg.org.*

Essays and discussion topics

1 Why are most small firms not interested in internationalising?
2 What are the advantages to a small firm of thinking about internationalisation sooner rather than later?
3 What are the global trends that push small firms towards internationalising? Which are the strongest and which are accelerating fastest?
4 What are the disincentives they face?
5 What is a 'global brand'? How likely is a small firm to achieve a global brand presence?
6 What are the problems facing a service business internationalising? How might they be overcome?
7 What are the problems facing a retail business internationalising? How might they be overcome?
8 What is the role of e-business and the internet in internationalisation?
9 Few dot.com start-ups were really international from inception. Discuss. Try to provide examples of those that were and those that were not and the reasons for this.
10 What are the barriers to an international start-up? How can they be overcome?
11 Why are high-technology start-ups more likely to be international from inception?
12 Do you agree with the stage model of internationalisation? Explain.
13 How important to internationalisation is network theory?
14 How important to internationalisation is learning theory?
15 Why might 'real' entrepreneurs – not necessarily just owner-managers – find that they are really good at internationalisation?
16 Why might immigrants find that they are really good at international entrepreneurship? Is there any evidence to suggest that they are?
17 The most important issue in the business plan is management. The most important issue in internationalisation is management. The most important issue in business is management. Discuss.
18 Can education and training help the process of internationalisation? If so, how can this be achieved?
19 Is the degree and speed of internationalisation related to the age and size of the firm?
20 Is increasing internationalisation good for everyone?

Activities

1 Find an example of an international start-up and write a report explaining what it did and why it did it.
2 Each year the United Nations Conference on Trade and Development (UNCTAD) publishes its World Investment Report on its website (see list above). Access the most recent report. What does this tell you about the most recent trends? What does this tell you about the role of SMEs? Write a report assessing the current position.
3 Using the websites listed above, examine the trends in globalisation and write a report assessing their impact on the international business environment.

Further reading

Dicken, P. (1998) *Global Shift: Transforming the World Economy*, London: Paul Chapman Publishing.
Giddens, A. (2000) *Runaway World: How Globalisation is Reshaping our Lives*, Andover: Routledge.
Leonidou, L.C. and Katsikeas, C.S. (1996) 'The Export Development Process: An Integrative Review of Empirical Models', *Journal of International Business Studies*, no. 27 (Third Quarter).
Zahra, S.A. and George, G. (2000) 'International Entrepreneurship: The Current Status of the Field and Future Research Agenda', in M.A. Hitt, R.D. Ireland , S.M. Camp and D.I. Sexton, *Strategic Entrepreneurship: Creating a New Mindset*, Oxford: Blackwell.

References

Aggarwal, R. (1999) 'Technology and Globalisation as Mutual Reinforcers in Business: Reorienting Strategic Thinking for the New Millennium', *Management International Review*, 2 (1).
Autio, E., Sapienza, H.J. and Almeida, J.G. (2000) 'Effects of Age at Entry, Knowledge Intensity, and Imitability on International Growth', *Academy of Management Journal*, 43.
Bryan, D. and Rafferty, M. (1999) *The Global Economy in Australia: Global Integrastion and National Economic Policy*, St. Leonards: Allen & Unwin.
Burns, P. (2005) *Corporate Entrepreneurship: Building an Entrepreneurial Organisation*, Basingstoke: Palgrave Macmillan.
Carson, D. (1990) 'Some Exploratory Models of Assessing Small Firms' Marketing Performance', *European Journal of Marketing*, 24(11).
Coviello, N.E. and Munro, H.J. (1995) 'Growing the Entrepreneurial Firm: Networking for International Market Development', *European Journal of Marketing*, 29(7).
Crick, D. and Choudhry, S. (1997) ' "Small Business" Motives for Exporting: The Effect of Internationalisation', *Journal of Marketing Practice: Applied Marketing Science*, 3(3).
Dicken, P. (1998) *Global Shift: Transforming the World Economy*, London: Paul Chapman.
Dubini, P. and Aldrich, H. (1991) 'Personal and Extended Networks are Central to the Entrepreneurial Process', *Journal of Business Venturing*, 6.
Hoon-Halbauer, S.K. (1999) 'Managing Relationships with Sino-Foreign Joint Ventures', *Journal of World Business*, 34.
Johanson, J. and Wiedershheim-Paul, F. (1975) 'The Internationalisation Process of the Firm: Four Swedish Cases', *Journal of Management Studies*, 12 (October).
Johanson, J. and Vahlne, J.-E. (1977) 'The Internationalisation of the Firm: A Model of Knowledge Development and Increasing Foreign Market Commitments', *Journal of International Business Studies*, 4.
Johnson, J.E. (2004) 'Factors Influencing the Early Internationalisation of High Technology Start-ups: US and UK Evidence', *Journal of International Entrepreneurship*, 2.
Karagozoglu, N. and Lindell, M. (1996) 'Internationalisation of Small and Medium-sized Technology-based Firms: An Exploratory Study', *Journal of Small Business Management*, 36(1).

Larson, A. (1992) 'Network Dyads in Entrepreneurial Settings: A Study of the Governance of Exchange Relationships', *Administrative Science Quarterly*, 37.

Leonidou, L.C. and Katsikeas, C.S. (1996) 'The Export Development Process: An Integrative Review of Empirical Models', *Journal of International Business Studies*, 27 (Third Quarter).

Litvak, I.A. (1990) 'Instant International: Strategic Reality for Small High-Technology Firms in Canada', *Multinational Business*, 2 (Summer).

Lord, M.D. and Ranft, A.L. (2000) 'Orgainisational Learning about New International Markets: Exploring the Internal Transfer of Local Market Knowledge', *Journal of International Business Studies*, 31.

McDougall, P.P., Shane, S. and Oviatt, B.M. (1994) 'Explaining the Formation of International New Ventures: The Limits of Theories from International Business Research', *Journal of Business Venturing*, 9.

Namiki, N. (1988) 'Export Strategy for Small Business', *Journal of Small Business Management*, 26 (April).

Oakley, P. (1996) 'High-Tech NPD Success through Faster Overseas Launch', *European Journal of Marketing*, 30(8).

Oviatt, B.M. and McDougall, P.P. (1994) 'Towards a Theory of International New Ventures', *Journal of International Business Studies*, 25 (First Quarter).

Oviatt, B.M. and McDougall, P.P. (1995) 'Global Start-ups: Entrepreneurs on a Worldwide Stage', *Academy of Management Executive*, 9 (2).

Reuber, A.R. and Fisher, E. (1997) 'The Influence of the Management Team's International Experience on the Internationalisation Behaviours of SMEs', *Journal of International Business Studies*, 28 (Fourth Quarter).

Selassie, H., Mathews, B., Lloyd-Reason, T. and Mughan, T. (2004) 'Internationalisation Factors and Firm Size: An Empirical Study of the East of England', in F. McDonald, M. Mayer and T. Buck (eds), *The Process of Internationalisation: Strategic, Cultural and Policy Perspectives*, Basingstoke: Palgrave Macmillan.

Sullivan, D. and Bauerschmidt, A. (1990) 'Incremental Internationalisation: A Test of Johanson and Vahlne's Thesis', *Management International Review*, 30 (January).

Vernon, R. (1966) 'International Investment and International Trade in the Product Cycle', *Quarterly Journal of Economics*, 80.

Welch, L. and Loustarinen, R. (1988) 'Internationalisation: Evolution of a Concept', *Journal of General Management*, 14(2).

Wilson, R.M.S. and Gilligan, C. (1997), *Strategic Marketing Management: Planning, Implementation and Control*, Oxford: Butterworth-Heineman.

17

Social and Civic Entrepreneurship

Contents

- The rise of social entrepreneurship
- Social enterprise and the social economy
- The social entrepreneur
- The growth and development of the social enterprise
- The civic entrepreneur
- The dangers of social entrepreneurship
- Summary

LEARNING OUTCOMES

By the end of this chapter you should be able to:

- Explain what is meant by the terms 'social entrepreneurship' and 'civic entrepreneurship';

- Explain what is meant by the terms and list the qualities required by 'social entrepreneurs' and 'civic entrepreneurs';

- Explain the rise of social entrepreneurship;

- Explain what is meant by the term 'social enterprise' and 'social economy' and its role within the economy as a whole;

- Explain how social capital can be built up;

- Describe the issues facing the social enterprise at different stages of its life;

- List the dangers of social entrepreneurship.

The rise of social entrepreneurship

There is a long history of entrepreneurs with social motivations – from the chocolate maker J. Cadbury & Sons with its Quaker values, to the jam maker Wilkin & Sons. More recently Body Shop and Timberland have managed to successfully combine business and social values – and in the process enhance their brand image. But always the commercial objective came first. In contrast, social entrepreneurship is about putting the social objective first and utilising commercial skills to achieve them, in an entrepreneurial way. This also has a long history from Victorian hospitals to the modern-day hospice movement. Civic entrepreneurship, on the other hand, is to do with putting entrepreneurial behaviour into the public sector. The two concepts have often been used in an almost interchangeable way, but they are different. The link is through the voluntary, community and not-for-profit sectors that straddle the public and private sectors.

There is a long tradition of voluntary and community sector involvement in charitable initiatives, working with the public sector, and more recently in the delivery of government programmes, particularly regeneration initiatives. In the UK the sector received almost £4 billion from government, local authorities and the National Health Service in 2000/01, with about a third going to Housing Associations. In 2003 about 6.6 per cent of the UK population are estimated to be involved in some sort of activity that has community or social goals at its heart either as a start-up or as a manager – higher than the rate of entrepreneurial activity at 6.4 per cent (GEM, 2004). But in an environment where there is reduced government spending, increasing social need and greater competition for charitable donations, it is little wonder that not-for-profit organisations have turned to entrepreneurship for a new way forward – sometimes called 'social enterprise' or the 'Third Way'.

> 'Our vision is bold: social enterprise offers radical new ways of operating for public benefit. By combining strong public service ethos with business acumen, we can open up the possibility of entrepreneurial organisations – highly responsive to customers and with the freedom of the private sector – but which are driven by commitment to public benefit rather than purely maximising profit for shareholders. Many social enterprises are already showing this can be done. But we recognise that they are currently only a small part of our economy. We want to build on this foundation and create an environment in which more people feel they are able to start and grow such businesses.'
>
> **Tony Blair**, Prime Minister of Britain
> Foreword to *Social Enterprise: A Strategy for Success*, DTI, 2002

Entrepreneurship has shown itself adept at dealing with, indeed thriving in, a changing environment, so why not adapt it to produce social entrepreneurship?

The social entrepreneurship movement can take many forms. *In extremis* it proposes the reconstruction of welfare by building social partnerships between the public, social and business sectors. This involves not-for-profit organisations undertaking entrepreneurial ventures and the pooling of government welfare funding under the control of local communities. In the UK, Leadbeater (1997) has called for a 'new philosophy, practice and organisation' of social welfare with social entrepreneurs in a pivotal role pushing through innovations. He concluded that the UK social welfare system is in need of radical reforms that empower disadvantaged people and encourage them to take greater responsibility for, and control over, their lives. The UK government sees this as part of its strategy for tackling long-term levels of deprivation and high rates of social exclusion. Such is the enthusiasm for this that it launched the Social Enterprise Unit within the Department of Trade and Industry in 2001 and a new Minister for Social Enterprise was appointed.

In the USA, the not-for-profit sector is much larger than in Europe and now represents some 7 per cent of GDP, probably twice the size of the UK. Philanthropy, or charitable giving, is also far larger and better established, and the so-called 'Welfare State' is an anathema. It is not surprising, therefore, that in the USA there is a subtle shift of emphasis towards the entrepreneurial management of not-for-profit organisations and how they compete for funds. Boschee (1998) talks about a 'tectonic shift' in the way that not-for-profit organisations see themselves, and are funded. Brinckerhoff (2000) actually says that social entrepreneurship is now one of the essential characteristics of successful not-for-profit organisations. And an important extra dimension to social entrepreneurship, particularly in the USA, has become fund-raising.

Social entrepreneurship is therefore an emerging but ill-defined concept. It can be loosely defined as the use of entrepreneurial behaviour for social rather than profit objectives. Social entrepreneurs therefore differ from business entrepreneurs in terms of their mission. Their primary purpose is to 'create superior social value for their clients' (Mort *et al.*, 2003). They 'identify under-utilised resources – people, buildings, equipment – and find ways of putting them to use to satisfy unmet social needs' (Leadbeater, *op. cit.*). They may work in not-for-profit organisations, ethical businesses, government or other public bodies. However, in practice the term social entrepreneurship covers two overlapping activities:

1 Combining an income-generating activity with a social goal – often called a 'social enterprise', but the this can also include entrepreneurial fund-raising activities undertaken by charities.
2 Creating social change at a community level – normally through voluntary or community groups – without necessarily involving income-generating activities. This is also sometimes called 'civic innovation', which Fowler (2000) defines as creating 'something different in the way citizens understand and solve a social problem. It is characterised by a new set of civic institutions or patterns of social relations.'

There is further confusion. As with business entrepreneurship, the literature on social entrepreneurship often confuses the act of starting a new enterprises, albeit social, with entrepreneurial behaviour. Mort (*op. cit.*) defines social entrepreneurship as 'leading to the establishment of a new social enterprise and the continued innovation in existing ones'. However, a social enterprise – whether old or new – may not necessarily act entrepreneurially. Continuing innovation is the defining characteristic of entrepreneurship. Some authors recognise this, for example Leadbeater (*op. cit.*) says that social entrepreneurs 'innovate new welfare services and new ways of delivering existing ones'. However, note in this definition the absence of income-generating activities. Finally, just like business entrepreneurship, there is a strong focus in the literature on the individual rather than the organisation (see, for example, Thompson *et al.*, 2000).

A further distinction is the use of the term 'integrated' as opposed to 'complementary' social entrepreneurship. The term 'integrated social entrepreneurship' is used when surplus-generating activities simultaneously create social benefit, with one objective not getting in the way of the other. The art of integration, according to Fowler (*op. cit.*), is to 'marry the development agendas with market opportunities and then manage them properly so that they are synergistic not draining.' One example he uses is the Grameen Bank. This bank provides micro-credit to the poor of Bangladesh (its name means 'bank of the villages' in Bangla). The example quoted uses micro-credit to establish a new sort of self-sustaining rural association between women. The examples he uses seek to 'reduce external financial dependency, increase development impact and spread risk.'

All too often, however, this is not the case and the one agenda 'contaminates' the other perhaps leading to reduced efficiency and effectiveness on the commercial side or dilution of the social objectives on the other. When surpluses from the commercial activity are simply used as a source of cross-subsidy for the social objectives, rather than producing social benefits themselves, this can more accurately be called complementary social entrepreneurship – which almost takes us back to companies like Body Shop and Timberland.

Social enterprise and the social economy

Social enterprises are often the innovative start-up that is the brain-child of the social entrepreneur and therefore the terms often go hand in hand. Social enterprises can take a number of forms including social firms, cooperatives, credit unions, community loan funds, mutual insurers, development trusts, intermediate labour market projects, community foundations and the trading arms of charities. Again definitions do vary, although the primary mission of a social enterprise is always social. In the USA a defining characteristic seems to be the ability to earn revenues and to reinvest them to achieve the social aim. In the UK there is emphasis on community involvement and separation from government.

'There is a gap in the market, and that gap has developed because no matter how much money we have as an economy, public services are never going to be able to fulfil all of society's needs and expectations in terms of health, education and social welfare ... Part of the problem is that socially entrepreneurial behaviour unsettles a lot of people. Social entrepreneurs by their nature are seeing gaps in the market, developing new ways of doing things, and challenging others to do things differently. People are suspicious of that and don't know how to see it as a constructive force.'

Adele Blakebrough, co-founder of **Community Action Network**
Professional Manager, March 2004

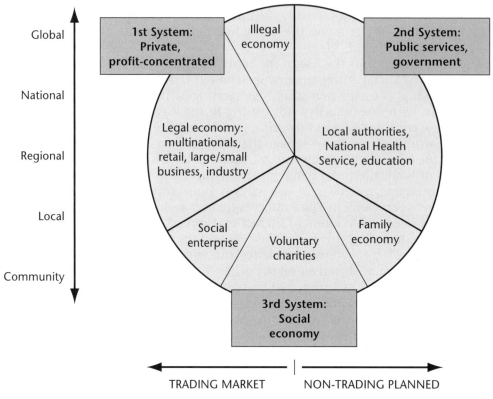

Source: Pearce (2003).

Figure 17.1 The three systems of the economy

Pearce (2003) characterises the social enterprise as:

- Having a primarily social purpose, with a secondary commercial activity;
- Achieving that purpose by engaging in trade;
- Not distributing profits to individuals but reinvesting profits either in the enterprise or new social ventures;
- Democratically involving members in its governance;
- Being openly accountable to a defined constituency and a wider community.

Pearce tries to explain this myriad of interlinking concepts by talking about three systems of the economy – private, public and social – delineated in two dimensions – trading/non-trading and global/community-based. These are shown in Figure 17.1. The first system is the private sector which concentrates on trading, with the objective of profit maximisation. But even this has its legal and illegal sectors. It operates on anything from a local to a global basis. The second is the public services and government, which operates in a planned, non-trading way. It is characterised as bureaucratic and inefficient. It also operates on anything from a local to a global basis. The third system is the social economy that includes social enterprise, voluntary and charity organisations and the family economy. This is far more

The **Big Issue** is probably the most prominent example of social entrepreneurship in the UK. Initially started up as a non-profit organisation by **John Bird** in 1991, backed by Gordon and Anita Roddick (of Body Shop fame), it is now a limited company that donates its profits to the Big Issue Foundation, a charity that addresses the problems of the homeless. Initially started in London, it copied a similar idea in New York.

The *Big Issue* is a magazine sold by homeless people on the streets of many UK towns and cities. Its aim is to allow them to work to earn a living – enabling them to address their personal poverty and retake control of their lives – and to campaign on social exclusion issues. The magazine sets out to sell to consumers on its quality rather than as a means of securing a charitable donation. However, the fact that it is sold by the homeless, exclusively on the streets rather than in magazine stores or by volunteers, makes the nature of the transaction not altogether straightforward. When they are asked to buy, consumers come face-to-face with beneficiaries and can see that they are trying to help themselves out of their situation. One key aspect of the transaction is that the consumer is asked for a limited and relatively small financial contribution (the cover price was £1.20 in 2006). This legitimises small donations. The round-figure price makes purchase easy in situations where time might be pressured. In this way giving small amounts to a morally justified and legitimate cause is made easy.

These factors have led researchers to conclude that 'the Big Issue is rarely bought for its own sake, simply as a quality product, but that its intrinsic value to the consumer does play a role in whether or not the initiative is supported. In other words, consumers buy it because they believe that they are helping the homeless (to help themselves)' (Hibbert *et al.*, 2002).

Questions
1 Is this an example of social entrepreneurship? If so, why?
2 Is the *Big Issue* a social enterprise? If so, why?
3 Is it an entrepreneurial response to a social problem? If so, why?
4 Is it the best response to this social problem? What problems do you see with it?

community-based and can be both planned and based upon market trading. The use of the word 'systems', rather than sector, in this context is deliberate as it is meant to imply that each system is not homogenous.

The social entrepreneur

As you might expect, the social entrepreneur seems to enjoy most of the character traits and behavioural characteristics as their business counterparts. Thompson (*op. cit.*) says:

They are *ambitious* and *driven*. They have been able to clarify and *communicate* an *inspirational mission*; around this they have *recruited* and *inspired* paid staff, users and partners, as well as an army of volunteers. They have known where they could acquire resources, some of which they have 'begged, stolen or borrowed.' But their vision has been for something which will *add value* for the underprivileged sections of the community. The development of *relationships* and *networks* of contacts has brought *trust*, visibility, credibility and cooperation which has been used as an intellectual base from which the physical and financial capital required to generate social capital could be found. *Creativity* invariably featured. By understanding and managing the inherent *risks* – the projects are often financially fragile with *limited resourcing*; and the targeted beneficiaries may be prone to stray – the social entrepreneurs have been able to overcome the inevitable setbacks and crises. (Italics in original)

Social entrepreneurs are often seen as leaders of public organisations who possess several leadership characteristics with significant personal credibility that allows them to generate followers' commitment in terms of social values which shows itself in strong collective purpose (Waddock and Post, 1991). Leadbeater (*op. cit.*) would add to the catalogue of characteristics the ability to identify gaps and related opportunity. He describes social entrepreneurs in similar ways to Thompson:

- 'Socially *driven, ambitious* leaders, with great skills in *communicating a mission* and *inspiring* staff, users and partners. In all cases they have been capable of creating impressive schemes with virtually *no resources*.'
- Creating '*flat and flexible organisations*, with a core of full-time paid staff, who work with few resources but a *culture of creativity*.'

In the UK, the GEM report (*op. cit.*) claims these social entrepreneurs are predominantly better qualified, older, employed and on higher incomes, although there are high levels of social entrepreneurship amongst disadvantaged groups. It also claims that women and ethnic minorities are much more likely to be social entrepreneurs than mainstream entrepreneurs. These claims should, however, be treated with caution because the definition of social entrepreneur is so broad that it includes anybody trying to start or managing alone or with others any form of social, community or voluntary activity.

In essence social entrepreneurs are entrepreneurs in a social or not-for-profit context. The difference is that their prime motivation, aims and mission are social rather than commercial. They still pursue opportunity and continually innovate, but for the purpose of serving their social mission. And in doing this they, perhaps, exhibit a longer-term planning horizon than the typical business entrepreneur. They can become entrepreneurial leaders, if they have or can develop the skills, but again their mission and values are social. Perhaps the skills they need to achieve their aims are slightly different. The School for Social Entrepreneurs identifies the basic tools of social entrepreneurship as fund-raising, marketing, finances, charity law and publicity. However, I would add the need to have a heightened sense of accountability to the wide range of stakeholders involved in the complexity of a social enterprise. And it is this that sets them apart.

Not-for-profit organisations are uniquely complex organisations that are set up to provide some sort of exchange that results in increased social value. They often have multiple stakeholders – clients, sponsors, donors, employees, government – and multiple service objectives. In a business the objective is usually far more simple – that is to maximise the return to the owner. Not-for-profit organisations also face a rapidly changing environment where they compete intensely with each other and even other commercial organisations for monetary donations. They therefore must pursue dual strategies that involve commercial success by developing sustainable competitive advantage in order to fulfil their social mission. It is this complexity that the social entrepreneur is somehow able to bind into vision that affects public attitudes (Waddock and Post, *op. cit.*).

Mort *et al.* (*op. cit.*) use this complexity to argue for the multi-dimensional nature of social entrepreneurship. They conceptualise the social entrepreneurship construct and depict it in Figure 17.2. They argue that, firstly, the social entrepreneur is driven by a mission of 'creating better social value than their competitors which results in them exhibiting entrepreneurially virtuous behaviour.' Secondly, they exhibit balanced judgement and an ability to see through the complexity of the situation they face. Thirdly, in a similar way to business entrepreneurs, they are able to recognise opportunities to create better social value that others can not. Finally, just like business entrepreneurs, they display innovativeness, proactiveness and risk-taking in their decision-making. Only when these four elements combine is social entrepreneurship created.

Virtue is a key element in the construct. It underpins the social entrepreneur's balanced judgement. The authors define it as 'positively good values such as love, integrity, honesty and empathy, which must be acted upon to become genuine virtues.' The social entrepreneur's attitudes and behaviours must have a virtuous dimension. This influences everything they do and gives them a 'coherent unity of purpose and action in the face of moral complexity.' And of course the similarities with the entrepreneurial leader, with their strong vision built on equally strong underlying values as described in previous chapters, are obvious. Only the context changes.

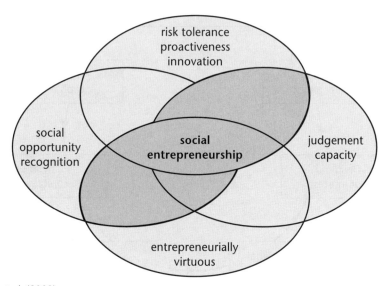

Source: Mort *et al.* (2003).

Figure 17.2   Multidimensional social entrepreneurship construct

The growth and development of the social enterprise

Leadbeater (*op. cit.*) places great store on the development of social capital during the life of the social enterprise. He calls this a 'virtuous circle'. It starts with an endowment of social capital – 'a network of relationships and contracts, which are tied together by shared values and interests.' The trick for the entrepreneur is to lever this up to gain access to more resources – firstly physical capital such as buildings and then financial capital to start the wheel turning and then human resources to start delivering the project. Organisational capital is generated as the project starts delivering its objectives and further resources are attracted, but this will only be achieved with greater formalisation in structures and financial controls and a stronger set of relationships with partners. Finally the project starts to pay dividends, such as the creation of permanent physical infrastructure that can be used by the community – new community centres, hospices or sports facilities. And the increased trust and cooperation generated by a successful project can lead to an fresh injection of social capital as the network of relationships and contacts expands. And so the cycle continues. This is shown in Figure 17.3.

To Leadbeater only this fusion of the public and private sectors produces this chemical reaction:

> The welfare state is blessed with a lot of physical and financial capital. Yet it destroys social and human capital as often as it creates it. It is too bureaucratic to generate the relationships of trust and goodwill, which can start to revive a sense of

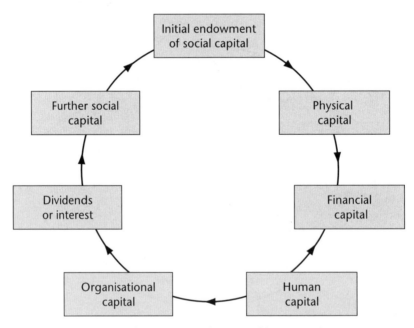

Source: Leadbeater (*op. cit.*), courtesy of Demos (www.demos.co.uk/openaccess).

Figure 17.3 The virtuous circle of social capital

community and solidarity ... The private sector relies on social capital, but all too rarely creates it. Private sector companies depend upon a relationship of trust with their employees, consumers and the communities where they operate. Yet all too often restructuring, delayering and down sizing have destroyed these bonds of social capital.

Leadbeater contends that entrepreneurial social organisations are driven to grow, but, like their commercial counterparts, they can run into a range of problems that can stunt their growth or even lead to failure at each stage. This stage growth model is shown in Figure 17.4. At each stage there are different imperatives and a need for different skills.

Stage 1 sees the organisation trying to establish itself. The key issue is to set the appropriate mission. But as the organisation grows this may have to be revisited as the scope of its activities expands. This needs to be handled sensitively with all the

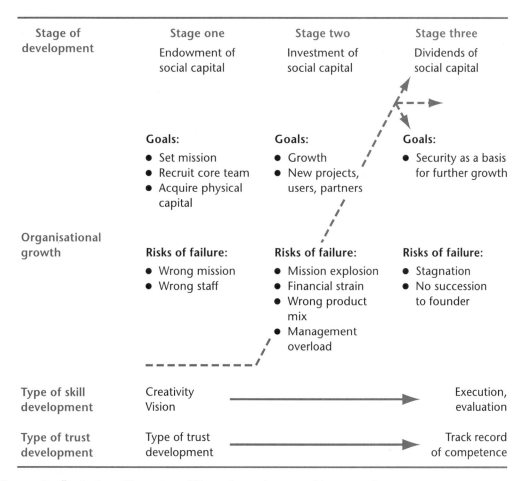

Source: Leadbeater (*op. cit.*), courtesy of Demos (www.demos.co.uk/openaccess).

Figure 17.4 The life cycle of the social entrepreneur

stakeholders. There is always the danger that one group of stakeholders may hijack the mission and revise it to meet its own ends, thus alienating others. This can be a risk for organisations that are short of funds and the funders therefore are able to set conditions that affect the mission. At the other extreme, too much influence by consumers may result in low prices and financial problems for the organisation that can threaten its survival. These are issues of governance, which become more complex as the organisation grows.

As social organisations grow they may have to change the products or services they offer because of changing social need. New products or services may displace existing ones and, without clear criteria to make these decisions, such as profit, the process can become very political. This means that the organisation needs to become very adept at evaluating the success of its work – developing appropriate measures of accountability is a significant issue in a not-for-profit organisation. At the same time it needs to become more professional and to develop the same entrepreneurial leadership skills outlined in Chapter 8. Effective, efficient delivery becomes increasingly important. The organisation needs to build a reputation based on its track record – in the commercial world it would be called developing a brand. And the final challenge is the same as for its commercial counterpart – how to manage succession.

The civic entrepreneur

The term 'civic entrepreneurship' is concerned with entrepreneurship within larger civic organisations in the public sector, or Pearce's 2nd System (Figure 17.2). It is about creating change in innovative ways. This may or may not involve income-generating activities. Leadbeater and Goss (1998) profiled five civic organisations that exhibited entreprenerial behaviour: a small school, a police force, a health authority and two local authorities. The school reinvented itself to become more of a community resource. The police force implemented a restorative justice system for youth crime involving a number of different local agencies. The health authority worked to integrate community services by encouraging general practitioners (local doctors) to plan strategically how to meet local health needs rather than concentrating solely on delivering their basic medical services contract. Both local authorities restructured to create more space for entrepreneurship, devolving powers and delegating authority. Leadbeater and Goss noted that 'all these organisations were inspired by a sense of mission, which focused on producing better outcomes rather than merely producing more output. They were guided by a goal of becoming more effective, not merely more efficient.'

Civic entrepreneurship involves a civic manager, head-teacher or other head of a organisational unit acting entrepreneurially. Kirby (2003) likens them to intrapreneurs in the commercial world. According to Ross and Unwalla (1986) the best intrapreneurs are result-orientated, ambitious, rational, competitive and questioning. They dislike bureaucracy – so they are less likely to be found in the 2nd System – and are challenged by innovation but have an understanding of their organisation and a belief in their colleagues. They are adept at politics and good at resolving conflict – and need to be because they will face a lot of it as they smooth the connections with 'conventional' management.

Pinchot (1985) also characterises intrapreneurs as goal orientated and self-motivated but, unlike entrepreneurs, he says they are also motivated by organisational (or professional) reward and recognition. They are able to delegate but not afraid to roll their sleeves up and do what needs to be done themselves. Like entrepreneurs, they need to be self-confident and optimistic, but may well be cynical about the bureaucratic systems within which they operate, although they do believe they can circumvent or manipulate them. In that sense they are good at working out problems within the 'system' – or even bypassing the system – rather than leaving the organisation. Like entrepreneurs they are strongly intuitive, but unlike entrepreneurs their corporate or civic background means they are willing to undertake research before they act. They are risk-takers but extremely self-confident, believing that, if they lose their jobs, they will quickly find new ones. However, they are sensitive to the need to disguise risks within the organisation so as to minimise the political cost of failure. They are adept communicators with strong interpersonal skills that make them good at persuading others to do what they want. In this respect they are somewhat more patient than entrepreneurs.

However, intrapreneurs work in the commercial world and civic entrepreneurs in the public sector and Leadbeater and Goss (*op. cit.*) have a slightly different view of the qualities needed for success. They would add that civic entrepreneurs know that they cannot succeed alone and are keen to involve other individuals or organisations with complementary skills. They are keen to work across traditional boundaries, within and outside their organisation. They also need to be extremely adept at dealing with complex, political situations and communicating with a wide range of stakeholders with differing objectives. To work effectively, a civic entrepreneur either needs to be highly placed themselves or, like an intrapreneur, to have a high-level sponsor to protect them when times are difficult or vested interests are upset and to help them to unblock the blockages to change as they occur. Sponsors will help secure resources, provide advice and contacts. They will need to nurture and encourage the civic entrepreneur, particularly early on in the life of the project or when things go wrong. They will need to endorse and create visibility for the project at the appropriate time and be good at managing the political and public dimensions of their work, building legitimacy as the project becomes successful. As Leadbeater and Goss (*op. cit.*) noted in their study of civic entrepreneurship:

> In most cases the process of revitalisation began with a joint effort by political leaders, managers, staff and users to rethink the organisation's goals and purpose. This strategic sense of purpose was not confined to senior managers. They understood that this sense of purpose needed to be shared, ideally from the outset, by politicians, staff and users.

The issue in civic entrepreneurship is the degree of risk that is acceptable within the services offered in the public sector. Many of these services – like health care and education – affect people's lives. Whilst innovation is obviously needed, otherwise organisations will stultify, what scale of innovation, with the related risks, should a civic entrepreneur be allowed to push through? Entrepreneurship involves the risk of failure, but if failure means that a person dies – as it might do in the context of health care – is that risk acceptable?

Case with questions

Ridgeway Primary School and Nursery is a large primary school on the outskirts of Croydon in the UK. It is an unlikely place to find an example of civic entrepreneurship but since 1998 it has defied the UK's national curriculum and not implemented the literacy or numeracy hours required of it. Instead it has followed its own strongly held philosophy that a primary curriculum is only made coherent through making creative links between subjects. The school's vision is to have a creative curriculum that inspires both children and teachers to learn. The school wants to create a real learning community based upon a genuine will to learn that encourages creativity in children and teachers alike. The literacy and numeracy hours did not fit with this philosophy.

Head teacher, **Anna House**, believes creativity is the thread that runs through everything the school does. She believes in motivating people rather than working through hierarchies and structures. Parents, governors and visitors are used as a creative resource. Teachers work in creative teams along with teaching assistants, each learning from the other. Even the school meals organisers are encouraged to think creatively.

There is a detailed 38-page teaching and learning policy which draws on research into effective teaching and learning to justify the school's policies. The school aims to create a holistic curriculum with certain sustained themes like 'spirituality', 'citizenship', 'water' or 'save the planet' running through it so as to create continuity and embed learning, thus avoiding the danger of short-term, easily forgotten experiences. There are three themes each year. The themes build up to provide a view of the world that fire the children's curiosity. There is detailed planning of the curriculum around these themes. Literacy or numeracy is encouraged because of the child's interest in the theme, rather than as an end in itself. So, for example, the theme of 'shoes' was the context in year 6 for learning about materials and developing different shoe designs. This 'enquiry-based learning' provides scope for individual creativity and the development of thinking skills. The curriculum is enhanced by lunchtime clubs in areas such as chess, drama and even Japanese (run by a parent). Creative activity is linked to opportunities to think, so as to turn the experience into learning. So, for example, children are encouraged to think about how and why certain types of shading on a drawing create the effect of texture. There is also an emphasis on developing independence and self-direction in learning. Children assess themselves against their own learning targets. In year 1 children are given their own Inventions Book in which to design creative solutions to problems. At Key Stage 1 (5–7 years old) there are no set playtimes. Children develop their own portfolios showing achievements in learning. One feature of this is the extensive use of digital photographs to record these achievements. Teachers also enjoy much autonomy. For example, they can choose when, and if, to take a playtime.

The risks faced by the school in not following the national curriculum were high. Ultimately, if there had been persistently poor Ofsted (the UK schools' inspectorate) reports the school may have been closed. But the risk has paid off. Not only has it passed all its Ofsted visits but Ofsted has describes the school as having a 'very high quality curriculum'.

Questions
1 Is this an example of civic entrepreneurship? If so, why?
2 Is this an entrepreneurial response to an educational issue? If so, why?
3 What are the risks posed by this form of action?

The dangers of social entrepreneurship

There are always lessons to be learnt when the activities of one sector are compared to another. Eikenberry and Kluver (2004) acknowledge the need for the public sector to work with not-for-profit organisations and community and voluntary organisations: 'They are more than just tools for achieving the most efficient and effective mode of service delivery; they are also important vehicles for creating and maintaining a strong civil society.' Alexander *et al.* (1999) underline the importance of their role as 'schools or laboratories of democratic citizenship' – training grounds for citizenship that involve people in socially beneficial activities that they would not otherwise engage in.

However, the 'Third Way' has been criticised from many quarters as ill-defined and not something that can be relied upon to deliver social objectives as a matter of policy, as it relies too much on the philanthropic motives of individuals. It has also been pointed out that, unlike its commercial counterpart, no economic case in terms of efficiency can be made to support a shift to social entrepreneurship and the market is not a legitimate benchmark to justify changes from a rights-based welfare system (Cook *et al.*, 2003).

The problem then is the mixing of social and economic objectives. There is no accepted framework to measure the two together and in particular the trade-off between them. What is efficient economically may be ineffective socially, and vice versa, but where does the acceptable trade-off lie, and who decides? Social enterprises can therefore all too easily avoid rigorous monitoring both because of the lack of an accounting framework and because of the complexity of the interests of their diverse stakeholder base. In the commercial world it is simple. Owners generally look to get the maximum financial return on their investment and, if one owner-manager has different, perhaps lifestyle, objectives, he has no other owners who can object to his decision.

Fowler (*op. cit.*) also has reservations, noting particularly that it is a risky framework for the development of the recipients of international development aid – the non-government development organisations. These organisations handle large amounts of public money. He doubts that they can handle the conflicts between social and commercial behaviour. He argues that retaining their moral underpinning and inspiration is vital and any involvement in income-generating activities will compromise this. He also fears that the social entrepreneur framework is not sustainable for their survival because they are so dependent on government aid. There is also the concern about what entrepreneurial activities the large amounts of public money they recieve might be put to. He is therefore more in favour of 'civic entrepreneurship' which he sees as providing 'civic, as opposed to public, legitimacy and economic viability from a broad base of citizen support.'

Eikenberry and Kluver (*op. cit.*) are particularly concerned about the problems of what they call 'the methods and values of the market' being applied in both the public and the not-for-profit sector and its detrimental impact upon democracy and citizenship in the USA. They put their point strongly: 'For the public sector, an emphasis on entrepreneurialism is incompatible with democratic citizenship and its emphasis on accountability and collective action for the public interest (King and Strivers, 1998; Box, 1999; deLeon and Denhardt, 2000; Denhardt and Denhardt, 2000; Box *et al.*, 2001). Furthermore, the market model places little or no value on democratic ideals such as fairness and justice (Terry, 1998). For the non-profit sector, marketisation trends such as commercial revenue generation, contract competition, the influence of new and emerging donors, and social entrepreneurship compromise the non-profit sector's civil society roles as value guardians service providers and advocates, and the builders of social capital.'

There are a number of strategic issues that run through the literature on social entrepreneurship. The first is that the mixing of social and economic objectives within a social enterprise can be dangerous. There are difficulties accounting for the two objectives and in particular making trade-offs between the two. The range of activities – everything from social services to shops – means that it is imperative to focus on the core business, or mission and realise what is peripheral, a means to the ultimate mission. Unless this happens, social enterprises can avoid rigorous monitoring and democratic accountability. But how do these organisations decide on what is their core mission and who decides? And even then, how do they arrive at a clear idea of what is 'performance', and then how it can be measured?

The likely complex nature of the stakeholders' interests in a social organisation mean that an understanding of these dynamics and how they might be influenced is important. With a lack of clear performance criteria, these dynamics take on an added importance. This raises the possibility of political influence leading to economic benefit, otherwise known as political patronage and other less savoury names. How do social enterprises guard against this?

Social enterprise is at the boundary between public and private sectors – and that boundary keeps shifting. There is an inherent conflict in the values and beliefs of the two sectors. It is a conflict we have seen before in the family firm (Chapter 15). And with an acknowledgement of the conflict can come ways of finding a resolution. The issues relating to social enterprise revolve around its efficiency and effectiveness on the one hand and its democratic accountability on the other. But the argument that the public sector itself – in all its many guises – can learn some lessons from entrepreneurship seems to have been won.

Summary

Social entrepreneurship is an ill-defined concept. It can be loosely defined as the use of entrepreneurial behaviour for social rather than profit objectives. Social entrepreneurs therefore differ from business entrepreneurs in terms of their mission. Social enterprises are the organisations social entrepreneurs set up to achieve their aims. The **Big Issue**, started by **John Bird**, is probably the best known example of social entrepreneurship in the UK.

A major confusion is whether or not they need to engage in income-generating commercial activities. If they do, the surpluses should be applied to their social mission. Integrated social entrepreneurship is when surplus-generating activities simultaneously create social benefit.

Social entrepreneurship happens when social opportunity recognition combines with risk tolerance, proactiveness, innovation and good judgement, and is applied towards a virtuous objective.

Social entrepreneurs have many of the same qualities as business entrepreneurs, however they also need a heightened sense of accountability to the wide range of stakeholders involved in a social enterprise.

The virtuous circle of social capital can lead to its growth and the building of capacity. But as the social enterprise grows it will face different problems, imperatives and the need for different skills. These are shown in Figure 17.4.

Civic entrepreneurship is concerned with entrepreneurial behaviour in the public sector. It is similar to intrapreneurship in the commercial world, although often the civic entrepreneur is also an existing head of an organisational unit – like **Anna House** at the **Ridgeway Primary School and Nursery**. The issue here is the degree of risk that is acceptable within many of the services offered in the public sector, when they might affect people's lives. What scale of innovation, with the related risks, should a civic entrepreneur be allowed to push through – for example in the area of health care or education?

The mixing of social and economic objectives within a social enterprise can be dangerous. There are difficulties accounting for the two objectives and in particular making trade-offs between the two. Social enterprises can therefore avoid rigorous monitoring and democratic accountability. This is particularly the case when the body is in receipt of large amounts of public money, such as non-government development organisations. It has also been pointed out that no economic case can be made for a shift to social entrepreneurship. Finally there is the fear that the increase in commercialisation of not-for-profit organisations will jeopardise their role as training grounds for democratic citizenship.

Useful websites

Ashoka Changemakers (a website of resources for social entrepreneurship):
   www.changemakers.net

Centre for Social Innovation (Stanford Business School website): www.gsb.stanford.edu/csi/

Demos (a political 'think-tank'): www.demos.co.uk

The Small Business Service Social Enterprise Unit: www.sbs.gov.uk, and select 'Social Enterprise'

Joshua Venture (a website of social entrepreneurship resources):
   www.joshuaventure.org/resources/soc-ent-resources.html

Social Entrepreneurship Monitor, UK:
   www.gemconsortium.org/default.asp, and select 'Documents' then 'UK'

The Institute for Social Entrepreneurs: www.socialent.org

The School for Social Entrepreneurs (UK): www.sse.org.uk

Essays and discussion topics

1 How would you define social entrepreneurship? Is the term misused?
2 Can social and business objectives mix? If so, how?
3 What are the cultures of the private and public sectors? How do they differ and why will they clash? Can this be resolved? If so, how?
4 Can not-for-profit organisations like charities be run entrepreneurially? Should they be?

5   How do you feel about the entrepreneurial – some would say aggressive – fund-raising activities of some charities? Does this affect their ability to meet their mission?

6   Most charities raise money, however little, for their causes. Does this make them social enterprises? What distinguishes the social enterprise? Does how much is raised or how it is raised affect your view?

7   How is a social entrepreneur different from a business entrepreneur?

8   How will social entrepreneurs know they have been successful?

9   'Virtue is in the eye of the beholder.' How might this comment apply to the social entrepreneur?

10 How different is the accumulation of social capital by the social entrepreneur from financial capital by the business entrepreneur at start-up?

11 Compare and contrast Leadbeater's life cycle model to the model by Greiner for a business.

12 How is a civic entrepreneur different from an intrapreneur?

13 How will civic entrepreneurs know they have been successful?

14 Is risk-taking appropriate in the public sector?

15 How can a social enterprise be held to account?

16 Should public money be given to a social enterprise?

17 Should public money be used to develop a commercial activity as part of a social enterprise? If not, why not? If yes, why and would there be any constraints on this?

18 In subsidising a social enterprise tax payers' money is being used to put other owner-managers of small local firms out of business. Discuss.

19 Where is the boundary between social enterprise and voluntary or charity organisations? Give examples.

20 Where is the boundary between social enterprise and commercial business? Give examples.

Activities

1   Go to the Demos website and download the report by Charles Leadbeater: *The Rise of the Social Entrepreneur* (it is freely available). It contains five case studies:

- The Bromley-by-Bow Centre
- The Mildmay Mission Hospital
- Kaleidoscope
- The Youth Charter for Sport
- The Eldonians

Select one case and write a report evaluating whether this is a legitimate example of social entrepreneurship. Note any dangers you see in the case. What do you think of the author's argument for civic entrepreneurship?

2   Go to the Demos website and download the report by Charles Leadbeater and Sue Goss: *Civic Entrepreneurship* (it is freely available). It contains five case studies:

- West Walker Primary School
- Thames Valley Police
- Kirklees Metropolitan Authority
- Dorset Health Authority
- South Somerset District Council.

Select one case and write a report evaluating whether this is a legitimate example of civic entrepreneurship. Note any dangers you see in the case. What do you think of the authors' argument for civic entrepreneurship?

3   Review the websites on this topic given in the chapter and prepare a list of resources that are available to someone thinking of setting up a social enterprise.

Further reading

Brinckerhoff, P. (2000) *Social Entrepreneurship: The Art of Mission-Based Venture Development*, Hoboken, NJ: Wiley.

Dees, J.G., Emerson, J. and Economy, P. (2001) *Enterprising Nonprofits: A Toolkit for Social Entrepreneurs*, Hoboken, NJ: Wiley.

References

Alexander, J., Nank, R. and Strivers, C. (1999) 'Implications of Welfare Reform: Do Nonprofit Survival Strategies Threaten Civil Society?', *Nonprofit and Voluntary Sector Quarterly*, 28(4).

Boschee, J. (1998) *Merging Mission and Money: A Board Member's Guide to Social Entrepreneurship*, Washington, DC: BoardSource.

Box, R.C. (1999) 'Running Government Like a Business: Implications for Public Administration Theory and Practice', *American Review of Public Administration*, 29(1).

Box, R.C., Marshall, G.S., Reed, B.J. and Reed, C.M. (2001) 'New Public Management and Substantive Democracy', *Public Administration Review*, 60(5), September/October.

Brinckerhoff, P. (2000) *Social Entrepreneurship: The Art of Mission-Based Venture Development*, Hoboken, NJ: Wiley.

Cook B., Dodds C. and Mitchell W. (2003) 'Social Entrepreneurship – False Premises and Dangerous Forebodings', *Australian Journal of Social Issues*, 38(1), February.

deLeon, L. and Denhardt, R.B. (2000) 'The Political Theory of Reinvention', *Public Administration Review*, 60(2), March/April.

Denhardt, R.B. and Denhardt, J.V. (2000) 'The New Public Service: Serving Rather than Steering', *Public Administration Review*, 60(6), November/December.

Eikenberry, A. and Kluver, J.D. (2004) 'The Marketisation of the Non-profit Sector: Civil Society at Risk?', *Public Administration Review*, 64(2), March/April.

Fowler, A. (2000) 'NGDOs as a Moment in History: Beyond Aid to Social Entrepreneurship or Civic Innovation?', *Third World Quarterly*, 21(4).

GEM (Harding, R. and Cowling, M.) (2004) *Social Entrepreneurship Monitor, United Kingdom*, London: London Business School.

Hibbert, S.A., Hogg, G. and Quinn, T. (2002) 'Consumer Response to Social Entrepreneurship: The Case of the Big Issue in Scotland', *International Journal of Nonprofit and Voluntary Sector Marketing*, 7(3).

King, C.S. and Strivers, C. (eds) (1998) *Government Is Us: Public Administration in an Anti-Government Era*, Thousand Oaks, CA: Sage.

Kirby, D. (2003) *Entrepreneurship*, Maidenhead: McGraw-Hill.

Leadbeater, C. (1997) *The Rise of the Social Entrepreneur*, London: Demos.

Leadbeater, C. and Goss, S. (1998) *Civic Entrepreneurship*, London: Demos.

Mort, G.S., Weerawardena, J. and Carnegie, K. (2003) 'Social Entrepreneurship: Towards Conceptualisation', *International Journal of Nonprofit and Voluntary Sector Marketing*, 8(1).

Pearce, J. (2003) *Social Enterprise in Anytown*, Calouste Gulbenkian Foundation.

Pinchot, G.H. (1985) *Intrapreneurship*, New York: Harper & Row.

Ross, J.E. and Unwalla, D. (1986) 'Who is an Intrapreneur?', *Personnel*, 63(12).

Terry, L.D. (1998) 'Administrative Leadership, Neo-Managerialism, and the Public Management Movement', *Public Administration Review*, 58(3), May/June.

Thompson, J., Alvey, G. and Lees, A. (2000) 'Social Entrepreneurship – A Look at the People and the Potential', *Management Decision,* 38/5.

Waddock, S.A. and Post, J.E. (1991) 'Social Entrepreneurs and Catalytic Change', *Public Administration Review*, 51(5).

18

Corporate Entrepreneurship

Contents

- Defining corporate entrepreneurship
- Building an entrepreneurial architecture
- The learning organisation
- Shaping the architecture
- The role of entrepreneurial leadership
- Constructing an entrepreneurial culture
- The role of size and structure
- Management and structure
- Freedom and control
- Summary

LEARNING OUTCOMES

By the end of this chapter you should be able to:

- Explain what is meant by the term 'corporate entrepreneurship' and the basic schools of thought that have contributed to its development;

- Explain what is meant by the term 'entrepreneurial architecture', how it might be shaped and how it might lead to sustainable competitive advantage in the appropriate environment;

- Explain what is meant by the term 'learning organisation' and how it underpins the entrepreneurial architecture in a larger firm;

- Explain what is meant by the term 'entrepreneurial management' and

the differences between it and traditional management;

- List the disciplines that contribute to this new area;

- Explain what an entrepreneurial culture means in an organisation;

- Explain how structures and size can encourage and contribute to the development of corporate entrepreneurship;

- Describe the balance between freedom and control needed in an entrepreneurial organisation and explain the dimensions on which it can be measured.

Defining corporate entrepreneurship

Greiner (1972) predicts that the final crisis facing a business is one of 'red tape' or bureaucracy – the loss of its entrepreneurial nature (see Chapter 8). And with the loss of entrepreneurship there is the danger that the firm will cease to change and innovate. But is this inevitable? Can it be delayed or even prevented? In fact, many truly successful innovations, particularly product innovations but certainly the ones involving large amounts of capital, originate from large not small companies. There are few Dysons in this world who successfully struggle to bring a genuinely new product to the market themselves, against all the odds. (James Dyson invented a completely new 'cyclone' vacuum cleaner and then successfully claimed against Hoover for infringing his patents with their 'vortex' cleaner.) There are just too many problems to sort out – not least of which is finding the finance. Moreover it is easier for a middle or large company to sort out these problems because it has more resources, more experience ... more of everything to throw at a problem.

Incremental improvements to products and services are one thing. They can be addressed systematically. But these changes, important as they are, do not conquer new markets. Often what is needed is the mould-breaking innovation and big companies can put bureaucratic barriers in the way of this. When the personal computer was first introduced it was considered simply a toy and the market leader in computers, IBM, ignored it for many years. However, the personal computer turned the whole computer industry on its head and nearly caused the demise of IBM. Not only did IBM not lead in this major innovation, it also tried to ignore it – and paid the price.

'Corporate entrepreneurship' is the term used to describe entrepreneurial behaviour in an established, larger organisation. The objective of this is simple – to gain competitive advantage by encouraging innovation at all levels in the organisation – corporation, division, business unit, functional or project team levels. Even as late as the 1980s some academics still believed it was difficult, if not impossible, for entrepreneurial activity to take place in larger, bureaucratic organisations (Morse, 1986). Nevertheless there is a large literature on the general phenomenon stretching back over 30 years. Despite this there is no real consensus on what the term means. Vesper (1984) suggested it was characterised by three activities:

- The creation of new business units by an established firm;
- The development and implementation of entrepreneurial strategic thrusts;
- The emergence of new ideas from various levels in the organisation.

Notwithstanding this, Zahra (1991) still defined corporate entrepreneurship as 'activities aimed at creating new businesses in established companies'. Guth and Ginsberg (1990) expanded this to include 'transformation of organisations through strategic renewal'. More recently Zahra *et al.* (1999) suggested that there are many facets to entrepreneurship at firm level which reflect different combinations of:

- The content of entrepreneurship – corporate venturing, innovation, proactivity.
- The sources of entrepreneurship – both internal and external.
- The focus of entrepreneurship – formal or informal.

These views cover a wide range. Trying to pull together the different strands, Birkinshaw (2003) identified four strands of the literature that he calls 'basic schools of thought': corporate venturing, intrapreneurship, 'bringing the market inside' and entrepreneurial transformation.

Corporate venturing

This is concerned with larger businesses needing to manage new, entrepreneurial businesses separately from the mainstream activity. It is concerned with investment by larger firms in strategically important smaller firms and different forms of corporate venturing units (Chesbrough, 2002). The reasons for doing so rarely involve short-term financial gain but more normally relate to issues of innovation and strategic foresight. Small firms are often good at innovation and larger firms therefore have to buy them out to capitalise on their 'first-mover advantage' in a critical area of new technology development. This happens far more in the USA than in the UK with firms like General Electric, Monsanto, Xerox, Apple, IBM and Kyocera particularly active.

Corporate venturing is also concerned with the organisational structures needed to encourage new businesses whilst aligning them to the company's existing activities (Galbraith, 1982; Burgelman, 1983; Drucker, 1985). It also deals with how companies can manage disruptive technologies (Christensen, 1997).

Case with question

Julian Metcalfe and **Sinclair Beecham** opened their first **Prêt A Manger** sandwich bar in Victoria Street, central London, in 1986. They made sandwiches in the basement from fresh ingredients bought every morning at Covent Garden market. They built Prêt on the simple concept of providing gourmet, fresh and organic fast food in modern, clean surroundings. The formula proved successful. By 2001 Prêt had 103 stores in the UK and one in New York, producing a turnover of £100 000 million and profits of £3.6 million.

But the pair had ambitious plans to expand Prêt overseas, particularly in Asia, and the experience in New York had taught them how difficult, time-consuming and expensive this could be. They also wanted to launch 'Family Prêt', a similar concept but with larger, less urban shops especially for children. The problem was that they needed both cash and world-wide contacts and expertise.

Nevertheless it came as a surprise to analysts when they sold a 33 per cent stake in Prêt to McDonald's in 2001 for an estimated £26 million. The motives were, however, simple enough. McDonald's could provide not only cash but also the support for Prêt's global expansion plans and they were happy not to change the Prêt formula in any way. McDonald's, who also owned the Aroma coffee bar chain, saw this as a strategic purchase that would advance their long-term strategy of gaining a greater share of the diverse informal eating-out market. By 2003 the chain had grown to 151 outlets, world-wide, with 123 in the UK.

Question
Using the Boston matrix, explain where Prêt fits into McDonald's product portfolio and why it is so important.

Intrapreneurship

This is concerned with individual employees and how they might be encouraged to act in an entrepreneurial way within a larger organisation. They are entrepreneurs in larger organisations. Rarely the inventor of the product, they work with teams to cut through the bureaucracy of the organisation to develop it for the market place as quickly as possible. They share many of the characteristics of the entrepreneur, and may ultimately become the managing director of a company set up by its larger parent to exploit the idea. However, essentially, like Art Frye with his Post-it Notes at 3M (see case at the end of this chapter), intrapreneurs work within the larger organisation and will have come from within it. They are therefore likely to be hybrids, having to work hard to create entrepreneurial structures and cultures around them, but always having to communicate with the more bureaucratic organisation that employs them.

The literature looks at the systems, structures and cultures that inhibit this activity and how they might be circumvented or even challenged. It is concerned with the character and personality of this strange hybrid of entrepreneur and 'company-man'. The term was introduced and popularised by Gifford Pinchot (1985) building on the earlier work of Ross Kanter (1982). In many ways it was this school that launched the idea that large organisations could change and be something different to what, all too often, they had become.

Bringing the market Inside

This focuses mainly on the structural changes needed to encourage entrepreneurial behaviour and argues for a market approach to resource allocation and people management systems using market-based techniques such as spin-offs and venture capital operations (Hamel, 1999; Foster and Kaplan, 2001). For example, Monsanto, Apple, 3M and Xerox use independent venture capital conduits to finance their spin-outs from in-house research.

Case insight

Xerox may have problems with its core copier business but it has managed to push through many innovations. Many were pioneered by its Palo Alto Research Centre (PARC). But initially few were taken up by Xerox, who left them to be exploited, often very successfully, by others. The one (major) exception was, of course, the laser printer. It was only when it set up a separate company, **Xerox Technology Ventures**, located almost as far away in the USA as you can get from both Xerox head office and PARC that things began to change. This company was to exploit technologies that did not 'fit' into Xerox's product portfolio.

If a product was turned down by head office it could be offered to the new venture group. Once a working model was perfected, the founders, who would be rewarded with a 20 per cent stake in the new business, were moved out of the plush PARC laboratories and into low-cost commercial premises and professional management put in to bring the product to market.

After ten years the company now has more than a dozen young firms established.

Entrepreneurial transformation

The premise behind this strand of literature is that large firms need to adapt to an ever-changing environment if they are to survive and to do so they need to adapt their structures and cultures so as to encourage entrepreneurial activity in individual employees (Peters and Waterman, 1982; Kanter, 1989; Tushman and O'Reilly, 1996; Ghoshal and Bartlett, 1997). According to this school individual behaviour is fashioned by the leadership, strategy, systems, structures and culture in the organisation – called the entrepreneurial architecture (Burns, 2005). To the writers in this school the previous three 'schools' are simply techniques that can help bring about the entrepreneurial transformation.

Building an entrepreneurial architecture

To create an entrepreneurial architecture Burns (*op. cit.*) claims the very DNA of the entrepreneur must, somehow, be replicated in the larger corporate entity. Entrepreneurial architecture is a strategic architecture that is sufficiently detailed to provide guidance about how it can be achieved, but not so prescriptive as to become constraining. Indeed one of the paradoxes of this architecture is that it cannot be prescriptive but it must evolve and develop – and yet the architecture needs to be such as to ensure this can happen.

Architecture is the term used by John Kay (1993) to describe the relational contracts within and around the organisation – with customers, suppliers and staff. These are long-term relationships, although not necessarily just legal contracts, which are only partly specified and only really enforced by the need of the parties to work together. Like all relationships, architecture is based upon mutual trust, although underpinned by mutual self-interest. This self-interest discourages one party acting in some way at the expense of another because it is important that they continue to work together. We have already stressed the importance of relationships in the way the entrepreneur does business.

Just as entrepreneurs use networks of relationships to help them operate in a way that allows them to seize opportunities quickly, architecture allows the entrepreneurial firm to respond quickly and effectively to change and opportunity. Developing organisational architecture is a systematic exploitation of one of the main distinctive capabilities of entrepreneurs. It builds in dynamic capabilities that are difficult to copy. It does this by creating within the organisation the knowledge and routines that enable this to happen smoothly and unhindered. Staff are somehow motivated in themselves to make this happen, knowing it is good for the organisation – what has been called empowerment. Architecture can create barriers to entry and competitive advantage by institutionalising these relationships. It is difficult to copy because it is not a legal contract and not written down anywhere, relying instead on the complex network of personal relationships throughout the organisation. Architecture is created partly through appropriate strategies, partly through appropriate structures, but mainly through developing the appropriate culture in the organisation.

Kay (*op. cit.*) emphasises the advantages of architecture:

> The value of architecture lies in the capacity of organisations which establish it to create organisational knowledge and routines, to respond flexibly to changing circumstances, and to achieve easy and open exchanges of information. Each is capable of creating an asset for the firm – organisational knowledge which is more than the sum of individual knowledge, flexibility, and responsiveness which extends to the institution as well as to its members.

Using examples of small and large organisations, Kay emphasises that architecture comprises patterns of long-term relationships which are 'complex, subtle and hard to define precisely or to replicate' and he observes that it is easier to sustain than to create and even more difficult to create in an organisation that does not have it in the first place. Individuals participate in these relationships voluntarily because of a strong personal feeling that it is in their interests because they are participating in a 'repeated game' in which they share the rewards of collective achievement. The relationships solve problems of cooperation, coordination and commitment. They set the rules of the game and if you cheat you would find it difficult to play the game again with the same players. These relationships are characterised as having a high but structured degree of informality, something that can be mistaken as haphazard, chaotic or just lucky. In this way the architecture is distinctive and difficult to copy because individuals only know or understand a small part of the overall structure.

Kay (*op. cit.*) continues:

> There is an expectation of long-term relationships both within the firm and between its members, a commitment to a sharing of the rewards of collective achievement, and a high but structured degree of informality. This informality is sometimes mistaken for disorganisation – in popular discussion of chaos, *entrepreneurship*, or adhocracy as conditions of innovation – but truly chaotic organisations rarely perform well, and a system of relational contracts substitutes an extensive set of unwritten rules and expectations of behaviour for the formal obligations of the classical contract.

With this description we start to glimpse reflections of the start-up entrepreneur in the middle of a spider's web of informal, personal relationships, recognising opportunity everywhere, trying to innovate and trying to replicate success, using networks, relying on personal relationships with customers, staff and suppliers. They prefer influence and informal relationships to formal contracts. They use these to secure repeat sales at the expense of competitors and to secure resources or competitive advantage that they might not otherwise have. Close partnerships with suppliers where information and knowledge are shared can lead to significant advantages in lowering costs, lead times and inventories. All these relationships are based on trust – 'my word is my bond' – and most involve a degree of self-interest. The challenge is to replicate these relationships across the organisation and develop that entrepreneurial architecture.

Kay (*op. cit.*) sees no conflict in the need for stability and continuity in relationships and the equal need for change and flexibility in an entrepreneurial firm:

> If there is a single central lesson from the success ... of cases developed in this book, it is that the stability of relationships and the capacity to respond to change are mutually supportive, not mutually exclusive, requirements. It is within the context of long-term relationships, and often only within that context that the development of organisational knowledge, the free exchange of information, and a readiness to respond quickly and flexibly can be sustained.

And here lies an important by-product of this architecture – it creates organisational learning and knowledge that can be used to create competitive advantage.

Case with question

Dell is a pioneer of e-business. What makes Dell special today is its 'fully integrated value chain' – B2B2C. Suppliers, including many small firms, have real-time access to information about customer orders and deliveries via the company's extranet. They organise supplies of hard drives, motherboards, modems and so on on a 'just-in-time' basis so as to keep the production line moving smoothly. From the parts being delivered to the orders being shipped out takes just a few hours. Inventories are minimised and, what is more, the cash is received from the customer before Dell pays its suppliers.

Dell have created a three-way 'information partnership' between itself and its customers and suppliers by treating them as collaborators who together find ways of improving efficiency:

'The best way I know to establish and maintain a healthy, competitive culture is to partner with your people – through shared objectives and common strategies ... Dell is very much a relationship orientated company ... how we communicate and partner with our employees and customers. But our commitment doesn't stop there. Our willingness and ability to partner to achieve our common goals is perhaps seen in its purest form in how we forge strong alliances with our suppliers ... Early in Dell's history we had more than 140 different suppliers providing us with component parts ... Today our rule is to keep it simple and have as few partners as possible. Fewer than 40 suppliers provide us with about 90 percent of our material needs. Closer partnerships with fewer suppliers is a great way to cut cost and further speed products to market.' (Michael Dell, 1999)

Dell's market place is highly competitive. Dell prides itself on good marketing of quality products but, most importantly, speedy delivery of customised products. Nevertheless, whilst it might not sell the cheapest computers in the market place, the price it asks must always be competitive and that means costs must be kept as low as possible.

Question
From what you know about the company, is Dell's competitive advantage based solely on its external architecture? What else might contribute to this?

Entrepreneurs learn by doing, and they learn quickly not to repeat mistakes but to capitalise on success. Because they are one person, knowledge and learning is transferred continuously, quickly and without barriers. As the organisation grows the challenge is for knowledge and learning to continue to be transferred in this way. But how do you translate what happens in the brain of one person into the operations of an entire organisation? And what does learning really mean? The answer to this lies in the concept of the 'learning organisation'.

The learning organisation

The person most associated with the concept of the learning organisation is Peter Senge. His book, *The Fifth Discipline: The Art and Science of the Learning Organisation*, published in 1990, was a loose collection of ideas about change, learning and communication drawn from an eclectic variety of sources. However the central concept was inherently attractive:

As the world becomes more interconnected and business becomes more complex and dynamic, work must become more 'learningful' ... It is no longer sufficient to have one person learning for the organisation ... It's just not possible any longer to 'figure it out' from the top, and have everyone else following the orders of the 'grand strategist'. The organisations that will truly excel in the future will be the organisations that discover how to tap people's commitment and capacity to learn at all levels in the organisation.

If the grand strategist is the entrepreneur, then you can see that the challenge laid down is one of making the whole organisation entrepreneurial. A learning organisation has been defined as one that 'facilitates the learning of all its members and continuously transforms itself ... adapting, changing, developing and transforming themselves in response to the needs, wishes and aspirations of people, inside and outside' (Pedler *et al.*, 1991). Writings on the learning organisation stress how it is flexible, adaptable and better equipped to thrive in a turbulent environment – the very environment that entrepreneurs and entrepreneurial firms inhabit. A learning organisation facilitates learning for all its members and continually transforms itself:

'There are countless successful companies that are thriving now despite the fact that they started with little more than passion and a good idea. There are also many that have failed, for the very same reason. The difference is that the thriving companies gathered the knowledge that gave them the substantial edge over their competition, which they then used to improve their execution, whatever their product or service ... The key is not so much one great idea or patent as it is the execution and implementation of a great strategy.'
Michael Dell (1999)
➜

- Encouraging systematic problem solving;
- Encouraging experimentation and new approaches;
- Learning from past experience and history;
- Learning from best practice and outside experience;
- Being skilled at transferring knowledge in the organisation.

Peter Senge (1992) even observes that learning organisations can only be built by leaders with fire and passion; 'Learning organisations can be built only by individuals who put their life spirit into the task.' The similarity to the entrepreneur is striking. Indeed the similarities can also be seen from the literature about entrepreneurs. Timmons (1999) says successful entrepreneurs are: 'patient leaders, capable of instilling tangible visions and managing for the long haul. *The entrepreneur is at once a learner and a teacher*, a doer and a visionary.' Being a learner and a teacher are two of the prime tasks for a leader in a learning organisation. Truly entrepreneurial organisations, therefore, are in fact learning organisations. This goes to the heart of their architecture.

A learning organisation thrives in turbulent and changing environments. It is fast and responsive. It requires unitarism – a belief that the interests of the organisation and the individual are the same. Shared values are at the core of this, as is being part of a team or an 'ingroup' (the terminology used by Hofstede in his analysis of culture, reviewed in Chapter 8). This results in staff feeling empowered to influence the direction of the organisation and believing that continually developing, learning and acquiring new knowledge is the way to do this.

Continually developing, learning and acquiring new knowledge is therefore at the heart of a learning organisation. But knowledge is about more than just information sharing. It is about learning from each other and from outside the organisation. It is about a better understanding of interrelationships, complexities and causalities. Daniel Kim (1993) suggests that effective learning can be considered to be a revolving wheel (Figure 18.1). During half the cycle, you test concepts and observe what happens through experience – learning 'know-how'. In the second half of the cycle, you are reflecting on the observations and forming concepts – learning 'know-why'. This is often called 'double-loop learning'. It is this second sort of learning that is of particular value to the organisation because it is at this point that root causes of problems are diagnosed and systematic solutions put in place.

So real learning is about application, continuous problem-solving, understanding the root cause of problems rather than being distracted by the symptoms. It is about continually challenging the mental models we hold – deeply-held beliefs about how the world works that are shaped by our experiences and shape our experiences. It occurs when people within organisations share, explore and challenge their mental models. When this happens the wheel of learning both affects and is affected by our mental models, as shown in Figure 18.2. Once we start to share our knowledge of know-how and/or know-why with others, organisational learning takes place. The difficulties in doing this increase with the size of the organisation. However, the constantly increasing amount of know-how and know-why, accumulated through years of turning of the wheel of learning and sharing of mental models, becomes part of the collective memory of the organisation. Although this accumulated knowledge is tacit, shadowy and fragile it is unique and can be part of the organisational architecture that underpins its competitive advantage.

Again, the similarities with how entrepreneurs operate is pronounced. The learning organisation literature stresses incrementalism and learning by doing on the job, rather than in the classroom. It stresses questioning of the status quo. What is more it explains why entrepreneurs are more comfortable continuously strategising and

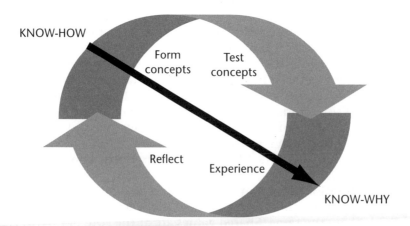

Figure 18.1 The wheel of learning

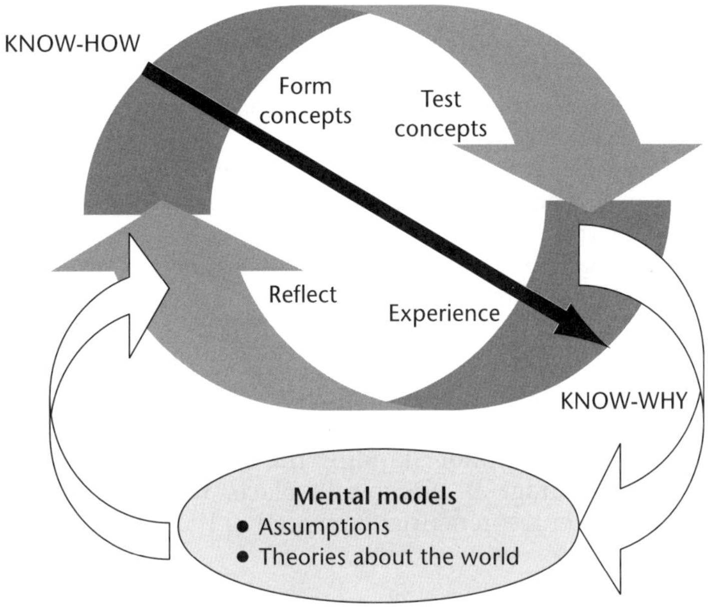

Figure 18.2 The wheel of learning and our mental models

why strategy tends frequently to emerge, based on the learning that is continuously taking place.

The ability to adapt is what makes the difference between survival and growth in an uncertain, turbulent environment and an organisation's ability to adapt is the direct result of its ability to learn collectively about the factors that influence it. Constant learning by organisations requires the acquisition of new knowledge and skill and the willingness to apply it to decision-making (Miller, 1996). It includes the unlearning of old routines (Markoczy, 1994) so that the range of potential behaviour is altered (Wilpert, 1995).

Some academics however, such as Symon (2002), are cynical about the concept of a learning organisation, arguing that the literature relies on 'metaphor, exaggeration and justification', observing that the concept was introduced when 'structural and political changes swung the balance of power in favour of the employer' and seeing it as a device to 'lure them (the workers) into their control'. Certainly Senge's 1990 book was a loose collection of ideas couched in mystical terminology and was light on practicality. But others have built on this in a more structured manner. Theoretical and empirical research does, however, show that many barriers exist to implementing the concept of a learning organisation and many academics would say that, in its extreme form, the learning organisation is indeed a utopian ideal and that it is a journey rather than a destination ever to be arrived at. Table 18.1 summarises some of the major concepts about learning organisations.

Our mental models, those deeply-held images of how the world works, are both shaped by our experiences and help shape our experiences. And from school onwards, all too often, conformity is rewarded, mistakes punished and too much questioning discouraged. How can we possibly make the leap of faith required to convince us things could be different? And how robust are our learning processes? Do we have the

Table 18.1 The learning organisation – major concepts

- True learning requires the acquisition of both know-how and know-why through the wheel of learning so that chains of causality can be identified;
- Mental models are shaped by experience and help shape experience;
- Learning occurs when individuals share, examine and challenge their mental models;
- The most important learning occurs on the job;
- The most effective learning is social and active, not individual and passive;
- The most important things to learn are tacit things – intuition, judgement, expertise.

skill, let alone the time, to reflect in this modern world? Can these learning processes ever be sufficiently robust to get us to see how information, action and results form a chain of causality – the key to understanding the root cause of a problem? And how can an organisation encourage all this to take place? Which brings us back to the challenge of building an entrepreneurial architecture that encourages these qualities.

Shaping the architecture

Entrepreneurial organisations thrive in changing, unstable or disruptive environments – even chaos. They thrive in environments where change is the norm and opportunities are constantly presenting themselves. These environments are characterised by high degrees of uncertainty – even contradiction – and difficulty in operating the firm. The environment influences the tools that can be used to shape the architecture of the organisation:

- The leadership and management of the organisation;
- The culture in the organisation;
- The design of the organisation – its structure, size and organisation.

The architecture helps determine the strategies the organisation adopts, however these strategies in turn influence the architecture. The environment also influences these strategies. The whole, delicately balanced and inter-related system is shown in Figure 18.3.

What the company does with this architecture depends on the strategies it adopts. Entrepreneurial architecture can create competitive advantages on which the organisation can build effective strategies for succeeding against competitors. However, how the organisation approaches strategy development will also influence, and be influenced by, this architecture. The interplay of these factors helps determine strategy in an entrepreneurial organisation and strategy development becomes part of its architecture – something difficult to copy because it is constantly evolving and adapting to the changing market place.

The degree and direction of entrepreneurial intensity – the frequency and scale of the entrepreneurial acts – has implications for the entrepreneurial architecture; its leadership, culture and structure. For example, infrequent major innovation is risky and requires a certain culture and structure that is different from that required for what might be described as continuous, incremental improvement, which is less risky.

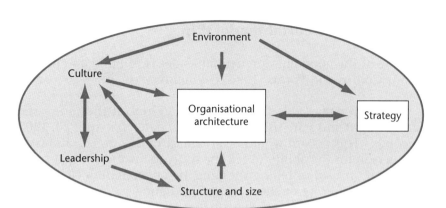

Source: P. Burns (*op. cit.*).

Figure 18.3   Influences on organisational architecture

Strong organisational architecture can be both internal and external. Internal focuses on the employees, generating a strong sense of collectivism rather than individuality and implying strong job security. This collectivism comes from shared objectives and commonly accepted strategies. And this brings with it potential weaknesses: 'Firms with strong *internal* architecture tend to restrict individuality and recruit employees of characteristic, and familiar type, inflexibility is a potential weakness' (Kay, *op. cit.*). These we also recognise as familiar potential weaknesses for entrepreneurs in growing firms. However, whilst adopting certain administrative traits is critical for successful growth (Cooper, 1993), both the entrepreneur and the organisation must also remain essentially entrepreneurial. Retaining a balance is crucial, building on the distinctive traits, skills, capabilities and approach to business of the entrepreneur and institutionalising elements of their approach – replicating their DNA within the organisation's culture.

External architecture is found where firms share knowledge with outsiders, which encourages flexibility and fast response times. It is based on deep relationships and is often found in networks or clusters of small firms in particular geographic areas where they depend on each other for various aspects of their commercial activity. For example, in the UK there is a cluster of small firms in South Wales which manufacture sofas. Around them is a skilled workforce and the infrastructure needed to support them. Italy has developed these clusters in numerous industries from knitwear and ties to tiles, all based in different geographic clusters. Some larger firms, such as Dell, have developed competitive advantage based upon the development of distinctive global supply networks – which are also based on effective external architecture.

Whether internal or external, architecture is based upon mutually supportive, long-term relationships. Any relationship is based upon trust, and trust can take a long time to build but can be lost very quickly. It is also based on mutual self interest – there must be something in it for both parties. It is based on knowledge and information and is essentially informal rather than formal. It can be planned and it can be engineered, but is not easy to achieve. It needs cultivating and managing and its roots lie deep in the interpersonal relationships in the organisation.

The role of entrepreneurial leadership

The primary role of the good entrepreneurial leader is to build an entrepreneurial architecture. As Collins and Porras (1994) eloquently explain:

> Imagine you met a remarkable person who could look at the sun or stars at any time of day or night and state the exact time and date: 'It's April 23, 1401, 2:36 am, and 12 seconds.' This person would be an amazing time teller, and we'd probably revere that person for the ability to tell the time. But wouldn't that person be even more amazing if, instead of telling the time, he or she built a clock that could tell time forever, even after he or she was dead and gone.
>
> Having a great idea or being a charismatic, visionary leader is 'time telling'; building a company that can prosper far beyond the presence of any single leader and through multiple product life cycles is 'clock building'. The builders of visionary companies tend to be clock builders, not time tellers ... And instead of concentrating on acquiring the individual personality traits of visionary leadership, they take an architectural approach and concentrate on building the organisational traits of visionary companies.

The emerging discipline of entrepreneurial leadership – the ability to lead and manage this larger entrepreneurial organisation – is about encouraging opportunity seeking and innovation in a systematic manner throughout the organisation, always questioning the established order, seeking ways to improve and create competitive advantage. It is about encouraging the qualities enjoyed by successful entrepreneurs such as vision and drive. It is about learning new ways to manage organisations involving relationships and culture rather than discipline and control. It is about new ways of dealing with risk, uncertainty and ambiguity so as to maintain flexibility – and allowing failure. It is about institutionalising a process of continuous strategising, learning from customers, competitors and the environment. It is about encouraging change and managing rapid growth. And it is about doing these things throughout an organisation so that it reflects the entrepreneurial characteristics of its managers – responding quickly and effectively to opportunities or changes in the market place. Entrepreneurial leadership

> 'There is a real need for corporate entrepreneurs at the moment. For too long the prevailing consensus has been "if it ain't broke, don't fix it" but entrepreneurs recognise that action and change are crucial for maximising potential and taking advantage of opportunities. You have to be tough and outgoing and not afraid of leaving calm waters to ride the waves of a storm. I consider myself to be a corporate entrepreneur. I have not created the company I am in charge of, but I have changed the way it is run and have made a real difference. I think times have changed and entrepreneurs don't have to be totally out on a limb. There are plenty of opportunities for entrepreneurialism in large companies too.'
>
> **Diane Thompson,**
> **Chief Executive, Camelot**
> (also founder of an advertising agency)
> *Sunday Times* 17 March 2002

Table 18.2 Traditional vs entrepreneurial leadership and management

Traditional management	Entrepreneurial management
• Encouraging control	• Encouraging opportunity seeking
• Encouraging discipline	• Encouraging innovation
• Encouraging uniformity	• Encouraging questioning of the status quo
• Encouraging conformity	• Encouraging vision
• Encouraging efficiency	• Encouraging drive
• Encouraging effectiveness	• Encouraging relationships within and outside the organisation
• Encouraging contractual relationships only	• Encouraging strategising at all levels in the organisation
• Encouraging long-term planning	• Encouraging learning
• Encouraging 'training'	• Encouraging the rapid transfer of knowledge and information
• Encouraging managing functionally	• Encouraging cooperation
• Compartmentalising knowledge and information	• Tolerating uncertainty and ambiguity
• Trying to create certainty and clarify ambiguity	• Taking risks
• Avoiding risk	• Allowing failure
• Discouraging failure	• Accepting and embracing change
• Seeing change as a threat	• Not controlling too strongly

and management is therefore about a different set of imperatives to traditional management. These are summarised in Table 18.2.

In short it is about creating and managing an entrepreneurial architecture – the network of relational contracts within, or around, an organisation, its employees, suppliers, customers and networks. Drucker (*op. cit.*) delineated the discipline as follows:

> Entrepreneurship is based upon the same principles, whether the entrepreneur is an existing large institution or an individual starting his or her new venture single-handed. It makes little or no difference whether the entrepreneur is a business or a non-business public-service organisation, nor even whether the entrepreneur is a government or non-government institution. The rules are pretty much the same, and so are the kinds of innovation and where to look for them. In every case there is a discipline we might call Entrepreneurial Management.

This entrepreneurial architecture creates within the organisation the knowledge and routines that allow it to respond flexibly to change and opportunity in the way the entrepreneur does. It is a very real and valuable asset. It creates competitive advantage and can be sustained. In reality the discipline of entrepreneurial management draws on and brings together many different business disciplines, some established and others emerging in their own right, and themes from them. These strands are shown in Figure 18.4.

Figure 18.4 Disciplines influencing entrepreneurial leadership and management

Constructing an entrepreneurial culture

Hofstede *et al.* (1990) looked at the different dimensions of organisational culture in an attempt to discriminate between entrepreneurial and administrative organisations. These were not so much dimensions as descriptors of what an entrepreneurial culture might look like compared to an administrative one. These descriptors are shown in Table 18.3.

Morris and Kuratko (2002) have a slightly different view of what an entrepreneurial culture might look like within an organisation. Based on synthesis of the work of Timmons (*op. cit.*), Peters (1997) and Cornwall and Perlman (1990), they say it would have the following elements:

- People and empowerment focus:
- Commitment and personal responsibility;
- 'Doing the right thing';
- Value creation through innovation and change;
- Hands-on management;
- Freedom to grow and to fail;
- Attention to basics;
- Emphasis on the future and a sense of urgency.

Table 18.3 Entrepreneurial vs administrative cultures

Entrepreneurial	Administrative
• Results orientation	• Process orientation
• Job orientation	• Employee orientation
• Parochial interest	• Professional interest
• Open system	• Closed system
• Loose control	• Tight control
• Pragmatic orientation	• Normative orientation

Source: Hofstede *et al.* (*op. cit.*).

Table 18.4 Cultures that enhance vs cultures that inhibit learning

A culture that enhances learning	A culture that inhibits learning
• Balances interests of all stakeholders	• Tasks are more important than people
• Focuses on people rather than systems	• Focuses on systems rather than people
• Empowers people and makes them believe they can change things	• Allows change only when absolutely necessary
• Makes time for learning	• Is preoccupied with short-term coping and adapting
• Takes a holistic approach to problems	• Compartmentalises problem-solving
• Encourages open communication	• Restricts the flow of information
• Believes in teamwork	• Believes in competition between individuals
• Has approachable leaders	• Has controlling leaders

Source: Derived from Schein (1994).

Entrepreneurial organisations are also learning organisations. Schein (1994) listed some of the features of a learning culture and compared them to a culture that inhibits learning. These are shown in Table 18.4. If you are starting from scratch you might be able to establish these features from the outset but to change an established organisational culture is altogether more difficult. Most established organisations inhibit learning. Schein concluded that to nurture these qualities you need to establish a 'psychologically safe haven' or 'parallel system' within the organisation where learning – as we have defined it – can occur.

The constant theme coming through both the entrepreneurship literature and the learning organisation literature is the need to empower and motivate employees to do 'the right thing', without having to be ordered to do so. This implies more of a consensus form of decision-making that can mitigate against speed of action. In some circumstances this might just not be possible if an opportunity is to be seized. This is when the organisation moves back from collectivism to individualism as entrepreneurs assert themselves. Often the different scenarios will already have been considered as the organisation continuously strategises and evaluates the options open to it. However, ultimately there may be a problem here that only considerations of size and structure can address. If the decision-making group is too large, the organisation may well not be able to react with sufficient speed to changing circumstances.

An entrepreneurial culture needs to motivate people to do the 'right things', in the right way, for the organisation as well as for themselves. It needs to help them cope with an uncertain future by giving them a vision and a belief that they can achieve it. Entrepreneurs

'Creating a culture in which every person in your organisation, at every level, thinks and acts like an owner means that you need to aim to connect individual performance with your company's most important objectives ... A company composed of individual owners is less focused on hierarchy and who has a nice office, and more intent on achieving their goals.'
Michael Dell (1999)

are naturally good at motivating staff by the example they set – 'walking-the-talk' – but as the firm grows the leader needs to find different ways of communicating with more people, infecting them with the entrepreneurial virus. The culture of a firm comes from the leader, it reflects their personal values and their vision, but it is made up of a lot of small items of detail. Cultures can come about by chance, but if leaders want to plan for success, they need to plan to achieve the culture they want.

Entrepreneurial culture is far harder to describe than it is to recognise – not unexpected given the lack of scientific measures available. Many of the detailed

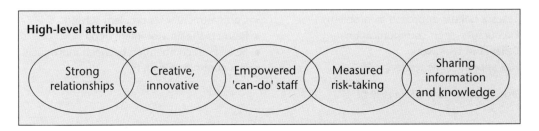

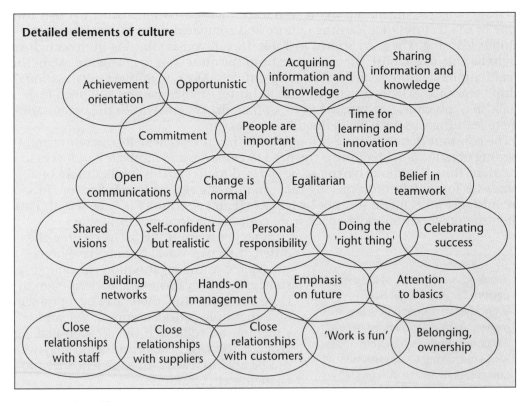

Source: Burns (*op. cit.*).

Figure 18.5 The cultural web hierarchy in an entrepreneurial organisation

elements described contribute to the recognition and are important in contributing to the overall culture. However many elements are just detail and can get in the way of the big picture. Burns (*op. cit.*) talks about five 'high level' elements that really set the culture of the organisation apart as being entrepreneurial:

- Creativity and innovation;
- Empowerment;
- Strong relationships;
- Continual learning;
- Measured risk-taking.

They represent the very DNA of the entrepreneur and are supported by 25 detailed elements, all shown in Figure 18.5.

Case with questions

Body Shop was set up in 1976 by **Anita Roddick**. It started out as a small shop in a back street in Brighton and the franchise chain enjoyed phenomenal growth in the 1980s. Whilst growth has now slowed as competitors have emerged, Body Shop has become a multinational public company and remains a major high street retailer.

The Body Shop brand is inexorably linked with its culture, which in turn is based firmly in its ethical and environmental beliefs and values. Based very much around the charismatic Anita Roddick's views that business can be a vehicle for social and environmental change, the firm has championed a number of key values and beliefs including environmentally friendly packaging and the use of natural ingredients not tested on animals. Store staff even get time off to work on local social projects. Body Shop has also championed numerous causes such as 'save the rainforests', 'trade not aid' and the reduction of Third World debt. These not only show themselves in window displays and PR activities, they also underscore everything the company does.

Franchisees are selected partly upon their 'fit' with Anita Roddock's ideas. Employees receive regular newsletters and videos concentrating on Body Shop campaigns and achievements. In 1995 the firm introduced in-store satellite transmitted radio. Body Shop takes every opportunity to put forward its values and beliefs which it believes sets it out as distinctive and different from its high street competitors. It also believes that the company brings together like-minded people and motivates staff in what otherwise is a sector with high staff turnover.

In 1998 Anita Roddick stood down as Chief Executive of Body Shop. In 2002 she and her husband, Gordon, resigned as co-chairmen, although she remains as a consultant to the firm. It will be interesting to see whether the culture of the firm and the brand continue to have the same strong identity now the founders have left.

Questions
1 How is the Body Shop culture perpetuated?
2 How important are environmental issues to the Body Shop brand? Based upon what you know of the shop, how does this 'fit' with the rest of the marketing mix?

The role of size and structure

Structures create order in an organisation but there is no single 'best' structure. The most appropriate structure depends on the nature of the organisation, the strategies it employs, the tasks it undertakes, the environment it operates in and its size.

Size does seem to matter. Large organisations are more complex than small and complexity impedes information flows, lengthens decision-making and can kill initiative. To be entrepreneurial, a large organisation needs to find ways of breaking itself down into a number of sub-organisations with varying degrees of autonomy. The span of control for management does seem to matter – 'walking-the-talk' only seems possible up to a certain size. But large organisations can structure themselves so that they comprise smaller 'units'. Again there are no prescriptive 'correct' approaches. However, large companies have been seeking to replicate the flexibility of the small firm and encourage entrepreneurial management by 'deconstructing' themselves – that is, breaking themselves down into smaller units – for some time. Peter Chemin, CEO of the Fox TV empire believes that 'in the management of creativity, size is your enemy' (*Economist*, 4 December 1999). He has tried to break down the studio into small units, even at the risk of incurring higher costs.

Small organisational units are more responsive to the environment and large firms have responded to the entrepreneurial challenge by experimenting with different organisational forms. There is an accelerating trend to downsize and deconstruct large firms – breaking them down to smaller components so that even the core is better able to act entrepreneurially. More firms are outsourcing non-core activities, downscoping and using project forms of organisation. They are developing strategic alliances with smaller firms and using them to 'outsource innovation'. They are flattening organisational structures, investing in information technology and new HRM techniques to make this happen.

Structures evolve as organisations grow and survival depends on swift adaptation. For larger firms, both hierarchical and matrix structures, or a combination, can be appropriate in different circumstances (see Chapter 8). However the traditional hierarchical structure tends to be mechanistic, bureaucratic and rigid. It is most appropriate for simple tasks in stable environments. Entrepreneurial organisations typically face a high degree of environmental turbulence. If the tasks they need to undertake are complex, they are best served by an organic organisation structure – one that changes and adapts to suit circumstances. Miller (1986) defines an organic structure as having 'limited hierarchy and highly flexible structure. Groups of trained specialists from different work areas collaborate to design and produce complex and rapidly changing products. The emphasis is on extensive personal interaction and face-to-face communication, frequent meetings, use of committees and other liaison devices to ensure collaboration. Power is decentralised and authority is linked to expertise. Few bureaucratic rules or standard procedures exist. Sensitive information-gathering systems are in place for anticipating and monitoring the external environment.'

So what will an organic structure look like? Unfortunately that is difficult to answer because, by its very definition, it is constantly forming and reforming to meet the changes it faces as it undertakes those complex tasks. Figure 18.6 is an example of one highly organic structure which comprises a series of spider's-web organisations within one large spider's web. There is no hierarchy. The organisation is flat. In this

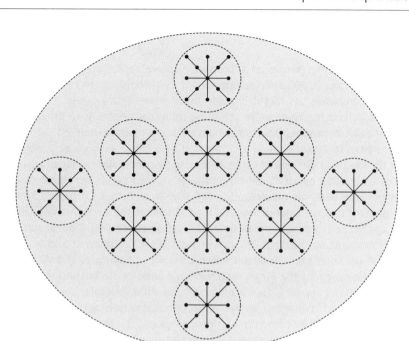

Figure 18.6 An organic structure

organisation the reporting lines between the smaller spider's webs are informal. Each operates almost autonomously and, in that sense, this may be seen more as a loose coalition of entrepreneurial teams, perhaps forming and reforming as opportunities appear. The danger is that each might operate with too much autonomy and too little direction, resulting in anarchy. In many organisations, particularly larger ones, more structure and hierarchy may therefore be needed.

Remember that it is unlikely that one organisational structure – even an organic one – will suit all situations. Greiner (1972) emphasised how organisations naturally change and adapt and Galbraith (1995) underlines the importance of change and variety rather than rigidity and conformity: 'Organisational designs that facilitate variety, change, and speed are sources of competitive advantage. These designs are difficult to execute and copy because they are intricate blends of many different policies.' So flexibility and ability to change quickly are the key. Like the chameleon, the entrepreneurial organisational structure will adapt to best suit the environment it finds itself in.

The common themes are that the organic structure will be flexible, decentralised with a minimum of levels within the structures. It will be more horizontal than vertical. Authority will be based on expertise not on role and authority for decision-making will be delegated and individuals empowered to make decisions. It will be informal rather than formal, with loose control but an emphasis on getting things done. Spans of control are likely to be broader. Team-working is likely to be the norm. There will be structures within structures that encourage smaller units to develop, each with considerable autonomy, but there will be structures in place that encourage rapid, open, effective communication between and across these units and through any hierarchy. The success of these units will depend on the degree of fit with the

---

Case with question

Richard Branson describes **Virgin** as a 'branded venture capital company'. He comments: 'Despite employing over 20 000 people, Virgin is not a big company – it's a big brand made up of lots of small companies.' In fact it is made up of some 270 separate, semi-independent companies and Richard has been adept at setting up in partnership with other firms or even selling off part of his companies' shares to finance Virgin's global expansion.

In the three years to 2002 he raised an estimated £1.3 billion in this way. Among these the biggest was the sale of 49 per cent of Virgin Atlantic to Singapore Airlines for an estimated £600 million, followed in 2001 by a £75 million mortgage secured on his remaining stake. He sold 50 per cent of Virgin Blue, the Australian low-fare carrier, to Patrick Corp. for £96 million. He also sold Virgin One to Royal Bank of Scotland for £45 million, the Virgin Active health clubs for £75 million and the French Megastore business to Lagardère for £92 million. In additon, he has raised smaller amounts by selling stakes in Raymond Blanc's restaurants and is looking for a partner in his Virgin Entertainment Group which comprises Megastores and V2 stores.

Richard Branson now runs the Virgin empire from a large house in London's Holland Park. Although there does not appear to be a traditional head office structure, Virgin employs a large number of professional managers. It has a devolved structure and an informal culture. Employees are encouraged to come up with new ideas and development capital is available. Once a new venture reaches a certain size it is launched as an independent company within the Virgin Group and the intrapreneur takes an equity stake. Will Whitehorn, Branson's right hand man for the last 16 years, says of Richard: 'He doesn't believe that huge companies are the right way to go. He thinks small is beautiful ... He's a one-person venture capital company, raising money from selling businesses and investing in new ones, and that's the way it will be in the future' (*The Guardian*, 30 April 2002).

Question
Do you agree that Virgin is just a 'branded venture capital company'? Explain.

---

mainstream organisation requiring a high degree of awareness, commitment and connection between the two (Thornhill and Amit, 2001).What is more, with such a loose structure, strong entrepreneurial leadership and culture will be needed to keep the organisation together and moving in the right direction.

Management and structure

Management is an art not least because the structures of the organisation affect how you undertake it – and vice versa. As an entrepreneurial firm moves away from centralised, formal hierarchies to flatter structures with more horizontal communication the need for managers and tight management control lessens. If you are looking for 'dazzling breakthroughs' then autonomy and flexibility are crucial. But if the degree and frequency of entrepreneurship is less, the need for controls will increase. Again, it is all a question of balance.

In this context, Covin and Slevin (1990) argue that entrepreneurial behaviour within an organisation is positively correlated with performance when structures are more organic, as shown in Figure 18.7. In reality the dimension of structure from

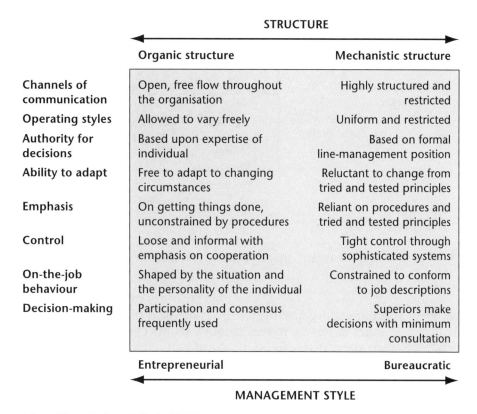

STRUCTURE

	Organic structure	Mechanistic structure
Channels of communication	Open, free flow throughout the organisation	Highly structured and restricted
Operating styles	Allowed to vary freely	Uniform and restricted
Authority for decisions	Based upon expertise of individual	Based on formal line-management position
Ability to adapt	Free to adapt to changing circumstances	Reluctant to change from tried and tested principles
Emphasis	On getting things done, unconstrained by procedures	Reliant on procedures and tried and tested principles
Control	Loose and informal with emphasis on cooperation	Tight control through sophisticated systems
On-the-job behaviour	Shaped by the situation and the personality of the individual	Constrained to conform to job descriptions
Decision-making	Participation and consensus frequently used	Superiors make decisions with minimum consultation

Entrepreneurial   Bureaucratic

MANAGEMENT STYLE

Source: Adapted from Covin and Slevin (1990).

Figure 18.7   Organisational structure and management style

organic to mechanistic is a continuum and ought to correspond to the managerial dimension from entrepreneurial to administrative. A mechanistic structure is appropriate for a bureaucratic or administrative style of management because it will result in an efficient albeit bureaucratic organisation. However, it will stifle, if not kill, an entrepreneurial style. On the other hand an organic structure facilitates an effective entrepreneurial management style. Organisations are much more problematic when there is an incongruity between structure and style.

Figure 18.8 shows the effects this incongruity can have. It demonstrates what Covin and Slevin call 'cycling', where a successful firm can move backwards and forwards between quadrants 1 and 3 as it moves from periods of opportunity, innovation and change to periods of consolidation and stability – when greater bureaucratic control is needed. This mirrors quite closely the strategy formulation cycle described in Figure 11.3 (page 311) and may give one reason why the transition from growth to consolidation is so often interspersed with a crisis – management style and organisational structures are out of sync and the firms get stuck in quadrants 2 and 4. Change, if it is to be successfully managed must be along both dimensions simultaneously.

It must be remembered, however, that it is quite possible to have different units, departments or divisions within an umbrella organisation that have different, but in

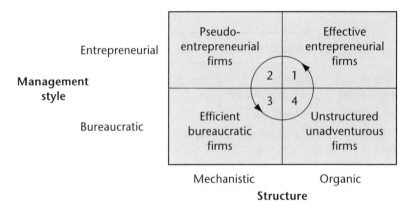

Source: Covin and Slevin (op. cit.).

Figure 18.8 Organisational structure, management style and the concept of cycling

their own way, appropriate organisational structures and management styles – particularly as a product or service moves through its life cycle. The only issue is that the interface between them needs to be managed carefully.

Freedom and control

Most organisational control systems are aimed at eliminating risk and uncertainty – something the entrepreneurial firm must tolerate – and promoting efficiency and effectiveness – which can be at the expense of innovation. Innovation requires organisational 'slack' or 'space' – a looseness in resource availability which allows employees to 'borrow' expertise, research, materials, equipment and other resources as they develop new concepts. 3M have built slack into the organisation by allowing researchers to spend 15 per cent of their time on their own projects. Garud and Van de Ven (1992) confirm that entrepreneurial activity in a large organisation is more likely to continue, despite negative outcomes, when there is slack in resource availability and a high degree of ambiguity about the outcomes. A highly efficient organisation has no slack. Everything is tightly controlled, every penny accounted for, all jobs are defined and individuals made to conform. This environment might lead to high degrees of efficiency but it does not encourage entrepreneurship and innovation.

The leader in an entrepreneurial firm, therefore, faces a crucial dilemma – the amount of freedom given to the management team. Too much and anarchy or worse might result. Too little and creativity, initiative and entrepreneurship will be stifled. It is all well and good talking about empowerment, but at what stage does it become licence?

The answer is a question of 'balance'. Birkinshaw (op. cit.) explains the model used by BP to help guide and control entrepreneurial action. BP's philosophy is that 'successful business performance comes from a dispersed and high level of ownership of, and a commitment to, an agreed-upon objective'. Within BP there are a number of business units. Heads of units have a 'contract' agreed between them and the top executives in the organisation. Once agreed they have 'free rein to deliver on their contract in whatever way they see fit, within a set of identified constraints'. BP's model uses four components to help guide and control entrepreneurial action:

- *Direction* – the company's broad strategy and goals;
- *Space or slack* – the degree of looseness in resource availability (monetary budgets, physical space and supervision of time);
- *Boundaries* – the legal, regulatory and moral limits within which the company operates;
- *Support* – the information and knowledge transfer systems and training and development programmes provided by the company to help business unit managers do their job.

All four need to be in balance. If they are too tight they constrain the business unit, but if too slack they might result in chaos. This is shown in Figure 18.9. These elements need to be looked at in the whole rather than individually. And balance is the key. Birkinshaw observes that most companies operate in the 'constrained' area in Figure 18.9 – direction defined too tightly, too little space, overtight boundaries and overly complex support structures – rather than the 'chaos' area, so most central management probably needs to 'let go' a little. The point is that management is an art, not a science, and it involves some fine judgements about the individuals you work with – their strengths and weaknesses – as well as their personal characteristics.

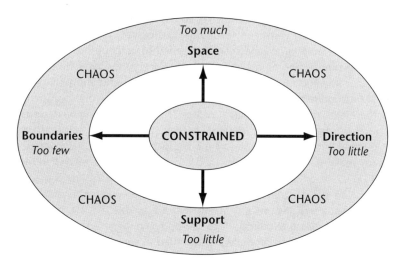

Source: Adapted from Birkinshaw (2003).

Figure 18.9 Freedom vs control

Case with questions

3M has been known for decades as an entrepreneurial company that pursues growth through innovation. It generates a quarter of its annual revenues from products less than five years old. 3M started life as the Minnesota Mining and Manufacturing Company back in 1902. Its most successful product – flexible sandpaper – still forms an important part of its product line but this now comprises of over 60 000 products that range from adhesive tapes to office supplies, medical supplies and equipment to traffic and safety signs, magnetic tapes and CDs to electrical equipment. Originally innovation was encouraged informally by the founders, but over more than a century some of these rules have been formalised. But most important of all, there has built up a culture which encourages innovation. And because this culture has built up a history of success, it perpetuates itself.

3M started life selling a somewhat inferior quality of sandpaper. The only way they could do this was by getting close to the customer – demonstrating it to the workmen that used it and persuading them to specify the product – an early form of relationship selling. This was the first strategic thrust of the fledgling business – get close to customers and understand their needs.

However, the company was desperate to move away from selling a commodity product and competing primarily on price and its closeness to the customer led it to discover market opportunities that it had the expertise to capitalise on. The first such product was Three-M-Ite^{TM} Abrasive – an abrasive cloth using aluminium oxide for durability in place of a natural abrasive. This was followed by waterproof sandpaper – an idea bought from an inventor who subsequently came to work for 3M. This was followed shortly by Wetordry^{TM} – a product designed for use by the car industry in finishing bodywork. And with this the second strategic thrust of the company was developed – to seek out niche markets, no matter how small, which would allow it to charge a premium price for its products. The company began to realise that many small niche markets could prove to be more profitable than a few large ones.

In the 1990s this began to change somewhat, to the extent that some technologies became more sophisticated and the investment needed to develop new products increased. Therefore the return required became larger and markets needed to be correspondingly bigger. Luckily the world was increasingly becoming a global market place. At the same time, competition was becoming tougher and the rapidity of technological change and shortening of product life cycles made 3M recognise the need to dominate any market niche quickly. Speed of response was vital. By the 1990s, many of the market niches 3M was pioneering were turning out to be not that small at all, particularly in the global market place. So, the approach remained the same, but the speed of response and size of market niche, world-wide, increased.

The company really started to diversify when it entered the tape market in the 1920s, but even this built on its expertise in coatings, backings and adhesives. What is more the way the first product evolved demonstrates perfectly how an entrepreneurial architecture works. By being close to its customers 3M saw a problem that it was able to solve for them through its technical expertise. In selling Wetordry^{TM} to car-body finishers, an employee realised how difficult it was for the painters to produce the latest fad in car painting – two tone paintwork. The result was the development of masking tape – imperfect at first, but developed over the years 'out-of-hours' by an employee to what we know it to be today and from that technology developed the Scotch^{TM} range of branded tapes. So, the third strategic thrust was developed – having identified a market opportunity through closeness to the customer, diversify into these

➡

related areas. Once 3M found a niche product to offer in a new market, it soon developed other related products and achieved a dominant position in the new market. In the 1990s 3M came to recognise that it did best when it introduced radically innovative products into a niche market in which it already had a toe hold.

This experience also taught 3M the value of research but in particular to value maverick inventors who were so attached to their ideas that they would push them through despite the bureaucracy of the company. It was in the late 1920s that it developed the policy of allowing researchers to spend up to 15 per cent of their time working on their own projects. To this day, it tries to make innovation part of the corporate culture by encouraging staff to spend 15 per cent of their time working on pet ideas that they hope one day will become new products for the company. They can also get money to buy equipment and hire extra help. To get an idea accepted, they must first win the personal backing of a member of the main board. Then an inter-disciplinary team of engineers, marketing specialists and accountants is set up to take the idea further. Failure is not punished, but success is well rewarded.

Perhaps the best known contemporary example of the success of this policy is the development of the Post-It® Note by Art Frye in the 1980s. He was looking for a way to mark places in a hymn book – a paper marker that would stick, but not permanently. At the same time the company had developed a new glue which, unfortunately as it seemed at the time, would not dry. Art spotted a use for the product but what was different was the way he went about persuading his bosses to back the project. He produced the product, complete with its distinctive yellow colour, and distributed it to secretaries who started using it throughout 3M. Art then cut their supplies, insisting that there would be no more unless the company officially backed the product. The rest is history.

So the fourth strategic thrust of the company was developed – to pursue product development and innovation at every level in the organisation through research. This was formalised when the Central Research Laboratory was set up in 1937, but maverick research continued to be encouraged. In 1940, a New Product Department was developed to explore the viability of new products or technologies unrelated to existing ones. In 1943, a Product Fabrications Laboratory was set up to develop manufacturing processes. In the 1980s four Sector Labs were created with a view to being more responsive to the market place and undertaking medium-term research (5–10 years); Industrial and Consumer, Life Sciences, Electronic and Information Technologies and Graphic Technologies. The Central Lab, renamed the Corporate Lab, was maintained to undertake more long-term research (over 10 years). In addition most of the Divisions had their own Labs undertaking short-term, developmental research (1–5 years).

3M has always been admired for its ability to share knowledge across the organisation and link technologies to produce numerous products that could be sold in different markets. One example of this is Scotchlite™ Reflective Sheeting used for road signs, developed in the 1940s – in fact as a result of failed research to develop reflective road markings. This combined research from three different laboratories to produce signs with a waterproof base onto which a covering of an opaque, light-reflecting pigment was added followed by microscopic beads. This was all sealed with a thin coat of plastic to ensure weather durability. Strategy five had emerged – get different parts of the organisation to communicate and work together and, most important of all, share knowledge.

→

This became formalised in the 1950s with the establishment of the Technical Forum, established with the aim of sharing knowledge across the company. It held annual shows. Out of this came the Technical Council, made up of technical directors and technical personnel, which met several times a year to review research and address common problems. Alongside this the Manufacturing Council and then the Marketing Council were established. At the same time Technical Directors and researchers regularly moved around the different divisions. The fifth strategy was in place – share knowledge.

The culture in 3M evolved out of its place of origin and has been called 'Minnesota nice'. It has been described as non-political, low ego, egalitarian and non-hierarchical as well as hardworking and self-critical. It has also, at least in its earlier days, been described as paternalistic in its approach to employees. Above all, 3M is achievement orientated and achievement, particularly in research, was rewarded, often through promotion. For example successful new product teams were spun off to form new divisions. The leader of the team often became general manager of the new division and this was seen as a great motivator. Lesser achievements were also acknowledged. Researchers who consistently achieved 'high standards of originality, dedication and integrity in the technical field' – as judged by their peers, not management – were invited to join the exclusive 'Calton Society'. The 'Golden Step' and 'Pathfinder' awards were also given to those helping develop successful new products. Achievement was lauded at all levels. Strategy six was emerging – encourage achievement through reward.

Today 3M faces many challenges to maintaining its reputation for innovation. As it becomes larger and more complex, involved in different markets with different products and technologies, at different stages of their life cycle, it recognises that different managerial approaches may be necessary. The 'maverick', high-risk approach to research and development may not be appropriate in certain sectors. The 25 per cent rule – the proportion of new product sales – may not be achievable by all Divisions. 3M also faces stiffer competition which means that cost economies have had to be made to maintain profitability. As a result the 15 per cent rule – slack time to research new products – is under severe pressure, to the point where it is described as more of an attitude than a reality. Nevertheless, 3M has for over a century successfully practised corporate entrepreneurship.

Questions

1 Describe the organisational structures and devices 3M uses to encourage entrepreneurial activity. Why do they work?
2 How does 3M distinguish between incremental and fundamental innovations?
3 Describe, as best you can from the case, the culture of the organisation. What does this depend upon?
4 Why has 3M been such a successful innovator for so long?
5 Can other companies just copy 3M's structures and culture and become successful innovators also?

A series of case studies on 3M, tracking its history and development since its inception in 1902, have been written by Research Associate Mary Ackenhusen, Professor Neil Churchill and Associate Professor Daniel Muzyka from INSEAD. They can be obtained from the Case Clearing House, England and USA.

Summary

Corporate entrepreneurship is the term used to describe entrepreneurial behaviour in an established, larger organisation. It is an emerging discipline. A more precise definition is difficult but there are four identifiable strands of literature:

1 Corporate venturing – for example the purchase of **Prêt A Manger** by McDonald's.
2 Intrapreneurship – for example Art Frye at **3M**.
3 Bring the market inside – for example the establishment of **Xerox Technology Venture**.
4 Entrepreneurial transformation – for example as practised at **3M**.

Entrepreneurial transformation is about adapting large firms through their leadership, strategies, systems, structures and cultures so that they are better able to cope with change and innovation. This is called creating entrepreneurial architecture. It creates within the organisation the knowledge and routines that allow it to respond flexibly to change and opportunity in the very way the entrepreneur does. It is not necessarily based on legal contracts and often only partly specified, therefore it is not easy to copy. It is based upon trust and mutual self-interest. Because it is complex, architecture can be a major source of sustainable competitive advantage. Strong architecture is based on deep personal relationships, either internal or external. **Dell** gains some of its competitive advantage from partnering with suppliers (external architecture).

Entrepreneurial management is about the ability to lead and manage this larger entrepreneurial organisation – a need endorsed by **Diane Thompson** of **Camelot**. It involves the development of an entrepreneurial architecture – the network of relational contracts within, or around, an organisation, its employees, suppliers, customers and networks – that encourages:

- Opportunity seeking and innovation;
- Vision and drive;
- Relationships and culture;
- New ways of dealing with risk and uncertainty;
- Institutionalising a process of continuous learning and strategising.

Learning organisations thrive in turbulence. Real knowledge means using the wheel of learning (Figure 18.2) to understand the root cause of problems so as to put in place systematic solutions to problems – 'knowing-how', 'knowing-why' and doing something about it. It means linking this to our mental models so as to challenge how things are. The most important learning occurs on the job. It is social and active. It is about learning tacit knowledge – intuition, judgement and expertise.

Entrepreneurial firms thrive in environments of change, chaos, complexity, competition, uncertainty even contradiction. The exact nature of effective entrepreneurial architecture depends on the environment. It can be sectorally and geographically dependent. It can vary with the nature of the entrepreneurial intensity. The point is that there can be no prescriptive blueprint for entrepreneurial architecture. However, generally entrepreneurial firms thrive in changing, unstable or disruptive environments.

Culture within an organisation is based on a firm set of enduring values. As **Michael Dell** says, it is the most important thing a leader creates. It can be transmitted individually by the entrepreneur or, as in the case of **Body Shop**, through PR activities, induction, training and good communications generally.

Figure 18.5 shows the cultural web of entrepreurship, but it distinguishes between 'high-level' attributes – strong relationships, creativity and innovation, empowerment, measured risk-taking and continual learning – and the detailed elements of culture.

Structures create order in an organisation but there is no single 'best' solution. The most appropriate structure depends on the nature of the organisation, the strategies it employs, the tasks it undertakes, the environment it operates in and its size.

Small organisational units are more responsive to the environment and large firms have responded to the entrepreneurial challenge by experimenting with different organisational forms.

An organic structure has limited hierarchy and is highly flexible, decentralised with a minimum of levels within the structures. It is more horizontal than vertical. Authority is based on expertise not on role, and authority for decision-making is delegated and individuals empowered to make decisions. It is informal rather than formal, with loose control but an emphasis on getting things done. Spans of control are likely to be broader. Team-working is likely to be the norm.

There are structures within structures that encourage smaller units to develop, each with considerable autonomy, but there are also structures in place that encourage rapid, open, effective communication between and across these units and through any hierarchy.

Richard Branson understands this, and his **Virgin** empire comprises some 270 separate, semi-independent companies, often set up in partnership with other individuals and organisations.

Managers must give up control to gain control. Entrepreneurial firms need loose control but tight accountability. Too much control stifles creativity, innovation and entrepreneurship. However, too little control can lead to chaos. Most firms place too many constraints and controls on managers. What is needed is 'balance', as in **BP**'s model which involves:

- Space or slack – a looseness in resource availability;
- Direction – the broad strategy and goals;
- Support – like knowledge transfer and training systems;
- Boundaries – not just rules but underlying morals and ethics.

The concept of space or slack – a looseness in resource availability – is important for entrepreneurship. Some slack is necessary for experimentation and innovation. Internal seed or venture funding is also needed to take ideas further.

For an organisation to work effectively, the organisation structure and the style of management need to be in sync. As an entrepreneurial firm moves away from centralised, formal hierarchies to flatter structures with more horizontal communication the need for managers and tight management control lessens. If you are looking for 'dazzling breakthroughs' then autonomy and flexibility are crucial. But if the degree and frequency of entrepreneurship is less, the need for controls will increase. Again, it is all a question of balance. Many successful firms cycle between organic/entrepreneurial structure and styles and mechanistic/bureaucratic as they grow – mirroring the growth → crisis → consolidation process noted in strategy development.

Essays and discussion topics

1 Can large firms also be entrepreneurial? Is it in their interests to be so? What pressures are there for them not to be entrepreneurial?
2 What is corporate entrepreneurship?
3 What do you think of the four 'schools' of literature identified by Birkinshaw?
4 What is corporate venturing?
5 What is intrapreneurship?
6 What do you understand by the term 'entrepreneurial architecture'? Why are relationships rather than legal contracts important?
7 What is needed to build long-term relationships?
8 How can entrepreneurial architecture be shaped?
9 Why can the architecture of a firm give it sustainable competitive advantage?
10 Is the learning organisation a romantic dream?
11 How can you spot a learning organisation?
12 How does an entrepreneur learn?
13 Is the entrepreneurial organisation really a learning organisation?
14 How do you really learn?
15 How do you spread learning and knowledge in an organisation?
16 Do you have mental models? How do these ever change?
17 Is there such a thing as an organisational mental model?
18 Should an entrepreneur find building this architecture easier than other people?
19 What is entrepreneurial management? How does it differ from traditional management?
20 Can a traditional manager become an entrepreneurial manager?
21 Why is the leader's role crucial in developing an entrepreneurial organisation?
22 Will an entrepreneurial organisation succeed in all circumstances?
23 In what circumstances might a bureaucratic organisation be more successful than an entrepreneurial organisation?
24 How might the geographic environment affect an effective entrepreneurial architecture?
25 What are the five 'high level' elements of entrepreneurial culture? Explain 'high level'.
26 Do you agree that the most important elements of an entrepreneurial culture are creativity and innovation, empowerment, strong relationships, continual learning and measured risk-taking?
27 What do you understand by an organic structure? Try drawing one.
28 Why does tight control stifle creativity, innovation and entrepreneurship?
29 Why is slack or space so important for creativity, innovation and entrepreneurship?
30 How do you achieve 'balance' between freedom and control? Who makes the judgement?
31 How can you have lose control but tight accountability? Give examples.
32 With freedom comes accountability. Discuss.
33 Freedom without accountability leads to anarchy. Discuss.
34 Is corporate entrepreneurship a discipline?

Activities

1 Identify two large organisations that you would describe as entrepreneurial and explain why you would describe them in this way. Are they commercially successful? Can you identify any clues as to why they might be successful?
2 List the type of organisations and market sectors or environments that face high degrees of turbulence. Select a particularly turbulent sector and research how the organisations within it are organised and the success, or otherwise, they have in dealing with it.

3 Select two organisations, one that you would describe as entrepreneurial, the other that you would describe as administrative or bureaucratic. Referring back to Hofstede's work (Chapter 8), describe their cultures in a brief report and evaluate on the five dimensions of creativity and innovation, empowerment, strong relationships, continual learning and measured risk-taking.

4 Give some specific examples of an industry where a hierarchical, bureaucratic structure should be the best way to organise. Select three companies in this industry and investigate their organisational structure. Explain why their structure conforms or does not conform to your expectations, taking into account the success of the business in that industry.

References

Birkinshaw, J.M. (2003) 'The Paradox of Corporate Entrepreneurship', *Strategy and Business*, 30, Spring.

Burgelman, R.A. (1983) 'A Process Model of Internal Corporate Venturing in the Diversified Major Firm', *Administrative Science Quarterly*, 28.

Burns, P. (2005) *Corporate Entrepreneurship: Building an Entrepreneurial Organisation*, Basingstoke: Palgrave Macmillan.

Chesbrough, H.W. (2002) 'Making Sense of Corporate Venture Capital', *Harvard Business Review*, March.

Christensen, C.M. (1997) *The Innovator's Dilemma: When New Technologies Cause Great Firms to Fail*, Boston: Harvard Business School Press.

Collins, J.C. and Porras, J.I. (1994) *Built to Last: Successful Habits of Visionary Companies*, New York: Harper Business.

Cooper, A.C. (1993) 'Challenges in Predicting New Firm Performance', *Journal of Business Venturing*, May.

Cornwall, J. and Perlman, B. (1990), *Organisational Entrepreneurship*, Homewood, IL: Irwin.

Covin, D. and Slevin, J. (1990) 'Judging Entrepreneurial Style and Organisational Structure: How to Get Your Act Together', *Sloan Management Review*, 31 (Winter).

Dell, M. (1999) *Direct from Dell: Strategies that Revolutionised an Industry*, New York: Harper Business.

Drucker, P.F. (1985) *Innovation and Entrepreneurship: Practice and Principles*, London: Heinemann.

Foster, R.N. and Kaplan, S. (2001) *Creative Destruction: Why Companies that are Built to Last Underperform the Market – and How to Successfully Transform Them*, New York: Currency Doubleday.

Galbraith, J. (1982) 'Designing the Innovating Organisation', *Organisational Dynamics*, Winter.

Galbraith, J. (1995) *Designing Organisations*, San Francisco: Jossey-Bass.

Garud, R. and Van de Ven, A. (1992) 'An Empirical Evaluation of the Internal Corporate Venturing Process', *Strategic Management Journal*, 13 (Special Issue).

Ghoshal, S. and Bartlett, C.A. (1997) *The Individualised Corporation: A Fundamentally New Approach to Management*, New York: Harper Business.

Greiner, L. (1972) 'Revolution and Evolution as Organisations Grow', *Harvard Business Review*, 50, July/August.

Guth, W.D. and Ginsberg, A. (1990) 'Corporate Entrepreneurship', *Strategic Management Journal*, 11 (Special Issue).

Hamel, G. (1999) 'Bringing Silicon Valley Inside', *Harvard Business Review*, September.

Hofstede, G., Neuijen, B., Daval Ohayv, D. and Sanders, G. (1990) 'Measuring Organizational Cultures: A Qualitative and Quantative Study across Twenty Cases', *Administrative Sciences Quarterly*, 35.

Kanter, R.M. (1982) 'The Middle Manager as Innovator', *Harvard Business Review*, July.

Kanter, R.M. (1989) *When Giants Learn to Dance: Mastering the Challenge of Strategy, Management and Careers in the 1990s*, New York: Simon & Schuster.

Kay, J. (1993) *Foundations of Corporate Success*, Oxford: Oxford University Press.

Kim, D.H. (1993) 'The Link between Individual and Organizational Learning', *Sloan Management Review*, Fall.

Markoczy, L. (1994) 'Modes of Organisational Learning: Institutional Change and Hungarian Joint Ventures', *International Studies of Management and Organisations*, 24, December.

Miller, A. (1996) *Strategic Management*, Maidenhead: Irwin/McGraw-Hill.

Miller, D. (1986) 'Configurations of Strategy and Structure: Towards a Synthesis', *Strategic Management Journal*, 7.

Morris, M.H. and Kuratko, D.F. (2002) *Corporate Entrepreneurship*, Orlando: Harcourt College Publishers.

Morse, C.W. (1986) 'The Delusion of Intrapreneurship', *Long Range Planning*, 19(2).

Pedler, M., Burgoyne, J.G. and Boydell, T. (1991) *The Learning Company: A Strategy for Sustainable Development*, London: McGraw-Hill.

Peters, T. (1997) *The Circle of Innovation*, New York: Alfred A. Knopf.

Peters, T. and Waterman, R. (1982) *In Search of Excellence: Lessons from America's Best-Run Companies*, New York: Harper Row.

Pinchot, G. (1985) *Intrapreneuring: Why You Don't Have to Leave the Company to Become an Entrepreneur*, New York: Harper Row.

Schein E.H. (1990) 'Organisational Culture', *American Psychologist*, February.

Schein E.H. (1994) 'Organisational and Managerial Culture as a Facilitator or Inhibitor of Organisational Learning', *MIT Organisational Learning Network Working Paper 10.004*, May.

Senge, P. (1990) *The Fifth Discipline: The Art and Science of the Learning Organisation*, New York: Currency Doubleday.

Senge, P. (1992) 'Mental Models', *Planning Review*, March–April.

Symon, G. (2002) 'The "Reality" of Rhetoric and the Learning Organisation in the UK', *Human Resource Development International*, 5(2).

Thornhill, S. and Amit, R. (2001) 'A Dynamic Perspective of Internal Fit in Corporate Venturing', *Journal of Business Venturing*, 16(1).

Timmons, J.A. (1999) *New Venture Creation: Entrepreneurship for the 21st Century*, Singapore: Irwin/McGraw Hill.

Tushman, M.L. and O'Reilly, C.A. (1996) 'Ambidextrous Organisations: Managing Evolutionary and Revolutionary Change', *California Management Review*, 38(4).

Vesper, K.H. (1984) 'The Three Faces of Corporate Entrepreneurship: A Pilot Study', in J.A. Hornaday *et al.* (eds), *Frontiers of Entrepreneurial Research*, Wellesley, MA: Babson College.

Wilpert, B. (1995) 'Organisational Behaviour', *Annual Review of Psychology*, 46, January.

Zahra, S.A. (1991) 'Predictors and Financial Outcomes of Corporate Entrepreneurship: An Exploratory Study', *Journal of Business Venturing*, 6(4) (July).

Zahra, S.A., Jennings, D.F. and Kuratko, D.F. (1999) 'The Antecedents and Consequences of Firm Level Entrepreneurship: The State of the Field', *Entrepreneurship: Theory and Practice*, 24.

Checklist of Regulations to be met in Setting up a Business in the UK

The following list summarises some of the main UK regulations. The Business Link website has an interactive tool which tells you what licences and permits your particular business may need in addition to these: www.businesslink.gov.uk/bdotg/ action/lfilter. The website also contains hyperlinks to relevant local authorities.

The checklist has been adapted from DTI (1998) *Setting up in Business: A Guide to Regulatory Requirements*.

Area		Requirement	Help & Advice
Business structure	Sole Trader	If trading with a name other than your own, must display name and address of owner at premises and on stationery.	www.businesslink.gov.uk
	Partnership	As above. Set up a formal deed of partnership (otherwise terms of the Partnership Act 1890 apply).	
	Limited company	Register name and office with Registrar of Companies (Companies House). If trading with a name other than full corporate name, must display name and address of owning company. Must file annual return.	www.companieshouse.gov.uk
	Cooperatives	*Either:* Register (as above) with Companies House. Name must be acceptable. *or:* Register under Industrial and Provident Societies Act Register of Friendly Societies. Must be bona fide cooperative and name acceptable.	www.icof.co.uk www.co-opunion.co.uk
	Franchises	Need contract with franchisor. Legal advice essential.	www.british-franchise.org
Tax	VAT	Check whether registration necessary because of turnover level.	www.hmrc.gov.uk
	Tax	Notify local Inland Revenue office on form CWF1 and submit P45.	
	National insurance	If self-employed, register for Class 2 contributions on form CWF1 at back of form CWL1 booklet.	

Area		Requirement	Help & Advice
Health and Safety	Health and safety	Most factories and workshops need to register with the Health and Safety Executive and offices, shops and other premises with the local authority. Processes causing pollution must register. If food is being prepared or stored contact the local authority Environmental Health Department.	www.hse.gov.uk
	Fire certificate	Fire certificate may be necessary (e.g. guest houses, hotels, residential nurseries). Check with local Fire Authority.	www.fire.org.uk, www.businesslink.gov.uk
	Environment	If business uses refrigeration, air conditioning, fire-fighting equipment or cleaning solvents legislation may apply.	www.defra.gov.uk, www.environment-agency.gov.uk
		If business produces, disposes of, imports or exports waste legislation may apply.	
Employees	Rights	Employment protection legislation applies. If an existing business is taken over, existing terms must be maintained.	www.dti.gov.uk
Premises	New	If new building or change of use is involved consult local authority Planning Department.	www.startinbusiness.co.uk
	Existing	If business involves plant or machinery installed within an industrial site but outside a building or the premises will require structural alteration consult local authority Planning or Building Regulations Departments.	

Licences		
	Cinemas, theatres, child minders, taxis, indoor sports venues, public entertainment venues, street traders, pet shops or kennels, scrap metal dealing, sex shops, residential care, nursing homes or agencies need to apply to the local authority Licensing Department.	
	Scrap metal processing, waste management, abstraction of water or discharge of effluent need to apply to the Environmental Agency.	www.environment-agency.gov.uk
	Hotels, restaurants, abattoirs, hairdressers, mobile shops (food sales), massage, skin piercing (including tattooing), work with asbestos need to apply to local authority Environmental Health Department.	
	Heavy goods or public service operators need to apply to the area office of the Vehicle Inspectorate Executive Agency.	www.vosa.gov.uk
	Companies involved in possession or sale of weapons need to apply to local police.	
	Sale of alcohol in shops, public houses, clubs, nightclubs, restaurants, hotels etc. need to apply to the local authority.	www.culture.gov.uk/ alcohol_and_entertainment
	Money lending, credit arrangement, debt collection, credit cards, credit reference agencies, hiring, leasing or renting goods all require a Credit Licence from the Office of Fair Trading.	www.oft.gov.uk/Business/licence
	If you keep information on people on computer you must be registered with the Data Protection Agency.	www.ico.gov.uk

Sources of Information, Help and Advice in the UK

There are many sources of help and advice in the UK. The most comprehensive single source is the British Library Business and IP (Intellectual Property) Centre in London (www.bl.uk/bipc). The free Reader Pass gives you access to the Library's collection of over 150 million items – books, manuscripts, maps, newspapers, magazines, patents, prints and drawings, photographs and more. You can find images and sounds to aid in the creative process, technical literature to aid in scientific discovery and market information to help develop your competitive strategy. There is information on market size, trends, competition and target customers including hundreds of market research reports from companies such as Mintel, Datamonitor and Frost and Sullivan covering a huge variety of industries. They offer free online access to databases giving company, financial and industrial information such as Fame, Amadeus, OnSource, Lexis-Nexis and Dialog. The British Library also houses the most comprehensive collection of patent specifications in the world – currently over 50 million specifications from 40 countries – and provides access to the most up-to-date literature on patents, trademarks, designs and copyright, together with access to extensive online search tools. It even has an inspirational entrepreneurial role model events programme.

Owner-managers might decide to join business associations such as the local Chamber of Commerce or Trade Association, membership of which gives them access to certain support and services, often financed by membership fees. These are largely self-selecting, self-regulating groups although the British Chambers of Commerce have developed their own rather onerous accreditation and quality assurance system. The services provided by these associations vary enormously. However, studies have shown that their services are predominantly low-cost, low-frequency and low-duration (Bennett, 1996, 1998) – in other words they can provide you with information and advice cheaply and quickly. Chambers generally attract a higher proportion of SMEs as members and are locally-based, thereby providing good opportunities for local networking.

Regionally-based Learning and Skills Councils and their Scottish counterparts, Local Enterprise Councils (LECs), are government-funded bodies with largely private sector boards of management. They provide advice, information, training (particularly in Investors in People), diagnostic consultancy and support to firms. They can also provide information and advice on grants and subsidies. The Scottish LECs are integrated into the networks of Scottish Enterprise and Highlands and Islands Enterprise. This provides more substantial consultancy, larger grant aids infrastructure and export support than English equivalents (Bennett *et al.*, 1994).

Local advice and consultancy to SMEs is offered in England through the Business Link network, in Scotland a similar network called Business Shop and in Wales through Business Connect. These organisations are designed as first-stop shops offering general advice on business and grant and subsidy availability through to specialist advice on topics such as marketing, exports, innovation and product design (Priest, 1999). The English Business Links tend to offer a greater range of services than Business Shops and Business Connects. All are financed mainly by government and are closely related to Learning and Skills Councils and LECs. Business Link has an excellent, practical website providing information, help, advice and hyperlink connections to other relevant sites (www.businesslink.gov.uk).

There are also some 200 locally-based, not-for-profit Enterprise Agencies around the UK. Their financial backing is variable – most are sponsored by local governments or LSC/LEC contracts, with large companies giving significant in-kind and financial support in many cases (Bennett, 1996). They offer advice and consultancy particularly to start-ups and micro businesses across a wide range of fields, but particularly business strategy and planning, and finance. They are also an invaluable source of information on local grants. They offer a personal service that is often free of charge; however, they have been criticised in terms of their quality control procedures and the impact they have on their clients (Bennett and Robson, 1999).

Across the UK, the Small Business Service provides information and advice via telephone and internet (www.sbs.gov.uk), working closely with Business Links and their equivalents. The Department of Trade and Industry can also be helpful. Many of the banks also provide free information and advice. For example, Barclays provides free Business Information Fact-sheets which give information on size of market, types of customers, competition, advertising, start-up costs, qualifications and legal matters relevant to particular fields of business. They also provide more general start-up information in the form of free booklets. However, do not forget your network of friends and colleagues who might be willing to help and advise.

See also the selected websites given in the Learning Resources section.

References

Bennett, R.J. (1996) 'Can Transaction Cost Economics Explain Voluntary Chambers of Commerce?', *Journal of Institutional and Theoretical Economics, 152*.

Bennett, R.J. (1998) 'Business Associations and their Potential Contribution to the Competitiveness of SMEs', *Entrepreneurship and Regional Development, 10*.

Bennett, R.J. and Robson, P.J.A. (1999) 'Intensity of Interaction in Supply of Business Advice and Client Impact', *British Journal of Management*, 10(4).

Bennett, R.A., Wicks, P. and McCoshan, A. (1994) *Local Empowerment and Business Services: Britain's Experiment with TECs*, London: UCL Press.

Priest, S.P. (1999) 'Business Link SME Services: Targeting Innovation and Change', *Environment and Planning C; Government and Policy*, 17.

Entrepreneurship Exercises

1 Are you really entrepreneurial?

1 Go to the electronic version of the GET test that is available on the website accompanying this book (www.palgrave.com/business/burns). Answer the questions and review the analysis provided. Do you have the character traits of an entrepreneur? Append a print-out of the analysis provided and outline why you agree or disagree with it giving concrete examples of your behaviour to support your views.

2 If for any reason you cannot obtain the test, try answering the following questions:

		Yes	No
1	Do you work hard at things that interest you?	☐	☐
2	Are you a self-starter, somebody who does not need pushing?	☐	☐
3	Are you the sort of person who frequently has new ideas?	☐	☐
4	Do these ideas usually get implemented?	☐	☐
5	Do you try to do things differently?	☐	☐
6	Are you willing to put in the extra hours to get things done?	☐	☐
7	Are you willing to do without holidays for the sake of your business?	☐	☐
8	Have you a supportive family that does not object to you putting in those extra hours?	☐	☐
9	Do you usually do your own thing rather than follow the crowd?	☐	☐
10	Do you set yourself goals and gain satisfaction from achieving them?	☐	☐
11	When things go wrong do you press on regardless if you believe in what you are doing?	☐	☐
12	Can you work alone, if you need to?	☐	☐
13	Do you like money?	☐	☐
14	Are you fairly stable – not too many ups and downs?	☐	☐
15	When you don't get your own way, do you shrug it off, not bear a grudge and just get on with life?	☐	☐
16	Can you motivate others to work with you?	☐	☐
17	Are you willing to take measured risks?	☐	☐

	Yes	No
18 Can you live with uncertainty about the future?	☐	☐
19 Are you willing to try your hand at most things?	☐	☐
20 Do others consider you a fairly good all rounder?	☐	☐
21 Do you really feel you can succeed with your own business?	☐	☐
22 Do you frequently have good ideas for business?	☐	☐
23 Did you do things to make money when you were a child?	☐	☐
24 Do you always want to succeed at what you do?	☐	☐
25 Do you really, really want to start your own business?	☐	☐

If you answered 'yes' to all these questions you certainly have the makings of a successful entrepreneur and anything over 20 is good. But are you really sure you answered the questions honestly? Why not ask someone close to you to rate you in these areas. Outline why you agree or disagree with these conclusions giving concrete examples of your behaviour to support your views.

3 List the advantages and disadvantages of:

- Employment
- Self-employment

4 List the reasons why you want to set up your own business. Are they good enough to motivate you to succeed? List the reasons why you should not set up your own business. Can they be overcome or, if not, are you prepared to live with the risk?

Based on this information, write a report on whether or not you are the right sort of person to set up and run your own business. Make certain you are as objective as possible. You can append the results of exercises 1 or 2 to your report. Remember to make certain that you give examples to support any character traits or behaviours you claim to have – otherwise it is just your opinion.

Whether or not you might be entrepreneurial, do you want to start your own business now or at some time in the future?

2 Generating the idea

1 Follow this four-step guide to generating ideas for a start-up, adapted from Timmons (2003). The aim is to generate as many ideas as possible so while generating ideas it is important not to evaluate them or get bogged down in the detail of how they may or may not work.

Step 1 *List ideas.* Think of unmet market needs, changes in technology or legislation or demographics, ideas you have seen in other regions or countries that you have not seen here, knowledge and information gaps.

Step 2 *Expand the list.* Think about your personal interests, experiences, desired lifestyle, values and what you feel you are likely to do well or would like to do.

Step 3 *Get feedback on the list from at least three people who know you.* Knowing you, they might be able to add to the list by interpreting it slightly differently.

Step 4 *Jot down insights, observations and conclusions about your ideas and personal preferences.*

2 Using the list generated from this exercise, evaluate each idea against the following eight criteria, using a score of 1 (very poor or very unattractive) to 5 (very high or very attractive).

- *Attractiveness of idea* – Would you enjoy doing it?
- *Ability to undertake* – Do you have the skills needed to do it?
- *Practicality* – Is it something that really can be done?
- *Potential market demand* – Will customers buy it?
- *Ability to combat competition* – Is there competition and can you combat it in some way?
- *Ability to differentiate* – Can you differentiate it in some way that can be sustained over a long period?
- *Price potential* – Can you avoid competing simply on price?
- *Resource availability* – Do you think you have, or can get, the resources you need to start up this business?

The top scoring three or four ideas might be worth exploring further.

3 List the critical factors that you would need to make certain were right in taking the top-scoring three or four ideas from the previous exercise further. Evaluate the ideas and select the one you want to take further. Be aware that the one you select may still prove not to be commercially viable and you may have to return to this list to research another idea.

Write a brief report justifying your selected business idea.

3 Evaluating the opportunity

Using the pro forma on the following pages, write a business plan for the selected business idea. (A copy of this pro forma can be printed off from the website.) Some points to remember are:

- Stress the benefits of your product or service to the chosen target market(s).
- Undertake the necessary market research. Estimate the size and growth of the market.
- Name your major competitors and evaluate their strengths and weaknesses. Evaluate the degree of competition in the market, using Porter's Five Forces.
- Evaluate the strengths and weaknesses of your business.
- Be clear about the basis for your competitive advantage over these competitors.
- Be clear about the marketing strategy you aim to adopt, giving details of any basis for differentiating your product or service and the marketing mix you aim to adopt.
- Be clear about your channels of distribution, if appropriate.
- Be clear about the selling price you have decided to set for your product or service and how you have arrived at it.
- Be clear about any particular launch strategy.
- Be clear about the implications for the business of the cost structure. What is the contribution margin? What are the fixed costs? What, therefore, are the business imperatives?
- Are you certain you can at least make your break-even point? How many units to you have to sell each day to achieve this?
- Are you certain you can survive on the cash flow generated by your business? Have you included necessary drawings?
- Keep your fixed costs and capital investment as low as possible. Can you borrow, rent or lease equipment, rather than buy it?
- What are the critical success factors and how will you make sure that you achieve them?
- Show the funding you will need for the business and where it might come from – remember the business plan you prepare for yourself could look very different from one you prepare to raise finance.

Business plan

Business name and address:

Proprietor's name and address:

Business form:

Business activity:

Aims:

Objectives:

Market size and growth:

Competitors:

	Names	Strengths	Weaknesses

Your business:

	Strengths	Weaknesses

Competitive advantages:

Proposed customers:

Advertising and promotions strategy:

Pricing strategy:

Premises:

Equipment:

Key people and job functions:

Background details of key people:

Financial highlights

12 months to:

Turnover:

Profit:

Break-even:

Funding requirement:

Source of funds:

Forecast profit and loss account

Business:

Period:

Sales:		£	(A)
Less direct (variable) costs:			
materials	£		
direct wages	£		
other	£		
Total direct (variable) costs:		£	
Gross profit/contribution:		£	(B)
Fixed costs (overheads):			
wages/salaries (including taxes)	£		
rent	£		
heat/light/power	£		
advertising	£		
insurance	£		
transport/travel	£		
telephone	£		
stationery/postage	£		
repairs/renewals	£		
depreciation	£		
local taxes	£		
other	£		
other	£		
Total fixed costs		£	(C)
Net profit		£	
Less drawings or dividends		£	
Profit retained in the business		£	

$$\text{Break-even point} = \frac{(C) \times (A)}{(B)}$$

Cash flow forecast

Month:												
SALES												
Volume:												
Value:												
RECEIPTS												
Sales – cash												
Sales – debtors												
Capital introduced												
Grants, loans etc												
Total (A)												
PAYMENTS												
Materials												
Wages/salaries												
Rent												
Heat/light/power												
Advertising												
Insurance												
Transport/travel												
Telephone												
Stationery/postage												
Repairs/renewals												
Local taxes												
Other _____												
Other _____												
Capital purchases												
Loan repayments												
Drawings/ dividends												
Total (B)												
CASH BALANCES												
Cash flow (A)−(B)												
Opening balance												
Closing balance												

4 Growth audit of an existing business

Select a local small firm that you are familiar with and, using the checklists on the following pages, evaluate its potential for growth.

1   Using Growth Audit Checklist 1 as a guide, evaluate the personal qualities of the owner-manager and their ability to handle growth and take the firm forward.
2   Using Growth Audit Checklist 2 as a guide, evaluate the management team and their ability to handle growth and take the firm forward.
3   Using Growth Audit Checklist 3 as a guide, evaluate the product/market offerings of the firm and the opportunities for growth. Use the checklist for each product/market offering. Represent the product/market portfolio in a Boston matrix.
4   Using Growth Audit Checklist 4 as a guide, evaluate the competitive environment and competitors facing the firm and evaluate how it might develop sustainable competitive advantage.
5   Using Growth Audit Checklist 5 as a guide, undertake a financial analysis of the firm and draw up your conclusions about how it is performing. If you are able to obtain projected or budgeted financial statements, repeat the analysis.
6   Analyse the results from steps 1 to 5 and summarise in the form of a SWOT analysis.
7   If the firm has projected or budgeted sales for next year, break them down into the four categories of the product/market matrix (below) and critically analyse how the firm proposes to achieve this increase.

  - List the ways the company intends to achieve greater market penetration.
  - Detail why the company is going into new markets and how it is going to do so.
  - Give details of any new product(s) it intends to sell and why existing customers are expected to buy.
  - Give details of and the rationale for any diversification. Explain how it will go about diversifying.
  - Give details of and the rationale for any mergers and acquisitions. Explain how it will go about making the acquisition or merger.

	% sales from:		% sales from:
Existing products/customers:		Product development	
Market development:		Diversification:	

8   In the light of the SWOT analysis, and after discussion with management, critically evaluate the risks associated with these four strategies and the safeguards put in place to provide early warning signs and deal with them. If the organisation has a number of different product/service offerings, repeat the exercise for each one, bearing in mind where it lies in its product life cycle and the generic marketing strategy being followed. Evaluate its overall portfolio strategy.
    Write up your findings in the form of a report.

Small Business Audit Checklist 1

Personal qualities of the owner-manager

- Why is the owner-manager in business?
  - are they push or pull factors?

- Is the owner-manager entrepreneurial?
  - are they opportunistic, innovative, self-confident and self-motivated, proactive with vision and flair and a willingness to take risks?
  - are they willing to make, and emotionally strong enough to endure, sacrifices and personal hardship for the sake of the business?

- What are the entrepreneurs long-term objectives?
  - is it capital gain, regular income, need for achievement, contribution to society, provide employment, produce something that is needed, build something that will outlive them, achieve status, have fun?

- Does the entrepreneur really want the firm to grow?

- Does the entrepreneur have the ability to change the way they manage the firm as it grows?
  - will they be able to delegate but control and coordinate?

- Does the entrepreneur have the ability to become a leader?
  - do they have vision and ideas, have the ability to undertake long-term strategic planning, communicate effectively, have the potential to create the right culture in the firm and will they be able to monitor and control performance effectively?

- What style of leadership will they adopt?
  - is it appropriate for the group they manage, the tasks they undertake and the situation they are in?

- Are they able to cope with crises effectively?

- Can they build a management team?

- Can they build an effective board of directors?

Small Business Audit Checklist 2

The management team

- Is there a management team in place?
- Does it have an adequate mix of outside experience?
- Do they have the right skills mix?
- Is there a proper organisation structure?
- Is it appropriate for the degree of task complexity?
- Are there any gaps in the structure?
- Is authority delegated to the management team?
- Are there proper controls in place to monitor their performance?
- Is there an appropriate culture in place?
  - influenced by appropriate organisational and cognitive processes and behaviours?
- Are they a cohesive team?
  - do they have the right mix of Belbin team roles?
- Are there any gaps in the team profile?
- How does this show itself in the way they operate?
- Do the team handle conflict in an effective manner?
- Is the management team cohesive?
- Is the management team motivated to succeed?
  - are they personally motivated, are there appropriate incentives in place?
- Is there a concern for staff within the firm?
- Is staff turnover generally low?
- Is the level of absenteeism, for illness or accident, average for the industry?
- Do staff see themselves as part of the firm, with adequate remuneration and career paths?
- Are there skill gaps in the firm?
- Do staff generally receive adequate training?
- Do staff understand the vision or mission of the firm and do they 'buy into' it?
- Are management and staff motivated to succeed?

Small Business Audit Checklist 3

The product/market offering

- Can the firm identify the target market segments they are selling to?

- Are customer needs understood?

- Are the benefits offered by the products/services understood?

- How loyal are customers?

- How frequent are customer complaints and are they properly followed up?

- Does the firm understand where each product/market offering is in its life cycle?

- Does the position for the firm mirror that of the industry?

- Is the portfolio of product/market offerings balanced?

- Are new product/market offerings planned to replace those coming to the end of their life?

- Does the firm understand the value chain for each of its product/market offerings?

- Does the firm have any benchmark information on how it compares or how its product/market offerings compare to those of competitors?

- Does the firm follow a definite generic marketing strategy for each product/market offering?

- Can it command leadership in this area?

- Does the firm understand its core competencies?

- Does the firm command operational excellence, product leadership or customer intimacy?

- Does strategy emphasise something that makes the firm as unique as possible and delivers as much value to the customer as possible?

- Does the strategy reflect the position of each product/market offering in its life cycle?

- If cost is important for any product/market offering, does the firm understand the economies of scale it faces and can it command cost leadership?

- If differentiation is important, does the product/market offering have a strong brand?

- If focus is important, does the firm undertake frequent and thorough market research, and does it have strong customer relations?

Small Business Audit Checklist 4

The competitive environment

- Does the firm regularly undertake market research?

- Does the firm regularly monitor trends in the industry or sector?

- Are there any trends in the market or industry that are likely to particularly affect the firm?

- How competitive does Porter's Five Forces analysis show the firm's industry to be?

- Relative to this, how well is the firm performing?

- Does the firm have any views about future trends (SLEPT) that might affect it?

- Does it have a strategic response to these trends?

- Does the firm have information on competitors?
  - size, profitability and operating methods?
  - benchmark performance for efficiency, quality and so on?
  - marketing strategies of competitors?

- Can the firm identify which competitors are successful and why?

- Does the firm know of any important changes that competitors will be making in the future?
  - marketing mix?
  - new markets or market segments?
  - new or developed products?

- What is the basis for the firm's competitive advantage?

- How sustainable is this?

Small Business Audit Checklist 5

Financial performance

Performance

Return on shareholders funds (%) $\dfrac{\text{Net profit (after interest)}}{\text{Shareholders funds}}$ ☐

Return on total assets (%) $\dfrac{\text{Operating profit (before interest)}}{\text{Total assets}}$ ☐

Profitability

Net margin (%) $\dfrac{\text{Net profit}}{\text{Sales}}$ ☐

Gross margin (%) $\dfrac{\text{Gross profit}}{\text{Sales}}$ ☐

Cost of materials (%) $\dfrac{\text{Cost of materials}}{\text{Sales}}$ ☐

Cost of labour (%) $\dfrac{\text{Cost of labour}}{\text{Sales}}$ ☐

Overhead cost (%) $\dfrac{\text{Overhead costs}}{\text{Sales}}$ ☐

Asset efficiency

Capital/Net asset turnover $\dfrac{\text{Sales}}{\text{Net assets}}$ ☐

Debtor turnover $\dfrac{\text{Sales}}{\text{Debtors}}$ ☐

Stock turnover $\dfrac{\text{Sales}}{\text{Stock}}$ ☐

Fixed asset turnover $\dfrac{\text{Sales}}{\text{Fixed assets}}$ ☐

Liquidity

Current ratio $\dfrac{\text{Current assets}}{\text{Current liabilities}}$ ☐

Quick ratio $\dfrac{\text{Current assets excluding stock}}{\text{Current liabilities}}$ ☐

Gearing

Gearing ratio (%) $\dfrac{\text{All loans + overdrafts}}{\text{Shareholders funds}}$ ☐

Short-term debt ratio (%) $\dfrac{\text{Short-term loans + overdrafts}}{\text{All loans + overdraft}}$ ☐

Interest cover $\dfrac{\text{Trading profit}}{\text{Interest}}$ ☐

Risk

Margin of safety $\dfrac{\text{Sales} - \text{Break-even sales}}{\text{Sales}}$ ☐

Learning Resources

Selected case studies

Chapter 3 or 5: Opportunity recognition

Ajay Bam
2 part case 805-009-1 and 805-010-1. Teaching note 805-009-8
Written by W. Bygrave and C. Hedberg, Babson College.

Chapter 3 or 18: Innovation and new product development

Domino Printing Sciences (A & B).
2 cases 602-031-1 and 602-032-1. Video: 602-031-3. Teaching note: 602-031-8.
Written by K. Goffin, D. Walker and M. Sweeney, Cranfield School of Management, Cranfield, England.

Chapters 5, 6 and 14: Business start-up

Fariba (A) and (B).
Cases 803-012-1 and 803-013-1. Video 803-012-3. Teaching note 803-012-8.
Writen by P. Clark, D. Molian and R. Brown, Cranfield School of Management, Cranfield University, England.

Michelle Mone and MJM International.
Case 803-044-1. Teaching note 803-044-6.
Written by F. Martin, University of Stirling, Scotland.

Chapter 7: Running a small firm – focus, priorities

Lemmings.
Case 397-033-1. No teaching note.
Written by F. Martin, University of Stirling, Scotland, and C. Craig, Carol Craig Associates.

Chapter 8: Individual entrepreneurs

Richard Branson/Herb Kelleher – Leaders Extraordinaire.
Case 803-005-1. Teaching note: 803-005-8.
Written by V. Sarvai, under the direction of A. Mukund, ICFA Center for Management Research (ICMR), Hyderabad, India.

Richard Branson's Leadership Style.
Case 804-019-1. No teaching note.
Written by D.G. Prasuna and K.B.S. Kumar, ICFAI University Press, India.

Michael Dell – The Man Behind Dell.
Case 402-015-1. Teaching note: 402-015-8.
Written by K. Subhadra, under the direction of A. Mukund, ICFA Center for Management Research (ICMR), Hyderabad, India.

Larry Ellison: A Samurai Warrior in Silicon Valley.
Case 402-038-1. No teaching note.
Written by M. Kets de Vries and E. Florent-Treacy, INSEAD, Fontainebleau, France.

Chapters 9 to 11: growing the business

Ebay.com – Profitably Managing Growth from Start-up to 2000.
Case: 301-017-1. Teaching note: 301-017-8.
Written by G.J. Stockport, D. Pudney and M. van der Merwe, The Graduate School of
   Management, University of Western Australia, Australia.

Dangdang.com.
Case 803-050-1. No teaching note.
Written by N. Rajshekar and K. Arun, ICFAI Business School Case Development Centre, India.

Branson's Virgin: The Coming of Age of a Counter-Cultural Enterprise.
Case: 495-014-1. Supplement: 495-014-4. Interview: 495-014-5. Video: 495-015-3. Teaching note:
   495-014-8.
Written by M. Kets de Vries, INSEAD, Fontainebleau, France.

The House that Branson Built: Virgin's Entry into the New Millenium.
Case 400-002-1. Teaching note: 400-002-8.
Written by M. Kets de Vries, INSEAD, Fontainebleau, France.

Body Shop.
Case: 9-392-032. Teaching note: 5-392-038.
Written by C.A. Bartlett, K.W. Eldererkin and K. McQuade, Harvard Business School, Boston, USA.

easyJet: The Web's Favourite Airline.
Case IMD-3-0873. Video: 300-036-3. Teaching note: IMD-3-0873TN.
Written by N. Kumar and B. Rogers, IMD, Lausanne, Switzerland.

easyEverything: The Internet Shop.
Case IMD-3-0874.
Written by N. Kumar and B. Rogers, IMD, Lausanne, Switzerland.

www.easyRentacar.com.
Case IMD-3-0875. Teaching note IMD-3-0875-T.
Written by N. Kumar and B. Rogers, IMD, Lausane, Switzerland

Ryanair – The Low Fares Airline.
Case 399-122-1.
Written by E. O'Higgins, University College Dublin, Ireland.

Chapter 10: Diversification

Snakes and Ladders: Cobra Beer's Defining Moments.
Case 803-066-1. No teaching note.
Written by M. de Rond, The Judge Institute of Management Studies, University of Cambridge,
   England.

Chapter 12: Failure

Leonardro and Co.
Case 803-045-1. Teaching note 803-045-8.
Written by F. Martin, University of Stirling, Scotland.

Chapter16: International start-up

The Celtic Tiger Moves to the Beat of the Reggae Boyz.
Case 805-014-1. No teaching note.
Written by I. Boyett, Nottingham University Business School, England.

Chapter 17: Social Entrepreneurship

The Big Issue.
Case 803-065-1. No teaching note.
Written by J. Lloyd, London Business School, England.

Cases on civic entrepreneurship free from www.demos.co.uk:
   Thames Valley Police
   Dorset Health Authority
   South Somerset District Council

Chapter 18: Corporate entrepreneurship

The 3M Company: (A) Building the Entrepreneurial Corporation (1902-1950).
Case 802-001-1. No teaching note.

The 3M Company: (B) Defining Strategy (1950-1990).
Case 802-002-1. No teaching note.

The 3M Company: (C) Dynamic Balance for the 90s.
Case 802-003-1. No teaching note.
Written by M. Ackenhusen, N. Churchill and D. Muzyka, INSEAD, Fontainebleau, France.

3M's Organisational Culture.
Case 403-041-1. Teaching note: 403-041-8.
Written by S Dutta, K Subhadra, ICFAI Center for Management Research (ICMR), Hyderabad, India.

Unless otherwise stated, cases can be obtained from the European Case Clearing House, England and USA.

North America: Tel: +1 781 239 5884 Fax: +1 781 239 5885
                    e-mail: ECCHBabson@aol.com.

Rest of the world: Tel: +44 (0) 1234 750903 Fax: +44 (0)1234 751125
                    email: ECCH@cranfield.ac.uk
website: www.ecch.cranfield.ac.uk

Selected further reading

Entrepreneurship and Small Business

Birley, S. and Muzyaka, D. (eds) (2000) *Mastering Entrepreneurship: Your Single Source Guide to becoming a Master of Entrepreneurship*, Harlow: Pearson Professional Education.

Bolton, B. and Thompson, J. (2000) *Entrepreneurs: Talent, Temperament, Techniques*, Oxford: Butterworth-Heinemann.

Bridge, S., O'Neill, K. and Cromie, S. (2003) *Understanding Enterprise, Entrepreneurship and Small Business*, Basingstoke: Palgrave Macmillan.

Bygrave, W.D. and Zacharakis, A. (eds) (2003) *The Portable MBA in Entrepreneurship*, 3rd edn, New York: John Wiley & Sons.

Kirby, D. (2003) *Entrepreneurship*, Maidenhead: McGraw Hill.

Kuratko, D.F. and Hodgetts, R.M. (2001) *Entrepreneurship: An International Perspective*, Orlando: Harcourt College Publishers.

Timmons, J.A. (2003) *New Venture Creation: Entrepreneurship for the 21st Century*, 6th edn, Singapore: Irwin/McGraw Hill.

Selected topics in alphabetic order

Corporate entrepreneurship

Burns, P. (2005) *Corporate Entrepreneurship: Building an Entrepreneurial Organisation*, Basingstoke: Palgrave Macmillan.

Morris, M.H. and Kuratko, D.F. (2002) *Corporate Entrepreneurship: Entrepreneurial Development within Organisations*, Fort Worth: Harcourt College Publishers.

Sathe, V. (2003) *Corporate Entrepreneurship: Top Managers and New Business Creation,* Cambridge: Cambridge University Press.

Culture

Guirdham, M. (1999) *Communicating across Cultures*, Basingstoke: Macmillan Business – now Palgrave Macmillan.

Schneider, S.C. and Barsoux, J.L. (1997) *Managing across Cultures*, Hemel Hempstead: Prentice Hall.

Economists' perspective on small business

Cosh, A. and Hughes, A. (eds) (1998), *Enterprise Britain: Growth Innovation and Public Policy in the Small and Medium Sized Enterprise Sector 1994–97*, ESRC Centre for Business Research, Cambridge.

Schumacher, E.F. (1974) *Small is Beautiful: A Study of Economics as if People Mattered*, London: Abacus.

Storey D.J. (1998) *Understanding the Small Business Sector*, London: International Thomson Business Press.

Entrepreneurial marketing

Chaston, I. (2000) *Entrepreneurial Marketing: Competing by Challenging Convention,* Basingstoke: Macmillan – now Palgrave Macmillan.

Family firms

Kenyon-Rouvinez, D. and Ward, J.L. (eds) (2005) *Family Business: Key Issues*, Basingstoke: Palgrave Macmillan.
Leach, P. (1996) *The BDO Stoy Hayward Guide to the Family Business*, London: Kogan Page.

Innovation

Drucker, P.F. (1985) *Innovation and Entrepreneurship: Practice and Principles*, London: Heinemann.
Peters, T. (1997) *The Circle of Innovation*, New York: Alfred A. Knopf.
Tidd, J., Bassant, J. and Pavitt, K. (2001) *Managing Innovation: Integrating Technological, Market and Organisational Change*, New York: Wiley.

International entrepreneurship

Dicken, P. (!998) *Global Shift: Transforming the World Economy,* London: Paul Chapman Publishing.
Giddens, A. (2000) *Runaway World: How Globalisation is Reshaping our Lives,* Andover: Routledge.

Social entrepreneurship

Brinckerhoff, P. (2000) *Social Entrepreneurship: The Art of Mission-Based Venture Development*, Hoboken, NJ: Wiley.
Dees, J.G., Emerson, J. and Economy, P. (2001) *Enterprising Nonprofits: A Toolkit for Social Entrepreneurs*, Hoboken, NJ: Wiley.
Ebrhim, A. (2004) *NGOs and Organisational* Change, Cambridge: Cambridge University Press.

Strategy

Johnson, G. and Scholes, K. (2004) *Exploring Corporate Strategy*, Harlow: Financial Times/Prentice-Hall.
Kay, J. (1998) *Foundations of Corporate Success*, Oxford: Oxford University Press.
Mintzberg, H. (1994) *The Rise and Fall of Strategic Planning*, New York: Free Press.
Mintzberg, H., Ahlstrand, B. and Lampel, J. (1998) *Strategy Safari*, New York: Free Press.
Wickham, P.A. (2001) *Strategic Entrepreneurship: A Decision-Making Approach to New Venture Creation and Management*, Harlow: Pearson Education.

Selected journals

There are a number of journals that specifically concerned with entrepreneurship and small business. Here are some of them:

Academy of Entrepreneurship Journal
Enterprise and Innovation Management Studies
Entrepreneurial Executive
Entrepreneurship and Regional Development
Entrepreneurship, Theory and Practice
Family Business Review
Franchise Review
International Journal of Entrepreneurial Behaviour and Research
International Journal of Entrepreneurship Education
International Journal of Entrepreneurship and Innovation

International Journal of Entrepreneurship and Innovation Management
International Journal of Entrepreneurship and Small Business
International Journal of Management and Enterprise Development
International Small Business Journal
Journal of Business and Entrepreneurship
Journal of Business Venturing
Journal of Developmental Entrepreneurship
Journal of Enterprising Culture
Journal of Entrepreneurship
Journal of Entrepreneurship Education
Journal of Research in Marketing and Entrepreneurship
Journal of Small Business and Enterprise Development
Journal of Small Business Management
Journal of Small Business Strategies
Journal of Small Business Finance
New England Journal of Entrepreneurship
Small Business Economics
Venture Capital

Articles on entrepreneurship in general also appear in most business and management journals, particularly in the subject areas of strategy and human resources. The easiest way to find academic articles on a topic related to small firms is to use a web-based search engine. Your library will advise you on the most appropriate one to use.

Selected websites

Do a *Google* search on 'entrepreneurship' and you will get over 40 million results. Do one on 'small firms' and you will find over 57 million. Investigating so many sites is virtually impossible. Probably the best place to find UK resources of any kind related to entrepreneurship or small business is:

Small Business Research Portal   www.smallbusinessportal.co.uk
This site provides information on academics, books, centres, conferences, government agencies, mega-sites, publications, reviews and has a useful research tools section.

The Checklist of regulations to be met in setting up a business in the UK (page 502) also contains websites that offer help and advice in meeting these regulations. Listed below are other sites that may prove useful. Remember they change rapidly, so always be willing to try a *Google* search for what you require.

Academic sites

Global Entrepreneurship Monitor   www.gemconsortium.org
The website of the consortium of universities that participate in the GEM project. Links to local sites.

Babson College Centre for Entrepreneurship   www3.babson.edu/eship/
This site provides papers and abstracts and details of various initiatives.

Information Centre for Entrepreneurship   www.bibl.hj.se/ice/
This site provides a collection of printed material from periodicals to working papers and describes itself as providing 'one of the world's largest collections in the fields of entrepreneurship, innovations and small and medium-sized enterprises'.

Center for Entrepreneurial Leadership Clearinghouse
on Entrepreneurship Education   www.celcee.edu
This US Department of Education site has been set up to disseminate information not normally distributed through the usual sources.

Sites with practical information, advice and help on start-ups

UK Business Link   www.businesslink.gov.uk
This is an excellent site full of practical information and advice about starting up, finance, international trade, growing the business and buying or selling a business in the UK. It contains hyperlinks to many other relevant sites.

UK Small Business Service   www.sbs.gov.uk
UK Small Business Service website.

United States Small Business Administration   www.sba.gov
US Government site full of practical information and advice as well as specimen business plans.

The British Library Business & IP Centre   www.bl.uk/bipc
The website for the British Library – which provides the most comprehensive business information resource in the UK (see page 520). Most resources can only be accessed by personal visit.

Business Help   www.bizhelp24.com
This provides UK business and finance information, news, help and services for small firms.

Enterweb   www.enterweb.org
As well as offering information and advice, this site provides a wide range of links to other sites around the world.

Livewire Young Entrepreneurs   www.shell-livewire.org
This site provides practical help and support for young entrepreneurs wishing to start their own business. It offers a free start-a-business toolkit and hosts an annual, national competition.

Prince's Trust   www.princes-trust.org.uk
The site offers practical help and support and low-interest loans to young entrepreneurs.

Start-up Magazine   www.startups.co.uk
A UK web-based magazine for start-ups also offering information and advice.

Start-up Journal   startupjournal.com
A US web-based magazine from the Wall Street Journal.

Business plans

Teneric	www.teneric.co.uk
Bplans	www.bplans.com
Businessplans	www.businessplans.org
Business-plans	www.business-plans.co.uk

All these sites provide free sample business plans, help and advice.

Benchmark performance   www.benchmarkindex.com

Finance

Finding finance   www.money-off.co.uk
A search engine for different sources of finance.

Fairinvestment   www.fairinvestment.co.uk
Provides an independent comparison of business banking services.

British Venture Capital Association   www.bvca.co.uk
The website of the British Venture Capital Association.

European Venture Capital Association   www.evca.com
The website of the European Venture Capital Association.

UK venture capital funds   www.growthbusiness.co.uk
This site provides a guide to UK venture capital funds.

Business Angels   www.bbaa.org.uk
The website of the British Business Angels Association.

Business Angels   www.venturesite.co.uk
A virtual network of business angels on which investment opportunities can be posted.

First Tuesday   www.firsttuesday.com
The website for First Tuesday business angels.

Creativity

Creax   www.creax.com
The site with hyperlinks to other creativity websites – an enormous resource.

Family business

The Family Business Network   www.fbn-i.org

International trade

The International Monetary Fund   www.imf.org
The IMF has a range of briefs on its website.

The World Trade Organization   www.wto.org

The World Bank   www.worldbank.org

The United Nations Conference on Trade and Development   www.unctad.org
UNCTAD publishes a World Investment Report annually. Highlights can be found on its website.

The International Chamber of Commerce   www.iccwbo.org
This is the ICC world business organisation website.

The Institute for International Economics   www.iie.com
This website contains numerous resources and links related to trade issues.

The International Forum on Globalization   www.ifg.org

Social entrepreneurship

Ashoka Changemakers   www.changemakers.net
This is a website of resources for social entrepreneurship.

Center for Social Innovation   www.gsb.stanford.edu/csi/
This is a Stanford Business School website.

Demos   www.demos.co.uk
Demos is a political 'think-tank'.

Joshua Venture   www.joshuaventure.org/resources/soc-ent-resources.html
This is a website of social entrepreneurship resources.

Social Entrepreneurship Monitor   www.gemconsortium.org/default.asp,
                                                     and select 'Documents' then 'UK'
This is the social entrepreneurship equivalent of the GEM website.

The Institute for Social Entrepreneurs   www.socialent.org

The National Center for Social Entrepreneurs (USA)   www.socialentrepreneurs.org/

The School for Social Entrepreneurs (UK)   www.sse.org.uk

The Small Business Service Social Enterprise Unit   www.sbs.gov.uk,
                                                      and select 'Social Enterprise'

WARNING
Information downloaded from websites is easily detected by specialist plagiarism software used by most universities. If you use any information from websites for your coursework assignments ensure that all direct quotes – text copied from the site – are placed in inverted commas and full web attribution is given. You may need to seek advice from your tutor on how much material can be used in this way. Failure to follow this advice may lead to your coursework being given a 'fail' mark.

Author Index

Subject Index